An Engagement with Time

An Engagement with Time

Winton Dean

Dynasty Press Limited
Ground Floor, 19 New Road
Brighton, East Sussex
United Kingdom, BN1 1UF

First published in this version by Dynasty Press Limited
ISBN 978-1-8380418-1-6

Copyright © Estate of Winton Dean and Stephen Dean 2024

The Estate of Winton Dean and Stephen Dean have asserted their right under the Copyright, Designs and Patents Act 1988 to be identified as the authors of this work.

All Rights Reserved. No part of this publication may be reproduced in any form or by any means without the written permission of the authors.

No AI Training: Without in any way limiting the authors' and publisher's exclusive rights under copyright, any use of this publication to 'train' generative artificial intelligence (AI) technologies to generate text is expressly prohibited. This book was authored by Winton Dean and Stephen Dean and not generated by any machine or artificial intelligence. This statement serves as a legally binding guarantee of authenticity and can be used to establish the true creators of this work should any doubt arise.

Cover design by Martyn Ridgewell

Typeset by Biddles Books Ltd., Castle House, East Winch Road, Blackborough End, King's Lynn, Norfolk PE32 1SF

Printed and bound in the United Kingdom

Introduction

by Stephen Dean

My father embarked on his memoirs late in life, put them aside to finish the second volume of *Handel's Operas* (published at the age of 90), then resumed work spasmodically, until extreme old age and infirmity brought an end to his labours. He stopped at the beginning of 1946. The succeeding chapters were written by me, culled from many sources, principally recorded conversations I had with my father very late in his life, letters from his ample files, including surviving letters to his great friend Philip Radcliffe and his mother-in-law Margaret Craigmyle, his pocket diaries (informative on appointments and the weather – when extreme), my mother's letters to me, and my own recollections. He read and approved my first paragraphs, encompassing the research trip to Paris with Philip Radcliffe in 1947 and the Master Musicians party the following year. Material towards the end of Chapter 14 was adapted from his late essay, 'Lennox Berkeley and his Operas', unpublished during his life. My father gave up his detailed diary at the beginning of 1938, but in the same year and the same volume began a music diary, recording his impressions of every piece of music he heard for the first time, and often his later reactions as well. He kept this up for sixty years. I have relied heavily on this source.

The memoirs conclude with his opening lecture at Berkeley, California, in April 1966, leaving the remaining 47 years of his long life unrecorded. The lectures, which he feared he would not finish in time, following a severe breakdown at the start of the year, were a triumphant success. They were published in 1969 as *Handel and the Opera Seria*, the first book ever devoted to Handel's operas. When he returned home he resolved, for a time at least, not to embark on any major work of scholarship, and to take up salmon fishing in Scotland. Only the second resolution was kept. Labour on the monumental *Handel's Operas 1704-1726* (with J.M. Knapp) was soon in progress, and occupied many years – interrupted by other projects, including a substantial chapter 'Beethoven and Opera' (in *The Beethoven Companion*, 1971) and many other articles and contributions to composite works (some reprinted in *Essays on Opera*, 1990). He edited and annotated Edward J. Dent's lectures, *The Rise of Romantic Opera* (1976); he supplied the Handel entry and numerous articles on singers for *The New Grove* (1980); he contributed three long chapters on French, Italian and German Opera (1790-1830) to Vol. VIII of *The New Oxford History of Music* (1982). *Handel's Operas 1704-1726* was eventually published in 1987. His edition of Handel's *Giulio Cesare* (with Sarah Fuller) appeared in 1998. Sharp disagreements with his collaborator ensured that *Handel's Operas 1726-1741* was published under his sole name in 2006.

During these years he wrote a great many opera notices (mostly for *The Musical Times*), reviewed books and records and reported on scholarly dissertations. In 1977 he returned to Berkeley (with Thalia) delivering lectures on Handel, Weber and Donizetti. He was in America again in October-November 1979, lecturing at Stony Brook, New York, Yale, Vassar College and Chicago. In June, at Halle, he delivered a lecture in German (in which he was by no means fluent). In 1981 he lectured at Wolfenbüttel and Maryland. In December 1984, he gave a talk (on Handel's *Orlando*) to the Friends of Scottish Opera at Yair – a fine eighteenth-century house opposite Fairnilee – the day after a successful pheasant shoot.

Introduction

The tercentenary of Handel's birth in 1985 saw Winton delivering lectures and papers all over the globe, at Keele, eight universities in Australia, Boston, Rome, London, Washington, Portland, Eugene, Vancouver and Leeds. In July he attended a grand concert in Westminster Abbey to mark the opening of the London Handel Festival. Afterwards, at a reception in Inigo Jones's Banqueting House, he was introduced to the then Prince of Wales, 'warmly indoctrinating him' (according to John Roberts) 'on the greatness of Handel's operas and the many indignities they had suffered at the hands of modern stage directors. Had Princess Diana not been attending a Live Aid concert that evening, she would surely have received equal treatment' ('Memories of Winton Dean (1916-2013)', *Newsletter of the American Handel Society*, Spring 2014).

Winton continued to give the occasional lecture well into his 80s. In his last years he became increasingly immobile and was eventually confined to his bedroom. But his mind remained clear. One incident near the end of his life perhaps throws light on his character. He was enjoying a late breakfast in the kitchen of our flat at Fairnilee when the Zimbabwean carer came in hurriedly: 'Mr Dean, Mr Dean, you must get up immediately – the house is on fire!' This was indeed true, and had he looked round he would have seen smoke and flames pouring from an upper storey. But Winton was not going to budge, whatever the emergency – until he had finished his breakfast!

Winton died at Hambledon on 19th December 2013, aged 97. Thalia, after enduring years of ill-health following a stroke in 1987, died on 10th December 2000 at the age of 82. They lie together in the peaceful churchyard at Hambledon.

I should like to thank Sir Curtis Price, Diana McVeagh and Bruce Phillips for reading the text of the whole book and offering many helpful comments. I am grateful to Diana McVeagh for offering her personal memories of my father and to Frances Abraham for allowing me to quote from her father Gerald Abraham's diaries. Sally Fuller, John Roberts and Charlotte Greenspan, Winton's former students at Berkeley, suggested many improvements and additions to the final chapter. I am grateful to Rufus Hale for his drawing of his great-uncle Winton (frontispiece). Nick Watson took the photo on the back flyleaf. Finally, thanks go to David Hornsby and to my cousin Tacita Dean for their help in bringing the project to fruition.

Contents

	List of Illustrations	xi
1.	Beginnings	1
2.	Early Life	38
3.	Sheppey	82
4.	Harrow	98
5.	Cambridge	151
6.	Family Troubles	177
7.	Salzburg and Greece	229
8.	Saul	260
9.	Clare	279
10.	Germany and Beyond	300
11.	Thalia	314
12.	Marriage	335
13.	War	364
14.	Milford	393
15.	The Dramatic Handel	420
16.	Hambledon	447
17.	Publication	498
18.	Romantic Opera	531
19.	Shakespeare and Opera	573
20.	Fairnilee	587
21.	Heading for Berkeley	620
22.	Berkeley	631
	Postscript	644
	Index	646

List of Illustrations

Frontispiece: Drawing of his great-uncle Winton Dean by Rufus Hale

Plate Section between pages 334 & 335

1. Joseph Dean (1816-1895)
2. Harding Hewer Dean c. 1880
3. Elizabeth Mary Winton, 1880
4. Nicholaas Laurentius Van Gruisen (1824-1898)
5. Joseph Isaacs, 1894
6. Sara Isaacs
7. Rufus Isaacs
8. Harry Isaacs
9. Alfred Sutro c. 1905
10. Essie Sutro
11. Basil's mother
12. Esther as a girl
13. Wilfred Van Gruisen
14. Basil
15. Basil joins up
16. Hambledon Hurst 1918, with Ruby
17. Esther, Winton, Gran at Hambledon, 1918
18. Hambledon Hurst, June 1923
19. Esther in Switzerland, 1926
20. Tommy and Gran on Blackdown, 1926
21. Winton at Warden, Aug. 1928
22. Joe, Haricot, Margaret, Martin at Sheerness, Sept. 1928

23. Grandparents' Golden Wedding, 1932. Front row: Winton, Madeline, Vernon, Dorothy. Back row (5th left) Esther
24. Alfred and Essie Sutro at Hambledon c. 1932
25. Joe, Winton, Martin at the bungalow, 1933
26. Dean grandparents visit Warden, with Winton, Vernon, Esther, Dorothy, 1934
27. Gran at Hambledon, 1934
28. Tommy at Hambledon with Tiger, 1934
29. Little Easton Manor c. 1934
30. Winton and Joe birds-nesting at the Manor, April 1934
31. Esther at Hambledon, 1934
32. Eugene Bagger at Hambledon, 1934
33. Eugene and Esther by the pond, April 1934
34. Vicky, Tessa, Basil at the Manor, Aug. 1934
35. Tessa, Winton, Joe at the Manor, 1934
36. Winton on Loch Sunart with a catch of mackerel, Sept.1934
37. Hilary at Wittering, July 1935
38. Winton and Brigid Bartley at Hamble, July 1935
39. Churches expedition, July 1936. Kenneth Harrison and Philip Radcliffe (in car)
40. Winton at Salzburg, Aug. 1936
41. The Theseion, Sept. 1936
42. Byzantine church at Plataniti, 1936
43. Winton at Daphni, 1936
44. Basil in 1930s
45. Clare Mallory c. 1936
46. Thalia as Anya, 1938
47. Alexander Shaw, 2nd Baron Craigmyle
48. Thalia's mother Margaret
49. Alexander at Fairnilee c. 1936

List of Illustrations

50. Thalia, Rosamond Berridge, Ruth, Halsey Colchester, Donald at Fairnilee, Sept. 1938
51. Winton and Thalia at Hambledon, June 1939
52. Brigid at Hambledon, July 1945
53. Gran at Hambledon, July 1945
54. Brigid and Thalia, Aug. 1945
55. Stephen with Shenka, Aug. 1947
56. Philip Radcliffe, Eric Blom, Thalia, Stephen, Molly Blom, Diana McVeagh at Milford, June 1949
57. Grouse shoot at Peel, Aug. 1949. Winton (left) with Margaret
58. Freda and Lennox Berkeley at Milford with Thalia and Stephen, May 1950
59. The White House, June 1950
60. Diana, Hercules, Stephen at Milford, 1956
61. Pat Abraham, Diana Bromley, Diana, Gerald Abraham, Frances Abraham, Thalia, Nigel Fortune picnicking at Hambledon, June 1957
62. Calfshaw Cottage, 1958
63. Frank Walker
64. Winton and Thalia at Calfshaw on their silver wedding day

CHAPTER 1

Beginnings

One of the motives impelling those who sit down to write about their own lives is presumably vanity. We think we are important, or sufficiently important for other people to want to read about us. Even if we have no thought of publication, we still hope to be read by friends or relatives, and perhaps by others after we are dead. We are attempting a justification of our lives, or in the classical sense of the word an apology. To change the meaning, nearly all of us have a good deal to apologise for. We may have more specific motives: an urge to get our own back on those who have done us an injury, perhaps on society for constricting our ambitions or (as we may suppose) warping our lives. Freudians say that most of us bear a grudge against our parents, all the more potent if we have endeavoured, consciously or unconsciously, to conceal it.

There is nothing abnormal or shameful about this. No one after all is obliged to read us. But there is also something to be said for even the humblest autobiographer. I have never forgotten an episode told me by my grandmother more than fifty years ago about her own youth. She was on holiday, I think in the Lake District, with her brother and youngest sister, my Uncle Rufus and Aunt Essie, both of whom will recur later in this story. Two schoolmasters were staying in their hotel, and engaged them in a long conversation. Most of the talking was done by the schoolmasters, who, finding at least one sympathetic listener, enlarged on their past experiences and present hopes and fears, which were in no sense exceptional. When they had gone Essie, a clever and gifted woman but inclined to intolerance, asked Rufus how he had the patience to listen to such tedious stuff. He advised her never to dismiss other people's experiences out of hand: something of value might be learned even from the most unlikely quarters. I recalled this incident when I was staying with Rufus and his second wife at Walmer Castle in 1934. He was then Marquess of Reading, and had been Lord Chief Justice, Ambassador to the USA, Viceroy of India and Foreign Secretary. I was a callow undergraduate of eighteen who had spent one term at Cambridge. Rufus asked me many questions about what I was doing and what I hoped to do. I talked freely; he made me feel that my views were not only of interest to him but in some obscure way important, though they can have been nothing of the sort.

Rufus's attitude confirmed him in my eyes as a great man; it also convinced me that he was right. There *is* something to be learned from everyone's experience. As Janáček put it in the epigraph to his last opera *From the House of the Dead*, whose characters are all convicted criminals, 'in every creature a divine spark'. I do not flatter myself that my experience is of much value, but I am encouraged to put it on paper. That however is a defence, not a motive. What chiefly impels me is not so much a desire to justify myself but the urge to discover why my life has taken the course it has, and why it seems to me at least in part a failure. Looking back from the age of seventy-two, I am aware of a long succession of wrong turnings and missed opportunities. What I have achieved has been largely the result of accidents, and it is not nearly as much as it could have been. This may be the experience of many men; but in my case the stakes were higher than the average. As a child, eager to understand and follow Christian principles, I was much perplexed by the parable of the talents. Why was the man entrusted with one talent rebuked for keeping it safe, whereas the men with two and five talents were acclaimed for profiting from their manipulation of the stock market and doubling the endowment with which they were born? Of course it is clear now. If I was endowed with, say, four talents, I have made good use of two of them but buried the other two. It is not as if I was unaware of them; again and again I have taken them out, looked at them, and hurriedly returned them to their hiding-place, whence they have generated an intermittent sense of uneasiness and guilt.

I always knew that I possessed exceptional powers. Indeed I could not be unaware of it, since my performances at school and the reports of my masters constantly emphasised the fact. The decision on how they were to be used was a matter for me, and it was a decision, or series of decisions, that I found increasingly difficult to take. At first there was no great problem, though the seeds of future troubles and embarrassments were laid very early. I had merely to do my school work as well as I could, and since I had a vivid and retentive memory and great powers of application it was the easiest thing in the world to win prizes and scholarships. It was when my emotions were deeply stirred and set off all manner of internal convulsions that it began to dawn on me that I had the temperament of a creative artist and as a consequence was not destined for an easy life. I did not think I could set the world to rights, but was quite certain that I could externalise my experiences and create something of lasting value out of them.

As a result of this discovery, from my later schooldays on I have been deeply divided. One half of me wished to launch out on the high seas of imagination and create things outside myself; the other half wanted to record, examine and criticise, to assess and pronounce upon the creative achievements of others. Both halves were very powerful, and for a long time they fought so furiously that they threatened to neutralise each other. I am not sure how it is possible to combine creative and critical activity on the highest level, though it can certainly be done at low and medium pressure. For me the pressure was always high, since I am incapable of following any course of action without carrying it to the extreme limit within the range of my abilities. This no doubt is an obsessive characteristic, and it may help to explain why the critical-intellectual side of my personality, which I fear has grown more and more obsessive with time, has nearly always been victorious. But it was not a bloodless or total victory; the underdog has continued to struggle and squirm.

Nor have I much doubt that the better side lost. It requires more courage and a thicker skin to pursue the career of a creative artist in a world that is likely to be more or less hostile than to pursue a life of scholarly research in study or library. The latter is not only easier; it is less beneficial. Even an artist of the second rank may be more useful to the community than a good scholar who feeds on the work of others. On the other hand the finest scholars and critics harbour a failed or potential artist within; it is the understanding derived from this that exalts them above the common run. I do not think I lack courage, but I do lack the extra protective skin, the impermeable self-confidence, that preserves the serious artist from discouragement when he meets misunderstanding and contempt. And such skins as I do possess have at crucial times been heavily battered by misfortunes that I had no means of foreseeing or avoiding. It is possible, though this is no ultimate defence, that the vital extra layer of confidence which might have developed was a victim of these early struggles.

But if in some respects I have had more than my share of ill luck, I have been equally fortunate in others, as this account will show. Bad luck should never be blamed for failure; it may offer an explanation, but never an excuse. Beethoven was one of the unluckiest men who ever lived. Moreover, as Gertrude Stein once observed, little artists can suffer all the agonies of great artists without the reward of belonging to their company. If luck is the aggregate of the impact made on our lives by outer circumstances and environment, an estimate of these forces can be interesting and revealing.

I am writing this at a time of enforced idleness, not with a view to publication but to clear my mind about what I have left undone, and to answer the question Why? Much of what I record will be of no interest to the general public; some of it could offend persons still living or appear to dishonour the memory of the dead. Nevertheless if this is to be an honest enquiry I must set it all down, even if it has to be suppressed or subjected to the equivalent of the thirty-year rule imposed on politically sensitive material.

* * * * *

It has often occurred to me that there were few limits to the eccentricity that could have sprung from the heterogeneous collection of genes I inherited. The attempt to identify the separate strains, though unlikely to prove anything, has always fascinated me, and may point the way to some of the contradictions in my character. Many of my forebears are interesting on their own account. They were a very mixed lot, in nationality, blood, background, temperament, profession, taste and almost every other imaginable respect. On any rational computation my parents should probably never have married or produced children, though that is not a point I am in a position to labour. They were both very gifted. My father, Basil Dean, was the second son and third child of a worthy, pious and (on the surface) rather dull Croydon family, which had no discoverable links with the arts, except that my father's Aunt Nellie married an architect, Arnold Dunbar-Smith. My grandfather Harding Hewer Dean, was named after the two doctors who brought him into the world, four of his elder siblings having died in infancy, as did three of their four successors. It is possible that the same principle of nomenclature was applied to others of the brood, one of whom was christened Pinkerton Jenns. I was however not to relish the thought of having an Uncle Pinkerton, for he died in 1854 at the age of two, long before the days of Belasco and Puccini. My great-grandmother also had an unusual name: she was born Philadelphia Haslock. This was evidently a family name, for she had an aunt, two cousins and a daughter all called Philadelphia. When in the 1960s I began to write a detective story I proposed to hide my identity under my great-grandmother's name, since most successful detective stories seemed to be written by women. Mine however was never finished.

My great-grandfather, Joseph Dean, one of many to bear that name, who appears in photographs as a venerable patriarch with a large spade-shaped beard, had twelve children and was himself one of twenty (the progeny of another Joseph, a baker at Deptford), several of whom emigrated to Tasmania in the 1830s. Although I had been intrigued by the postscript to my grandparents' 1882 wedding announcement, 'Tasmanian papers, please copy', I knew nothing of my Australian relatives until quite recently, when a third-cousin in Sydney, Ken Dean, wrote to me out of the blue. (He was descended from the second Joseph's brother, William Boswell Dean.) We subsequently exchanged much genealogical information.

The discovery of the Australian Deans threw quite a new light on the family. They were pioneers and, in the best sense, adventurers. William Boswell must have been a formidable figure. By trade a baker like his father, he had in his youth manufactured ships' biscuits or hard tack at the Royal Arsenal in Deptford. On emigrating he set up Australia's first biscuit factory at Launceston, and then branched out into mining (coal, gold and tin), saw-milling, ship-building, horse-breeding and many other commercial activities. He was credited with establishing the coal-mining industry in northern Tasmania and opening up the port of Devonport and its hinterland for trade. He exported wheat and flour to England, Tasmanian products to the goldfields of California, and sheep to the Sandwich Islands (Hawaii), and fitted out a ship for sperm-whaling. At the Great Exhibition of 1851 he was awarded a medal, though it is not clear which of his products was so honoured. With all of this he was a strict teetotaller, who helped found a paper, *The Teetotal Advocate* (which ran for two years at a considerable loss), wrote many letters to the press in favour of immigration, and promoted other worthy causes. One of these was the establishment of Government Savings Bonds, another led to the abandonment in 1853 of the transportation of convicts to Tasmania.

William Boswell was described as a tall and very powerful man who covered immense distances on foot, and once knocked out a prize-fighter hired to break up a temperance procession. His voice, said to have carried from his bakery to the wharf at Launceston, proved useful before the invention of the telephone. Though often in financial difficulties and bankrupt at least once, he died a respected citizen and left a book, *Notorious Bushrangers of Tasmania*, published posthumously in 1891 under the pseudonym Cabby. I was startled to find this in the British Library catalogue listed with my works under W.B. Dean, but the copy proved to have been destroyed by bombing during the War. My cousin Ken sent me some xeroxed pages, which suggest that the title was partly camouflage. It is a polemical work directed not so much against bushrangers, who behaved no worse than anyone else, as against the early settlers, soldiers as well as convicts, and the absurd and criminal negligence of the British Government, the transporting authority, in omitting to strike a balance between the sexes. The whole final section of the book deals with the escape to America, assisted by William Boswell, of Irish prisoners sentenced for sedition and rebellion in 1848.

Three of William Boswell's sisters, like him, married in Tasmania and did much to populate the young colony. The eldest, Catherine (Aunt Kate), who never married, was co-founder of the first Sunday School in Launceston and became a pillar of the Methodist Church, living a life as rich in educational and philanthropic work as it was long in years; she was born before Waterloo and died after the Boer War. Their cousin, another William, became a prosperous farmer and a magistrate in the Derwent valley near Hobart. One of his sons joined the California gold rush in 1850 and wrote about his experiences in a book (of which I possess a copy). A grand-daughter, Amy Sherwin (Mme Hugo Gorlitz), seems to have been a predecessor of Joan Sutherland; she was known as the Tasmanian Nightingale. According to Australian tradition all these Deans, and therefore my branch as well, descended from a landowning family that played a prominent part on the Roundhead side in the Civil War. One of them presumably was Admiral Richard Deane, who was killed in battle against the Dutch off the North Foreland in 1653.

Ken's enthusiasm for genealogy led me to explore some old legal documents of the late eighteenth and early nineteenth century left by my father. These not only tied in neatly with the Australian branch but extended the family tree two generations further back, revealing one or two skeletons in the process. One relative in 1792 was the subject of a writ *de lunatico inquirando*, whereby his brother-in-law was required to produce him at 'the Orange Coffeehouse in Chelsea aforesaid near Ranelagh' for examination by the Commissioners, 'to inquire whether [he] be a Lunatick or not'. This brother-in-law, James Jones, uncle of Joseph Dean I, was both a publican and a sinner. He kept a tavern, the Mermaid in Royal Hospital Row, Chelsea, and in a prolix Will made elaborate financial arrangements for the maintenance of 'my natural child James Millin begotten on the body of Elizabeth Millin' – who was less than a year old when Jones died in February 1802. The Mermaid evidently did good business: Jones's wine-merchant's bill for 1797 specifies 142 gallons of cognac, 122 of bordeaux, 276 of port, and no fewer than 537 of rum. Perhaps it is not surprising that some cadet branches became addicted to temperance.

Another relic is a heavy album full of old studio photographs, leather-bound with metal clasps, weighing seven pounds and adorned with seventeen coloured engravings of flowering shrubs and a lush quotation from Longfellow. It bears a copperplate inscription: 'Presented to Mr H.H. Dean with best wishes for his happiness & prosperity from his friends and fellow teachers at St Saviours Sunday School Croydon 6th January 1882', eleven days before his wedding. Ken sent me photographs of several of William Boswell's and Joseph II's sisters, remarkable for the exceptional length and massiveness of their noses, with a view to my matching them with those in the album. One or two were unmistakable, but although my grandparents had scrupulously filled every space, with rare exceptions they omitted to supply identifications. Nose-growing seems to have been a function of the Tasmanian climate; photographs of Aunt Kate at different ages show that organ developing most impressively with the passage of years.

The album and its contents convey an aroma of musty Victorianism that reminds me vividly of my paternal grandparents' house – or houses, for they moved more than once – as I remember it in my childhood. The rooms were always rather dark; the windows were seldom open; an unmarried aunt usually hovered in the background; above all, there was a lack of emotional warmth, all the more perceptible by contrast with my maternal grandparents. I seemed to have stepped back into another age, utterly remote from that in which I lived at home. The atmosphere of piety, though not oppressive, was something I did not understand. When I was about five – I think when I was sent down to Croydon while my brother Joe was born – my grandfather took me to a children's service, probably the first time I had entered a church since my christening. He told me to kneel down and stand up when he did, and in general to follow his example. Observing that he uttered the word 'Amen' in a loud voice at more or less regular intervals, I concluded that this was the right thing to do, and when the parson paused in the course of what seemed a very long speech I interjected my own 'Amen'. He looked faintly surprised; I had interrupted his sermon.

My grandmother came from a rather higher rank of society than her husband. She was Elizabeth Mary Winton, the eldest child of a Kent family claiming descent from the Huguenots; there was also a Dutch strain – Dunk or Van Dunk. Her father had died young, in mysterious circumstances, at the age of thirty-two. The family had a coat of arms, and early in the century possessed a smart coach, whose horses were adorned with the family crest, a wheatsheaf (years later my father gave me a small brass emblem, the only relic of those accoutrements). But they had come down in the world, owing to an uncle's misappropriation of trust funds. Even so Mrs Winton took strong exception to her daughter's proposed marriage, and for a time cut off her allowance. There was financial stringency in the new household too. My grandfather, who was in the tobacco business, had a partner who absconded with the firm's funds, and considered it his duty to repay the creditors out of his own pocket, a process that took at least ten years. Even to my eyes as a child my grandmother, the older by two years, was the dominant partner in the marriage. She may secretly have despised her husband (my father heard her say 'All that praying wears out his trousers'); certainly he was relegated to second place.

It seems possible that there was some genetic weakness in this branch of the family. Of my great-grandparents' twelve children, only four grew up, only two married, and Harding Hewer alone had children. Of his five, four grew up, only the two older sons married, and my father alone had issue. The eldest, Vernon, became a tea-planter in India, where he contracted syphilis. He was thought to be cured, married a wife (Violet, shortened to Vie) whom we all liked enormously, and when I first remember him appeared to be a jovial country squire with no artistic or intellectual interests of any kind. His subsequent decline, due to a recurrence of his disease, became inextricably entangled with my life and will be narrated later. The youngest of the family, Duncan, died in infancy. My grandmother preserved his memory by having him photographed in his cot after death, surrounded by cut flowers. This touch of mawkishness was somehow typical. Neither of the daughters, Madeline and Dorothy, married. Dorothy suffered from ill health – rheumatic I think – and lived at home; I never saw her after the death of her parents. She horrified my father and me by giving the family Bible – from which I had fortunately copied most of the details above, dating back to the early 18th century – for salvage during the War. Madeline was a portent. She taught English at Bedford College for Women and was the epitome of a schoolmistress, emotionally repressed and without a touch of humour. When at the age of sixteen I had some Wordsworthian verses about the scenery round Geneva printed in *The Harrovian*, she demanded to see them, adjusted her pince-nez at an aggressive angle and pronounced her verdict: 'Just as I thought. Not an original line in the whole thing'. Quite true - but what did she expect? In one of my early letters of thanks for a Christmas present I horrified her by spelling her name 'Magdalene'. She became mentally disturbed towards the end of her life, and complained that people insisted on sticking bodkins into her. The psychologist would have a word for this.

* * * * *

I knew all four of my grandparents, the first of whom did not die until I was twenty-one. Both couples achieved golden weddings, but that was about the only thing they had in common. My mother's father, Albert Van Gruisen, came from a musical family in the north Dutch province of Friesland. His great-grandfather, Albertus Van Gruisen (1741-1824), was a distinguished organ-builder, responsible for many organs in Friesian churches and later in other parts of the country. The family was Roman Catholic, but he worked for churches of all denominations. I have a list of eleven organs built or renovated by him, of which the eighth (1811) was recorded as the twenty-ninth built by the firm. The climax of his career was perhaps the restoration of the famous organ in the Grootkerk at Alkmaar in 1822. His third son, another Albertus (1786-1831) followed him in the business, which was carried on in the next generation. He died of a chill caught when visiting his eldest son, who had been wounded in the war in which Belgium gained her independence from Holland. His third son, Nicolaas Laurentius (anglicised as Nicolas Laurence), migrated in the 1840s to Liverpool, where he founded an organ and piano business and married a Staffordshire girl, Anne Clegg Jenkinson. He was evidently something of a live wire. At his funeral in 1898, six years after the death of his wife, the family was disconcerted by the appearance of a strange woman in deep mourning. They had never suspected the old man of taking a mistress.

My grandfather Albert Henry Van Gruisen was the fifth of a family of nine, two of whom died in infancy. He had two brothers; both were musical and entered the firm. I never knew either of them. Nicholas, who was my mother's godfather, died before I was born. He interested me as the only Van Gruisen to venture into print; in his youth he published a curious little book describing a holiday in Iceland. This appeared in 1879 and is one of the earliest volumes to feature in the family library which I began to collect before the war, and which now contains 160 volumes by nearly 40 authors. The youngest brother, Horace, was never mentioned during my childhood. I was given to understand that he had gone to the bad. This of course raised my curiosity; I learned eventually that he had two grave weaknesses, which caused his dismissal from the firm. They were Women and Drink. My mother visited him once and said he was perfectly charming, with a delightful sense of humour, and much more relaxed than his brothers and sisters. The example of Uncle Horace was largely responsible for the horror expressed by my grandfather whenever as a schoolboy I came within striking distance of a glass of wine or even beer. His fears were increased by the fate of a nephew by marriage, who lived up to his name of Beveridge and died of alcoholism.

For sufficient reasons, no doubt including the fact that he was tone-deaf, the piano business was not considered a suitable career for my grandfather. He was apprenticed to a fruit-broker, proved a hardworking and successful business man, and rose to become senior partner in the Liverpool firm of Connolly Shaw and Company. I knew three of his four sisters. They were all very short, as stiff as ramrods in their carriage, and to every appearance highly conventional. Aunt Aggie (Agatha), the eldest, I only met once, at her grand-daughter Myrtle Adamson's wedding reception, when she seized a large plate of cakes, placed a glass of champagne in the midst of them, led me into a corner, and sat down on a diminutive chair which had been made for me as a child. Here she held a kind of court, her sharp gestures alternating with the consumption of refreshments. I was told that at my mother's wedding she was the only relative who made catty remarks. Aunt Kate and Aunt Emmy, who lived to be 97 and 87 respectively, I found much more congenial, especially when they went out of their way to supply me with facts and dates for the family tree.

My grandmother's family was much more exotic. When the second Marquess of Reading was preparing to write his father's biography, he employed a genealogist to enquire into his forebears. This produced some interesting results, and further research added others. The primeval Isaacs, recorded only as Isaac, came apparently from Germany in the early eighteenth century and settled at Chelmsford. His great-grandson Michael Isaacs founded the firm of M. Isaacs and Sons, fruit-brokers, in London and married Sara Mendoza, from another Jewish family which had already produced a ritual slaughterer (author of a book on his craft which he seems to have written in Hebrew and translated into Spanish in 1732), a woman described as an exorciser of evil spirits, and two prize-fighters, one of whom, Daniel Mendoza (1764-1836), who sired 11 children, was the most celebrated pugilist of his day and the author of an autobiography. I once saw him enacted in a film about William Pitt. Among his direct descendants was the comedian Peter Sellers. The Mendozas were supposed to be related to Disraeli; the connection was not proved, but the younger members of the Isaacs family referred to the statesman familiarly as Uncle Ben.

Michael and Sara Isaacs had two sons, Henry, who in 1889 became the first Jewish Lord Mayor of London and received the customary knighthood, and Joseph, my great-grandfather, who married Sara, eldest of the fourteen children of Daniel Davis, china and glass merchant, and his wife Frances Marks. My grandmother and her elder sister Nellie told me many amusing stories about the Davis clan, which produced two novelists, two dramatists, two criminals and the author and journalist J.B. Morton (Beachcomber). Daniel Davis was a vain old man who used to dye his hair and dry it before an open window. When his wife had borne him fourteen children, she said: 'I've had enough. If you want any more you can go elsewhere'. And he did – if indeed he had not done so already, for whenever his wife was about to give birth he went off to Paris to enjoy himself. It was generally assumed that he had a girlfriend there. The Davis sons were all remarkably handsome, and much pursued by women. Two of them went to South Africa and were involved in gold and diamond mining. One at least, Godfrey, was a shameless philanderer who made an unhappy marriage and was always in debt. His only daughter, Beatrice, had the misfortune to 'marry' a Portuguese bigamist. She had a daughter, Adrienne Leonie, by Leoncavallo's brother and a son (father unidentified), George John Seaton, who was sent to Devil's Island as a persistent criminal and wrote a book about it, ghosted by a journalist from *The People*. Although I never met him, he made several attempts to extract money from me. Beatrice settled in Paris and lived to the age of 97.

Of the Davis daughters, Fanny had the looks of a Spanish gypsy. She lived for some time in Peru and came back with a parrot which had a remarkable gift for song, pausing at intervals to remark 'Shut the door, Laura' (its own name) and 'Go away, you nasty children'. Phoebe, who lived to be 98, was a frivolous coquette. Her eldest son, Victor, was reputed to have been murdered in South Africa, but according to another account he died after colliding with a drunken waiter carrying a tray of knives. Her youngest son, Edgar, swindled his cousin Rufus Isaacs out of a large sum of money. Since he was a relation Rufus did not prosecute, but destiny caught Edgar in the end: he was killed in 1941 in a London air raid. Lizzie was an extravagant numbskull who refused £500 a year as insufficient compensation when her business collapsed in South America, and lived to regret it. Jane, who never married, was short and fat, and always willing to help her nephews Harry and Rufus when they got into a scrape and were afraid to go home. When Epstein's carving Rima was unveiled, she was heard to observe: 'I could strip better than that!' She enjoyed her glass of whisky to the end of her life, and like Phoebe died at 98.

Three of the sisters married two brothers. Henry Miller married Phoebe; William Miller married first Esther, who died in childbirth, and then her younger sister Lizzie. Each of William's marriages produced a writer of fiction, though of a very different kind. Esther's son Leonard took the name Merrick and was well known in his day; a collected edition of his novels and stories was published in 1918-22 in 14 volumes, each with an introduction by a well-known author. He and my grandmother were the same age, and close friends in their youth. His wife and daughter also contributed to the family library. Lizzie's daughter, another Esther, wrote serial thrillers for trashy papers and at least one book. She made a good deal of money, but was exploited and overworked by her mother and finally went out of her mind. The William Millers lived at 19 Belsize Park, next door to the Isaacs family at 21. Miller, according to my grandmother, was a horrid little man, full of fads, who refused to let the Isaacs children play in his garden. They took their revenge by tearing up all the newspapers in the house and on a Sunday morning, when Miller was about to invite his friends to admire his spick-and-span garden, discharged the fragments over the wall. They were duly punished, but could see from their parents' expressions that the sympathy was on their side.

Joseph and Sara Isaacs had nine children, of whom my grandmother, Florence Angela (she was known as Florrie and detested her second name), was the sixth. They were all exceptionally gifted. Two of the sons died young, one as the result of an accident at school. I knew six of them and can just remember a seventh (we are a long-lived family; two of the Isaacs forbears and one Davis topped the century, and quite a number reached the nineties). I recall being taken to see my great-grandmother, who then lived at Dulwich with a companion called Miss Jones and retained traces of her formidable youth. She had been a veritable matriarch. She had no intellectual interests, no women friends and an uncertain temper, took no exercise, read worthless novels and played endless games of cards, but kept her easy-going husband and her exuberant brood under firm control by sheer force of personality. They were a close-knit and sociable family. In the 1860s they lived at 1 Belsize Park, Hampstead, then for more than twenty years from 1869 at 21 Belsize Avenue with grandmother Marks, Uncle Henry and (after her marriage) Nellie nearby in a little colony.

The eldest daughter Frances (Fran) dramatised Tolstoy's novel *Resurrection* and wrote an authoritative book on French household cooking. The second, Nellie, was a competent journalist. Esther (Essie), the youngest of the family, was a talented painter, especially in pastels, wrote a book about Poussin, and married the dramatist Alfred Sutro: there will be much to say about both of them later. Florrie was also a painter; she and Essie studied professionally in Paris. The sons all suffered from being thrust into the fruit-broking business as soon as they left school at sixteen; none went to university. The eldest, Harry, was considered the brightest of the family, much more so than Rufus, who was a year younger. The fourth son, Godfrey (always known as Jack) was a successful businessman who achieved fame, or notoriety, as managing director of the Marconi company at the time of the scandal in 1912. Fred, the youngest, had literary tastes; he wrote plays and translated Lope de Vega. After several disappointments in love he rather went to pieces, lived wildly and died in his thirties from tuberculosis contracted in Spain.

Several of the children had musical talent. In this they took after their parents. Joseph possessed an artistic temperament and a beautiful but untrained tenor voice as well as a natural ear. Since his wife was a contralto, his brother Henry a bass and his sister-in-law a soprano they formed a natural quartet and used to sing excerpts from Italian opera, including the *Rigoletto* quartet, in impromptu home concerts. Henry and his wife both had some musical training.

Fran and Nellie gained diplomas from the Royal Academy of Music, one as a pianist, the other as a singer. Rufus was a light baritone. Florrie loved music but was no great performer. She told me that on one occasion her mother asked her to sing, and when she had finished said: 'Ah, you should have heard *me* sing when I was young.' She did have literary leanings, and wrote a story about a knight who returned from many years in the Holy Land with stirring tales of his adventures; to which his wife replied 'I too have not been idle' and exhibited a row of small children. The laughter that greeted this may have extinguished her literary ambition. The family had a box at Covent Garden, and my grandmother recalled an occasion when the tenor missed a top note and her father gave it him from the box. The parents particularly disliked Meyerbeer's *Le Prophète*; whenever it was performed they sent two or more of the children, till my grandmother was heartily sick of the three Anabaptists. This must have been in 1878-83, when the opera was given each season. The family regularly attended the original productions of the Savoy operettas.

Harry was not musical; indeed he took pride in being a Philistine. I remember the glee with which he shocked his sisters by denouncing Van Gogh and the Impressionists. As a young man he was always the leader, full of irrepressible high spirits; he often led Rufus into mischief. His weakness was that he preferred to be king of a small castle rather than a subordinate in a big one. Even in old age he was a man of extraordinary vitality. He lived to be 91 and only died because he said he was tired of life and refused to eat; after the death of his first wife, when well into his eighties, he married the nurse who had attended her and then apparently thought better of it. He was all his life an incorrigible joker. My grandmother told me many stories about him. One Christmas he invited the waits up to the dining-room and asked them to play, having previously stuffed the bells of their instruments with loaves of bread. When all the family

Beginnings

except the two eldest girls were still living at home he came down to breakfast to find on the sideboard a ham which had reappeared, as hams sometimes do, for several consecutive mornings, without being sensibly diminished. 'Don't you think we've had enough of this ham?' he said, and picking it up tossed it to his nearest brother. It was passed on round the table until it came back to Harry, who pitched it through the window into Belsize Park.

In later life he answered the telephone one morning to be greeted by a strange voice, who evidently had the wrong number: 'This is your tailor, sir. Have you any orders today?' 'Yes', said Harry at once, 'make me a new dress suit as quickly as you can', and put the phone down. On one occasion the joke was on him. He dozed off after dinner with the radio on, and shot out of his chair on hearing the announcer say: 'Harry Isaacs will now play Beethoven's Moonlight Sonata'. There was a well-known pianist of the same name. When at the age of about eighteen I became interested in the family and began to construct genealogical trees, I consulted all available great-aunts and uncles. Harry gave me a number of biographical particulars and character sketches. I remember the relish with which he described one of his nephew Marcel's three wives: 'She was a spicy tart!' Marcel Isaacs's career was nothing if not adventurous in other respects than matrimony: according to a press cutting of 1933 he had been agent to the King of Italy's equerry in the Turko-Bulgarian war of 1911-12, was badly wounded on the Somme, spent eighteen months in Canada as 'everything from picture show singer to mining-camp cook' (he described this in a book, *Adventures and Misadventures, or An Undergraduate's Experiences in Canada*, by 'Lofty'), became a playwright and journalist, studied art in Paris, and was proposing to retire to a tiny cottage in Devon and devote the rest of his life to painting.

Rufus was a charmer and the peace-maker of the family, constantly patching up quarrels between his parents. He had many interests, and put his sister Florrie on to reading J.S. Mill. The story of his early life with its many failures, his first sight of India as a humble ship's boy and his second as Viceroy, is familiar from the biographies. I do not need to detail his career, but he took more than an avuncular interest in mine. His grandson Michael, later the third marquess, was born in the same month as me and was pursuing a rather lowly career at Eton while I was winning a succession of classical prizes at Harrow, and Rufus and Gran jokingly suggested an exchange. My visits to him at Deal and Walmer Castles will be described later. He was a most impressive man, and developed a refreshing habit of honouring me with £5 notes. When his son Gerald published the first volume of his father's life in 1942, my grandmother told me that his account of Rufus's engagement and marriage, presumably obtained from Lady Reading, was romanticised and false. She gave me the following account, which I wrote down at the time.

Rufus was privately engaged to the daughter of a diamond millionaire named Ochs. Alice Cohen was a close friend of this girl, and through her came to know Rufus. She suggested to him that Miss Ochs, who had shrunk from asking her father's consent to the marriage, was playing with him, and that he should ask her to marry him without this consent. He did so, and was refused. Later Miss Ochs went back on the refusal, but by this time Rufus, who could never resist a pretty girl, had drifted into an engagement with Alice. It was not the Cohens but the Isaacs's who were opposed to the marriage, on the ground that Rufus (a) had no money and few prospects, and (b) was changeable in his affections. Nor was Rufus at all happy about the engagement. Finally he wrote to Alice breaking it off and went away, leaving his address with his sisters Florrie and Essie and telling them to communicate with him only in case of serious emergency. His excuse had been that Alice and her sister had been stricken with a form of deafness (which was true) and that his parents considered it inadvisable for him to contract a marriage in such circumstances (which was not true). On receiving the letter Alice suffered a nervous collapse, and her condition was described as serious. Florrie went to see the doctor to satisfy herself on this point, and then sent a telegram recalling Rufus. He renewed the engagement, strongly urged and supported by the Cohens, who allowed the couple £500 a year for two years until such time as Rufus should make good. The marriage was very happy, though Alice suffered all her life from deafness.

Essie, by some years the youngest of the family, was very spoiled as a child, which permanently affected her character. She and Florrie used to fight like cats as children, but became close friends when they found a common interest in painting, and remained so until Essie's death fifty years later. They were however very unalike in temperament. At the age of sixteen Essie insisted on leaving school and learning to paint professionally, which Florrie already did. Their parents agreed to their attending an art school in Paris provided they paid their way. They raised the money by copying pictures at the National Gallery. This single-mindedness astonished their parents. Essie promptly fell in love with Paris and persuaded Florrie to join her in a vow: they would never marry, but would live for ART. It was on one of her early visits to the continent, either in Paris or Brussels, that my grandmother caught sight of the benign white-haired figure of Liszt, who made an impression that she never forgot.

Alfred Sutro was introduced to the family by Florrie about 1880, and for years she was supposed to be engaged to him, which indeed was his wish. (The daughters took pleasure in concealing the true situation from their parents, who never knew which boy friend belonged to whom.) The family found Alfred amusing, but could not bring themselves to take him as seriously as he took himself. He was vain and a little pompous, dressed like a dandy, and possessed a curiously patchy sense of humour (I was to verify this nearly fifty years later). Florrie despised him because he played cards with elder members of the family and recommended French novels to the Mater, as Mrs Isaacs was always known. Harry in particular liked to pull his leg. On one occasion he contrived, without being noticed, to extract Alfred's hinder shirt-tails before he went riding; on another, having induced Alfred to climb up a creeper to the first-floor window, he slammed the window and left him suspended.

Essie was never really in love with Alfred, but could not bear anyone else to have him. During one of her off-periods Alfred proposed to Marie Cathcart, later Harry Isaacs's first wife, and was accepted; but Essie rushed back to Alfred, and he had to explain to Marie that it was all a mistake. His first proposal to Essie was also accidental; they were all trying to persuade Essie to go to a dance, and Alfred in desperation said he would propose to her if she came. She did, and took him seriously. He subsequently confided his embarrassment to Florrie, but once having made the proposal thought he ought to stick to it. After she had kept him on a string for seven years they were married in Paris in 1894. A year or two later Essie fell violently in love with A.B. Walkley, a friend of Alfred's and later dramatic critic of *The Times*, who was staying with them at Studland, where C.F.A. Voysey had built them a house. She wanted to run away with Walkley, but as a family man he preferred to keep his job at the Post Office. However they enjoyed a clandestine love affair which lasted more than twenty years and wrecked her marriage. Essie was happy with Alfred only in the last few years before his death, when she bitterly regretted her earlier refusal to have children. I remember her pointing to me and my brothers and saying pathetically: 'These are all I have'.

* * * * *

My grandparents first met through Harry Isaacs. My grandfather told my mother how it happened. He was a man who planned his actions with his head and then, as often as not, allowed his heart to get the better of him. He had decided to marry; he was thirty, in a sound financial position, and had met and liked a girl called Betty with a good background – always an important consideration with him – who he thought would make him a satisfactory wife. Knowing that the Isaacs family had taken a house on the Thames for the summer, and that Betty was due to stay with them, he persuaded Harry (a colleague in the fruit business) to invite him down from Liverpool for a weekend. 'When I got there, she had a little sore on her lip, so – well, I thought I would wait a day or two. And then – I SAW YOUR MOTHER!' Her vow to sacrifice marriage to art went by the board, and Essie never forgave him; she constantly referred to him as the Philistine (which in a sense he was).

They were married six months later, on 23 January 1890. Sir Henry Isaacs, then Lord Mayor, laid on a wedding breakfast at the Mansion House; my grandfather gave me a copy of the menu, which was positively Lucullan in its proportions, but I lost it along with photographs of him as a young man when my wallet was stolen many years ago. The young couple were more than once entertained by their distinguished relative. Sir Henry subsequently put together a strange book called *Memoirs of my Mayoralty*, of which there is a copy in the British Library. He had it published privately, with no title page, imprint or index and the many plates uncaptioned. It was a scissors and paste job, comprising press reports, minutes of meetings, and the speeches of political and church leaders and other functionaries, including Sir Henry himself. From it we learn that Florrie and Essie, together with Sir Henry's daughter, were Maids of Honour to the Lady Mayoress at his inauguration. On 6 October 1890 the Lord Mayor gave a banquet for the delegates to the Congrès Littéraire et Artistique Internationale, at which the list of guests included Mrs Lynn Linton, Professor Max-Müller, R.D. Blackmore, James McNeill Whistler, Augustus Harris, Frank Harris, Max Nordau, Edmund Gosse, Henry Arthur Jones, Oscar Wilde and Mr and Mrs A. Van Gruisen.

The marriage surprised both families. Although the Isaacs children had recoiled from the strict Jewish faith of their parents Florrie was the first to marry a Gentile. Moreover they seemed to have nothing in common; all her friends thought she was making a foolish mistake. My grandfather had no interest in the arts. Despite his family's profession, he was not only unmusical; he was tone-deaf. He told me that he had only once been to a concert and once to an opera in his life. The concert was given by Sousa and his band in Liverpool; he could not remember the name of the opera, but it was the silliest stuff – the hero was pulled on to the stage by a goose. The opera was evidently *Lohengrin*.

He was a successful businessman of striking honesty and the most upright standards. It was this rocklike sense of values on which the marriage was based. My grandmother often told me this, pointing out that her artistic and cultural interests could always be satisfied by friends and relatives. Nor was she infatuated with him; she was not much interested in sex and derived little pleasure from it. She married him because she could rely on him absolutely. As she put it, common tastes are a luxury; principles are what count. In his family he was known as Bertie, and that was how she addressed him in the only love letter that survives (they kept all their letters to each other, but despite my violent protests my mother destroyed nearly all their papers as well as her own shortly before her death). She soon decided that Bertie was not a suitable name. At first, when her friends asked her what she called him, she replied that she did not have to call him – he was always there. Then she settled on Tommy, and Tommy he became, not only to contemporaries but to his children and grandchildren. He was also known as the Colonel, on account of his upright bearing, firm handshake and trim little moustache; for a long time I thought he really was a colonel. He had his formidable side, particularly as a young man. He had been educated partly at Jena soon after the Franco-Prussian War, and perhaps retained a touch of Prussian rigour, though this was leavened by a delightful sense of humour. Whenever there was an emotional upset in the family, for example over the growing unhappiness of my mother's marriage and the steps leading to her divorce, my grandmother's first reaction was: 'We must keep it from the Colonel'. When the time came for revelation, it was generally found that he knew about it from the beginning.

Alfred Sutro had been furious when Florrie began to show an interest in Tommy. When he and Tommy were both staying with the Isaacs family on the river, and Tommy was waiting for the chance to propose, Alfred refused to leave them alone and made a thorough nuisance of himself. Later, when they were married and living in Birkenhead, he visited them and shocked old friends of Tommy's by flirting outrageously with Florrie at dinner. Tommy refused to leave them together when it was time to go to bed, and when Alfred again came north refused to put him up, although it was the weekend of the Grand National and he knew there would be no accommodation in the Liverpool area. He never discovered where Alfred spent that night, and subsequently felt guilty. However friendly relations were restored after Alfred's marriage to Essie, helped perhaps by the fact that for the first two years the Sutros lived in Paris.

I was devoted to both my mother's parents, and their homes in Birkenhead, London and Hambledon in Surrey were always a source of great happiness and a haven of security. This as it turned out was very fortunate. My grandmother, quite apart from the liveliness of mind and breadth of interests characteristic of all the Isaacs family, had a remarkable flair for treating everyone of whatever class or generation as equals. Her servants stayed with her all their working lives; the cook and the housemaid whom I knew when I was nearly grown up had been with her during my mother's childhood. When I was at Cambridge she encouraged me to invite my friends down for weekends. Gran treated us as if we were her contemporaries, and there was no subject that could not be discussed or in which she failed to show an interest. I once found her engaged in a detailed discussion with two of my friends about sex life in Newnham and Girton.

My grandparents had three children, of whom my mother was the eldest and the only girl. The younger son, Wilfred, was by common consent the brightest and most gifted, besides possessing great personal charm. He joined the army in 1915, won the Military Cross during the Battle of the Somme for an act of great gallantry (saving the lives of sixteen of his men by digging them out under heavy fire) at the age of 18½, and died of wounds soon after his nineteenth birthday. With modern antiseptic drugs his life could have been saved. His elder brother Harry was something of a puzzle to his mother and sister. He inherited his father's lack of interest in the arts – he was even more of a Philistine than his uncle Harry Isaacs – but neither his business brain nor his mother's vivid intelligence. Gran and my mother both expressed surprise that the combination of Jewish and Dutch blood could produce such a typically phlegmatic Englishman. He became a director of Connolly Shaw and a Birkenhead town councillor, but although everyone liked him he never seemed to achieve much. He always struck me as genial, companionable and a little stupid. I discovered later that his life had been blighted by a stroke of cruel ill-luck. He married a Scottish girl, the daughter and niece of family friends, only to discover on his honeymoon that she was a confirmed lesbian. He eventually obtained a legal separation, but damaged his liver by over-indulgence in gin and committed suicide at the age of nearly 77. He did however leave a son to carry on the Van Gruisen name; the only two other bearers of it in his generation had both lost their lives in the 1914-18 war.

My mother, Esther (named after her aunt Essie), was more like Wilfred than Harry, but in her too the balance of genes seems to have been imperfect. She was basically an intellectual with a good brain and a feeling for the arts, especially literature and music, but little creative talent. She published one novel and wrote at least one more, *Feather in the Wind*, which also existed as a play (I forget which came first). Her critical faculty was well developed, and she was useful to my father and Alec Rea as a reader of plays submitted to their management. I sometimes read them too, and remember at the age of twelve or thirteen feeling sorry for the authors doomed to have their work rejected. For some years she also contributed a column on London theatrical affairs to *The Sheffield Daily Telegraph*. (She complained later when the tax authorities discovered this and demanded payment of the arrears due.) When her novel *Rule of Three* was published in 1923, St John Ervine told her that it was far better constructed than anyone had a right to expect from a beginner but the dialogue was dull and the characters insufficiently interesting. She accepted this judgment. Earlier, in 1918, she had a short story published in the New York magazine *The Smart Set*. The editors, George Jean Nathan and H.L. Mencken, said they would be delighted to have her as a regular contributor, and there was no reason why she should not sell them a story every month. But she never followed this up. In one respect Esther was unlucky. As in many a middle class family then and later Gran, accustomed to leading a full and active social life, entrusted the care of her children to a nanny. Her choice was a red-headed German woman called Amelia Becker, who exhibited some of the less amiable characteristics of her race and proved to be a tyrant of no mean order, as I was to discover many years later. She demanded absolute subservience to her rule in the nursery, and much preferred dealing with boys rather than girls.

As will presently appear, my relationship with my mother was subject to strains and swung between extremes at different periods of my life. It was closest when I was about eighteen, and again thirty or more years later. She suffered grievously from her marriage to my father, who went out of his way to humiliate her and undermine her precarious self-confidence. Her second marriage restored this on one level, and led indirectly to her reception into the Roman Catholic Church, but created havoc in her family relationships and cut her off from many of her old friends. The changes in her personality at this time were so extreme that it may be difficult to make some of her actions appear credible. After the death of her second husband most of the fences were mended. She established friendly relations with my father, who submitted most of the chapters in his two volumes of autobiography for her criticism, and regularly visited her or rang her up for advice and encouragement. He even invited her to lunch on what would have been their golden wedding day. A few years later, to their mingled amusement and embarrassment, their children celebrated their golden divorce.

Although both my parents mellowed in old age, they were not in agreement over the past. When my father sent my mother the chapter in *Seven Ages* containing his first references to her, she told him he was on the wrong track. He refused to listen, and withheld the parts of the book dealing with the marriage. His published account is so obviously distorted – he had a great capacity for deceiving himself about his motives – that I asked her, for our private benefit and instruction, to write down her account of the relationship from the beginning. This document, which I christened *The Basiliad*, struck me at once as accurate, penetrating and very fair. (Later, also at my request, she drafted an account of her relations with Alfred and Essie Sutro, known as *The Sutroad*, which proved equally fascinating.) As an act of justice to her memory, and because it bears intimately on my own life, I include a summary of her narrative here.

According to her, Basil's account of his childhood in *Seven Ages* is heavily romanticised. She said – and my observations confirm this – that he was ashamed of his home with its air of genteel poverty, and particularly of his father. He disliked its religious aura: the first thing he said to Esther after my birth (he was away on military duties at the time) was 'I hope you're not going to have the boy baptised'. (I was baptised, at the insistence of my Van Gruisen grandparents, but my brothers were not, until many years later.) He grew up with a driving ambition and a variety of chips on his shoulder. He was educated as a day boy at Whitgift, a perfectly respectable school but for some reason a source of shame, somewhat mitigated in later life when one of his contemporaries rose to eminence as Air Chief Marshal Lord Tedder. An even stranger source of shame was the fact of paternity; he refused to put his full name to the announcement of my birth or my brothers'.

He left home and a clerkship in a city office shortly before his eighteenth birthday and joined a repertory company as an actor. A year later he was with Miss Horniman's company in Manchester, and by 1911, at the age of 22, was directing the newly established Liverpool Repertory Company after a very successful trial season in the spring. It was in that year that my mother first met him, at the Birkenhead house of a family friend, Charlotte (Mrs Sewell) Bacon, who was an amateur philosopher, a dabbler in the occult, and a born match-maker. She proceeded to throw them together in what she considered the most promising places, a wild patch at the bottom of her garden, a remote pub in North Wales with the ominous name of Loggerheads, the beach at Abersoch on the Welsh coast; she even retired strategically to the loo to leave them together. Basil had at once fallen in love, and proposed regularly; Esther, who wanted only intellectual companionship and resented Mrs Bacon's manoeuvres, as regularly refused him. During a summer holiday at Abersoch Mrs Bacon proposed that they should spend the night on the beach to watch the sunrise, chaperoned by herself and Gran. The chaperones then left the young couple to wander about alone. After a picnic breakfast in the sandhills Basil read Keats's *Endymion* aloud, and sent Esther to sleep. In the spring of 1912 he was allowed to join the Van Gruisen family on holiday at Fasano on Lake Garda, and Esther became engaged to him by mistake. By this time she wished she could fall in love with him. In the end the trick was accomplished by his production of Hauptmann's *Hannele*, which she found profoundly moving.

For six months the engagement was kept secret lest it should provoke an explosion from Tommy. When he was eventually told he merely grunted, having no doubt long suspected the truth. Aunt Aggie's response to the news was: 'Has he got good teeth?' Her equally old-fashioned sister Lottie sent for Esther and scolded her fiercely for proposing to marry into the theatre, which she did not consider respectable (this situation was to have a parallel in my life). Towards the end of the year's engagement Basil grew surly and quarrelsome; he was always a great scowler, as Dodie Smith remarked in one of her volumes of autobiography fifty years later. Gran attributed this to subconscious resentment at having been so persistently refused, and she was almost certainly right. Only a week before the wedding, while on a short holiday in the Lake District, Esther suggested a postponement. Basil rushed up to Grasmere, and a reconciliation was effected before a cosy kitchen fire.

They were married on 30 April 1914 in Bidston church, just outside Birkenhead. Neither of them was a Christian; they agreed to a church wedding only because marriage in a registry office would have shocked Tommy and scandalised Basil's parents. In the vestry Essie Sutro, coming face to face with the vicar (the father of George Leigh-Mallory) and wanting to make polite conversation, said: 'Not much doing in your line, is there?' On the previous day a gypsy who called at the house had told Esther that her husband would leave her, a prediction repeated by the stars two years later when she tried to cast my horoscope. There was apparently a misprint in the key to the position of the stars, for they predicted that I would be a brewer. This would have been correct for my first cousin Michael Van Gruisen.

There was an odd incident on their honeymoon, spent at Fasano. Basil had been working with enthusiasm on James Elroy Flecker's play *Hassan*, but had not met the poet, who was living in Switzerland suffering from tuberculosis, of which he was soon to die. A proposed meeting at Locarno fell through; but when Flecker suggested that the couple should join him at Davos, Basil refused - secretly, on the ground that 'this was a decision no bride should be asked to share'. My mother's later reaction was 'Why on earth not?' She would have been delighted to go. In the event neither of them ever met Flecker.

When they returned to a little flat in Abbey Court, St John's Wood, Basil solemnly informed his wife that 'the theatre would always come first'. Basil, who was then working as assistant producer to Sir Herbert Tree at His Majesty's, needed her constant assurances that he would be a success, which she was very happy to give. At first they were ideally happy, spending many evenings that summer in the gallery at Drury Lane for Diaghilev's Russian opera and ballet season. All too soon the outbreak of war disrupted their lives. Basil volunteered for the army and joined the Cheshire Regiment, but saw no active service on account of poor eyesight. He was soon organising entertainment for the troops at Oswestry; his scheme for garrison theatres was eventually taken over by the government under NAAFI, and became the prototype of ENSA in the later war. Inevitably there were separations, but the implication in *Seven Ages* that Esther preferred the sanctuary of her parents' home to living with him, and later refused 'to come into the market-place to join the battle', is misleading. It was true that she lacked domestic skills, having no experience of cooking or running a household, and – as a result of this and Miss Becker's iron rule in the nursery – was deficient in self-confidence. But Basil was always one to exploit the weakness of others (the result of his own insecurity no doubt) and to address people in an inferior social position with withering contempt. I was to witness many instances of this later. And the more they retreated or showed signs of fear, the more aggressive he became. That was certainly the pattern of his marriage to Esther. It also accounts for his notorious unpopularity in the theatre.

He once said to her during the engagement: 'Perhaps one of these days I will present you with a child'. The form of words was somehow characteristic. But he never showed any further desire to be a parent. When I was born he became intensely jealous, resenting the time my mother spent with me, as if it detracted from her love for him, and quite unable to understand that two such loyalties could co-exist. She was then staying at a farm at Pant on the border between Wales and Shropshire in order to be near his camp at Oswestry. Assuming he would eventually be sent to the front, she handed me over to the landlady whenever he came home on leave and hid every sign of my existence. She always intended to have another child, partly because at the age of three I craved the company of other children, and prepared to face Basil's opposition. He considered it 'provincial' to have a family, and an encumbrance on the free life he felt was due to him as an artist. But she did not tell him soon enough, and for ever afterwards he thought she had deliberately deceived him.

Martin was born on my fourth birthday ('My God, what a technique!' was the comment of Eugene Goossens's wife). Basil was not in the house; he had rented a flat 'to be near the theatre' and spent more and more time away from home. Joe was born only thirteen months later, conceived unintentionally after my uncle Harry's wedding. When he was due, Basil was in America on theatre business. He rang up on his return and asked 'Has that baby been born yet?' When she said 'No' he replied 'Then I'm not coming home'. She had a haemorrhage at Joe's birth, and the doctor asked where the husband was. No one could tell him; Basil had never given Esther the address of his flat, and she had never asked for it. Two days later he came to see her, held her hand, and said gently: 'I have just been unfaithful to you for the first time'. She remarked that it did not break her heart, but it stopped her milk. She also told me, though she did not put it in *The Basiliad*, that Basil tried to persuade her to have an abortion.

With three young children at home, two of them babies, she was naturally unable to attend his rehearsals. This was the time of his greatest success, culminating in the production of Flecker's *Hassan* in September 1923. His dissatisfaction with her increased in proportion to the success of his career. When he did not sit silent and glowering throughout their meals together, he would criticise her as 'provincial and schoolmistressy'. Her lack of worldliness, which he had once admired, he now deplored. Her diffidence made her unable to answer back. He made her feel that by his standards – always those of an 'artist' – she was inferior. She tried to accept this and adapt her way of life to his, but inevitably it did not work. I can see how her diffidence was likely to irritate a man whose thrusting ambition made him more and more a public figure; but this does not excuse his insensitiveness to her feelings.

Another symptom of his insecurity was the extent to which he was influenced by other people's opinions, especially if they were in any way derogatory. One of his friends put it about that Esther was the wrong sort of wife for him and would be no help in his career. In fact from the first she had done her best to support him. It may not have been much, and he makes no mention of it in *Seven Ages*, but it does not deserve to be forgotten. In the days of the Liverpool Repertory Theatre she had undertaken various small backstage jobs, and collaborated at least once with the scenic artist George Harris, who became a close friend of both my parents and whom I remember as a delightful man. This was over patterns for the Dream Merchant's costume in *Fifinella*, the Christmas fairy play that Basil wrote with Barry Jackson. Later she edited the printed version of the play, which carries her name on the title page. Basil encouraged her to write reports on the plays submitted to the theatre, though the official reader was the poet Lascelles Abercrombie. She helped to cut the lengthy manuscript of *Hassan*. She was even cast for a small part in a war-time comedy to save expense, but never played it because news came that her brother Wilfred was dying. Her final job for Basil was in the Knightsbridge office of the Entertainments Branch of the Navy and Army Canteen Board, where she interviewed potential lady managers to take the place of men.

When Basil began his affair with Nancy Parsons (the stage name of Lady Mercy Greville, daughter of the Countess of Warwick) Esther felt only a sense of relief; at last there was a chance to end her anomalous position and begin a new life. Basil's sentence in *Seven Ages*, 'After months of indecision my wife was about to sue for divorce', turns the truth on its head. It was he who could not make up his mind. He left their house in Queen's Road, St John's Wood, for the last time in the autumn of 1923. In August the following year he rang her up at Selsey, where we were on holiday. She thought he had at last agreed to the divorce; on the contrary, he wanted her to go away for a trial weekend. She knew this would be no guarantee for the future and refused. The next move was an appointment with solicitors, and she had to spend a day in London. This led to a comic anticlimax. The friend with whom she was staying (Roger Bacon, the son of Charlotte and Sewell), a worthy but humourless barrister, jibbed at her being away for a whole day. She did not want to explain, not wishing to throw a cloud over the company, but he was so persistent that at last she said she was going to divorce Basil. 'What a pity', he replied, 'it will spoil our four at tennis'.

It was still necessary to break the news to Tommy, who had not been told that anything was wrong; indeed a few months earlier, impressed by the triumphant reception of *Hassan*, he had wanted to give Basil a gold watch and had been dissuaded with difficulty. My mother was with her parents on the loggia at Hambledon when the phone rang. Gran answered it and came back looking apprehensive: 'It's a solicitor for you. What does that mean?' 'It means I'm going to divorce Basil.' Gran went back into the house and was sick. Esther was left with Tommy, and – as she put it – by sheer good luck said the right thing. 'Everyone knows he is living with Mercy Greville'. Tommy replied calmly: 'In that case it's the only thing you can do'.

The divorce caused quite a stir in the press. Basil's reference in *Seven Ages* to 'the Judge of the High Court trumpeting my domestic faults as he granted my wife her Decree Nisi' is pure imagination: the Judge, in Esther's recollection, said nothing, but when her maiden name Van Gruisen was mentioned he gave her a penetrating look. He had met her parents many years before when he and Rufus Isaacs were on the Northern Circuit. About three months later Basil asked to meet her, and for fear of the King's Proctor a secret assignation had to be made at the house of Mrs Alec Rea. She was completely taken aback when he implored her not to implement the divorce: he regretted his attitude to his sons and promised to behave differently in future if she would agree to start again. When she refused, he had to be revived with brandy. He may have been afraid that the divorce would damage his career; we had it on good authority that it cost him a knighthood. More personal matters were involved too. On the day the decree was made absolute he went to see my mother and said: 'I've got to get married tomorrow and I don't want to!' As she truly wrote, 'Basil has always tended to undervalue things, even to denigrate them - until he has lost them'. This was true of his marriage and of his relations with his sons. It was also true of his beautiful house, Little Easton Manor, which Lady Warwick bestowed on him on his marriage to Nancy and on which he spent a fortune; he sold it at the beginning of the last war, and never ceased to regret it.

My parents continued to meet after the divorce, usually in connection with us children. On one occasion they went to a Delius Festival concert at the Queen's Hall and sat in the second row of the circle, just behind the blind and paralysed composer in his invalid chair, who acknowledged the tumultuous applause regardless of whether it was for him, Sir Thomas Beecham or the orchestra. Some years later, after he had divorced Nancy, Basil visited us at our holiday bungalow in the Isle of Sheppey (where he filmed us acting an impromptu scene from *Beau Geste*) and indicated clearly to Esther that he wished them to remarry. He had had affairs with at least two leading actresses (Frances Doble and Madeleine Carroll), and said that he could not stand the strain of such a relationship. However strange it may seem, he was by taste and inclination monogamous. Although he married for a third time, and would have liked to do so yet again, he never achieved a satisfactory relationship with a woman.

The Basiliad closes with a touching tribute. 'It is difficult to believe now how Basil could have caused me so much unhappiness in the past, though I can still see that he would never have been an easy person to live with. In old age and poor health he has grown gentle and considerate. I have the greatest admiration for the courage and resignation with which he faces not only material difficulties but the shameful lack of recognition in this country of his achievement in the theatre. Now that we are both lonely and have outlived so many of our friends it is a solace and a pleasure to us both, I think, to have found each other again.'

CHAPTER 2

Early Life

I was born on 18 March 1916 at 10.30 in the morning in my grandparents' house in Birkenhead. The Abbey Court flat had been shut up when Basil joined the army, and Esther returned to Birkenhead, where she had a war job at the Town Hall, indexing pink Army Forms for the National Register of men qualified for service. She also helped her mother to run a day-nursery. (Gran was always active in social work; she later became treasurer of an institution called the Sun Babies Nursery, and was on the central committee of the National Union of Townswomen's Guilds.) A miniature pink card was filled up for me, giving my occupation as 'looking after mother' and excusing me from national service as 'said to be indispensable at home'. A caption to this effect accompanied a photograph of me, looking rather contemptuous, in *The Birkenhead News* ten months later.

My grandparents' address was 37 Bidston Road, but they called the house Alcira after the town in the south of Spain where they had spent their honeymoon. This struck me later as a happy omen. Change one letter, and it becomes *Alcina*; change another, and it is *Alzira* – the titles of operas by two of my favourite composers, Handel and Verdi. I was very fond of this house, which had a large garden, at the bottom of which were two symmetrically placed buildings, both painted green, one a garage, the other a studio where Gran retired to paint. The house was Victorian and of no great beauty, but in 1902 my grandparents had employed the architect C.F.A. Voysey to enlarge and alter it. He remodelled the dining-room with wooden panelling, adding a conservatory and a large room that jutted into the garden, with two steps leading down from the hall. Originally a billiard room, it was used for parties and dances. In my time Gran used to sit there in the afternoons, dispensing tea from a silver tea-pot and playing Duo-Art rolls on a pianola. This fascinated me; I cannot remember what the music was, but long afterwards when I was hearing a piece as I thought for the first time the music would be vaguely familiar. The slow movement of Schumann's piano quintet was very familiar indeed, and I can only assume I heard it as a child in the drawing-room at Alcira.

I always looked forward to our visits to Birkenhead, and was very distressed when the house was sold on Tommy's retirement in 1925 and the grandparents moved to a flat in London at 82 Portland Place. The whole environment of Alcira acquired a kind of sanctity in my memory: the garden with its summerhouse, sundial and croquet lawn, where I first learned to recognise a wallflower and a toad; the walks to the windmill on Bidston Hill and the steep bank covered with gorse and sandy tracks, known as Thermopylae, which commanded a superb view over the Wirral peninsula; above all, the trams. I was always fascinated by trams – not so much the vehicles themselves, though they made a distinctive and agreeable clanking, as the fact that they ran on lines and you could trace on the ground where they would have to go, with the delicious uncertainty as to what they would do when they reached a set of points. I examined with interest the long-disused tracks of the horse trams in Palm Grove, where my grandparents lived on their marriage and my mother was born.

Railways had a similar attraction, and still have. One of my earliest memories is of a disused railway on the sea shore, still equipped with signals but the rusty tracks half buried in sand. I believe this was at Wallasey, but have never been able to identify the spot. The rail journey from Euston was a great thrill. I used to look out of the window, try to catch the names of stations, and record them in a notebook. The best trains, in my opinion, stopped only at Rugby, Crewe and Chester; each had an elaborate track layout that provoked me into trying to memorise it but always defeated me. If the train stopped anywhere else, it was decidedly inferior. The terminus, Birkenhead Woodside – now abolished as a result of the pettifogging activities of Dr Beeching – also had a tram terminus outside, with a pleasingly complex layout of tracks. Sometimes the journey provided less welcome adventures. Once I was nearly left behind on the platform at Crewe. The train started before the advertised time, and a smart porter picked me up and pitched me into the carriage, where my mother, who had been in her school cricket XI, made a neat catch. On another occasion I travelled when suffering from whooping-cough, and vomited repeatedly into a small cup, the only receptacle available; most trains then had no corridors. Awful warnings from my mother kept the carriage free from other passengers.

Occasionally we went to Liverpool, crossing the Mersey by a ferry steamer which emitted a loud admonitory hoot when about to start. Liverpool had larger and more sumptuous trams, but they lacked the character of their plebeian Birkenhead counterparts. It also had an overhead railway, another casualty of modern economy, which ran above the docks and afforded a splendid view of shipping and the river. On my last visit to Alcira, in April 1925, Tommy took me over its full length. That last visit was a bitter-sweet occasion. I knew the house was to be sold, and determined to savour the delights of the place to the utmost. I went on all my favourite walks; one was to a railway station in the country (?Upton), visible from Thermopylae; I stood on the bridge watching the trains pass beneath, and came back by a muddy track known as Boot and Shoe Lane, where celandines bloomed in profusion.

As a child I possessed a phenomenally vivid and retentive memory, both aural and visual. My mother swore that I described accurately a scene at Pant when I was six months old (it included a railway line). This seems improbable, but I have several clear memories of the year 1918. One is of an air raid during the first war, when I was woken up and hidden under what I took to be a staircase at 10 Abbey Court. Others are of a visit to Bournemouth, where Tommy was recuperating after a severe attack of rheumatism or lumbago. There was a public garden with a little stream running through it, on which I tried to sail a toy boat but lost it under a bridge. To keep me quiet when I woke up early in the morning my mother gave me a packet of paper-wrapped chocolate cigarettes to play with. This worked well, until one morning only a neat pile of paper remained: I had discovered that the contents were edible. Most vividly of all I remember a Christmas party at Birkenhead in 1918: the excitement of being taken out after dark in a car, the Christmas tree let down through a hole in the ceiling, a boy trying to sit on a wooden locomotive which repeatedly shot away from him and deposited him on the floor. Very early in 1919 I accompanied my mother and grandparents on an expedition to Queen's Road, St John's Wood (now Queen's Grove) to choose a house. They settled on number 30, and we moved there in February, but before that we inspected a house towards the bottom of the road on the other side. Gran condemned it as damp. I rather liked the idea of a damp house, not having the faintest notion what it meant.

I have many recollections of the house and garden at Hambledon in Surrey before it was enlarged, an event that took place in 1919, as the date on a chimney records. This house, my home for the last fifty years, will figure constantly in my story. I was first taken there at the age of six weeks, and have spent part – if sometimes only a small part – of every year of my life there. My grandparents rented it in the early summer of 1916 in order to be near the Sutros, who had a country house a mile away at Sandhills, near Witley. Hambledon Hurst had been built in 1895 by two literary spinsters, Edith Sichel and Emily Ritchie, in the style of an old Surrey cottage. It was itself no more than a cottage; water came from a well and there was no bathroom (I used to be bathed in a metal tub in the back parlour, now part of the hall); but it possessed the luxury of two staircases, one leading down to a maid's sitting-room. This has since been removed and replaced by an airing cupboard. My grandparents fell in love with the place, rented it again in 1917 and bought it the following year. Edith Sichel died early in the war: Miss Ritchie published a charming collection of her letters, which mention visits to Hambledon by Fanny Davies, Ellen Terry and others. Miss Ritchie was a near relative of Thackeray; the house was full of his drawings and caricatures, which unfortunately she took away. But it still contains part of an old dinner service dating from her time.

The garden was small and full of flowers, and included a little sunk rose-garden that now lies buried under my study. I remember the old gardener, Denyer, who seemed to belong to the remote past, and the grim housekeeper Mrs Telford clumping down the backstairs and unwinding a long bandage from her rheumatic leg. The alterations, which doubled the size of the house and added a garage, were again entrusted to Voysey, who designed furniture for the new bedrooms and the cloakroom. Since my grandparents intended to spend only the summers there, and those first summers were very hot, they had the entire ground floor of the new part of the house laid out as a single room with tiny windows high up in the south wall and heavy oak beams for a ceiling. It made a cool room in hot weather, but when in 1939 Gran and Tommy gave up their London flat and moved permanently to Hambledon it proved a white elephant, especially as the open fireplace, intended more for appearance than use, smoked abominably. When we acquired the house in 1956, we divided the big room into a music room and a study, separated by a wall of oak bookshelves on both sides, enlarged the windows to the south, removed the heavy beams which, having been built of half-seasoned timber, had begun to sag ominously, and added an entrance to the study from the front garden. Previously the house had no central heating; for many years there was no electric light, and a telephone only in the cloakroom. Voysey had a number of fads: locks secured not by keys but by wooden wedges on a leather string, lavatories flushed by handles at the sides set in hollows that proved a trap for spiders, and ventilators in the walls of the bedrooms that creaked in the wind and frightened me as a child. We had all these taken out, and felt slightly guilty later when students of Voysey's architecture asked permission to inspect the house.

The garden was greatly enlarged in 1919, taking in two adjacent fields. For a whole summer it was a muddy wilderness full of workmen manoeuvring wheelbarrows precariously over planks. One of the fields was devoted largely to fruit and vegetables, with a toolshed and a greenhouse which had to be concealed behind a clump of laurels because Tommy had a rooted objection to such utilitarian features being visible from the house. The other field in due course contained a rock garden, a rose garden, a grass tennis court, a bowling green (surrounded by a yew hedge), a small pond full of water-lilies, a dell and a grove of nut trees, most of them on different levels, which made the garden seem larger than it really was. The pond was stocked with goldfish until they caught the eye of a passing heron. There was also a red oak, spectacular in the autumn, and two dwarf cypresses framing the approach to the tennis court. At least they were supposed to be dwarf; but they grew to enormous size, and eventually fell victims to gales – the second of them, together with the red oak, in the great storm of October 1987. A replacement pair of supposedly dwarf cypresses has since outgrown their statutory dimension. More successful was a bank of rhododendrons of many species and colours, which for years showed a coy reluctance to develop but then, like the cypresses, broke free, swamped everything that grew near them, including part of the rose and rock gardens, and now make a glorious display, blooming in succession, in May and June.

In my grandparents' time two gardeners, Bert and Ernie Jeffery, were kept fully occupied. Now, despite constant efforts to preserve horticultural decorum, the kitchen garden has shrunk to barely a quarter of its size and much of the rest has gone wild. Gran herself was an enthusiastic gardener, who for so long as she was able cared lovingly for the rock and rose gardens and kept the house full of fresh cut flowers. She was an artist in their arrangement; it was a matter of pride to me as a child that I was one of only two persons permitted to assist her. I cannot remember Tommy doing much in the garden, except stab dandelions on the lawns with a pointed implement. But he liked walking round it, and had a habit, which horrified Gran, of relieving himself at a certain point behind the bowling-green hedge. Although only the upper part of his body was visible, it was obvious what he was doing. In 1932 he bought the lordship of the manor, which carried with it 150 acres of common land (technically 'manor waste') and according to the documents a number of strange medieval rights over neighbouring properties, extinguished by Act of Parliament only in the 1920s. When later I told my next-door neighbour that they included the right of best beast at Michaelmas, he replied: 'Which would you prefer, my dog or my wife?' The manor waste, since registered under the Commons Act, is a picturesque stretch of wild wooded country which suffered grievously in the 1987 storm.

Early Life

Until the outbreak of war Hambledon Hurst was unoccupied during the winter months. Ruby, Harry and family would stay for a fortnight in late March or early April. After that we came down, depending on school holidays. The grandparents' summer season at Hambledon lasted from mid-April to early October, with a break in August for staff holidays, when Gran and Tommy would go to France, where Tommy took a cure in the thermal baths at Mont-Dore. Bicarbonate of soda, iron and arsenic were the principal ingredients of these waters, apparently.

There were three members of staff. Lizzie Briggs, the cook, a friendly woman who talked with a lisp, had been with the family at Birkenhead in my mother's childhood. She stayed for at least thirty years. Margaret Dunovan, the elderly housemaid, had also begun at Birkenhead. She was a nice old thing. Gran was a sociable person and often had guests for the weekend, such as the portrait-painting couple George and Maud Hall-Neale. A younger maid, in uniform, served at table. Later this post was filled by a tall, stroppy Welsh lass. Margaret was succeeded by Gertrude, a quiet, delightful girl, whose duties included dusting, laundry and ironing. The three of them slept in the two hot attic rooms at the top of the house. After Lizzie's retirement Dorothy, a woman of enormous proportions, took her place as cook.

For many years Gran kept bees at Hambledon. Three hives were set out on the grass under the lime trees. A small wooden shed in the hedge behind housed her equipment, gown, hood, smoker, etc. As a child I remember seeing her going to tend the bees. She was very professional about it. I watched from a safe distance as she extracted the honeycombs. Occasionally a comb would have two different coloured honeys, partly light and partly dark, from different flowers. I remember the humming of the bees in the lime trees and the dripping, sticky honeydew, secreted by aphids. Gran produced a lot of lime honey, which I liked, and dark heather honey later in the year. In the winter Bert or his wife Fanny kept an eye on the hives.

Hambledon has been at all times a place of happy associations. The house in Queen's Road, which was our home from 1919 to 1930, also carries mostly pleasant memories. It was not large – after my brothers' birth and when my father was still at home it became inconveniently crowded – but it had a spacious drawing-room overlooking the small garden with a balcony and an outside flight of steps leading down to a stone playground. The most unusual interior feature was the bath, which had at one end a remarkable apparatus for squirting water in every imaginable direction, controlled by a series of pipes and stops like some crazy organ. The garden had a small lawn and a flower bed on each side, but I cannot remember many flowers except a deep purple clematis growing on a trellis. A fig-tree grew in one corner and every year produced a multiplicity of small figs but they never ripened. My brothers and I were each allotted a little patch in which we grew mignonette, stocks, bright red daisies and other simple flowers from seed. I always enjoyed gardening, more so than my brothers at that time, though Martin later developed green fingers and established conservatories full of exotic blooms in each of his successive residences. My earliest ambition in life was to be a gardener, Martin's to be an engine-driver, Joe's to be a muffin man - so that he could eat the muffins. In those days the muffin man, walking the streets with a tray of muffins covered by a green cloth on his head and ringing a bell, was a characteristic feature of St John's Wood. Another was the lamp-lighter, who at dusk turned on each of the gas lamps in the street with a long pole. A third was the troop of Household Cavalry exercising through the streets from their barracks in Ordnance Road (now Ordnance Hill).

St John's Wood was then a residential area of early Victorian villas in white stucco, something of a backwater between Finchley Road

Early Life

with its busy buses on one side and the smarter and more imposing Avenue Road on the other. Most of them have since been pulled down and replaced. St John's Wood Park had been built as a private estate, and its northern end near Swiss Cottage was closed by gates. A few of its houses were very large indeed, with massive gate posts and sizeable gardens. One belonged to some friends of my mother called Muspratt, who on one occasion gave a large children's party, each child being accompanied and fussed over by a nurse. I can only have been five or six years old at the time. After tea the daughter of the house, who was about my age, went into a back room for a certain purpose, and I followed her. When she sat on a pot, with a posse of nurses fluttering round, I told her that was not the right way to do it, and proceeded to give a demonstration. 'Oh', she said, 'I haven't got one of those'. I refused to believe her and insisted on ocular proof, while the nurses tried to shoo me away. When I met the girl again, she was a rising barrister. I did not dare remind her of the incident.

When Martin was born in 1920 there were two further additions to the household. One was Margaret Miles, a country girl from Chieveley in Berkshire, who came as housemaid and, after a spell elsewhere, returned to cook. She was good-natured but had a violent temper. On one occasion she threw me down the steep flight of stairs from the attic, and I hit my head with a bang on the door at the bottom. Later, in the Sheppey bungalow, we had a tremendous fight, which left me in disgrace and Margaret covered with black bruises and a bite on the arm. I cannot remember the cause of this, but there was no permanent ill-feeling. The other newcomer was a major influence on all our lives. Her name was Laura Harrison, known to us first as Nurse and then as Haricot. She was apparently an illegitimate addition to a large and poor family in Liverpool, where her father maltreated her and she nearly died of appendicitis with complications. She was minute, well under five feet in height, but had great spirit and one of the sweetest and most generous natures I have ever encountered. She was devoted to us, and used to spend her entire wages – only ten shillings a week – on birthday and Christmas presents for us. In troubled times later she was a tower of strength. While she was with us I probably owed more to her and her loyal affection than to anyone else, not even excepting my mother. When she left we never lost touch. We were never quite sure of her age; she once told me she was 38, but as she remained 38 for a number of years we found the exact calculation difficult. She was over 90 when she died in 1976, having spent her years of retirement in the Reading area, first with Margaret and her husband, then from 1972 when her mind began to fail in Wokingham Hospital, where she talked constantly of my brothers and me and begged visitors to the ward not to disturb us when we were trying to sleep. She asked nothing of anybody; when in her last years we made her a small allowance she was touchingly grateful.

When I was four years old my father decided it was time for me to see one of his productions. This was *The Blue Lagoon*, a dramatisation of H. de Vere Stacpoole's novel about a boy and girl, wrecked on a South Sea island, who grew up to discover the facts of sex by instinct – a singular choice for a child of my age. I cannot remember how my mother explained this, but she did tell me about certain spectacular scenes for which my father and his designer George Harris had devised new theatrical techniques. I remember these very well. There was a scene on a ship, which caught fire; another in which an old sailor rowed the children in a boat on a sea that heaved most realistically while the blazing ship sank in the distance; and a hurricane on the island that bent the palm trees double. I was most impressed but also puzzled; I sat in the stalls asking countless questions: what were the man and woman going to do, and why? I did not connect this with the arrival of the baby, and demanded in a loud voice where it had come from. The girl as an adolescent was played by an actress called Faith Celli, about whom Basil tells a very funny story in *Seven Ages*. Years later I came upon her tombstone in the churchyard of the little Border church where I was married. She had left the stage to marry a local landowner who subsequently became the third Viscount Elibank. When Basil stayed with us at Fairnilee for Christmas in 1964 he walked down the road and visited her grave.

That was not my first visit to the theatre. The previous Christmas my parents had taken me, aged three, to the children's play *Fifinella*. This begins with an old-fashioned pantomime scene, interrupted by children in the audience demanding proper fairies. I protested loudly, thinking they were trying to spoil the show. It must I think have been a dress rehearsal, for I remember being on the stage surrounded by dancing fairies, who greeted me as they whirled past. I was taken to meet the Man in the Moon, but shrank back and refused to shake hands. My father said 'Perhaps it is something about the eyes'. It was his strange costume that frightened me, though I could not put this into words.

By far the strongest emotion of my childhood was fear. For this my father was partly but not wholly responsible. I was certainly afraid of him, but, fortunately for me, he was often away, and I was chiefly aware of him as an uncomfortable force in the background. He left finally when I was seven; my brothers do not remember him at home at all. One incident is particularly vivid. I was playing in his dressing-room and found a box of Beecham's pills, which I took to be sweets. He allowed me to sample one, with drastic consequences. My mother was furious. He also alarmed me by cutting a corn on his toe with a razor and making it bleed. During the second war, when my mother was in the Bahamas, I wrote to her of my delight in my daughter Brigid, remarking that she was not at all afraid of me.

It had never occurred to me that very small children were not afraid of their fathers.

A more potent instrument of fear was the nurse who was in charge of me for a few months before Haricot arrived. In 1918-19 I had a nurse called Dicky Mills, whom I liked; she allowed me all sorts of liberties. At Hambledon one day I took off her stockings and unwittingly received my first experience of erotic pleasure. She was young and said to be very pretty; she attracted all the men and began to neglect her duties, so she had to go. In the emergency my mother recalled her tyrannical old nurse, Amelia Becker, known as Nan. If I found my food unpleasant, it was forced down my throat, even if it made me sick. Every day I had to recite my bad deeds, which included failure to visit the lavatory after breakfast. She was only with me for one winter until just after my fourth birthday, but she left a mark. Haricot told me later that when she first arrived she found me cowering in a corner in abject terror. My mother, whom I only saw briefly once or twice a day, Nan being in complete control, had no idea of what was happening.

For years I was terrified of being left in the dark. When Joe was born I was moved out of the night-nursery which I had shared happily with Martin and Haricot and made to sleep in the attic, where the roof or the chimney creaked and the wind made sudden mysterious noises. A night-light was allowed after a while, but that created shadows that advanced and retreated without warning. I used to lie awake, wondering whether it was safer to remain thus or to risk the horrors of recurrent nightmares. In July 1923 there was a tremendous thunderstorm that seemed to last all night (its devastating effect on the University cricket match can be read in the 1924 Wisden). I was terrified until my mother came up and sat with me. When Basil left, I was moved to his dressing-room, where I used to dress very slowly, counting the numbers of men, women, dogs and cats I could see from the window. Other causes of fear were rats, spiders and, for some unfathomable reason, the King of Diamonds in a pack of cards. I thought he had a nasty look on his face, and once when he went temporarily missing I was sure he was planning to do me some mischief. More menacing than these, because unquestionably real, was a boy not much older than me who lived in a run-down terrace at the other end of Queen's Road. I never knew who he was, but he took a delight in threatening and chasing me whenever he saw the chance, and I would run desperately to the comforting warmth of the nursery.

When Joe was expected, in April 1921, I was sent to stay with my paternal grandparents, who then lived in a house called Glenmore at Sanderstead near Croydon. It was one of their more hospitable residences and had a patch of wild woodland in the garden, where I ran down paths imagining all sorts of adventures. There were several railways in the district, and the steam locomotives were an inexhaustible source of interest. Locomotives also featured on the postcards my mother sent me regularly when I was away from home; no other pictures were considered adequate. I still have one announcing Joe's birth. I remember my first sight of him, a small wriggling object, born with masses of black hair. I took a dislike to the maternity nurse, a brisk efficient woman called Hoggard, upon whose arrival I was always sent out of the room.

That summer of 1921 we took Hawthorn Cottage at Hambledon on the other side of the cricket-green, the grandparents' house being full. The weather was exceedingly hot. Once in the middle of the night I was woken up by my mother coming into the room with Haricot and declaring that there was a strong smell of hats (*sic*). I cannot account for this; it was definitely not cats. I could smell nothing, never having possessed a sense of smell, though my sense of taste is acute. My mother had a sense of smell in childhood, lost it during an illness when she was at Girton, and recovered it when I was born; I used to accuse her of stealing mine. When later I told the family doctor of my deficiency, he opened various bottles and placed them under my nose. I was aware of nothing. He tried another bottle; I took a deep breath and passed out; it was chloroform. Years later the subject came up at a musical party given by John Makower. A somewhat sententious girl declared that if I could not smell I could not taste. I disputed this. 'Very well', said the host, 'We'll put him to the test'. I was blindfolded, given four or five glasses of wine, and asked to identify them (not the precise vintage, of course, and I was allowed a biscuit in between). I did so correctly, though nearly caught out when one of them proved to be a repeat.

To revert to 1921 at Hambledon, there was a major crisis one afternoon when Martin vanished. He was barely eighteen months old, and a search party was hastily organised. He was not in the garden, or down the well. Eventually he was found on the common outside the gate, happily browsing off a blackberry bush. He was always an enthusiastic, indeed a voracious feeder. When seated in his high-chair he would never address a bottle of milk until he could see a second one placed ready for the follow-on. When he had finished one he would pitch it out, giving Haricot plenty of fielding practice. Blackberries caused a genuine casualty that year. We were busy collecting them in paper bags from a hedge, when Margaret trod in a wasps' nest. She let out a piercing scream, threw down her bag, and ran about in all directions. The village was roused and searched for some stuff called blue-bag, and Margaret was treated and put to bed. My first encounter with rats occurred at this time. Hawthorn Cottage had no lavatory, only an earth closet in the garden over a ditch, which attracted a congregation of rats. I was given a stick to frighten them off by banging on the door, but this was hardly conducive to easy evacuation.

Except in 1928, we always spent part of our summer holidays at Hambledon. My mother stayed with the grandparents and their guests at the Hurst. Martin, Joe and I and Haricot lodged at Malthouse Farm just beyond the top of the garden. It was occupied by a retired naval man named Hawkins with a parrot whose language we were discouraged from imitating. He was succeeded after a year or two by Arthur Ashdown, a builder whom Tommy engaged as a bailiff when later he bought the manor. Ashdown also ran the small farm with a few cows, and on one occasion was fined for watering the milk. Martin was responsible for a few alarms and excursions, walking one night in his sleep and on another occasion falling downstairs while blowing a wooden whistle and cutting his mouth with a splinter. One night an aircraft in difficulties clipped a chimney and came down in a field below the Parkers' house at Feathercombe. After a few years I was promoted to dinner at the Hurst and had to make my way back to the farm in the dark.

Like most families we had our euphemisms for the natural functions. If we wanted to pass water, we were 'going to be tidy' (introduced by Nan when I could not pronounce the word 'lavatory'). After breakfast we 'did our business'. This produced some comic situations. When Haricot asked Martin, as a very small child, to put his shoes tidy, she found them arranged in pairs outside the lavatory. A dog's turd was referred to, by extension, as 'business'. My first image of a business man was of my father sitting on the loo. When Tommy left the Birkenhead house after breakfast and I was told that he had gone to business, I put the wrong construction on it, knew that it was necessary but was puzzled as to why he had to go to Liverpool to do it.

Children's minds pick up all sorts of strange associations. There was a newsagents' stall outside Marlborough Road Station, where Queen's ran into Finchley Road, served by a man and a boy; I was convinced that the man was W.H. Smith and the boy his son. Even ordinary words acquired pictorial connections. For some reason, perhaps by assonance with 'hot water', the word 'daughter' evoked to my mind a small jug with a metal lid. My first idea of 'God' was an oldish man sitting on a gate with a top-hat on the side of his head. A friend, Peter Joseph, told me that his was a small country railway station.

* * * * *

In the autumn of 1921 the time came for me to go to school. Instructed by my mother, I had learned to read and write before I was four; neither accomplishment caused me much difficulty. When Haricot arrived my only problem was in distinguishing between lower-case b and d. The school chosen, which took day-boys between the ages of five and thirteen, was Sheringham House, at 11 Belsize Road just below Swiss Cottage. On the first day my mother took me all the way and introduced me to Mr Holmes, the headmaster. After that she escorted me as far as the Finchley Road crossing, and I walked the rest of the distance. We wore blue and grey caps inscribed with the initials SHS, which I later associated with some early Jugoslav stamps. Mr Holmes was a kindly man, but I disliked his wife, a plump blowsy woman who took us for singing. She wrote in my report that I was afraid to hear my own voice, which embarrassed me acutely when it made my mother laugh, probably because it was true. The lowest form, in which I was placed, was taught by a bespectacled spinster called Miss Brett, who proved less severe than her appearance led me to expect. We studied no fewer than fourteen subjects, including Natural History and Botany, Conversational French, Poetry, Drawing and Singing, as well as Writing, Reading, Spelling and Dictation, but no Latin. Most of my memories are concerned with reading and spelling. A boy with a stammer, asked to spell 'steeple', began it with a letter 'stee', which clearly should have existed (my son Stephen was to resuscitate it in his turn). His name was Sprague; when in due course I came across the word 'ague' I assured my mother that it must rhyme with Sprague and could not possibly have two syllables. I had to read a passage about a 'guilty Scotsman', which lodged so firmly in my memory that for some time afterwards I instinctively associated Scotsmen with guilt.

My mother preserved all my school reports, which make strange reading. My conduct was always excellent, though in the first two terms I was 'very talkative'. My first term was not impressive for my place in form, but Miss Brett said that I wrote well for one so young and Mr Holmes commented on my memory and anxiety to learn. In my second term I was top of the class in French, Geography, and Natural History and Botany – not the subjects I should have expected; in the third term in English Grammar and Composition. In my fifth term I was top of the form, taking the lead in Reading, Spelling and Punctuation, Geography, Natural History and all forms of Mathematics – again a surprising assortment.

In May 1923 I was moved up to the second form and came third out of 19, though nearly two years below the average age. I was 'a wonder' at my age in Mental Arithmetic. But my writing and drawing were criticised for untidiness, and a term later the form master, Mr Hawkins, remarked pungently that 'economy in use of ink would make his work look better'. However I came top of the form and won a prize. I was 'an infallible little worker' even in Scripture, on which my first report had been 'weak', and – more surprising still – came second in Science, which was added to the curriculum in the second form. Mr Holmes summed it up: 'The report speaks for itself. Has amazing powers of retention'. And in the following term, my last at Sheringham House, when I came second: 'A wonderful little boy at work – has a great future before him'.

Mr Holmes noted in July 1923 that I had a serious rival of my own age. This was Arnold Kettle, who was my senior by one day. We used sometimes to have tea at each other's homes, and I met him again at Cambridge. He subsequently became a Marxist Professor of English; his death was the occasion of a diatribe from Bernard Levin and some angry correspondence in *The Times*. I can remember the names of dozens of my contemporaries at Sheringham House; the disadvantage of a retentive memory is that it retains a mass of useless information. I was emotionally attracted to one or two of them, and used to follow them home at a distance in the afternoon, without ever speaking to them, before making my way back late to Queen's Road. After reaching the second form I had lunch at the school; on the day after the great thunderstorm of July 1923, which turned the University cricket match at Lord's upside down, a second helping of a certain pink pudding was awarded to the only boy who slept through it.

There were no sports facilities in Belsize Road, though there was a playground where we used to kick footballs around. For organised games we travelled out on the Metropolitan Line to playing-fields in less built-up areas. The cricket ground seemed to me very large, with plenty of space for 3 or 4 games. Anyone who committed a misdemeanour was ordered to walk all the way round it, a mild punishment once inflicted on me. We were taken occasionally to the Finchley Road swimming baths, where an elderly attendant laughed at me and made me feel inferior because I could not swim. One of the sports days was the occasion of my first (and so far only) brush with the law. Three of us were returning home along Finchley Road; one of the others irritated me so much that I gave him a hearty bash with my cricket bat and made his hand bleed. The third, a rather self-important individual, fetched a policeman, who gave me a solemn warning. Sheringham House was the only school I attended where I was not subjected to some form of bullying, perhaps because it was a day school. My worst experience was at a prize-giving at the Finchley Road baths, where the whole school marched in order of seniority and was drawn up in a square. I was not paying much attention, when I suddenly thought I heard my name called. Rather surprised I advanced towards Mr Holmes, only to be sent scuttling back. I felt covered in shame.

The most enterprising features of the curriculum were the expeditions out into the country on Saturday afternoons in summer. These were voluntary; we were asked to bring money for our rail fares, and perhaps for the bottles of fizzy lemonade which were opened by pressing a round ball of glass into the neck of the bottle. On one occasion I sallied forth armed with two half-crowns, but accidentally dropped one of them through a grating at the end of Queen's Road. Afraid to mention this and full of trepidation, I proffered my remaining coin. All was well: 'That's right, two-and-fourpence'. I enjoyed these expeditions, on which the atmosphere was very relaxed. On one of them, I think near Chorley Wood, two of the boys wandered off and got lost. There was a general hue and cry. We eventually found them sitting on the platform of a little terminal station which I have never been able to identify. On a similar occasion, after I had left, I was told that Joe was found drunk in a ditch after consuming two bottles of ginger beer.

There was a school magazine, *The Blue and Grey* (motto 'Possunt qui volunt'), which appeared once a term and was edited by the boys, who supplied most of the contributions. I still possess some copies, covered in my childish hieroglyphics. They contain such titbits as the definition of a vacuum as a large empty space where the Pope lives. On glancing through the issue for the summer term of 1922 I was startled to find this sentence at the end of a report on an outing to Northwood: 'Dean and other juveniles asked so many questions that the poor Sergeant-Major must have arrived home with a bad head-ache, and longing for the dispersal of the party'. I have no idea who the Sergeant-Major was, but I do remember that expedition and the apparently fortuitous appearance of Mrs Holmes and Miss Brett on bicycles at a café where we were having tea.

I was very attached to my brothers, though my diary at a somewhat later period is full of impatient and probably unjust comments on the inadequacy of one or other of them. They were very unalike in character (then and later); my preference between them varied at different periods. Martin, who was large for his age, was supposed to have delicate nerves. Two men, child psychologists of some kind, used to come to talk to him, and Joe and I were sent out of the room. Martin also had the advantage of a godmother (Mrs Alec Rea) who always gave him birthday and Christmas presents, whereas Joe's and mine did not. This was the cause of some envy. We went for walks every day with Haricot (seldom with my mother), generally to Primrose Hill or Regent's Park, where we fed the ducks and geese on the lake and the grey squirrels (not yet unmasked as a pest) on the Broad Walk and inspected animals in the Zoo, some of the paddocks being visible from the park. Our favourites were two Mongolian Wild Horses. They seemed anything but wild; indeed they craved attention. Whenever we moved on they would kick the wooden palisade of their paddock to summon us back. There was also a llama, which spat, and a creature called a takin, a species of yak, which lived by itself and never took any notice of anyone but for some reason intrigued us, perhaps on account of its rarity.

On these walks we were generally accompanied by Tiger, Gran's wire-haired terrier, who spent the summers at Hambledon and the winters at Queen's Road. One day he disappeared in Regent's Park and was missing for a fortnight. Since we were all very fond of him we were greatly distressed. Then one day when we were walking down Avenue Road he rushed out of a garden in a state of great excitement, furiously wagging his tail. We concluded that he had been stolen and tied up, but had picked up our scent and broken free. Though anything but a model by Cruft's standards, he was a great character, an important member of the household, and could do no wrong – except one summer at Hambledon when he had an affair with a Pekingese bitch. The result was a creature of weird aspect, like something out of Greek mythology, which haunted the village for some years after Tiger's death. We called it a tigon, after the tiger-lion cross in the Zoo. Martin too on one occasion was lost in Regent's Park, and became the object of a frenzied search; but he reappeared later in the evening, looking very important in charge of a policeman.

Since Tommy and Alfred Sutro were both Fellows of the Zoological Society with the right to issue free tickets, we had unlimited entry to the Zoo and were familiar with almost its entire population. I always had to visit the reptile house – surely an eccentric taste – but disliked the parrots because they made such an infernal noise, and was not particularly taken with the lions and tigers, which were either asleep or paced endlessly up and down their cages. We were more interested when Alfred persuaded a keeper to take us backstage and show us a litter of lion cubs playing like kittens. The monkeys were entertaining, especially when they picked fleas out of each other's hair and scratched their bottoms. Once when I offered one of them a nut it pulled off my glove and carried it into the cage. The keeper was called, and administered to the erring monkey a couple of smacks and a verbal lecture such as might be addressed to a disobedient schoolboy. The giraffes were an obvious attraction; I saw one extend its neck over the high fence and take a bite at the ornamental cherries in a woman's hat. What the keeper said on this occasion I cannot recall. Another interesting creature was the giant ant-eater, which never did very much but appeared to have a tail at both ends. We were given rides on elephants and camels. I did not appreciate the latter, which walked in an ungainly manner as if they had five legs. Someone's definition of a camel as a horse designed by a committee has always seemed to me much to the point. The aquarium when it opened offered a whole range of new interests. After our first visit Martin informed Haricot with delight that he had seen a kipper swimming around, and a lot of 'little interestings', his name for insects.

I had an extraordinary obsession with counting, which no doubt has some occult psychological significance. I would count the number of animals in each cage and the number of dogs we met on walks; large dogs such as greyhounds and Great Danes were known as camel dogs. Walks on wet days were rendered more tolerable because the rain brought out the worms and enabled us to make a good count. I even counted the number of times my brothers cried and wrote it down in a book.

Children's parties never appealed to me, and I positively loathed the communal games such as Musical Chairs, Grandfather's Steps and Nuts in May that were an almost invariable feature of these occasions. Fancy dress parties – not that we went to many – were even worse. There was one at A.P. Herbert's house when I was six and Martin two; Joe was too young to be invited. I was dressed as a pierrot, which was not a great success as there were several other pierrots. Martin went as Father Christmas with a specially designed scarlet costume trimmed with some sort of white fur and was much admired, though he was too shy to utter a word. On the way home I was sick in the taxi, to the voluble indignation of the driver. The Leopold Sutros – he was Alfred's elder brother – gave a party for both adults and children, special provisions being laid out for each group. I did not care for jellies and trifles and detested marzipan, but my eye was caught by a plate of plovers' eggs on the adults' table. My mother pointed out that they were for grown-ups only, but I insisted that I wanted one and eventually, with the connivance of our hostess, obtained my wish.

If I felt neglected when my mother was preoccupied with my brothers, I have no recollection of it, probably because Haricot gave me extra attention. My mother was not naturally at ease with children after they had passed the baby stage, and could not have coped with us unassisted. We used to visit her in her room after breakfast, which she had in bed, and spend an hour or so with her downstairs after tea; otherwise our habitation was the nursery. This routine seems strange today, as does the presence of three servants in the house. That should not be taken to imply that we lived in luxury. We certainly never went in want, but the need for economy and the avoidance of waste were constantly impressed on us, especially after Basil's departure. He had to pay £600 a year alimony by court order, and was expected to cover our education. This responsibility he constantly evaded, pleading poverty, though he lived on a far more luxurious scale than we did. Looking back, I think my mother coped with the situation remarkably well. She never attempted to turn us against him. He used to visit us at fairly long intervals, when his presence was acceptable, but more as an occasional uncle than a father. His attitude to his children was peculiar. After his early jealousy, followed by neglect, he assumed an air of detachment, not hostile but treating us as encumbrances he had somehow acquired by accident, much as a tom-cat might regard the kittens he had unwittingly sired. Behind this always was the feeling that an artist ought to be free from domestic responsibilities. I soon got used to this situation (Martin and Joe of course had known no other. Joe later told me that for years he never knew he had a father), but it gave rise to some awkward developments later.

My mother played a great deal of bridge in those days, often with people she did not greatly like, because it helped to take her mind off her troubles. I was sometimes allowed downstairs to watch, and by the age of seven knew the rudiments of the game. Whenever she played away from home, she would bring back at my request the markers on which she had recorded the score, which I studied with interest. Soon I aspired to play, at first a two-handed game with her. On one regrettable occasion, when she was called to the telephone, I stacked the cards for the next deal. But I miscalculated, and she made a small slam. This taught me a lesson I never forgot. Soon I graduated to family bridge with the grandparents, which was most enjoyable; needless to say, I was not allowed to play for money. Gran was an erratic player with a propensity to overcall and go cheerfully down by many tricks. Tommy was steadier. You always knew when he was about to produce a trump or a master card, for he rose slightly in his chair and brought down the card with great emphasis. Martin and Joe when they grew older showed less interest in bridge. Joe, when he was dealt the ace of trumps or some other key card, was apt to put it on his chair and sit on it. Eventually I became a good player, but was forced to give up the game on marrying a wife with no card sense.

* * * * *

In May 1924 I was removed from Sheringham House and sent to my first boarding-school, at Elstree. It was chosen on the recommendation of John Galsworthy, a friend of my father's, who had known the headmaster, E.L. Sanderson, since they had been at Harrow together, and had been best man at his wedding. Sanderson had introduced Galsworthy to Joseph Conrad many years before on a cruise somewhere in the Pacific. Elstree was a well-known preparatory school with a high reputation for scholarship and games, especially cricket. Sanderson's father had taken it over in 1869 and greatly raised its reputation. It was carried on by a third generation. It still exists, after moving from Elstree to Woolhampton in Berkshire at the beginning of the last war, but there is no longer a Sanderson in command.

My memories of Elstree are very mixed. The standard of teaching was high, and I benefited greatly from this. In some other respects I think the experience did me harm. I hated being away from home, in an atmosphere that was strange and soon became hostile. I was very small for my age, and easily frightened; this and my exceptional success in work were enough to make me a butt for larger and lazier boys. The English schoolboy is like the jackal; he may be harmless on his own, but he hunts in packs, and when the pack is in full cry it turns on weaker creatures and harries them mercilessly. At the beginning of my second summer term I developed measles and was put in a sickroom for a month with a boy of my own age and two a good deal older, both aggressive types, who made my life a misery, though whenever the matron entered they were as good as gold. As a result of this and similar experiences I began to wet my bed at night, which of course made me an even easier target. The authorities transferred me to a dormitory with three or four others, all younger than me, who suffered the same affliction. The pack treated us as pariahs, and I felt as if I carried the mark of Cain. A few years later I recalled in my diary that during the three years 1926-28 I did not have a friend in the world.

The sick room, which was known as Egypt and had a large photograph of Kitchener over the fireplace (all the dormitories were named after military and naval leaders in the first war), struck me as a place of correction rather than recuperation. I disliked the school doctor, a huge man called Martin, known as Blob; he exuded an insensitive heartiness that seemed to blame us for being ill. I had several illnesses at Elstree, not only measles but nephritis, conjunctivitis and occasional bouts of flu. The only one I found tolerable was conjunctivitis or pink eye: I did not feel ill, but was off work and allowed to wander round the large garden and look for birds' nests. The school was afraid of epidemics; our parents were adjured not to take us to theatres or cinemas within three weeks of the beginning of each term (except in the summer holidays this left only the first week free, the period when we least craved such entertainment). Some parents I believe ignored this; but once my mother admitted taking me to a film. She received a formidable lecture from Sanderson, and some of the backwash devolved on me.

Sanderson, while at heart a benevolent and generous man (as I discovered later), was a schoolmaster of old-fashioned type. He did not believe in sparing the rod, which was more than once laid on me. The whole school stood in awe of him; he probably considered this an attitude of proper respect. He was known behind his back as Bags; if anyone called out 'Bags is coming', we scuttled away like rabbits or became as mute as mice. He was not however the source of authority with which we came most frequently in contact. There were three matrons: Miss Tate, the housekeeper, Miss English, who looked after our clothes, and Sister Cox, in charge of our health. Miss English was comparatively humane, but Miss Tate was a bossy woman constantly enforcing punishments for minor misdemeanours. She was known as Botter; her first name I think was Beatrice – a name I have disliked ever since. I had met Sister Cox before; she had been nurse to a family whose son was at Sheringham House, and went to Elstree the same time as I did. The acquaintance was to bring me no advantage. There was a sadistic streak in Sister Cox. If we said we felt ill, she gave the impression that she thought we were malingering. She once thrust a thermometer into my mouth with such force that it broke. When I complained of giddiness, she ascertained that my temperature was normal, then sent me to bed in a darkened room for three days with nothing to read or play with except a box of studs and very little to eat. I was then sent straight back to work, feeling giddier than ever. It slowly dawned on me that this treatment was designed to punish me for feigning illness. Much later my occasional feelings of giddiness were attributed to low blood pressure.

Bad circulation accounted for the most grievous affliction of my schooldays, chilblains. This may sound a childish complaint, but I have never known anything so persistently painful. Each winter every one of my toes and fingers swelled up to twice their normal size, some of them boasting two or three chilblains. Putting on shoes or boots was an agony, and every time I came near a fire the pain and irritation threatened to drive me frantic. I hope modern medicine has managed to devise a cure. I also suffered from spots and small boils which were irritated by the hairy underclothes we had to wear. My mother in one of her rare mistakes used to make fun of me for this, telling people that on being taken to Peter Robinsons I cried out 'O God, don't give me Wolsey pants'. Whether for this or other reasons I had a horror of trying on clothes and still cannot abide hairy underclothes. As soon as I could I gave up wearing a vest, and have never worn one since.

The régime was not deliberately inhumane; but few school authorities are (or were) alive to the unhappiness inflicted on some of their charges by their fellows and sometimes by the staff. The Sandersons assured my mother that I was as happy as a lark. Mrs Sanderson had a very attractive personality, but we saw little of her. On Sunday evenings she read to the junior school in the drawing-room while her husband read to the seniors in the study. How they all fitted in I cannot recall, for the rooms were not large and there were eighty boys in the school. Most of us sat on the floor. I enjoyed *King Solomon's Mines* with Mrs Sanderson, but was less enthusiastic about *Nicholas Nickleby* in the study; it seemed intolerably verbose, even though Sanderson skipped bits he thought we would find tedious. I made several attempts to read Dickens; *David Copperfield* defeated me more than once. Nor was I much more successful with Scott; even abridged versions of *Ivanhoe*, *The Talisman* and *Quentin Durward* failed to hold my attention. The only novel by either author I have read from cover to cover is *The Fair Maid of Perth*, when after the war I needed to compare it with Bizet's opera.

The school dining-hall was a large room with a high table, at which the senior master and the prefects sat. The Sandersons did not eat with the school. The rest of us were accommodated at four long tables, with one of the assistant masters at each end. They moved round week by week in rotation. One or two would toss a piece of cheese to the boys sitting next to them (cheese was supplied only to the masters), and this became to some extent an index of their popularity. There were solitary tables at the side to which boys who misbehaved were banished by Miss Tate. I was constantly the victim of this sentence. The chief sin, so far as I remember, was talking when we had been put on silence. We had to be silent at the beginning of the meal; when the senior master struck a bell once we could talk; if we made too much noise he struck it twice and we had to hold our peace till the end of the meal.

The food varied between the palatable and the disgusting. Irish stew, which looked like something dug from a farmyard midden, was suspected to contain the remains of all the meals of the preceding week. My dislike of onions probably dates from my objection to this. There was an unpleasant concoction of currants and suet known as spotted dick, or in the vernacular dead man's leg. Other horrors were tapioca and bread-and-butter pudding. Worst of all was the revolting custard, mixed with slabs of tepid skin. This once made me literally sick. There was no way of escaping the inquisition of Miss Tate, who stood over us until we had consumed every morsel. On the other hand macaroni cheese and treacle tart were general favourites, and we had lemonade in the summer and plenty of fruit.

The walls of the hall were covered to the roof with wooden boards on which was carved the name of every boy who had attended the school since the 1860s. One large board carried the names of all who had won scholarships to public schools or been accepted by the naval colleges. In idle moments I would memorise the names and can still recite some of them. To my mind the earliest names belonged to a remote and primitive age; I realise now that many of them could have been still living in 1924.

The senior master was a man named Harker who wore a surgical boot. We believed that his foot had been run over by a tram. He had white curly hair and seemed to us very old, the more so when we discovered in the library lists in his writing with dates in the nineteenth century. However he survived at least till the last war. He had a habit of pulling our hair when we did something wrong, and was not very popular. For two of the assistant masters I had considerable respect, not only because they offered me cheese. J.F. Walmsley, who became senior master when Harker retired, taught mostly English, History and Geography, and made them interesting by relating them to recent and contemporary events. He had been wounded in the trenches by a mortar bomb, and told us it was his own fault for arguing with a fellow-officer when he should have taken cover. When prominent politicians or soldiers died, he would bring their achievements into his lessons. I still associate the deaths of Asquith, Haig and Foch among others with Walmsley's class-room. Every week he wrote on the blackboard a poem which we had to learn; his choice was generally excellent, going up to Flecker and

Rupert Brooke, and he gave me an interest in English poetry that I have never lost.

Like everyone else, he was impressed by my memory, accuracy and enthusiasm for work, and he always gave me good reports; but he soon probed my weakness. His verdict on my first term was: 'He expresses himself well, but shows little imagination as yet. He obviously prefers facts to fiction'. In June 1927 my composition work was 'still rather infantile'. A year later, while my essays had 'greatly improved', I was 'often at a loss in dealing with abstract ideas'. By the end of 1928 I was expressing myself 'readily on any subject' and 'beginning to develop a taste for good literature'. In my final report (July 1929) Walmsley wrote: 'He has written some good essays; but is more at home dealing with facts than with theories'. This was true. So much school work consisted of learning by memory, and since that faculty never let me down – all through the school I had the disconcerting habit of getting close to 100% in exams – I doubtless relied on it too much. But there was also a mental block. I remember sitting down to write an essay on the film *Ben Hur* and being quite unable to put a word on paper beyond naming the author of the novel on which it was based. It was not that I lacked imagination: I had if anything too much, but was terrified of using it.

Walmsley wrote on one occasion that I was 'content with no place but the first'. This was true, and it did not make me popular. I was intensely competitive. In my first term I was first, both in term work and exams, in all subjects except Scripture, and although I was moved up every term until I reached the top form at the age of 10½, two years below the average, I seldom failed to come out first or second, especially in Latin. As a result I won a whole library of prizes.

The other master who impressed me was J.M. Christie, a dour Scot with a reputation for ferocity; his nickname was Kibosh. I did not encounter him for several terms, and was prepared for the worst; yet his reports were extraordinarily encouraging and generous. When I reached his form for Latin at the age of 9½ (the average age was nearly 12) he wrote: 'His work is rather wonderful and he is possessed of an amazing memory. I have not tried to push him on, but rather to repress him – yet he comes out first. His written work is untidy – the only fault, and one easily accounted for by his tender age'. (Others made this point; one said that I presented my work 'in a most unattractive fashion'.) Christie took the top form in Mathematics and French, and carefully prepared me for a public school scholarship. He remarked perceptively that I had 'the brains but not the inclination for Maths', and wanted me to read French in the holidays. I don't think I did; but I managed at least once to come first in both subjects, though Christie thought that music was interfering with my French (piano lessons had to be taken out of the time allotted for other subjects). He initiated me into stocks and shares, on which I probably knew as much then as I do now. Christie was a very lively teacher, who invented two characters called MacSplutterage and MacMudd to whom malefactors were likened. He had been a special constable during the war, and vividly described the destruction of a Zeppelin shot down in flames near Elstree. I was told later that he led a rackety life. He made a late marriage, and on one of my subsequent visits to Elstree introduced me to a wife much younger than himself.

Sanderson taught Classics to the top form. A Classical scholar himself, he insisted on the most rigorous standards. He soon decided that I was a born Classic, and set me to learn Greek before I was ten. I won a special annual prize for Latin prose composition at the age of eleven and repeated the feat in the next two years, which was a school record. At Greek I was still more successful – Sanderson said it was my best subject – and came first in all my last seven terms. I certainly owed much to his skill as a teacher.

The most critical features of my Elstree reports were Sanderson's comments under the heading General Conduct. After my first term he criticised my manners and said I was far too selfish even for a boy of eight. Presently there are references to 'far too many punishment drills and a nuisance in dormitory. Since he has been moved to a single room, he has improved in one respect' (December 1925). This was an allusion to bed-wetting, which was considered a sin rather than a misfortune. Later my conduct was described as good, sometimes with qualifications. 'Inclined to be a nuisance in dormitory. Otherwise good' (November 1927). Being a nuisance in this context meant talking after lights out when I was in the pariah dormitory, whose lights were put out first. I was subjected to painful corporal punishment at least once for this, and once for something I had not consciously done. Another boy had reported me for 'showing sights' – in other words indecent exposure – of which I was quite unaware.

A good deal of importance was ascribed to organised games. While not particularly good at games, I came to enjoy them when I grew stronger. Football had one advantage over cricket: if you made a blunder you could retrieve it, whereas in cricket, once you were out, you had to wait till the next game for another innings. I reached the second XI at football and played at least twice in away matches. Once I was left behind by mistake and had to be rapidly transported by car, running on to the field when the match was already in progress. Another day I was suffering from lumbago but did not report it for fear of missing the match; I remember the agony of having to turn quickly.

I developed a curious passion for cricket – curious because it was not exclusively or even primarily concerned with my own performances. Although I reached the first XI and played one or two stubborn innings, I was not awarded my colours. I was a somewhat strokeless defensive batsman, but refused even to try to bowl. One spring I was taken to the nets at Lord's, and missed the opportunity of being instructed by Walter Brearley, a great fast bowler of the past. I took an intense interest in first-class cricket, eagerly studying the scores in the newspapers. I remember Sanderson commenting on the enormous total of 511 for 2 wickets made by England against South Africa in the Lord's Test of 1924, and later that summer I held long discussions with a man at Selsey about the South African team. Once or twice each summer an Elstree Staff XI, supplemented by outside help including one or two professionals from Lord's, played a match against one of the amateur touring sides, whose team often included ex-County players sporting exotic caps and blazers. What I particularly enjoyed was scoring, and I was sometimes appointed to this office. I remember one match in which the Staff XI included the school carpenter, a dashing left-hander called Wilkins, the cricket master Geoffrey Greig, who had played as a fast bowler for Worcestershire, and Major Brierley, the Sandersons' son-in-law, who opened the innings. The visitors were led by Lord Dalmeny, captain of Surrey early in the century and later Earl of Rosebery, and included Lord Grimthorpe, a tall dark man who played with a very straight bat. Lord Dalmeny at one point grew decidedly testy, though I cannot recall what provoked him.

There was a popular game called dab-cricket. Whether this was peculiar to Elstree or universal among schoolboys I do not know. It required the preparation of a pad marked with numerous circles containing numbers for the runs scored from each stroke, extras, methods of dismissal, and so on. You then closed your eyes and dabbed with a pencil or sharp point, six times for each over, recording the results in a score-book. Most boys picked two county teams from the papers for their competitors. I invented a number of teams of my own, giving each player strongly individual characteristics, and developed the game to a fantastic degree of elaboration, both as the preparation of the pad (with a 'caught' circle close to a six, a 'bowled' at each end, and so on) and in the manner of dabbing, which could imitate the action of bowlers of different types. There were few subtleties in the game of cricket that could not in some way be represented by an equivalent. As well as at Elstree, Martin and I played this game in the holidays for hours on end and obtained immense pleasure from it, though quite why this world peopled by imaginary cricketers was so satisfying is not clear.

At Elstree we indulged in plenty of other games in our spare time, from chess and Mah-Jongg to L'Attaque and battles between armies of pen nibs on a board; you moved a nib in turn and knocked out an opponent by turning him upside down. There was a craze for growing mustard and cress on wet flannels in tin boxes, and radishes in a little earth; this had the advantage that the products were edible. During breaks we played in a large gravelled yard, which contained a number of squash courts of unorthodox design, with sloping sides and no back wall. I do not remember much serious squash, but a friend and I devised a ball game of our own involving various hazards, which could only be played in one court. Among the hazards was the metal exhaust of a stove in the adjacent boot-room, which protruded from the roof and had a little cap on top. This was known as the timtootle, and if you hit it and kept the ball in court you won the game. More often the ball shot over into the road, whence it could only be retrieved if the master on duty was not looking. On the far side of the yard was the gymnasium, presided over by Sergeant Stubbs (who had a bullet in his wrist which he invited us to feel), and the school lavatories, rudimentary earth-closets of venerable antiquity and very cold in winter. At the General Election of 1929 the Conservative candidate made a speech in the yard, and Sanderson told the head boy, Hugh Martin, to call for three cheers. As the candidate had recently changed his name from Lloyd-Graeme to Cunliffe-Lister, Hugh not unnaturally became somewhat confused, despite Sanderson's loud prompting, and we were not sure whom we were cheering. He won the seat, but Sanderson was filled with gloomy foreboding when the Labour Party made many gains and formed the next government.

One term three of us decided to start a magazine, called *The Fortnightly*. I have a copy of the first issue, dated 22 October 1927; there never was a second. It contains an article on pedometers, the first scene of a play (to be continued), a problem, jokes and some general information (supplied by me): the Nine Muses, the Seven Wonders of the World, and Groups of Animals. The Editor's Note states: 'The only difficulty about the magazine is the printing and that is why we cannot produce more than three copies', signed D.C. Thompson: Printer. The 'printing' was done in two colours on his new typewriter.

Various entertainments were laid on for our benefit and instruction. During my first term we were conveyed to the British Empire Exhibition at Wembley; the only thing I recall, apart from a number of large pavilions bearing the names of different Dominions, is a brand-new Great Western locomotive of the Castle class. The lectures with slides, chiefly during the winter terms, have made little impression. Not so the performances of two ventriloquist-conjurors, Frederick Chester and Ernest Sewell, who also sang songs. The words and tune of one of Chester's songs, 'Jemima's the name of our cat', still remain in my head, though I have never heard it since. Every three years there were school plays, one performed by seniors and one by juniors. They too contained songs, and were produced by Miss Davies, the music mistress. The first in which I appeared was called *The Little Men*, based on William Allingham's poem. I had one line to speak and one piece of business to perform, the theft of potatoes from someone's bag. At the performance Miss Davies put so many potatoes in the bag that I had no time to empty it before my exit. My mother came to this, with Martin and Joe wearing new white sweaters.

The summer play three years later was a version of *Chu Chin Chow*, the popular musical of the 1914-18 war. I was cast as a slave-girl and had to sing a song about soup. Mrs Sanderson said I looked the image of my mother. Again some of the music lodged permanently in my head. We had occasional films, presented on a rather primitive apparatus in the Big Schoolroom. They were two lengths, two reels and ten reels, and were very popular, especially those featuring Charlie Chaplin. There was a whole series about the Napoleonic Wars, full of battle scenes, the Bridge of Lodi and Austerlitz among others, which I found gripping.

On Guy Fawkes Day we had a fireworks display, first in the school yard, later on the playing field. The fireworks were released by Woodgate, the gardener, who on one occasion was nearly beheaded by a recalcitrant rocket, which shot over his shoulder and embedded itself above the window of the music room, to be greeted by the surprised head of Miss Davies. Another open-air event was the school sports, which took place annually in July and in which I never distinguished myself. I could never run fast or jump high, and when placed in a sack on the ground for the sack-race was unable to get to my feet. Every year there was an air display at Hendon, including a race, for which one of the turning points was the Aldenham Reservoir, just beyond the Elstree playing-field. We were thrilled by the sight of so many aircraft flying so low, though probably no schoolboy of today would turn a hair.

One Easter term was so warm that we played cricket in March, using improvised equipment. Another – in 1929 I think – was so cold that all football was cancelled and we were taken to the frozen Aldenham reservoir for skating. This was another sport that defeated me; as soon as I tried to move, the ice would rise up and hit me on the nose. On a later occasion, as Martin informed me in a letter, Joe fell through the ice and put half the reservoir out of bounds. While I was at Elstree there was a total eclipse of the sun, for which we were prepared with scientific information and smoked glass. The event was a disappointment; the sky was heavily overcast, and no eclipse was visible except, so far as I can remember, at Giggleswick in Yorkshire, the only occasion on which that doubtless estimable place has impinged on my consciousness.

Elstree had its own chapel, which like the playing field was approached by a subway under the road (Watling Street, now the A5). Two services every Sunday were compulsory. I had had no religious instruction, and was soon rebuked by a prefect for not bowing in the Creed. The words of some of the psalms and ten commandments puzzled me considerably. 'And there was that Leviathan' suggested only the image of a four-funnel passenger liner. I concluded that adultery must be what grown-ups did after the children had been put to bed, but was not clear why it was forbidden. Sermons, preached by the chaplain, the Reverend Norman Ashby, who had a long pointed red nose, were rather a bore, except occasionally when there was a special preacher on behalf of such initiatives as the Missions to Seamen (the name of the Reverend Vibart Ridgeway sticks in my mind). On these occasions there would be special collections, for which we gave sixpence; on ordinary Sundays we gave a penny. The coins were issued to us; we were not allowed to hold any money. I am ashamed to say that on one Sunday I only pretended to put a penny in the offertory bag, and on the following Sunday, when there was a special collection, I put in the penny I had saved and kept the sixpence, which I hid in the lining of my coat.

One preacher made a point that impressed me. Arguing that we must say our prayers every day, not only on Sunday, he told a story about a man who complained on Monday morning that he had been given no breakfast. 'But, sir', replied the cook, 'you had breakfast yesterday'. When Mr Greig joined the staff, his father, the first Bishop of Guildford, was invited to preach. I had never seen a bishop before, and assumed that this venerable bearded figure was so old that someone had to carry a big crooked stick in case he fell over. I once fainted in chapel and woke to find myself on the floor of the headmaster's study. We had evening prayers daily in the Big Schoolroom and sang a hymn accompanied by a wheezy old harmonium which had been there since the middle of the nineteenth century. It had a hole at the back, and once in prep I put my foot through this and played a loud chord. I was certainly no advertisement for a religious education. When studying the Greek Testament with Sanderson I translated the Holy Ghost as the Holy Wind, the literal meaning of the Greek. 'Irreverent little boy!' he exclaimed. Perhaps he was not far wrong.

In my early days in chapel my ear was caught by a peculiar roaring noise proceeding from the back of the choir. This proved to be Sanderson and Walmsley singing bass, almost two octaves below everyone else (Christie never attended chapel; perhaps he was a Presbyterian). The treble voices were supplied by the best singers among the boys, coached by Miss Davies, who played the organ; it had to be pumped by hand, a duty that occasionally fell to me. My voice was not exceptional, but I could sing accurately; during my last two years I was in the choir, and generally put on to sing descants. The great advantage of being in the choir was that we had an extra half holiday each winter term (and a special tea) and a whole holiday in the summer. For this we were taken to Lord's to see a first-class match. I enjoyed this enormously, and can remember many details of the matches between Middlesex and Somerset in 1928 and Middlesex and Yorkshire in 1929. Somerset were the underdogs, and their fielding struck me as poor, but M.D. Lyon hit a splendid six. In the Yorkshire match what impressed me most was the guileful slow bowling of Wilfred Rhodes, who had played for England against Australia in the nineteenth century. It was the only time I saw him play.

My interest in music was awakened in a curious way, and had nothing to do with Elstree or the choir. Although my parents both liked music, they did not play an instrument and made no move to have me taught one. We had a gramophone in the nursery, but its repertory of records was limited. There were sentimental ballads (including 'Home sweet home'), hearty songs by Ketèlbey sung by Peter Dawson, *The Lost Chord* played on the organ, an orchestral piece called *A Bit of the Ocean*, and *The Entry of the Gladiators* by Fučik, which was a great favourite of Martin's. We all liked songs called *Valencia* and *Barcelona* and a ditty that ran 'I had a little drink about an hour ago, and it went right to my head' (of course I missed the point of this) and items called *The Floral Dance* and *Side by Side*. None of this stirred me much. One day when I was visiting the paternal grandparents in Bloomsbury I heard, through the window, a street organ playing a tune that set some nerve vibrating deep within me. It was a strange sensation, as if it came from the remote past. The tune began to haunt my memory. A few months later I heard someone whistling it in the street. In March 1927 I had a serious illness at Elstree, diagnosed as nephritis. I did not feel ill, but began to pass blood in my urine. I was kept in bed for two or three weeks, forbidden to move and fed only on milk and water. Two other boys had the same complaint, and a very pleasant nurse was hired to read to us. We were not even allowed to raise our arms above the bed-clothes. Someone produced a kind of musical box which played metal records slotted as for a barrel organ. Most of them played traditional or folk tunes, but to my amazement one of the records played my tune. It was labelled *Carmen Polka*.

An Engagement with Time

As soon as I was well, I rushed to a gramophone shop, but there I had no luck. I found *Carmen saeculare*, but no polka. The following term I told my story to Miss Davies. She asked me if it was out of the opera; but I had no idea that *Carmen* was an opera. She took out a vocal score, opened it, and at once played my tune. It was the wordless song that Carmen sings to José in Act II when she dances for him, accompanying herself on the castanets – not a polka, but at least a dance. I tingled all over with excitement, and resolved to learn the piano in order to play it as often as I wished. By a devious succession of events that moment determined my future career.

When I asked my mother if I could learn the piano, she consented, provided I gave up carpentry. They were both additional subjects, for which extra fees were charged, and there was only enough money for one of them. I had been learning carpentry for about a year and greatly enjoyed it; instructed by Wilkins, the school carpenter, I made a wooden box, which I still have, and a bookshelf, which has disappeared. Operating a saw and a plane gave me considerable satisfaction, though once the saw slipped and exposed the tendon in my left thumb. I still carry the faint scar. I pondered long over the enforced choice between carpentry and music; after much heart-searching I decided on music.

I should of course have begun the piano much earlier. My fingers were stiff, and I had great difficulty in co-ordinating movement between my two hands, as Miss Davies remarked in her always encouraging reports. I struggled on and learned a piece which, thanks to the operation of the pedal, sounded much more difficult than it was. I even composed little tunes, which Miss Davies helped me to write down. During my last term Dr R.S. Thatcher came over from Harrow to inspect the music at Elstree, and we were all warned to have our pieces ready. I was sure I would dry up, and was terrified of being asked to play. Fortunately I was not. I had not made any great progress when I left Elstree, but could play my *Carmen* dance. The last time I saw Miss Davies was on a visit to Elstree in its new home in 1953; she was reading my book on Bizet. She has been dead for many years, but I shall always feel grateful to her for identifying that tune.

It was assumed that I would try for a scholarship at a public school; I think I had been put down for Charterhouse and one other school, possibly Eton. But the Harrow scholarship exam came first, at the beginning of March. Although I was not yet thirteen, and would still be eligible a year later, Sanderson decided that it would be good practice for me to enter. The exams lasted for three days, 5-7 March 1929. Hugh Martin (my rival in form), another boy and I were driven over to Harrow each morning by the Sandersons' chauffeur and collected in the evening. There were six papers, three Latin, one Greek, one French, and one History and English. I did not think I had done well. The task of turning sixteen lines of Samuel Daniel's poem 'Come, worthy Greek, Ulysses, come' into Latin Elegiacs completely baffled me; but it baffled the other candidates as well.

A few days later Sanderson sent Hugh and me over to see the results pinned up on the school notice-board (he must already have known them): Hugh was awarded the top scholarship, I the third. There was great rejoicing at Elstree and at home; three telegrams were brought to me during a game of football. Sanderson, himself an Old Harrovian, suggested to my mother that I should accept the scholarship offered and not try for another school; I suspect that this had been his plan all along. But I had not been entered for Harrow. Sanderson settled that by taking me over one afternoon to see the headmaster, Dr Cyril Norwood. Norwood, after a conversation with me alone, told Sanderson that he would take me into his house in September the same year. As a bonus I was given a day at Lord's for my first Eton and Harrow match, in which the Harrow innings was opened by the distinguished combination of Terence Rattigan and Victor, later Lord Rothschild. When I met him years later (he married one of my Cambridge friends) I reminded him of the shot that caused his dismissal in the second innings. He looked amused: 'It was a cow-shot', he declared.

I was never made a prefect at Elstree, a fact I greatly resented. Mrs Sanderson told my mother that it was for my own sake, to spare me the weight of responsibility. If so, it was a psychological blunder. It made me feel (acutely) inferior, the more so as it gave certain of my juniors authority over me, a position of which one or two were not slow to take advantage.

The last event of my Elstree life was a little talk that Sanderson gave individually to all boys who were leaving. This was intended to prepare us for the problems of puberty. I was very innocent, and knew nothing of such matters. Instead of simply explaining the facts, Sanderson loaded them with a heavy patina of moral injunction. He warned me against two great evils. The first was masturbation (though he did not use that word), which if indulged in could lead to insanity. The second he did not explain: it involved two individuals, and no decent boy would have anything to do with it. This puzzled me considerably. A year or two later, when I began to have nocturnal emissions, I thought I had committed a dangerous sin. While we were staying at Little Easton Manor, with only my little half-sister Tessa and her nurse in the house, this occurred on two consecutive nights. I woke up in a panic, and was on the point of dashing up to London to ask my mother how I could avert the consequences. The whole subject became a source of acute fear and anxiety.

It would be wrong to give the impression that life at Elstree was predominantly brutal, or that I never enjoyed myself. It was without doubt an admirable school, but better suited to extroverts, especially if they were athletes, than to the timorous and insecure creature that I was. Probably I would have fared the same or worse at any other boarding school, and a day school would have suited me better; but my mother can hardly be blamed for not predicting this. The Sandersons I know were genuinely fond of me, not only because I was a good scholar and a fine advertisement for their teaching; but they were unaware of what went on in my mind outside school hours. I did not bear any resentment; on one occasion when Sanderson beat me I surprised him by admitting afterwards that I deserved it. After leaving I often returned to Elstree to play cricket or football, either from Harrow or London, and was always warmly welcomed. At Harrow Speech Days, after I had received a prize I regularly went to sit with the Sandersons for the rest of the entertainment. More than once in later years I noted in my diary how odd it was that although I was unhappy at Elstree I always enjoyed going back.

CHAPTER 3

Sheppey

After divorcing Basil in 1924/5 my mother, who was still young and obviously attractive to the male sex, had plenty of admirers. I was doubtless not aware of all of them (for the greater part of the ten years from May 1924 I was at boarding school) and have no idea how far the relationships went, but three at least were serious, lasted a number of years, and necessarily impinged on my life. Looking back, I was inclined to divide the time into the Woodham-Smith period, the Mitford Brice period and the Bagger period.

G.I. Woodham-Smith, known as Bobby, was a lean, handsome and hungry-looking solicitor who had the reputation of steering rather close to the wind. My mother met him I think through the Bacons. His signature appears with hers in the Hambledon visitors' book during the years 1925-27, and he was responsible for our link with Warden Bay in the Isle of Sheppey. In 1926 Mother learned to drive a car. Her teacher (in the years before tests) was a friend of Woodham-Smith, an exuberant Irishman called Fitzgerald with a long pointed nose and an extraordinary laugh that began at a low pitch and ran *crescendo* up the chromatic scale like a rocket; I likened it to a musical corkscrew. She bought a second-hand Rover two-seater with a dicky seat just large enough to hold my brothers. In this little vehicle she made her first long journey in September that year from Hambledon to Warden Bay (between Minster and Leysdown), which Woodham-Smith and others, following a trend of the times, were trying to transform into a popular holiday resort by buying up land and building cheap bungalows. She took me with her, and we stayed for ten days in a down-at-heel hotel, run by a couple called Richards. The enterprise was already in full swing, with bungalows springing up round the bay and up a low hill towards Warden Point, which had one small shop that doubled as a post office and offered bed and breakfast for three or four persons. Beyond it the road disappeared over the cliffs. The sea encroached steadily every year and had already carried away two successive churches; the remains of the second, which appeared to be a cheap wooden affair, could still be detected half way down the cliff. A few concrete pill-boxes survived from the 1914-18 war until they too toppled into the sea.

Our only previous experience of a seaside holiday had been in 1924 at Selsey, where there were lots of children, plenty of sand – enough for a light aircraft to land one day – and other orthodox pleasures, including fairs and a semi-derelict railway. I recall the excitement of watching the four-funnelled liner *Aquitania* making for Southampton, and on a different level the pleasure of discussing with an adult enthusiast the merits of the South African cricket team on their first tour since the 1914-18 war. Memorable too was the four-year-old Martin's response to his first sight of the sea: '*Please don't put me too near the taps!*'

Even at the time Warden seemed an odd place to choose. The beach comprised more shingle and mud than sand, and behind it the cliffs were crumbling. That part of Sheppey – like most of the island – had few trees and no tourist attractions apart from one or two old churches and the fragment of a castle. The land consisted chiefly of scattered sheep farms and bleak expanses of marsh, with an airfield at Eastchurch, the scene of some of the earliest powered flights before the first war. It is now a prison. The inhabitants, apart from farmers, seemed to be either retired people living on small pensions or – as I was to learn later – shady characters who had slipped out of London to escape their creditors. Woodham-Smith, who was living in an old army hut, and Richards seemed to be in charge of the enterprise, for which the most ambitious plans had been drawn up. Something about Richards filled me with mistrust, but I could not define what it was. Others more or less involved were Fitzgerald, his sister Cecil Taylor and her husband, and a monosyllabic architect named Heygate. I was encouraged to play with Richards's son, a year or two younger than me, whom I did not much like. There was also a Greek family called Avgherinos, one of whom arranged to play cricket with me and then failed to turn up. I was taken out fishing in the Bay in a small boat. I can't remember if we caught anything, but the rocking motion of the boat made me sick.

The result of this visit, reinforced perhaps by countless pictorial advertisements of Sunny Warden Bay plastered on hoardings all over Kent, was that my mother persuaded Tommy to invest in one of the new bungalows as a base for our summer holidays. From 1927 to 1934 it served as such, and occasionally for two or three weeks in the spring, but only in 1928 did we spend the whole summer period there. It was pleasantly situated on a small hill my mother called Smuggler's Beacon, then Thorn Hill, though I don't remember any thorns. It was of somewhat ramshackle construction, and at first had only three small bedrooms. Martin, Joe and Haricot slept in one (until this was considered improper), Margaret in what became my room, I in my mother's, and she on a divan in the living-room. Later Margaret was despatched up a narrow wooden stair into the roof-space. I can't remember where Haricot slept eventually, unless it was in the kitchen. We ate in the hall, from which three steps led down via the front door to a small veranda and thence to a stony path. I remember my mother struggling to carve a recalcitrant leg of mutton, which leapt off the table, through the front door, down the steps, across the veranda and on to the path. We spent much of our time on the beach, where we had a hut for changing, and it was a matter of pride that we always had a picnic tea. This meant that Haricot and Margaret spent a great deal of time every day cutting sandwiches; mine always had to contain marmalade. It does not seem to have rained so frequently in those days. We also climbed the cliffs, bathed, caught shrimps in a net, and captured crabs in the intestines of a dilapidated jetty which was covered at high tide. For some reason we regarded these creatures as evil and cut off their claws as trophies, until they smelt so bad we were ordered to bury them.

We did not see a great deal of our neighbours. The nearest were an elderly couple called Fielder, who had lived in South America. He could occasionally be prevailed upon to give demonstrations with a whip; she was an enthusiastic but indifferent bridge player who hated losing. Once when we were playing, Joe put his head round the door and asked: 'Mummy, are you letting Mrs Fielder win, as you said you would?' A little further away a kindly old lady, Mrs Campion, lived with her sister Miss Copeland and possessed a tennis court on which she allowed us to play. She had two daughters, one very dark, the other very fair, both married to naval officers serving in the Mediterranean; they kindly augmented my collection of Maltese stamps.

We sometimes walked to Eastchurch across fields where there was supposed to be a right-of-way, but the farmer, a Mr Beale, denied this and threatened us, brandishing some agricultural implement. It was at Eastchurch that 'V. Hann Family Butcher' plied his trade. I wondered what the difference was between a family butcher and an ordinary butcher, such as we had in St John's Wood. He could hardly butcher whole families, unless the reference was to sheep or cattle. There was also a garage, where on one occasion when the Rover or its successor had got into difficulty, my mother asked if she could borrow some pliers. 'Sorry, Madam', came the reply, 'we don't stock cigarettes'. Just outside the village, on a little hill, stood the battlements of Shurland Castle, which presented a formidable façade but little behind. One day an aircraft crashed just in front of it, killing the two occupants. We walked over with Haricot to view the wreckage. By some quirk of memory I recall that the pilot's name was E.L. Wilson, and that at the inquest his father complained bitterly about his treatment in the service.

One feature of interest was the long since vanished Sheppey Light Railway, which ran from Queenborough via Sheerness East, Minster and Eastchurch to a miniature terminus at Leysdown in the NE corner of the island. Though of standard gauge it was decidedly primitive. There was scarcely a bridge on the island, but several level crossings. When the little two-carriage train pulled by a small tank engine approached one, the driver would hop out, open the gates and after crossing the road close them again before remounting his engine. I don't remember any buses; if we needed to go to Sheerness in a hurry, we could for 8 shillings hire a taxi operated by a Mr Fox, who resembled his name.

There was not a great deal else to do, but we never had much difficulty in amusing ourselves, often with variants of cricket. We laid out a rough pitch in what would have been the garden of the bungalow if any attempt had been made to cultivate it. We bowled to each other under-arm, using hard balls but stumps as bats and scoring on a very recondite system. When one of us was out, he could always come in again, batting under another name and in a different style. The scores were recorded in a book. This occupied many hours, until one day I hit the ball on the half-volley with more strength than I intended and narrowly missed my mother's head as she sat in a deckchair reading a book. After that we were banished to even rougher ground behind the bungalow, where it was impossible to produce anything approaching a level pitch. There was an indoor version for wet weather in which we each played our own match. Setting up matchboxes as wickets and various small boxes as fielders, we bowled a marble with the left hand and batted with a ruler in the right (or vice versa). The boxes were so positioned that they could make catches. This was played on the bare boards of the attic. There was a space between them and the rafters of the roof, down which a good many marbles disappeared and were lost. I sometimes wondered if they were still there, but I later heard from Joe that the entire bungalow had disappeared.

For these games we invented a whole series of imaginary teams and cricketers, usually with outlandish names, each of whom had his individual style and character, just as in dab-cricket; but for some reason the two hierarches were kept apart. Cricket even invaded our journeys in the small 4-seater that succeeded the Rover. Scoring was governed by the vehicles we overtook: we scored one for a bicycle, two for a horse and cart, three for a bus, four for a private car, six for a motor-cycle. If anything overtook us, whoever was batting was out. Hence one of us was constantly urging the driver to overtake anything in front and not to allow anything behind to pass, a procedure hardly conducive to safe or comfortable driving.

The year 1928 was not a happy one for me. In March, towards the end of his first term at Elstree, Martin was seriously ill with complications after measles. In May my mother went on a month's cruise in the Mediterranean, paid for by Ernest Makower, a kindly friend of the grandparents. It was thought that Martin needed a period of recuperation, and he was sent to Hambledon for the whole month of May, together with Haricot and Joe, who was withdrawn temporarily from Sheringham House to keep him company. I felt bitter at being left out of this arrangement and sent back to Elstree, the more so when I discovered that we were to spend the entire summer holidays at Warden instead of dividing them with Hambledon, as we did in all other years. In 1928 I spent a single day at Hambledon, less than in any other year of my life. Two other families whom we knew were persuaded to spend the summer at Warden – Kitty Wallace (who had been my mother's bridesmaid) with four sons aged 1, 2, 4 and 8 and two nurses, and Lewis Bacon, daughter-in-law of the match maker Charlotte with a daughter and son of about Martin's and Joe's age. I was the odd one out, since Martin and Joe naturally played with their contemporaries. The weeks dragged past, and I became heartily sick of Warden. It is strange how after eighty years I can still taste the tang of bitterness when I think of that summer.

The vividness of my imagination in childhood broke through in dreams of alarming realism. I had a whole series that summer in Warden, in which either I or someone close to me was murdered, and can still recall some of them. In one Margaret was strangled in the hall next to the room where I was sleeping. In another I was on a long walk and met a sinister man who stared at me. Whenever I looked I could not avoid his stare, and I knew that he had a knife which he would throw at me as soon as my back was turned. I then began to faint, a sensation reminiscent of being anaesthetised by ether (I had experienced this twice and found it peculiarly unpleasant) and thought I would never wake up. Then I lost consciousness, but woke up (still in the dream) and found that I was dead. This propensity for nightmares was accentuated by reading detective stories which my mother obtained from the library; everything I read presented itself to my mind as reality. So to a rather less degree did plays and films. During our first summer at Warden, when I was sleeping in my mother's room, I was woken up by returning revellers – Fitzgerald's corkscrew laugh, and his voice calling 'Get your gas-masks!' – and was seized with momentary terror, as if a new war had broken out. When we were at Hambledon during this period we stayed with the farmer at Malthouse Farm, since there was no room at the Hurst: but I had dinner with the grandparents. Afterwards I had to cover about 200 yards back to the farm, mostly through the garden; I used to run all the way in case some dangerous thing attacked me in the dark. Even when out with my mother I was once terrified by the bloodcurdling cry of a fox in the woods.

Our later summers at Warden were rather more tolerable, though I still found it difficult to find companions of my own age. Mrs Waghorn, who gave highly entertaining Christmas parties in St John's Wood with guests of all ages, came with her children Anne and Mark. My mother later claimed that I was smitten with Anne, who was nearer my age, but I don't recall any emotional attraction. Much more welcome were occasional visits from the Muirheads, Litellus and Benedetta (always abbreviated to Tellie and Ben) who almost alone managed to remain on friendly terms with three generations of our family. Tellie, son of the founder of Muirhead's Blue Guides and a relative of the Reas, was a walking encyclopaedia with an extraordinary fund of knowledge on any subject you liked to mention, as well as a rich sense of humour. For years we had evenings of paper games with them, usually a compound of consequences with general knowledge tests of our own invention. I remember them coming to Queen's Road in the 1920s; Ben, who was born in 1900 and all but outlived the 20th century, saying that she was 26; and the difficult birth of their son Simon more than 80 years ago. They attributed the success of their marriage to the fact that they were not afraid to quarrel and advised Thalia and me to follow their example. Their visits to Warden, always provided interesting discussions, and sometimes trips to neighbouring places of interest.

There were occasional group expeditions in several cars to some spot on the mainland, where we had a mass picnic. These were arranged by Miss Fry, the brisk spinster who kept the post office at Warden Point. She was a compulsive organiser, who was always trying to make us play rounders. I disliked this game, and devised methods of outwitting her, on one occasion leading a secessionist party to inspect the ancient church at High Halstow. On our return to the cars a battle royal developed with squashy plums as missiles, one of which scored a direct hit on the forehead of a lady of strikingly exotic appearance who went by the (possibly apt) name of Mrs Lawless. Miss Fry was not amused.

One enjoyable event was associated with our journeys to Warden, whether from London or Hambledon. We used to spend the best part of a day at Rooting Manor, Little Chart, near Ashford, the house of my father's elder brother Vernon. His wife Vie was one of the kindest and most generous people I knew, and like Gran she had a gift for establishing happy relations with children. We were regularly let loose in the fruit cage and encouraged to consume as much as we could contain. Once or twice I stayed at Rooting by myself. I was allowed to play an elaborate card game of my invention, involving warfare between two or more packs of cards spread face downwards all over the drawing-room floor, a thing never permitted at home. Michael and John Balkwill, Vie's sons from her first marriage, had many of their mother's qualities and were great favourites of us all. Another memory of Rooting is my first hearing on a gramophone record of Dvořák's *Humoresque* in G flat, which at once captivated me. The house was very old, and reputed to be haunted. The atmosphere was certainly spooky at night, when a strange glow appeared which looked like moonlight – except that it persisted when there was no moon. It was said to be phosphorescence caused by decaying vegetable matter.

In London during the winter, as at Warden, we were constantly evolving new games, many of which featured lead soldiers and civilians, pieces of artillery (firing metal shells propelled by a spring) and forts, sometimes combined with a clockwork railway layout and various vehicles and constructions built from Meccano – using our own designs, not those offered by the booklet that went with the set. We did not compete against each other, but each conducted our own battles, accompanied by a running commentary that sometimes drove Haricot or Margaret to protest. There were various rules or conventions governing the lead civilians. Each had his own name, and if there were two or more of the same design they had to share the name. Some of the names came from books, others were of real people, others purely fanciful. I had a porter called Collapsible and two others called Conception and Contraception, though I had no idea what the words meant. Martin, whose imagination was distinctly earthy, had a station master called Mr Piss. There was a golfer called Colonel Killiecrankie, and knights in armour with different coloured shields called Interpretators. The black Interpretator was always more powerful than the red, green or pink, and a knight with a helmet more dangerous than one without.

These persons were put through the most sanguinary battles, known as consputes, which only ended when most of the participants were considered dead or unconscious. A certain figure of an elderly woman was always known as Mrs Van Gruisen – never Gran or Grandma – and a young workman was Ernie, the under-gardener at Hambledon. Margaret once came in and protested against Ernie repeatedly knocking down Mrs Van Gruisen. We were fond of both originals, and there was no question of our working out our resentments on the substitutes, though perhaps in some obscure way these imaginary fights, which we greatly enjoyed, may have released hidden aggressive instincts. I doubt if there is any parallel with the vicarious pleasure modern children reputedly derive from television. There was of course no television in our childhood, and very little radio, at least in the nursery. When I was about twelve, Gran gave me a crystal set, which involved earphones and the manipulation of a metal whisker. Although it seemed a miracle that this could produce any sound at all, its operation was apt to be frustrating, since it was necessary to keep on fiddling with the position of the whisker in order to keep on the wavelength. We envied the few friends who owned a radio with a loudspeaker.

There was something theatrical about these improvised games, a kind of childish *commedia dell' arte*. We also operated toy theatres, for which Martin and I wrote plays. Joe, who was something of a loner – he played less with soldiers and cricket games – decorated his theatre with elaborate lighting effects and miniature furniture (the beds had little chamber-pots underneath), but never went so far as to perform a play. Martin and I used to collaborate: I generally wrote the play, he controlled the theatrical effects, and we both spoke the dialogue, moving the characters (the same lead figures with wires attached) as we did so. From about 1930 we gave performances at Christmas with my mother, Gran and Uncle Alfred Sutro as audience. One of the programmes survives, and one of my plays, which was called *Oysters for Dinner*. Alfred declared this an excellent title and laughed most encouragingly at the jokes. This was a comedy; I had by that time written some gruesome schoolboy thrillers, in which most of the characters were killed off before the end, and in my first term at Harrow a full-length pseudo-Elizabethan tragedy called *The Hand of Fate*. (I thought it so appalling on coming across it a few years later that I hastily destroyed it.) This came of reading the complete works of Shakespeare, which I had chosen as a school prize, at the age of twelve and thirteen. I cannot have understood more than a very small fraction.

I had already seen *A Midsummer Night's Dream* acted by puppets, which kept breaking down, and a full professional performance of *Othello*, to which Gran, waving aside protests from other members of the family, took me in 1926. It gripped me completely; I can still remember what the actors looked like (the Othello I think was Matheson Lang) and how they pronounced some of their lines. We were taken to pantomimes or children's plays like *Where the Rainbow Ends* and *Peter Pan* at Christmas, and occasionally to the circus or a film. I did not greatly care for pantomimes, and positively disliked the convention of a female principal boy – too often a mature woman with bulges in the wrong place – which seemed to me a silly idea. Films were more enjoyable, since they usually contained plenty of action. I particularly recall the chariot race in *Ben Hur*, fights between first-war aircraft in *Wings*, and a glorious locomotive chase in *The General* with Buster Keaton in the uniform of the American Civil War.

In April 1929 I stayed in Whitehaven with one of my few Elstree friends, Pim Ormrod, and was introduced to the beauties of the Lake District. I also played badminton for the first and only time in my life, and found it a singularly frustrating game since the harder I hit the shuttle the less far it seemed to travel. I got into hot water for accidentally discharging a blank-cartridge pistol in the car. This was a new toy, which added an impressive touch of realism to our games. In the same month I paid my first visit to Little Easton Manor, the beautiful old house that Lady Warwick bestowed on my father when he married her daughter Mercy. I took to her at once; indeed I found both my stepmothers easier to get on with than my father. Unfortunately I was in bed with flu for most of the visit, but on the last afternoon went birds-nesting with Mercy in the park of Easton Lodge, her mother's home. The Manor, especially before my father altered it, was a distinctly spooky house, full of creaking boards and dark corners. Edward IV was said to have spent his honeymoon there. Part of it dated from the 15th Century, and the remains of the moat could be seen in the garden. There was also, hidden behind a bush, the entrance to a secret passage that once led to the church. As at Rooting, I took care not to go out after dark, and was tempted to sleep with the light on.

In 1931 and again in 1932 I persuaded Mother to drive us to Canterbury to watch a day's cricket in the first-class match between Kent and the visiting team from the Dominions. We were particularly lucky in the former year, when Frank Woolley made a double century, twice hitting two sixes in consecutive balls, and Leslie Ames, who made over 100, driving a six that pitched on the rim of the concrete stand where we were sitting. In the following year the Indian captain C.K. Nayudu was bowled for 99. On one or both of these occasions I was fascinated by the sight of C.S. Marriott bowling his leg-breaks with an air of detachment, looking like the schoolmaster that he was. He played only one Test Match for England, against the West Indies in 1933, but then took 11 wickets. He might have been picked more often had he not been a useless batsman and a liability in the field. I hoped to see the Canterbury match that year (when Marriott took another ten) but for some reason Mother refused to take us, and we had no chance with the Australians in 1934.

* * * * *

My mother certainly hoped to marry Woodham-Smith. It may be that the prospect of inheriting three young stepsons proved too great an obstacle, or perhaps that was an excuse. At all events in 1928 he married Cecil Taylor, who later under her married name became a distinguished historical writer, author of books on Florence Nightingale and the Crimean War. Vie told Joe that when Woodham-Smith withdrew, Mother took an overdose of some drug, fortunately without fatal effect. I heard that Taylor turned up at Hambledon and made a scene, apparently in the belief that Esther was responsible for the break-up of his marriage.

She was said at one time to have been very keen on John Archibald, a lawyer friend of the Sutros, whom I never met. That could have been at this period (or perhaps earlier); he was twice a weekend guest at Hambledon, accompanied by his Italian wife. There were several eligible bachelors, including Wilkie Calvert and Philip Davis, who used to take her out to dinner and / or the theatre, before which she would appear in glamorous evening dress to say good-night to me; but she always laughed when I asked if she proposed to marry any of them.

A more serious candidate was Mitford Brice, whom she met at the Fielders' bungalow at Warden in I think 1930, along with a wife and a bull-terrier. The wife may have been a misnomer, but the bull-terrier was genuine. He was addressed as George but his official name was Mitsu Dannebrog. Brice was a retired Major in the Buffs, with a distinguished record in the Great War (he was awarded the Military Cross), who stood for Parliament as a Conservative at West Willesden in 1924. He was a member of the Kennel Club. As well as breeding bull-terriers he published a number of books on canine subjects, including *Our Princesses and Their Dogs* (1936). For a time he used the pen-name Michael Chance, anticipating that of a well-known countertenor. He too spent a number of weekends at Hambledon (in 1931-2) and I often saw his handwriting on letters addressed to my mother. Like Woodham-Smith, who gave me a copy of Stevenson's *Kidnapped* as a Christmas present in 1927, he treated me well. I still have three letters from him.

Brice arranged for me to have cricket coaching from Joe Hulme, the Middlesex cricketer and Arsenal footballer, at the Alexandra Palace. He took me to my first Test Match, between England and New Zealand at the Oval in August 1931, in which I saw Sutcliffe and Duleepsinhji on the way to centuries and Bakewell, the other opener, run out through refusing to answer Sutcliffe's call for a short single. There was one odd incident on this occasion. Play was interrupted by rain, and Brice left me in my seat, saying he would be back soon. After a considerable time I became bored and went in search of him. I looked in at the bar and saw him, as I thought. But he looked right through me, and I wondered if he had a double. I went back to my seat, and presently he returned as if nothing had happened. I heard later that my mother had broken off relations with him after discovering that gifts he had bestowed on her had been charged to her account at Selfridge's or (as noted in my diary) that she had lent him a large sum of money which he failed to repay. There may have been some truth in this, for Basil, who heard about it from Vernon, made it a pretext for trying to reduce his alimony.

Many years later I was astonished to catch sight of Mitford Brice's name in a *Times Literary Supplement* article of 16 May 2003 that I would normally not have read. The author, A.D. Harvey, had come across Brice while trawling through Metropolitan Police and Army records and outlined his extraordinary career. In 1936 Brice had been convicted of indecent assault on a boy (we heard something of this at the time). His military career was decidedly chequered. In 1909 in Hong Kong as Second Lieutenant he 'frequented houses of ill-fame and squandered his money besides seriously damaging his health'. In the First World War Brice was wounded at Loos, promoted to Major and awarded the MC for his part in the storming of the Schwaben Redoubt in October 1916. After this, 'having concussed himself by falling into a shell hole when drunk, he began taking veronal for post-concussion insomnia, became addicted, went on a bender in Paris, passed a number of dud cheques, promoted himself to Lieutenant Colonel, was arrested, jumped train to escape his guard and finally obtained a discharge from the Army on medical grounds'. The Deputy Adjutant General noted: 'The man is an absolute waster' who only escaped trial by Court Marshal because he was sick. He is last heard of, as Major Michael Brice MC, in 1941 as 'something in the Home Guard'. The village bobby at Chalfont St Giles reported 'local gossip as to Boy Scouts'.

CHAPTER 4

Harrow

My Harrow career began in September 1929. In some respects it duplicated my experiences at Elstree, but in more extreme form. School work presented no difficulty; I was even more successful than at Elstree, and had great respect for all my form-masters and for most of those who taught subsidiary subjects. Life outside teaching hours was a very different matter. The Head Master's was the largest house in the school, with about 85 boys. For games and competitions it was divided into two parts, known as HM A and HM B, which were smaller in numbers than any of the other principal houses. (As a result the house seldom won any of the major competitions where numbers counted; but the term before my arrival the two halves astonishingly had reached the final of the knockout cricket tournament, and the Cock House Match became a purely domestic affair.) The house itself was physically divided into two main staircases, Old and New, with the kitchens and the Head Master's quarters in between, joined by a long passage through the kitchen quarters. I was put in a room at the top of the Old staircase with two other boys, both Exhibitioners in Classics. This was a bad arrangement, since two will always gang up against the third. Although I later became friendly with both these boys, they gave me a grim time during my first year.

Nor did we see a great deal of Norwood. The running of the house was entrusted to an Under-Housemaster, a bachelor in his thirties called Bostock, who had many virtues but one or two blind spots, as I was to discover later. A great deal of authority was wielded by the house monitors, through the system of fagging, which was supposed to inculcate a sense of responsibility. They did not have personal fags; the younger boys served all the monitors, two at a time in daily rotation (one for each side of the house), and were at their beck and call at almost all times of the day, including meals. Among their duties was to clean the monitors' shoes and in the winter to light fires in their rooms and make sure they did not go out. The monitors could send them on any errand, including messages to boys in other houses, and some of them seemed to take pleasure in devising footling tasks. They could also inflict extra days' fagging as a punishment without informing Bostock. The head of the house, David Stewart-Brown (later a distinguished Q.C.), was also Head of the School and a member of the school team in all three principal sports, Rugby, Harrow football and cricket. He was far more formidable than any master, especially as we were continually under his eye. For some reason I seemed to antagonise him; he was constantly pouncing on me and giving me 'extras' for small accidental misdemeanours, what he called 'slackness', on one occasion three at a time because I had been given several 'extras' by other monitors. One monitor gave me an 'extra' when he heard me say jokingly that whenever he approached his room his fire went out, another because I did not answer his call at a time when I was not supposed to be on duty. I complained to Bostock about this; but he felt he had to support the monitor and told me to serve my sentence. I made a vow that if ever I became a monitor I would never abuse my authority. There was a strict hierarchy throughout the house, with a whole range of privileges, on a printed sheet, to which members of each year – and especially house monitors – were entitled. Most of them were utterly trivial; but in addition to other rules and regulations they underlined the servile status of new boys.

Games, which of course were compulsory, were at first another sore trial. Harrow was still to a considerable extent in the grip of the old tradition which rated toughness in games above almost anything else. In the autumn term we played rugby, which was a new experience for me. Since HM B, to which I belonged, was weak in numbers, boys of all ages and sizes had to play in the same team. For some reason authority decreed that I should play as a lock forward in the second row of the scrum. I was still small and light for my age (five feet and under six stone, according to my report), and I found myself alongside another lad of similar displacement, with the largest and heaviest boy not only in the house but in the school shoving behind us in the middle of the front row. Inevitably the scrum was liable to collapse, and I found myself kicked almost as frequently as the ball. Bostock remarked in his report that I was 'physically rather timid … We would like to see a little more grit'.

As a result of these and other stresses the bed-wetting which I had overcome two years before recurred, causing me the most acute shame and embarrassment. My room-companions seized on this all too easy occasion for ridicule, and it no doubt contributed to Bostock's pronouncement at the end of my first year that I was still rather an infant, years younger than my contemporaries. It was cured with some difficulty by our doctor in St John's Wood, to whom I went up once a week, by a quasi-hypnotic treatment. A more unfortunate result of the stress in the long run was my abandonment of the piano. Both practice and lessons had to come out of spare time, which in view of the extra fagging I had to do was none too liberal. In his first report Thatcher wrote that I had musical intelligence but needed to be 'more reliable both in practice and attendance at lessons'. He was no doubt right. But though an excellent teacher he was a nervy, highly strung man and was apt to discourage me with withering remarks like 'If Mozart could compose this at the age of six, you should be able to play it at thirteen'. His tense manner communicated itself to me. I would practice for hours, and then at my next lesson my fingers would be quite unable to do what they had done quite adequately in private; whereupon he would accuse me of not practicing. On one occasion when the second music-master took his place I got on much better. Thatcher's report on my fourth term was: 'Still very slow, and unless he really enjoys it I would recommend discontinuance'. I was not enjoying it, and did discontinue it, a decision I have regretted ever since.

There was an ironical sequel. After the war, when I began work on Bizet, I discovered that the only full scores of his early operas in the country were in the Angelina Goetz collection at the Royal Academy of Music, where Thatcher was then Warden and subsequently Principal. I wrote to him asking permission to see them, adding that he might possibly remember me as one of his most incompetent pupils at Harrow. He was perfectly charming, made the scores available, and took me to lunch with the Principal. When I thanked him after finishing with the scores, he said: 'It's strange to find you doing this sort of work'. Evidently he did remember. My few subsequent meetings with him were very cordial; there was no allusion to the past.

Thatcher conducted the school choral society, in which I took part as a treble during my first year. His manner when displeased with us was devastating, but he obtained a good performance at the concert. The programme consisted of a potted *Meistersinger*, the Hallelujah chorus from *Messiah* and Balfour Gardiner's setting of Masefield's *Cargoes*. This contains some tongue-twisters, including the line 'Dirty British coaster with a salt-caked smoke-stack', which had to be sung rapidly and was apt to emerge as a series of spoonerisms.

Thatcher also officiated at House Singing, an event that took place in each house two or three times every winter term. On the first such occasion every new boy had to sing, solo, a verse from *Men of Harlech*, an assignment that filled me with dread. After a string of us, all piping trebles, had surmounted this hurdle, it was found that a senior boy, a member of the Seligman family, had somehow evaded it. He was accordingly required to sing, and began in a sepulchral double-bass voice that sent Thatcher scurrying down the piano to find the appropriate pitch. The whole house had to rehearse several songs from the School Song Book, after which senior boys in turn could nominate any individual or group to sing a verse of their choice, stating a reason. This would be subtle form of revenge and a source of considerable merriment. The Harrow Songs were famous – justly so. Though some of the words have dated, most of the tunes are excellent and have stood the test of time. *Forty Years On*, in which words and tune are happily mated, can communicate a thrill to the least faithful of old boys and even to outsiders. During my time at Harrow Norwood and Thatcher added several sterling specimens to the book.

Every second year the school, with the assistance of masters' daughters and others, mounted a stage production of a Sullivan operetta in Speechroom. I found *The Mikado* and *The Gondoliers* easy to enjoy; but when the Webber-Douglas School gave a performance of *Così fan tutte* with two pianos I was baffled, despite a lucid preliminary talk from Thatcher. I was clearly not ready for Mozart. *Hansel and Gretel*, performed by the same forces, was more accessible, though the story did not appeal to me. By a strange chance this was the occasion of the first appearance on any stage (in the chorus) of my father's future third wife, her name misprinted in the programme as Victoria Hooper.

My unfortunate experience with Thatcher put me off music altogether for several years. There were piano and song recitals and an occasional orchestral concert, but apart from a recital by John Cross and the London Singers in October 1931 they made little impression on me, and I have lost most of the programmes. Among the artists I heard were John Coates (an elderly and dignified figure), Helen Henschel, Smeterlin and Ethel Bartlett and Rae Robertson. Nevertheless music continued to nag at me in my own despite. In September 1933 I tried to account for its curious impact: it made me feel pensive and uneasy, sad, even morbid. When it did not impel me to write verse, it was apt to cut off the pleasures of daily life. On one occasion at Harrow a tune came to me in my sleep, and I tried to write it down; I identified it later as a confused recollection of Nicolai's overture to *The Merry Wives of Windsor*, which I was quite unaware of having heard. In January 1934 I went to a concert in Liverpool conducted by Nikolai Malko, and decided that Russian music made me even more restless than other kinds. The break-through came on 20 February that year, when the LSO performed Elgar's *Enigma Variations* in Speechroom, preceded by an explanatory talk by Thatcher, illustrated at the piano, which I found enthralling. He mentioned that the composer was seriously ill. The music carried me away completely. Three days later Elgar died, and Thatcher played the Nimrod variation as an organ voluntary in Chapel. I heard the variations again on the radio a few days later, and have never lost my enthusiasm for them.

For the most part I remember the plays more clearly than the concerts. There were performances of *The Tempest*, with Donald Wolfit as Caliban grovelling with reptilian realism, and *Henry V*, which I thought insensitively cast. John Gielgud brought a company down for what we thought would be a production of *Hamlet*. Instead he gave a sort of lecture recital, illustrated by scenes from the play. This was interesting, but I would have preferred the whole play; I was going through a passionate Shakespeare period, and had already seen Gielgud as Mark Anthony and Romeo at the Old Vic. A company consisting largely of Old Harrovians brought a spirited production of *Saint Joan*, my first experience of Shaw, and the masters enacted a most entertaining double bill consisting of Barrie's *Shall We Join the Ladies?* and Galsworthy's *The Little Man*, in which two of my future form-masters distinguished themselves, Plumptre as Galsworthy's central figure and Moir as an explosive German station-master who kept tripping over the luggage. *Le Barbier de Séville*, given in French by a company from the Comédie Française, was more educational than entertaining, since few of us were able to follow the dialogue. There were occasional films, of which I particularly enjoyed *Brown on Resolution*, based on C.S. Forester's novel about the navy in the 1914 War, and *The General*, the classic comedy featuring Buster Keaton and a hilarious locomotive chase set in the period of the American Civil War. When I saw this again more than forty years later I found that I remembered the locomotive episodes vividly but had totally forgotten that throughout his adventures Keaton was accompanied by a girl. Another film, whose name I forget, was so stilted and old-fashioned that the tender scenes were greeted by the whole school with howls of laughter.

Classics of course was my main subject, and I spent a year in each form, Remove, Lower Fifth and Upper Fifth, and two in the Sixth. My form masters for the first three years were T.E.J. Bradshaw, Philip Boas and James Moir, all of whom I liked. They were very different. Bradshaw could roar, but his bark was greater than his bite, and so far as I remember he never barked at me personally. One day he set us to imitate a terse epigrammatic sketch of G.K. Chesterton, taking as subject anyone we liked. Hugh Martin chose Bradshaw himself, featured as Jupiter Touans distributing his thunder round the Old School. Bradshaw was much amused. Boas, recently down from Oxford, had certain mild eccentricities. He used to bring a bulldog into early school; it usually sat motionless on the platform, but occasionally scratched itself or made what we took to be a comment on our efforts or those of its master. That was the year we took School Certificate, for which the English set books were *Macbeth* and Coleridge. It was possible to draw Boas off the subject into long digressions, sometimes very remote from the work in hand. We enjoyed doing this, and one or two of the class were specialists at it. Boas would suddenly pull himself together and say 'Now, Roper, you are trying to lead me astray again', only for someone else to take up the running and lead him in another tangential direction. Moir was a precise and witty Scotsman, an excellent scholar liked by everyone. He and Bradshaw both died sadly young – Bradshaw soon after his wife after many years of marriage had unexpectedly produced a son and thereby given the school a half-holiday.

They all gave me marvellous reports. Bradshaw called me a brilliant performer after one term and was talking about open scholarships at the university after three. Moir remarked, as Walmsley had done at Elstree, that 'facts play rather a large part, to the exclusion of general discussion, of a subject', but two terms later applauded 'some clever renderings of Aristophanes into English verse'. I almost invariably came first in Latin and Greek, and often in other subjects too, including French and even Mathematics. At first Mathematics were rather a trial. I could often produce the right answer, only to be told that that was of minor significance: I ought to have shown all the steps by which I reached it. I had doubtless done these in my head, and was never convinced that the right answer did not matter. When in my second year I had a sympathetic teacher, A.P. Boissier, I shot ahead. He wrote: 'He has imagination and is not afraid to use it' – though I am not sure what scope there is for imagination in fairly elementary mathematics – and 'His progress and conduct have been all that could be desired'. Boissier's daughter used to appear in the school's Gilbert and Sullivan productions, and later, as Marchioness of Aberdeen, did stout work for opera in the Scottish Highlands.

One of the English masters, T.F. Coade, later Headmaster of Bryanston, was an enlightened teacher who introduced discussion of the other arts; I remember a whole period devoted to a picture by Van Gogh. He found my style 'just a little long-winded' and advised me to practice economy of words. J.F.M. Holland (History) made similar points and said that I had not yet discovered how to write on paper what I wanted to say. In School Certificate I gained credits in seven subjects and narrowly missed one in the eighth, Additional Mathematics. This was no surprise: I was baffled by elementary mechanics and the mysterious functions of a factor called dy-by-dx, which was written like a fraction dy/dx but meant something different. The fact that I missed this credit put me below some of my peers in the school order; Norwood readjusted this by promoting me to the Classical Sixth while I was still working with the Upper Fifth, a sensitive move for which I was grateful.

I enjoyed games a good deal more after the first term. I played a good deal of squash and Eton fives, at which I eventually became quite proficient. The organised sport in the spring term was Harrow Football, a hybrid and esoteric game that employed a very large ball flattened at the poles like a grapefruit. Two referees were required but there were no penalties; if a player was offside, one of the referees (and probably the opposition) shouted at him and he was expected to desist. The rules for handling the ball were unlike those in any other kind of football. The goalposts had no cross bar and were considered to stretch to infinity. Bostock said that I played 'with good pluck' in my second term, 'and we hope that this is the first step towards manliness'. This was a recurring theme – manliness was a physical rather than intellectual quality – but I evidently improved in Bostock's estimation, for by my seventh term I was 'a useful member of the house' and by my eighth I seemed to have lost my timidity. In December 1932 he even wrote 'He seems to enjoy life here and has a cheerful wholesome influence' (I had distinguished myself on the rugby field). Norwood always added a postscript to my report, and he was never less than encouraging. In July 1931 after my second year his verdict was: 'The report does him credit in every way: we are all very pleased with him.'

About this time, like everyone else of my age, I was compulsorily enlisted in the O.T.C. (Officers Training Corps). This was a feature of Harrow life that I most detested. We had parades twice a week, a long one on Wednesday afternoons in place of sport and a shorter one on Friday mornings, besides extra parades for the inter-house competition. We were dressed in uncomfortable uniforms and put through marching, arms drill with rifles, and other soul-destroying manoeuvres. There were numerous strict rules and regulations involving the polishing of boots, belts and chin-straps and the exact arrangement of puttees: what would have been called bullshit if the term had then been invented. The Corps was organised as a battalion of three companies, each drilled by a sergeant-major, an old regular soldier. Their names as I still remember were Banks, Gudgeon and Kimber. Each house supplied a platoon, commanded by an under-officer, one of the senior boys, with corporals or lance-corporals in charge of sections. Since no one then imagined there would be another war, this 'playing at soldiers' seemed a pointless operation which brought the worst out of the under-officers and NCOs, and out of Bostock, who was the adjutant and obviously loved shouting orders and the whole set-up. On the other hand Banks, our company sergeant-major, was a very pleasant man, more humane than anyone else in authority. Fixing bayonets was a distressful operation and not without danger; at one parade my neighbour stuck his bayonet in my thumb, and I had to remain smartly at attention with blood poring over my uniform. On another occasion I was forcibly shaved before the parade by Jock Colville (later Sir John, Churchill's secretary), our under-officer; this was probably when I first began to shave on alternate days.

There was an inspection by a general once a year, when we were kept at attention for long periods and usually one or more boys fainted and had to be removed, and a field-day once a term. For this we were conveyed in buses to Aldershot or Bagshot or some other military locality, and engaged in operations in open country, equipped with blank cartridges, haversacks and water-bottles, which – a pleasant surprise – contained lemonade. I found that the only way to be comfortable was to wear pyjamas under my uniform; but the field-days were a good deal more tolerable than the parades. On one occasion we marched back to the embussing point behind a pipe band; it was astonishing how this quickened our step. I have a photo of this occasion.

After a certain period we had to take an exam called Certificate A. This was in two parts, practical and written. In the former we had to drill a squad, which was instructed to follow our orders exactly, even if they were obviously wrong. One candidate, seized with panic, had the squad marching right off the parade-ground and down a grassy slope until it reached a fence, whereupon the rear ranks closed in and all continued marking time, until the CSM demanded: '*Nah*, what are you going to do about it?' A large landscape target was produced, and the examiner, pointing to some prominent feature, told us to give proper orders for Lewis-gun or rifle fire, specifying the position, nature and estimated range of the object. I learned that the army knows only two kinds of tree, fir trees and bushy-top trees. The written paper was chiefly a matter of map-reading, which I found easy. After passing in November 1932 I found myself eligible for consideration for a commission in the Supplementary Reserve, Territorial Army, the TA Reserve of Officers, or the Active

Militia of Canada. I was promoted to lance corporal and ordered to help with the instruction of later Certificate A candidates, but was heartily glad to be let off Corps for most of my last term.

At the end of the summer term the whole battalion went into camp on Salisbury Plain. This occupied the first ten days of the holidays, which I thought iniquitous. In 1932, when I was first due to go, I heard that a few boys had received permission to attend a League of Nations Union summer school at Geneva instead. This appealed to me, and I spoke to my mother about it, arguing that it would be more profitable to study peace than war. She went to see Bostock, who said that camp would do me more good. He described it to me as 'an unpleasant duty', 'part of your education', which 'separates sheep from goats'. In this connection I was quite content to be a goat. My mother appealed to Norwood, who overruled Bostock and released me. Bostock was furious, and said to my mother with what she described as a snarl: 'I'll have my pound of flesh next year'. In the event he was disappointed. After endeavouring to escape and appearing before a medical board – whose proceedings, consisting of a few irrelevant questions and the perfunctory application of a stethoscope, I described as a farce – I reconciled myself to the inevitable; whereupon a timely epidemic caused the whole camp to be cancelled. (Norwood had urged the parents of a friend of mine to leave a few germs around so that he could cancel camp and all the trouble it caused.) The relief I felt was immeasurable. In 1934, when I was leaving, I was not obliged to attend.

The expedition to Geneva, my first journey abroad, was interesting and enormously enjoyable; a little later I looked back on that fortnight as the happiest of my life. After a few days I sent to my mother a letter of titanic length, asking her to preserve it in the family archives; it has confirmed and supplemented my recollections. There were about 150 of us, boys and girls, from a wide variety of schools. In charge, together with officials of the League of Nations, were several schoolmasters under the command of the Headmaster of Rugby, P.H.B. Lyon. The officials included J.C. Maxwell Garnett, a lean and forceful character 'rather inordinately fond of protruding himself into other people's lectures'; Frederick Whelan, who was short and stout and lectured in a highly melodramatic manner (he had theatrical connections and is mentioned in my father's autobiography); Lieutenant-Colonel Forty, 'One of those mild-absentminded-looking-retired-colonels ... Suitably attired in a rucksack and an old mackintosh', who I think was the treasurer; and Miss Anne Tynan, the secretary, a large lady who looked formidable and no doubt would have been had occasion arisen. One of the masters, B.A. Fletcher, had recently been round the world and told us how 'he came upon a human sacrifice apparatus in an Indian jungle'.

We crossed by night from Newhaven to Dieppe and were battened down below decks on account of the rough sea, each issued with a basin. I described the sequel to my mother: 'I made the discovery that as the journey advanced the less became the increase per half hour in the basin and the more the noise of regurgitation grew. I was afraid that this performance would wake up anyone who happened to be asleep, but I found myself quite unable to suppress it, and all that happened was that a fat man a few berths away sat up and scratched his head.' Eventually I 'fell asleep, but was woken up by the French steward emptying the basin, and the business began over again'.

I soon recovered and remember with pleasure the fresh taste of half an apple given me by Fletcher in the train and the crisp croissants of our breakfast at the Gare de Lyon, somewhat spoiled by revolting slabs of skin in the coffee. Our guide across Paris was a man in a green uniform who turned out to be a Russian prince. We watched the Parisians hurrying to work and remarked on the difference in tempo from London. I was struck by the strange appearance of

French and Swiss locomotives, and the unfamiliar rhythm and ostinato pattern of continental trains travelling over the tracks. The journey across France took a whole day, during which we were served with a lunch of eight or nine courses and I began to read my first Dorothy Sayers, *Have His Carcase*. We changed trains at Bellegarde near the Swiss frontier and had to wait some time on the platform. Here I was accosted by a jeering and perhaps obscene old man, a workman or porter, who talked through a drooping moustache in a French dialect that defeated me. 'Eventually I began shrugging my shoulders, whereupon he shrugged his too, so we didn't get very far.'

At Geneva we lodged at the Collège de la Grande Boissière, a comfortable hostel ('food very good and rather out of the ordinary'), two to a room. It happened that there was an odd number of Harrovians and Rugbians, and I found myself sharing with Peter Joseph, two years my senior, who had just left Rugby. This was a very happy arrangement: we made friends at once, found we shared a similar brand of humour, and spent much time laughing at the strange assortment of humanity among whom we were placed. He was about to enter a family firm of solicitors with the sonorous title of Tamplin, Joseph, Ponsonby, Ryde and Flux. This was the beginning of a lasting friendship.

The atmosphere of the school was delightfully relaxed, with no disciplinary regulations or tiresome restrictions. But we were expected to work quite hard, attending numerous lectures on different aspects of the League's activities, and had to walk nearly two miles six or more times a day, sometimes up a long and steep hill. I took copious notes on the lectures; unfortunately they disappeared in circumstances to be described later, together with the programme of events and a list of all those attending. The lecturers I remember most clearly are Frederick Whelan, Konni Zilliacus ('nationality doubtful – certainly partly English'), later a prominent left-wing M.P., who wore a white suit and sweated profusely, and an expert on the Far East who talked about 'the yellow brain'. Whelan addressed us frequently in the different buildings of the League Secretariat and Assembly, recalling with grand gestures events that he had witnessed 'in this very room' and world statesmen who sat 'in that chair just there'. Also present were parties of schoolboys from Holland, France, Germany and the United States. The Americans 'wear extraordinary shirts of bright colours with inscriptions on them, and usually eat with their mouths open'. I particularly liked the Germans; a meeting was arranged at which one of them talked to us about his country in very good English. I remember him saying that the Nazis were Germany's only hope, and trusting that he was wrong.

Geneva struck me as a very clean city, sanitary, reasonably quiet and conspicuous for hotels, trams and hordes of bicycles, but everything in the shops was very expensive. The tram layout was complicated and fascinating, with different systems criss-crossing each other. We were shown over a great many buildings, ancient and modern, including the cathedral and the impressive Renaissance Monument with statues of Calvin and other Protestant reformers. One day a party of girls got lost, and a fleet of taxis was sent to search for them, organised by Colonel Forty, 'who was always on the spot but never appeared to be doing very much'. My regrettable verdict on the girls was that they were 'rather a mushy lot, even allowing for the fact that they are girls'. Sexism had not yet been proclaimed a sin.

There were various side-shows, including a boat trip on the lake to the Castle of Chillon, a day at Chamonix, where we went on a funicular railway and explored the Mer de Glace with canvas socks over our shoes, and I nearly fell down a crevasse in trying to leap over it, and an expedition to climb the Salève, a small mountain nearby. Some of the more adventurous spirits indulged in a race to the top; one of them started off at tremendous speed and was found half way up at the side of the track, gasping like a stranded whale. The view from the top was superb, and inspired me to the pseudo-Wordsworthian poem mentioned earlier. On the last evening there was a party to which each of the larger school contingents contributed songs or sketches. The Harrow group staged a parody of an LNU meeting addressed by each of the officials in turn. This was largely my idea, and I wrote a Whelan speech in trochaic tetrameters containing literal quotations. This was brilliantly delivered by Claude Marks with all the authentic gestures. Whelan laughed so much that he rolled off his chair. Antony Part (later knighted as a distinguished civil servant) played Maxwell Garnett and contrived to look remarkably like him. I played Miss Tynan in a hat and coat borrowed from one of the girls and yellow stockings belonging to a boy from Christ's Hospital.

* * * * *

From December 1932 until January 1938 I kept a detailed diary, at first in infinitesimal writing in ten small red notebooks, later in larger ones. It must amount to at least a million words. I cannot remember what induced me to start it – possibly a fear that time and my life were slipping away before I had obtained a grasp on them. I gave it up because it was making me too introspective; I was spending far too much time scrutinising and analysing my own motives and actions. It seems to me now, re-reading it after more than fifty years, a most depressing document. Much that I recorded is utterly trivial, and I heartily dislike the character it reveals, especially in the first two years. On the other hand it preserves many details and incidents that would otherwise have been lost, some of them amusing, others of interest for a variety of reasons. It helped me to sort out my thoughts and put them, in so far as I was able, into coherent form. And it covers some of the most difficult and critical years of my life. It has no literary value, but it has helped me to see what went wrong and why things turned out as they did. Without it, relying only on my memory, I might have foreshortened or unintentionally distorted a good deal that still seems to me significant.

What emerges most clearly is the overwhelming emotional pressure under which I lived during the last two years at Harrow. I was very intense in my friendships, and though at least half aware of their homosexual undercurrents was unable to view them with any kind of detachment. I was strongly attracted to two boys in turn, both of my year, with neither of whom I had much in common. I scarcely knew that it was perfectly normal for boys of my age to have homosexual feelings, especially in a closed male community like a house at a public school. I knew little about sex, and what I did know was deeply coloured by Sanderson's moral imperatives, reinforced by certain remarks of Bostock's to the same effect. I thought of masturbation, even when involuntary, as a vice, and referred to it as such in my diary. There was never any question of active homosexual practices – indeed I was never aware of them occurring at Harrow, though no doubt they did – but the emotional tension was enormous and perhaps all the greater; and since the whole subject was tinged with acute feelings of guilt and shame, it is scarcely surprising that I drove myself nearly frantic and on more than one occasion came near to throwing myself out of windows. One or two of the masters, notably Holland and Watkins, who lodged with Bostock at the Head Master's, may have suspected some of this, but although they were sympathetic and gave good general advice, I could not bring myself to confide in them. Nor could I tell my mother; my father, even if I could have talked to him, was far too remote.

My psychological make-up cannot have helped. I was subject to huge swings of mood, between wild elation and the blackest depression (cyclothymic I believe is the term), and the slightest things could drive me within seconds from one extreme to the other. I took every minor disappointment far too much to heart; when my plans went awry I was apt to assume that the world or destiny was conspiring against me, and seethed with bitterness and resentment. The fact that other people's misfortunes affected me only a little less deeply was no great help. The demands I made on my friends must have been quite intolerable, though I was convinced that they were fair and reasonable. Partly no doubt as a result of bullying at Elstree, I was never – or very seldom – able to lose my temper. The superego was far too strong: my feelings of frustration were bottled up and turned inwards. All this is reflected in my diary, which presents a most unhealthy mixture of self-righteousness, confusion and self-pity, with occasional flashes of surprising objectivity.

All this was complicated by physical ailments. In March 1933 Bostock wrote in an otherwise favourable report: 'Chilblains, colds in the head and such-like afflictions reduce him to a state of ineffective misery'. They did indeed, and I am not surprised. I seem to have had about three heavy colds each winter term and others in the summer, as well as boils, head-aches and infectious rashes, known as Burmese itch. Far worse were chilblains. I have never in my life suffered anything so painful. Every finger and toe swelled like a young beetroot. Often I could hardly get my shoes on; Corps and football were agony. While the root cause must have been bad circulation, conditions at Harrow, where we were not allowed fires until evening and seemed always to be cold, can only have accentuated it. I consulted the house matron, a much more sympathetic soul than Sister Cox, and the school doctor, but no ointment or pills were of the slightest use. It was years before I outgrew chilblains; and they returned in full measure during the bitter winter of 1946-7, when the coal shortage inhibited adequate heating.

Another source of inner struggle, on a different level, was religion. I wished ardently to acquire a firm faith, but my efforts were only intermittently successful. I listened attentively to the sermons in Chapel, and commented on them regularly in my diary. Norwood, though not in orders, preached two or three times each term, and I generally found his sermons inspiring. One of the chaplains, D.B. Kittermaster, who was also a housemaster, likewise had the gift of putting his message across to schoolboys. I was impressed by the Bishops of Hull, Croydon and Ripon, and interested in the Reverend P.B. Clayton's account of Toc H. I described him as 'an odd man, short and tubby, with a face like a crinkly cheese, a hollow drawling voice and a most pronounced sense of humour'. We read Bishop Gore's book *The Reconstruction of Belief* in Norwood's divinity class, and I reproduced some of it in one of my scholarship papers at King's. My only report for Divinity, in July 1932, said that my written work was extremely good, but I was very diffident in expressing my opinion.

I tried to regulate my conduct according to Christian principles; but something in the public school atmosphere was antipathetic to religion. My efforts to discuss it with friends and contemporaries got nowhere and were sometimes rebuffed. I was continually bothered by the contrast between their reverent behaviour in Chapel and their total abandonment of anything approaching Christian behaviour as soon as they got outside. Bostock advised me to be confirmed, but I refused to take this step without the certainty that I was a true believer. I did not wish to take it because it was the done thing, which seemed to be the attitude of my contemporaries. At Bostock's suggestion I attended Norwood's confirmation classes at the beginning of my last year, although I was two years or more older than most of the candidates. But I never was confirmed. It seems that I was waiting for a call that never came. My next crisis over religion was to be very different and far more disastrous.

We had House prayers every evening, together with a reading from the New Testament by the house monitors in rotation. It is perhaps significant that my chief recollection of this is decidedly secular. A boy who was known for his enquiring and sceptical mind (his father was an M.P.) had to read St Mark's account of the cure of the man sick of the palsy, containing the words 'And when they could not come nigh unto him for the press'. He pronounced this in such a way as to evoke a picture of newsmen with notebooks and cameras, and the house, including Bostock, collapsed with laughter.

In view of all these stresses it now seems astonishing that I somehow contrived to keep my school work in a separate compartment. We had three Classics teachers in the Classical Sixth. Our form master E.V.C. Plumptre, always known as Plum, was a delightful man, free from all pomposity and with a rich sense of humour. Besides being a good scholar and an outstanding teacher, he was very musical, and used to accompany the Head Master's representatives in school singing competitions. When I told him how much I admired the *Enigma Variations*, he played them through for me on the piano. I met him occasionally at Covent Garden after the war, and he once stayed with us at Hambledon. I saw him far less after leaving Harrow than I would have liked. I sometimes felt that Ronald Watkins disapproved of my character, but he was never less than fair, and gave me most complimentary reports. He had a great knowledge of poetry and drama, and after I left used to produce Shakespeare plays annually in Speechroom. He also read poetry over the radio in a voice at once mellow, fruity and rather world-weary. I was told that after hearing one of his broadcasts an old lady in Clapham committed suicide, whereupon he gave them up. Our third Classics teacher was Norwood, a formidable figure of whom we stood in awe. In his presence we never ventured on the jokes and little leg-pulls that we tried with the others. But he was an inspiring teacher and could be very entertaining in a dry way. He told us that to this day Gaelic shepherds counted their flocks in Greek; more than half a century later this was unexpectedly confirmed by the title of Harrison Birtwistle's opera *Yan Tan Tethera*.

The Classical side gave up Mathematics after School Certificate, but we continued to take one foreign language. About 1932 this was changed from French to German. Our first German master, who later entered the diplomatic service and emerged as Sir Herbert Marchant, rightly doubted whether I had a flair for the language (although I came first) and declared: 'I do not know whether he will ever be fluent, but he will certainly be accurate'. I remember his amusement when someone coined the word 'Eine Fehlerin', meaning a female mistake. Marchant's successor was H.D. Samuel, with whom we read Goethe's *Iphigenie auf Tauris*. In January 1934 I decided that I wanted to give up the language when we were given a textbook of Nazi propaganda to study, complete with pictures of Hitler and other obnoxious leaders. Bostock persuaded me to continue, but my protest and that of others got the textbook changed. I am thankful now that I yielded; my German is not good, but at least I understand something of the language.

In the Upper Fifth our English master was D.C. Whimster, who had some good ideas. He set us to write a modern comedy after the manner of Aristophanes. Since the style of Aristophanes embraced puns, indecency and satirical attacks on contemporary politicians (and others) we had quite a field day. My piece, called *The Taximen*, was written in blank verse and various Greek metres, and satirised Churchill, who had recently been run over by a taxi in New York, and the Labour leader George Lansbury, who was said to bathe every day in the Serpentine. He became the leader of the Parliamentary Bathing Party. Churchill denounced him as 'a mere idle whimster', which earned a question mark in the margin.

From Whimster we moved to Stewart Mason, later a distinguished educationalist in Leicestershire, who also proved an enlightened teacher, besides, with his American wife, entertaining us hospitably out of school hours. He took a considerable interest in the prose and verse I wrote of my own volition as well as in his class, and made helpful comments on my style. At first he found it insufficiently concise and exact ('too much facility with words and metre'). By December 1932 he noted 'great facility with the technique of literature, especially of verse', but in his next report wanted more concrete imagery. In the Easter term of 1933 he set us to write, in our own time, a short biography of a major historical figure. Already fascinated by military history, I chose Marlborough. Mason found my effort 'adequate, but too much concerned with external events', a fair criticism. I doubt if it was even adequate, for it was largely a précis of Sir John Fortescue's Life.

In March 1933, one of my most unhappy periods, I took the Leaving Scholarship exam for practice a year early, and was one of only three Classics placed in the first class by the outside examiner, a Cambridge don; one of the others was Michael Grant, a year my senior. For this I received a special prize. Watkins, who previously had found little trace of imaginative intelligence, said a term later that in composition I had improved in power of expression and in history showed 'a new faculty of criticism. If he can develop these, his habitual accuracy and portentous memory will carry him to great success in the scholarship season'. He credited me in April 1934 with 'one really beautiful copy of Greek Iambics'. Plum in one of his reports said I could afford to be more tolerant and listen to other points of view, but had no doubts of success 'if he can refrain from overworking at the expense of his health', a significant comment in view of later events. Bostock in his house report for the summer term of 1933 mentioned difficulties and misunderstandings (a reference to O.T.C. camp), but 'he need have no fears, unless he allows himself to lose his head. He is not really a selfish boy, but he needs an enthusiasm which will make him forget himself'. This seems to me eminently fair.

There were a number of voluntary clubs and societies which contributed a good deal to our wider education. The Dramatic Society naturally attracted me. Play-readings were held in one or other of the masters' houses, and were often lively; I remember particularly *The Barretts of Wimpole Street* and *Berkeley Square*. In February 1933 the Society mounted a stage production of John Drinkwater's *Abraham Lincoln* in the Music School, produced by a retired actress living in Harrow called Miss James. This was most enjoyable and achieved notable success. The cast included a singular variety of talent. Lincoln was played by Dorian Williams, a very good actor who embarked on a professional career (I obtained an interview for him with my father, who came to the show and was impressed by his performance), but ultimately achieved fame as a BBC commentator on show-jumping. Lincoln's Minister for War was Jack Profumo, who was to hold the corresponding post in the British cabinet. He had a gift for comedy which threatened to make cabinet meetings funnier than Drinkwater intended, but spoke the last line of the play ('Now he belongs to the ages') very movingly. Michael Denison played a female part, a woman in deep mourning for her son. The rival generals Grant and Lee were Hugh Martin and Charles Laborde, the school rugby captain, who cut a most impressive figure in Confederate uniform. My part, as Lincoln's secretary Slaney, required me to read Prospero's final speech in *The Tempest* and to fall off a bench in my sleep, which always raised the biggest laugh of the evening. A friend, Philip Tallack, who played a perspiring and dust-covered messenger, insisted on throwing himself downstairs before every performance in order to achieve verisimilitude. In one scene everyone not on stage, in a weird miscellany of costumes, had to march round behind the scenery singing 'John Brown's Body', led by Laborde manipulating a box full of sand labelled 'Marching Men This Side Up'. It was said to be very moving. We all assisted the enterprise in various ways, including the printing of bills, under the supervision of the treasurer, a stage-struck Siamese prince. A little later I was startled to receive a cutting 'From a Women's Notebook' in a Birkenhead paper stating that I was busy producing *Lincoln*: 'I have myself not seen him since his perambulator days, but even then he was an exceptionally bright youngster'. The play chosen for the following year was *Shameless Wayne* by Mordaunt Shairp; but I disliked it and resigned my part.

About this time I joined an architectural society, started by Mason the previous year, which organised expeditions to view old churches on half-holidays in the summer term. An introductory lecture by Samuel with slides stimulated my interest. The party usually numbered about fifteen, travelling in four cars each driven by a master. We visited three or four churches chosen for their special architectural interest and consumed a lavish picnic tea at some suitable spot, such as the river at Oxford or the top of Ivinghoe Beacon; once when it rained we borrowed a barn from the Duke of Buckingham. Every one of these expeditions produced a crop of comic incidents, duly recorded in the minutes, which we wrote up in turn. Almost always one car broke down or ran out of petrol and one or more got lost. The expedition to Oxford was our most ambitious; we spent most of the time in Merton Chapel and had a hilarious picnic on three punts moored together against an island, during which various important objects accidentally fell in the water. One of the party was enlisted as a diver to retrieve a silver spoon. The steep and slippery descent from Ivinghoe Beacon caused two of the masters to lose control of their feet and go careering down the slope frantically waving the hampers that had contained the provisions. These had been sensibly diminished by Samuel's Corgi, deprived of its lunch to prevent it being sick in the car. The proceedings were a very happy blend of education and informality. On one occasion I contrived to deprive a master of his braces and convince him that he had left them behind. These expeditions were not only a marvellous change from school routine; they gave me such an enthusiasm for ecclesiastical architecture (I filled my diary with technical details) that I followed it up in the holidays, infected my brothers and later many friends at Cambridge, and over a period of years visited hundreds of churches and took more than a thousand photographs.

I also developed an interest in archaeology as a result of spending a week in September 1933 at the excavation of Salmonsbury Camp at Bourton-on-the-Water. This was organised by Whimster, and again combined education and entertainment. There were about six of us, including two masters. We slept in various lodgings in the village, but our headquarters was a small inn kept by one A.E. Yearp, who combined the occupations of family butcher and nocturnal fisherman. One morning he appeared with a massive trout, on another with some delicious crayfish; whether they were poached or lawfully apprehended we never discovered. Mr Yearp seemed to possess the only lavatory in the village; the queue for it stretched down the stairs and into the street. The archaeologist in charge of the dig, G.C. Dunning, could be severe with his assistants but possessed the saving grace of a sense of humour. He claimed to have discovered an Anglo-Saxon flea in one of his excavations and exhibited it in a Cambridge museum, where it was found to be a hen flea. Two middle-aged spinsters staying at the inn registered disapproval of our high spirits. Dunning decided that they were ripe for shock treatment and approached the dinner table one evening through the window in pyjamas. We all dined at one large table.

During a rare moment of silence as the coffee went round one of our party picked up a lump of sugar with the sugar-tongs; but the tongs slipped, and it shot into the air, described a lazy parabola, and landed in the full cup of one of the ladies on the other side of the table. This incident seemed typical of the week, during which one of the Harrow boys, returning to his lodging on a dark night after a visit to the pub, fell into the stream that flows beside the village street, and another became strongly enamoured of a girl assisting at the dig. Another girl – Miss Fell – became an archaeologist, and years later I read her obituary in *The Times*.

The participants in the dig were an amusingly varied bunch, including a distinguished retired civil servant, Sir Edward Harrison, an excitable local colonel, and Toty de Navarro, a Cambridge don and son of a famous actress (Mary Anderson), who was very good company. We excavated seriously all day, unearthing fragments of Roman pavement, a Belgic rubbish dump (my discovery), the skeleton of a baby, and a beautifully constructed well, last used apparently for drowning a dog with a Civil War cannon-ball attached to its neck. There was some competition as to who should be first to descend. The lot fell on Haines, a local workman and general factotum; no sooner had he disappeared than a stream of rich Gloucestershire oaths accompanied a demand to be hauled up quick owing to the abominable smell. A week later we had a reunion dinner in London and went to see James Bridie's play *A Sleeping Clergyman*. Plans were made for more digging the following year, but I was unable to go. The following term we paid an interesting visit to Mortimer Wheeler's dig at Verulamium, where his wife showed us round the spectacular ruins. This led me to study a number of books on Roman Britain.

About this time I was fascinated by J.W. Dunne's book *An Experiment with Time*, which put forward a theory that past, present and future are a single continuum, and it is possible to tap the future when the conscious mind is occupied elsewhere or not functioning, for example in dreams. This is not recognised, for we forget almost all our dreams immediately. I have been told that the theory has been exposed as nonsense; nevertheless for a time I made a practice of recording my dreams as soon as I woke up, and found that they did sometimes contain references to incidents that occurred two or three days later, though these were never of the slightest consequence. When I heard of the sudden and most unexpected death from tetanus of a young master who had been with us at Bourton three months before, I was shocked but somehow not surprised, and concluded that I must already have dreamed it. The passage of time, its seemingly irregular rhythm and tempo, its mysteries and strange ambiguities, has haunted me all my life, and found its way into several of my writings. It has often seemed that only a slender barrier prevented me from moving into another period, whether of my own life or of some place with which I had close associations. On a number of occasions I have had the most vivid presentiment of events yet to come, as well as telepathic knowledge of things happening elsewhere, and they have proved astonishingly accurate.

One of the healthier aspects of Harrow life was the frequency with which eminent speakers were invited to address either the whole school or one of the senior clubs on current affairs, political and social as well as artistic. At club meetings anyone who wished was encouraged to ask questions. Many of these occasions I have forgotten, though I commented on them in my diary, sometimes at considerable length. I also read the first leader in *The Times* every day, Tommy having agreed to pay for the paper on this condition. My denunciations of Hitler were predictable enough; more surprisingly a lecture on Mussolini's Italy, which I much enjoyed, roused in me sharp disagreement on some points. I considered Mussolini an ill-balanced man, a great patriot perhaps in the eyes of his countrymen but contemptible in the sight of God. This was in 1933, before he had begun to attack his neighbours. Partly as a result of seeing some horrifying film footage of the 1914-18 War I held strong pacifist views, hoped one day to write an article or book on the subject, and did in fact write such an essay in my entrance scholarship for King's. Some speakers I do clearly remember: Ivor Brown on drama, Geoffrey Lloyd, an Old Harrovian M.P. on the House of Commons, Lord Halifax on India, and Sir Bernard Pares on Russia. I described Pares as a curious abrupt sort of man with a mind like Thucydides, who talked continually in antitheses and answered questions very snappily. On the other hand I have totally forgotten the evening of Sir John Thompson's talk on the Indian White Paper (1934), though I asked several questions and had a pleasant conversation with him afterwards about my uncle Rufus and aunt Stella, and another with Captain Dugdale, Under-Secretary at the Colonial Office. In my estimation he was a delightful man but a typical politician, able to speak at length on a subject about which he knew nothing.

At the beginning of my last year I conceived an ambition to win house caps for all three of the principal sports, partly to demonstrate to Bostock and others – and to myself – that I could do it. I threw myself into the rugby games (now playing as a flank forward, my proper place), sustaining several injuries in the process, and distinguished myself in the first round of the House matches, a tremendous game that I still remember in detail, which gave us our first victory for three years. It was the last game of rugby I ever played. A week later, after a few days at home, I went to Cambridge to take the scholarship exam for King's, in weather so appallingly cold that I had to wear a thick pullover at night. It left me totally exhausted. When the telegram came announcing that I had won a major scholarship I rushed over to find Norwood and the other resident masters either in the bath or dressing. Plum emerged from the bathroom and danced a jig in his underpants. Norwood announced at supper that the House had won all the Classical form prizes in the school, that all four of its candidates had won university scholarships or exhibitions, and that it was no wonder I was successful since the examiners could not possibly read my writing. In fact the entire Classical Sixth won university scholarships, an emphatic tribute to the teaching. While waiting for my result I had been awarded a rugby cap, despite inevitably missing the second-round match. What stands out in my memory of that exciting week is that I was far prouder of the cap than of the scholarship. I knew that, barring accidents, the latter was within my powers; the former was a very different matter, for which I had to strive against inner and outer obstacles.

I was less successful in the other two sports. Throughout the Easter term I was unwell, suffering from boils, head-aches and swollen glands in the neck and ending with a heavy bout of flu. I was taken to a heart specialist, who apparently found something slightly wrong, but I never heard what it was. To my intense fury the school doctor forbade me to play in the House Match (though I was passed fit for Corps the following day); we lost narrowly, so that I could not be considered for a cap (or a fez as it was called), though Harrow football was probably my best game. After this, winning a Leaving Scholarship was little consolation. In the summer term (my last) I won no fewer than nine prizes, including three gold medals (subsequently stolen from the grandparents' safe) and a scholarship to Rome, which I was never able to take up, first on account of illness and later because Mussolini's invasion of Abyssinia was thought likely to result in war with Italy. It was more than fifty years before I was able to visit Rome.

I would gladly have traded several of these prizes for a cricket cap. But cricket is a game in which a slight error or a momentary attack of nerves can reduce all one's hopes to dust. Moreover the boy with whom I was emotionally involved was captain of the team, and the resulting cross-currents, apart from making me miserable, put me right off my game. For the third consecutive summer I opened the innings in House matches, but fell below the moderate achievements of previous seasons. My job was to take the shine off the new ball rather than make a large score; I succeeded in doing neither. Only in fielding was I a success; as a result of constant practice with Martin and Joe (with a tennis ball) I very seldom missed a possible catch. That was not enough. On 22 May, acknowledging that the longed for cap had almost certainly slipped out of reach, I wrote despondently: 'I love cricket and what it stands for more than any other game or sport – but by a brutal irony I am a failure at it'.

At the beginning of the Easter term I had been made a House monitor. It transpired later that I owed this to Bostock, who overruled the existing monitors; they were always consulted about such appointments. The effect was wholly beneficial. I took my duties seriously; they included giving help to younger boys in work and games, and I felt that I was doing something useful. There were regular monitors' meetings with Bostock, who also from time to time invited two or three of us to supper or to drink beer, when we discussed the affairs of the House. These seemed to us immensely important; the narrow world of a public school constituted a miniature universe, imposing its own sense of values and insulating us from events outside, which we saw as it were through a glass and with the security of distance. I became aware of this false perspective during my last term. At the same time I remembered my vow of four years before and was careful to keep it. It was customary for those leaving to say goodbye to every member of the house individually; when I came to do this at the end of my last term, more than one of them told me that I was the only house monitor who remained human, a complement I much appreciated.

By the middle of the summer term I was in a bad mental state, subject to black depressions and quite unable to cope with emotional difficulties. I felt that my brain and memory were becoming impaired, and that any further stress would send me out of my mind. On 10 June Norwood sent for me; he said he had seen my face twitching in Chapel and other signs of overstrain, and that Bostock had heard me pacing up and down like a caged animal on the roof. If this went on, it might lead to a very serious breakdown. He wished me to go away into the country for a few weeks' holiday, to avoid having to take several months off later; and he invited me to stay with him in Scotland before going up to Cambridge. I was as astonished by his perception as by his kindness, but he probably knew much more than I imagined about what was going on. Although there were still things I wanted to do at Harrow, I at once felt an overwhelming sense of relief. Most of the next month I spent at Hambledon with my mother and the grandparents in a state of unalloyed happiness such as I have seldom felt before or since, returning to Harrow only for Speech Day and the last week of term.

I always looked back on my Harrow career with mixed feelings, but can see now that, with the important exception of my first year, it was not responsible for my troubles, which were due to my own temperament or ill health or both. They could have occurred in any other environment. I feel nothing but gratitude for those who taught me; the curriculum was not unduly restricted, and was supplemented by numerous extracurricular activities, from which I learned much. Even the high place allotted to games probably did me more good than harm. Norwood did his best to prepare me for the future, and discussed possible careers as early as March 1933. There seemed to me objections to all those he mentioned except (astonishingly) the Colonial Service. My interest in the life of my uncle Rufus led me for a time to consider the bar, but law held few attractions, though it claimed both my brothers. I was convinced that an important destiny awaited me, and that I would be a writer of some kind. But I needed to hurry up: a boy at Elstree who claimed to tell fortunes from cards had prophesied that I would die in 1949. He must have caught me at a credulous moment, for I could not dismiss the idea from my mind, and even felt a superstitious relief at the arrival of January 1950.

My final report from Bostock could hardly have been more enthusiastic. 'His countless prizes bear witness to his phenomenal success in work, and in games his keenness has never flagged, and it is not surprising that he got overtired ... His high standard of endeavour has set an example to all'. Norwood added: 'He takes with him my friendship, and sincere good wishes for his success'. Watkins, a Kingsman, wrote: 'It seems that he has been cheated of his opportunity of seeing Harrow from a deck-chair', and wished me all good fortune 'at the ideal college in October'.

* * * * *

In November 1930 we had left Queen's Road for 13 Cumberland Terrace on the other side of Regent's Park. My mother made the move in the middle of term without giving us any warning; I was taken aback and rather indignant. It was strange, at the start of the Christmas holidays, having to direct a taxi to a home I had never seen. However I was soon reconciled to the house, whose only inconvenience was the inordinate number of stairs. It occupied four floors and a basement, with only two rooms to a floor (except on the top storey, which had three); but they were fine large rooms, and the whole terrace was (and is) a noble specimen of John Nash's architecture, looking on to Regent's Park at the front and Albany Street at the back. The previous owner of number 13 had christened it Cumberland House; but my mother was impatient of superstition and changed it back. I learned later that one of the two immediately preceding occupants had gone bankrupt and the other (father of a boy at Harrow with me) had shot himself in the hall. Margaret subsequently found a mass of unpaid bills blocking the flue of the kitchen range. Perhaps we should have taken this for an omen; but at first all was well.

My great-uncle and aunt Alfred and Essie Sutro lived in Chester Terrace, and my grandparents during the winter within walking distance at 82 Portland Place. Since the Sutros had a country house at Sandhills, less than two miles from Hambledon, we saw a great deal of them at all times of the year. Alfred was avuncular in every sense of the term. Having no children of his own, he took a great interest in my brothers and me, and was constantly offering my mother advice about our education, manners and general conduct – advice that was not always welcome. Once after taking Martin and Joe out to tea he made a great song and dance because they transferred cakes directly from the dish into their mouths, without as it were bouncing them on their plates first. My mother, who at the end of her life wrote an account of her relations with the Sutros at my request, said that there were two Alfreds: one kind, urbane, generous and witty, the other hypercritical, pernickety, easily shockable and sometimes peevish. This agreed with my experience. Alfred I had a delicious sense of humour, as he showed in some of his comedies; he could laugh at himself, and was humble about his success in the theatre. Alfred II was intolerant and totally humourless. Unfortunately one could never predict which Alfred would be in the saddle. It was all too easy to say the wrong thing. Towards the end of his life I made some remark about being unhappy during the holidays. He took this as a slight on my mother, abused me roundly, told all the family how ungrateful I was, and demanded an apology both to her and to himself. He wrote me a letter animadverting on my 'ingratitude' and 'rude and aggressive manners'. I tried to explain that he had got hold of the wrong end of the stick. For some weeks he remained angry and implacable, but eventually declared himself appeased by my 'charming letter'. I have no idea what I wrote; and I was so annoyed by the injustice of his letter that I foolishly destroyed it – after cutting off the signature.

Alfred used to take me to lunch à deux at the Garrick Club. On these occasions he discoursed most interestingly about his early life in the city and the theatre, and introduced me to distinguished friends who happened to be in the club. In this way I met Seymour Hicks, Nigel Playfair, Frederick Lonsdale and others. Unfortunately my diary is more explicit about the food than about the conversation. I could see that Alfred was immensely popular at the Garrick, and this is confirmed over and over again by the many cordial letters he received from eminent writers and theatrical people which subsequently came into my possession. He can scarcely have approved of D.H. Lawrence's opinions, but when he heard that Lawrence was in straitened circumstances early in the 1914 War he sent him £50 as a gift. Lawrence later returned it with expressions of astonished gratitude. Alfred kept a touching letter, congratulating him on one of his successes in the theatre, from 'the old man you befriended'. There were many instances of his kindness to struggling authors. He also did much charitable work running working-men's clubs in the East End.

From quite early on he concerned himself with my reading and presented me with a number of books from his library, adjuring me to read them for half an hour each day. I duly followed his advice with Herbert Paul's *Men and Letters*, Turgenev's *Sportsmen's Sketches* and J.W. Mackail's *History of Latin Literature*, but got hopelessly stuck in his translations of Maeterlinck. Alfred had of course been a successful dramatist, but his last few plays had failed and he was something of a back number. I think he felt this acutely, though he never spoke of it. This may account for the intense vigour with which he denounced the current state of politics and education, citing examples from his experiences when canvassing for Rufus many years before. He ran down the public schools without knowing anything about them, and was particularly disgusted when he heard I was learning German instead of French (he and Essie were both strong Francophiles). He set himself up as an arbiter of public morals. Once on returning with me from a walk in Regent's Park he stopped a motorist in the Outer Circle and, brandishing his walking-stick above his head, denounced him for exceeding the speed limit, which was then absurdly low. For a dramatist he could be strangely imperceptive. When my mother complained that after her divorce men thought themselves entitled to make advances to her in taxis, Alfred declared sternly: 'No man makes love to a woman unless she asks for it'. When he published a book called *About Women*, Gran remarked that of all subjects that was the one about which he knew least.

During his last months Alfred convinced himself that my parents were about to remarry. He had disliked Basil from the beginning, endeavoured to blackball him when he applied for membership of the Garrick, and never invited him to Chester Terrace even when he was married to my mother. Alfred died after a week's illness in September 1933 while I was at Bourton-on-the-Water. I was told that had he lived much longer he might have gone out of his mind, but since he died of leukaemia this seems improbable. His charming book of reminiscences, *Celebrities and Simple Souls*, on which he had been working with obvious enjoyment, was published a week later and made me regret that I had not asked him more questions when he was alive. The Readings came over to see Essie, and had dinner at Hambledon. I was much impressed by their conversation, by their promise to assist me over my career, and by the gift of a £5 note, the first I had seen. My comment was: 'Truly a remarkable day – and a remarkable uncle'. I had first met them two years before, when they were just married (Stella was his second wife) and he was Foreign Secretary.

Essie and Gran, though very close throughout their lives, were totally unlike in character. Where Gran was impetuous, generous and witty with an irrepressible sense of humour, and also unworldly and highly unconventional, Essie was reserved and something of an intellectual snob. She had the stronger will and the more aggressive personality, and conformed much more to the recognised way of the world. She must have possessed qualities that were not readily apparent, for her friends had included Henry James and other persons of fastidious taste. She also had a practical side; she loved gardening and had once taken a course in plumbing. But she gave the impression of being restless and unsatisfied, and had a mischievous, even a spiteful streak; she could squash people with a word. Her voice had a rather whining tone that suggested the key of E flat minor. Though her marriage had never been happy, in its last years she became dependent on Alfred, and she was left stranded by his death. She fell into a state of lethargy from which nothing could rouse her, refusing to go out or see her friends yet afraid of being left alone. We all tried to cheer her up; I raised a wan smile by foolishly proposing to put a firework under her chair. But nothing had the slightest effect.

In happier times the Sutros used to walk over to Hambledon on summer week-ends, sometimes with their house guests, either to talk or to play bowls or bridge. On one occasion, soon after Contract bridge replaced Auction, the bridge party fell short of a fourth player. There was a book in the house called *Contract Bridge in Twenty Minutes*. I told them if they waited twenty minutes I would play. Gran was all for letting me try, but Alfred vetoed the idea.

A neighbour of the Sutros at Sandhills (at first their landlord) was Graham Robertson, a man of quite exceptional charm and individuality. When very young he had known many of the Pre-Raphaelites, as well as Ellen Terry and other actresses and actors of that generation, and I think always regarded himself as belonging to their world. A sworn enemy of scientific progress, he refused to have electric light, running water or a bathroom in his house, much less a telephone or a radio, and he never admitted the 1914 War into his conversation or consciousness. Sargent painted a famous portrait of him as a young man, tall, slender and elegant with a touch of the dandy; when I knew him he was stoutish and anything but elegant, tramping across country in a shoddy old cloak and white tie accompanied by one or more of his beloved Old English sheepdogs. He was a talented painter and book-illustrator with a rich vein of humour; he presented Alfred with three delightful water-colour caricatures of himself and Alfred, with sheepdogs, which now hang in my study. His house was full of paintings by Blake, which he collected long before they became fashionable. He became an expert on the subject, and the collection, which he was always happy to show to friends (he once spent hours explaining the symbolism of the pictures to me), was by far the largest in private hands. He was also a great and practical lover of the theatre; he organised pageants at Guildford and Chiddingfold which he wrote and produced himself, and was the author of a popular children's play, *Pinkie and the Fairies*, and an enchanting book of reminiscences, *Time Was*. Better still were his letters; his friend Kerrison Preston published a volume of them after his death, and I have some written to my mother and me as well as to Alfred. One of his letters to my mother began: 'Dear Esther. I'm *so* glad you are a born fool. I am too and I owe a very happy life to this simple fact. It is the greatest boon & blessing.' He was most helpful when as an undergraduate I planned a book on Alfred, a project which graver events sadly nipped in the bud.

Always a lover of children, he took a great interest in me from my birth. He produced a donkey for me to ride, and designed a little wooden cart, painted red with my initials on the side. When I was three, I was taken round the garden of Tigbourne Court, a Lutyens house on the outskirts of Hambledon belonging to the Wethered family. It contained a lily pond, where the gardener, Albert Jeffery senior (two of whose sons were to become gardeners at Hambledon Hurst), pointed out the goldfish and tadpoles, and caught a tadpole in his hands. I tried to do the same and fell in headlong. He soon pulled me out by the foot, and Dicky Mills hauled me home in Graham's cart while my clothes were spread out to dry in the sun. The cart was still at Hambledon during the second war (I photographed my daughter Brigid in it), but has since disappeared. Graham also designed a bookplate for me. My mother sent him some verses of mine written at Harrow, on which he made sage but kindly comments, prefaced by the sentences: 'Do young people really feel that the world as at present is an ugly and unpleasant place? I hope not, because it's true and it is *so* bad for the young to know the truth about anything'.

Graham often came over to Hambledon. I remember him with a long pole knocking walnuts off a tree in the front garden for me and another child to catch. He sometimes accompanied the Sutros, and sometimes Sir Hedworth Williamson, a cheery old baronet with an enormous stomach and thin spindly legs like an Edward Lear caricature. (He was the ninth baronet; all Williamsons of his family seem to be christened Hedworth, just as all Earls of Shaftesbury are Anthony Ashley Cooper.) Once or twice the grandparents took me to visit Sir Hedworth at his house on the Isle of Wight, with a garden full of exotic shrubs. One of them had tightly closed flowers which, Sir Hedwoth told us, Queen Mary delighted to squeeze until they made an audible pop. Sir Hedworth took me for a swim in a rather rough sea; he was an even more remarkable shape in a bathing costume than in his usual breeches.

While I was at Harrow Basil began to take rather more interest in his progeny. We usually spent some days at Little Easton Manor in the spring and summer holidays. He was not always there himself; on the whole we preferred this, since his influence was apt to be convulsive. By this time however we had evolved a *modus vivendi*: we refused to take him seriously. There was a large lake in the grounds, with an island encircled by trees. We used to boat and bathe, and for a time indulged in a little coarse fishing (the fish, roach and perch, were regarded by the staff as too coarse for the table). On one occasion, when we had all bathed from the island, Basil took off his striped bathing-trunks and proceeded to rub himself down with a large bath-towel. By unspoken consent we rowed the boat ashore, taking Basil's bathing-trunks, which we propelled to the top of a tall tree by the front gate. They flew there like an admiral's flag on a battleship, while Basil roared like a bull on the island. His friend the actor George Curzon arrived at this point and increased Basil's fury by collapsing with laughter. When we released Basil he threw our clothes into a patch of brambles and subsequently lodged a complaint with my mother: 'I don't know why your boys seem to regard me as a joke'. When we did something of which we disapproved we were 'Your boys'; when we won scholarships or in any way gained credit we were 'My boys'.

I think he was proud of us up to a point, so long as he did not have any responsibility, financial or otherwise. On the other hand he was genuinely devoted to Tessa, his daughter by his second marriage. So were we all: she was a delightful person, both as a slight and wispy child and as a grown woman. The discovery that we had a sister greatly increased the pleasure of our visits to the Manor, though she was younger than me by nearly eleven years. I noted pompously in April 1934 that 'her erratic parentage is beginning to make itself felt, and she will be a real rip one day'. I was quite wrong. Though the product of two highly temperamental and unruly parents, she grew up one of the most sensible and balanced people I have known. Indeed all four of Basil's children made wholly happy and successful marriages, though I would not urge this as an argument in favour of broken homes.

Tessa was left for long periods in the charge of her nanny, Millicent Tresham, who must have played in her life something like the role that Haricot played in ours, though the two were utterly unalike. Miss Tresham, a gaunt and venerable figure, had spent some time in the east and acted as a kind of retainer in the Greville family. She used to regale us with long and sometimes lugubrious stories of their various doings that seemed to stretch into the remote past. I considered her 'a very patient woman, though a trifle snobbish'. She was devoted to Tessa, and on her death many years later bequeathed to her a little cottage at Elstead, a few miles from Hambledon, thus bringing the family into convenient and happy proximity.

By the early thirties Basil and Mercy were divorced, and she soon acquired two more husbands with the not inappropriate names of Gamble and Marter. Lady Warwick, having installed her and her second husband in a house on the other side of the Easton Lodge estate, drew the line at a third, declaring that she was tired of having her estate littered with Mercy's ex-husbands. We were sometimes invited to Easton Lodge, a large house with a strange exotic atmosphere: peacocks in the garden, a cage of monkeys near the stables, and signed photographs of Edward VII and other exalted persons all over the interior. Lady Warwick was a remarkable character. She had grown enormously fat, and used to drive round the estate very slowly in an ancient Austin 7, whose two front seats were just sufficiently wide to accommodate her ample haunches. She dispensed hospitality with the air of a *grande dame*, but she could be formidable. At lunch one day she offered Martin the choice of two puddings; Martin rashly asked for both, and she came down on him like a ton of bricks. Later she was to treat me with great kindness in a time of need.

On our spring visits we spent most of the time birdsnesting, a hobby now frowned upon. Although I kept one egg of each species, what we most enjoyed was the search, which involved climbing trees, exploring crevices of buildings, and trying to penetrate the thick reedbeds on the lake in a boat. The Manor was one of our favourite hunting grounds, since all manner of aquatic birds nested there, including Canada geese. There was a swan's nest every spring, but we hesitated to approach it after hearing reports of the ferocious male bird breaking intruders' legs. Eventually we found an addled swan's egg floating in the water and carried it in triumph to the house. When I attempted to blow it, the stench (to which I was impervious) nearly caused a revolution among the staff. When Basil came in, his nose went up like that of an offended thoroughbred, and paternal rumblings continued for some time. He disapproved of our taking eggs, but had no answer when we pointed out that our trophy was of no further use to the swan. One spring day the two dogs disappeared, and Basil ordered us out to search for them. We walked for miles, alternatively calling the dogs and looking for birds' nests, at first together, then separately. Having lost ourselves and suffered inconvenience from a bull, which chased each of us in turn, we arrived back in a bedraggled condition to find that the dogs had returned hours before.

Basil spent much time and money enlarging the Manor, a process that took several years. He incorporated two adjacent cottages and installed what we considered an astonishing number of bathrooms. I was glad to see some of the mustiness disappear – it 'no longer stinks of past ages' – but was still disturbed later by 'the halo of depression which seems to surround the place'. In April 1934 we found it looking like a palace, the cocktail bar (in a crypt approached by a flight of stairs in the middle of the drawing-room) adorned with wall-paintings of successive inhabitants from Edward IV to Basil himself. (A later owner had all this painted out.) The dining-room contained a lovely little stained-glass window of Tessa, dressed in blue.

On the first evening of this visit Basil produced a bottle of champagne, and informed us that he was going to be married again, to Victoria Hopper. He was a little taken aback by Martin's immediate reference to Henry VIII. I was surprised but pleased for Basil's sake, having long thought that the Manor needed a hostess, but also 'a little apprehensive for his new wife' and of possible complications if he had any more children. Complications of another kind soon supervened: the engagement was broken off a week later. On 14 May, back at Harrow, Martin and I were astonished to read in the paper that the marriage had taken place secretly after all. A few days later Basil wrote me a letter complaining of persecution by certain business acquaintances, apparently a reference to Sydney Carroll, with whom Vicky had a contract. We met Vicky for the first time in August. I don't know exactly what I expected, but I wrote that 'to my astonishment I was favourably impressed by her character as well as her appearance'. I had already seen her on the stage in plays and Basil's production of *Hansel and Gretel* (his single venture into opera), but thought her even prettier off it and, after her initial shyness wore off, completely natural and without affectation. That is how I have always felt about her. She was not a great actress, and her singing voice was apt to curdle, but she had a spontaneous youthful charm that perfectly fitted her for a limited range of parts.

The Ealing film studios had recently been built, with Basil as the first director. He often invited one, two or all three of us down to watch films being made. I went with Joe once when the office-boy had apparently been told to expect only one of us. 'Are you *both* Mr

Dean's sons?' he asked suspiciously. 'More or less', replied Joe, to the confusion of the office-boy and the amusement of the studio. The process of filming seemed to me a veritable representation of chaos, and also wasteful: dozens of people scurrying about for two hours like ants whose nest had been disturbed, to produce about three minutes of film, which might never be used. The most interesting things were the trick shots, involving at the same time life-size features, small models and mirrors with the backing partly stripped off. I witnessed the filming of a manned auto giro apparently crashing through a roof. We had lunch in the canteen with the stars, among whom I particularly remember Gracie Fields and John Loder. Gracie was delightful, wholly unselfconscious and happily indiscreet. She swore that Basil had eyes in the back of his head, and said she hated film-acting, as mechanical and destructive of imagination, and found the glare of the lights intolerable. For all my efforts and loyalty I never greatly enjoyed Basil's films. He seemed to me to be playing down to his audience instead of inviting them to meet him on his own level, as he had done in the straight theatre.

In January 1932 my paternal grandparents celebrated their Golden Wedding with a large party of family and friends at Croydon. It was a decidedly elderly gathering; I was the sole representative of my generation, wearing my first dinner-jacket, acquired for the occasion. There was a dinner with speeches and toasts (that of the old people proposed by a very tall man with the inappropriate name of Chick) but a marked shortage of alcoholic liquor; either someone had miscalculated or (more probably) my grandfather's well-known addiction to temperance and good works was thought to require a statute of limitations. Basil, after grumbling throughout the meal, went out to refresh himself at a pub and as a result missed the group photograph. Since he was the family's one celebrity this did not go down at all well. The photograph shows the old couple enthroned like Darby and Joan, all but upstaged by Madeline wearing a spectacular gold dress that seemed wholly at odds with her character.

* * * * *

For some time I had been an assiduous visitor to art galleries, whether to view the regular collections or special events like the Italian and Chinese exhibitions at Burlington House, both of which made a profound impression. I went generally with my mother or Gran, sometimes with Essie and later with Martin, who developed a great interest in painting and collected a large number of books on the subject. When I was not more than eleven Gran took me on a round of visits to the private views of various Royal Academicians, some of whom she knew personally. I remember particularly Russell Flint and Sir David Murray, a very old Scottish painter who specialised in Highland cattle. As he sat massive and motionless in his chair, he needed only horns to resemble a Highland bull himself. He had a remarkable signature which I found later in the Hambledon visitors' book. I became familiar with the National Gallery and the Wallace Collection, and also the Natural History Museum, where skeletons of dinosaurs fascinated me. At the National Portrait Gallery I was struck by the very odd faces of many artists and writers. When I met J.B. Priestley for the first time at a sherry party my only comment was that he was a most peculiar shape.

Honor Northcott, a lively friend of the Sutros, took me on my first visit to the British Museum Reading Room, where I wanted to discover biographical details about obscure South American statesmen to annotate a portrait stamp collection. I had begun to collect stamps in 1930, and as with all my interests I pursued it with immense enthusiasm. At first I concentrated on British Empire issues, but soon expanded to cover portraits, American precancels, complete envelopes and parcel wrappings from all over the world, and other sidelines. The pursuit of information to illustrate the portraits increased my general knowledge in a number of surprising directions. For some years almost all my pocket money went on stamps, and I would pester my friends and relatives for any envelopes they received from foreign parts. Stella regularly sent me fascinating specimens sent to the Readings. I still cannot resist adding to this accumulation, though I never seem to have time to put it in order. The other collections were gradually crowded out over the course of years.

Another interest was genealogy. With the assistance of grandparents, elderly aunts and uncles and others, supplemented in one case by family Bibles, I compiled a series of family trees covering all branches of the family. Tommy lent me an elaborate document compiled by a relative in Holland before the 1914 War, which traced one branch back to the seventeenth century. Later my cousin Michael got in touch with living Van Gruisens, and, as mentioned earlier, an Australian cousin of whose existence I was unaware supplied details of the Deans in Tasmania. I try to keep all these tables up to date, but have not yet discovered a method of restraining distant relatives from marrying and breeding at such a rate as to baffle my efforts to accommodate them.

Most of my recreations other than cricket and birdsnesting seem to have had a more or less intellectual or at least an indoor basis. We were indefatigable collectors, of cigarette cards (which also contributed out-of-the-way information with their 'Do You Know?' and 'Struggles for Existence' series), coins and even bus tickets as well as stamps. For a time Martin and Joe added matchbox labels. We also had a family museum containing all sorts of curiosities, some of them of genuine interest, from a piece of shrapnel dating from the 1914 War to the attenuated single-sheet newspapers published during the 1926 General Strike. As a family we were incorrigibly addicted to paper games of various kinds, either involving general knowledge or deriving in some way from the old game of consequences. We evolved many variants of this, including a genealogical type, beginning with two or more rounds of historical characters and ending with someone we all knew. I can still recall some of the results. 'Beethoven married Aspasia and begat Epstein' seems to have a crazy logic, but 'Daniel Defoe married the Virgin Mary and begat Sir Stafford Cripps' was considered too near the knuckle. There was a poetical type, in which each participant completed his neighbour's rhyming couplet, concealing it and adding the first line of another, and so on round the table. Played with the right people, this could reduce normally sane individuals to a condition of helpless laughter.

A more dangerous game, called Qualities, was to choose a friend or relative, especially one who was present, and write down the food, drink, flower, colour, character in fiction and moral quality that the person suggested to our minds, ending with the name and address we considered he or she ought to have. This was a severe test of the victim's sense of humour. My uncle Vernon (before he lost his reason) was quite content to be 'Sir Robert Trumpington, Trumpington Hall, Pants', but his sister Madeline bridled at the name chosen for her, 'Miss Priscilla Masterman'. I cannot recall her address, but when 'Hips' was proposed for the county she rose in her wrath, exclaimed 'If you must play this silly game I'm going to bed', and swept out of the room.

The friends with whom we most delighted to play these games, and who visited us for this and other purposes two or three times during every school holiday, were Tellie and Ben Muirhead. They were a little younger than my mother, and we had known them since the early 1920s; I first remember them at 30 Queen's Road about 1925. Tellie had a mind like an encyclopaedia, as befitted the editor of Muirhead's Blue Guides. It was impossible to mention a subject about which he did not possess recondite or specialist knowledge. He collected stamps, liked children, and was such good company that he was always welcome, at Cumberland Terrace, Warden or Hambledon. Ben was no less so, though she was a little put out when the food I proposed for her was lard. Tellie could be short-tempered, especially towards his own family, and most of all when playing bridge with Ben as his partner. Once in their house, at the height of a bridge argument, he picked up an ashtray and threw it at Ben, but his aim was poor and he hit my mother on the shoulder. Since Ben had cut her finger profusely into the oysters she was preparing for dinner, that evening was a rare failure. I have never liked oysters. When I was staying with the Muirheads on a later occasion Tellie had a furious argument with his son Simon over the breakfast table. Since they looked incredibly alike, I seemed to be witnessing a battle royal between two Tellies, and had to retire to prevent myself laughing. Another dear friend of those days was the actress and dramatist Dorothy Massingham, who used to lodge at Cumberland Terrace while we were at school. I described her in my diary as intelligent, rather absent-minded and immoderately fond of salad. Her suicide while I was at Harrow came as an appalling shock.

Since we lived near Lords (especially when we were in Queen's Road) we sometimes watched Middlesex home matches when they fell during the holidays. I remember games against Leicestershire and Warwickshire (when both sides were dismissed for about 60 on the first day), and more than one against Surrey. My boyhood hero Andrew Sandham hit two fours through the covers that I recall vividly. In this or another match Middlesex produced one B.G.W. Atkinson, a clumsy and heavy-footed batsman who held up the Surrey attack in a long stand with Hendren. In exasperation Surrey's fast bowler Alf Gover delivered a bouncer, whereupon Atkinson stepped back towards the wicket, raised his bat like a club, and struck the ball with a kind of tennis-smash full-pitch into the upper reaches of the pavilion, an unbelievable stroke that sent a buzz of astonishment round the ground. After the war, when I knew both Gover and Sandham, I asked Alf if he remembered this. He did indeed: seldom can a bowler of his pace have been hit for 6 back over his head. My most memorable visit to Lord's was on the third day of the Australian Test in 1934, one of the most sensational in the history of the game. On a rain-affected wicket Verity bowled the Australians out twice, taking 14 wickets in the day and giving England her first victory over Australia at Lord's for 38 years, and the only one between the Wars. I can recall how almost every batsman was out. The ground was so packed that I had to stand or lean against a parapet at the Nursery end, and went without lunch and tea in order not to lose this coign of vantage. In later years I more than once saw Bradman slaughter the bowling; on this occasion Verity tied him in knots and made him look like a rabbit.

I always attended both days of the Eton and Harrow match, for which we had an exeat from school. The Leopold Sutros, who lived in St John's Wood within walking distance of Lord's, gave large lunch parties for twenty or more people on both days every year, though they had no connection with either school. I met some surprising people there, including the actress Anna May Wong. Violet Sutro, who loved dispensing hospitality, which she did very well, insisted on our regarding her as an extra honorary aunt and loaded us with presents at Christmas.

In the early 1930s Ben had a clerical job at the Embassy Theatre, Swiss Cottage, and my mother and I saw a number of plays there. One in particular, in 1931, made an immense impression on me, partly perhaps because it activated my subconscious obsession with time. This was *The Macropulos Secret* by Karel Čapek. Its strange theme and atmosphere haunted me long before I knew that it had inspired what I have always considered the greatest of Janáček's operas. Another play that moved me was Gordon Deviot's *Richard of Bordeaux*, which gave John Gielgud one of his most congenial parts. We enjoyed all Dodie Smith's comedies, which Basil produced, but it was a long time before I met the author. Her volumes of autobiography, published long after the war, have a good deal to say about Basil. The portrait she draws seems to me true and fair (he usually figures in theatrical reminisces as an ogre); I wrote to tell her so, and this led to a very happy meeting. I began to develop an interest in Bernard Shaw, and surprised my mother by asking to see his new play *Too True to be Good*. I enjoyed it, but thought there was far too much talk in the last act.

The greatest theatrical thrill of those years was my first *Carmen*. Ever since I fell in love with the music (or what I knew of it – I had records of a number of excerpts, which I played again and again) my mother had promised to take me to the first performance that fell in the school holidays. The opera was in the Old Vic repertory, but they always seemed to put it on just after term began. At last an opportunity came, in the first week of January 1931. By chance this was the very first opera performance given at the new Sadler's Wells Theatre, and the proceedings closed with speeches from the stage by Lilian Baylis, Clive Carey (I think) and others, possibly including Dent. I was too excited by the opera to listen to the speeches. This is the only one of countless operatic performances I have attended of which I do not have the programme. When I mentioned this to George Harewood a few years ago, he promised to have the theatre's copy xeroxed for me, only to discover that they did not possess it either.

The books that most impressed me were also in some way concerned with the lapse of time, though I have only just spotted the connection: *Wuthering Heights*, the only Victorian novel I have enjoyed sufficiently to read it twice; Clemence Dane's *Broome Stages*, the story of a theatrical dynasty; *The Count of Monte Cristo*; above all, *The Forsyte Saga*. It is now fashionable to decry Galsworthy, but I suspect he may outlive many current idols. My parents knew him well, and I was about to be introduced to him when he died. I fancied I saw much of my own character in Jon Forsyte. My brother Joe had been christened Jolyon after the Forsyte family name. When my mother told Galsworthy this, pronouncing the name Jŏlyon with a short first o, he corrected her: 'But it is Jōlyon'. BBC and others, please copy. *Eminent Victorians*, which I had chosen as a prize at Elstree, interested me for its style: I instinctively distrusted it as history.

Most of my time at Harrow was occupied with Greek and Roman authors, whose style we were expected to recreate in our exercises. I did not find this particularly difficult, and except in one or two instances it did not inhibit my enjoyment of them as literature. I always preferred the Greeks to the Romans, especially Homer, Aeschylus, Aristophanes and the poets of the Greek Anthology, though at Cambridge I developed great admiration for Lucretius and Catullus. The occasion of my first visit to Cambridge (from Harrow) was a production of the *Oresteia* of Aeschylus with music by Armstrong Gibbs. When I was working on Handel more than twenty years later I could still read the *Trachiniae* of Sophocles (the source of Handel's *Hercules*) in the original, a task far beyond me now.

Although Tommy was still active – he took us all to Whipsnade Zoo and at least twice visited me at Harrow – his social life was increasingly inhibited by deafness. This sometimes produced comic results. For a time he used an ear-trumpet, but was apt to apply it to his ear when speaking but take it out when his turn came to listen. He tried other forms of hearing-aid, including a species of headphone that enabled him to hear the ticking of a grandfather clock for the first time in years. ('What's that little noise?' Gran and

I were puzzled until we realised that we were so used to the clock that we no longer noticed it.) Once at a banquet Tommy's replies seemed more than usually inconsequent. It turned out that the device was tuned to the conversation at the table behind him. But he often could not be bothered to put the apparatus on. Like other deaf people he sometimes picked up things he was not intended to hear. At dinner one evening my mother, Gran and I were discussing a play we had seen, and mentioned the actress who played the prostitute. 'The what?' asked Tommy suddenly. 'The prostitute.' 'Institute?' 'PROSTITUTE.' 'Can't hear you.' 'The tart!' 'Part?' 'The sort of girl you took out before you married me,' Gran shouted. 'Oh!' said Tommy with a beaming smile, 'The tart!' Their old friends the Makowers came over to lunch one day, and Ernest Makower began to tell, in French, a long and rather risqué story about a cardinal visiting a nunnery. Tommy sensed that he was missing something and asked to be put in the picture. Since he was no linguist, Rachel Makower took him to a seat outside the open French window and began the story very loudly in English. The narratives then proceeded in two languages, in a sort of canon. The story, just this side of indelicacy in French, sounded utterly obscene in English.

When Tommy, Gran and I were on a long car journey, Tommy suddenly called out to the chauffeur, an elderly man almost as deaf as himself: 'Monk!' Silence. 'MONK!' 'Yes, sir?' 'I want to pumpship.' 'Beg pardon, sir?' 'I want to PUMPSHIP.' 'Very good, sir. I'll find a tree, sir.' Monk, generally a silent man much in awe of a dominating wife, told me that in his opinion the only use for Belisha beacons was to prevent dogs using door-posts. He was apt to be vague about names, and referred to Philip Radcliffe's mother as Mrs Ratworthy. In March 1934 we all drove down to the wedding of my second cousin Myrtle, the grand-daughter of Tommy's eldest sister Aunt Aggie, at Chiddingfold. Since he was her nearest surviving male relative, he was asked to give her away. He somehow contrived to escort her up the aisle on her right side instead of the left. The clergyman failed to notice this and began the service: there seemed a real danger of his marrying Myrtle to Tommy. Gran's frantic whispering failed to penetrate Tommy's ear, whereupon she leaned out of her pew and pulled the tail of his morning-coat. 'What the devil's the matter?' he exclaimed, far more loudly than he intended. I have seldom attended a wedding, my own not excluded, at which some hilarious incident did not occur.

We always spent Christmas Day with the grandparents at 82 Portland Place, fetched by Monk in the car. One Christmas while we were still at Queen's Road there was a fog so dense that visibility was reduced to barely a yard. Monk drove very cautiously at walking-pace, but even so collided head-on with a lamp-post; we thought this a splendid adventure. Christmas dinner, at mid-day, was naturally an occasion for excessive eating and drinking, and was regularly followed by Martin or Joe – usually Martin – retiring hurt and reclining on a sofa before the end of the meal. One year Martin came equipped with rubber walnuts which squeaked when picked up and lumps of sugar made of chalk which he secreted in suitable places. His biggest success was a metal fly on a pin which he stuck into the turkey. When the time came for Tommy to carve the bird – a matter of some ceremony – he first tried to drive the fly away by brandishing the carving-knife, and then, declaring it to be dead, began carefully to cut it out. (He was responsible for occasional happy slips of the tongue, complaining at dinner at Hambledon that the gardener had let the peas and broad beans grow too old, and declaring weightily 'that he ought to use circumcision'.) There was always a monumental fug in the flat, since Tommy refused to have a window open in the belief that fresh air increased his catarrh; for the relief of this he kept a spittoon strategically hidden behind a large photograph of Essie on a side table.

When Martin's turn came to be considered for a public school, Sanderson did not think he had much chance of a Harrow scholarship owing to lack of imagination. (On another occasion he said that Martin was a very good worker but an incompetent head of the school.) My opinion was different, and fortunately I was right: Martin won the fifth scholarship. Joe's case was much more problematical, since he had convinced himself that the task was beyond him. Sanderson told me that he was improving beyond all expectation, but did not want to enter him the following years since he did not consider him up to scholarship standard. Again I disagreed, and undertook to coach Joe in the holidays, especially in Greek and Ancient History. It was not easy to interest him in Xenophon, least of all during the summer, and sometimes I despaired of getting him to concentrate; but eventually our efforts were crowned with success.

CHAPTER 5

Cambridge

The last six months of 1934 were a very happy period in my life. That summer at Hambledon I listened to a good deal of music on the radio with Gran (who like all the Isaacs family was very musical). I particularly remember enjoying a performance of Mozart's *Entführung*, which two years later was to be the first opera I saw at Glyndebourne, again with Gran. I went to the theatre with my mother, revelled in the beauty of Hambledon and the sociable week-end parties at which Gran was a superb hostess, and began to play cricket regularly for the village, whose picturesque little ground lay just outside the front gate. This was the type of cricket I most enjoyed, for social as well as sporting reasons. Hambledon had a genuine village team, consisting almost entirely of gardeners and workers at a local brickyard, with a carpenter and an electrician, who was the captain. All lived in the village. I had known most of them for years, since I had followed the fortunes of the team from early childhood (and at Elstree had described one particularly exciting match in an essay which Walmsley praised for its vividness). There were four Jeffery brothers, all gardeners, two of whom, Bert and Ernie, were employed by my grandparents and later by us for their entire working lives. It was Bert, the vice-captain and formerly captain, who introduced me into the team. He was a tall man and a very fine bowler, with a high action and a natural lift from the pitch; he could move the ball away in the air and bring it back off the wicket, though I don't think he knew how he did it. I once heard him apologise to a batsman after bowling him with a vicious breakback. It was the opinion of a number of distinguished cricketers that he would have had a successful career in the first-class game. His batting, usually at number 11, conformed more to the recognised pattern of village cricket. He had only two strokes, a dead bat and an almighty heave, which depending on the angle of contact would send the ball anywhere, sometimes for 6 over the slips or third man. Both methods on occasion won matches for Hambledon. During the war, towards the end of his career, Bert made two appearances at Lord's for the Surrey Home Guard against the Sussex Home Guard. On the first occasion the match was abandoned when the old Surrey player Andy Ducat fell dead at the wicket. On the second Bert earned a paragraph of appreciation from the correspondent of *The Times*, not for his bowling but for his batting: he presented a masterly negative bat while his partner (a former Harrow captain) made 50.

The standard of the cricket was remarkably high, especially in the half dozen seasons before the war. We played against teams with a far larger population to draw on, such as Godalming and Merrow (a suburb of Guildford) and quite frequently beat them, nearly always after a titanic struggle. We owed our success to three things. Half the team were good bowlers and all could bat (in very different styles) so that we could go in in any order. We were an excellent fielding side. And, perhaps as a result of long familiarity with each other's strengths and weaknesses, we developed a remarkable team spirit, such as I have never known elsewhere. When the best players failed, there was always someone to step into the breach. Again and again we would pull lost matches out of the fire, achieving improbable victories by one wicket or fewer than ten runs. 1935 was a vintage season in this respect, and the most successful in the history of the club. After a defeat and a lucky draw in the first two games we ran through the rest of the season unbeaten with 17 victories and two draws due to rain. Yet several of the victories were by infinitesimal margins, three in succession, all against strong sides, by 3, 7 and 7 runs. In one of these matches, on a dreadful wicket, we were put out for 35, of which 16 were scored by the last pair, including three leg-byes off Bert's bottom; at tea the opponents' score was 9 runs for 7 wickets. My contributions were generally confined to holding catches at critical moments, though occasionally I played a useful innings. My very first match for Hambledon, at Puttenham on the Hog's Back in August 1933, began with me being stung by a wasp and letting a boundary through my legs at cover. The batsman, looking for easy runs, slammed the next ball at me ankle high; fortunately I caught it.

One of our keenest fixtures was against Feathercombe, a country house eleven named after the residence (in the village) of Eric Parker, the well-known naturalist and writer on sporting and country themes, who had four sons well spaced out in age. The Parkers were a very hospitable family, who over a long period organised boys' matches for different age groups for the benefit of their sons, their friends and the village boys. I first played in them at the age of about ten. Martin and Joe were contemporary with the youngest Parker; in the matches for their age group I was sometimes called upon to umpire. In those days there was a deep muddy ditch running round the green inside the boundary. In one of the boys' games, I remember, someone hit a ball into the ditch and Hambledon ran 9 before 'lost ball' was called.

For the Hambledon matches Feathercombe used to put out a strong team containing one or two men who had played first-class cricket (one of them a relative) and occasionally young professionals from Lord's. It was against such a team that Bert Jeffery once took four wickets with consecutive balls in the first over of the match. Feathercombe played their home matches on the beautiful private ground at Busbridge Hall, where South African and other touring teams sometimes began their season with a one-day game. This had an excellent wicket, and the scoring was generally high. In 1938 during the Munich crisis we played two games there on consecutive Saturdays. Both were epic struggles: each side in turn declared with a total well over 200, yet lost the match. It was a perfect if temporary antidote to Hitler. After the war, when Hambledon were trying to raise money for a new pavilion, I published a short history of the Hambledon-Feathercombe matches. For my own amusement I wrote a brief account of every match in which I played for Hambledon.

The matches were played in a keen and very competitive spirit, watched by half the population of the village, who were not afraid to give tongue at critical moments. The proceedings ended in the convivial relaxation of beer and darts at Hambledon's one pub, the Merry Harriers. For away matches we travelled in a hired coach; in those days no one in the team possessed a car. On Bank Holidays there was an all-day match, with a marquee for the sale of beer and sometimes a band, which played for dancing till long after the sun went down. These were happy and moving occasions; I felt as if I were part of some age-long ritual. Comic incidents were not infrequent. During one match a swarm of bees crossed the pitch, just as the bowler was running up, circled round and settled on the stumps. The bowler and most of the fielders threw themselves full-length, pointing out that it was the duty of the umpires to deal with the situation. Fortunately the queen decided that her situation was precarious and moved off. Once when I was batting an exquisitely dressed woman on a smart horse trotted gently along the road at square-leg. The bowler served up a juicy full-toss, which I hit in the meat of the bat straight at them. Suddenly one or other saw the danger and leapt into action; the ball passed between the seat of the woman and that of the horse, and the pair disappeared down the road at a healthy gallop.

Late in August 1934 I spent a fortnight with the Norwoods on the west coast of Scotland, my first visit to that surpassingly beautiful country. Their house was on the Ardnamurchan peninsula, the most westerly part of the mainland. The journey there took a night and the best part of a day, involving at least three trains, a long wait at Glenfinnan, a motor-boat to the far end of Loch Shiel, and a car over the hump of peninsula to Loch Sunart. Norwood on holiday was a different being from the solemn and formidable headmaster of Harrow. He wore old clothes that did not match and spent much time messing about in boats. Apart from Mrs Norwood's brother I was the only guest, two other boys having fallen out at the last minute. When the weather permitted (there were frequent violent storms) we lived and picnicked in the open air, either exploring the country or fishing from a boat in the loch. The lobster-pots, which we visited daily, yielded not only lobsters but edible crabs, dogfish and other creatures, and we caught pollack and mackerel in surprising numbers with rod and line. We also baited something called a paternoster with mussels for flatfish, but I do not recall any being caught. I took the two dogs on the hill, where they brought back young rabbits. We lived mostly on such products, and having enjoyed some success with mackerel taken on a spinner – not an exacting task – I had a flattering sense of contributing to the commissariat. The views from the top of a nearby hill were staggering: Mull to the south, Rhum, Muck, Eigg and a distant Skye to the north, with Homer's wine-dark sea all around, constantly changing colour from claret to rosé and back according to the appearances of the sun. There were seals and great northern divers on an island, and in the course of exploring a glen full of moss, boulders and noisy cascades I caught sight of a group of red deer and attempted to stalk them, to the detriment of my trousers. The way of life was new to me, and I revelled in it.

Towards the end of my visit Norwood had to address the British Association in Aberdeen and inspect the site of an even more remote holiday home that he was contemplating near Lochinver in Sutherland. I thus had the rich experience of a five-day tour of the Highlands from coast to coast: we spent one night in Fort William, one at Ellon near Aberdeen, one at Inverness and two at Lochinver. Not surprisingly I was overwhelmed by the beauty, variety and wildness of the country, especially the weird shape of Coulbeg, Suilven, Canisp, Quinag and other mountains, which stuck up at all angles and appeared in unexpected places as the car followed the winding roads. The climate also made its contributions, including a whirlwind that covered us with bracken and spray near Loch Assynt and a triple rainbow resting on the hills on either side of Glencoe and lighting up the waterfalls like stained glass in a cathedral. This followed a storm of unbridled ferocity that turned the road into a river-bed. More exotic phenomena were a pair of elephants, presumably from a circus, grazing on the roadside near Dalwhinnie and a cheese at Ellon so alive with maggots that it threatened to leave the table.

While staying with the Norwoods I had the first of a number of telepathic or psychic experiences that befell me at this period. On one of the few really sunny days – it was 2 September – I was overcome with sudden lassitude and acute depression. There seemed no reason for it, and though I went for a walk on the hill I could not shake it off. A little later I learned that two people I knew had met unexpected deaths that day: the recent head of my house at Harrow was killed in an aircraft accident, and the eight-year-old only son of our friends Philip and Lorna Rea died of polio. During my first year at Cambridge several other incidents defied a natural explanation. I met a future friend whom I was convinced I had known in the past, until this was proved to be impossible. After a lecture by Professor Ifor Evans on poetry and criticism, which had greatly stimulated me, the chairman rose to make an unexpected announcement (not to express conventional thanks); I found I had dreamed the whole incident the night before, and knew precisely what he was going to say. I can only connect such things with my hypersensitive mental condition; it was as if time had somehow slipped out of sequence. There was to be an even more striking instance a few months later.

On my return from Scotland we paid our last brief visit to the bungalow at Warden, which had been sold earlier that summer. Not all of us however: Joe had been taken ill with acute appendicitis and rushed up to Guy's Hospital, and my mother did not appear till the last day. I had assumed she was with Joe, but she was so preoccupied, evasive and unlike her normal self that I knew something was on her mind, and this made me anxious. When she produced a brand-new cigarette case I suspected that she intended to marry again, but could not identify the lucky man. I had an overwhelming feeling 'that our present position is coming to an end, that some great change is being engineered somewhere'.

Joe had been seriously ill, but soon recovered. He wrote me a very funny letter about his operation, with illustrations (quite a feature of his correspondence at this time); when I visited him in Guy's I found him much entertained by the proximity of Dame Clara Butt in the next ward. All that final week at Warden the weather was beautifully sunny and hot, but the place seemed curiously dead. On the last evening I was invited to play bridge with four neighbours. I had often played with them before, but this was a particularly enjoyable occasion, about which I wrote in my diary: 'I could not have been with four nicer people ... I am afraid this may be the last game of bridge that I will play with them'. I never saw any of them again.

Two days before going up to Cambridge I found myself falling in love, with a girl I had known for eighteen months. I first met Hilary at the Muirheads' house in January 1933, when I was seventeen and she a year younger. I found her far more interesting and amusing than the many other girls I met at parties, and liked everything about her except her name, Hitchcock. In the following May I spent two or three days with her family at East Wittering, where they had an attractive thatched bungalow. We found we had countless interests in common; we both wrote verse, had the same tastes in literature, and laughed at the same things. We began a boisterously cheerful correspondence; from a 'florid and affectionate' letter of hers in October I suspected that she was growing 'embarrassingly keen on me', a situation which for some reason caused me much amusement. In December the boot was on the other foot: after two meetings at which we talked for hours and I found her amazingly pretty, I felt myself 'in grave danger of falling for her completely, and I don't know at all how right or wrong that would be'. This qualification seems very odd. During the summer and autumn we talked with such animation that we lost the time. 'She always seems to like the things I like.' We used to have meals at the Quality Inn in Upper Regent Street and speculate at length and in detail about the private lives of the people at adjacent tables. The climax, such as it was, came on 6 October, a deliriously happy evening when I showed my feelings quite openly, and her response convinced me 'that she may feel a little the same as I do'. However in a letter the following week she denied this and urged me to restrain my affections, though she had enjoyed my timid advances and wished to retain our friendship. Though very upset for a time, I respected her wishes and our friendship continued as before – if anything, even more happily. In late April 1935 after three hours of complete contentment I wrote: 'I'm not, I think, in love with her; but if I am – well, I have good reason to be'. I learned later that she had written the crucial letter at the urging of her mother, an interfering and unintelligent woman and a member of the Oxford Group, whose action was to have a sad sequel. It seems to me now, after more than fifty years, that Hilary and I were an almost perfect fit. But while one of the fates was

Cambridge

bringing us together, another was preparing a very different future for both of us.

* * * * *

My first term at King's brought an immense release of emotions and inhibitions. The contrast between the narrow circumscribed world of a public school and the relaxed climate of a university is of course a commonplace experience. I felt it in an extreme form. The sense of freedom went to my head and intoxicated me. I threw myself into social life with an eagerness and enthusiasm that knew no bounds. Sometimes I seemed to be burning the candle not only at both ends but in the middle as well. Inevitably there was a conflict between social activities and the exercises I had to produce for my Classical supervisors; but I was a fast worker with considerable powers of concentration, and for a long time I managed to balance the account without showing a loss, though I probably spent considerably less time working than my contemporaries. One Gordian knot I cut very soon, by ceasing to go to lectures. At first my attendance at several courses was regular; but they took up time, and I was not long in finding that they told me nothing that I did not know already or that I could not learn from books. I informed my supervisors, who accepted the decision without demur. At the beginning of my second term I did attend two or three lectures by A.E. Housman, the Professor of Latin, on the early manuscripts of Horace, more out of curiosity than anything else. Like everyone else, I found them extraordinarily dry for a lyric poet, though not without interest. Housman was a small insignificant-looking old man; I saw him for the last time, passing in the street, a week before he died.

I soon made countless friends, among undergraduates (especially those of senior years) and the younger dons. Some of these friendships were of comparatively brief duration; others lasted until departure from Cambridge or – more decisively – the War enforced a separation; some, for instance with Philip Radcliffe and Oliver Zangwill, were lifelong. There were family links with Oliver, whose father Israel Zangwill had been a close friend of the Sutros, and also with David Hubback, whose mother Eva was Principal of Morley College and had worked for many years with Gran on Townswomen's Guilds and other voluntary work. The friend I saw most during the first two years was Francis Kitto, a Wykehamist classical scholar a year my senior, a wild, passionate individual; though homosexual at King's, he later married and with his wife started a school for difficult children in the West Country. The last I heard of him was that his marriage and the school had broken down, and he was taking jobs as a municipal gardener in Cornwall. He was one of the best chess players in England. He had rooms near the river, and used to feed the tame ducks, on one occasion making them drunk by lacing their milk with whisky. The sight of 3 or 4 ducks trying to walk accompanied by much quacking and repeatedly falling over their feet was exceedingly funny. Francis died of cancer in 1964 without fulfilling his potential. A few friendships were resumed in later years. None that I recall came to a sticky end. Attempts were made, chiefly by members of other colleges, to revive old acquaintanceships from Sheringham House and Elstree days; but though I was amused to see how my contemporaries had changed and grown up, and saw quite a lot of them during my first year, these relationships seemed to fizzle out, no doubt because we had too little beyond accidental circumstances in common.

I joined no University societies (apart from the English Club during my first term, which offered a few interesting lectures from distinguished visitors) and took part in no organised sports, even cricket. My exercise, apart from long walks, was confined to fives and occasionally squash in the winter terms and tennis in the summer. One of those with whom I played regularly was Alan Turing, already known as a brilliant mathematician and later renowned for his work with computers. Though friendly, he was one of the most introverted and buttoned up men I ever met, and I never got beyond his reserve. I played a good deal of bridge; but most of my time was spent in talk, endless talk on all manner of subjects. King's took pride in its reputation as the most tolerant and broadminded of colleges (a position that changed markedly after the War), and certainly every kind of outrageous opinion would be maintained without murder or violence being done, though one of my friends, Neville Bewley, did have his long hair forcibly shorn by members of the Boat Club in their cups. In my first year I acquired a reputation for being forward and rather assertive, but this was placed to my credit rather than the opposite.

Two of the most popular subjects were politics and sex. I was not a natural rebel, except possibly against father figures, and held no strong political views; I was doubtless too preoccupied with trying to sort out my personal problems and relationships to take much interest in worldly events. Many of my friends were politically active, all strongly inclined to the left. It very soon struck me that they were approaching the subject with singularly woolly minds, and I repeatedly told them so. The recurring trials of engineers and others in Moscow, obviously rigged, were alone enough to put Soviet Communism out of court. I did not know any of the notorious Cambridge traitors, though I met Anthony Blunt occasionally at parties (and later when we were both Fellows of the British Academy) and was on speaking terms with Alister Watson, the mathematician, then a Fellow of King's. Two or three years later the outbreak of the Spanish Civil War, which seemed to me a clash between two evil systems, caused great excitement among my Cambridge friends and acquaintances. Three of them, Henry Pearson, Julian Bell and the poet John Cornford, enlisted on the Republican side and were killed. Henry had been at Sheringham House; he was excellent company, and we used to go together to plays at the Festival Theatre. It was said that he lost his life because he was too tall to be accommodated in Spanish trenches. I was deeply moved by the spirit in which they were willing to fight and die for their convictions, but had no respect for the convictions themselves.

By a long-established tradition sex at King's meant homosexuality; those who had intellectual pretentions looked down on heterosexuals as hearty toughs; most of them seemed to be members of the Boat Club. This tradition had been a great deal weakened by my time, but traces of it remained. There was much gossip in the College as to who was in love with whom. To my intense relief I had now outgrown this phase. Although at least two of my friends were attracted to me, and one (Francis Kitto) pressed me very hard, I was unable to reciprocate. Fortunately this did not destroy our friendship.

What most interested me was literature, especially poetry – much more than music at this juncture. I had endless arguments, especially about Ezra Pound, whose personality I found as distasteful as his verse. My sympathies were entirely with John Sparrow's book *Sense and Poetry*. It took me a long time to come to terms with T.S. Eliot, and Auden irritated me by his style as well as his politics, but I admired MacNeice and especially Wilfred Owen. Eliot and Auden came to lecture at Cambridge in the same week, and I met them briefly. Eliot's lecture, before a large audience, seemed to me vague and inconclusive, like his criticism, though he did say that Hopkins would not be a permanent influence and that the blank verse tradition was exhausted. At the end when questions were invited Eric Hobsbawm, then a Freshman with a strong North Country accent, broke the ice by asking him to tell us what he had been talking about. (When many years later I asked him if he remembered the occasion, he put his head in his hands and said: 'Do I not?') Eliot, who had considerable charm, took this very well.

Auden disappointed us by refusing to talk about poetry at all; he preferred to read two short stories by Edward Upward. It seemed unnecessary to invite a well-known poet down for this. I thought Auden unaffected and amusing, but far from prepossessing: 'he has a face like a sick sheep'.

King's was rich in Classical dons: J.T. Sheppard, the Provost, producer of the triennial Greek plays and a prize eccentric if ever there was one; F.E. Adcock, Professor of Ancient History, a little bald man with gold-rimmed spectacles who could not pronounce his r's but always seemed to choose words that emphasised them, like wepwehensible; H.H. Sills, a Yorkshireman, who wore high stiff collars and exuded an aroma of the nineties, if not earlier; Nathaniel Wedd, who was even older – he had published an edition of Euripides' *Orestes* in 1895 – but had a well-deserved reputation for dry anticlerical witticisms; Donald Lucas (younger brother of my later supervisor F.L. Lucas, known as Peter), whose air of gloomy resignation was perfectly complemented by the extrovert cheerfulness of his buxom wife; and Patrick Wilkinson, a great lover of scandal in his early days but a distinguished Latinist and later the University's Public Orator. The first two had retired from College supervision, but were active lecturers. The others all supervised my work at one time or other. I got on well with all of them. They each had distinctive mannerisms, which we delighted to imitate and parody.

Sheppard's manner amounted almost to self-parody, both privately and in his lectures. The first time I heard him lecture, my reaction was that there could be no such person. I likened him to a clown preaching a sermon. In private we were always 'dear boys' and subject to constant blessing and laying on of hands. When lecturing 'he sits on top of the desk instead of behind it; he spends much of the time in buffoonery and play-acting, and behaves in a manner which, if he were an ape, might be called human. Yet all this in a delightful, perfectly natural manner, though his love of pictorial and gesticulating illustration will often lead him off the subject and render quite unintelligible the thought he is pursuing'. Much of this of course was camouflage; he was no fool.

Adcock used to invite Classical Freshmen to dinner, two at a time with one senior or a younger don. It was a rather stately occasion for which one had to wear evening dress. Adcock did most of the talking, in an epigrammatic style such as he employed in his lectures on Thucydides. He declared that Norfolk roads were constructed on the principle that one good turn deserved another, and, on the suggestion that the *Hippolytus* should be chosen for the Greek play: 'I don't know any undergraduate capable of playing Phaedra, and if there is one he ought to be sent down'. Adcock liked to invite his particular favourite, of whom I was never one, to play golf at Brancaster; this was always a great success, provided Adcock did not lose.

Sills lived on a hill at Shelford and seldom if ever came to social events in College, but from time to time invited his students out to lunch, where there was always a choice of five or six puddings. He had a sabre-toothed daughter and a wife who seemed to belong to an even earlier generation than Sills himself. There was something anachronistic about his driving a car, which he did very slowly; it should have been a carriage and pair. His style of lecturing was idiosyncratic, often including an imaginary conversation between himself and the subject of the lecture. I remember one fragment. 'Now, Herodotus, there is just one more question I should like to ăsk you. What about your religion?' 'Ah, Sills, I wish you hadn't ăsked me that question.' He was a north-countryman and always used the short ă.

Wedd was a particularly delightful man, who looked as if at some time in the past a heavy weight had been hung from his chin. His aphorisms were much prized, but their flavour depended on his particular tone of voice, at once ruminative and assertive. 'Modern poets are like animals that have got an itch, which they can't scratch because their legs are too short.' 'The Greeks had a special word for drunkenness in women, and they were right.' 'Yes – the Oxford Group – yes – a mission for the rich; they never had a mission before, poor chaps.' Wedd's name had been familiar to me at Harrow and even at Elstree, when we had to take down his fair copies of passages we had been required to translate into Greek or Latin prose. I had imagined him long dead. Meeting him in the flesh was rather like an encounter with Tennyson or Browning.

There were many other rich characters among the dons. The Dean, Eric Milner-White, moved rather in his own circle, consisting of the comparatively few religious undergraduates. There was a gulf between them and the rest of the College, whose temper was overwhelmingly secular. The Chapel, while admired and accepted as part of the establishment, seemed to be taken for granted. Scholars, in rotation, were required to read the lessons on Sundays and at the early weekday services, where attendance was very small. I always seemed to be confronted with the Hittites and the Jebusites and other tongue-twisters. Milner was said to be strongly antifeminist and to dislike officiating at weddings. On one occasion he was reported to have dropped the ring down a grating, on another to have intoned 'Those whom God has joined asunder let no man put together'. A shy man, he once began a conversation with an even shyer undergraduate: 'I see, Mr – ah, I see – ah – I see that you have a moustache'. His speech, full of breathy sibilants, positively asked to be imitated: Philip Radcliffe used to read the part of Bull, the canting chaplain in Vanbrugh's *Relapse*, in a Milner voice, to devastating effect. When Milner discovered that I was interested in church architecture, he offered to drive me round. At one church there was an awkwardly placed brass near the sanctuary which I wished to photograph. I was afraid that Milner would object to the moving of church furniture, or even to photography. Far from it: 'Ah – let us tear down the altar-rails' he cried enthusiastically, and proceeded to do so. When my book on Handel's oratorios was published, long after we had both left King's (he was then Dean of York), he wrote me the most charming letter, full of praise and appreciation.

Donald Beves, the Tutor (responsible for admissions and discipline), was a man of generous circumference (except during the War, when his clothes hung despondently about him as if from a scarecrow). He had a delicious sense of humour and was completely without self-importance. At a charade party at the Claphams', when called upon to enact Odysseus turned by Circe into a swine, he went on all fours without his trousers and snorted his way round the room. His name was a dissyllable, except when contracted for poetic or other reasons, as in the terse clerihew that appeared in an issue of *Basileon*, a licentious and anonymous periodical generally edited by Kingsmen in their last term:

> Beves
> Heaves and heaves
> Beer
> I fear.

He was not, I think, unduly addicted to the bottle, though my memory is haunted by the cry of the High Table drinks waiter going his rounds every night in hall: 'Drink, sir, please sir, Mr Beves sir?' A monosyllable again, of course.

Donald had a great love of the theatre, and was a marvellous actor – a born Falstaff – and a successful producer of many University plays. In the staged Handel oratorios he always appeared as a high priest, on one occasion dressed entirely in fish scales. The climax of the 1935 festival celebrating the 250th anniversary of Handel's birth was a scene representing the apotheosis of the composer, crowned with a laurel wreath by Apollo and acclaimed by a chorus of Muses. Donald played the part of Handel in gorgeous eighteenth-century costume and full-bottomed wig, and looked exactly like the portraits as he advanced sedately across the back lawn of King's to the strains of the Minuet from the overture to *Berenice*.

Apollo's oration on that occasion, in resonant Shakespearian verse, was composed by George Rylands, universally known as Dadie, an ornament to the College in more than one sense. He was a man of striking appearance which hardly changed over the years. A leading Shakespeare scholar, he too was involved in countless University productions, especially for the Marlowe Society, which put on an Elizabethan play every spring term. I often wondered why he published so little, for there seemed to be nothing he did not know about English literature, of which he was a trenchant teacher. His lecturing style, full of orotund epigrams, suggested to me a mixture of Dr Johnson and Oscar Wilde. I recorded one specimen sentence: 'Walpole's hoarse laugh was famous and much favoured by Queen Caroline; he hunted with his beagles in Richmond Park and talked bawdy after dinner'. Dadie could be formidable, as I found when I began to read English, but after receiving a few crushing criticisms I decided that it was no good feeling downcast: I must either admit their justice or fight back with vigour. In earlier years what struck me most about Dadie was his hospitality. He was always giving parties, at which one found just the people one wished to see. There were select lunches in his rooms for three or four persons, at one of which I met Maurice Bowra on a visit from Oxford. Epigrams flew in all directions, and I almost expected to find some of them adhering to the walls.

King's seemed to be full of parties, especially during my first year, and I revelled in them. It was some time before I ventured to give one of my own, partly because I was afraid of running short of money. Tommy gave me an allowance of £200 a year, on which, together with my scholarships, I was expected to live, paying my own College bills and all expenses during the holidays. This was a good education in economy, but it meant that I had to live fairly frugally, especially after leaving home in circumstances presently to be related. I decided that one commodity on which I would not stint myself was coal; Cambridge winters can be bitterly cold, and the miseries I had suffered at Harrow must be avoided at all costs. I became quite adept at cooking simple meals for my friends, mostly built round omelettes.

The College had a number of feline inhabitants. The most distinguished was a neutered Siamese called Ming, which belonged to third year Oliver Zangwill. Having observed that College regulations forbade undergraduates to keep dogs but said nothing about cats, he quietly established Ming in his rooms at the beginning of one term. Being a cat of character, charm and humour, like his master, Ming quickly won the affection of Oliver's friends, then of the authorities, and finally of the whole College. He accompanied Oliver to parties and behaved with scrupulous decorum. Oliver used to sign his letters with little drawings of Ming in characteristic poses. When Oliver went down, one half expected Ming to present himself at the Senate House for a degree. One day someone left a diminutive black kitten in my rooms shortly before Sills was due to give a College lecture. It insisted on accompanying me to the lecture and began by playing havoc with the attention of the audience; then, after a short nap on my knee, it took up a position on the front desk and paid careful attention to Sills's learned disquisition on the Ionian revolt.

Cambridge

In October 1934, just after I went up to King's, my Aunt Essie fell out of a window into the area of her house in Chester Terrace, broke her arm and nose, and sustained cuts and severe shock. No one ever discovered whether this was a suicide attempt or an accident resulting from her suspicion that her paid companion Enid Bagger, who had just left the house, was making off with some of her property. She drifted towards insanity and would unquestionably have been certified had she not died at the beginning of December. The last time I saw her she gave me one of her pastels, a village scene in France, for my rooms at King's. A year earlier, at her request, I began sorting the hundreds of letters from well-known authors, painters and others that Alfred had preserved. I found them fascinating. When I told Essie this, she gave me a few of the less valuable and promised to leave me the rest in her will. But she died intestate, and Gran was left with the task of dividing her property equally among her five surviving brothers and sisters and their families. She gave me the letters, since I had been promised them, and many gramophone records, including Haydn's *Clock* Symphony, Mozart's *Jupiter*, Beethoven's *Archduke* trio, a potted *Pelléas et Mélisande* and a number of operatic excerpts, mostly on single-sided records, and – most memorable of all – four of Beethoven's last five string quartets, to which I soon added the fifth. Later Gran added Alfred's commonplace book, from which he used to read to me; but his handwriting, notoriously difficult to read at the best of times, was here indecipherable.

The Sutros, who in the early years of their marriage lived in Paris, among a society of writers and painters, possessed a small bronze of a horse by Degas and many fine pictures. One of them, an Utrillo, was presented to the Tate Gallery in their memory. The pearl of the collection was a Van Gogh which they had bought in Paris for two or three hundred francs early in their marriage in the 1890s, when the painter was scarcely known, and carried home unframed. It was a café scene in Arles with yellow chairs in the foreground and a splash of red from a wine-bottle on a table. Whenever I went to Chester Terrace I used to gaze at it in wonder. I implored Gran to see that it was kept in the family, not for its value but for its extraordinary beauty; but it was considered too valuable for one person's share, and was sent to be sold. It disappeared into some American collection. Today of course it would be worth millions.

During the next six months I began to decipher, file and type copies of the letters, and to collect information about Alfred's career. (Gran appalled me by saying that she had destroyed four letters from Henry James because they contained nothing of interest.) My first idea was to publish the letters in a book, and in April 1935 I went to see the publisher Hamish Hamilton, who had known Alfred and was a friend of my mother's. He said the letters, though of great interest, were too disconnected to make a satisfactory book, and suggested a full biography making use of the letters. I consulted Graham Robertson, Alfred's brother Leopold and his nephew John Sutro, who offered to give me introductions to many of the writers, including Maeterlinck. I took down some reminiscences of Alfred's youth, chiefly from Gran, began a systematic examination of Alfred's plays, and read a number of books containing references to him and the theatre of his day, intending to spend at least a year on the job. But more pressing events supervened, and my work slumbered for nearly 50 years (though I lent the Shaw letters to Hesketh Pearson for his biography). It remained at the back of my mind – though I was periodically distressed by the fact that Alfred's correspondents from whom I should have obtained information were gradually dying off – until quite recently, when Lewis Sawin, an American Professor of English at the University of Colorado, wrote to me out of the blue. He became interested in Alfred over his dramatisation of *The Egoist*. After some discussion my son Stephen and I deciphered the remaining letters and made the collection available to Sawin for a biography.

In December, after my first term at Cambridge, the Readings invited me to stay at Walmer Castle, my uncle's official residence as Lord Warden of the Cinque Ports. Two or three years earlier I had visited him at Deal Castle, further along the coast, where we spent much of the afternoon on the terrace looking at the shipping in the Downs through a telescope. As he showed on this occasion, Rufus never lost his boyish enthusiasm for the sea dating from his year as a ship's boy in early youth. While I was at Deal Sir Johnston Forbes-Robertson and Lillah McCarthy (Lady Keeble) called unexpectedly, he very frail, she very self-possessed and looking more like a headmistress than a famous actress. My stay at Walmer began inauspiciously; my letter announcing the train I intended to take had been delayed in the Christmas mail, and the butler, having received no orders, refused at first to admit me or to credit my identity. Whether for this reason or because I was overawed by the constant flow of guests and visitors (who included Rufus's former chief A.D.C. in India, the general commanding the troops at Dover, and other people whose names were familiar from the newspapers), I remained tongue-tied almost throughout the visit, though perfectly content to listen. Stella, herself a brilliant talker, later complained to Gran about this, but I cannot feel much surprise or guilt. What struck me most, apart from the liveliness and interest of the conversation (in which my great-uncle Harry Isaacs took a prominent part), was the extreme happiness of Rufus's second marriage. He and Stella would even sit holding hands like a pair of young lovers. He talked to me helpfully and at length about careers, without attempting to press me in any one direction. At this stage, strange as it seems now, I felt inclined towards the Treasury.

Three months later the Readings invited me to a sumptuous dinner party (seven courses and champagne) at their London house, 32 Curzon Street (it now carries a blue L.C.C. plaque, which gives me a strange feeling when I pass it), and afterwards to a charity ball in aid of the Jewish Free Reading Room (I never discovered what this was) at a private house in Albert Gate. I had been taking dancing lessons, from a very pretty girl, and trying to cure the habit of stepping off smartly with the left foot, as in the O.T.C. In the event all was well, and I had a hilarious evening, which I described with gusto in my diary.

At the beginning of my second term at King's I was elected to membership of the Ten Club, a College play-reading society founded before the first War which regarded itself as the most exclusive club in Cambridge. We met once a week in the winter terms, each member in turn acting as host, and sometimes had a light-hearted excursion into the fens in the summer. The play-readings were highly entertaining, provided the secretary exercised sufficient skill in the casting. The appropriateness – or inappropriateness – of the reader to his part could be the occasion of great merriment, and so could the secretary's minutes of the previous meeting, which were often satirical and sometimes scandalous. I was generally given blustering Blimpish parts such as Lord Porteous in Maugham's *The Circle* and Sir John Brute in Vanbrugh's *The Provoked Wife*. The reading of this play disintegrated into helpless laughter when it transpired that many of us had different texts with varying degrees of expurgation. Restoration comedies were always popular, especially *The Relapse*, in which the casting of Donald Beves as Sir Tunbelly Clumsy was a *sine qua non*. There were serious readings too; I remember a gripping *Othello* with Dadie in the name part. After the reading the party became social, with beer and other refreshments dispensed by the host. In my second year I was elected secretary, and later president.

My interest in music was beginning to increase, but it was a gradual process, not a sudden revelation. A year earlier Gran had taken me to a chamber music club in St John's Wood, where string quartets by Haydn, Brahms and Beethoven played by the Blech Quartet made little impression, and a little later, at an Ernest Makower concert with Beecham and the LPO, I was bored by a Mozart piano concerto played by John Hunt but entertained by Beecham's 'quaint gestures'. (On an earlier occasion at the St John's Wood club a work by a living composer, I think a piano trio, was played twice. The composer, a thin elderly man with a fringe of white hair, was present, but I have never been able to identify him.) The change was initiated partly by my friendship with Philip Radcliffe and partly by Essie's records, which I played again and again. This had the curious consequence that I became familiar with Beethoven's late quartets before hearing any of the earlier ones, and never found them at all difficult. The Lydian mode movement of the A minor quartet made sense to me while Philip (who was of course vastly more experienced) was still trying to come to terms with it. I hired a piano and began to play again, at first with great application, but never got very far. At the same time my interest in the Classics began to slip, though at no time have I regretted the time spent on them. There is still no doubt in my mind that a Classical education is the best possible training for clarity of thought and expression. I forced myself to enter for the John Stewart of Rannoch Classical scholarship at the beginning of the summer term, and was not at all surprised when I failed to win it, though in Mays, the preliminary exam at the end of my first year (the same term) I was told that I only just missed coming first in the University.

I first met Philip at a cocktail party given for freshmen during my first term, and our friendship soon began to flourish thanks largely to his initiative. He was a shy man, a College Fellow in Music, and a non-practising homosexual who revelled in the relaxed atmosphere of King's and took a strong liking to me. I hardly need say that there was no physical relationship (my homosexual urges were long past), but we shared many interests besides music, a background in Classics (his father was a Classics master at Charterhouse), a very similar sense of humour, and – ever increasingly on my part – a boundless interest in the art of music. We soon began to go to concerts together, and he constituted himself as a kind of tutor, initiating me into every aspect of the art, in taste and technique. To a lesser extent I influenced him, notably in my expanding fascination with opera as a combination of the arts. I soon infected him with an enthusiasm for *Carmen* – and much later with the operas of Benjamin Britten. I had no suspicion of course that my future career lay in music, but from very early on Philip constantly encouraged my interest in the art and was always on hand to enlighten me as technical problems confronted me with increasing complexity. This is certainly not a conventional method of imparting or acquiring musical knowledge, but it proved mightily effective. The one thing it did not teach me was to play an instrument. In a sense that was hardly essential, but it would have been useful. In course of time I learned to read a score – and on a later occasion spotted a missing accidental in Walter Leigh's *Frogs* music that the composer had missed.

Through my great aunt Nelly, my paternal grandfather's only surviving sister, I obtained an introduction to Sir Sydney Cockerell, the Director of the Fitzwilliam Museum. Aunt Nelly, a sterling and generous character, easily my favourite among my father's relations, was the widow of the architect Arnold Dunbar-Smith, who had designed the new wing of the Fitzwilliam in the 1920s. (He was a reserved but very pleasant man, whom I only met once, at the grandparents' golden wedding. He and Aunt Nelly had no children, but adopted a daughter who won some distinction as an expert on folk music under the name Margaret Dean-Smith.) Sir Sydney, a little bird-like man with a short pointed white beard and a penetrating eye, had the reputation for being a tartar, but, perhaps because he had a high opinion of my uncle Arnold, he treated me with extraordinary kindness, invited me to his house, showed me all manner of treasures, and even sought out nearly 100 envelopes with foreign stamps to enrich my collection. He had been a friend of the Pre-Raphaelites and many writers at the beginning of the century, and had a wonderful collection of autographs of Shaw (*John Bull's Other Island*, not in shorthand), Francis Thompson (*The Hound of Heaven*), Hardy and others. He also showed us (Jock Colville was with me) many beautiful illuminated manuscripts, some ancient, others done by Lady Cockerell, who was an invalid. He invited me to return whenever I wished, but alas! after two meetings I never availed myself of the opportunity. My life had become too crowded.

Often at this period my hyperaesthesia led to moods of extreme, almost manic exhilaration. The slightest stimulus, perhaps from a piece of music, a play or a poem, would set every nerve in frantic vibration. I became an emotional volcano. The mere awareness of being alive gave me an intense thrill, and I felt that nothing was beyond my powers. At such moments the poetry of Blake seemed to have a special kinship with my feelings, especially the quatrain:

> To see the world in a grain of sand,
> And a heaven in a wild flower,
> Hold infinity in the palm of your hand
> And eternity in an hour.

I thought of all the little actions performed by countless men and women that seem so important for the moment but are destined to be consumed by time and totally forgotten, and conceived an intense pity for the human race. One such occasion was the evening of George V's Silver Jubilee in May 1935, when with a companion (Neville Bewley) I was caught up in the collective emotion of the crowds celebrating on Midsummer Common with brass bands, torchlit processions and fireworks. My mind went back to the dancing on the cricket green at Hambledon the previous summer, when the whole village seemed to be celebrating as the sun set on one horizon and the moon rose on the other. I wondered what everyone, everywhere, was doing at this particular moment in time, and wished I could know and share it. As we wandered round Cambridge Neville kept humming Tom Moore's 'Believe me if all those endearing young charms', endowing that sentimental ditty with a vicarious potency that has never quite worn off.

I tried to channel all this excess emotion into verse, but had neither the control nor the technique to bring it off. I would pace round the College at night and endeavour to express my thoughts and feelings in conversation with friends, lasting into the small hours and regularly defeating my resolution to go to bed at a reasonable time. These exalted moods would be succeeded, sometimes very abruptly, by bouts of black depression and disillusionment at the thoughtlessness and stupidity of the human animal, when I would exist in a dark haze unable to take an interest in anything. In January 1935 I ascribed this, rather awkwardly, to 'starvation of a vital need for discussing all the problems of life with someone of the opposite sex, for overhauling my whole system of relative values'. Whether as effect or cause, I suffered a good deal of physical ill-health in the form of indigestion, swollen glands and persistent head-aches. I consulted the Tutor, who sent me to a doctor. Somewhat prosaically he diagnosed the after-effects of flu, which while doubtless a contributory factor was hardly the root of the problem.

CHAPTER 6

Family Troubles

IT IS CLEAR, LOOKING BACK, that I was ripe for some major experience, if indeed I had not sensed it in advance. But I was certainly not prepared for the series of domestic crises that now supervened, piled one on top of another. All my close relatives became involved in a number of interlocking quarrels that caused untold anguish to many people over several years and finally split the family asunder. The first of them, which had begun a year earlier, concerned me only indirectly, though it soon became entangled with the others. My Uncle Vernon, Basil's elder brother, had married in middle life Violet Balkwill, a woman with two sons by a former husband. They seemed a very contented family. We thought of Vernon as a hearty extrovert, not particularly imaginative but of a rocklike reliability. His wife, known as Vie, who was my mother's closest friend, struck us all as the most kind-hearted, generous and caring person we knew, and both her sons, who were some years older than me, had inherited her qualities. Their beautiful old house, Rooting Manor near Ashford in Kent, was second only to Hambledon in my affections. Apart from our visits on the way to Warden, I had stayed there myself more than once when recovering from an illness. Early in 1934 Vernon went down to Rooting with a girl of 23, whom he claimed to have met at a fortune-teller's but who turned out to be a prostitute, proclaimed that he had at last found happiness, freedom and a woman who could give him children, sent all Vie's personal belongings up to London, and refused to maintain her. At the same time he poisoned the minds of his parents, so that they disowned her.

It was soon apparent that Vernon was out of his mind. His decline over the next few years need not be related in detail, though cross-currents from it continued to muddy family waters. At various times he was arrested for debt, declared bankrupt, and imprisoned for contempt of court. There were sexual scandals too. When he was indigent Vie supported him by taking jobs. Convinced of his omniscience, he began to write letters of advice to world statesmen and other public figures, including Hitler and the Archbishop of Canterbury, and at the beginning of the War was arrested for attempting to dismantle beach defences on the south coast. He was then certified, and died in an asylum in 1963, still hale and hearty but incurably insane. During these years I met him only once, by chance in 1936, and the only difference I could detect was that the pitch of his voice had risen by about a minor third.

We were all appalled by Vernon's behaviour, my mother most of all; but Basil, without making any attempt to discover the facts, took his brother's side. He invited me out to lunch, delivered a long diatribe on the limitations of the female sex (a favourite theme), declared that in Vernon's place he would have brought an action for slander (presumably against Vie), and said he would be deeply offended if I did not make a date with Vernon, which of course I refused to do. Basil's self-interest was involved as well. Before my mother had any reason to distrust Vernon, she confided in him that she had lent a substantial sum of money to a friend (Mitford Brice) who had not repaid it. Vernon told this to Basil, who tried to make it an excuse for discontinuing his alimony. This was not to be the only argument he deployed for that purpose.

Family Troubles

In April 1934, when Essie's health was deteriorating rapidly, Gran engaged a companion, introduced as Mrs Enid Bagger, a stout and not unamiable woman. Since Essie wished to be near her sister, they rented a neighbour's house at Hambledon which happened to be vacant. Presently the woman's supposed husband, Eugene Bagger, established himself nearby and appeared frequently at the Hurst for meals. In fact his name was not Bagger, and Enid was not his wife. He was a Hungarian Jew, born in 1892, whose father's name was Schoen; the family changed this to the Magyar Szekeres in 1900. Baptised a Roman Catholic at the age of 17, he soon relapsed. In 1913 he moved to Copenhagen, where he married an older divorced woman with two daughters called Palline Bagger, whose name he took, describing it as 'one of the family names of my relations' (*sic*)[1]. In 1915 the family sailed to the United States, where Eugene worked as a journalist and took US citizenship in 1920. He published three books, including a Life of the Emperor Franz Joseph, which he later repudiated. He left Palline after six years and returned to Europe, spending three years in Vienna, then settling in the South of France (Saint Raphael), where he lived (?with Enid) 1927-32, presumably on her money, for he had little of his own. He was still legally married to Palline. Some of this I discovered later by mere chance; an old friend[2] of my wife's turned out to be a friend of Palline, who she said was a delightful person and had a very raw deal.

This was the man with whom my mother fell in love. When on 23 September 1934 she told me this in confidence (only Vie was in

1 According to his sworn affidavit on marriage to my mother at Montreux on 29 April 1938.
2 Phyllis Green, the mother of the writer Roger Lancelyn Green, who had become friends after meeting Thalia and her mother on a Hellenic cruise in 1937. Mrs Green wrote to Thalia after seeing the *Times* announcement of her engagement to the son of 'Mrs Eugene Bagger' in February 1939. In a letter to Thalia (23 February 1941) she enlarged on Eugene's reputation in America.

the secret) I was delighted for her sake. I was fully aware that her marriage to Basil had been a disaster, that she had brought us up well without ever attempting to turn us against him, and that fate surely owed her some recompense. I was not only prepared to accept Eugene; I was prejudiced in his favour. My first impressions were wholly favourable. During a walk on the Common on 17 August 1934 we had 'a most interesting and abstruse discussion on modern psychology', during which he described himself as a follower of Adler, not Freud. My diary records that 'we got on extremely well ... He has a most intriguing mind, and I am looking forward to our next talk, when I hope to ask about the personal application of psychology'. On the appointed date (24 August) he disappeared with my mother for the entire day and nothing was said about a further talk. I believed everything my mother told me about him, that he was a trained psychologist, an expert on music and all the other arts, could speak five languages, and had long been writing a *magnum opus* on the philosophy of history, which was sure to startle the world. I also was led to believe that the obstacle to their marriage was Enid's intolerable behaviour, which had done him incalculable harm and was now blocking a divorce; as soon as that difficulty had been overcome, and he had made some money by the publication of his book, all would be well. In fact the book was never finished, much less published, and it seems doubtful if much of it was ever written; it became known in the family as Penelope's web.

My first conversations with Eugene were about psychology. He ascribed Vernon's troubles to his strong-minded mother oppressing her male children and producing symptoms of defeatism, contempt for women and inflated self-importance. Signs of friction first appeared in December, when he gave me a long and pompous lecture on what he admitted was a tiny matter, saying that it indicated neurotic tendencies. I had already been put off by his manner, especially towards the grandparents and their guests. He laid down the law on every subject that arose, declaring that Catholics were the only religious people in the world, and Europe had only two alternatives for survival, Catholicism and Nazism. He never tired of disparaging everything English: the English Christmas, the English love of toleration, the English sense of humour, English conductors (Adrian Boult was a particular target), the flabbiness of the Church of England. 'Why then did he come to England?' Gran used to enquire. It was not so much his opinions that gave offence, but the way he voiced them; he treated any opposition with sneering contempt. His method of arguing seemed to me full of fallacies, especially the familiar one of proving his assertions by assuming his premises; but I soon ceased to argue with him.

What disturbed me much more was the effect on my mother. It was not merely that she invariably took his side and echoed his opinions, which were often the opposite of what she had hitherto believed. She became completely absorbed in his personality, to an extent that I would not have believed possible in anyone, least of all in her. She lost her sense of humour: when I described in a letter, with an obvious twinkle, a series of misadventures that had befallen my luggage on a journey to Cambridge, she roundly ticked me off for being sorry for myself. She became aggressive and ready to pounce before any occasion arose. This was the consequence of Eugene's professed policy of encouraging her to stand up for herself, not a bad thing within limits. Presently anything that went wrong in the household, however trivial, was ascribed to some delinquency of mine, or occasionally of the servants. She even withheld some of Essie's gramophone records and demanded one of Henry James's letters to Essie, saying that I had plenty of others. I gave it to her to keep the peace.

I consulted Vie about this. Both in person and in letters she emphasised the point I already appreciated, that having for years found little emotional satisfaction in life my mother was bound to seem preoccupied. Vie repeatedly urged me to keep a level temper and be content with an unselfish place in the background, and never to give them a handle. I stress this, because Vie was presently accused of deliberately subverting my allegiance. I was glad to return to Cambridge, and began to dread going home.

The climate was more cordial at the start of the 1935 Easter vacation – but not for long. There was a most enjoyable sherry party at Cumberland Terrace for my nineteenth birthday, for which many of my friends were invited. I spent as much time as possible away from home, staying with Francis Kitto's family in Hampshire, visiting many cathedrals and churches, and after an adventurous journey joining a reading party at the Hubbacks' cottage near Padstow on the north coast of Cornwall. On the evening before my return to Cambridge a casual reference to the adjustments needed as a result of Eugene's entry into the family (not that he had any status – his marriage to my mother was three years in the future) led him to make a violent and prolonged attack on my character, accusing me of wanting my mother to myself, resenting her having a life of her own, unscrupulously pursuing my selfish ends at the expense of other people, then hiding behind them when I felt in danger, and a great deal more. I was the worst case of neurosis, barring Essie, that he had ever encountered. My mother sat by and agreed with everything. I felt like a murderer being tried for his life under the lash of bullying Counsel at the Old Bailey. I dreamed that night that a madman had run riot through my brain with a pneumatic drill. Martin and Joe, aged fifteen and fourteen, had been mentioned incidentally; on the following day my mother called the three of us in and asked them if they had any complaints about the holidays. To her astonishment they both replied in the affirmative and made precisely the same points as I had done, if anything with even greater emphasis. I was almost as surprised as she was, since at that time we had not exchanged one word on the subject. Some very disagreeable correspondence followed, including a venomous letter from my mother accusing me of corrupting not only Martin and Joe but the servants, betraying her confidence, treating her with contempt, and doing all I could to make her life unbearable. She had spoken to the grandparents, who threatened to stop my allowance and have me turned out of the house unless I mended my ways. I am sure they never contemplated any such thing. I destroyed nearly all her letters of this period, since their hysterical, almost paranoiac tone simply did not reflect her true character. There was little doubt who had inspired or dictated them.

Such was the background to the next major event. On 18 May I attended the wedding of Michael Clapham and Elizabeth (Leeby) Rea in King's Chapel. I knew both families. The Reas had been friends of my parents and the Van Gruisen grandparents since before the first War, when Alec Rea, a Liverpool business man and Leeby's uncle, had been one of Basil's strongest supporters in the Liverpool Repertory Theatre. After the War they formed a famous theatrical partnership, ReandeaN, in London. Michael's father, J.H. Clapham the economic historian, was Vice-Provost of King's and had two or three times invited me to his hospitable house, Storey's End. Michael had a small printing-press and had published a little book of Leigh Hunt's letters edited by Tim Munby, a friend of mine in his third year and after the War the librarian at King's. There was some question of his publishing some of my poems. I was in two minds about this, being anxious to appear in print yet afraid of adding to the mass of mediocre verse on the market. Perhaps fortunately the scheme came to nothing; but Tim was a helpful go-between, and presented me with an autograph letter from the Duke of Wellington.

The wedding produced a crop of comic incidents and the most startling of my psychic experiences. There were nine bridesmaids, including two small children who carried the bride's train. When they reached the steps half way to the sanctuary they stopped abruptly, half-wrenching the other end of the train from the bride's head. The twelve-year-old bridesmaid who came next, like them a niece of Leeby's, lifted them up the steps but unfortunately put them down on top of the train, bringing all movement to a standstill. Presently the length of the service proved too much for one of the little girls, who called out to her mother in the nearby stalls: 'Mummy – mummy – I want to wee-wee!' 'Can't you wait?' 'NO.' 'Then do it in your pants and say nothing!' Their stage whispers carried easily to me in the choir-stalls. My attention however was distracted by one of the grown-up bridesmaids. Looking at her I was visited by a series of extraordinary sensations: That I had not only seen her before but had known her in some remote past, that she was destined to play a crucial part in my life, and that some link united us that could never be broken. Strongest of all, I knew exactly what sort of girl she was, not just in outward appearance but in character. All this before I had spoken to her or knew her name, and before she knew of my existence. Except that I cannot have known her before, all these impressions proved to be correct, though not always in a way that I could have expected. I cannot account for this, unless my over-excitable condition, by some telepathic process, for a moment contrived to annihilate time.

That evening the Claphams gave a small party and dance at their house Storey's End. There were only 25 to 30 people there, including the bridesmaids, and we were told to introduce ourselves to anyone we did not know. I was far too timid to approach my particular bridesmaid, and half-inclined to dismiss my vision as a hallucination; but destiny took a hand. During a pause in the dancing to gramophone records I stepped back and found I was treading on the hem of someone's dress. I looked round to apologise, and saw Brigid smiling at me. Before I had time to think I asked her for the next dance. We were together for the rest of the evening, either dancing or sitting out talking, and she gave me a lift back to King's in a microscopic Austin 7 without a roof. A tune to which we danced, called *Easter Parade*, became hallowed in my memory. We found we had many interests and friends in common – she had been a contemporary of Leeby's at Newnham and was four years my senior – but what struck me most, apart from the fact that she was a delightful dancer, was the extraordinary sympathy that seemed to unite us from the very first moment. This was instinctive, not a matter of thought or calculation. I had never felt anything like it before.

By chance Hilary was in Cambridge that weekend. I had given her tea on the day of the wedding, and she came to a little party of mine on the Sunday. This was smaller than I intended; my mother had refused to come up for the wedding, and had dissuaded the grandparents from attending; Tellie Muirhead, who was related to the Reas, was kept away by the sudden death of his father. I had asked Brigid and Clare Mallory, daughter of the climber lost on Everest, whom I had met for the first time two days earlier at a party of David Hubback's; had they been able to come, all three girls to whom I was deeply attached before my marriage would have been present together – a piquant thought. That evening I dined with the Guillebauds, with whom Hilary was staying, and afterwards wrote a comic poem, *The Ballad of the Vice-Prepostal Daughter*, about the vain advances paid by John Saltmarsh, a King's history don, to Jana, the youngest Clapham daughter. Four or five days later I received a passionate, agonised letter from Hilary, full of cancellations and broken sentences, declaring her love for me, just after I had written in my diary that any attraction she may have had for me was quite gone. I felt stunned by the irony, and also guilty, since it must have been my joyful words about Brigid that forced the letter out of her (I subsequently destroyed it, for her sake). However our friendship survived, and two years later we had a happy little fling, after which she had an abortion – to my considerable alarm, though I was not responsible. Her emotional life at that time was stormy. However she married happily, and her son Jeremy is my only god-son.

It is not easy to give a coherent account of the year that followed, when on several fronts crisis followed crisis. However it began with a lull: for most of the summer months, spent chiefly with the grandparents at Hambledon, I was happier than I had been for a long time. The day before the Mays exam I went to the Derby with Hilary and her family, in a strange party that included several heavy-weight aunts and a Russian prince, and enjoyed surveying the weird mixture of humanity assembled on Epsom Downs. I had my fortune told by a gypsy, who declared that my present attachment would come to nothing, but my marriage would be very happy. She was right on both points. I was making plans to visit Rome on my scholarship, and received helpful information and advice from various people, including Michael Grant, Patrick Wilkinson and Plum ('Don't get conscripted for Abyssinia'). My family were worried about political risks, and when Mario Lamberti, an Italian research student at King's who became a dear friend, wrote that there was typhus in Rome, they put their foot down.

I kept up a lively correspondence with Martin and Joe, who were both entertaining on paper. Martin wrote very long letters, all in one paragraph, divided between satirical comments on the masters at Harrow and complaints that all his money went on food; but he was clearly proud to be described by a member of his form as 'Greed personified'. However he was growing more and more interested in art and had collected 173 books on painting, including 40 that had belonged to Essie. Essie had published a book on Poussin, and left another unfinished, about the influence of Constable on the French school. It was to be called *From Constable to Cubism*; she had written chapters on Constable and Modigliani, and started one on Whistler. Martin, encouraged by Gran, proposed to finish the book. I read his chapter on Whistler and the Victorians – presumably the one Essie had started – and thought it remarkably good, only needing a certain amount of compression and rearrangement. The book was never finished, either because Martin lost interest in the subject or as a result of the horrors that were about to overwhelm the family. At the same time Martin gave it as his decided opinion that music was the greatest art, and sent intelligent comments on the concerts at Harrow. He was entertained by the peregrinations of Beecham on the platform, but objected to the bass Arthur Cranmer, who 'made a foul scooping noise'. At House singing 'Joe made an extraordinary noise singing *Men of Harlech*, and got quite a good clap!' It was becoming apparent that Joe had inherited Tommy's tone-deafness; he could not sing the National Anthem in tune even when I played it on the piano. About this time the two of them wrote a letter to *The Times* criticising Sir Reginald Blomfield for depreciating and pulling down Nash's Regent Street, Joe supplying the ideas and Martin the language. The editor thanked them, but did not publish it.

The Cambridge Handel Festival in June, organised by Professor Dent to celebrate the 250th anniversary of the composer's birth, was rich in delights and comic incidents. The oratorio *Susanna*, preceded by *The Choice of Hercules*, was performed with action on the back lawn of King's on a temporary stage erected against the central arch (Jumbo) of Gibbs Building. In fine weather the effect was idyllically beautiful. The two choruses in *The Choice of Hercules* approached across the lawn from opposite sides, Pleasure's attendants accompanied by greyhounds and other exotic attractions. At one performance the wind suddenly got up, played havoc with the orchestra's music, removed a hat from a lady in the front row and deposited it neatly on the head of another lady six rows back. When Frederick Woodhouse, playing the Second Elder in *Susanna*, compared himself to 'The oak that for a thousand years Withstood the tempest's might' and pointed to a property tree standing high on the platform, it promptly toppled over and bounded down the steps into the orchestra, felling several music stands. Another performance was interrupted by a deluge, and after a helter-skelter chase had to be concluded in Hall. The last was at night, and floodlit. David Hubback and I had been to *A Midsummer Night's Dream* at the Festival Theatre (I saw many plays there this term, from *See Naples and Die* to the second half of Goethe's *Faust*) and arrived back in King's for the later stages of the Handel programme. This concluded, as already mentioned, with the apotheosis of Handel: Donald Beves, a superb actor endowed by nature with Handelian proportions and elaborately costumed, approaching from behind the audience with a nice mixture of timorousness and pomposity to the strains of the *Berenice* Minuet, Apollo (Hubert Langley) reciting Dadie's sonorous verses and crowning him with a laurel wreath, while the chorus sang the finale of *Ariodante* to new words by Dent, an address to the Muses beginning 'Ye learned virgins, haste'. The whole episode was intensely moving; the flood-lighting seemed to give it a timeless quality.

There were various church expeditions, including a three-day tour of East Anglia with David Hubback, partly on foot, of which I wrote a long and lively description. We spent the nights in very varied accommodation at Norwich, Bury St Edmunds and Bures. On the way back to Cambridge by a now long defunct railway line I walked several miles to Kedington church accompanied by an old man, a child, a dog and an exuberance of birdsong, and had to run nearly all the way back to catch the next train. A kindly porter revived me with water. I was just in time for the King's May Week Ball, to which I went by invitation in a party of Claphams as Jana's partner. This was a very merry occasion, lasting all night and involving a 1.30 a.m. supper, at which we tried to intoxicate the Provost to discover my Mays results, a group photograph at 6 a.m. and a vast breakfast of coffee and sausages in a pub at Grantchester. In the small hours one of the party tossed off half a (small) bottle of brandy and promptly shared a decanter of sherry, all of which he subsequently denied; we made him laugh at breakfast, and contaminated coffee poured from all his facial apertures.

I went straight down to Hambledon and spent most of the next ten weeks there in a state of absolute contentment, gardening, reading (mostly Cicero), talking, and playing tennis and cricket. There were some particularly thrilling Hambledon matches; the team attributed two of our most impressive victories, over Godalming and Feathercombe, largely to my fielding, which was an exaggeration but highly gratifying. I had watched several of the University matches, seen Larwood and Tate bowl, and went to one day of the Lord's Test Match against South Africa, when the England batsmen were bamboozled by a Greek googly bowler named Xenophon Balaskas. I continued to work at the Sutro letters, lunching with John Sutro at the Garrick, visiting Graham Robertson, and attempting to decipher about fifty letters from Alfred to Israel Zangwill during a very happy weekend with Oliver and his mother near Angmering. The reason why so few of Zangwill's letters to Alfred survived now emerged: Mrs Zangwill had asked Essie to destroy her letters, and in her confused state she had destroyed Israel's as well. I made a firm decision to devote my life to writing: 'Whether I am gifted for it I know not; but I don't think I'm gifted for anything else'. The one sad note was the illness and death of Tiger, Gran's very intelligent wire-haired terrier, who dated back to Birkenhead days and to whom all the family were devoted.

Eugene took a room in Chiddingfold, and was much in evidence. For some time the climate was less heated, though there were plenty of arguments. He damned the whole Romantic movement in art because it was rooted in subjectivism, and declared that I could not be musical because at that time I disliked Brahms. He was constantly ramming Mahler down my throat – surely a subjective composer if ever there was one – but that was not the only reason why I have always detested Mahler's music. One evening Eugene denounced Henry James and then turned on me, accusing me of wasting time, opportunity and a first-rate mind on irrelevances. These included my stamp collection and the life of Alfred. Though he returned to this theme more than once, I refused to be provoked but noted plaintively: 'I wish I knew just *where* I am wrong, and *how* I could be happier'. Once or twice he even said something in my favour.

I saw Brigid twice in London, on the first occasion ringing her up on the spur of the moment between two parties. We talked for hours, and I was blissfully happy. In the middle of August I spent two days with her and three friends on a house-boat in the Hamble river. One evening we talked for two hours on deck, and I could no longer conceal that I was hopelessly in love with her. She knew it already, of course, and treated me very gently, saying she was very fond of me but still in love with someone else (Roland Bourne), who had jilted her when she was at Cambridge. My emotions were in a complete turmoil, then and for some time afterwards. I did not know whether to go on seeing her, hoping against hope that she would change her mind, or to break it off at once. I soon found I could not do this; if I did, I would probably throw myself under a train. Fortunately Brigid was a person of rare understanding. She managed to convince me that she valued my friendship very greatly and wished it to continue, but could offer no hope of anything more. I accepted this; perhaps there was no choice. In all that followed I was as moved by her absolute honesty in all her dealings with me as by her generosity and obvious affection. She could so easily have either pretended to feel more than she did, allowing me to take her out and give her a good time, or pushed me off on the ground that my emotional affairs would be an intolerable burden to her – as indeed they very soon were.

At the beginning of September the grandparents left Hambledon for three weeks, as they usually did, to give the servants a holiday. The rest of us, including Eugene, moved to a guest house at North Lancing. The town was a sorry expanse of ugly bungalows, but the Old Forge, an attractive Elizabethan building just below the Downs, was comfortable, the food was good, the atmosphere pleasant, and we were the only guests. Eugene however took against it, complained that the noise from builders along the road prevented him working (he always had excuses for this), grumbled at the accommodation (only one bathroom), rejected the food as insufficient and was extremely offensive to the staff. My mother echoed him like a tame poodle. I felt acutely embarrassed and ashamed of them. We had booked for a fortnight, but they decided to return to London, leaving the three of us to stay till the end of the second week. In the evening Eugene lost his temper and abused me at some length in public. Next morning they left after a final vicious row with the manageress over the bill. We spent the rest of the week happily walking on the Downs and looking at churches. Joe climbed a high wall to photograph the remarkable Saxon tower at Sompting; the photo came out well, but missed the tower completely.

Towards the end of the month I went to Paris for a week by myself, unwillingly but determined to prove my independence. Eugene had dared me to do so, implying that I did not have the guts. I spent the whole time sight-seeing and was predictably overwhelmed by the pictures in the Louvre, but not by Versailles. I decided to do it all on foot ('No short cuts to experience') and walked every day for miles, visiting churches, museums and art galleries, until laid low by an acute attack of gastric flu. The pictures evoked pages of comment and appreciation in my diary. My companions in a lift ascending the

Eiffel Tower were 'three Dutch, three hearty Germans, three Slavs who resembled by-no-means-Aryan cods, two very self-conscious clergymen of the Church of England, a young Frenchman with the face and manner of a pickpocket, two American girls who wrote hundreds of postcards, and a man of undefined nationality who emitted exactly the noises one might have expected from an amorous warthog'. I reached the doubtful conclusion that these sounds indicated satisfaction. I visited some relatives, including Aunt Fran, Gran's eldest sister, who was very spry for an octogenarian and wore a flowing red wig but had lost her memory. She lived with her elderly bachelor son Louis, whom she seemed to treat as a tame dog. I rather disconcerted Gran by describing her as an Isaacs gone to seed.

Back at Hambledon things began to boil up. My mother became very aggressive and demanded a grovelling letter from me, confessing to rudeness and other supposed misdemeanours. Gran told her and Eugene that they were heartless brutes, but was caught between two fires, and relations became very strained. Nevertheless humour kept breaking in. A new wire-haired terrier puppy appeared and was reported to run after anything in trousers – 'which is all right in a dog', said Gran, who considered buying a pair. When told that I spent my evenings in Paris writing up my diary, 'Not the thing to go to Paris for', she remarked, 'but it's cheaper'. Tommy recounted a nightmare in which he had dealings with a 'bogey', which tried to get into his bed. When pressed he became embarrassed and refused to divulge its sex, but finally admitted that he would like to have known more about it. Bert, asked to explain why he took only one of two eggs laid by a hen in the woodshed, replied 'If I leaves one, he lays another'. 'Why *he*?' 'We always calls them he.' His world was rich in personification; about the only thing I heard him refer to in the neuter was my mother's old car. A vivid memory of these days is a sunset of quite spectacular brilliance, which gave the Surrey hills the appearance of wild mountains.

Family Troubles

On 6 October Honor Northcott invited me to lunch. I had described her in July as 'perhaps the most perceptive and sympathetic person I have ever met'. She now showed a different face. She pressed me to tell her how things were going; when I began to explain she interrupted before I could finish and launched the most ferocious diatribe I have ever received from anyone, calling me among much else a coward, a weakling, a traitor, a cad, and accusing me of being responsible not only for my own troubles but all Mother's as well (out of jealousy of Eugene) and even by implication of setting up as a pretty boy at King's. I ought to obey blindly every expressed wish of either of them. This went on for at least half an hour. It soon became obvious that it was a trap, a put-up job: they had all met beforehand and agreed to confer on the following day (when Honor told two blatant lies, that I had gone to her complaining of my fate, and that she had done her utmost to stop me). She ended by trying to extract a promise that I would never again mention the subject to anyone on any occasion. Later I heard that she was to regret the whole episode. Her relations with my mother ended several years later in a bitter quarrel.

However the damage was done. Having nearly been sick in Honor's flat, I wandered distraught round Regent's Park, upset most of all by the behaviour of someone I had trusted as a friend. Fortunately I had arranged to dine that evening with Vie, who said at once that I looked ghastly and brought me back to sanity. Ten hours with Brigid the following day completed my recovery, for the moment at least. It was obvious now, if not earlier, that Eugene's object was not only to humiliate me but to break my spirit, and that my mother would do nothing to stop him. I learned later that the three of them invited Vie to a meeting. Her reward for her kindness was to be lectured, taunted and abused for four hours by Eugene and Honor while my mother sat in silence. She told me that on leaving the house in Cumberland Terrace she was sick in the street.

Looking back over fifty years, I have often tried to understand Eugene's motives and his character. He was certainly jealous of the happy and companionable relationship recently established between my mother and me. But that did not threaten him at all. He was equally prepared to run down her old friends, often criticising them with searing contempt. He produced glib psychological explanations for their deficiencies, as well as for mine and those of the grandparents (later, in letters to Joe, he referred to Gran as 'the Gorilla'). There was an element of megalomania in his behaviour: on every imaginable question he, and he alone, was right. When he was in good form we used to tease him about this. I once summed up his method of argument as follows: 'You know philosophy; philosophy is everything; therefore you know everything. Why then are we arguing?' I think he really believed this. One day at dinner Honor began to extol his brains and personality to his face in the most extravagant terms – so much so that I had to pinch myself to prevent myself laughing – and told him how wonderful and brilliant her Irish friends thought him. All he could say was that he was glad there were some sensible people in the world.

The key to his character obviously lay in the past. For a short time after the first War he was a person of consequence in journalistic circles in New York. He had then thrown this away to live at Saint Raphael, apparently at the expense of the woman with whom he set up house. I learned later that he was notorious in America for sponging on women, and have little doubt that, believing Tommy to be richer than he was, he proposed to treat my mother in the same way. This does not mean that he did not care for her. I believe he did; but he had to monopolise her and convince her and her family and friends, over and over again, that he was a great man whom the world had despised and rejected. Presumably he had to compensate for a gnawing sense of failure. He was a classical case of a vastly inflated inferiority complex.

In all this he sabotaged his own interests. Had he behaved with even a modicum of restraint, he could have had us all eating out of his hand. I was quite prepared to welcome him at first as a great writer and thinker, and to acknowledge plenty of imperfections in my own character. Tommy, who had a mildly chauvinistic attitude to foreigners, disliked him heartily from the start and regularly referred to him as Fritz. Gran, if only for her daughter's sake, was always trying to see the best in him. There was however much that she could not swallow, notably his aggressive attempts to score off other people and his dogmatic assertions about religion. About this time Charlotte (Lota) Bacon, the old Birkenhead friend mentioned earlier in connection with my parents' marriage, and a regular visitor to Hambledon, published a woolly would-be philosophical book entitled *Traveller, What of the Road?*. Eugene seized on this with relish, repeatedly denouncing the book and its author as 'Lot o' Tripe' in the presence of my Grandparents and visitors. One day at breakfast Gran told me she had been 'fulmigating' all night about his sneering references to the Church of England (of which she was not a member), thereby adding an expressive new word to the language. His contempt for everything English was no doubt influenced by the fact that he was not accepted at his own valuation. A Catholic convert is likely to take a poor view of the Church of England, but the manner in which he stated his case seemed to me to weaken it. He confused and undermined my fumbling attempts to discover a religious faith, chiefly by ridicule, and not only put me against Catholicism for many years; he convinced me that if he was a representative specimen of true Christianity it was no religion for me. Nor could I see how he reconciled his Catholic principles with his manoeuvres to obtain a divorce. His politics were equally offensive. Although as a Jew by birth and a Catholic by conversion (though for a time he had temporarily lapsed) he loathed Nazism and Communism, he strongly supported Mussolini's invasion of

Abyssinia and Franco's side in the Spanish Civil War. Italy and Spain were Catholic countries; 'Let the dirty blacks be gassed, what do I care?' This from a professed Christian.

My mother's attitude was easier to understand in one respect, if incomprehensible in another. From a very early stage her personality was totally absorbed in his; she accepted everything he said as the literal truth, and no one – nothing – could shift her. Had he told her that the moon was a triangular cheese full of maggots, and assured her that he meant it, she was capable of believing it, just as she believed everything he said about me. She told me that when they were married he would be justified in beating me physically. It was the total surrender of her judgment to his where I was concerned, which she furiously denied, that for long made reconciliation impossible. When Martin and Joe, followed by Haricot and Margaret, who had been with us for fifteen years, and a number of her friends either expressed some sympathy for me or agreed with something I had said, she was incredulous and assumed that I had suborned them – long before I had even raised the subject. In course of time her inability to keep off it alienated nearly all her old friends (except the Muirheads, who cried 'A plague on both your houses'; when later I told Tellie what had been happening he said I ought to have thrown the crockery about). In fact she did precisely what she accused me of doing. In December 1935, when I was in a nursing-home, she invited Philip Radcliffe to lunch alone (after refusing to have him to dinner with me), informed him that I was behaving outrageously and in danger of losing my sanity, and said that for the sake of my health he was on no account to raise the subject with me. Since this was the first he had heard of any trouble, and I seemed to him to be behaving quite normally, he was utterly baffled as well as upset. I only learned of this some time later.

All her life my mother took pride in being absolutely straight and truthful, with regard to herself as well as other people. On every other issue her claim was justified, most notably over her marriage to Basil. I could not help recalling Shakespeare's line 'Lilies that fester smell far worse than weeds'. By another irony, although from the time she met Eugene she proclaimed the Catholic cause in season and out, it was not he but a priest in the Bahamas during the War who was responsible for her conversion. When my relationship with her was restored, and after Eugene's death in 1955, I refused ever to argue with her, either over Catholicism or over Eugene; if she began to talk about either, I said nothing and as soon as possible steered the conversation in another direction. For the last thirty years of her life, so far as I could tell, she remained devoted to his memory. Whether she had any misgivings over the past I do not know; but I fancy that in the last resort her religion meant more to her than her second husband.

* * * * *

On returning to King's in October 1935 I made a firm resolution to live a social life and not allow myself to overwork or grow introspective. On the whole this worked, though I was unwell for much of the time with constant head-aches and digestive troubles. However long I slept, I always seemed tired, and was sometimes painfully aware of being 'a nuisance to my friends and a plague to myself'. The Ten Club gave me much pleasure; we had successful readings of *The Vortex*, *Young England* – an extraordinary play intended seriously but, to the distress of the author, a success with the London public who laughed at it as a burlesque – *Heartbreak House* and *Macbeth*; but I thought Maugham's *For Services Rendered* a strained and feeble play. Feeling a little more self-reliant, I began to make plans for the future; I would be a creative writer, supported perhaps by a Fellowship in English at King's.

My friendship with Philip Radcliffe ripened; we went to many concerts together, followed by a lively discussion of the music, generally over a glass of beer. There was an institution called the Informal Music Club, run by a formidable lady with the apt name of Mrs Hackforth, who organised three or four recitals or chamber concerts each winter term in the Masonic Hall. The informality lay in the seating arrangements; the audience sat in easy chairs of various types grouped round tables. The artists were front-rank professionals, as in the public concerts held in the Guildhall. This term I heard piano recitals by Moiseiwitsch and Egon Petri, the Budapest Trio, a song recital by Kipnis with Gerald Moore, and three Beethoven concerts given by the Pro Arte Quartet, which transported me completely, especially the Lydian mode slow movement of Op. 132. For a time I was Beethoven-mad, or Beethoven-drunk. My comments, mostly subjective, are of no particular interest, though I singled out Gerald Moore's exceptional skill as an accompanist.

After Petri's concert Philip took me to a small party given by Edward Dent, the Professor of Music, who usually offered hospitality to visiting artists. I came to know Dent quite well over the next few years, and found his company immensely entertaining as well as instructive. He was a great leg-puller and took delight in making provocative remarks to shock his more solemn listeners. Though a great academic scholar himself, he liked to poke fun at academic establishments, conventions and received opinions, in the not unreasonable belief that this would compel people to think for themselves. At a time when Bach was all the rage he would maintain that Handel was a much more interesting composer, and he never tired of making satirical remarks about Wagner. I once heard him declare that German composers whose names ended in

-er – not only Wagner, but Bruckner, Mahler, Reger and Pfitzner – seemed doomed to degenerate into long-winded bores. He would have included Elgar, who along with God and women was among his principal pet aversions. But he was no mere buffoon: he would jump to the rescue of Bach and Wagner if they were having a rough passage, and I heard him say of Vaughan Williams 'He embarrasses me sometimes; he shows up the falsity of my nature'.

Dent's manner of speaking could make even quite commonplace remarks sound funny. He talked rapidly in a rather high-pitched voice with his head inclined slightly to one side, and would continue without pause as he poured wine for his guests. At the Petri party there was an animated discussion about Liszt and Busoni, whose rhapsody on themes from *Don Giovanni* Petri had just played as an encore. Suddenly the buzz of conversation stopped, and Dent's voice came floating across the room: 'And I had the greatest difficulty in getting my pyjamas washed'. On a similar occasion it was 'stomach trouble of some kind, I believe'. He told me he had composed the words for the *Ariodante* chorus at the Handel apotheosis in his bath (being a Yorkshireman he used the short a). They began 'Ye learned virgins, haste'. Dent added that he was not at all sure that the Muses were virgins, but hoped to be excused on grounds of poetic licence. His mind would seize on the least suggestion of scandal, the more pornographic the better, wrap itself round it, and serve it up with embellishments.

About this time, also through Philip, I met J.B. Trend, the Professor of Spanish. He and Dent, old friends, were an incongruous pair, one (Dent) very tall and thin, the other short with a shiny bald head which he used to slap excitedly as he spoke. His speech was rapid and explosive, and not at all easy to understand until you found the wave-length. My first conversation with him was a series of *non sequiturs*. After concerts he would often invite Philip and me to his rooms in Christ's, where we usually drank tea. Once I wanted a pee, and asked Trend where this could be done. With much spiffling he disappeared into his bedroom and emerged with a chamber-pot, saying that the lavatory was inconveniently remote. At one of the Informal concerts Webern's Five Movements for string quartet, regarded then as the height of avant-garde obscurity, were down for performance. Just as the players were about to begin, and the audience were bracing themselves for the ordeal, Trend sat through a deck-chair and subsided spluttering to the floor. The players had to retune their minds, if not their instruments. The Second Viennese School seems to have had a rather drastic effect on the seating arrangements at the Masonic Hall: during a subsequent performance of Schoenberg's *Verklärte Nacht* (described by Dent as a series of codas) *two* people sat through their chairs. When I began to write about music after the War, both Dent and Trend gave me much encouragement and helpful advice.

Another musician whom I first met this term was Boris Ord, the organist of King's. He invited me, much to my surprise, to make an English translation of the choruses and solos in *The Frogs* of Aristophanes to fit new music by Walter Leigh, which was to be performed at the end of the Easter term. My translation was for the published score; the performance as usual would be in Greek. The music was still in manuscript, and I had no opportunity of hearing it at this stage. After some floundering – I did not find it at all easy – I did the job to Boris's satisfaction, though I wanted to make changes to my words, especially in the parodies, when I came to know the music well. This was my first published work of any substance, but it was delayed for nearly a year as a result of Boris mislaying the material.

Boris, a fine musician and a superb keyboard player on the harpsichord as well as the organ, who had trained the King's choir to a very high standard, was something of a rough diamond in other respects. Owing to ill-health his temper was short, and his tongue could be blistering – never, fortunately, at my expense. Like many musicians he had an earthy if not coarse sense of humour. He told me many stories about the 1922 production of Cyril Rootham's folk-based opera *The Two Sisters*, which like all C.U.M.S. enterprises drew on a mixture of professional and local amateur talent. One act took place in a forest and required a chorus of singing trees, the choristers, who included a number of dons' wives and daughters, being encased in canvas tree-trunks. The tenor lead was played by Steuart Wilson. When the curtain fell on this act Boris came on and asked 'Are you all right, Steuart?' Wilson, forgetting that he was not alone on stage, replied in a high-pitched voice 'I want to shit like a horse'. The reaction of the trees is not recorded. One of the cast, a baritone, had to sing the word 'stupidly', descending an octave for the last two syllables. The note was below his compass, and after trying various expedients Rootham laid on a group of six basses behind the scenery; the soloist sang 'stu-' and they added the '-piddly', the process being known as 'keeping a piddly'. Boris used to amuse himself by inventing clerihews and conundrums, of which I recall two: 'Bizet / Picked up ladies in the Champs Elysées; / Gounod / Was – you know'. 'Why did Adrian Boult? Because Henry Wood Landon Ronald.' Boris often gave parties for the choir to which other members of the College were sometimes invited. I have a characteristic memory of him sitting back in an armchair beaming contentedly with a tankard of beer at his elbow and two choral scholars happily perched on either knee.

This term saw the first of many happy expeditions to the superb churches in the area of marshland between Wisbech and the Wash. They were the brainwave of Peggy Wilson, a friend of Clare Mallory at Girton and the daughter of the rector of West Walton. She organised a Girton friend with a car; her parents entertained us to lunch and tea, and we visited as many churches as possible on the way up and in the interval. On the way back a tin containing a cake, which had been left on the running-board by mistake, fell off into a ditch. Clare and I, who were travelling in the open dickey, managed to retrieve it, but got so wet and cold in the process that we took off as many clothes as possible, huddled together, and sang all the songs we knew to keep up our spirits.

There was a hilarious charade party at the Claphams', at which Donald Beves played the parts of God, Herod, Odysseus turned into a swine, a chariot and a wall. I had to represent Enoch, who 'walked with God'; Donald, wearing an expression marvellously compounded of omnipotence and self-satisfaction, led me in attached to a dog-chain. I paid a brief but crowded visit to Oxford, and decided that the selection of Old Harrovians there was a good deal more interesting than that at Cambridge. Brigid came up for the day, which I described as the happiest in my life. As usual we talked for hours, and she kissed me with great affection at the end. I had been too shy to think of kissing her. I think it was on this occasion that at my request she gave me an account of all the men who had been in love with her, beginning with a tall, blond and very proper Wykehamist and ending with a man who, to her great amusement, signed off by sending her a cactus. She awarded him the victory (but not the prize). We invited ourselves to tea with the Claphams and reminisced happily about the wedding. That evening, at a concert in Hall, I heard Handel's lovely cantata *Apollo e Dafne* for the first time.

* * * * *

On returning to Cumberland Terrace in December I found on the hall table a long and ominous letter from Eugene, couched in the most offensive terms: 'You were only asserting the naughtiness of a fatally undersmacked little boy'. (Did he really think this was the way to win my submission? Apparently he did; my mother claimed that this was a wholly reasonable and helpful letter.) He repeated the old charges of disloyalty and stirring up trouble, and appended a long list of things I was expected to do and not do. 'People who consistently disregard these rules ... usually find their way into the prisons and mental institutions which society is compelled to maintain for the benefit of their kind.' In future I was to consider myself on probation, for not having come up to the standards expected of a grown up and civilised being. The insufferably pompous tone of the letter might have been that of Jehovah addressing the worshippers of Baal, though Eugene's position in the household was, to say the least, anomalous.

I decided to ignore this document, follow Fabian tactics, go out as much as possible in the evenings, and behave with model politeness. This worked well for a time, though I was conscious that he was waiting to pounce, and once or twice the atmosphere was sulphurous. He came to dinner nearly every night, behaving as if he owned the place, and amused himself by making snide remarks about me to Martin, who had shown signs of swallowing his doctrine whole. Joe, who at that time felt exactly as I did, told me just before Christmas that whenever I was absent Eugene made every possible insinuation against me, blaming me among many other things for my mother's indisposition after my party. When Basil sent some wine for Christmas he had sniffed it, saying sulkily 'Not bad'. Although there was no explosion at this time, I began to feel driven into a corner.

There were many parties, including a very good one for my friends at Cumberland Terrace. Unfortunately the emotional pressure from two different directions, accentuated by a violent recrudescence of chilblains, inability to sleep and much abdominal pain (I was suffering from subacute appendicitis throughout the winter but did not yet know it) made me touchy and difficult with Brigid. I knew perfectly well how I ought to behave, fully accepted the position between us, and for much of the time was wonderfully happy. Then my mood would swing the other way, I imagined some coolness or preoccupation on her part, and fell into the profoundest depression. This would be succeeded by bitter self-reproach, when I confessed that I had betrayed all my good resolutions and begged her to forgive me. This pattern repeated itself several times, and it is clear in the light of what followed that my defences were breaking down under the combined stress. We went to several shows, including Dodie Smith's *Call It a Day* and that marvellous film *The Ghost Goes West*, and there was one supremely happy day when, after she had a polyphoto taken for me, we played squash at the Ladies Carlton Club, dined with the grandparents at Portland Place, and went on to a dance given by the Hubbacks in St John's Wood. I took Brigid back to South Kensington in a taxi at 3 a.m., whispering endearments all the way, then returned to Cumberland Terrace, only to find that I had not quite enough money for the taxi fare, let alone the tip. I was about to go into the house to find some, when the driver told me not to bother, gave me a friendly grin and drove away. This little act of generosity from a stranger made a perfect conclusion to the day; I have often thought of that taxi driver and blessed him.

Shortly before Christmas the brother of a close friend of Brigid's (Frances Wiggin) committed suicide in Japan. Although I told myself again and again that I must expect Brigid to concentrate on caring for her friend and have little time or energy for me, I failed lamentably to live up to this resolution. On Boxing Day a large party of us, including Martin and Joe, drove down to a meet of the West Kent Hunt. Brigid said very little to me and once seemed to turn her back. I assumed, quite wrongly, that she was angry over my earlier derelictions, as she had every right to be, and was punishing me for my selfishness. Suddenly the world went blank, and I lost control. Not caring whether I lived or died, I threw myself over a small cliff, only to land ignominiously in a thorn bush, whence I was rescued and revived with brandy. Brigid coped with this magnificently; only two days later I wrote that I was getting all the happiness and exhilaration of love without any hope of it being returned. My mother however decided to call in a mental specialist, convinced not that I was ill but that I was insane.

On 30 December my uncle Rufus died. Seldom though I saw him, I felt that I had lost a wise friend. Gran, who was devoted to him, was shattered. I assumed from my mother's absence that she had gone to Portland Place to be with her, only to discover that she was much more concerned over Eugene, who had eaten some beans that disagreed with him. This left me speechless. The next day I had a violent gastric upset and vomited all night, for which she actually reprimanded me in the morning. Eugene alone had the privilege of being ill. I attended Rufus's memorial service in a synagogue, a harrowing and moving occasion on which for the first time I heard the Dead March from Handel's *Saul*. Astonishingly all through this period I continued to read Cicero's *De Officiis* and to visit art galleries, including the Chinese Exhibition at Burlington House, making detailed and lucid comments on all I saw.

On 3 January I was taken to see Dr Lewis Yealland in Harley Street. He was I believe a neurologist or an alienist, not a psychiatrist. He was very sympathetic and arranged for me to go into a nursing home the following day. I spent the evening with Brigid and, whether or not because a harbour was at last in sight, the clouds suddenly lifted and I was overwhelmed by a feeling of serenity and elation such as I had never experienced before and have seldom approached since. I wrote a lot of vaporous nonsense in my diary, but also two sentences that went to the root of the matter. 'Even if she got married tomorrow and I never saw her again, it would have been amply worth while …. What will become of us? *Whatever* it is, it cannot take this evening from me.'

Our relationship puzzled Dr Yealland, who evidently expected that my first objective would be to take her to bed and told my mother that I was probably impotent. Sexual satisfaction in that sense never seemed to me the most important thing; which may explain why, apart from adolescent homosexual urges, I have never been able to fall in love with anyone whose character I did not admire and respect.

* * * * *

On my last evening at 13 Cumberland Terrace Eugene was particularly surly, and when he began to dictate, Joe and I both stood up to him. Joe was later rebuked for this, but half excused on the ground that I had set a bad example. Next day I went into a nursing home in Queen Anne Street. Although I was still subject to perilous swings of mood, the rest and quiet began to do me good, and so did visits from my friends. But outside the tension mounted. My mother tried to make Vie promise not to see me. Joe smuggled out a note inside my gramophone and came to see me privily, saying that he had no one to talk to at home. Dr Yealland assured me that although my reaction was extreme I had indeed been through a devilish time. Presently he had an interview with Eugene and my mother that brought things to a head and ended with him telling Eugene in no uncertain terms what he thought of his behaviour. He considered him positively loathsome and the atmosphere of the house poisonous, and I must never return to it. My mother paid me a short visit alone, and I felt nothing but love and pity for her; there was no mention of Eugene.

Dr Yealland of course was dismissed from the case, and it was arranged that I would go to another nursing home, in Courtfield Gardens. For the intervening three days Brigid invited me to stay with her and her mother in Sydney Place. Before moving there I paid a brief visit to Cumberland Terrace to collect luggage. To my amazement when I tried to speak to Joe I was followed round the house as if I were a criminal. Joe wrote on an envelope that he had been forbidden to see me alone. I beckoned him into the morning room and locked the door. A frightful scene ensued, until I convinced my mother that it was absurd to prevent me seeing my own brother. Joe was in a bad state of nerves, having been alternatively bullied and pampered; I could only counsel him to lie low. At Brigid's I was visited by my mother's doctor (Cregan), who said I was to have a new doctor, a psychiatrist of the Adler school. When he tried to censor my visitors, I flatly refused and won my point.

The new nursing-home saw many extreme ups and downs in my condition, beginning with what meteorologists call a deep low. It was by no means the only one; I had days of abject terror and much physical pain, and I could not sleep. My new doctor, H.C. Squires, was at first so cautious and non-committal that I doubted his powers of understanding. However he gradually won my confidence. He had of course been primed by Eugene. He told me a little later that he could see the sort of person Eugene was, and that he found me utterly different from what he had been told to expect. He agreed with Yealland that I must never again live at home, advised against an early return to Cambridge, and wanted me to do no work of any kind for nine months, until the beginning of the next academic year in October.

I was in that nursing-home for a month. Many of my friends brought me gifts and the pleasure of their company. Gran brought me a radio, and I played my favourite records again and again. To this day the slow movement of Beethoven's Ninth Symphony, Schubert's B flat trio (of which Philip brought me records) and Mozart's clarinet quintet, especially when I hear them unexpectedly, can bring back the bitter-sweet flavour of those weeks with extraordinary vividness. I read an odd selection of books, from Dorothy Sayers to Stephen Spender. My mind continued to swing between wild elation and suicidal depression.

Even many decades later I find it difficult to put into words the horrors of these weeks in Courtfield Gardens, when I was plunged into what was then called a nervous breakdown but is now listed as acute depression. I was after all still a teenager and in no condition to face a world that seemed to be falling to pieces around me. There were happy moments, generally associated with Brigid, but attacks of sheer panic when I was alone, and tempted to end everything by jumping out of the window. Thought of suicide alternated with moments of wild exhilaration – and there was no knowing when one would give way to the other. Strange events stick out in my memory – the deaths of Kipling and George V, the latter resulting in Brigid appearing in a black dress, and Hindemith, who was on a visit, being locked up all night by the BBC to compose an Elegy. At least a dozen friends and relatives did their best to cheer me up, but the beneficial effects were only temporary, and I never knew when the panic attacks were liable to return.

Early in February Basil appeared on the scene. He had at last broken with Vernon, whose partners had excluded him from his business (he had informed Vie that his 'present wife' was about to have a baby, and he considered Christmas a suitable time to communicate this information), but this did not bring Basil closer to Vie, especially as he had been listening to my mother. To me he was in one of his most gracious moods. He talked of taking me to Paris (for the first showing of his Mozart film, in which Vicky played Constanze) and to America, and invited me to make my headquarters with him and Vicky, going there whenever I wished. He would do anything for me, even give me work. I was grateful, but (rightly as it turned out) could not suppress a fear that his mood might change without warning. Not for the first or last time I tried to analyse his character:

'He was as bland and charming as I have ever seen him. And how disarming he can be! When he really wants to, he can win anybody …. He delivered himself of much worldly advice, some of it sensible, some of it not. He is for independence and experience, and says that suffering, combined with a sound outlook, brings nothing but good to a man; this I believe. But he is unfair to women and calls them grasping … He said one or two remarkable things: that if he had had more experience in youth, he would have hurt fewer people. This argues, if not confession, at least consciousness of a wrongful past. He says he has had the hell of a struggle, but has at last achieved happiness … He talked of marriage (from my point of view) and seemed to think "experience" first would do me good, but must not be sought for its own sake. He is a very strange man. He talks to me like this today, yet will be brutally unfair to Vie; he will give me a fiver and in the same breath damn the servants black for something he knows they haven't done; he leaves Mother when Joe is born and returns three days later saying he has been unfaithful to her – yet a year or two afterwards begs her in tears not to divorce him (the divorce cost him a knighthood when George V exercised his veto); he can charm or horrify at will; he has the vilest faults, and is aware of them. Perhaps his battle with himself came too late. I saw today more plainly than ever what a great man he might have been.'

It seems to me now, long after the event, that there was an element of tragedy in his career. He rose so high so rapidly that there must have appeared no limits to what he could achieve in his profession. He was a brilliant producer of plays, especially in his early days. By the age of 35 he had reached the top of his profession. His career began to go down hill, in the opinion of my mother among others, with the break-up of his partnership with Alec Rea (the ReandeaN management), which more or less coincided with that of his first marriage. It has been suggested that his success went to his head, and that his boundless ambition overthrew his judgment. If so, it was combined with personal failings; certainly he was his own worst enemy. His move to Drury Lane was a tactical error and a financial disaster. His move into film-making – he was the first director of the Ealing Studios – was surely a step backwards. He may have believed that the cinema offered a brave new world ripe for conquest, but I suspect that (perhaps unconsciously) his motives were partly financial, and that this may account for an incontestable lowering of his artistic standards. He had developed expensive tastes; the extravagant rebuilding and enlargement of Little Easton Manor, a process that took several years, points to a marked *folie de grandeur*. Although he made some successful films, with Gracie Fields and George Formby as the stars, his finger was a little too obviously on the public pulse at the expense of his earlier ideals in the theatre. He never abandoned the straight theatre, but for a long time it took second place (inevitably during the Second War when his energies were concentrated on ENSA); while his later stage productions were as technically skilful as ever, they somehow failed to capture the imaginative vision of his earlier work, or for that matter the acclamation of the public.

One of Basil's strongest and least agreeable characteristics was his total lack of consideration for the feelings of other people, especially social inferiors and professional subordinates. I remember him more than once abusing a taxi-driver for driving too slowly in heavy London traffic. He was intensely unpopular in the theatre, as the memoirs of Noel Coward and others attest, not only for his tyrannical manner (which up to a point might be excused on artistic grounds) but because he seemed unable to obtain what he wanted without humiliating those he sought to correct. On one of my visits to Ealing

Studios Carol Reed, the assistant director, committed some minor misdemeanour or error of judgment whose nature I forget. Basil gave him the most appalling dressing down in the presence of all the actors and technicians, until the poor man blushed scarlet. When afterwards I asked Basil why he had to make such a scene over such a small matter, he replied that it was the only way to keep the man in his place. He ruled by fear; I am sure that behind this lay some dark fear – a fear of inadequacy perhaps. On another occasion he took me to the first night of Emlyn Williams's play *The Corn is Green*, in which the author played the leading part, and we went round to see him afterwards. All through the evening Basil had been muttering about the feebleness of the play, but as soon as he saw Williams he overflowed with fulsome praise and honeyed compliments. When I remarked on this, he said he had to do it; it was expected of him. That may have been so; but this was one of several incidents that gave me a horror of hypocrisy and devious behaviour of any kind, a trait that has sometimes complicated my own life.

A lively account of Basil's character, as man and stage director, appears in the third volume of Dodie Smith's four-volume autobiography, *Look Back with Astonishment* (1979). He had directed her first four plays, all of which achieved considerable success, and she saluted him as a highly creative director, a master of psychological detail, but sometimes reluctant to abandon ideas or modifications that were anathema to the author. He could drive her to fury, yet she clearly retained some affection for him, as shown in a note added after his death in 1978. Like my mother in the *Basiliad* that she wrote at my request towards the end of her life, Dodie demonstrates many inaccuracies – and not only of detail – in the two volumes of autobiography that Basil wrote towards the end of his life. One subject on which all agree – and I was to encounter it in my turn – was the pettifogging interference of the theatre censorship, which by a happy coincidence was abolished on Basil's eightieth birthday.

An Engagement with Time

In the middle of February Brigid and I spent ten days staying with Michael and Leeby Clapham in Bradford, an arrangement engineered by Brigid. I was still feeling shaky, constantly at war with myself, and oppressed by increasing symptoms of appendicitis and other physical ailments, and must have been an infernal nuisance to everybody. The weather was bitterly cold. Brigid used to rub my spot-infested back every night with some special lotion, and even changed bedrooms with me after I had woken up shivering. We did have some good times, including visits to York and Ripon Cathedrals and Fountains Abbey. After that Brigid went for a skiing holiday in the Black Forest, and I returned to Cambridge under strict injunctions to do no work.

The next three weeks were very happy, apart from splitting head-aches and constant stomach upsets. Rehearsals for *The Frogs* were beginning, and I was given a silent but spectacular part as the priestess of Demeter with a gorgeous pink and gold costume, a white wig and a tiara. I was not required to do much except walk on in a stately and female fashion, carrying a sheaf of corn and attended by four 'handmaidens' (casts were still all male), gaze proudly around, and hobnob with Kenneth Harrison as Iacchus. The rehearsals were chaotic in the extreme. The producer, J.T. Sheppard, improvised all the movements on the spur of the moment, and was for ever changing his mind. The broth was stirred by an ungainly number of supernumerary chefs: Dadie and Camille Prior (assistant producers), Donald Beves (stage manager), Geoffrey Wright (designer), Walter Leigh (composer), Boris (conductor) and Christopher Barlow (producer's secretary). Sometimes there seemed to be more producers than actors. Thanks to Sheppard's methods, no one had a clear idea what he or anyone else was supposed to be doing. Tempers sometimes ran high, especially between Boris and Christopher. The calmest person was Walter Leigh, a delightful man who looked more like a prize-fighter than a composer; his death in action in 1942 was a major loss to British music. There were some amusing contretemps. The Bishop of Lincoln, Dr Nugent Hicks, who was the College Visitor (and whom I had met at Harrow, where he was one of the school's Governors), tried on one of the huge green frogs' heads worn by the chorus, and could not get it off. The sight of his bandy-legged figure capering round the room clad in black episcopal gaiters and a frog's head was too much for everybody. The donkey, played in pantomime style by two persons, was the source of much merriment. It was required to dance, and the front legs kept tripping over the back legs. The attempts of Mrs Prior, a very small woman, to rehearse it were met by clumsy nods of comprehension and the raising of the ears in pained surprise. When one of the frogs jumped on the creature's back it collapsed, collected itself and ran full tilt into Donald Beves's ample stomach.

The first of the two dress rehearsals lasted 7½ hours and reached the middle of the second act. Some of us did not know whether we were to appear in the third, and Sheppard, incapacitated at frequent intervals by volcanic attacks of sneezing, could not enlighten us since he had not made up his mind. When the scenery arrived, all the movements of the chorus were thrown out and had to be rethought from the beginning. For the second dress rehearsal Donald, clad in a titanic striped rugby vest, made me up and complained about my prolific eyebrows; he finally painted them out and gave me a new and very elegant set higher up. The first two acts went fairly well, but the third was pandemonium (admittedly it followed an adjournment to the bar, after which the bishop became slightly tipsy); half of it was never rehearsed at all. For the timing of entrances and exits we trusted to luck and the fates. The first performance was a matinee, attended by Greek royalty in one of the boxes, with a lavish display of purple carpets and Sheppard wearing an exotic decoration. It went better than might have been feared, though the scales in which the verses of Aeschylus and Euripides are weighed at first refused to budge and then came down on the wrong side, and Charon, played by a lanky classical scholar in King's (Ossie Dilke), ferried his party across the Styx sporting a conspicuous wrist-watch. The evening performance was a triumph, and the standard continued to improve for the rest of the week, though Sheppard seemed to alter our movements every day.

It was a very amusing show, described by *The Spectator* as the best dramatic entertainment in England. When Sheppard's ideas worked he was an inspired producer. Aeacus and his henchmen drilled like a squad of Nazis, complete with Hitler salutes; the corpse spoke with an American accent, and the two landladies were dressed as bedmakers. Best of all was the music. The straight parts were very attractive – Walter Leigh had a rare gift for melody – and the parodies brilliant. In the play each of the poets, Euripides the modern and Aeschylus the traditionalist, utters two verse parodies of the other's style. Leigh gave Euripides two songs with catchy tunes in an old-fashioned Italian style, after Donizetti or early Verdi. For Aeschylus he surpassed himself: his first song was a mixture of Hindemith and Schoenbergian *Sprechgesang* with 'Pop goes the weasel' in an inner part, his second a delicious jazz take-off with a saxophone in the orchestra. This was encored at every performance: there was something irresistibly funny about jazzy music sung in Greek with an American intonation but a straight face by the imposing figure of Dick David, later a distinguished luminary of the University Press and the husband of a prominent Labour peeress.

The performances were given in the brand-new Arts Theatre, which had been launched with an Ibsen season only a fortnight before, when I saw Jean Forbes-Robertson as Hedda Gabler (magnificent) and Lydia Lopokova in *The Master Builder*: I thought she would have been a superb Hilda if 30 years younger. Basil, whose Mozart film had one of its first showings at the Arts, came to one performance of *The Frogs* and released my inhibitions with a bottle of champagne at dinner. A Harrow contingent, including Joe and Plum, came to another. I had only one difficult moment, when my sweeping cloak knocked down the altar; it was dexterously fielded by one of my handmaidens. We evolved some extra touches for the last night. The donkey vomited three carrots; the frogs' heads kissed at the back; Xanthias, about to be beaten by Aeacus, secreted a large exercise-book in his pants, from which Aeacus withdrew it with proctorial suspicion; when Aeacus knocked at the gates of Hades the bass drum was replaced by a tinkle on the triangle. The curtain-calls seemed to go on for hours. On the following day the entire cast was entertained to lunch at the University Arms by Mr Caclamanos, the Greek Minister, with a menu printed in Greek. Two days later Sheppard invited us all to a performance in the theatre by Ruth Draper, followed by a sumptuous supper, after which we sang most of Leigh's music, solos and choruses, accompanied by Boris at the piano. When further action was demanded, Sheppard took the part of Xanthias in the beating scene, and Dionysus, uttering the line 'where is the pot?' (in Greek) pointed unerringly at Donald's stomach. The expression on Donald's face and the reaction of his eyebrows made this irresistibly funny.

There were many other parties, at one of which Arthur Marshall, still a master at Oundle, did some of his incomparable girls' school sketches, a feature of Cambridge parties in those days. Dent gave a lecture on Leigh's *Frogs* music, full of academic humour, and told me that undergraduates could act only three types of women: the middle-aged mother of a family (their own mothers), the bed-maker and the screaming whore. I was greatly touched by the warmth of the welcome given me after my absence, and made a number of new friends, among them Derek Clifford, a King's contemporary known for his flamboyant manners, his poetry and his seduction of women. I was a little suspicious of him at first, but we became firm friends. I had met him the previous term at a lunch given by Kenneth Harrison, who went out of his way to provoke lively argument, himself acting as a kind of electric hare. Derek persuaded me to submit some of my poems for publication in a volume sponsored by the Spenser Society, which had been founded in reaction against the school of Pound and the political poets of the Thirties. By this time, my style or taste having begun to develop, I suspected that the reaction had gone too far. In due course four of my pieces appeared (not in my opinion the best), two mellifluous but unoriginal Georgian sonnets and two little translations from Sappho written during my first week at King's. I would still stand by these, and back one of them against either of Housman's versions (*More Poems* X and XI). The volume, *Thirty-One Poems from the Spenser Society of Cambridge University*, came out in June with a preface by Quiller-Couch, who was apparently very struck by my contributions and singled out one of them for quotation.

For the first ten days of the vacation I stayed with Basil and Vicky at their London flat and at the Manor. Neither of them was in good health, nor was I (I could hardly keep food down), but Vicky was charming to me. Brigid and I had long before made an arrangement to meet on my birthday (18 March), and Basil had invited her to dinner, after which we were to go dancing. Now she said she had another engagement. I felt betrayed, but she convinced me that it was a mistake, and for once I managed to keep my nerves under control. My birthday was a wretched day. Basil, who had altered his arrangements for the evening, thought Brigid rude. This gave him an opening for one of his favourite gambits, a denunciation of the female sex *in toto*; he said they all behaved like that sometimes, even the best of them, and could not help it. I then saw Dr Cregan, who said my appendix must come out; this was confirmed in due course by the surgeon, Sir Lancelot Barrington-Ward. At tea my mother and the grandparents argued depressingly about who was to pay the bill. In the evening Basil, Vicky and I went to the H.G. Wells film

Things to Come, and did not think much of it. Basil gave a lifelike imitation of Raymond Massey in the taxi (he was a brilliant mimic), and retired to bed rather grumpily with a plate of oranges.

At the Manor there was a spirited tea party with Lady Warwick and the Philip Guedallas; I had a long talk with Guedalla, whom I had met at Harrow, and felt I had learned much. Meanwhile the family rows continued to erupt like a volcano from several craters. Vie was savagely attacked by Tommy, whom my mother had primed with false information, and was sick in the street. Tommy's outburst upset Gran for a whole week. The Dean grandparents blamed Vie for my breakdown; I was horrified to learn that my mother was going to see them. Basil now declared that he had the fullest confidence in me. He considered both Vernon and Vie antisocial and refused to see either of them, called Eugene a bastard, and said he would write to Mother that something must be done about her anomalous position. For the first time he talked to me about the failure of his marriage to her, taking the same line as in *Seven Ages*.

On the 23rd I entered my third nursing-home in three months, in Fitzroy Square, not relishing the prospect in the least. It was found that I had lost a stone in weight since early February. Brigid had promised to visit me at 6 o'clock, but nothing happened. Eventually she rang up to say that she had been driven into the country and stayed late. This was so utterly unlike her that I knew something serious must have happened. I went under the anaesthetic hoping not to wake up (the nurses told me that I sang vigorously in Greek). For the first two or three days I was in great pain and very ill; even with morphia I could hardly sleep. This was accentuated by my nervous condition, which worried the doctors more than the operation, though my appendix was found to be inflamed, twisted and very long, and entangled round the gut. External events did not help. I learned that Mother had compelled Martin and Joe to return the money which Vie had sent them for their birthdays, had written Vie a filthy letter, and had spent an 'instructive hour' with the old Deans, who denied writing abusive letters about Vie – although she and I had both seen some of them.

Brigid sent me flowers, but put off coming to see me for four days. By that time I was desperate and at the end of my tether. I could see that she was holding something back; although she was reluctant and said that it was nothing that mattered to me, I forced her to tell me. She was in love with someone else, a fact she had discovered about ten days before, and he with her. Almost before I had time to react to this she said quietly that she could never marry him; he was a clergyman who had taken a vow of celibacy. At this I broke down completely and tried to tell her through my tears that I could not bear her to suffer that. She looked at me with an expression I can never forget, a mixture of affection and astonishment, said 'Oh, you do love me, don't you', threw her arms round my neck and kissed me. Extraordinary as it may seem, I never felt any jealousy of Lorimer; I simply knew that he was essential to Brigid's happiness. The story has a happy ending. Two years later he was released from his vow and they were married. As I write they have just celebrated their golden wedding, and mine is rapidly approaching. For more than forty years they were the dearest and closest of all our friends.

Not all that followed that evening was plain sailing – far from it. I was kept in the nursing-home longer than was expected, and described this period as the loneliest and bleakest of my life. With Brigid I was mostly light and cheerful, as I had promised. The one bad moment was when she went back on a long-standing promise to come with me to the King's May Week Ball. I had been looking forward intensely to this as a kind of lighthouse in a murky future, and would have done nothing to hurt her. Although very upset at first, I understood her reasons. I had many visitors and presents, including a book from Tessa (aged 9), by which I was very touched. Peter Joseph made me laugh so much that I had to beg him to be quiet in case my stitches burst. Joe told me of the slanders being perpetrated at Cumberland Terrace, mostly about Vie; the most grotesque was that I had been devoted to Eugene heart and soul until Vie, to gratify a private grudge, turned me against him. I realised the Martin and Joe would be subjected to continuous and probably intolerable pressure.

The Grandparents took me for a week to Ramsgate, a charmless and tedious town. Gran and I spent most of the time visiting superb churches, of which as usual I wrote copious and detailed descriptions. We ranged as far afield as Canterbury and St Margaret's Bay. Stella came over to lunch one day and impressed us with her courage and wisdom. She lived the rest of her life with the example of Rufus always before her, and was certainly worthy of him. She was often kind and helpful to me, but I never quite overcame a feeling of awe that her self-confidence and strength of character inspired. When we returned to London there was an 'incident' at Cumberland Terrace, where Gran took me to pick up a change of clothes. Eugene was there, though he always claimed to work all day. I did not see him, but Mother told me that there would be no tea for me and I was not wanted. I replied that I would gladly have tea in the kitchen, where I was always welcome. Eugene evidently decamped, for I was told I might as well come down to tea now. Mother spent most of the time telephoning and made no attempt to talk to me. She had invited me to lunch the following day but rang up later to say that on account of my rudeness she would not be present herself. This precipitated a row between her and Gran, who had been abused for bringing me round the previous day. Dr Squires was not in favour of my taking the Tripos exam at the end of May – he thought I was not nearly well enough – but was impressed by my determination to do so and agreed on condition that I did not worry about it and did not attempt to work at full pressure. He advised me, among other things, to remove all my property from Cumberland Terrace at the earliest moment. I then spent a very relaxed week-end at Hambledon with Bert the gardener and Fanny his wife. They looked after me with great care. We went to an air display by C.W.A Scott's circus at Witley Park, but Bert firmly refused to let me go up in a plane, an experience I was not to have for another 28 years.

On returning to Cambridge I had barely a month in which to prepare for the Tripos after five months in which I had done no work at all. Though Squires advised against it, I was desperately keen to get a First, which normally would have been well within my powers, but was still feeling weak in body and insecure in mind. There were days when I felt supremely confident, others when I could not work at all. During the exam I took whisky in Hall and strove to keep my mind and body in separate compartments. In the first paper (Greek Prose) I had fifty minutes of sheer panic, in which not a word reached the paper. A day or two later a heavy dose of flu assailed me, and by the end of the week I was completely played out, the exam no more than a hazy memory. In the event I missed a First by the narrowest margin, a fact that has irked me ever since, but received very sympathetic letters from all my supervisors, which in the bitterness of the moment I scarcely appreciated at their full value. Patrick Wilkinson wrote: 'In the circumstances it was a most plucky performance to get so near ... Your stock has risen here no end by your having done it.' Sheppard said the same. Donald Lucas thought it was probably to the discredit of the examiners that they did not give me a First; Sills said they very nearly did. Brigid, who knew better than anyone what I must be feeling, assured me that I had done marvellously well. I had already decided to read English in my third year (my mother considered this an awful blunder; when Joe told Plum 'the sad news, he made a noise through his teeth like the whistling of the wind down a Classical chimney'), and had my first meeting with Peter (F.L.) Lucas, Donald's brother, my new supervisor.

Many of the events of this term have been blotted from my memory, even when prompted by my diary. My emotions were growing numb, which was perhaps as well, but physically I seemed little better for the loss of my appendix. My digestive system in fact never recovered from the disturbances of this period, and has troubled me more or less continuously ever since. I saw Brigid three or four times between mid-April and June, but we somehow got at cross purposes. It was largely my fault; I was anxious to offer her support, but went about it the wrong way and was snubbed for my pains. Another promised visit to Cambridge was postponed and finally cancelled, and I concluded sadly that it was better for me not to see her. In one respect I tried to live up to her standards by inviting Peggy Wilson to take her place at the May Week Ball, knowing that Peggy longed to go and that it would be her only chance. I did not much enjoy it, but Peggy did; her gratitude was the evening's one rewarding feature.

Joe came to King's as my guest for a few days at the beginning of May. He was most companionable and a great success with my friends, especially Kenneth Harrison, whose distinctive manner of speech he mimicked to perfection. New carriages with exceptionally large lavatories were being introduced on the Portsmouth line. 'Delectable rolling-stock' declared Joe, and suggested that the new King should be invited to pass the first water. I took Joe to a charade party at the Claphams', where he played half of one of Hannibal's elephants. We spent most of the daylight hours looking at churches, including Peterborough Cathedral; he was then as interested in the subject as I was, and we even planned to write a book together.

I visited more churches that year than any other, sometimes by bicycle alone or with Peggy, more often by car. The West

Walton expeditions continued. In March we had battled against a snowstorm, and I was frozen in the dickey; in May a mishap to Robin Hammond's eye (she was the only driver) nearly landed us at West Walton for the night. At Castle Acre we were entertained by a friendly little guide, who informed us that 'here they lifted the lady eighteen inches and squared her off so'. Other expeditions were with Susan Radcliffe, Philip's sister, with Milner-White, with Vie's sister Lady Hollis, who boasted the succinct address 'Widdington, Essex', with Jana Clapham, and others. In July Kenneth, Philip and I managed to visit twelve churches in four counties in a single day, despite the car coming to an abrupt halt in the flooded river Nene and having to be manhandled out. Kenneth, the son of an archdeacon at York Minster, against whose beliefs he reacted with extreme violence while remaining fascinated by the ceremonial, reduced us to helpless laughter by preaching a mock-Milner sermon from the pulpit of Fotheringhay church. Fortunately the incumbent did not appear.

I was listening to more and more music, in concerts and on the radio, and with Philip's assistance began to teach myself to read a score. He took me to my second hearing of *Carmen*, at the old Vic, and we attended the first performance of Vaughan Williams's attractive but ungainly opera *The Poisoned Kiss* (a work killed by its libretto), after which I briefly met the composer. I did not think much of Basil's Mozart film, *Whom the Gods Love*; Margaret Kennedy's dialogue seemed trite, and even the direction none too good. Nor did T.S. Eliot's *Murder in the Cathedral*, which I described as a mixture of Aeschylus, St Paul, Bernard Shaw and the less creditable elements in Eliot's other work, make much of an appeal. I passed through a mild phase of balletomania, attending several performances by Russian companies in London and the Vic-Wells at Cambridge, where they gave a week's season at the Arts Theatre. There was a party for them at King's, where I had a long talk with

Constant Lambert, and Frederick Ashton regaled the company with a series of very funny and none too delicate imitations of various singers and ballerinas, ending one of them stark naked.

I spent a day at the Manor and played a peculiar game of tennis with Basil and Vicky, who grew angry when they missed the ball and accused each other of cheating. There was a comic moment when Basil, crouching at the net, was struck smartly on the posterior by his partner's drive, and the ball sailed high in the air out of court and into the bushes. We visited R.D. Blumenfeld, a sharp-witted old Jew in a bath-chair who had been a prominent Fleet Street editor. A more exotic experience was a weekend with Lady Warwick at Easton Lodge. On hearing of my troubles she had offered herself as a supernumerary grandmother, and she treated me with great kindness. I began inauspiciously by missing my train, but was soon carried off into the remote world of the 1880s. Apart from Lady Warwick's companion the other guests were three old ladies with minds as acute and tongues as sharp as any I had encountered. One was a Canadian with enormous ears who repeatedly bridled when one or other of the party mistook her accent for American. The other two, Mrs Gardner and Lady Augusta Fane, talked of the distant past as if it were the day before yesterday, expressed moderate opinions with great violence, and constantly interrupted each other. On the first evening we consumed an eight-course dinner, during which Lady Warwick discoursed liberally about the ghosts of Warwick Castle. Otherwise the conversation was mostly concerned with county councils, agriculture, market-gardens and the deterioration of the countryside; I had no idea that so many points of view were tenable on the subject of manure.

Most of the Sunday I spent wandering round the wild picturesque garden, looking for birds' nests (this was the only occasion when I found a cuckoo's egg) and encountering some of the twenty peacocks, seventeen dogs and numerous cats, geese and other creatures that lurked in the undergrowth. One evening, when the others had gone to bed, Lady Warwick talked to me alone. She told me that she had made liberal allowance for Tessa in her will, and spoke kindly of Vie and Miss Tresham, whom Basil or Vicky had dismissed. (Miss Tresham was very bitter about this, and blamed it on Vicky.) I don't think Lady Warwick liked Basil. She said that he talked of sinking vast sums of money in the barn theatre and turning it into a second Glyndebourne, 'a mad scheme if ever there was one'. He had created this theatre, which was minute, about the size of a village hall, out of one of the Manor outbuildings; my brothers and I sometimes performed little plays of our own composition there before Basil and the staff. Basil's attitude to Lady Warwick was one of cautious admiration. He once identified for me the fathers of her children; they included Lord Charles Beresford, Edward VII (I believe this is questionable – perhaps untrue) and General Laycock, who he said was the love of her life and Mercy's father. At the end of our conversation Lady Warwick told me to regard her as an old friend and invite myself to the Lodge whenever I was at a loose end. Unfortunately the opportunity never arose. The following week she sent me a £5 note. I used it to buy records of Mozart piano concertos.

I spent little time at Hambledon that summer and played in only three cricket matches. There was a Bagger plan to keep me away, and Gran, who disliked Eugene and was out of sympathy with Mother, again found herself between two fires. I was informed that Eugene considered himself the injured party and demanded a letter of apology or at least conciliation; also that Mother had made an approach to Vernon and considered him a grossly maligned man in great need of sympathy, though 'not the Vernon he was'. A meeting was even arranged between him and Martin and Joe, but apparently he missed his cue and soundly denounced Eugene.

At this time I was often depressed and haunted by forebodings of a European war. There were compensations, however, notably a delightful evening with Gran at Glyndebourne, where we were captivated both by the performance of the opera (*Die Entführung*) and by the surroundings: 'it was as if we were being entertained in a private house, with the music specially arranged for our enjoyment'. The experience of course was far more novel then than it is now. Mrs Anning Bell, the French widow of the painter Robert Anning Bell, came for a week-end and insisted on drawing my portrait. The sittings were a trial, since nothing could stop her talking. This was tolerable when she uttered such exclamations as 'Dear me, what a tiny nose it is!' but more often I was expected to take notice. I was reminded of a friend of Alfred's who divided bores into two types, the bloody and wilful and the helpless and God-damned. Mrs Anning Bell belonged emphatically to the former class. She prattled endlessly about all the titled people she had met and, knowing a little about a great many subjects, considered the whole world her conversational oyster. In the evenings she insisted on talking through music on the radio; we tried to quash her by telling vulgar stories, but this merely stimulated her to tell vulgar stories of her own. My portrait was not quite finished: unable to stand any more, I invented a fictitious appointment and fled. She promised to finish it later and did so, but Gran said she spoiled it and refused to buy it.

Both the Radcliffe and Mallory families lived in Godalming, and there was much coming and going between our respective houses, continuing contacts made in Cambridge. We had other links with the Mallorys: Clare's paternal grandfather had been the clergyman who married my parents at Bidston in 1914, and Gran had met her father, the climber, who was a master at Charterhouse. Clare herself was addicted to climbing; we had to restrain her from mounting the scaffolding on King's Chapel. She was also an exuberant tennis player, very musical, an enthusiast for old churches, and at this time a supporter of the Hambledon Cricket Club. She had what I described as 'a reforming, almost a missionary spirit' and was always taking up good causes. Her other grandfather, Hugh Thackeray Turner, whose house at Westbrook the family shared, was reputed to be the rudest man in Surrey. He reminded me of Captain Shotover in *Heartbreak House*. A bearded patriarch, he had been a well-known architect, but was now virtually blind. His abrupt manner of speech was inherited by most of his descendants.

The most dramatic event at Hambledon this summer was the appearance of two huge policemen demanding access to Tommy. They announced ominously that the body of a murdered baby had been found on the common, next to a paper bag with Tommy's name on it. They insisted on inspecting all three of the female staff, who were nearly if not wholly beyond child-bearing age, and eventually concluded that the baby was a stranger and the bag had been deposited by Frisky, Gran's exuberant new terrier puppy.

One day in June Eva Reading, wife of the second Marquess, rang up and invited me to the Balliol Ball that same evening. I just managed to make it, collecting necessaries in London on the way. I enjoyed the company of my cousins Michael and Joan and danced a rousing polka with Eva, who put tremendous spirit into everything she did. I described her, somewhat impertinently, as 'an amusing intelligent woman, with too many teeth in her mouth', but wished I could have her a little less diluted; she always seemed to be the centre of a crowd of people. The Readings asked me to two more dances the following week, one of them for Joan's coming-out. I seldom found much in common with the people I met on these occasions, but liked one girl, who proved to have a sense of humour. When I said that everyone I danced with appeared to be the daughter of a Scottish peer, she replied with a grin that her father was a Scottish peer (Lord Forres, I think). Little did I know what was in store for me.

In July, when Mother and Eugene had demanded my absence from Hambledon, I spent a week with the Wilsons at West Walton, a week at King's during the Long Vacation term, when I assiduously did no work, and a week with Professor Pigou in the Lake District. The Wilsons took me to many churches, including Lincoln and Southwell Cathedrals (the latter one of the most beautiful buildings in England), and we had music in the evenings. Mrs Wilson was a violinist who had studied in Germany. I had hardly arrived when she roped me in to assist at a Women's Institute bazaar. I made quite a sum for charity at a bagatelle board, and appeared in the local press as judge of a flower show. One night I dreamed that I had found one of the keys to the universe, enshrined in a sentence that I must at all costs remember on waking. It was 'There is no such thing as a collective parson's wife'. 'Oh', said Mrs Wilson, 'glad to hear that'. She was always very brisk at breakfast, whereas I tended to be sleepy. She delighted to relate how one morning she greeted me with: 'Now, Winton, porridge or cornflakes?' to which I replied 'Probably'. Her liveliness complemented the absent-mindedness of her husband, a charming elderly clergyman who had been headmaster at Ardingly but was later found to be suffering from Alzheimer's. It must have been hereditary: Peggy and one of her brothers were to die of it many years later, Peggy in her mid-nineties after I had lost touch with her.

Pigou, the Professor of Political Economy at Cambridge, was a Kingsman and an Old Harrovian who had asked me to breakfast as soon as I went up. He had a house on Buttermere to which he regularly invited undergraduates, generally two at a time, a routine that had begun before the 1914 War and was scrupulously recorded in his visitors' book. He had been a fanatical climber, but a weak heart now kept him on the level. This did not prevent him from vicariously despatching his guests on long treks all over the Lake District. The first duty laid on everyone was to climb Fleetwith Pike, a hill above Pigou's house, and record the time it took in the visitors' book. David Hubback and I logged very moderate times. On a later visit my companion was Peter Joseph, whose good-humoured charm was equalled only by his congenital lethargy. He achieved the slowest time ever recorded, having fallen asleep for two hours on the way. It rained for much of the week, and there were tremendous winds, which blew me off my feet on Fleetwith Pike. In the intervals David and I, under Pigou's instructions, went for enormous walks, climbing a whole range of peaks, ruining our boots and lacerating our feet in the process. One day we took a boat half way down the stream to Crummock Water and had the greatest difficulty in getting it back. Pigou was a most gracious host. He was a notorious antifeminist, never tired of declaring that 'women are the source of all evil', and that they are all alike, even to their handwriting. He complained, on looking at some of my photographs, about the hosts of young women who insisted on creeping in front of the camera. The only thing they were good for, in his opinion, was writing detective stories; in that respect he ranked them above men.

CHAPTER 7

Salzburg and Greece

From the last day of July until the first of October I was out of England, for the whole month of August in Salzburg. Philip travelled with me and remained for three weeks. My attendance at the Festival was largely engineered by Gran, who gave me £35 towards expenses. We lodged in the suburb of Parsch with a Count and Countess Manzano, with whom Michael Isaacs had stayed the previous year. The Countess was young and charming; we were less taken with the Count, who was flashy, something of a womaniser, and said to be a secret Nazi. But he amused us by telling a story about an epileptic governess in a mixture of three languages. He and Philip, having no language in common, attempted to converse in laborious French. During the annual Festival the Manzanos turned their home into a guest-house, mostly for English speakers. We were an oddly assorted crowd: a heavy blond Englishman from Cambridge, a handsome dark Scotsman from Oxford with his mother (who had a room next to the bathroom and was repeatedly roused by the stormy entrance and shame-faced exit of young men in pyjamas, but otherwise made little mark), two English girls, one weighty and silent, the other as spritely and superficial as a butterfly, and Cushing Toppan, an exuberant middle-aged bachelor from Boston, Mass. Most of them were present for social rather than musical reasons, and with the possible exception of Toppan none had anything in common with Philip. Later arrivals were five Australian sisters, a talkative and restless American family name MacMurray (he was the U.S. ambassador to Turkey), two Jugoslav sisters from a place called Tržič, one of them an excellent pianist who gave a concert, and an Austrian couple who did not mix with us but exercised a baneful influence by occupying one of the two bathrooms for an hour and a quarter each morning. I was never clear how many bedrooms the house contained; they occurred sporadically all over the building, two of them opening out of the drawing-room and dining room. Some of the party slept in neighbouring houses, as did the Manzanos' engaging three-year-old son Toto, who once favoured us with a song after dinner.

Our social life was uproarious and far from intellectual. Toppan appointed himself everyone's favourite uncle; it was difficult to be dull or depressed in his presence. The Count once reduced him to embarrassed silence by asking his age at lunch, and he dropped a brick by mentioning fly-buttons in the presence of Mrs MacMurray, a heavy New England mother. One of his funnier exploits was to seize the weighty English girl's knitting, drop one of the needles down someone's back, and laboriously transfer her half-knit garment on to a pen-holder. When three of the party insisted on talking politics (the Spanish Civil War had just broken out) he earned general approval by locking them in an alcove. Toppan was a kind-hearted man. He was most considerate when I was intermittently ill with gastric trouble, and besought me to take piano lessons while I was in Salzburg; I did go so far as to practise on his hired piano. Gerda Schallgruber, the Yugoslav pianist, got me into a private seminar given by Bruno Walter for some American students at the Mozarteum. This was about Brahms's Second Symphony, and I found it most instructive but cannot recall what I learned, except that he conducted vertically, dealing with all that happened in each bar, rather than horizontally, devoting attention to the individual entries of each instrument.

The weather alternated between extreme heat and torrential rain. We bathed regularly on the hot days, and most of the girls turned pink. Philip and I explored the city, visiting Mozart's birth-place and the summer-house in which he composed *The Magic Flute*. I took a photograph of this, and of the caretaker informing us with much gesticulation that it was 'verboten'. The plan of the city seemed chaotic, and the Baroque churches did not much appeal to me, but the romantic and impregnable-looking castle and the wooded hills that cropped up in the most unexpected places had a peculiar fascination. In the evenings and after concerts we went the rounds of all the bars and restaurants we could find, and I encountered numerous acquaintances from London, Cambridge and Harrow. I could sit for hours observing the countless variations on the common theme of humanity. The city was full of celebrities from all over Europe, in addition to the participants in the Festival. I narrowly missed Edward VIII, Umberto of Italy and the Duke and Duchess of Kent, but saw Chaliapin and Grace Moore at close quarters and twice came face to face with Marlene Dietrich in the street, pursued by a trail of autograph-hunters. David Hubback had given me an introduction to Egon Wellesz, whom I met for the first time, little thinking that he would end his days as a refugee in Oxford. Towards the end of the month I took the younger MacMurray daughter Lois, known as Bisi, out dancing, having appeared before her mother to be vetted as a responsible person. She was only thirteen but looked several years older and generally seemed to be left behind when the others went out. I thought her the most sensitive of the family. She was excellent company and touchingly grateful, and repaid me for her first glimpse of Salzburg night life by giving me stamps from her father's correspondence. I have often wondered what became of her.

An Engagement with Time

The main attraction of course was the Festival itself. I had never consumed such a rich and concentrated diet of music, and my education benefitted accordingly. I went to nine operas and more than a dozen concerts of various descriptions, including open-air serenades and chamber recitals in the hall of the Residenz. Two or three times the weather compelled artists and audience to decamp hastily into the building, where the acoustics were deplorable. The programmes were mostly Mozart, with a little Haydn, Schubert and Wolf's Italian Serenade. Three major concerts were conducted by Pierre Monteux (French music), Bruno Walter (Mozart) and Toscanini. My comments were mostly on the music, but I thought that Monteux let the brass get out of hand in the *Benvenuto Cellini* overture and the finale of Franck's symphony, and that Walter sentimentalised the first movement of Mozart's G minor symphony. Toscanini's Schubert C major symphony disappointed me; everything was crystal clear, but dry, academic, almost clinical. No doubt I approached it in the wrong spirit. In the second half, though Beethoven was promised, Toscanini conducted a commonplace suite by Goldmark, Smetana's *Vltava* and the overture to *Semiramide*, the last with such panache as to convince me for ten minutes that Rossini was the most exciting composer who ever lived. The magnificent orchestra was the Vienna Philharmonic. Mozart's C minor Mass and Requiem were given in churches; I found both profoundly satisfying, but would have preferred the Mass without the Benedictus. The most eccentric concert was a recital by Gigli with organ accompaniment in the cathedral. I admired his voice, but not his technique or his taste. The programme consisted of music by Mozart, Handel, Stradella, Perosi, Nicolai, Bach-Gounod, Verdi, Bizet, Bruckner, Franck, Wagner and Michael Haydn in that order.

The operas were *Der Corregidor* (Wolf), *Don Giovanni*, *Orfeo* (Gluck) and *Tristan und Isolde* conducted by Walter, *Così fan tutte* and *Figaro* conducted by Weingartner, and *Die Meistersinger*, *Falstaff* and *Fidelio* conducted by Toscanini. Nearly all of them I was hearing for the first time in the theatre. My comments therefore can have little value. I thought *Der Corregidor* under-rehearsed and not too well sung, and was critical of the visual aspect of nearly all the productions, especially *Don Giovanni* and *Tristan*. Of the former 'the production, as such, hardly existed – the scenes seemed to have been rehearsed separately and then casually strung on one after another. There was always too much stuff on the stage, and too much use made of certain theatrical effects, so that by the time they were really needed we had got tired of them'. However the hell that devoured Don Giovanni was realistic and terrifying. I considered the scenery in *Falstaff* tawdry and the staging of *Tristan* abominable, but had plenty of praise for the singers, especially Stabile (Don Giovanni and Falstaff), Borgioli (Don Ottavio), Elisabeth Schumann (Despina and Susanna), Ludwig Hofmann (King Mark), Lotte Lehmann (Leonore) and Alfred Jerger (Pizarro). Kerstin Thorborg I admired as Brangäne but not as Orfeo, where she cut an awkward figure. Jarmila Novotna was a good Fiordiligi and a very moving Countess in *Figaro*, though I was struck by her acting and her beauty as much as by her voice. In *Tristan* Anny Konetzni sang eloquently but looked like a she-elephant. Josef Kalenburg (Tristan) I thought could neither sing nor act; perhaps he was having an off-night. When these lovers embraced, their bodies collided amidships well before contact could be established elsewhere. I made some heretical remarks about this opera, wishing that out of fairness to Wagner the last act could have been cut. All three acts were played in a grey Celtic twilight. Afterwards in a restaurant I gave a public demonstration of how a Wagnerian hero would eat a piece of cake.

I did not much care for Weingartner's Mozart (as opposed to his Beethoven, which I knew from gramophone records); Act I of *Figaro* seemed spiritless, and his treatment of *Così fan tutte* lacking in sparkle and lightness of touch. Walter impressed me, especially in *Orfeo* and *Tristan*, but Toscanini was a revelation. All three of the operas he conducted bowled me over completely. His rhythmic precision, absolute clarity and control of pace over the entire score struck me as beyond criticism. A charge of electricity seemed to run through his performances, including the stage action, as if a thousand-watt bulb had been turned on, and they negated the passage of time. After five hours of *Die Meistersinger* I still wanted more; the scenes I had thought relatively weak moved me as much as the rest. *Falstaff*, which I had never heard before, began by running me off my feet (Toscanini took the second scene at a tremendous speed), but as soon as I had recovered my breath I was utterly captivated and had to be led numb from the theatre. The cast was excellent except for the Nannetta, Augusta Oltrabella, whose name flattered her. *Fidelio* was the best of all. I remember particularly the opening of the prisoners' chorus and the *Leonora* no. 3 overture, played between the scenes of Act II. This practice is strictly to be deplored, since it kills the finale, but I doubt if anyone who heard Toscanini's performance would wish it away. The tension as the main theme of the Allegro entered, first a whisper in the distance, then a blaze of triumph, had the audience on the edge of their seats; at the end of the overture they created such a commotion, standing up, shouting, stamping and banging on the seats that it was some time before the opera could be resumed. The cast was very strong; even the plump Hungarian Koloman von Patáky, whom I had heard in *Die Entführung* at Glyndebourne and whose figure reminded me of Eugene, made one overlook the fact that he was far too well nourished for a prisoner long immured in a dungeon. The performance of these three operas set my standards for life; I can still hear long stretches of them in Toscanini's tempi.

There were two interesting excursions from Salzburg. Vie had given me an introduction to Clifford Curzon, then a rising young pianist still in his twenties. He and his wife, the American harpsichordist Lucille Wallace, had a house at Litzlberg on Attersee, a picturesque lake in the Salzkammergut. Philip and I had a most enjoyable two days. Although Clifford and Lucille had never met either of us before, they made us feel at home from the first moment; we got on so well that we never seemed to stop talking. We had delicious meals on a terrace in the open air, and regularly sat talking till it was nearly time to eat again. We discussed and argued about every musical subject under the sun. I wish I could recall the details, or that it would have been possible for someone to preserve the conversation on a tape-recorder. I do remember Clifford's hearty agreement with me over Walter's conducting of Mozart's G minor symphony, his half-ashamed confession that the composer of popular ballads Albert Ketèlbey was his uncle, and a notable instance of Philip's encyclopaedic knowledge of the entire classical repertory. Clifford, after repeatedly failing to catch him out, asked if he knew d'Indy's variations for piano in E flat minor. 'Yes', replied Philip, 'but aren't they by Dukas?' Nina Milkina, aged seventeen and very shy, was a fellow-guest and played us the pieces she was preparing for one of her early recitals. The house was full of keyboard instruments; even I was let loose in a (padded) room containing a clavichord and a harpsichord as well as a piano. We bathed at intervals from a landing-stage built through the reeds at the bottom of the garden. Philip was a very slow and deliberate breast-stroke swimmer; when induced to put on a pair of rubber frog's feet he astonished everyone, not least himself, by shooting through the water like a torpedo-boat. Before dinner I used to row out into the lake and watch the play of the twilight on water, clouds and mountains. It was an idyllic existence.

The second excursion was to St Gilgen on the Wolfgangsee, another lovely lake girdled with mountains, where a peasant wedding was celebrated at the expense of the state. The crowds were enormous; we had to jostle desperately to obtain any view of the proceedings. The picturesque wooden houses were decorated with all manner of flags and bunting; brass bands and processions in elaborate national costumes and municipal regalia, some of them weird and wonderful, marched down the street; and many celebrities attended, including the Austrian Chancellor Schuschnigg, Toscanini, Lotte Lehmann and the Crown Prince of Italy. By holding the camera above my head and those of the crowd in front of me I took a number of photographs, including an excellent one of Toscanini. The only people who seemed totally mystified by the whole business were the little bride and bridegroom.

As a joke I began to compose a High Table overture, allotting a familiar and appropriate melody and a suitable instrument to each member of the King's High Table, and then having them converse, amicably or indignantly, in a contrapuntal argument. It was amusing to discover how the opening of Schubert's C major symphony and the *Meistersinger* overture, the Toreador's song, the march in Tchaikovsky's *Pathétique* and *The Red Flag* could be variously combined, sometimes in diminution and inversion. The piece was never finished. At the same time Philip was more worthily engaged with a set of orchestral variations, broadcast later in the year by the BBC Northern Ireland Orchestra, conducted by Peter Montgomery.

I was sorry to leave Salzburg. The inhabitants of Parsch 168 had somehow risen by several degrees in my estimation. I reflected that in a week's time we would be distributed between Greece, Turkey, Italy, Switzerland, Hungary, Jugoslavia, France, England and the United States, while one English girl remained with the Manzanos. 'It seems difficult to believe that some of us may never meet again, and that all of us certainly will not ... What a fortuitous inconsequent world it is! Any one of us might so easily have met an entirely different set of people'.

* * * * *

On 1 September I travelled by train from Salzburg to Desenzano on Lake Garda, changing at Innsbruck and Verona. The journey took 13 hours, but its various discomforts were mitigated by superb scenery, especially in the neighbourhood of the Brenner Pass. Above Bolzano the mountains stood up a wonderful vivid pink at sunset. My travelling companions were a taciturn young American and an exceptionally garrulous Canadian lady who had taken two years to go round the world and had every intention of telling us all about it. Our locomotive refused to function outside Innsbruck, and when another was attached one of the carriages came off the rails. Otherwise the only incident of note was that my fountain pen fell down the lavatory on to the line and perished.

At Desenzano I stayed for three days with my Italian friend Mario Lamberti and his parents. Mario had been a research student at King's, and on leaving had made me promise that if ever I visited Italy, whether in one, five or thirty years' time, I would visit him without fail. This was the only occasion on which I was able to take advantage of his invitation. Except briefly when he visited Cambridge I never saw him again; he perished mysteriously during the war while working for the resistance movement. He was a man of great charm, and his mother was a most spritely lady with whom I had lively conversations although neither of us could speak the other's language. Meric Dobson, another King's friend, arrived next day. We visited Fasano, where my parents spent their honeymoon, Riva at the head of Lake Garda, by a picturesque new road that tunnelled in and out of the mountains, and the little peninsula of Sirmione, which boasts a 13th century castle, the hefty remains of a Roman villa said to have belonged to Catullus, and countless lizards and enormous dragonflies. Unfortunately there were also mosquitoes, whose depredations were apt to keep me awake for much of the night both in Italy and Greece; our hotel in Venice had mosquito nets, but they seemed to keep out the air as well as the mosquitoes. The sun went down impressively behind tall cypresses and shot myriads of colours over the lake. The Italian landscape has indescribable warmth of its own; its familiarity puzzled me until I realised where I had encountered it before, in countless old Italian paintings.

Meric and I spent two days in Venice, one on the way to Greece and one on the way back. My first sight of the city, through which we made a wide tour in a gondola, far exceeded my expectations; all the glorious things I had heard seemed flat when set beside the reality. We spent much time on the Piazza, suffering high-level bombardment and near-decapitation by flying pigeons. St Mark's, though impressive from a distance, struck me as too heavy and over-encrusted with detail for its size, especially the interior; the thing I most admired was a little Byzantine carving built into the outer wall. I preferred the exterior of the Doges' Palace, and spent a long time inside trying to study the pictures and suffering a stiff neck from having constantly to look at the ceiling. Did Renaissance Italians have eyes on top of their heads? I came away profoundly impressed by Veronese's sense of perspective and convinced that Tiepolo was underrated.

We travelled down the Adriatic in a small crowded steamer, the S.S. *Quirinale*, a journey that took three days. It was quite comfortable in the second class, but there was no room to be alone and, with a contingent of fidgety Balilla on board, little hope of quiet. I shared a cabin with two pleasant Americans, one short and thick, the other lanky and bespectacled, on their way to teach in Istanbul. Meric, who was travelling deck class to save money, fetched his food from the kitchen and his drink from a room containing a dead sheep (in half). His companions were four light-headed Americans (three of them female), a hawk-eyed and monosyllabic German lady, and three very shop-soiled Greeks. We were the only British on board. The other nationalities gradually sorted themselves into groups, easily distinguished by their behaviour. The Italians never remained in one place for five minutes; the French read suspicious novels and muttered behind newspapers; the Germans lay coarsely and copiously on deck chairs, at least one of which collapsed under the weight; the Turks were heavy and sombre but polite; the Americans played deck games and got into difficulties with the stewards; the Greeks frequented the windows of first-class cabins to watch ladies, and even gentlemen, undressing.

The sea was beautifully calm, the sun grew hotter and hotter, and most of our energy evaporated. I competed with five Americans and two Turkish girls at throwing hoops over rings and was acclaimed champion. We called at Brindisi late one night; this yielded another American in our cabin and even more overcrowding above. Meric and I walked about on shore for an hour; we found a huge Roman column, one or two carvings, a 17th century cathedral, numbers of thin cats, and various nocturnal happenings of a more or less edifying nature. Most people suffered stomach upsets; there was a wholesale consumption of pills by the Americans. Once I came upon Meric and the entire American contingent, now augmented to ten, collaborating in the consumption of a gigantic water-melon. By the last afternoon we were among the Greek islands, which by a trick of the mist, seemed to be floating in mid-air. As we passed the lights of Patras the band, a tired-looking trio hired to entertain the first-class passengers, incongruously struck up the waltz from *The Merry Widow*.

We passed through the Corinth Canal and reached the Peiraeus early in the morning. After a crazy taxi-drive through clouds of dust we arrived at the house of the Mesdemoiselles Dmitrov, two bulky middle-aged ladies from Smyrna with whom two of our friends had lodged a year or so before. They welcomed us effusively as if we were long-lost nephews, and fed us well, though the bottles of wine were apt to yield a deposit of earwigs among the grounds. The method of taking a bath in their house was peculiar. We were provided with two large metal pans, one full of water, the other empty, and a bailer. The procedure was to convey the water by means of the bailer out of Pan 1 via our bodies into Pan 2, in which it was just possible to squat. This was explained by the Mlles Dmitrov, who explained everything in great detail. They told us exactly what we were eating and why we were eating it. Their manner suggested that of a matron showing members of the Royal Family over a hospital. They spoke of the horrors of the Turkish attack on Smyrna in 1922, in which they lost all their possessions.

We stayed in Athens for a week, not nearly long enough to see all we wished to see, and divided our time almost equally between the buildings and the museums. We first approached the Acropolis at night, and my initial step on the holy ground was ominous: a vivid flash of summer lightning behind Lycabettus lit up the whole city, a band far away on the left struck up the prelude to *Carmen*, and I began the ascent. Of course the gates were shut; we had to postpone our full inspection till the following day. It would be pointless to repeat my rhapsodical and far from coherent reactions. I felt as if I had been dosed with a powerful drug and ran about with my hands to my head, unable to think or speak. The Erecktheion moved me even more than the Parthenon. Most striking of all was the effect of the sunset. The Parthenon was orange one moment, then white, then crimson, then purple, then orange again. The hills, the city and the sea continually revealed fresh facets and more daring colours – tantalising because they changed all the time and never waited long enough to be savoured in full. No sooner had one impression fixed itself in my mind than it became something else. I took many photographs, but not being in colour they convey only a fraction of what we saw. After the gates were shut we sat for fully an hour silent on a stone. On a later visit the sunset threatened to be even more spectacular, but at the crucial moment was obscured by clouds. We then came upon a party of palpable British colonels being shown round by a Greek guide, who enlarged on the beauty of each feature with ever more extravagant ventures into hyperbole. He was nonplussed by the growing scepticism of the colonels.

We explored many other buildings in the city: the delightful little Doric temple, almost complete, miscalled the Theseion (actually the temple of Hephaestus), the temple of Zeus, the pillar of Lysicrates, the Roman agora with its striking Tower of the Winds, the arch and stoa of Hadrian, the two ancient theatres, in one of which a chaotic rehearsal was taking place. I was delighted by the lovely little Byzantine churches with their sprouting domes, especially the early 9th century metropolitan cathedral, only 34 feet long – half a cricket pitch – but covered with carvings. Beside it the new cathedral, a top-heavy 19th century parody of the same style, stood like a cow to its new-born calf. Having few windows these old churches are very dark inside, so that it is scarcely possible to see the mosaics. In one of them a lady, apparently mistaking us for Greek priests, asked us in French to say a mass for her. It was some time before we could make her understand that we lacked the qualifications.

On our first visit to the National Museum we concentrated on the Mycenaean antiquities. I had not imagined that they had reached such a high degree of artistic refinement so early. No wonder Homer talked of 'golden Mycenae'. The later exhibits were quite as memorable. Many funeral carvings seemed lapped in the peace of eternity. Some of them moved me so much that I felt I had always known them, or had always been searching for them. I also fell for the joyous little Tanagra statuettes. But there was far too much to take in; after a while the pottery began to appear repetitive. The museum on the Acropolis was if anything even more overpowering because it was smaller and more concentrated; almost every item seemed to attain the ultimate in beauty. What were these Greeks that they could achieve this? And how many more such treasures have perished or been swallowed up by the earth or the sea? A carving of Athena looking down at her spear, and the whole world shrinks to a little egg in comparison.

We had afternoon journeys to Daphni and Sunium, on each occasion by bus. The 11th century monastery at Daphni harmonises perfectly with the surrounding country, whose purple-brown ruggedness was something quite new in my experience. It is full of superb mosaics, hiding in all the alcoves and under every arch, with a huge head of Christ beneath the central dome. The journey was entertaining; we were soon on the friendliest terms with the other passengers, mostly workmen, one of whom pointed out a lunatic asylum with the words "In there we have a thousand foolish – how say you in English?" That was as nothing compared to the journey to Sunium. The bus was full when we arrived, its complement for the most part comprising unshaven men with curly moustaches who had not finished their lunch; they continued for some time to consume about 75% of what they put in their mouths. There was also a supercargo of dogs, hens, babies, bicycles, bedsteads and other packages, stuffed partly on top of the vehicle but mostly into any available space between the passengers. This had happened some time before we arrived, but we were not permitted to start until a number of heated and violent arguments had taken place between the driver, the conductor, three or four passengers, a hen and several bystanders. For some minutes the air was full of grunts, noises, epithets, percussions, lamentations and portions of lunch. Suddenly it all stopped, and with a jerk that shot me out of my seat the bus started.

On the way we picked up more packages, dogs and moustaches, most of which deposited themselves around and on top of the driver.

From Karitea to Laurion the road was under repair; but instead of taking it up in strips the workmen had dug up the full width and diverted what could hardly at best be called a track over the bare hillside. We had perforce to follow, jolting, rolling and pitching, over banks of stones and the dry beds of streams, our wheels never at the same altitude on both sides. Having regained the track we met, right across our front, a Morris Commercial lorry into which three or four desultory workmen were shovelling stones. They refused to move it: abuse, jeering, loss of temper by both parties; suddenly, as everyone ran out of breath, calm returned and, accompanied by vague mutterings, the lorry waddled slowly off the road. This procedure was repeated a few hundred yards further on, first with a mule, then with a horse and cart. At Laurion, an unpleasant grimy village, there was a welcome pause while we changed buses. We expected something more of the famous site of the Athenian silver mines. From there to Sunium was an anti-climax. The road was perfect; but it had taken us 2¾ hours to travel some twenty-odd miles.

Sunium on the southern tip of Attica is a lovely spot, high on a cliff with a view of mountains, sea and islands in almost every direction. Aegina and the site of the Battle of Salamis lie below. The temple of Poseidon, built of very white marble, is an imposing fragment, but has been mutilated by the weather and generations of name-carvers, including Byron, whose verses rang constantly in our heads. This was presumably the rocky brow on which he placed King Xerxes. Our return journey was less eventful, though we paused repeatedly to pick up sportsmen's trophies, and once the conductor stopped the bus, jumped out and shot a quail himself.

We had planned a fortnight's tour of the Peloponnese, to be undertaken partly on foot, partly by such transport as we found available, but avoiding conducted tours. This was both for reasons of economy and to give us a better view of the country. Had we known what we were in for, we might have been less bold. Our start was inauspicious. We rose at 5.30 and then found ourselves at the wrong railway station, an easy mistake to make. In the desperate rush that ensued I caught my foot in a wire and fell down a five-foot drop on to some sharp stones, with much resulting bloodshed, bruising and bad temper. Travel by train, like all travel in Greece, is (or was) crowded, noisy and uncomfortable, though partially redeemed by the countryside and the numerous openings it afforded for comedy. Neither of these was I in a position to appreciate at the time. We found ourselves in a packed third-class carriage with little air, hard seats and no lavatory. The other travellers, from men down to dogs and flies, soon began to take an unhealthy interest in my bloody knee; the men even poked it. They also asked innumerable questions.

There were only two trains a day on this not unimportant line, and each was an event. At every station the villagers surged round with grapes and melons for sale; for the next few miles it was doubly dangerous to put one's head out of the window for fear of flying refuse. On one stretch we were entertained by an old man and a boy with banjos, who squatted and played on the carriage floor. They got out at the next station, then presumably repeated the performance on the next train in the opposite direction. Badinage and gossip were exchanged between the passengers and the men who worked the level crossings. The train was always late; if the journey lasted an extra hour, that was reckoned an advantage. The locomotives seemed to share the same spirit; they were to be found sometimes at one end of the train, sometimes at the other, and sometimes at both, and from their appearance they might have been the fruit of one of the earlier experiments of George Stephenson. All drivers of vehicles in Greece (trains, trams, buses, taxis) had one joy in common, their horns or whistles. These boasted every variety of pitch and tuning: some sounded like a grating saw, some like a sick cow, some like the last trump; and needless to say they were brought into action on every possible occasion. The best-equipped vehicles boasted two, three or even four different notes; when these all sounded it really was advisable to get out of the way.

We reached Examilia, the station for Old Corinth, after 3½ hours, though it was no great distance from Athens. Here, standing forlorn among the alien corn, we espied a lavatory – full of lizards, lice and other inhabitants and without water, but none the less a lavatory. In due course we climbed the great rocky lump of the Acrocorinth, where we saw massive and complex medieval fortifications, admired the wide views, and drank refreshing water from a spring. For the equivalent of sixpence each, of which a penny was tip, we obtained a hefty lunch of bread, cheese, wine, grapes and coffee, and watched the local inhabitants playing a mysterious form of billiards. The old town, some distance from the modern city, has Roman ruins, seven columns of a squat and massive Doric temple of very early date, a couple of pleasant little medieval churches and a museum, whose modest contents helped to place in perspective the glorious art of Attica. On our way back to Examilia we got hopelessly lost, hit the railway at least three miles from the station, and sprinted along the line to collect our rucksacks and arrive, dripping and panting, a minute before the train was due. We need not have hurried; it was 45 minutes late.

We travelled to Mycenae with two weedy-looking but friendly French youths and put up at La Belle Helène de Menelas, the only inn in the village. It was kept by one Orestes, whose sister, aptly named Helen, had recently been carried off to the United States by some American Paris. The beds were unexpectedly comfortable; the verdict of the *Guide bleu*, 'rustique mais propre', stated the case admirably. The inn had quite a zoo attached to it. Two huge dogs and three slender cats, with the hungriest expressions on their faces, attended all meals and consumed the crumbs that fell from the rich man's table; they were apt too to leap on the rich man's lap and threaten to devour him as well. At the back, besides every imaginable type of cattle, were hens with extraordinary figures, turkeys, guinea-fowl and a black rabbit.

The ruins impressed me not for their beauty but for their extraordinary massiveness and grandeur, and for an atmosphere that could be felt. One was somehow aware of the pressure of 3,500 years. The bee-hive tombs had a queer echo; their silence was a positive, not a negative thing. We went down a subterranean staircase whose steps were worn, the sides polished, by the passing of countless generations. The citadel, approached by the lion gate and standing on a rocky eminence commanding a strategic view of the Argive plain, inspired a sense of wonder at the Mycenaean architects' achievement on a site calculated to deter all but the most intrepid builders.

We decided to sample every brand of Greek wine we could find, and by the second evening had tried several. The lighter white wines were the most agreeable; a heavy dessert wine called Mavrodaphni tasted unpleasantly like syrup of figs and had much the same effect. After dinner we embarked on a long and exhaustive argument about the value of art, selfishness and the improvement of the soul, surely appropriate for two students of the Classics in such a place as Mycenae. My ideals, though expressed awkwardly and at great length, seem to me more mature than I might have expected.

In the morning we sat under the trees observing the arrival of an extraordinary caravanserai of tourists, of all shapes and sizes in every imaginable type of conveyance. One car carried seventeen persons, followed by ten in a cart and a gigantic man riding a microscopic donkey. We had bargained for a car to drive us round all day, and obtained a bright and efficient little driver. Armed with a vast picnic lunch supplied by Orestes, we set out over a road that rivalled that to Sunium in irregularity. The Argive Heraion offered little but the groundplan of a temple, littered with shards; the ancient Greeks certainly knew how to choose a site. The citadel at Tiryns is very different from that at Mycenae, since it was a military fortress, not the centre of a civilization. The tremendously massive walls of undressed stone, worn to a glassy polish by hundreds of generations of sheep, the roofed galleries, the secret staircase within the thickness of the wall leading to a postern gate, and the bath with drain and holes for erecting curtains are astonishingly well preserved. Our driver showed us a Mycenaean bridge, a lion carved on a mountain, and four exquisite little Byzantine churches. That at Plataniti must be one of the tiniest anywhere; those at Midéa and Koroni concentrated more interest and beauty per square foot than any building I had seen. The superb theatre at Epidaurus, carved out of the hillside and retaining nearly all its original seating, would serve splendidly for a dramatic or operatic festival if it were not so remote; I believe it has been used for modern productions. The acoustics are so perfect that when one of us whispered on the stage, the other could hear perfectly in the remote top row of seats. There was also a little Odeon - a Glyndebourne to the big theatre's Covent Garden – and extensive ruins of a stadium and tholos (circular temple).

As we drove through the villages we were received almost like the King and Queen on Jubilee Day. All the children and many of the adults waved and shouted greetings, which we acknowledged with such dignity as we could command. At one place two or three children threw stones at the car. Our driver sprang out, made an emphatic demonstration, and returned the fire in kind. One or two men in the fields protested. We drove on before an international incident could develop. At another village we removed the tail from a dilatory cock; the villagers took this in their stride. I began to love the Greek countryside with its rugged hills and expanses of brown rock, despite the dust and the absence of greenery. It had a reserve, as if it held the keys to many secrets, inviting scrutiny but baffling it at the same time. Owing to the absence of distinct landmarks it confused our sense of orientation. I would carefully work out to which point of the compass we were travelling, only for the sun to appear a minute or two later in an impossible place and make nonsense of my calculations.

We put up at the Grande Bretagne in Nauplia, where we were the only guests and treated with great respect; the water-melons were delicious. Nauplia looked an attractive place, and I should have preferred to stay longer instead of sweltering in intense heat at Argos. We began by searching for the museum, but no one seemed to know where it was; or rather, everyone had his own idea, but no two opinions coincided. We located it in the end in a ramshackle barnlike building with the plaster peeling off the ceiling. It offered only a few pots and scarcely repaid a visit. We explored two theatres, one of them tolerably well preserved, a Roman building and some temple relics inhabited by many green lizards, and climbed the Aspis. This offered a fine view but exhausted our energy. In the narrow streets the children ran after us and hailed us as lords; we were even offered a minute kitten scarcely three inches long. We ate a curiously assorted picnic lunch on the platform of Argos Junction, photographed a primitive locomotive, and observed a number of gentlemen entering the ladies' lavatory, presumably because it had seats. We also studied the art of spitting, in which the Greeks are unrivalled in distance, volume and frequency, if not always in accuracy.

The train journey to Tripolis was rendered hazardous by the man sitting opposite, who uttered heart-rending groans and insisted on having all the windows shut; but we passed through some of the wildest mountain scenery. So we did in the bus between Tripolis and Sparta, but that was still more uncomfortable owing to the awkward arrangement of seating and the attention of our old enemies the mosquitos. At Sparta we repelled a murderous assault of men and boys recommending the Hotel Mistra, and put up at the Panhellenion. This was kept by a man whose name, literally translated, meant Christ Chestnut, and proved quite comfortable.

The antiquities of Sparta amounted to little except a half-excavated Roman theatre and, in the museum, some queer masks and little lead figures, austere and primitive by comparison with Athenian art. We set out on foot for Mistra, where a small boy served us with the most vicious goat's milk cheese and the most glutinous pudding we had yet encountered, and shook up a bottle of beer which he then squirted in Meric's face. Old Mistra astonished us: a complete Byzantine town of the 14th and 15th centuries built on the side of a steep hill, devoid of inhabitants. Most of the buildings, including a large palace, were in ruins, but the churches had been kept in repair. There were eight of them, apart from sundry small chapels, all constructed on the same general plan, with one large cupola and several smaller ones, but none precisely identical. The size, number and position of the cupolas varied, often governed by the slope of the ground. All the churches were rich in frescoes and mosaics. We were most impressed by the unusual tower and frescoes of the Peribleptos (built right into the rock), the cloisters and lovely arcaded tower of the Pantanassa, and the glorious central cupola of St Theodore's. The old archbishop's palace and courtyard remains attached to the cathedral. We climbed up to the Frankish fortress crowning the hill, which has a view commanding the whole Eurotas valley; this must have been an impregnable spot if ever there was one. The only inhabitants of the old town were seven nuns in the Pantanassa, who received us politely in French and supplied us with guides from their number. The guardian of the Peribleptos proved to be a microscopic lady with a stentorian voice, whose piercing tones disturbed all the bats in the building.

The next part of the journey was not pleasant. It involved first a two-hour walk to the village of Trypi over the roughest and stoniest track that constantly traversed steep ravines. We lost our way more than once; our rucksacks grew heavier and heavier; only after a lavish distribution of money to the peasantry did we reach Trypi, to discover that there was no inn. We eventually found quarters, which it would be too polite to call squalid, in the house of one Aspiotis. There was no light, no cleanliness, no privacy; and a nasty little Greek with an oleaginous manner who spoke bad English with an American accent informed us that we must get up at five in the morning for the journey to Kalamata. I flatly refused to start before 8. Moreover he wanted a fearful price for the hire of a mule. We got rid of him at last, though he made a second attack reinforced by his brother-in-law. Then another muleteer arrived. He could speak no English, but managed to convey to us that he was a fine fellow, that he could write, that he was 32, and many other things; and he undercut the first man by 100 drachmas. We told him to come at 8 in the morning. I had to attend to various injuries before retiring; the beds were of the consistency of paving-stones and for hours defied our exhausted efforts to sleep; and it transpired that our room also served as a hen-house.

There was a fine altercation at 8 o'clock. The first man called the second spiteful and lowered his price in disgust. Each blew his own trumpet with vigour. When breath ran short they appealed to us to decide between them. We chose the second man, and had no cause to regret it. Our tramp across the steep and rugged Taygetus range, a distance of some 20 miles, took ten hours, including one for lunch. The scenery was superb; we travelled up rocky gorges, round the flanks of mountains, through pine forests, along the beds of streams, passing the crest of the Langada Pass at 2 and reaching Kalamata soon after 6. I walked for as long as I could, but in time the rocky paths and steep ascents had their effect, my wind began to give out and my blisters to multiply. Then I mounted the mule, a most intelligent creature, whose principal task was to carry the rucksacks; we named him Ferdinand. Riding a mule is rather like bestriding a table; the animal seems as broad as it is high. I stood it for an hour or so, but the pain in my thighs became so unbearable that it was all I could do to sit still. So for the last two hours I limped along on foot in the rear of the caravan, more and more exhausted. There were brighter moments, as when I was assaulted by a locust (?); this was when I was riding, and required some skill in negotiation. But for much of the way I cursed the day I was born. Even the music of the goat-bells high on the mountains – and it is music, not mere noise – was lost on me. I was half-dead when we reached Kalamata, and feeling horribly sick. Meric, who was very helpful and sympathetic, was in rather better case. With great difficulty I dragged myself up the stairs of the hotel, the White House, and at the earliest available moment enjoyed the luxury of a hot bath, the first since leaving Athens.

Our condition forced us to prune some of the activities planned for the next day or two. We took a train to Valyra and ate our lunch in a café under close observation from the entire village, men, women, children, cats and dogs, who offered liberal comment, criticism and advice. The Greeks, besides being very hospitable, must be the most inquisitive people on earth (in this respect at least they have not changed in 25 centuries), and their curiosity is apt to outrun their manners. They asked us if we had come with the King, who had recently sailed in Greek waters. It took us all afternoon to reach the Vourcano monastery, half way up Mount Ithome, partly because Meric had to carry both rucksacks and partly because we were misdirected. Also I stupidly picked a cactus fruit, and it took 45 minutes to extract the spines. The monks received us with great courtesy and put us in a fine large room, where we were served with bread, cheese and wine. A gross unshaven man, a servant who said his name was Kyriakos, paid court to us, gave us walnuts, and in the end became so embarrassingly affectionate that we had to turn him out. We attended part of a service, which sounded like a race between three monks to see who could finish first, and were shown a miraculous icon found on top of the mountain. Our beds were a little prickly; nevertheless we would have slept soundly but for the bell ringing for service at all unearthly hours; in due course a fine pig joined the symphony just outside our window.

In the morning we climbed Ithome, after surmounting ten sleeping bodies stretched out on a straw mat outside the lavatory; apparently they betokened a festival. It was a steeper climb than it looked, but rewarded us with another superlative view. At the top was a little monastery, where a hermit refreshed us with brandy and Turkish Delight, an incident that might have come from the *Morte d'Arthur*. He pointed out various gates and remains of ancient Messene, and showed us frescos of great beauty in his church. We reached Valyra station just in time for a very sluggish train, which took the best part of 4½ hours to jolt us to Megalopolis, where it arrived an hour late. We beguiled the time by consuming innumerable bunches of grapes and conversing with a kindly old man who had been in America and gave us the benefit of his experience in great detail. The guards and other officials seemed to spend the entire journey walking up and down the footboards outside the carriages; to judge by their behaviour, they might have been paid according to the number of punches administered to each ticket. One of them told us that the train would be '25 centimes late'.

The journey from Megalopolis to Andritsena scarcely bears thinking about. It took two hours, over roads as bad as that to Sunium with the addition of a precipice on at least one side throughout; and the driver repeatedly took one or both hands off the wheel as he turned to address someone in the back. There were ten of us in a small springless four-seater, including an enormous fat man who sat beside me. A tremendous argument arose, complicated by language difficulties. The subjects of dispute were: which hotel should we patronise at Andritsena, and by what means should we proceed to Olympia? We wanted to take a direct route by car; they told us this would cost us 1400 drachmas, and we ought to take a roundabout route involving horses as well as cars. Eventually we gave in over the hotel, sorry to miss a landlord calling himself Christ Christson, provided we could find someone able to speak English. Only then did it transpire that the fat man, one Ambariotis, was the landlord of the hotel we had been persuaded to patronise – though hotel was perhaps too strong a word. Even so, as at a number of other places, we found the signatures of many English friends in the visitors' book. The English-speaker duly appeared, and proved to be another enormous man who looked like a retired policeman. He was very garrulous and quite helpful.

We stayed two nights at Andritsena, much persecuted by insects; on the second night I fell through the bed with a splintering crash, to be retrieved with tender care by Meric. The intervening day gave us one of the most memorable experiences of our trip. Led by a guide, we walked for about eight miles across the wild, pathless and beautiful mountain landscape of Arcadia to Bassae. Here Ictinus, the architect of the Parthenon, built a temple in 420 B.C. to celebrate a treaty between two local states. It stands complete except for the roof and the frieze, its blue stone merging harmoniously with the surroundings, miles from the nearest human habitation. (This may be the case no longer; a road has apparently been built since the war. I am thankful to have seen Bassae before it was smutched by civilisation.) Our first view of the temple was breath-taking; I thought it quite as beautiful as its sister on the Acropolis. On our return we found Andritsena in the throes of market-day. The town was full of errant pigs, hens, goats, horses, donkeys, mules and their owners of all ages, every one seemingly giving tongue at once. I learned for the first time to what depths of its being a pig detests a change of masters.

We left Andritsena in a taxi, delayed by a puncture and (on my part) a violent attack of diarrhoea. At a place beginning with Z we found two horses awaiting us and continued our journey on these, reaching Olympia at 5 p.m. The path lay along the lovely and fertile valley of the Alphaeus, which flowed plentifully even in autumnal heat. We plucked the ears of sweet-corn and met with no adventures except a forest fire in some pines. A glimpse of the pediments from the temple of Zeus in the museum induced us to spend an extra day at Olympia. These half-archaic sculptures possess immense vigour; the expressions on the faces, purely formal at first sight, begin mysteriously to haunt the memory like the statues on Etruscan tombs. I detected a hint of sentimentality, as well as abundant natural grace, in the Hermes of Praxiteles. The ruins of the stadium and temples rather disappointed us. While the ground plan is extensive and doubtless of value to archaeologists, two columns in the temple of Hera alone remain standing. We could see the arch leading to the stadium, the starting line for the races, the shell of Nero's house and of a Byzantine church, some mighty pillars of the temple of Zeus felled by an earthquake, and a great many foundations; the rest had to be reconstructed in the mind. Among the ruins we met a number of tortoises and a Dutchman, with whom I had a long architectural argument after lunch. He and Meric bathed in the Alphaeus, which was shallow, swift and muddy. We talked with a couple of young Germans in the evening. The hotel boasted two water-closets, both emanating from England, bearing the names Niagara and Tornado. Niagara worked, but Tornado did not.

We rose at an unearthly hour and spent more than 17 hours travelling, though the distance covered was not great. I would have liked to see more of the country round Olympia, which was exceptionally green for Greece, but the heat forbade it. The train journey to Patras took six hours and was remarkable only for a violent row between me and an old woman through the lavatory door at Pyrgos. Fortunately each of us was incomprehensible to the other. At Patras we wasted several hours and ate a gigantic lunch, during which I was pestered by a man who wanted to clean my shoes and a cat that tried to eat the straps of my rucksack. Cleaning shoes and selling lottery tickets are (or were) prominent industries (and nuisances) in Greek towns. Our little steamer came in an hour late and departed an hour and a half later still. The voyage across the Gulf of Corinth to Itea, the port of Delphi, took another six hours. We did not arrive till after midnight, but were compensated by a wonderful sunset, in which the mountainous coasts of the gulf displayed a beauty beyond any dream, and by the antics of our fellow-travellers. Several of them, seeing my camera, clamoured to be photographed; they all asked us who we were, where we came from, where we were going, and why. There was great excitement when a scraggy hen, tied by the leg to other scraggy hens, laid a microscopic egg. We put in at Aegion and all but collided with another vessel, whose captain sprang out on deck gesticulating, clad only in pyjama trousers. Our greatest trial was the ship's siren, which made the most piercing and terrifying noise I ever heard before the days of jet aircraft, and one never knew when it was going to open up. The man so obviously enjoyed blowing it that he let it off indiscriminately; waiting for it was like standing under the blade of a guillotine. Reaching Itea at last, we betook ourselves to the Hotel Hermes and ravenously attacked hunks of so-called roast lamb as rebarbative as shoe leather.

The first thing we saw on the way to Delphi was a caravan of camels; what their business was we never discovered. Scenically Delphi was the most beautiful place we saw in Greece – and that is saying a lot. Lofty mountains on two sides, the rocky home of eagles; a deep valley falling away in front of which runs a river of olive-trees, leading to Itea and the Gulf at one end, to the mountains of the interior at the other; and the light constantly changing. We put up at the Pythian Apollo, easily the most comfortable hotel we had encountered; the signature before ours in the visitors' book, occupying a page to itself, was that of Dr Josef Goebbels. The stadium, almost complete, with judges' tribunal, both starting lines, most of the original stone seats, and a little arched grotto where once was a spring, was the most evocative thing we saw. There were countless other ruins of all dates from archaic to Hellenistic and Roman, the Treasury of the Athenians (cleverly restored, using old material), the gymnasium with a fine bath, and several temples, one of them, in the sanctuary of Athena, retaining three stufa columns; twelve more were destroyed by an unnecessary landslide in 1905. We drank reverently from the Castalian spring and penetrated a tunnel where we disturbed a nest of furious buzzing insects. The museum was being cleaned, and the exhibits lay around in desperate confusion. There was much to see, especially from the early period: the statues of Cleobis and Biton, a bronze charioteer, an incredible Sphinx-like object set up on a pillar by the Naxians, statuettes, pots and lamps in profusion, and an inscription with one of the few surviving specimens of ancient Greek music. I spent a long time on my back trying to make this out, a proceeding which so impressed the officials that they let me have a transcription at half price.

We were nearly stranded at Delphi. It took a great deal of firmness on our part, aided by the not inconsiderable weight of the manager of the Pythian Apollo, to obtain seats on an already crowded bus; only in Greece would it have been possible at all. The journey back to Athens was long and cramped, but afforded glorious views of Parnassus, a noble mountain. We stopped at Levadia, where we found grapes but no lavatory, and at Thebes, a dull and disagreeable town where we ate pomegranates. During our tour, including the week in Athens, I read almost the whole of *Morte d'Arthur*, a good deal of Boswell's *Life of Johnson*, *A Passage to India*, *The Testament of Beauty* and six cantos of *The Faerie Queen*. Meric, who was still reading Classics, set himself to read Edgar Wallace in Greek.

Our departure from Athens, after a final visit to the Acropolis and a touching invitation from the Dmitrovs to return, was a frantic scramble. We were running low on cash; I had left an Austrian 20 schilling note with the agents as a reserve, but found that they had changed it into drachmas on their own responsibility and refused to give me any other currency. Having now learned how to argue in Greece, I made a great scene. Had I not just got rid of all my drachmas? What possible use would they be in Italy? Did not my boat leave in less than an hour's time? I would be hanged before I would take drachmas, etc. Four British shillings and three lire centesimi were produced, illegally I was told; the rest I had to take in drachmas. But twenty precious minutes were lost. We rushed to the Peiraeus, where all was confusion. Where was the man who stamped the passport? Here, there; no, that man dealt with the money and you had to go to him afterwards, by which time a long queue would have assembled. We found the right man behind a tiny hole in the wall, and twenty people fighting for precedence. Forms must be filled in; they must have our fathers' names and could not spell them when we told them. The stamping of each passport took a good three minutes. The boat sailed in five minutes, and there were still numerous barriers through which we had to pilot ourselves and our luggage. We forgot we were Englishmen and gentlemen, and pushed, scrambled and shouted like the rest. I doubt if we would have caught the boat if it had left on time.

Life on the *Quirinale* was much as before, except that the weather was colder and the sea rougher, with a high wind. One night we passed through a cycle of storms, which flashed crimson lightning; next morning, by a curious phenomenon of light, a string of islands seemed to be floating in mid-air. My cabin companions were a bearded Swiss clergyman who read devotional books in paper covers and a nervy rabbit-faced Englishman named Reynolds who looked as if he belonged behind a grocery counter; his piety required a reading from the New Testament in the early hours of the morning. We lost him at Brindisi, but this did not facilitate conversation with the Swiss clergyman. However I had pleasant talks with a young German architect from Munich and a Turk studying ethics at London University. The one unusual event was the sudden and mysterious vaccination of Meric by the ship's doctor.

In Venice we purchased a stock of provisions for the train journey, including a two-litre bottle of chianti, which reduced our Italian funds to 1 lira 45 centesimi between us. We travelled by the Modane route with stops at Milan and Turin. After Greece Milan seemed a refreshingly clean city, and I admired the cathedral, especially the tracery of the three eastern windows: Gothic gone mad, as it might well in Italy, with a riotous profusion of detail. The interior, too high for its length, was atrociously lit – to conceal the fact (I was informed) that the lacework of the roof is nothing but wallpaper. Our carriage-companions for the night were two charming little Italian girls and their nurse, a considerable person who belched. Having revived ourselves with coffee at the Gare St Lazare, we found ourselves almost broke and could only buy for our lunch two ham sandwiches and one banana, which used up our last centime. We consumed these on the boat, though the French customs, who were looking for gold, were very loth to let the banana out of the country. At Newhaven, knowing the ropes, I was first through the customs. Just as I was stepping into the train an official seized me. What was that in the pocket of my raincoat, which I was carrying over my arm? A book. What book? (rubbing his hands together). I tried to extract it, but it stuck. The tip of his nose quivered. At last it emerged – the Poetical Works of Edmund Spenser.

CHAPTER 8

Saul

Family affairs became even more inflamed in the winter of 1936/37. On the day of my return to King's I went to Cumberland Terrace for the last time, and was confronted with an ultimatum: I must break off relations with either Mother or Vie, apologise to Eugene and confess that my breakdown was my own fault. Vie was 'a thorough liar, hypocrite and humbug', deliberately responsible for the break between Mother and me, and for poisoning relations between her and the Dean grandparents and even between her and Basil. I proposed that we should wipe out the past and never mention Vie, but that was clearly not enough. A fortnight later I received a most distressing letter from Mother, begging me for the sake of her health and happiness not to meet her any more. It was obvious that this cost her much agony and that she loathed the idea of a split which I feared might be final. I could only comply with her wish, while noting that Eugene stood to gain either way: if I submitted to his terms he would get his pound of flesh (and never let me forget it), if I refused he would be rid of me for good. I doubt if he seriously considered her feelings.

Early in December the battle was renewed, and both Gran and Basil were now deployed against me. I was to be banished from the traditional Christmas Day at Portland Place, Mother declaring that she, Eugene, Martin and Joe would not attend if I were there.

According to her, Gran 'knows that the family are in the right and you are in the wrong'. Gran did not say this, but she appealed to all that was noble and generous in my nature to save Mother from a breakdown by (i) writing to Eugene confessing that I had misjudged him, and (ii) admitting that Vie was wholly responsible for the break. Whether or not some compromise was possible on the first point, the second was simply not true and I refused to consider it. I felt the weight of Atlas on my shoulders, and in danger of alienating the sympathy of everyone.

I spent Christmas in Birkenhead with Gran's old friend and contemporary Dalziel McKay, a stalwart person whom I much admired. Her philosophy of life, which she called the psychology of human relationships and the religion of the future, made a strong appeal to me. She was very kind and sympathetic, but with the best of intentions reinforced Gran's appeal. I agreed to write to Eugene, registering good will if nothing else, and we concocted a draft letter. During this visit I explored all my old haunts, including the garden of Alcira, went to plays in Liverpool and enjoyed the company of my uncle Harry Van Gruisen and his family, who made me very welcome on Christmas Day. I consulted Squires, who advised me not to write to Eugene. He was a very cautious man, naturally anxious not to lose his *locus standi*, but he said he could not conceive how Eugene, after all that had happened subsequent to, if not consequent on, his entry into the family, did not make an offer to withdraw. He had told Mother that I would not have had my recent breakdown but for Eugene, though I might have had another. They took that to mean that I would have had a breakdown in any event.

Basil, who in October, in a very benign mood, had given me lunch at the Ivy and feasted me like an oriental potentate, and in November had taken me to *Boris Godunov* at Covent Garden, now abruptly changed his ground after a meeting with Mother. He refused to have me for Christmas because my differences with her were still unsettled: 'You have apparently expressed the strongest preference for the friendship of a married relation who is not persona grata with either side of your family'. A fortnight later he took strong exception to my consulting doctors. 'That a young man of twenty, normal and healthy with a career to make in life, should do so strikes me as quite fantastic ... Break away from excessive woman's influence, and discover where the ground lies and the microscopic importance of your own ego. You haven't done so yet, and you won't do work of any value, no matter what its nature until you do.' This was scarcely helpful, especially as he was going entirely on hearsay. In January I had Martin to lunch. He clearly hero-worshipped Eugene, and I could not keep him off the subject. The following day he wrote me a letter in the Bagger idiom. 'I am writing to say that I shall not be able to see you again until you have changed your attitude. Yesterday you told me a number of lies and I am not prepared to stand for it. [These were mostly statements about Vie, who sent him documents of proof and a solicitor's letter] ... I will have no more dealings with a liar. That is all I have to say. For God's sake don't be such a damned fool and admit that you are wrong.' This put the lid on my intention to write to Eugene. I tried to put the whole thing out of my head.

Meanwhile Cumberland Terrace had been sold, and at the end of January Mother and Eugene left for France, though they were not married for another two years. In the next dozen years, apart from the first Christmas of the War at Hambledon, I saw her only twice and him not at all. Most of my possessions were sent to me in packing-cases, but some of my books (including one or two school prizes), part of my stamp collection, my material on the German visit and a good deal else disappeared for ever. Haricot told me that Mother threw out a lot of stuff without looking at it, including the family museum. This contained, apart from odds and ends, some things of considerable interest, including copies of the single-page newspapers published during the 1926 General Strike and a collection of Victorian and Edwardian silver coins. Haricot, looking for a new job after 17 years, wrote me some touching letters. She was sorry for Mother at the parting ('had to run in quickly before I broke down'), but thought Martin was 'going potty' and was positively vitriolic about Eugene. She thought that Joe was equally under his influence, though Joe and I had just spent some pleasant days going round city churches.

My Dean grandmother died at the end of February at the age of 84. Basil took Martin down to the funeral as representative of our generation; this was reflected in a letter he sent me a fortnight later. 'I am told that, in addition to severing relations with both sides of your family you are repeating insulting remarks about my family which, for good or ill, is also your own! I have not been told what the remarks are, but that you can descend to such snobbery or caddishness, according to the nature of the remarks, passes my comprehension. It is at least some indication of the sort of influence to which you have submitted yourself. The fact that your maternal grandmother apparently condones your attitude towards your mother in no way excuses it.' He therefore felt unable to celebrate my 21st birthday. I replied that I had not severed relations with anybody. Two days later Mother took a similar line, in a tone of disapproval rather than rebuke, refusing to see me when she returned to England in May because of what I said about Martin's 'facts'.

It is scarcely surprising that the intermittent crises and unending stress did my health no good. The removal of my appendix seemed to make little difference to the chronic gastric disturbances, vomiting and diarrhoea alternating with constipation. The brainstorms of the previous winter – a terrifying condition of blind panic – recurred at intervals, though with rather less frequency, and I became a more or less permanent victim of insomnia. For a time I felt that my mind was permanently impaired. All the symptoms of course were closely connected. Although I eventually outgrew the brainstorms, my digestive system has been the cause of endless trouble ever since, going out of order at the slightest provocation, and I have scarcely ever been able to sleep through a night without the assistance of some drug.

There were compensations, however. Many friends of my mother's generation, notably the Muirheads and Philip and Lorna Rea, went out of their way to show me kindness and hospitality. So did my aunt Nelly Dunbar-Smith (who hoped that I would not go on the stage) and the Hugh de Selincourts, parents-in-law of Vie's son Michael Balkwill, though I was not able to take advantage of their invitations. I had many good friends at Cambridge. Here the most significant development was my growing interest in music, sedulously fostered by Philip. I went to more and more concerts, and began to exercise my critical faculties instead of using music as an emotional drug. At this time I ranked Haydn as second only to Beethoven and was surprised at the neglect of his piano sonatas. I proposed to protest to the BBC about the habit of performers in 18th century music of ending every period with a rallentando and omitting repeats. Clifford Curzon's use of the pedal particularly impressed me; I travelled from Cambridge for a number of London recitals given by him and Lucille, and always received a warm welcome when we met. Myra Hess, 'a tremendous Semitic woman with a face like the full moon', clad in 'a sort of purple table-cloth', greatly moved me in Beethoven (Op. 109), but her way of pounding the piano with immense violence seemed ill-suited to Haydn and Schubert. I heard a very early performance of Alban Berg's violin concerto at the Queen's Hall (December 1936), and found it a rewarding experience; the intellectual effort in trying to grasp it somehow cleared my mind.

I saw Dent frequently and more than once invited him to my rooms, where he discoursed at fascinating length about opera. He gave a public lecture on Tudor music, imparting much information and not eschewing a dig at the Church. He quoted a bishop to the effect that, whereas the Huguenots sang psalms in the fields, the Catholics either remained silent or sang songs of notable obscenity. Trend was beginning to concern himself with the rescue of scholars and composers from Franco's Spain, some of whom settled in England as refugees. Among them was Roberto Gerhard, with whom I had many interesting talks in the next few years. Kenneth Harrison was always good value in a discussion; he affected to be suspicious of any music that was not Bach or a fugue, and would talk treason about Beethoven, who was then my god. The Pro Arte Quartet gave another series of recitals. The F minor quartet (Op. 95) affected me like strong drink, and I could not be restrained from chasing cats and knocking down bicycles. After op. 135 I was too moved to speak, then suddenly overflowed with sensations of love and benevolence for the whole world.

In November the Dresden Opera played for a week at Covent Garden, including a single performance of *Ariadne auf Naxos* conducted by the composer. Boris, who had studied in Dresden and knew many of the orchestral players, organised a party from King's, including Dadie and A.F. Scholfield, the University Librarian, a man with beetling brows and biting wit and a brilliant raconteur, who invited Philip and me to dine with him beforehand at the Athenaeum. We duly presented ourselves, to find no Scholfield but a club full of obvious generals and colonels. It slowly dawned on us that we were in the wrong building. We hastily put this right, and encountered Scholfield dining in grim and solitary state; fortunately the brows soon relaxed. I found the opera charming, apart from the Wagnerian duet at the end, though perhaps not a great masterpiece, but was surprised by Strauss's detached method of conducting, at the opposite extreme from that of Beecham or Furtwängler. He sat calmly in a chair, beating time with no show of emotion, but obtained a thoroughly committed performance. The orchestral playing was superior to the singing and the production, which I thought rather tawdry. Erna Sack as Zerbinetta climbed to B flat in alt, but made us all feel uncomfortable. The tenor looked like a prize-fighter, not perhaps unsuitably for Bacchus. Afterwards we went to the Café Royal and drank beer with Strohbach, the producer, and other members of the Dresden company.

There was a happy sequel two days later, when at Boris's invitation the orchestra's leading string players gave a concert in King's, including Schubert's C major quintet and Brahms's sextet in B flat. Afterwards Boris gave a party at which spontaneous music-making continued into the small hours. Philip, who knew the piano part of most of the Beethoven and Brahms violin sonatas by heart, played the opening bars of several of them, and Roth, the orchestra's leader, joined in. This continued until the memory of one or the other failed; Philip's generally outlasted Roth's. The proceedings closed with the first movement of Beethoven's violin concerto, Boris playing the orchestral part on the piano from a full score. I had a long and friendly talk with Kratina, the cellist, more about politics than music.

About this time my interest in opera quickened appreciably. Shortly after *Ariadne* I saw *Boris Godunov* at Covent Garden, conducted by Albert Coates, and was struck by the immense difference in impact between a stage and a radio performance. The exact appropriateness of each musical phrase to the dramatic action, the pull between lyricism and realism and between voices and orchestra took on a new significance. Apart from Harold Williams (Boris) and the chorus, I was critical of the performance: 'the tenor rasped like a saw and the Marina yelled like a kitchen-maid'. The critic of *The Times* roused my particular indignation by calling the music of the third act dull. I went with Basil, whose hat was misappropriated in the cloakroom; his reflections on this were voluble and unprintable, and lasted all the way back to his flat in Lowndes Square. In January I went in succession to *Figaro* at Sadler's Wells (which in many respects I preferred to the Salzburg production on account of the company's team spirit), and *Manon Lescaut, Gianni Schicchi, Salome* and *Un ballo in maschera* at Covent Garden, generally sitting in the gallery. I admired Constant Lambert's conducting in *Manon Lescaut* and enjoyed both halves of the Puccini-Strauss double bill, though Hildegarde Ranczak, the Salome, wore a dress that made her look twice her size (which so far as I remember was not inconsiderable in the first place). I was again vituperative about 'such utter rubbish as the *Times* dished up for a review in the morning', attributing it to Frank Howes. The music of *Ballo* thrilled me, but I thought the conductor (Salfi) commonplace, the costumes foul and the production not much better. In those days the producer was often not named in Covent Garden programmes, and I was almost invariably critical of the visual aspects of opera, to which little attention seemed to be paid; the modern reaction in the opposite direction had a good deal to be said for it initially, until it got disastrously out of hand. Of the singers in *Ballo* I admired Borgioli (Riccardo) and Constance Willis (Ulrica), but thought Brownlee a dull Renato and Eva Turner a rasping Amelia.

My decision to leave Classics for Part I of the English Tripos gave me no cause for regret. I got on very well with Peter Lucas, who repeatedly expressed delight at the content and style of my weekly essays. Two in particular pleased him, on Milton and Malory; he said the second made him want to read the whole *Morte d'Arthur* again. When we disagreed, as on Pope and Johnson's view of Gray, a stimulating argument developed. Needless to say, I greatly enjoyed writing for such an appreciative reader. In November I was awarded second prize (a small sum of money) in a College essay competition, founded in 1786 by Dr Thomas James, a former Fellow and Headmaster of Rugby. We were given a choice of half a dozen subjects. One I remember was Dr Johnson's pronouncement 'Why, sir, public affairs vex no man'. Another was 'Decadence', my choice. I identified the decadent with the neurotic, the man who clings to outworn modes; the idea seemed to me interesting and provocative, if perhaps unsound. I lent the manuscript to Gran, who passed it on to Mother. When I asked for its return I was told that it had been posted back to me, but it never arrived. Vie was convinced that Eugene destroyed it. In March, on Peter Lucas's recommendation, the College gave me the Rupert Brooke Studentship, offered to the best student reading for the English or History Tripos. It amounted to £20 to be spent on foreign travel, and helped to pay for my second visit to Salzburg.

There was one unhappy event. My comic verses about Jana Clapham and John Saltmarsh had gone the round of the College, and I had been persuaded to give them to the *Basileon*. The Clapham family had been as amused by them as everyone else. I now discovered that the publication had given great offence to Mrs Clapham, who had told Jana to ask me to withdraw them. Mrs Clapham's reaction was understandable, but Jana had never passed on the message. I wrote at once to apologise, but Mrs Clapham never forgave me; I was never again invited to Storey's End, though Clapham and his daughters showed no hostility to me, and Saltmarsh went out of his way to be friendly.

The Frogs had been so successful in Cambridge that a special matinée, largely for schools, was arranged at the Chiswick Empire Theatre at the end of November. The whole cast travelled up in a special carriage, rehearsed as chaotically as usual in the morning, and had lunch at the Town Hall. The performance began with a characteristic speech from Sheppard, and the first two acts went well, especially the second; but the third was a disaster. At the rehearsal Boris, whose temper was always liable to be uncertain, had had a row with Christopher Gandy (Euripides) about the tempo of his first parody. There were faults on both sides; but instead of making some accommodation Boris markedly quickened the tempo and soon had Christopher floundering two or three bars behind the orchestra. He became flustered and forgot his words; Sheppard shouted something from his box; and from that point everything went wrong. Several of the cast confused their lines and jumped whole passages. Once Boris failed to bring the orchestra in on cue, Sheppard shouted 'Get on with it!' and Boris answered back. What should have been a happy occasion ended in horrible anti-climax. Sheppard regained his good humour next day, after sending a grovelling apology to Boris, and told me that my costume turned me into an apotheosis of the bedmaker. The programme advertised my translation, but spoiled the effect by spelling my name wrong.

* * * * *

Since January 1936, having no home, I had stayed during the vacations sometimes with the grandparents at 82 Portland Place, where I slept on a camp bed in Tommy's study, sometimes with Basil, and sometimes with friends. For the Christmas vacation Vie arranged for me first to lodge with her friends Christopher and Penelope Wheeler in Mecklenburgh Square and then to occupy a small house, temporarily vacant, in Marsham Street, where I inherited a genial but very talkative house-keeper. In addition to Birkenhead I paid visits to the Dobsons at Bristol and the McBurneys at Brockenhurst; Charles McBurney, another King's contemporary, became a distinguished archaeologist, and we renewed our friendship many years later when we were both Fellows of the British Academy. The Wheelers, a cultured elderly couple, were very kind to me and made me feel 'that there is some point in my existence on earth'. Theirs was 'the sort of house where you pick up absorbingly interesting books in casual places. I found T.S. Eliot on the stairs and Keats in the bathroom'. Christopher, a retired doctor, had collaborated with Vie in a most interesting play about a doctor who killed his best friend's lovely but selfish wife because she obstructed her husband's work for humanity. This had a single Sunday night performance at the Royalty Theatre on 13 December under the not very happy title *Death Asks a Verdict* by 'Christopher Vye'. Nicholas Hannen and Coral Brown played the leading parts. The play, which I thought a little too subtle for most of the audience, was rather in the tradition of Granville Barker. I was enormously impressed by the ideas and the dialogue, but felt that there was something not quite right about the end. Unfortunately no theatre could be found to give it a run.

Two days later I saw Granville Barker's *Waste*, with Hannen again in the lead and a superb cast including Felix Aylmer, Gibb McLaughlin, Harcourt Williams and Cecil Trouncer. This moved me in much the same way but even more, and inspired an ambition to write plays with serious ideas and true complex characters. My dramatic fare this month was nothing if not varied. Hilary was having a prolonged row with her parents about a new boyfriend of whom they disapproved. To give her some relief she and I went to the Windmill Theatre with Rupert Bailey, a friend of her family who by coincidence had been a contemporary of mine at Elstree. He was a decidedly prim young man (he described Hilary as 'a decorative girl on a dance floor'); on catching sight of the nudes he blushed to the roots of his hair. I enjoyed the Dorothy Sayers play *Busman's Honeymoon*, with Dennis Arundell as a surprising but not unsuccessful choice for Lord Peter but a Bunter who could never have been an army batman and seemed to me totally miscast.

This was the month of the abdication crisis. I was very critical of Edward VIII, 'a second-rate man' who should have thrown Mrs Simpson over or refused the throne in January. I missed his notorious broadcast, which coincided with a party I was giving at the house of two of Vie's friends. It was a very successful party, after which six or seven of us went to a film and a restaurant, where we drank coffee and burnt an effigy of Boris constructed from cigarettes. We went out into Piccadilly Circus, and John Davison had just launched into a pompous speech about the constitutional crisis, when Boris appeared in person. He must have been astonished by our speechlessness and open mouths.

There were many other parties, including a particularly enjoyable one at the home of Hugh Miller, the actor who produced Vie's play. His wife Olga, who wrote political epigrams for *The New Statesman* under the name Sagittarius, made a great impression on me with her rare compound of wit and charm. Many interesting people were there, including the John Drinkwaters and Dorothy Sayers. The latter, in a great flurry over her recent first night, amazed me: 'she looks like a cross between a boy scout and an inspector of schools, dresses entirely male in black and white, with hair brushed straight back, wears pince-nez and seems not so much to have grown fat as to have consolidated the space in her immediate vicinity'. I liked Drinkwater, who reminded me of a Canadian farmer rather than a poet, but took a violent dislike to his wife, the red-haired violinist Daisy Kennedy: 'noisy, ignorant, haughty and assertive: a combination of qualities which I so much loathe that I had to refrain from speaking to her for fear of being downright rude'.

At the end of the month I was an usher at the wedding of Vie's younger son John Balkwill to Barbara Davison. There had been a preliminary party two months before at which I first met John Davison, Barbara's brother, and also Adrian Boult, whose friendly manner completely disarmed my shyness. I argued with him about Bruckner, whose music then seemed to me useful only as a soporific, and doubtless talked nonsense. Frank Howes, then second music critic on *The Times*, played the organ at the wedding and perpetrated a wrong note in Mendelssohn's Wedding March at every appearance of the tune – much to my glee, for I was seething with indignation at his rather supercilious opera notices. At the reception I had a much longer talk with Boult, who treated my opinions with more consideration than they probably deserved. This was typical of him, as I discovered from later acquaintance. He never pulled rank on the young and ignorant; later, after my book on Bizet was published, he astonished me by his humility. The reception closed with two memorable incidents. One of the bridal suitcases burst when being carried to their car and distributed a fine selection of pyjamas and underwear over the pavement. An ill-directed barrage of rice, preferred to confetti as making less mess, hit several people in the eye and made a strange pattering noise behind me; I looked round and saw the grains bouncing on Adrian Boult's bald head, the loftiest object in view.

I had been writing poems feverishly since the summer, including several of some length, and made a determined effort to get them into print, sending different specimens to *The Observer*, *The London Mercury* and T.S. Eliot. Christopher Wheeler and Vie, who thought highly of some of them, put me in touch with Mrs Harold Monro, editor of several anthologies, and Richard Church, reader for J.M. Dent. None of this produced any tangible result, and I lost heart – much too easily. Every rejection slip seemed a slap in the face. In fact the comments of the last two were less discouraging than I thought at the time. Mrs Monro wrote to Christopher Wheeler: 'I feel that their author quite certainly has the stuff of a poet within him, but I'm not sure that he really gets it into these that I have read'. She found a want of 'direct communication between the mind, the hand and the pen', and thought my 'natural expression constricted by some kind of self-consciousness that forces him to use words and phrases that do not actually convey what is in his mind'. Church also mentioned self-consciousness and images too sought after. In one of the longer poems (*Crusade*) he saw clever, reasoned sophistication, the working of a civilised mind in its natural state; one passage came near to a fusion of image, phrase, rhythm and meaning, 'but then the <u>argument</u> is resumed'. In one or two of the shorter poems (he and Mrs Monro differed in those they thought best) he found progress towards mastery of 'that most difficult of all things – the poetic paragraph'. 'I think you have many gifts; perhaps too many.' But he ended by suggesting that I might not have suffered enough; this – illogically perhaps – led me to devalue his judgment.

Pigou urged me to enter for the Chancellor's Medal, but I found it difficult to write to order on a set subject. I added some lines to an earlier poem about Memory, trying to make it look as if they were about the Thames, but found the result unsatisfactory and felt rather as if I had forged a cheque. Needless to say, I did not win the medal. In addition to writing verse I tried to satisfy the creative urge, which took the form of intense excitement for hours on end, by composing music at the piano, though aware that with my lack of the requisite training it was unlikely to have any value.

The Spenser Society held a number of meetings, readings and debates, in which Derek Clifford and John Manifold took a prominent part. John was 'Australian in blood and in personality' and something of a boaster; he produced an axe with which he claimed to have killed a Nazi in Munich. He wrote vigorous and rather formal verse, abjuring emotion as an irrelevance. Surprisingly he also played and wrote about the recorder. He liked eighteenth-century music, especially Mozart, and maintained that Beethoven must have been mentally ill as well as physically deaf to have written such things as the late B flat and A minor quartets. I found his personality strange but refreshing, at one point considering him the most healthily stimulating man I knew, at another the vainest and most selfish. I was not altogether surprised when he announced his intention of renouncing poetry in favour of the more important claims of Australian nationalism. Derek was more sympathetic, and I was convinced that he had genuine poetic gifts. Indeed each of us felt this about the other. He puzzled me by saying that my verse reminded him of Browning, a poet I had scarcely read. We made a plan to publish a joint volume, but this too fell by the wayside. He later published a collection of poems on his own, as well as at least one novel and books on such varied subjects as pelargoniums, a history of garden design and, with his son Timothy, the Norwich school of painters.

Humbert Wolfe, Drinkwater and others came to address the Spenser Society. I had dinner with Drinkwater, but found him stodgier than before and was not over-impressed by the poems of his own that he read. A plan to discuss the Sutro letters – he had corresponded at some length with Alfred – was overtaken by his sudden death only a week or two later. Wolfe got in some stinging blows at the Leavises and Gertrude Stein, and declared (very questionably) that all poetry was a compound of distance, solitude and song.

The great event of the spring term was the production of Handel's *Saul* by the University Music Faculty in the Guildhall, produced by Camille Prior and conducted by Boris. Like all C.U.M.S. enterprises it was largely the work of students and amateurs with some professional stiffening, chiefly in the solo parts. Any weakness or lack of expertise was more than compensated by immense enthusiasm. The staging of Handel's oratorios had become something of a Cambridge tradition, launched by Cyril Rootham and greatly encouraged by Dent; it began with *Semele* in 1925, followed by *Samson* and *Jephtha* as well as *The Choice of Hercules* and *Susanna*. The idiosyncrasies of the wide curtainless Guildhall stage necessitated a permanent set built up on several levels, the different locations of the action picked out by lighting. The chorus was divided between a large contingent of about 100 seated at low level on either side of the orchestra and a smaller but quite substantial body on stage, reinforced by supers and dancers for the spectacular wedding, feast and battle scenes. The choral contribution could thus be varied, semichoruses being sung by the stage group alone, weighty pronouncements such as 'Envy, eldest-born of hell' by the seated chorus (this was immensely effective, with two dancers miming on a darkened stage), and the massive finales by the full body. This ensured that the chorus emerged in its true role as the protagonist of the drama while also carrying the weight of commentary in the manner of Greek tragedy. It made total nonsense of the criticism, voiced by people who have never seen one of these productions, that Handel's big contrapuntal choruses are antipathetic to stage performance.

The principal parts were sung by David Franklin (Saul), Hubert Langley (Jonathan) – with whom I struck up a firm friendship – Peter Evans (David), Mabel (later Margaret) Ritchie (Michal) and Ena Mitchell (Merab). Franklin, just beginning his professional career as an operatic bass, sang well and looked magnificent, but was inclined to be surly; at rehearsals this produced some lively backchat with Boris, a fine conductor but something of a martinet. I had two parts, the first during the Minuet of the overture, when I appeared as Jesse with a long grey beard, shepherd's crook and a large brood of children, including eight sons, from whom Samuel selected David; the second as an anonymous elder of Israel. I was given various bits of business in the crowd scenes and picked up the music by ear, joining lustily in the choruses, generally as a bass but occasionally as a tenor when the pitch seemed more convenient. At the dress rehearsal – when Boris was heard to address the sopranos in his earthy voice as 'imprudent women' (David's words in the libretto) – I caught Dent out in a musical question, whereupon he offered to appear as one of my sons.

The performances were immensely impressive, musically and dramatically. Gwen Raverat designed some spectacular costumes, and Mrs Prior surpassed herself, devising some brilliant business for the five C major symphonies that represent the outer events of the story and frame the action. These and the overture, apart from its initial Allegro, were mimed. The second Allegro, shifted to follow the Minuet, served to depict David's fight with Goliath, played by the tallest man in the University, built up to a height of more than eight feet by special boots and a lofty plumed helmet. This made a superb introduction to the Epinicion with its apocalyptic entry of three trombones, their first appearance in Handel's music. The carillon symphony was a dance for 'the daughters of the land'. At the wedding Donald Beves as the High Priest of Israel, clad in a bejewelled purple blanket and a tall black hat, officiated in a manner that irresistibly recalled the operations of Milner in Chapel, including what was taken for a little homily on fornication. He was likewise in charge at the feast, distributing a lavish supply of genuine and property fruit. The armies were made up of large men from the King's boat club, commanded by Patrick Wilkinson in a black beard and a burnished coal-scuttle helmet. The battle, though short, was nothing if not realistic. After this the Dead March, the two coffins followed by a long procession winding across the upper stage down a flight of steps to the footlights, was extraordinarily moving – so much so that a catch in the throat prevented me singing at the start of the finale. Another great moment was the rising of the Ghost of Samuel, lit from behind by an eerie green light and sung by a local bank manager with a sepulchral voice.

Saul

There was a rich crop of amusing incidents, many of them associated with Franklin, who was somewhat deficient in humour. In an interval of one of the rehearsals, when I recognised something he was singing as 'Eri tu' in *Un ballo in maschera*, he gave me a peculiar look as if indicating that no mere undergraduate ought to know such a thing. Saul is twice required to throw his javelin in a furious rage, first at David, then at Jonathan, with the stage packed with chorus and supers. A special space was cleared for him in front of one of the side entrances, but Franklin was no marksman and the chorus lived in fear of their lives. Several spare javelins were prepared; he needed them all. After nearly impaling one of the sopranos through the ear, he decided to aim high and struck a spotlight, setting it audibly rocking and shattering the javelin. At another performance he judged his throw perfectly, but the javelin, after passing through the exit and down a short flight of stairs, hit a wall on the half-volley and shot back on the stage in half, landing at Saul's feet. The look that Franklin gave made this even funnier. When bouquets were distributed after the last performance an attendant presented him with a set of darts. On the first night there was a titter when the lights went up on Saul in his tent, shortly before David's harp solo. Franklin glared round and gingerly felt his costume, unaware that a large pair of scissors had been left under his throne.

There were parties every night after the show, and sometimes before it as well. At one of these, between the matinée and the last performance on Saturday, members of the boat club, who had notoriously weak heads, refreshed themselves too liberally; there were hiccups at the feast, and the battle left the stage littered with unplanned casualties, withdrawn only with difficulty. The final performance had a sensational start: the trombones' first C major chord blew down the framework of a door behind one of the exits. It fell in a cloud of splinters and dust, weakened perhaps by Saul's javelin. During the feast symphony the one surviving non-property orange, sniffed suspiciously and rejected up stage by the captain of the guard, passed down the ranks of the army to the footlights and was tossed into the orchestra; only a feat of goalkeeping by the percussionist prevented an unauthorised entry of the timps. Among the cascades of flowers and fruit during the curtain-calls was a very prickly pine-apple for Boris.

The production had an excellent press, with enthusiastic and perceptive notices from Jack Westrup in *The Daily Telegraph* and Francis Toye in *The Morning Post*, though Frank Howes in a *Times* Friday article could not resist lecturing Dent for poking fun at the Victorian tradition of oratorio performance. In this connection it was very appropriate that Bernard Shaw was among the audience. What most astonished me, and many others, was the overwhelming dramatic power of the music and its unfailing aptness to character and incident. I knew nothing then of Handel's career as an opera composer, and was puzzled to account for the impact. It was this production of *Saul*, followed by that of *Solomon* under the same auspices after the war, that impelled me to seek an answer and to devote ten years of my life to the study of Handel's oratorios.

CHAPTER 9

Clare

During this winter I saw more and more of Clare Mallory. I had first set eyes on her at a performance of *Love's Labour's Lost* by the first year at Girton, in which she played Rosaline, looked delightful, but babbled so much that many of her words were inaudible. She was a brilliant girl, in personality and intelligence; despite recurring emotional crises she obtained a double first in History. She was vivacious, impulsive, nervy, and appeared to lead a somewhat scatterbrained existence, for ever taking up new causes and chasing hares of every kind. Her reforming spirit and pursuit of unattainable ideals was subject to periodical disappointment when they inevitably collapsed. This extended to her personal relationships. Her vitality made her immensely attractive; but it disconcerted her to find that her most trusted male friends, whose support she craved, spoiled everything by falling in love with her after she had unwittingly led them on. Among those most smitten was my close friend David Hubback. Clare was very fond of him but not in love; their constant proximity (they were both reading History and shared the same circle of friends) irked them both in different ways. All her friends were concerned about this and anxious to bring some steadying influence into her life.

Clare and I had a great deal in common, intellectually and temperamentally, including an absorbing interest in all the arts. She was very musical, played more than one instrument, was fascinated by old churches, and at one time (I think later) took up sculpture. Her energies were even more widely dispersed than mine; I could not share her enthusiasm for climbing and left-wing politics. We both swung between over-confidence and intense self-criticism, and indulged in too much theorising and self-analysis. We seemed to be on the same wave-length, and she came to confide in me more and more. In the week of *Saul* I suddenly realised that I was beginning to fall in love with her. I told her at once, and she begged me to stop it: the last thing she wanted was to lose my friendship. It was the same old story, sex threatening to spoil a very happy relationship. We talked it over, and although the furniture of my mind seemed to be upside down and standing on the walls the situation was saved – for the moment. She was surprised and delighted that I did not demand everything of her; I rejoiced in her implicit trust and the obvious relief she found in talking to me. I felt as firm as a rock – no less a rock if the seas occasionally broke over it.

After a Schnabel concert in the Guildhall Clare missed the last bus to Girton, and I escorted her back in a taxi, trying to calm her flustered nerves. Schnabel played a mammoth programme of five Beethoven sonatas, including the last two; I thought his approach over-intellectual and rather pedantic. Dent in the interval compared him unfavourably with Busoni, and told me that Schnabel greatly objected to playing in the Guildhall 'between the emergency exit and the ladies' lavatory'. When informed that Cortot, Fischer and Petri had not complained, he had grown pompous and scornful; whereupon Dent teased him for adhering to the German habit of glorifying the virtuoso at the expense of the music. Schnabel burst into a loud harangue in defence of 'Die Kunst', and Dent narrowly refrained from telling him he was talking rubbish.

Soon after this Dent invited me to lunch, charmed me with his talk on opera, especially Verdi, with a characteristic digression at one point about Italian prostitutes, and flattered me by welcoming Philip's suggestion that I should do a new translation of the *Carmen* libretto. Philip and I had exhaustive musical discussions after the many concerts we attended, and began a habit, which was to continue for decades, of running through at the piano the scores of works we were about to hear, especially operas. Since he was no great pianist and neither of us could sing, this was strictly a private exercise, but I found it most instructive. At a concert by the Léner Quartet on a bitterly cold evening I perspired so much during Beethoven's A minor that Philip said it made him quite warm. I went repeatedly to London to hear recitals by Clifford and Lucille. They gave a joint historical concert at the Wigmore Hall on five keyboard instruments ranging from virginals to a concert grand. When I went round afterwards they broke free from a crowd of worshipping dowagers and welcomed me with open arms.

A new acquaintance at this time was Mrs Gordon, the elderly widow of an Anglo-Indian colonel, who lived at the Malting House by the river and was said to have the best cuisine and the finest collection of gramophone records in Cambridge. She entertained many visiting artists, and gave dinner parties at which musical undergraduates could meet and talk to them. I often enjoyed her hospitality. Among the many interesting people I met there were Boyd Neel and Gerald Moore, whom I had admired since first hearing him at Harrow.

Another of my interests at this time was Ibsen. I was immensely impressed by a stage production of *Ghosts* and a reading of *The Wild Duck* at the Ten Club, but could never quite reconcile myself to Ibsen's technique, in particular the flatness of the dialogue and his habit of beginning his plots in the middle, or even towards the end, and working backwards and forwards at the same time. The emotional climate of *Ghosts* struck me as bearing an uncanny resemblance to that of my family, with the late Mrs Alving a combination of Basil and Vernon. The Ten also read *The Voysey Inheritance* and *Outward Bound*, 'a sugary play' which had thrilled me at the age of sixteen. At the end of term, the Marlowe Society put on *The Revenger's Tragedy*, said to be its first production since 1607. The performance, in which Vindice was played by Bobby Holmes, a good actor who as Cecil Holmes had contributed to *Thirty-One Poems* and was later to be a B.B.C. announcer, and Lussurioso by Noel Annan, veered abruptly between horror and farce, redeemed at intervals by the poetry. I was so moved by Tess Mayor's Castiza that I composed a little piece of music for her.

Gran and Tommy gave me a splendid party for my birthday, which quite made up for the coolness of both my parents. Although not all the friends I invited could come, twenty-four of us, from three generations, dined at the Berkeley, after which we danced till 2 a.m. I had put Hilary and Derek next to one another, to see what happened, and was much amused by the result. After dancing intimately for some time they left together in a taxi; Derek's comment was 'My God! What a sex-machine! She nearly raped me'. My Philistine uncle Harry Van Gruisen, rather out of his depth for much of the evening, suddenly blossomed when a cabaret came on with a song called Nellie the Nudist Queen and a comedian sang a song, 'Twenty years a chambermaid in a house of ill-repute', to the tune of the Lincolnshire Poacher. I was showered with presents, including two volumes of Tovey's *Essays in Musical Analysis* with a flattering inscription from Clifford and Lucille.

The vacation provided a happy interlude, though distant rumbles in the form of letters inspired a sense of physical disgust with my family and a desire never to see some of them again. A week with

Pigou in the Lakes, with Peter Joseph a most congenial companion, was chiefly remarkable for the bitterly cold weather, sleet and snow. I earned credit for running to the village and back before breakfast; one of the party surpassed this by bathing in the lake. Pigou and I were both taken ill, he with a slight heart attack, I with a gastric chill. We both grew beards; his was a remarkable compound of white and red, enhanced by his appearance in a 'Peloponnesian dressing-gown'. We played the qualities game and gave him the name and address Sir Thomas Gadshackleton, Bart, The Great Gables, Much Fetlock, Fruits. A week-end with Vie and her mother at Worthing followed, and a visit to the Mayor family at Steyning. Of all my friends Tess (later Lady Rothschild) seemed to get most enjoyment out of life, and her high spirits were infectious. Like me, she was always being asked how old she was. Our relationship was exceptionally happy – all the more so because, though she was very attractive and broke many hearts, I was never in danger of falling in love with her.

A week's walking-tour in the Berkshire Downs and upper Thames valley with John Davison was a great success, both for the churches we saw and for the amusing characters and adventures we encountered. We began at Lambourn and ended at Cricklade, staying in pubs and lunching generally off cheese and biscuits and pints of beer. At one remote village there was no pub; we consumed tinned veal and tongue and a quart of Cydrax ('a vapid and gaseous liquor not to be recommended') in the shadow of a vivid red telephone booth, which seemed to be the only post-1850 edifice in the place, and intoxicated a quantity of hens by giving them the remains of the meat dipped in the remains of the Cydrax. At Letcombe Regis a dear old woman in a woollen cap gave us tea and chattered away with great animation about her old aunts and uncles who lived to the age of 90 and her experiences at a tea party in a Norwegian church; her favourite expressions were 'class people' and 'I *never*! I *never*!!' – a register of extreme surprise. At Childrey we conversed with a shaggy-bearded old man who had worked in the Liverpool and Birkenhead docks and smoked the filthiest imaginable tobacco. John exchanged ecclesiastical scandal with a churchwarden. We were received by an antediluvian little vicar at Inglesham, and treated to a thrilling display of bell-ringing at Fairford; at Kempsford, while endeavouring to take a photograph, I fell off a wall into the vicarage garden. We walked many miles each day, glorying in the beauty of the countryside; once we were given a lift over a dull stretch by a cheery Welshman.

At Uffington, where we arrived very wet after a shower of rain, there was no room in the inn, the landlord having just died (his wife and daughter were very apologetic about this), so we put up at the post office. We were received very hospitably – though John caused a sensation by coming down to supper in apricot pyjamas, having no dry trousers – but had to share a bed, an ungainly piece of furniture, high at the sides with a deep depression in the middle. We kept rolling into this and waking each other up. However there was compensation in the shape of a very pretty girl who called us in the morning. Two days later we had to negotiate a winding muddy stream, just too wide to jump, which turned out to be the infant Thames. We were punished for our lèse-majesté in assaulting it. I got across with the help of a log; John, having immersed his leg to the depth of several inches, began to jettison his property, throwing across first his camera, then his rucksack. This landed on the bank but bounced back into the water and began to drift away. When it was retrieved, we found that the only things to suffer were my pyjamas, which John had been carrying under protest all morning after the maid at Fairford had packed them in the wrong rucksack.

No less enjoyable was a week at the Hubbacks' cottage in Cornwall, with David, his sister Rachel, Charles Rycroft and two of the Simon family, Brian and John. This was a reading party; we were there to work, and it was astonishing how much, in the intervals of church expeditions, horseplay and other hilarious activities, we managed to achieve. I was reading voraciously, not only for the Tripos but for the Charles Oldham Shakespeare Scholarship which I proposed to attempt in the summer, studying all the plays in preparation. At the same time I was deep in Chaucer, Langland, Henryson, and the essays of Dryden, Addison and Johnson. I enjoyed them all except Addison, in whom I found something bloodless: 'He gives you bowdlerised Dryden in a gilt binding, like Cydrax in a wine glass'. The weather produced a succession of storms and wonderful sunsets. In investigating a pool sparkling with sea anemones I slid a considerable distance over slippery rocks on my bottom, so that my trousers became a laughing stock. Everything we did turned to laughter, including the church expeditions (which produced much aesthetic pleasure as well); on one of them David drove the car into a very wet bog. We found a memorial to the Reverend Vicesimus Lush (was he really the twentieth child?) and a bishop of Exeter called Offspring Blackball. The agents through whom the cottage was to be let in the summer were Messrs Button, Menhesnit and Mutton. Eyloshayle church had a monument to a lady with the happy legend: 'To deliver to posterity a description of the beauty of her mind would be equally vain as the sculptor's attempt in the above resemblance of her face. The one was superior to art, the other to imagination'. Brian addressed a letter to Tess absent-mindedly giving the county as 'Simon', whereupon we decided that 'Sussex' was a contraction of 'Simon-sex'. He also declared blandly at breakfast: 'It's appalling the way David comes into my room at 8 and says I'm awake when I'm not'.

April 16th I described as a Herculean day. Brian and I rose at 5.15 a.m. and set out for London in his small car, stopping at Glastonbury, Wells, Bath and Bradford-on-Avon on the way. Each of these places we explored in detail and with high appreciation.

There was a dinner party at the grandparents' flat in Portland Place, after which I set out for Philip Tallack's 21st birthday party at Sunbridge Park near Bromley. The dancing lasted into the small hours, and I got to bed, feeling remarkably fresh, at 4.15 a.m. Next came a relaxed week-end with the Jefferys at Hambledon. Bert and I went on a pub crawl in Guildford and had a long conversation with a girl from the Salvation Army. Gran and I went with Harry V.G. to see Shaw's *Candida* – an amusing evening that ended with a lively critical discussion (which I recorded at length in my diary). Harry's reaction was characteristic: 'I can't understand why you keep criticising. I've had a jolly good evening'. On the last day of the vacation I had a delightful lunch with the Curzons and tea with Stella, who gave me much wise advice, speaking of the importance of self-discipline in Rufus's life and inspiring me with an ambition to emulate his example.

* * * * *

During the May term Philip and I paid some rewarding visits to London: *Hugh the Drover* at Sadler's Wells ('a pleasing and comfortable work, typically English and typically Vaughan Williams, rising to no great heights' but not well performed), Gluck's *Alceste* at Covent Garden ('a very beautiful production from Paris' conducted by Philippe Gaubert with Germaine Lubin outstanding as the heroine), a joint recital by Clifford Curzon and Elena Gerhardt, 'a great whale of a woman with a dressing-gown cord round her middle' but a marvellous artist (she sang in Cambridge later in the term), Beethoven's Ninth Symphony conducted by Furtwängler with the Berlin Philharmonic, and two Toscanini concerts with the BBC Symphony Orchestra. I had mixed feelings about Furtwängler, a superb Wagner conductor from radio performances but too self-indulgent and melodramatic in Beethoven. The first movement of the Ninth emerged as a series of incidents rather than a unity; the Scherzo, oddly balanced, threatened to turn into a drum concerto; but the Adagio was wonderful and parts of the finale scarcely less so – though he brought in the big tune so quietly that it was scarcely distinguishable – until the closing bars, which were totally obliterated by the cymbals. When Furtwängler's convulsive gestures subsided, the audience began to applaud, stopped, and then, realising that the work must have ended, resumed their applause. Exactly the same thing happened when three months later I heard Furtwängler conduct the symphony in Salzburg with the Vienna Philharmonic.

Toscanini impressed me much more. His programmes included Brahms's first symphony, Shostakovich's first (then wholly unfamiliar) and Beethoven's *Coriolan* overture and Eroica as well as some makeweights. He not only generated intense energy; he presented a coherent view of the works as wholes, never allowing details to protrude or incidents to grow out of proportion. His beat, like Strauss's in *Ariadne*, was absolutely precise and clear; while everything was under absolute control, one felt that the music was held together by some coiled elastic spring that might at any moment break free. Furtwängler seemed a posturing bandmaster by comparison, as if his own emotions were of greater moment than Beethoven's. The turgid element that had hitherto bothered me in the scoring of Brahms's first movement dissolved completely. The Shostakovich came over as a great modern masterpiece, a rank that I felt his overblown later symphonies never quite attained. Best of all was the Eroica, a shattering experience.

Two of these expeditions, in the first week of May, ended in our missing the last train back to Cambridge, a misdemeanour for which I (though not of course Philip) had to appear before the tutor and keep extra nights in College at the end of term. On the first occasion we had plenty of time, but a bus strike and the invasion of the capital by half the population of Sunderland to see the Cup Final caused such a jam on the tube that we were stuck for 20 minutes and found King's Cross in a state of siege, with noisy engagements between policemen and drunks. Philip spent the night in a waiting room, a prey to a greater concentration of 'fooks' and 'booggers' than he had ever heard in his life; I returned to Portland Place, where Gran let me in privily and let me sleep on the hall sofa, next to Frisky's basket. Frisky was a little puzzled by this but raised no objection; when Alice the maid appeared in the morning and saw a strange body she woke me up with a piercing shriek. I slipped out early; neither Tommy nor Mother, who was on a visit from France, ever knew I was there. The odds against this happening twice must have been enormous. Yet five days later, after waiting some minutes for a tube we reached the barrier at King's Cross in time to see the 11.40 steaming out. A frantic rush in a taxi to Liverpool Street, and the 11.50 played the same trick. After a sleepless night in a hotel we rose at 5 a.m. and caught an early train, since Philip had to conduct an exam at 9 a.m. The tutor (Donald Beves) was more amused than censorious.

The enterprise of the Arts Theatre brought a number of interesting shows to Cambridge. The Auden-Isherwood play *The Ascent of F6* seemed to me a disappointing muddle, with plenty of ideas, none of them developed adequately in dramatic terms, and an incoherent plot. The best poetry in the written text was cut in the theatre. Nor was there much to admire in the performance. I met Rupert Doone and Robert Medley, the producer and designer, at lunch; Doone struck me as a vain little man and his production as deplorable. They spoke of Auden in reverent terms as if he were Shakespeare. Later in the term the Sadler's Wells Opera and Ballet each came for a week. The operas were *Figaro*, *The Barber of Seville*, in which only Arnold Matters as Figaro could make Rossini's patter convincing, and *Madam Butterfly*. After the thunderstorm in the last act of

The Barber we emerged to find a real thunderstorm of tremendous violence raging outside; torrential rain compelled us to shelter for 20 minutes.

Butterfly I saw twice on consecutive nights. Dent had invited me to dinner and *Rigoletto* on the Saturday, but the illness of the baritone, Redvers Llewellyn, caused *Butterfly* to be repeated instead. Dent, who loathed Puccini, kept up a *sotto voce* running commentary almost throughout, with scandalous conjectures about the relationship of Butterfly's child to Tudor Davies, the rather elderly and wooden tenor. At dinner, where we consumed a large bottle of Burgundy between us, he kept me in constant laughter about past dramatic productions in Cambridge, notably *Doctor Faustus* in 1908, and related the diseases that all the great composers died of, most of them venereal (two different kinds in the case of Schubert). He revealed a surprising weakness for the conducting of Landon Ronald and confessed that he adored Mendelssohn. I found him the queerest contradiction in character. The night before he had given a party for the company, at which I had enjoyable talks with the conductor Lawrance Collingwood and several of the singers. Llewellyn applauded my suggestion that they should do *Simon Boccanegra*, which they did after the war. Dent flattered me by asking me to translate *Der Schauspieldirektor* as well as *Carmen*. Boris came out with a riddle: Why is Joan Cross? Because Arnold Matters. He quoted Lydia Keynes (Lopokova) whispering to a man who came in late at a Paderewski concert and sat on a radiator: 'Look out, or you will burn your two halves'. She was renowned for her malapropisms; she said at a party that she had been upset to find barristers in her bed, and they attacked her all night. 'I think you mean harvesters, my dear', Keynes replied drily. An elderly don at Trinity was said to have remarked that many coroners were coming over for the fornication.

I wrote my first opera notice and my first musical article, both for the *Cambridge Review* at the suggestion of the editor, Frank Thistlethwaite, a contemporary at St John's who became a lifelong friend. The notice, of *Butterfly*, was spoiled by a subeditor introducing a new paragraph where I had placed a comma. The article was a deliberately provocative attack on musical fashions, snobbery and worship of virtuoso performers, adducing evidence from Pope (*Essay on Criticism*), Beddoes and 'Mr Ezra Pound and certain other of the more excremental modern poets'. I poked fun at a friend (?Kenneth Harrison) who left a concert after a minor work of Bach and before a major work of Handel, and who was carried away when I played him a piece of Handel which he thought was Bach. Frank proposed that I should succeed him as editor of the *Review*, but this was vetoed by the Trinity dons who dominated the committee; they refused to consider a Kingsman because the last King's editor had been so bad. Other literary efforts at this time were two book reviews for the scientific periodical *Discovery*, then edited by Tellie. One was a stiff work by W.F. Jackson Knight on anthropological ritual, taking its start from the Sixth *Aeneid* – I entered a protest against the seeming immunity of technical works from the laws of English prose – the other a study of bees in folklore. I also wrote a parody of *The Ascent of F6* for the *Basileon*, which caused much amusement but now seems barely comprehensible; and there was a positive diarrhoea of poems, mostly inspired by Clare. I had recently condemned everything I had written before the previous summer, one or two lines excepted, as trash. My essays for Peter Lucas continued to meet with enthusiastic approval: he told me I was his only pupil who knew how to construct an essay, and borrowed a piece about the metaphysical poets in order to copy some of my quotations. I was reading T.S. Eliot (not one of Peter's favourites), now enjoying the poems but contemptuous of *The Use of Poetry and the Use of Criticism*, which seemed a monument of woolly thinking.

On the Saturday of Coronation week I took down a cricket team to play against Hambledon, their fixture having fallen through. It was difficult to raise enough players; my fast bowlers let me down at the last minute, and I had to fill up with friends who had not played since their schooldays. We drove down in three cars, and managed to reach Hambledon on time from three different directions. Hambledon, who the week before had beaten Godalming away (a match that made the *Evening Standard*), gave us a dreadful hiding, but the match was voted a great success and we received an effusive welcome. There had been alarums and excursions earlier. Mother, home for three weeks and refusing to see me, had induced both Grandparents to write to me, cancelling the match. Fortunately better counsels prevailed, and she went to Harrow for the day.

The family quarrels were beginning to recede a little so far as I was concerned, but there were distant rumblings. Gran had occasion to rebuke Eugene for gross bad manners. Vernon had an interview with Tommy and talked like a raving lunatic; soon he was to be in prison for contempt of court. I heard that Martin and Joe had made contact with him, only to encounter a denunciation of Catholicism, the whole Bagger relationship and Mother's treatment of me. Tommy had a financial row with Mother, flatly refusing to make up the alimony she would lose if she married Eugene. Although Joe wrote solemnly repudiating anything critical he might have said about Eugene in Cambridge the previous year, he said he had no intention of throwing me over. He wrote many amusing and delightful letters from Harrow, describing a harpsichord recital by Boris, interspersed with funny stories about great composers ('We regard him here as a typical King's product') and lectures from L.S. Amery, Sir William Rothenstein ('He kept us waiting for 15 minutes, and talked for 20'), Sir Samuel Hoare ('pathetic – his nasal twang scarcely ever emitted anything that was not stale') and Charles Morgan (an excellent talk on 'The Mind of the Artist'). On Speech Day 'our Father, which art in Ealing, was going to come down cum wife, but he never answered the invitation'. 'The Holy Ghost was engaged in a Korda film, or rather the Father was, and Vicky turned up alone … She was very nice indeed.' He wanted me to get a new camera, offering to develop and print for me (enclosing a specimen), and was very concerned for my health. 'Have the bowels anything to do with it? … If you don't get better immediately I will – do something drastic, anyway.' 'Our Father came down yesterday and was much taken by Byron's relics, including his bedroom slippers.'

My overwhelming preoccupation this summer was my relationship with Clare, which went through all manner of vicissitudes. She told me early in the term that I was the most fundamentally cheerful person she knew, and that I alone had overcome her dislike of being touched and kissed because I was somehow pure. (She had had a frightening experience the year before and was not sure she was still a virgin.) Indeed she often kissed me first and was so affectionate and responsive that it was inevitable I should fall completely. I resisted for a time, feeling guilty about David, till he assured me that he had found comfort elsewhere. At the end of May Clare had to take her final exam, Part II of the History Tripos, whereas I had only Mays since I was staying up a fourth year. After I had not seen her for nearly a fortnight the tension became too great and I suddenly collapsed. Apart from mental terrors, my arms and feet became paralysed and I feared I was about to have a stroke. The doctor diagnosed complete exhaustion of my nervous system, told me not to take the exam or the Shakespeare Scholarship, and gave me a strong soporific. When I woke up, I wrote to Peggy imploring her not to tell Clare till she had finished her Tripos, and was escorted by Philip to Hambledon, where cuckoos were singing all day, sometimes two or three at once, and nightingales all night, and all the flowers in the garden seemed to be blooming at once. In two days I felt much refreshed.

Clare

The next two weeks were chaotic, both in the event and in my memory, though at the time I described them in extraordinary detail. On returning to King's I found Clare waiting. She threw herself into my arms, saying she was much fonder of me than she thought. For the next two months she was more than half in love with me, and I could hold back no longer. For much of the time I was in seventh heaven; but there were agonising brainstorms and unfathomable depressions as well. It was a period of wild turmoil. One day we would be making love happily and talking about everything from contraceptives to climbing trees; the next she might suddenly bite my head off. On one such occasion, in the interval of a performance by the Vic-Wells ballet, I received a violent shock: I ran into Leeby, who told me that Brigid was to marry her clergyman. I was fully prepared for this and had no possible reason to be upset, but felt as if I had been struck in the stomach by a ram-rod. It transpired that Glenn Millikan, an American research student in Trinity ten years older than us, was also in love with Clare. I liked Glenn, and took this in my stride – till one day Clare told me she loved him more than she had ever loved anybody, though she soon went back on this and said she loved me as much as ever. In fact she could not decide between us, a situation that was to persist for months.

We were both overwrought and overtired, burning the candle at both ends and in the middle as well. We rushed about in a whirl of parties, dances, church expeditions, and much else. Clare went to three consecutive all-night parties, and two more a little later. We each gave parties of our own; my chief recollection of mine, on a very hot evening, is of Trend squatting on his haunches like a Buddha listening to records of *Dido and Aeneas* and spiffling with approval. The Ballet supplied some distraction; *Les Patineurs*, arranged by Constant Lambert from Meyerbeer, sounded like diluted Rossini and Chopin played on a brass band, to irresistibly comic effect. Hurrying back from a church expedition to get to a party, Clare lost control of

Glenn's car, whose brakes were defective, and collided with the wall of St John's, destroying a bicycle in the process. Fortunately no one was hurt; but there was no drink left at the party when we eventually arrived. The next evening was even crazier. Between a party and a dance Clare's car was stolen, which tipped her off balance and cost me a fortune in taxi fares. I was additionally distracted by an incident on my staircase, when a mad fascist held up four of my friends with a revolver. Derek was reduced to cheering us up by telling indecent stories. We danced till dawn, but I remember nothing about it.

Three days later I was having breakfast with Philip when suddenly the fried fish began to fly round my brain like a weight at the end of a piece of string. The doctor, not very impressed, gave me a sedative, and I allowed Philip to take me to *The Flying Dutchman* at Covent Garden. This was a mistake. Three times I was seized with blind panic; the last time, in the middle of the second act, I could no longer bear the music and rushed out into the street. At Liverpool Street I rang up Gran and asked her to arrange an appointment with Squires. The next day, incredibly, I travelled to Hambledon and played in a splendid and most enjoyable cricket match at Cranleigh, even batting well in a crisis and feeling perfectly relaxed in the delightful company of the villagers. But the black dog promptly returned. Unable to sleep and subject to violent digestive upsets and more and more frequent brainstorms, I had to cancel engagements with Stella and Vie, a Toscanini concert and *Così fan tutte* at Glyndebourne.

Squires sentenced me to another spell in a nursing home, but was very helpful and sympathetic. He said I had a remarkably good brain and courage that anyone might admire but was far too much a prey to my emotions, and my brain was so agile that it exhausted both itself and my body. Clare had planned a week's holiday climbing with friends in Wales, which she offered to cancel for my sake. I knew she needed a change and was determined that she should go.

Squires told Mrs Mallory that it would be a fine thing if I had the strength to live without her, but it was a very great risk. Later he said he was astonished at my decision. However the decision gave both Clare and me strength, and we went to the King's Ball as planned. Apart from an agonising period when Clare went to change her dress and disappeared for over two hours (I feared an accident, but she had merely fallen asleep) we had a wonderful evening.

My three weeks at Stoneycrest, the nursing-home at Hindhead, were inevitably a period of sharp ups and downs, but I began to recover more quickly than Squires expected; he told Gran that I should be there for at least five weeks. I was well fed and looked after by a kindly staff under a matron who reminded me alternately of an elderly Louis XV marquise and a bull-necked modern locomotive. The desperate struggle between good intentions and overpowering emotional demands were gradually leading to increased self-knowledge, though still subject to disturbance by a panic that I could not control. In one period of 24 hours I lost a pound and a half in weight. At best I felt desperately lonely, in a kind of spiritual coma. My visitors were a great help, especially Gran, with whom I could discuss anything, even the pros and cons of young people sleeping together with special reference to Cambridge. One day she brought my 84-year-old great aunt Kate, Tommy's elder sister, a wonderful character with a deep gurgling laugh like a double bassoon. Mrs Mallory was unexpectedly sympathetic. We could discuss Clare dispassionately from every angle; she was surprised that so highly-strung a character had got through Cambridge without a breakdown. She gave me much sound advice on how to bring up children; the eldest was nearly always self-centred. Philip returned from a festival of contemporary music in Paris, and I caused him to do the nose-trick twice in ten minutes by making him laugh just as he was drinking tea. I had a kind letter from Cushing Toppan (who had appeared in Cambridge at the time of the Coronation, characteristically showing a young German round the university), offering to come over from Paris at once if he could do anything to help. There was also a letter from Mother saying, on the strength of my *Cambridge Review* article, that she could see me as one of the leading music critics of the age.

Squires came three times and uttered many wise words; I can appreciate them now even more than at the time. He identified two ineluctable facts that every man and woman must face, death and the utter isolation of the human soul, and ascribed most mental breakdowns to evasion of them. In his opinion everyone had a guiding principle which regulates his or her life, and to which they return when events tend to draw them away. His was a passion for perfection; mine was a passion to be loved, to be all in all to someone. He assured me that my extreme swings of mood were perfectly normal, since I was born with a cyclothymic temperament. So indeed was Clare, but our swings often failed to coincide. He applauded the fact that I was conscious of the pitfalls and my own weaknesses, even if I could not always avoid the one or get a grip on the other. We talked about sex and my experiences at Harrow, which he called a typically ironical comment on the educational system of the country.

One remarkable event fell in this period. This was a cricket match, arranged by Eric Parker, between the two Hambledons, ours and the Hampshire village famous for its supremacy in the 18th century. Unhappily I was not considered well enough to play, but Monk drove me over to the Hampshire Hambledon to watch. It was a struggle worthy of the pen of Homer, and was featured in the national press. I wrote a full account in my diary, and give only the highlights here. The Hampshire team reached 143 for 4, but were bundled out after tea for 166. Surrey began badly, made a partial recovery, then collapsed; we were 80 for 7 and, after a brave little stand, 104 for 8 with Eric Parker junior, a powerful left-hander, going strong. At this point our captain, with a rare stroke of genius, promoted Bert Jeffery, number 11 on the card, to number 10 and told him to block up one end. He did, while Eric hit the bowling all over the field. A bus-load of our supporters had supplied themselves with a nine-gallon barrel of beer, and it became evident that the content had reached its appropriate destination, for they applauded every run and gave copious (and sometimes unprintable) advice to each batsman between the overs. At 138 Eric was bowled for a gallant 64. Amid awful silence the last man, Fred Edwards, a fast bowler, went in, while Bert's old father invoked the aid of heaven and it was found that the ladies were absent-mindedly frequenting the gentlemen's lavatory, sending the gentlemen into the ladies'. Fred, who had a good eye, played the natural fast bowler's game and hit out at everything. The bowlers and fielders panicked and began to drop catches. Amid the wildest excitement 160 went up, and it was announced that the ladies' lavatory had gone irretrievably out of order. The last over was called; the bowler rearranged his field and bowled a fast bouncer. Fred hooked it over the pavilion for 6, tried to do the same with the next ball, which was pitched further up, and was comprehensively bowled. The match was adjudged a tie, though the scorers were so confused by the excitement that they announced three different results in ten minutes. Bert, who had obeyed instructions and defended doggedly while 62 runs were scored, seldom hitting the ball more than five yards, was left not out 1.

That day Clare returned from Wales, where she had received the news of her First from my ecstatic telegram before the newspapers arrived, and visited me after dinner. We were blissfully happy. Once a nurse burst in to find Clare sitting on my knee with her arms round my neck: 'Are you ready for your dinner? Oh, evidently not!' My little Scottish night nurse showed me how to arrange the screens so as not to be seen from the door. I was determined to give Clare a glorious summer. In the autumn she was going for a year to Mills

College in California, so she resolved to live for the moment in what we called our honeymoon summer. Not that this prevented us on one occasion from planning the details of our imaginary wedding. We kissed and made love endlessly, only stopping short of the final act. This would assuredly have relieved my tension, but I had too much respect for her to press it. Her mother, who understood my difficulties and appreciated the efforts I made for Clare, described her with acute perception as half a Puritan and half a flirt; I would add a touch of the wild animal as well.

For much of July I was so ecstatically happy that I wanted to do the whole world a good turn. But there were times when her uncertain temper and unpredictability – she was always erratic in keeping appointments – plunged me into despair, and I had horrid visions of a black future without her; after which I would be overcome with shame and guilt, and form resolutions of unselfishness, humility and self-discipline. The continued alternation between uninhibited joy and peevish irritation, which afflicted us both in equal measure, seemed frankly ridiculous, even at the time; yet it was difficult to know how to break free. I was haunted by a fear that we were not right for one another and never would be, and that underneath both of us knew it. This was followed by the most loving reconciliation of all, but it was the truth. We parted at the beginning of August with fond promises to live for each other during the year of separation. My feelings were of pain, regret and remorse; I did not feel that I had given her as good a time as she deserved, and there was nothing more I could do about it.

A number of things helped to preserve my sanity, not least the conviviality of the cricket matches and the company of the village people and their wives and families, who always welcomed me as a friend. There were tennis parties, at one of which I met Robert Birley, the Headmaster of Charterhouse, whose enormous reach

– he was 6 foot 6 inches tall – made him a positive Verdun at the net. The Grandparents were very good to me, and allowed me to invite my friends for week-ends. Peggy, Tess, John Davison, Oliver Zangwill, Peter Joseph (now a budding solicitor in the formidable firm of Tamplin Joseph Ponsonby Ryde and Flux) and Rosemary Freeman came, and Gran seemed to take delight in all of them. A number of amusing incidents remain in my memory: Gran in the rose-garden exclaiming about 'the profligacy of nature', revealing that Tommy took a surreptitious interest in advertisements for female underclothes, and saying 'Now I must go and take my God for a walk'. Peter Joseph told a story about a little boy of four jealously watching attention being lavished on his new-born sister. Suddenly he burst out: 'When I'm married I'll walk behind my wife and stamp on all the eggs'. Tommy's deafness produced a contretemps when gales of laughter were heard from the next garden where our genial neighbour Brodie Hoare was entertaining two blonds. Tommy asked what was going on; when I whispered 'Brodie Hoare' he looked very shocked and told me I must never use such expressions. He thought I said 'Bloody whore'.

CHAPTER 10

Germany and Beyond

My second continental summer had an inauspicious start. Rupert Bailey intended to drive to south Germany via the Hook of Holland, and we arranged to go together, taking a leisurely route up the Rhine valley in the hope of enjoying the scenery. Rupert duly called for me at Hambledon; but when we reached Harwich we found that the papers for the car had not arrived as promised, and we were stuck for 24 hours. I was frantic with frustration, not least because I might have had another day with Clare. Luckily the sight of Rupert, normally the most timorous of men, stamping up and down the station platform purple with rage and threatening to burn Harwich to the ground, restored my sense of humour. We spent the extra day looking at the churches and antiquities of Colchester and its neighbourhood, but had to hurry our journey through Holland and Germany. All manner of extraneous obstacles held us up: Rotterdam proved to be a labyrinth; at Dordrecht we had to wait for a ferry and were nobbled by a crowd of small boys; we went round in futile circles at Breda; at Roermund we got hopelessly lost and drove ten miles back on our tracks. We soon began to get on each other's nerves. Rupert was obstinately convinced that he knew the way; although I had the map. He invariably doubted my directions, and when the map was ambiguous refused to stop and ask. He was also one of those irritatingly cautious drivers who slow up when intending to overtake and in consequence seldom overtake at all. Even on the German Autobahns he never exceeded 45 m.p.h.

Things went rather more smoothly after the German frontier. We stopped to look at Cologne Cathedral, then drove via Bonn, Koblenz and Bingen to Mainz, where we spent the night. Countless level crossings and lumbering lorries with trailers held us up, but what I most regretted was the need to pass through beautiful scenery that invited us to linger. On the next day near Stuttgart we ran into what looked like the entire German army on manoeuvres. The people were very friendly. The hotel proprietor at Mainz, who spoke English, went out of his way to please us; a garage hand who sold us petrol near Moenchengladbach told us he had been a prisoner in England during the first war and seemed to regard his treatment as a form of hospitality. We solemnly shook hands, expressing the fervent hope that there would be no repetition of hostilities. I have often wondered if he survived the second war. At Augsburg Rupert and I had a row. We proceeded to Munich in glum silence, and there Rupert stopped, though he had spoken of taking me to Salzburg. The only train started an hour late, and reached Salzburg just before 1a.m. I was so tired that I talked complete nonsense to the customs officers in a mixture of three languages. Fortunately they let me through, and a providential taxi took me to the Kreuzbrücklhof.

If this festival was on the whole less enjoyable than the previous year's, it was due partly to the weather, which for days on end was cold and wet, and partly to the fact that I was ill, culminating in an attack of dysentery, a debilitating experience that kept me intermittently in bed. Geoffrey Heath, a Cambridge friend with whom I had agreed to lodge at the Kreuzbrücklhof, had broken free from a constricting family background and was conducting an affair with a married woman at Berchtesgaden over the German frontier. Perhaps as a result of this he was not only preoccupied but inclined to be sententious and intolerant. But the city was full of people I knew, friends and acquaintances from London, Harrow, Cambridge and the previous year, and I made plenty of new friends. The Hubback family were in force, David having found happiness with Judy Williams whom he was subsequently to marry. Beryl Eeman, a Newnham friend of mine and Derek's, an intensely intellectual girl much given to self-analysis, confided in me about her love affair with John Berryman, whom she met at Cambridge. Most of us found him uncommunicative in the extreme; we made jokes about Beryl and her beard, little thinking he would become famous as a poet. Boris, much more relaxed than at Cambridge, was very good company. He introduced me to a young American friend of Sibelius, who, he said, was prevented from composing by a nervous disease of the hands. But his brain was nimble, capacious and full of appreciation for his contemporaries; he would talk of everything except his future and unfinished compositions.

Toppam and some of the Australian sisters were again at the Manzanos'. Toppan, a good Samaritan and a truly disinterested philanthropist, did much for my self-confidence and proved a good antidote to incipient panic. More than once I had been tempted to return to England. On one of my visits to the Manzanos I arrived in a great sweat and at once sat down to the piano, to play duets with the four-year-old Toto Manzano, who had an excellent sense of rhythm but could only operate in one key. When I stood up, there was an ominous rending sound, reminiscent of a certain moment in *Peter Pan*, and a circular patch from the seat of my trousers remained attached to the piano-stool. Among those staying with the Manzanos were the wife and daughter of the Swiss Minister in London, who presently set out for Hungary. But their car came in several pieces; they gave it away on the roadside and returned none the worse. Their daughter, Livia Paravicini, I described as 'a stately creature, with a weakness for pocketing every visible matchbox'.

There were convivial parties in restaurants after the concerts, at one of which I was induced to take part in an Austrian peasant dance to the huge amusement of the natives. Boris charged me with disgracing my country, my university and my name, but for nothing more serious than hitting him with a beer-mat.

The most impressive of the concerts were the two conducted by Toscanini: the Verdi Te Deum and Requiem and a Brahms programme including the Haydn variations, *Liebeslieder Walzer* and First Symphony. Both seemed to me beyond criticism. The Verdi Requiem, with a superb team of soloists – Zinka Kunz (later Milanov), Thorborg, Roswaenge and Kipnis – was another performance that established a firm standard in my memory. Furtwängler's Ninth Symphony, with a different orchestra, satisfied me even less than before; he dawdled depressingly in the trio of the Scherzo, with a concluding rallentando that suggested a gramophone running down. I had a spirited argument with Clifford Curzon about a Mozart concert conducted by Bruno Walter (the Prague and 39th symphonies and the piano concerto K. 467, in which Yvonne Lefèbure seemed to have a tug of war with the conductor over tempo). Clifford fumed at Walter for not keeping a steady rhythm and ignoring the first beat of the bar; he called the performance one long rubato. A string quartet concert at the Residenz suffered from the acoustics, as did the Mozart Requiem in the cathedral: a poor performance in any case, not improved by people walking about the aisles in squeaky shoes.

Four of the seven operas I heard were conducted by Toscanini: the same three as in 1936 and *Die Zauberflöte*. *Falstaff* with the same cast moved me even more than before, *Die Meistersinger* considerably less, partly because it was less well sung with a weaker Eva and Walther. I was also irritated by the opera, especially the second act, but that may have been due to incipient dysentery. *Fidelio* also seemed to be less well sung, except by Kipnis as Rocco, and the horns had a dreadful off-night. My memory of *Zauberflöte* is oddly at variance with what I wrote at the time. I clearly recall feeling uncomfortable about Toscanini's tempos – sometimes too fast but in 'O Isis und Osiris' so slow that Kipnis was forced to take a breath in the middle of a phrase. Yet I recorded nothing but enthusiasm for the conducting and the singing, apart from the Queen of Night. It was a very strong cast, including Novotna, Hilde Konetzni, Thorborg, Roswaenge, Dermota, Jerger, Domgraf-Fassbaender and Kipnis. I particularly admired the last two as Papageno and Sarastro.

Walter conducted *Figaro* with another marvellous cast: Pinza (Figaro), Stabile (Count), Rautawaara (Countess), Réthy (Susanna), Novotna (Cherubino), Lazzari (Bartolo) and Cravcenko (Marcellina). Pinza was the most dangerous Figaro I have ever heard, outdoing even Stabile's Count in menace; they might have been indulging in personal rivalry. But although the singing was superb, the total effect was scrappy, owing to poor scenery, a production all over the place, and some slipshod conducting by Walter with extreme rubato and unmotivated changes of tempo. I was bothered by the slow pace of the recitatives, and felt that the Sadler's Wells production, though inferior vocally, came nearer to the spirit of the work. I suppose it was reaction against productions like this that led modern producers to go head over heels in the opposite direction.

Two operas new to me were *Electra*, conducted (very well) by Knappertsbusch and *Euryanthe* under Walter. I was intermittently thrilled by *Electra*, whose peaks seemed to me superior to *Salome*, despite outbreaks of empty ranting and moments that suggested 'O sole mio' orchestrated by Wagner. But the production and the costumes were unspeakable, Electra (Rose Pauly) and Chrysothemis (Hilde Konetzni) – admittedly not well shaped by nature – looking like bedmakers and Orestes wearing a coat and skirt suitable for a highbrow funeral. There was an unfortunate moment when Electra planted her feet and stuck out her ample bosom just when the double bassoon emitted a distressingly human grunt. *Euryanthe* appealed to me so much that I bought a vocal score in the interval, but I was baffled by the style, which appeared to vacillate unpredictably between Mozart, German folksong and strong anticipations of Wagner, especially in recitative-arioso passages. I was not yet able to appreciate Weber's genius in going so far to reconcile these elements in the face of a 'footling' libretto. Again I had nothing good to say of the scenery and costumes, and not much for the two principal singers, Karl Friedrich and Maria Reining. Thorborg and Alexander Sved as Eglantine and Lysiart were much more convincing, but they had the strongest and most interesting parts.

Toppan introduced me to Newell Jenkins, a young American studying music at Freiburg and planning to mount a production of *Dido and Aeneas* there during the winter. We struck up an immediate friendship. He took me to the beautiful park at Hellbrunn with its curious waterworks, whereby puppets play dramatic scenes activated by water power alone, and a rock theatre where in 1613 opera was first performed on German soil. Three days later Newell and I and a monosyllabic Scotsman called Graham set out on the spur of the moment for a tour of the Salzkammergut. Continuous rain prevented us getting very far. We dined at St Gilgen, spent a night at Strobl, and then settled at Nussensee, a lovely little mountain lake surrounded by pine forests off the road to Ischl. The only house within two miles was the restaurant at one end where we stayed, kept by four women of various shapes and sizes and a microscopic simian waiter called Josef. The only other inhabitants were a large but docile St Bernard whose hoarse barks resounded among the pines, a mis-shapen hen with chicks, and a cat with one tabby and one black kitten. We were housed comfortably, hospitably and cheaply, and apart from two short trips to Ischl lived for three days in total idleness. During the few fine intervals we went for early morning bathes and rowed on the lake, which must be one of the most beautiful in Austria. Its icy clear water reflected mountains and woods and produced miraculous draughts of fishes, great and small; the banks were covered with ferns, gentians and other Alpine flowers; the stillness echoed the most distant sounds. When it rained, apart from singing *Dido* through from the score, we lay in the hay-loft, smoked and talked, and I read Rosamond Lehmann's *Dusty Answer*, a disturbing book, and Bradley's *Oxford Lectures on Poetry*. It was a wonderfully relaxing existence. During this week I came to know Newell quite well, yet through force of circumstances it was 48 years before we met again, though we were each aware of the other's career. He came up to me after I had given a lecture at an Early Music festival at Boston, and we celebrated with a special lunch. After that I never saw him again.

Newell dropped me at Litzlberg, where I spent four more happy days with the Curzons. Clifford and Lucille were both preparing for concerts and practiced most of the day; I was given a sound-proof room with a piano where I made a horrible noise trying to play excerpts from *Euryanthe*. We met again for meals, where the conversation flowed with immense spirit and plenty of argument. Clifford and Lucille had little time for the Salzburg Festival, apart from Toscanini's part in it, and loathed the fashionable people who patronised it. Their particular bêtes noirs were the London critics, especially those of the *Times* and *Daily Telegraph*, and I was inclined to agree. Clifford urged me to take up music criticism; he flattered me by rating my *Cambridge Review* article very high, and still more by asking my advice on a performance he was preparing for an Ernest Makower concert at the London Museum. I felt I must know a great deal more before undertaking such a career, and certainly had no such intention at this stage. We discussed the contrasted qualities and drawbacks of the Makowers and the Robert Mayers, rich Jews who gave free concerts in London. The Makowers emerged slightly

Germany and Beyond

less scathed, but we agreed (correctly) that the odds on a knighthood favoured Mayer. We had a splendid argument about opera, which I suspected that Clifford did not dignify as an art form at all. His attack roused me in its defence, and we all talked at once, Lucille interjecting a stream of semiquavers and Mrs Wallace, Lucille's mother, contributing an occasional sforzando. One evening after dinner Clifford played Brahms's D minor concerto with Lucille supplying the orchestral part on a second piano. I could not judge the performance, but was completely converted to the work. When Mary Piggott, another Newnham friend, and her mother came to stay, we tried our luck with a horoscope book, which told us that Lucille was to regret her first marriage all her life (she had only one) and Mary, a very proper girl, 'is inclined to be delicate about the lower organs'. Although the weather was less kind than in 1936, we managed one or two swims and I returned to Salzburg wonderfully refreshed.

The staff at the Kreuzbrücklhof gave me a touching send-off when I left on 1 September, and begged me to return next year. The train journey to Budapest took all day and involved a change at Vienna. Here I was sitting in the carriage when I heard a familiar voice talking English in the next compartment. It proved to be my cousin Michael Isaacs, who by chance was making the same journey by the same train on the same day; neither of us was aware that the other was out of England. We travelled together in great good fellowship and at the Hungarian frontier bought small bottles of local brandy. This made me merry and Michael quite irrepressible. He held forth in several languages at once, slapped the other passengers on the back, sang the *Blue Danube*, drank the health of the customs officers, and triumphantly declared a bottle of Eno's Fruit Salts. We parted firm friends with the other passengers, an Austrian girl, a young Hungarian, and an old Austrian resident in Egypt. I never met any of them again.

At Budapest I met John Davison, who was attending (and not enjoying) some kind of international conference with many English, French and Danish students. The atmosphere was grimly political, except after a wine-tasting expedition to the state cellars at Budafok, when the French in particular rolled into dinner very drunk. Even the spaniel-faced Hungarian woman who was our interpreter spoke faster than usual. At the Imperial Pension most of the students were sleeping several to a room, but I had one to myself with running water and taps inscribed in Hungarian; it took me some time to discover which meant hot and which cold, as cold water usually came out of both. I spent much time sight-seeing, walking for many miles in intense heat, inspecting numerous churches, including a sullen eighteenth-century cathedral, and the art gallery (where many pictures captivated my enthusiasm, notably a wonderful Vermeer of a woman in a lace collar), with intervals for bathing on St Margaret's Island. The Danube, incidentally, is not blue.

Despite a magnificent situation Budapest struck me as a sad city, noisy, dirty, full of ugly suspension bridges, yellow trams, painted women and bad language. The architecture had an air of monarchic decadence superimposed on heavy and fidgety Hungarian baroque, symbolised by the half Gothic, half baroque Parliament buildings on one side of the Danube and the vast deserted eighteenth-century palace on the other. One could understand why the first ambition of every Hungarian was to see the Treaty of Trianon revised. The most exciting aspects were the sunsets and, from the Coronation church behind its battlements on the Buda side of the river, the superb views up and down the Danube and over the whole city. We heard what purported to be a Tsigány orchestra, but the sound bore a close resemblance to bad Tchaikovsky. For once I was relieved when they burst into a Liszt Hungarian rhapsody.

Germany and Beyond

Roused by a little porter who looked like Charlie Chaplin with tooth-ache, John and I left by train for Ljubljana in the north of Jugoslavia. The journey was interesting: in Hungary past blue lakes and fields of Indian corn interspersed with sunflowers, the sunlight playing tricks over the plains; in Jugoslavia along wonderful wooded gorges with waterfalls and grotesque rock formations. We travelled with a young Czech called Kafka, immaculately clad (except when eating, which happened fairly often) in yellow gloves. He talked interestingly on politics and said that Salzburg was the ideal town in which to fall in love, especially for intellectuals. At Ljubljana we were nearly arrested – or so we interpreted the gestures of a uniformed official. No one spoke English, so we had to rely on German, at which John was even more incompetent than I, helped out by gesture. This worked well at the Hotel Štrugel, where we identified the meat on the menu by imitating various animals. One dish baffled us until, not familiar with the voice of deer, I made a gesture indicating horns; the waiter was delighted and brought us some excellent venison.

The town, clean and relatively quiet with comfortable wide streets, was a refreshing contrast to Budapest. We looked into one or two baroque churches, dodged between green trams that careered down the streets at a terrifying pace, and dined pleasantly in the open air under a grove of horse-chestnuts; then went for a walk, wrapped in earnest conversation about modern poetry, and promptly got lost. The inhabitants seemed to be ardent film-fans, to judge from numerous placards bearing succulent photographs and attractive titles such as *Spijonka Suzy*. On the following day we found a spacious park full of the most gorgeous flowers, climbed through thick woods to the top of a hill, and explored a castle, which sits romantically on a rock rather like that at Salzburg and commands the whole city. It proved to contain a chapel and a beautiful square of old buildings, used as alms-houses, with chestnut trees in the middle. We voted Jugoslavia as supreme in two respects, its scenery and its cigarettes.

We had intended to make for the Dalmatian coast, but found that this would have taken us through a corner of Italy, which our visas would not permit. So we moved to Bled by bus, another beautiful but dusty journey, varied by pauses for refreshment like the return from a village cricket match, and enlivened by a jovial flat-footed conductor, a talkative man with gold teeth and fuzzy hair who stopped the bus by running in front with a pumpkin, and a sinister unshaven figure who looked like a political agitator. We were captivated by Bled, a place of fantastic beauty on a deep blue lake set in a ring of mountains that changed colour as the sun played on them. On one side stood a fortress on a tall rock rising precipitously from the water; in the middle was a little conical island covered with trees with a church on top. We put up, comfortably and cheaply, at the Pension Mon Plaisir, whose garden ran down to a private bathing beach. Our fellow-guests were an amusing assortment. A fair girl with lovely hair but a hard mouth, with her mother; John kept meeting her emerging from the lavatory and called her Flouncy, for she seemed to possess only one garment, a long pink affair with flounces that served for morning and evening dress, dressing-gown and bathing-wrap. A middle-aged woman regularly pinched the Pension boat and exposed too much of her pendulous person. There was a lank man with a black moustache and a black dog; we were doubtful which we disliked more, and decided on the dog, noting how dogs tended to resemble their masters. And a sinister bald man who stared at us; whenever he came down to meals, and when he left the table after meals, he stared – always at us. We began to think we were under the evil eye.

The first three days were gloriously hot and sunny, and we spent most of them on or in the lake. We visited the island, whose church has a superb tower and the best baroque pulpit I had seen. Some sort of festival was in progress; bells were tolling, beggars crying, people filed round the altar in procession and were shepherded to and from the island in fat gondolas with striped awnings. The fortress contained an attractive little chapel and old houses with wide eaves and fantastic chimneys, the walls studded with coats of arms, carved and painted, reputedly of erstwhile bishops. The view across the lake was almost too 'picture-postcard': mountains tipped in pink and shaded in blue, clouds statuesque with golden fringes.

We decided to explore the country and walked to Zasip, a dirty little village on a slope, over a ridge with a gem of a chapel on top, through pine-woods alive with the tinkle of cow-bells, and into a deep ravine called Vintgart. This was a place of astonishing beauty, a cleft in the mountain with precipitous rock sides 100 feet high, trees clinging wherever physically possible, at the bottom a little river bubbling among boulders and tearing down waterfalls into clear blue pools of mysterious depth. A path, built out for most of the way on boards, crossed from side to side of the stream. We were about half-way up when a sudden storm of thunder, lightning and torrential rain struck with cataclysmic violence. We sheltered for a while, but the downpour seemed likely to continue for hours, if not days; so we trudged the four miles back, drenched to the skin. Since we had left much of our luggage at Ljubljana, I had perforce to appear at lunch in a pyjama top and the trousers whose seat had been left at Salzburg, edging my way sideways round the wall and provoking strange looks from the other guests.

For the next 24 hours it rained in buckets and turned so cold that we put on every available stitch of clothing. The landscape was transformed: snow appeared on the peaks, deep rich colours in the woods, a winter nip in the air, and low fingers of cloud cancelling the mountains. The season seemed to jump from summer to winter without the intervention of autumn. John and I worked, he struggling with Berdyaev while I took enormous drafts of Spenser. We had great arguments about history and art. I could not agree with him that Shakespeare's principal importance lay in the fact that he consummated Renaissance thought, nor in regarding art as subordinate to politics. His political views were not far from mine; we were both opposed to the emotional socialism then prevalent in the universities (John was at Oxford), but I understood his being shocked by Harry V.G.'s narrow championship of Franco – though he liked Harry personally.

The mystery of the evil eye was solved. The sinister bald gentleman spoke to us one day after dinner. He proved to be German, and perfectly harmless and charming. His odd behaviour was occasioned by the fact that he suspected us of being actors. He told us that the food problem in Berlin was pressing, and there was a lot of discontent with the government. We listened to the first act of *Tristan* together; but I was sick in the middle. I made great efforts to get in touch with the Schallgrubers, who lived not far away at Tržič. Unhappily the dates did not fit; they invited us to stay with them the week after we had to leave. I never saw them again.

We travelled back through Austria, rising above the snow line near Bad Gastein, where the sun turned the mountains a wonderful pink, and spent a day and a half in Munich. Somewhere on this journey I lost the silver pencil that Brigid gave me on my 20th birthday, which I regarded as my most precious possession. We thought Munich a very pleasant and spacious city, but spent most of the time in the art gallery, the Alte Pinakothek. As usual I recorded my preferences and criticisms in great detail; the Dürers and Goyas impressed me most. We stayed at the Würthemberger Hof, where I made the waiter laugh by unintentionally referring to a fork as 'eine Goebel'. Presently a hoarse ranting began to hold forth on the radio, and everyone fell silent. I asked the waiter what this was. 'Only Hitler', he replied with a shrug; certainly the Germans in the restaurant showed little enthusiasm or even interest.

The night journey by train was not comfortable. We were continually woken up, kicked and trampled by ebullient Nazis returning from the Nuremberg rally; as soon as one lot departed, another and noisier group got in. In addition I was afflicted by a large abscess which appeared like an angry beetroot on my left ear, apparently the result of an insect bite; the mosquitos had been the least attractive denizens of Bled. It discharged matter for 24 hours, and it was several days before my face and neck glands resumed their normal shape. At Ostend four trainloads of people were concentrated on a small boat, penned in like sheep throughout the crossing; it was impossible to move without touching someone else. But the customs gave us no trouble, although I was covered with contraband goods, chiefly Jugoslav jewellery.

CHAPTER 11

Thalia

After staying briefly with the Davisons in Kensington, I spent a very happy and peaceful fortnight at Hambledon, despite an attempt by Mother to have me turned out in favour of Martin and Joe. Gran said they could come, but refused to send me away. The reply was that Martin could not forgive my behaviour, so he and Joe went on a bicycling tour. There were a couple of hilarious cricket matches; Claude Duveen, one of the Feathercombe stalwarts, a long-legged barrister who bowled leg-breaks that pitched occasionally, contrived to solve much of the *Times* crossword while fielding. Tommy had his accountant down and kept the poor man deep in figures for the whole week-end. Tommy's accounts were a perennial source of anxiety and unintended humour. Every summer, ignoring Gran's attempts to dissuade him, he would spend evening after evening trying to make them balance according to the most rigid system, all the time muttering the most explicit obscenities. 'Really', said Gran, 'I didn't know he knew such words'. Certainly they escaped him on no other occasion.

At Cambridge my attempts to achieve emotional independence and self-sufficiency, to pull myself up by the bootstraps, were at last beginning to achieve some success. I was determined to live for others (especially Gran) and suppress my 'spidery unsatisfactory self', and counted and listed my blessings. It was a lonely period, despite the warmth and kindness of friends, especially Philip and Tess, and there were setbacks, notably when Glenn came to lunch in King's and informed me in his brash manner that Clare never had any intention of marrying me but was seriously considering him. It was true that she was considering marriage to him, as she told me in a very generous letter in November (she had two epistolary styles, one as impersonal as a *Times* leading article, the other sensitive and affectionate). She was fully aware of Glenn's faults, in particular his insensitivity, and said that I had given her many things he never could, and she could never marry him but for the existence of people like me; but he alone was sufficiently tough and insensitive to control her waywardness. I took this with complete calm and lack of bitterness and offered, if it would help, not to see or write to her. Though remaining as devoted as ever, I knew that what she said was true. Just after this Clare's sister Beridge and a young scientist came in turn to confide in me: they were in the same situation as Clare and I during the summer. I gave them what advice I could, feeling a strange mixture of sympathy and detachment.

A close friend of Brigid's whom I encountered at this time said that I was such a different person that she hardly recognised me. I went to see Brigid, hoping to test my strength and dispel illusions, and partly succeeded. She seemed to second my efforts, for she spoke to me impersonally as if I were a man in the street, though I knew that she did not feel like this in her heart. It was an odd meeting that left me confused and unhappy. I went away and composed a poem in the lavatory and a fugue in Regent's Park, but finished neither.

That was generally the result of my attempts to compose music. I could not resist the urge, but on looking at the product found it invariably so bad that I threw it away in disgust. My essays for Peter Lucas were more successful, and brought me many compliments. I discovered Landor and could scarcely stop reading him; Peter said

I made a point about classicism and romanticism that he had never encountered before, and was full of enthusiasm for my essays on Emily Brontë, Spenser and Sir Thomas Wyatt among others. The last I thought was the best. Peter was a very shy man; people said that he came out with me more than with any of his other pupils. By this time I had accumulated an enormous amount of information about parish church architecture and taken nearly a thousand photographs. Gran arranged for me to write a series of articles on the subject, illustrated by my own photographs, in *The Townswoman*, organ of the Townswomen's Guilds, of which she was the national treasurer. The plan was eventually to publish them in a book. I wrote eleven of a projected fourteen over the next year and a half, but the series was broken off by the outbreak of war, and the project lapsed. This was my first work of any substance to appear in print.

My comments on music, and on plays, were becoming more pointed. *French Without Tears* led me to prophesy that Terence Rattigan would one day write good serious plays. I was asked through Trend to review a revival of Handel's *Susanna*, now staged at the Arts, for *The Monthly Musical Record* – my first appearance in a serious musical journal – and wrote about a CUMS choral concert for a university paper. There were some fine concerts in Cambridge this autumn, including a Czech performance by the Prague Philharmonic under Rafael Kubelík, Beecham and the LPO in a programme of Mozart, Sibelius (7th Symphony) and lollipops, with a speech from the conductor 'in his best mountebank manner', and a recital by Casals and Horszowski, whose performance of Beethoven's C major cello sonata excited me so much that my watch stopped. At Christmas I heard *Messiah* complete for the first time, conducted by Beecham with an enormous orchestra at Covent Garden, and was more impressed by the work than the performance. The serried ranks of the chorus reminded me of Gran's story about the lady who found it an amusing piece. When asked to explain, she replied:

'Well, a lot of elderly women got up and sang "Unto us a child is born", whereupon a lot of elderly men got up and sang "Wonderful!"' Most thrilling of all was the Brahms Requiem at the Queen's Hall under Toscanini, with Isobel Baillie and Alexander Sved as soloists. Toscanini dispersed all the stodginess I had associated with that work. I heard him conduct Beethoven's First and Ninth Symphonies on the radio, and noted that he took the first movement of the latter and the second subject of the Adagio faster than usual. Boult I considered a finer conductor than he was given credit for, on the strength of his performance of Schubert's Great C major.

My operatic experience was enlarged by *Aida*, *La Bohème*, *Die Walküre* and *Faust*, all at Sadler's Wells. I had little time for *Faust*, least of all the dreadful soldiers' chorus, made worse by some of the audience whistling it simultaneously in a different key, but made enthusiastic though not uncritical comments on the other three, two of which I saw with Gran, a perfect companion on such occasions. *Aida* was done with great spirit and a voluptuous ballet led by Margot Fonteyn with almost nothing on. The company's team spirit and zest, 'as infectious as an autumn cold', carried *La Bohème* to great heights; I ranked it above *Butterfly*, and greatly preferred the committed audience at Sadler's Wells to that at Covent Garden. *Die Walküre* was a revelation ('Damn it, Wagner *was* a great man!'), though weakened by reduced orchestration, especially among the strings. I had always shied away from Wagner, having heard him mostly in 'bleeding chunks', and was never able to wallow in the chromatic style of *Tristan*, but my ambivalence was quite conquered on this occasion. Intelligent staging was a great help, though Siegmund was sung by a stiff tenor; when Sieglinde lay asleep between his legs, he stroked her hair with the gestures of a cellist.

The Ten Club provided some fine entertainment. It could always be relied on to make the most of coarse plays like *The Country Wife*, but gave a superb reading of *Othello* (Noel Annan as Othello, Dadie as Iago) and a very funny one of *Peter Pan*, inevitably burlesqued, with Donald Beves in the name part ('One of the queer things about Peter is that he is no weight at all. But it's a forbidden subject'.) When I had to say of Peter 'He is not really our father. He did not even know how to be a father till I showed him' Donald gave me a look that convulsed the company and threatened to terminate the proceedings. Philip took me to the biennial dinner of the Musical Association (not yet Royal), my first contact with that august body. There were a great many speeches, and we annotated the programme accordingly: Professor Percival Kirby 'in the Dorian mode', Sir Percy Buck 'Andante pontificale ma grazioso (sempre con sordino', Benjamin Dale 'Allegro salubre G major', Captain Evelyn Broadwood 'Allegro comodo ma discursivo: tema con variazioni D major', Stanley Marchant 'Andante aperto ma non troppo adagio', Sir Donald Somervell (Attorney General) 'Giocoso e risoluto, un poco ponderoso'. One night I dreamed that Dent found me eating snails in Regent's Park. He poked the shells with a stick, craned his neck as only he could, declared 'Ah yes, that's Urdubarbilis prognosticans, it's only found in the Himalayas', and engaged a tree in earnest conversation.

Church expeditions with meals at West Walton continued to refresh my spirit, 'like a gust of fresh air in a greenhouse'. I continued to give gramophone parties, one of them for the 99th anniversary of Bizet's birth, and read the only English biography of Bizet, by D.C. Parker, a dismally inadequate work. *The Testament of Beauty* seemed to me 'the most invertebrate of poems'. I was contemptuous of Stephen Spender's *Vienna* and very critical of Gerald Abraham's book on Borodin, a composer I greatly admired. There was something about Abraham's style and approach that put my back up: when his book *A Hundred Years of Music* came out in the following year I plastered the margin of Philip's copy (now mine) with vituperative comments. After the war he was to become a close friend.

In December, moved by the unhappiness of Gran and Tommy, I wrote Mother a conciliatory letter suggesting that we buried the past. It was no good: she accused me of moral cowardice, of knowing that I was wrong but refusing to admit it. So long as I refused to do that, reconciliation was impossible. She said I had made England so unpleasant for her that she had to leave the country and could not return. It never seemed to occur to her that the obstacle was the equivocal position in which she was placed by Eugene, who boasted that he could command £1,000 a year but made no move towards marrying or keeping her. Meanwhile the hapless Vernon, on the verge of bankruptcy with the contents of Rooting sold by order, had thrown himself on Vie's mercy. Refusing the advice of doctors and laymen to make a move towards having him certified, she had taken him for a holiday in Wales – where apart from the total degeneracy of his moral fibres and his conviction that he could set the world at rights he was reasonably normal – and was keeping him and his Leicester Square prostitute (who was devoted to her). This produced a complete volte-face from Basil, who wrote in September: 'I consider you are doing a very plucky thing in sticking to Vernon in this way. I also think I must have done you an injustice by accepting so readily his point of view in the past. For this I am sincerely sorry.' Vie's suggestion that he might have misjudged me too evoked a letter that seemed, like Shakespeare's equivocator, to swear in both the scales against either scale. 'I am interested in what you say of Winton's efforts to be reconciled to his mother. But I'm afraid my own attitude in the matter is not yet fully appreciated. Whilst I strongly disapprove of Winton's breach with his mother, I also think it quite impossible to approve of the conduct of Esther's friend. I hold most strongly that it is impossible for Winton to condone the conduct of the man in leaving Esther in such an equivocal position for so long. I thought I had made all this clear to Winton. It is for him to put the matter right with his mother, whilst making it quite clear he cannot accept any conditions whatever from the man whose behaviour has robbed him of any respect and any locus standi.'

How I was expected to reconcile these two objectives was not made clear. But Basil's attitude to me once more changed course. He wrote in January 1938: 'I have decided I cannot any longer maintain my attitude of tacit support of your mother in this matter. We must assume she is quite under the influence of this man, who obviously does not love her in a genuine way ... You are entirely right – in the light of actual events – to refuse an undignified surrender. Surrender to what? An obvious hanger-on!' And a few days later, after asking to see the correspondence: 'Mr Bagger strikes me as rather bumptious. He writes to you as a father of a singularly flatulent nature, which is surprising in view of his evident reluctance to assume the responsibility of such a relationship, even in a vicarious sense ... I do not detect any of the accents of a mother in your mother's letter at all ... The time will surely come when you can get some of your own back. And don't be priggish about feeling that way; it's quite justifiable.' He asked me to report on an actress appearing at the Arts, and made me an executor of his will. (He later cut me out of it altogether.)

I spent Christmas and the New Year with Bert and Fanny Jeffery at Hambledon. This was a most refreshing experience; some of my happiest hours at this period were spent with the village people. I had the highest admiration for Bert's character, and could discuss anything with him. He spoke a good deal about his experiences in France during the first war; he had a rough time, from which he characteristically derived much humour and no bitterness. But Fanny told me they still sometimes caused him to cry out in his sleep. Bert's father lived in a tiny cottage on the cricket green (Rose Cottage) where his family, four sons and a daughter, had been brought up. They were all present with their spouses on Christmas Day, which was spent in the cottage eating, drinking, talking and playing games, though the weather was so mild that someone suggested a game of cricket. I was received as one of the family and made to feel thoroughly at home. Every one of them was richly endowed with humour; stress and anxiety melted away in their presence. I even drafted an entire play in ten days. The excitement kept me awake at night, but I could only have done it in such a thoroughly congenial atmosphere.

We paid a couple of visits to cinemas in Guildford, played darts in the pub, went ferreting (a curiously exciting experience), and were shown the technicalities of brickmaking by the foreman of the local brickworks. The children of the village school gave an amusing Christmas entertainment, a sort of folk opera based on *Old King Cole*, the idea being to bring in as many nursery rhymes as possible, which were then repeated by the chorus. There was a New Year singsong and dance, accompanied by much horse-play, at the British Legion hut, ending with an orgy of kissing under the mistletoe. I had never kissed so many women in one evening in my life. The only casualty was Tom Hammond, husband of Bert's sister and the very efficient secretary of the cricket club, who was forced to retire with a bleeding nose; which hen pecked him was never discovered. As a contrast to this I visited the Radcliffes in Godalming and dined with Clare's family at Westbrook, where Fielden, the music master at Charterhouse, induced the party after dinner to give an impromptu and highly inaccurate performance of the choral finale of Beethoven's Ninth Symphony, clustering round two miniature scores while he beat hell out of the piano.

* * * * *

On 4 January 1938 my detailed diary ceased abruptly. I had been considering dropping it for some time, and remember a sense of relief. It had become a tedious duty as well as an encouragement to introspection, though it served a useful function by affording constant practice in the manipulation of words and ideas. I may not have been conscious of this at the time, but on re-reading it after more than fifty years I am struck by the gradual development of a style. Henceforward I kept a pocket diary, little more than a register of engagements. This is useful for dates and as an aid and corrective to memory; it brings back much that I had otherwise forgotten, and sometimes reveals that events which seemed years apart in my recollection in fact took place on the same day. Yet I regret the loss of immediate impressions, and wish that, for some periods at least, I had reverted to the old method.

In a limited sense I did. In the same year and the same volume I began a music diary, recording my impressions of every piece of music I heard for the first time and often my later reactions as well. I kept it up for more than sixty years and it must contain millions of words. My motives for starting it did not include deliberate preparation for a musical career. I wanted to clarify my responses by putting them into words, and to fix them so that they would not slip away down the sink of forgetfulness. This had one unexpected result: the act of reading words written years before not infrequently brought back melodies and harmonies, even of works which I had no recollection of having heard. There was an element of self-education on more than one level; I wished to train myself not only in musical understanding but in the ability to express my thoughts in the most articulate and economical form. This would be valuable even if my career had no connection with music, as I still intended to devote my life to creative rather than critical labour.

None of this was undertaken with a view to publication; I should hate to think that any of these lucubrations, often hastily written in note form, would be printed, even after my death. They were nothing more than raw material. Since I always tried to write down exactly what I felt, and since, especially in the early years, my musical knowledge and my experience were limited, I often voiced opinions that now seem worthless and perverse. My estimates of modern music which I did not understand were apt to be callow and reactionary. Sometimes they were contradicted in later entries, but often they were not. What I wrote about Schoenberg, Stravinsky, Bartók and even some earlier classical composers by no means represents what I think today. I was learning all the time, but the results of this process appear only intermittently in the diary entries.

I was greatly encouraged, both in keeping this record and in the general pursuit of music, by Philip Radcliffe, with whom I discussed every musical question endlessly over a period of more than fifty years. We must have played and sung through many thousands of works at the piano, including hundreds of operas. Some of my early diary entries no doubt reflect his opinions, which tended to be conservative. He was extraordinarily knowledgeable about the entire repertory from the sixteenth century to the end of the Romantic period, and had an astonishing amount of it literally at his finger-tips. No one else of my acquaintance was able to quote so much from memory, though he was by no means a technically accomplished pianist. He was a more than competent teacher of classical harmony and counterpoint, as well as of musical history, with an outstanding gift for imparting his knowledge to the young. On all music which he loved and admired his enthusiasm was infectious, and he was never impatient of the inadequacy of his pupils provided they possessed the spark of enthusiasm. He was suspicious of much twentieth-century music; I don't think that Schoenberg and the Second Viennese School ever gave him any pleasure. He complained that he could not hear atonal music in his head. But he strove always to keep an open mind; he considered it his duty to listen to the most rebarbative modern works, and genuinely regretted his inability to enjoy much that his juniors admired. It was the almost universal opinion that he was the best teacher in the Cambridge faculty; new students clamoured to be supervised by him, and he went on teaching individual pupils long after his official retirement.

Philip and I were by no means always in agreement, even in the early days. Generally it was my dislikes and prejudices that had to be overcome. I went through a phase of hostility to Brahms, and also to Fauré, one of Philip's favourites, whose harmonic restlessness I found unsettling, even disturbing. With his assistance I overcame this. For a time I nourished a curious antipathy to the key of G minor. Not possessing perfect pitch, I could not account for this logically, but it was not an affectation. It was balanced by an even stronger susceptibility to certain keys, especially D flat and E major, to which I reacted with instinctive pleasure. When I tried to rationalise this, and build up a coherent system in my head, the ability to distinguish even these keys would disappear.

Occasionally the boot was on the other foot. When I first knew Philip, he was inclined to regard much of Handel as an inferior substitute for Bach, and eighteenth-century music by composers other than the very great seemed to him dry and bloodless. What he liked most, as he was willing to admit, was a good Romantic wallow. While his favourite composer was Schubert, he had a particular weakness for Schumann and Tchaikovsky. For a long time he was irritated by Britten's music and disposed to acquiesce in Paddy Hadley's contemptuous references to Benjamin Brittle; later he confessed his inability to understand his earlier coolness. My reactions to Britten were much more favourable from the start; a performance of the Frank Bridge Variations early in 1939 led me to expect a great future.

My appetite for music was insatiable. Between January 1938 and the outbreak of war I attended more than a hundred concerts, 65 in 1938 alone, as well as many ballets and about twenty operas, and heard innumerable radio performances as well. While many of the concerts were in Cambridge, I constantly travelled to London during term, more often than not with Philip, and frequented the Queen's Hall and other venues when I was there during vacation. The total would have been higher had I not been in the country for weeks on end. Many of the orchestral concerts were conducted by Beecham, Boult or Wood: I also heard Weingartner ('Unfinished', Brahms 4), Albert Coates (a mainly Russian programme in Liverpool with Kentner playing the Scriabin concerto), and Toscanini several times (Jupiter, Schubert G major again, Beethoven 5 and 6, Missa Solemnis). The solo artists, a veritable galaxy of talent, included Landowska, Rachmaninov, Petri, Hess, Kathleen Long, Schnabel, Curzon, Edwin Fischer, Busch and Serkin, Yehudi and Hephzibah Menuhin, Kreisler, Suggia (in the Elgar concerto), Szigeti, Rubbra (a programme of violin sonatas with his wife), Britten, Pears and Sophie Wyss, Poulenc and Bernac, Mark and Michal Hambourg, the Brosa, Griller, Menges and Pro Arte Quartets, and many more. The Pro Arte played a complete Beethoven cycle in Cambridge which I considered one of the great experiences of my life.

Many of these left a permanent mark on my memory. Toscanini's Beethoven combined intense energy with a transparent clarity of detail, especially in the woodwind writing, that revealed countless new beauties. He took the Scherzo of the Pastoral with tremendous gusto and none of Walter's tiresome rubato, the slow movement rather faster than usual, and gave the storm a terrifying menace. Rachmaninov played the first Beethoven concerto and his own

Paganini Variations with Beecham and the LPO; his manner at the keyboard was detached, even phlegmatic, yet the music seethed with a romantic passion all the more overwhelming for the contrast. The programmes contained a great deal of Elgar and even more Sibelius, including all the symphonies, most of them in a series of concerts given by Beecham late in 1938. I vividly recall the delicacy of the incidental music to 'Swanwhite' – in the music and the performance – and the intensity of 'The Death of Mélisande' in Sibelius's music to Maeterlinck's play, where it was sometimes difficult to distinguish the cries of the woodwind from the hortatory yells of the conductor. Beecham had a marvellous touch in music of this kind, as well as in Bizet's newly discovered symphony (a particular delight to me) and Delius's *Appalachia*, which in his hands sounded like a major masterpiece. Kreisler's concert in Cambridge was a curiosity; he played beautifully, but with an indifferent pianist who evidently felt it incumbent on him to remain in the background. The programme included the Franck sonata, with an ostentatious interval for applause after the second movement, and a number of scrappy arrangements. I was asked to review this in the undergraduate paper, and let myself go in a notice that verged on the libellous, accusing the pianist of trampling upon his instrument in obsequious mezzo forte.

During the last two seasons before the war a group of young musicians, with the co-operation of the agents Ibbs and Tillett, organised an enterprising series of Sunday-night monthly concerts at the Cambridge Theatre in London. Since they were not designed to make a profit, prices were very cheap. The programmes centred first on Mozart, especially the concertos, but were extended later to embrace Haydn and Schubert. The artists were mostly young, and included a number who subsequently achieved fame in rather different fields, among them Jack Westrup, Mosco Carner, Reginald Goodall and William Glock. Boris conducted two concerts, in one of them performing a remarkable rescue act when Betty Humby (later

Beecham) got lost in Mozart's K. 271. There were I think nineteen concerts in all, of which I attended fourteen. In little more than a year I heard at least twenty-six Mozart concertos, many of them two or three times, and began to do some research on them, with special reference to the scoring for wind instruments and the persistence of certain rhythmic patterns. This project was never completed. I preferred Clifford Curzon's interpretation of K. 537 to Landowska's. The latter introduced what I described as Chopinesque twiddles into the slow movement, but this may have been justifiable ornamentation of passages left plain. I welcomed the chance to hear a good deal of music not at that time often performed in public, including a Haydn Mass and several works by Schubert for small choral groups. Two of the series were chamber concerts and one a Schubert recital by Schnabel, who took the late B flat sonata by the scruff of the neck and made it sound like Beethoven at his most unbuttoned.

Early in 1938 Boris asked me to translate the libretto of Weber's *Abu Hassan* for performance in a triple bill at the Arts. I at once consulted Dent, who advised me to make it lively and played through the vocal score, singing each part in a high cracked voice and interspersing irreverent comments ('What wretched stuff these classics did write!') between the vocal entries as he went on playing. I greatly enjoyed the challenge, and managed to fit the most unsingable vowels to the roulades in the parodies:

> Fatima.   I will sing you now a ditty.
>   With Aurora's dawning light –
>
> Abu Hassan.   That will kill me, have some pity!
>
> Fatima.   No, it softens hunger's bite!

The performances, conducted by Boris with Margaret Field-Hyde, Morgan Jones and Douglas Craig-Jones (whom I was to meet again as Douglas Craig in Handel productions after the war), were very lively. The other operas were Mozart's *Der Schauspieldirektor*, translated by Eric Blom, and *Riders to the Sea*, which I have always considered the best of Vaughan Williams's stage works. Gran and Dalziel McKay came up for the occasion, and I gave a party at which I introduced them very successfully to Peter Lucas. This was quite an achievement, since he normally never attended parties. Boris invited me to breakfast to meet Eric Blom. He was charming and gave me a very nice notice in the *Birmingham Post*, though he disapproved of my introducing slang. There were plans for several later productions of *Abu Hassan* in my translation, including one at Sadler's Wells in 1941 in a double bill with *Dido and Aeneas*. In the event it had to wait till 1974, when I revised the text for a production at the State University of New York, Stony Brook. It was also revived in 2007 by West Riding Opera under Martin Binks.

Shortly after this I saw by chance that Mozart's *Idomeneo* was to receive a single performance at the little Century Theatre, Notting Hill Gate, in a production by the Falmouth Players, with Geoffrey Dunn as the King. I had barely heard of the opera, which was then quite unknown except in Germany; this was in fact its London première. I hastened up alone to see it, and was bowled over by its intensity and tragic power and the subtlety of the characterisation: why was it the accepted view that Mozart could only write comedies? Boris also saw it and was so impressed that he determined to do it in Cambridge. Finding the Radford translation unsatisfactory, he invited me to make a new one if Dent did not want to undertake it, but eventually decided on modified Radford. In May 1939 the C.U.M.S. put it on for a week at the Arts, conducted by Boris with mostly professional singers and the University chorus. The impact was overwhelming. The part of Idamante, written for a soprano castrato, was sung by Elizabeth Darbishire, who was very moving. I have never been able to stomach the substitution of a tenor, as in all three Glyndebourne productions. Anthony Bernard conducted a revival, with the same Idamante and others of the Cambridge cast, at Haslemere in 1943, and a production at Oxford followed soon after the war. The opera's success in England dates from the Cambridge performances, though the credit has been claimed quite wrongly by Glyndebourne, as I have more than once pointed out in the magazine *Opera*.

In May 1938 I saw two other rare revivals, Handel's *Belshazzar* staged at the Scala Theatre in London and the British première of Verdi's *Macbeth* at Glyndebourne. The *Belshazzar* production, mounted by a body with Communist leanings, was perverse. It began with 'The people shall hear' from *Israel in Egypt* (why draw on another oratorio when several of the grandest choruses in *Belshazzar* are cut?) The words were absurdly modified to convey the chosen political message; 'All empires upon God depend' became 'All empires upon force depend', making nonsense of the context. Nevertheless nothing could dim the dramatic power of the music, especially the scene of the writing on the wall. I was more than ever convinced that Handel's genius demanded the theatre. *Macbeth* was musically thrilling, but strangely the producer pushed it back towards oratorio by dropping the curtain before the finales of the first and last acts. This took much of the dramatic stuffing out of the former and was quite ludicrous in the latter, where an obvious marching song was delivered by the whole cast standing at attention and looking silly. The programme is interesting for the appearance of some well-known names, including Peter Pears, among the chorus. The performance I attended was graced, not inappropriately, by a tremendous thunderstorm, which was audible during the opera and soaked the audience to the skin when they came out.

At this period the straight theatre interested me a much as opera; I was not sure that my future did not lie in writing for it. I saw a great many plays, from light comedy (*George and Margaret*, *French Without Tears*) to classics of every age: plenty of Shakespeare and the Elizabethans (*The Revenger's Tragedy*, *A New Way to Pay Old Debts*), Shaw, Chekhov (*The Cherry Orchard*, *Three Sisters*), O'Neill (*The Emperor Jones*, *Mourning Becomes Electra*), Priestley (*Time and the Conways*, *When We Are Married* and many more, some produced by Basil), Turgenev's *A Month in the Country*, Granville Barker's *Waste*, Schnitzler's *Professor Bernhardi* and many others. Basil gave me tickets for an excitingly dramatic play called *Autumn*, in which Vicky played opposite Flora Robson, a nice antithesis of innocence and blazing intensity. The Curzons took me to Giraudoux's *Anphitryon 38* with the Lunts, which I did not much like; the dinner and the convivial company more than made up for this.

One of these plays was to change the course of my life. In January 1938 Clare finally decided to marry Glenn, and Brigid married Lorimer. Though fully prepared for both, I felt that the fates were implacably opposed to my happiness. One evening, for the first and only time in my life, I made myself deliberately and disgustingly drunk. A very thick head duly punished me in the morning. A week later Philip took me to *The Cherry Orchard*, performed by the University Mummers. The first thing he said on opening the programme was 'There can't be such a person as Thalia Shaw', pronouncing the name in the old Greek style (Thaleia). He was soon to learn better. She played the part of Anya, the central character's younger daughter. What struck me most about her, apart from a pretty face and a delightful speaking voice, was a trait of character not easy to define: a kind of spontaneous impulsive generosity, totally without guile, which I detected instinctively much as I discerned Brigid's character in King's Chapel three years before. It is odd that of the three girls I wished to marry I first saw two on the stage and the third in an almost theatrical situation. There was another telepathic incident with regard to Thalia. The previous summer I had read the *Times* obituary of her grandfather the first Lord Craigmyle, and it remained vividly in my memory though the name then meant nothing to me.

Soon after the performance I asked Tess, who like Thalia was at Newnham, to arrange a meeting. This duly took place at a small tea party, and was a slightly disconcerting experience. Thalia was much quieter and more reserved than I expected, and not at all impulsive. Was it Chekhov's character rather than the actress who had moved me? Luckily I pursued the acquaintance; my vision had been correct, but it revealed what she was to become rather than what she was then. By the end of the term, after four or five meetings, it was clear that the attraction was mutual. But I was by no means sure it was the real thing. My feelings were very different from those inspired by either Brigid or Clare, much calmer and more detached. I was afraid I was not feeling enough, and uneasily aware that had I not seen her as Anya I might have felt nothing for her.

The vacation soon brought a crisis. So far I had no idea who her parents were. Thalia spoke rather incautiously to her mother, who jumped to the conclusion that things were more advanced than they really were and at once became protective. When I first went to their palatial flat in Lowndes Square, I found myself treated with suspicion, which turned to active hostility when they discovered that we were meeting every day. I was staying at Portland Place, sleeping as usual on a camp bed in Tommy's study, and the Grandparents gave a delightful dinner party on my birthday, with Tess, Hilary and Philip as well as Thalia. I introduced her to other friends, including Vie and David Hubback. We went to plays and concerts, including the B minor Mass at the Queen's Hall, and a very chaste dance at Cecil Sharp House with my cousin Margaret Dean-Smith. It was all perfectly respectable.

There was one strange evening when I was invited to dinner with the Craigmyles, very much aware I was on approval. Beforehand I had a drink with Philip and Lorna Rea, old friends of Gran's and Mother's who went out of their way to be hospitable to me. They plied me with good cheer till I begged them to stop: I must not be even a little drunk, since I was dining with a peer of the realm. 'Never mind that', said Philip. 'He'll probably be drunk too. They say drunk as a lord, after all.' The idea of Lord Craigmyle in his cups kept haunting me during dinner, which was a sticky meal; the victim of misfortune however was not me but Thalia, when a maid accidentally tipped a whole plate of soup down her new dress, which was never the same again. After the meal we saw *Three Sisters*, keeping up the association with Chekhov. The bomb fell a day or two later. Thalia was forbidden to see me in London and ordered to keep away from me in Cambridge.

The explanation lay in the character of Lord Craigmyle. By any standard he was a most formidable man. He had a brilliant intellect but poor health, which had compelled his resignation from the posts of Chairman of P&O and a director of the Bank of England. The only son in a family of girls, he had been very spoiled in his youth. He went from success to success: President of the Union at Oxford, a Member of Parliament for eight years, High Sheriff of the City of London, and director of many companies. He married a wealthy wife, the eldest daughter of the first Earl of Inchcape. Except for ill health he had never known a check. He had position and power, not least over his family, who all stood in awe of him. He had been known to ignore his wife for a whole weekend with the house full of guests, refusing to speak to her at meals on account of some fancied slight. Since he had a very violent temper, and could create an atmosphere of disapproval and hostility as oppressive as the sultry calm before a long-delayed thunderstorm, it was more than anyone's life was worth to stand up to him. He had had his way all his life over important issues, and generally over lesser ones as well. Moreover he was given to violent and irrational prejudices, especially where other people were concerned.

Thalia was the second of three sisters; her only brother Donald, the youngest of the family, was then 14, a schoolboy at Eton. They had all learned to keep out of their father's way when he was in one of his moods, and none had yet challenged his will. Thalia had escaped some of the pressure by going to Cambridge, on the urging of her teachers at St Felix School; she was the only one of the girls to attend a university. Ruth, the youngest, was at a finishing school in Switzerland, and I did not meet her until later. Jean, more than three years older than Thalia, had obviously had her spirit crushed; at that time she was nervous and introspective, though she developed a sturdy independence later. Lady Craigmyle too, with the heaviest burden to bear, had long ago surrendered the initiative on all major issues to her husband.

It was probably inevitable that Lord Craigmyle should resent the first potential suitor brought home by one of his daughters – and his favourite daughter too, as I subsequently discovered. He took an immediate, violent and inexpugnable dislike to me. This was totally irrational, though he soon found reasons, as will presently appear. Nothing was admitted in my favour, even the fact that my uncle Rufus had been a very close friend of the first Lord Inchcape. It was clear that Lord Craigmyle claimed a prescriptive right of veto against his daughters' friends; there was no question of anything more at this stage. Since Thalia was only 19 there was little we could do about it except lie low. The Craigmyles clearly hoped to frighten me off; but the course they took was the one most calculated to sabotage their own interests. Any doubts that Thalia or I may have entertained about our relationship were at once driven to the wall. Lord Craigmyle was the third father-figure with a domineering and intolerant temper whom I had encountered, and I had no intention of being cowed.

We refused to submit to the ban, and planned to meet in secret. The first occasion on which we put this into effect had its comic side. Thalia was going to spend a few days with her school friend Rosamond Berridge in Leicester. Knowing that she would be escorted to St Pancras, I went ahead, concealed myself in one of the train lavatories (a wise precaution, since she was accompanied to the station by Craigmyle family emissaries), and emerged when the train had started. Rosamond's parents were very hospitable and allowed me to spend the day with them, but her father, a clergyman, did not think it proper to put me up for the night. For the rest of the vacation I was away, staying with the Wilsons in West Walton, where I read the lessons in church, with the Davisons at Dingle in Suffolk, and with the Jefferys at Hambledon. I was co-opted into the Merry Harriers darts team and took part in a tournament against the Guildford police at their station headquarters. It was amusing meeting them coming off the beat and reporting on my fellow citizens' encounters with the law. Towards 10 o'clock they slipped out to make sure that the pubs were duly closed, then came back to reopen the station bar for at least another hour.

Plates

1. Joseph Dean (1816-1895)

2. Harding Hewer Dean c. 1880

3. Elizabeth Mary Winton, 1880

4. Nicholaas Laurentius Van Gruisen (1824-1898)

5. Joseph Isaacs, 1894

Plates

6. Sara Isaacs

7. Rufus Isaacs

8. Harry Isaacs

9. Alfred Sutro c. 1905

10. Essie Sutro

11. Basil's mother

12. Esther as a girl

13. Wilfred Van Gruisen

14. Basil

15. Basil joins up

16. Hambledon Hurst 1918, with Ruby

17. Esther, Winton, Gran at Hambledon, 1918

An Engagement with Time

18. Hambledon Hurst, June 1923

19. Esther in Switzerland, 1926

Plates

20. Tommy and Gran on Blackdown, 1926

21. Winton at Warden, Aug. 1928

22. Joe, Haricot, Margaret, Martin at Sheerness, Sept. 1928

23. Grandparents' Golden Wedding, 1932. Front row: Winton, Madeline, Vernon, Dorothy. Back row (5th left) Esther

24. Alfred and Essie Sutro at Hambledon c. 1932

25. Joe, Winton, Martin at the bungalow, 1933

An Engagement with Time

26. Dean grandparents visit Warden, with Winton, Vernon, Esther, Dorothy, 1934

27. Gran at Hambledon, 1934

28. Tommy at Hambledon with Tiger, 1934

29. Little Easton Manor c. 1934

30. Winton and Joe birds-nesting at the Manor, April 1934

31. Esther at Hambledon, 1934

32. Eugene Bagger at Hambledon, 1934

33. Eugene and Esther by the pond, April 1934

34. Vicky, Tessa, Basil at the Manor, Aug. 1934

35. Tessa, Winton, Joe at the Manor, 1934

36. Winton on Loch Sunart with a catch of mackerel, Sept.1934

37. Hilary at Wittering, July 1935

38. Winton and Brigid Bartley at Hamble, July 1935

39. Churches expedition, July 1936. Kenneth Harrison and Philip Radcliffe (in car)

An Engagement with Time

40. Winton at Salzburg, Aug. 1936

41. The Theseion, Sept. 1936

42. Byzantine church at Plataniti, 1936

An Engagement with Time

43. Winton at Daphni, 1936

44. Basil in 1930s

An Engagement with Time

45. Clare Mallory c. 1936

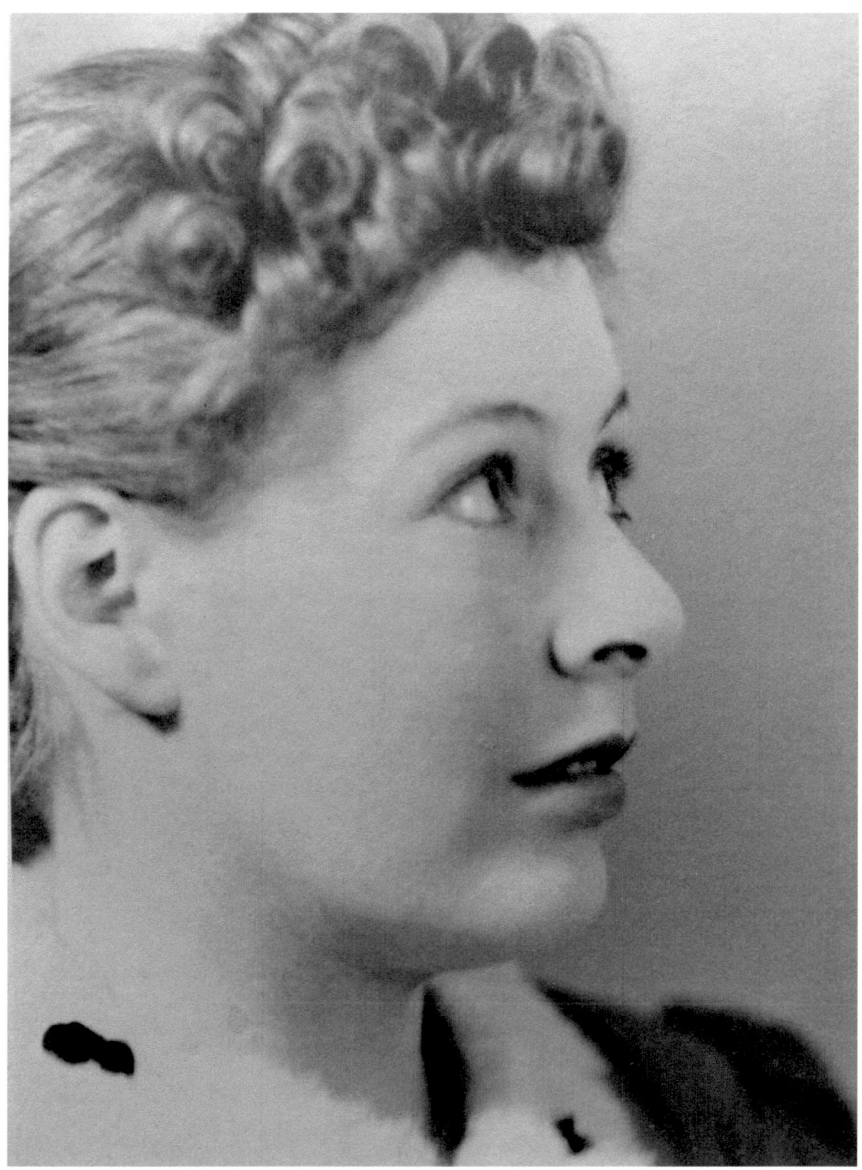

46. Thalia as Anya, 1938

An Engagement with Time

47. Alexander Shaw, 2ⁿᵈ Baron Craigmyle

48. Thalia's mother Margaret

49. Alexander at Fairnilee c. 1936

Plates

50. Thalia, Rosamond Berridge, Ruth, Halsey Colchester, Donald at Fairnilee, Sept. 1938

51. Winton and Thalia at Hambledon, June 1939

An Engagement with Time

52. Brigid at Hambledon, July 1945

53. Gran at Hambledon, July 1945

54. Brigid and Thalia, Aug. 1945

Plates

55. Stephen with Shenka, Aug. 1947

56. Philip Radcliffe, Eric Blom, Thalia, Stephen, Molly Blom, Diana McVeagh at Milford, June 1949

57. Grouse shoot at Peel, Aug. 1949. Winton (left) with Margaret

58. Freda and Lennox Berkeley at Milford with Thalia and Stephen, May 1950

59. The White House, June 1950

60. Diana, Hercules, Stephen at Milford, 1956

An Engagement with Time

61. Pat Abraham, Diana Bromley, Diana, Gerald Abraham, Frances Abraham, Thalia, Nigel Fortune picnicking at Hambledon, June 1957

62. Calfshaw Cottage, 1958

63. Frank Walker

64. Winton and Thalia at Calfshaw on their silver wedding day

CHAPTER 12

Marriage

February had been marked by a rather sad event. Hitherto Joe, while (as I put it) 'completely embaggered', had maintained friendly relations with me. In January, spending the holidays with Mother and Eugene in Switzerland, he had an operation for a cist on the testicle, of which he sent me an amusing description (I had described my own operation for an abscess in the groin in 1927, and sent him my first two church articles). 'Nothing vital was removed … Most of the nurses speak English, e.g. "Would you like to pusswater?" Which is a somewhat painful process!' He drew illustrations of a Swiss bedpan 'with a barrel-vaulted apse' and commode: 'Prix: 100 frs, constructed in lacquered steel, white, blue or dun … I too … had a bit of tube in my belly. It made a noise like a champagne cork when the doctor pulled it out.' Less than a month later I received a letter similar to Martin's a year before, accusing me of 'filthy lies and insinuations … vile brutality and caddishness … obstinate intellectual conceit', etc, etc, and repeating the old charges of poisoning the minds of Mother's friends and driving her out of the country. It ended: 'It is impossible for me to hold any more communication with you, until you have undergone a complete change of heart'. Joe maintained that it was his own decision, and although Mother had written in January 'You will undoubtedly lose Joe's friendship if you do not change' I believed him; but the language and the sentiments were all too familiar in other mouths. Philip, the mildest of men, remonstrated as gently as he could, but received two very pompous letters animadverting on my 'brutal instincts' and declaring that 'a nervous breakdown is a fundamental act of cowardice'.

When Basil heard of this he was 'deeply shocked' but advised me not to take it seriously. 'After all Joe is only a schoolboy. I admit that is no excuse for writing in the style of Alexandre Dumas. I'll write and tick him off properly.' He evidently wrote not only to Joe but to Martin, Mother and Tommy; when during the summer I made another attempt to straighten things out everything Basil said, for example about Mother's equivocal position, was put down to my evil influence. She was amazed that I did not want to beg forgiveness for the terrible things I did. If I had any loyalty to her, I would never want to see Vie (a 'false friend', guilty of 'spite' against Eugene), would 'express regret to Martin and Joe for landing them in an almost insupportable situation with their father', and tell Basil that if Martin and Joe quarrelled with me it was because I was in the wrong. Under pressure, I had offered to withdraw anything I might have said detrimental to Eugene or reflecting on his motives, but denied that my past actions implied wrong-headedness and moral degeneracy; the blame was perhaps fairly evenly divided. This brought Eugene into action with a demand for 'a <u>public</u> reparation, in the form of admitting to your father (to mention only him) that your account was distorted'. My 'account' had amounted merely to showing Basil the correspondence, beginning with Eugene's letter of December 1935. Eugene admitted that I had 'made an effort, however inadequate, to mend things', but my attitude '<u>stinks</u> of mental reservations'. Feeling now emotionally more secure, I was tempted to reply 'Let it stink!' I was not prepared to acknowledge that I had behaved like a cad, and I was not prepared to abandon Vie, who had supported me through thick and thin.

Marriage

Back at Cambridge for the summer term, Thalia and I met every day and soon reached the point of no return. We wished to establish some sort of *modus vivendi* with her parents. To this end her first cousin Tom Wheeler, who was much in favour with the Craigmyles, came to Cambridge for a week-end. He was very sympathetic and agreed to act as an intermediary. Since he was or had been more than a little in love with Thalia himself – though I did not know this at the time – his attitude was generous. This was a very happy term, free from the emotional convulsions of the past. We had an active social life, and I met Thalia's Newnham friends, who were all prosecuting more or less successful love affairs. We went to many plays and concerts, generally with Philip, and numerous parties. Once we were involved in a curious piece of pageantry organised by Mrs Prior in the Market Square. I cannot recall what it was in aid of, but Philip celebrated his birthday by appearing as a sixteenth-century Vice-Chancellor with me as one of his bulldogs, and a number of girls performed a country dance in costume. All this took place in a high wind, which must have caused anything we said to be inaudible. Towards the end of May I took my Tripos exam, and Thalia, reading English in her first year, took Mays.

This term I was the representative of my year on the committee organising the King's May Week ball. The duties were very light, and concerned chiefly with selecting the brand and vintage of champagne to be purchased. Since a great deal would be consumed, competition for the order was strong; twenty-one specimen bottles were submitted for trial. Dadie, who was the chairman, gave three dinner parties in his rooms at weekly intervals. Each of us had seven numbered champagne glasses by his place, and we sampled the contents of seven bottles in the course of each meal. The two best were chosen from each batch, and further bottles ordered. From these at a fourth session we made the final choice. This was the most agreeable committee on which I have ever served.

Thalia and I of course went to the Ball together. I was wearing a purple sash as a badge of office. It was a particularly joyful occasion because I heard that morning that I had been awarded a First Class in the Tripos. In congratulating me Patrick asked: 'Is it a record, as the papers say, for a Harrovian to get a First in English? Anyhow it's superb.' Since English was regarded as an easy option, the standard was set very high and few Firsts were awarded; Frank Thistlethwaite was among them. The Mummers Dance a week before had been less happy: we had spent the whole day on a church expedition with Kenneth Harrison, and Thalia was so tired that she arrived two hours late, bringing back painful memories of my experience with Clare the previous year. On the day after the King's Ball we paid a visit to Oxford. Thalia missed the train; on arrival I was astonished to find her already there; she had taken a taxi the whole way. She had already paid her first visit to Hambledon, arriving at a critical point in a cricket match against Godalming, which ended dramatically in a tie. She was often there throughout the summer, and Gran again allowed me to invite my friends; Beryl, Derek and Anne Clifford, Hilary, Tess, Oliver Zangwill, Peggy, John Davison and Peter Joseph came for week-ends. Clare and Glenn came over from Godalming just before their wedding; my gift of books on church architecture elicited a handsome letter from Glenn, thanking me for my attitude during the last year, saying he thought I behaved pretty consistently better than he had, and apologising for being boorish and backward in his treatment of me. This was generous, and perhaps more than I deserved.

Basil was very affable this summer, making 'a very belated presentation' for my 21st birthday and letting us use his flat for clandestine meetings. His letters contained pithy asides about the family. 'Do not concern yourself with Mr Bagger. He is an alien to our English ways of thought and feeling. If he had been trained at an English College he would have been "de-bagged" long ago.' 'I hear Martin has "embraced" the Catholic faith. '"Embrace" is a euphemism, for the embrace is a bear's hug, quite stifling the independent mind.' As a result of Tom Wheeler's diplomacy Lady Craigmyle invited me to a party for dinner and dancing at the Dorchester, with Thalia, both her sisters, Tom and others. It was a strange evening, much of which Tom spent trying to get off with Thalia. Some Cambridge friends put on an open-air performance of *The Tempest* in Lord Horder's garden at Steep near Petersfield, with Donald Beves as Stephano; never was there a more convincing drunken butler. The following year he was an even more memorable Falstaff in *The Merry Wives*. Peter Joseph's sister Anne, who played the bassoon in the orchestra at the Royal College of Music, got me tickets for a performance of *The Bartered Bride*, an opera I have always loved, to which I took Hilary. Fortunately this was the only day of the week when there was a late train to Witley, the station for Hambledon. I remember walking back from the station with the polka ringing in my ears.

During the Long Vacation term Thalia and I spent a fortnight in Cambridge, mostly playing tennis and looking at churches and doing very little work. I had decided to try for a Fellowship at King's with a dissertation on Landor, and had been awarded a College Studentship, later renewed for a second year, which would make this financially possible. There was a festival of sixteenth- and seventeenth-century music, organised by Dent, who introduced it with two characteristic lectures. The most entertaining event was an open-air Pageant of British Music in Neville's Court, Trinity, organised as usual by Mrs Prior: various historical scenes, from the Field of the Cloth of Gold to the Great Plague and Charles II's return from Newmarket in 1682, were enacted and illustrated with appropriate music. Many persons played suitably congenial parts: Philip as a French music master, Lady Clapham as Queen Elizabeth, Boris as Nicholas Staggins in a black full-bottomed wig quaking before Charles II. In one scene Philip, Boris and Donald Beves appeared among a group of seedy Puritans singing metrical psalms in a nasal whine. On a previous occasion Philip had had to register terror before Lady Clapham as Queen Elizabeth; he said he did not have to act at all, since she terrified him off the stage. The Madrigal Society, seated in punts anchored in the Cam below King's bridge, gave a concert of madrigals at dusk, at the end of which the punts were released to float downstream to the strains of Wilbye's 'Draw on, sweet night'. The audience were requested not to make a noise by rushing away, as the concert was to be broadcast. In the event radio listeners were puzzled by gales of laughter; a punt bearing six chamber-pots adorned with candles, released upstream, bore down on the singers.

In August Thalia went to France for a month while I undertook a walking tour up the west coast of Scotland, in the company of Peggy and a Dutch couple whose acquaintance she had made on a continental holiday. We took a train to Fort William and began by fording a stream and ascending Ben Nevis, then moved north as far as Ullapool, staying in youth hostels. Apart from occasional lifts from helpful lorry drivers when we happened to be on a road, which for the most part we were not, we proceeded on foot carrying rucksacks. The scenery was glorious, except on two days when rain and fog blotted everything out, but the expedition was not an entire success. The Dutch proved lacking in humour, and made a great fuss when the vagaries of my digestion imposed slight delays. The accommodation was often primitive. One remote hostel (either Carn Dearg or Badbea) was a tiny cottage with only two bedrooms, each fitted with eight bunks. The would-be occupants amounted to eleven men and five girls; but the warden, a Highlander with a sensitive moral conscience, flatly refused to allow the sexes to mix, though the girls raised no objection. Three of the men therefore had to doss down in the sparsely furnished kitchen. Early in the morning

Marriage

I awoke to the strains of the finale of Elgar's Second Symphony hummed cheerfully below; they came from a man who had spent the night on the upturned kitchen table. Elgar's tune never fails to evoke memories of this incongruous occasion. From Ullapool after a chilly bathe in Loch Broome we obtained some sort of transport to Inverness, where we stayed with a friend of Peggy's, a monosyllabic but friendly Highland general with shaggy blond eyebrows. In the evening we went to a circus, where a bored-looking lion trotted round the ring till it reached us, gave us a dirty look, turned its back, lifted its tail and discharged a copious jet of liquid at our feet. We returned to Fort William on a steamer through Loch Ness and the Caledonian Canal; I opened the first paper we had seen for a fortnight and read that Hutton had made 300 not out against the Australians.

After a privy meeting with Thalia in the empty Lowndes Square flat, I went with Philip to the Three Choirs Festival at Worcester. The programmes were mostly traditional: *Elijah*, *Messiah*, *The Dream of Gerontius*, selections from *Saul* (paralytically performed) and the Fauré Requiem, all in the cathedral, an orchestral concert in a cinema, and a very miscellaneous chamber concert that began with Delius's third violin sonata and ended, after numerous songs and piano pieces from all periods, with the Brahms horn trio. We cut the *St Matthew Passion* in order to visit Hereford and Gloucester Cathedrals. There was a great deal of Elgar, including *Enigma*, the violin concerto and *The Music Makers*, which has always seemed to me underrated. I could not understand why Elgar was not acknowledged as a great composer, and resolved to challenge Dent's heretical views on the subject. Two recent works that made a strong impression were Kodály's *Budavári Te Deum* and Vaughan Williams's *Dona Nobis Pacem*. Beethoven's Fifth Symphony was performed in the cathedral, where it sounded almost as much at home as a tiger in a drawing-room. The performances were not good; Ivor Atkins, a clumsy conductor, contrived to beat an extra bar after the end of Rachmaninov's second concerto. There were two new works, *An Hymn of Heavenly Beauty* by Harold Darke, which I found spineless and composed largely of crotchets, and the psalm *Domini est terra* by Lennox Berkeley, conducted by the composer, whom I saw for the first time. I did not much care for it, finding it fidgety except for one lovely entry for the sopranos near the beginning. I have been unable to check my impressions, never having heard the piece since.

The ambience of the festival was almost as entertaining as the music. The audiences, in which clerics, dowagers and country squires seemed to preponderate, were unlike any other in my acquaintance. I was reminded of a misprint alleged to have occurred in the programme of an earlier Three Choirs Festival: 'O ruddier than the clergy', from *Acis and Galatea* (which I once saw advertised on a Cambridge poster as *Acis and Gala Tea*). Philip and I found ourselves in the same hotel as all the London critics, who seemed a stodgy lot. In this opinion we were seconded by Jack Westrup, then a junior critic on *The Daily Telegraph*, with whom we struck up an instant friendship. He was much more relaxed than his later reputation as a stiff academic might lead one to suppose. Avoiding his colleagues, he joined us over a beer after the concerts, and we gossiped and pulled our elders to pieces to our hearts' content. One of the most conspicuous of these was Edwin Evans. He boasted an immense *massif central*. Unlike Donald Beves, a man of similar but less overwhelming proportions, he had an air of lordly self-importance. He always seemed to be holding forth in a voice like a foghorn about what Stravinsky or some other celebrity had said to him in 1920 or thereabouts. He would enter the gentlemen's lavatory, shoulder his companions to one side, and open fire like a howitzer from a considerable distance without interrupting his discourse. Philip heard him open – and nearly terminate – a meeting of the British section of the International Society for Contemporary Music, of which he was chairman in succession to Dent, with the sentence: 'Of course, as you all know, we never were a very large body'. He may not have been as witty as Falstaff, but he was the cause of much merriment in others.

On the Saturdays before and after this visit to Worcester I played in two memorable cricket matches, both between Hambledon and Feathercombe at Busbridge. They remain vivid in my memory partly on account of the exceptionally high scoring and thrilling finishes and partly because they afforded welcome relief from the grim negotiations taking place between Chamberlain and Hitler. The second match indeed was arranged at short notice for that very purpose. In the first match Feathercombe made 225 for 8 wickets declared, and Hambledon won by three wickets off the fifth ball of the last over. I was batting at the time; the winning run was a leg-bye, the ball travelling to short-leg, where two fielders competed for it and one picked up the other's foot. In the second match Hambledon declared at 211 for six wickets and lost by five wickets after another scramble against time. Political events also impinged on two Queen's Hall Proms which I attended later in the month. A note in the programme on the 27th announced that the Prime Minister's speech would be broadcast in the auditorium.

Meanwhile I had paid my first visit to Fairnilee, the Craigmyles' seat on the Tweed near Galashiels, a massive house in the Scots Baronial style. I first saw it early in the morning, having been met at Galashiels station by a chauffeur at 6.10 a.m. I was deposited in a bedroom and informed that Thalia was ill; she slipped in to tell me that she had been ordered to bed with a temperature. I spent the morning being driven round the countryside in search of a cub hunt that we never found, and the rest of the day with the sensation that I had strayed into a den of dangerous wild beasts.

The whole scale of the establishment was strange to me. The outside staff comprised five gardeners, three foresters, two gamekeepers, two chauffeurs and a groom. There were seven cars, including a Rolls Royce, a horse-box, an estate lorry and a shooting-brake, and several horses. Inside were a butler, a footman, a cook, at least four categories of maid, the children's old nanny, Miss Peakall, who acted as a kind of housekeeper and buffer-state, a riding instructor and Lord Craigmyle's secretary, Mr Huckle. The latter occupied a small cubby-hole in the basement and did not appear for meals; on two or three visits I don't think I ever set eyes on him. There were house guests too, as well as neighbours who dropped in for meals. Their conversation seemed to be mostly about horses.

Thalia and I went out as much as possible, driving round the countryside and visiting the Border abbeys. In the house I was very much aware of being under observation. One day there was a grouse shoot on Peel Moor, a nearby estate which the Craigmyles had recently bought. All the family and guests went up to join the shooting party for a picnic lunch, after which we had to climb a steep bank in order to reach the next line of butts. I helped Thalia up and was rebuked by Lady Craigmyle for allowing her to touch me. My first acquaintance of grouse-driving did not greatly impress me. The man in whose butt we stood seemed more interested in chatting, though every now and then he picked up his gun and shot a grouse.

The atmosphere lightened a little when several guests of our generation arrived, including Tom Wheeler and Halsey Colchester, a charming Oxford undergraduate whom Thalia had met through her aunt Lady Effie Millington-Drake. Now a new complication arose. It transpired that Halsey had fallen in love with Thalia, without her knowledge. He had been thrilled by the invitation, and was naturally appalled to find me in possession of the field. I liked him, and could only offer the cold comfort that I had recently been

Marriage

in his position. A school friend of Donald's called James Fish was also in the party. After he left I was startled to hear Lord Craigmyle making fun not only of his name but of the fact that his father was a dentist, evidently not a top-class profession. My departure evoked a more pungent comment: Halsey heard him say 'Thank God! Scotland is now a cleaner country'.

I went straight from Fairnilee to another walking-tour with John Davison, this time in the Cotswolds, starting at Burford. It was as convivial as before, and even more artistically fruitful: we hit on a whole range of splendid churches. From Stow-on-the-Wold we sent Tommy a telegram of congratulation on his 80th birthday. At Northleach we challenged an enormous lorry-driver to a game of darts, to be comprehensively humbled when he put almost every dart into the double or treble twenty. Thalia spent the last week-end of the vacation at Hambledon, leading her parents to believe she was in Leicester, and Monk drove us both back to Cambridge.

The most memorable event of this autumn term was the visit of the Group Theatre for the first performance, at the Arts, of the Auden-Isherwood play *On the Frontier* with music by Benjamin Britten. I did not think much of the play, but greatly enjoyed the social events surrounding it. Basil came up for the week-end, staying in College as Keynes's guest, and so did Lennox Berkeley, who was sharing a windmill with Britten at Snape. I had long talks with him and Britten, including some lively musical arguments. I was then inclined to be sniffy about Stravinsky; Lennox gently put me in my place. Basil, who like me thought more of the music than of the play, said to me afterwards, a propos of Britten: 'I want you to introduce me to that young man'. I effected the introduction at my new lodgings at 7 Peas Hill (I had moved out of College at the end of my fourth year); the result was a commission for incidental music to Priestley's new play *Johnson over Jordan*, which Basil was to produce in February 1939. I met Britten several times at this period. Once we happened to travel from London to Cambridge by the same train; we argued all the way about the relative merits of Brahms and Mahler. I found him thoroughly friendly and unaffected, but shrank from pushing myself into his company.

Clare and Glenn were now living in Cambridge. They came to one of my gramophone parties, at which Clare and I tried to teach Glenn to follow in a score. Though very willing to learn, he was not particularly musical. I remember him pointing to the first violin part and asking, 'Would that be the bassoon?' When Thalia and I dined with them, Clare banged her head on the oven door, then turned and swore at Glenn. He took it better than I would have done; she was quite right in supposing that I was not tough enough to cope with her wayward moods. They went to America early in the following summer and stayed there throughout the war, after which, ironically like Clare's father, Glenn was killed in a climbing accident. When Clare returned temporarily to England with three young sons, our friendship was resumed and lasted happily until her death on New Year's Day, 2001. She was the last to die of the girls I loved, all four of whom were my friends for life.

At another gramophone party I celebrated the centenary of Bizet's birth by playing the whole of *Carmen*. Martin Cooper's book on Bizet came out at the same time; Philip gave me a copy inscribed 'in eager expectation of a bigger and brighter work on the same subject', though I am not sure how seriously I was considering this. These parties had been going on now for more than two years, and I had a regular clientele, to which new faces were constantly added. Philip and Trend were regular attenders, as were Peggy and several Girton friends until they went down. On one occasion Peggy brought her mother. I decided to open with the Toscanini recording of the overture to *L'italiana in Algeri*, which begins with an extreme contrast of dynamics, a series of detached *pianissimo* chords followed by a very loud *fortissimo*. Mrs Wilson was just settling on her seat, and may not have taken in the *pianissimo* chords, which are very quiet indeed. At the *fortissimo* she shot straight up in the air like a startled rabbit, and for ever afterwards accused me of playing a trick on her.

An unfortunate contretemps marred the end of the term. At Salzburg the previous year I had introduced Clifford Curzon to Boris, who expressed a hope that he would play at one of the King's Music Society Sunday concerts. A date was finally fixed for early December, but nothing had been said about terms, nor did Boris send a formal invitation. In November Clifford wrote to me enquiring about arrangements. Boris asked me to reply, saying that the Society had little money and could only pay a nominal five guineas for expenses. This elicited an outspoken letter from Clifford, cancelling the concert, saying there had been no indication that he was expected to give his services, and pointing out that he was a professional whose musical education had cost thousands of pounds; he did sometimes give his services for charity, but this was always made clear from the start, and Cambridge University could hardly come under that category. It is clear that I had acted thoughtlessly and ought to have insisted on Boris making the arrangements. Unhappily I took Clifford's statement 'I find friendship impossible except on a basis of complete honesty' (which must have referred to his own letter) to imply that I had been dishonest, and was very upset. Although somewhat offended, he certainly bore no resentment. We met on a number of occasions after the war, and Thalia and I went to meals and parties at his house in Highgate. I sent him copies of my books and wrote to him on his sixtieth birthday; his replies were wonderfully cordial and full of enthusiasm for my work and career. He and Lucille both wrote with particular appreciation about *Handel and the Opera Seria* – they are among the most gratifying letters I have ever received – and more than once recalled our happy meetings at Litzlberg. Yet some residue remained at the back of my mind, not of anger but of fear. I longed to invite them to our house in the country, but was afraid that it would not come up to Clifford's immensely high standards. This seems absurd, and doubtless is so; it is not the only instance of a timorousness that presumably derives from the uncertainties of my childhood. Sadly it meant that I saw much less of Clifford and Lucille than I should have liked.

A few days after the end of term Thalia sailed for New York, where she remained for six weeks. This was a plan concocted by her parents to remove her from my reach. The distance they were prepared to travel in that direction is indicated by a letter from Lady Craigmyle to the American friend with whom Thalia was staying, which that lady left lying about, evidently intending Thalia to see it. It contained these sentences: 'It is *so* kind of you to have given her that lovely invitation. I think it is just what she needs to lift her out of the Cambridge atmosphere. That young man is a trial and we have to be *so* tactful. We pray that she may find someone to take his place'.

Although I did not feel any great danger of being supplanted, the strain caused by secret meetings and the need to be constantly on our guard was beginning to tell. At a dance in Berkeley Square two days before Thalia sailed I had a moment of sheer panic. Something she said seemed to indicate that she might want to be released. At once all the horrors of two and three years earlier threatened to return. We agreed that nothing should be decided until her return. Throughout these months I drew strength from recalling my relations with Brigid. When I first met her I had been only nineteen, very immature and insecure, with my home base in the family rapidly breaking down and no firm faith in anything. Brigid's generosity and patience had brought me through, by a very narrow margin. When I met Thalia, it was she who was nineteen, immature, quite as insecure as I had been, with no support or sympathy from her family. It was my duty to play Brigid's part and supply a rock, however slippery, to which Thalia could cling. The future of our relationship depended on me; the border between failure and success would be uncomfortably narrow. But, thanks largely to Brigid and also to Vie, whose letters and advice were full of wisdom and encouragement, I had learned a little.

On the day Thalia sailed I went to Elstree and for the last time played in a football match. Then I plunged into social activities, of which I have forgotten all but the concerts. One of these was distinctly curious. Hubert Langley had been trying to revive a dying Handel Society, and stimulated it into giving a concert at the Royal College. The conductor, he told me, was a good musician but unfortunately had little liking for Handel. His name was Reginald Goodall, and the programme must have been one of the oddest he ever conducted, three unaccompanied motets by Palestrina, Tchaikovsky's Fifth Symphony (which Hubert loathed, muttering that one tune reminded him of a bird caught in a net) and the first act of *Semele*, heavily cut. I loved this and wanted more. This was the last concert given by the Society.

Hubert was an amiably eccentric figure whose spiritual home was the eighteenth century; his presence in modern life seemed something of an anachronism. He had made commercially issued recordings as a treble choirboy at Eton before the 1914 war. A bachelor with private means, and an actor as well as a singer, he took part in amateur or semi-professional productions all over the country, many of them rarities like Dryden's *Aureng-Zebe*. He sent me a very funny description of playing Tristan in Masefield's tragedy opposite Violet Vanbrugh on a Cornish cliff top, dying twice nightly on wet grass with the wind blowing his skirt over his head and reciting death speeches against the full force of Atlantic waves dashing against the rocks. He wrote the first book on Arne (1938) and was a great lover of Handel. Early in 1939 he gave a performance of *Theodora*, hardly ever heard at that date, at the Foundling Hospital in Brunswick Square, the first of a series continued after the war. He said he had far more trouble in persuading the governors to let him do it than in organising the concert. His performances were apt to be unpredictable, not least in the movements he chose to cut. I had great arguments with him because he played down the dramatic element. He accused me of being nurtured on stage productions and therefore a stickler for realism; but he was quite right in preferring a contralto Didymus, which I then questioned. He was the only conductor I can recall who held the baton in his left hand. He had another peculiarity: he was allergic to nuts. When he stayed with us during and after the war we always made sure there was not a nut in the house. Nevertheless one morning he was taken acutely ill. We were all baffled, until we discovered the only possible cause, a pip in the marmalade.

Once more I spent Christmas and New Year with the Jefferys at Hambledon. This time the weather was bitterly cold, and the countryside under deep snow – one of only three or four white Christmases I can remember. I wrote my last serious poem, thinking of Thalia among the lights of New York. Philip later set it to music. Bert and I went to films and professional football matches, including a goalless draw between Portsmouth and Arsenal in a snowstorm. This was an entertainment I indulged in surprisingly often in those days. Generally we patronised Guildford City in the Southern League; but at Birkenhead the previous year I attended a cup-tie between Tranmere Rovers and Portsmouth, which I clearly remember Portsmouth were exceedingly lucky to win. Otherwise we played darts at the Merry Harriers or the British Legion hut, though some days I took time off to listen to music on the radio, a proceeding that puzzled Bert not a little.

Marriage

Thalia returned from New York several days after the beginning of the Lent term, and after a rather sticky first meeting relations were happily restored. Early in February, feeling rather like a character in a Victorian novel, I presented myself in Lord Craigmyle's study and asked his consent to our engagement. The interview was something of an ordeal, but at least free from explosions. He naturally enquired about my prospects and intentions, and pressed me to enter a respectable profession like the bar or the civil service. I could not promise this, but told him my intention of applying for a fellowship at King's in a year's time, after which I hoped to write and possibly teach. He was not really satisfied, but agreed to the engagement, provided we did not get married without consulting him further. I could not complain about this.

Our engagement was announced in *The Times* on 16 February, the anniversary of our first meeting. Gran came with me to choose an engagement ring. I received some delightful letters of congratulation, notably from Rosamond Berridge (with a moving encomium on Thalia's character) and Halsey Colchester, who thanked me for 'all the things you have done, both for me and for Thalia'. Vie wrote: 'It seems only the other day that you were making duckweed sandwiches at Rooting, and now I've got to be respectful to "Benedick the married man".' Stella wished us both 'all that is perfect and good and lovely and may your happiness approximate mine – which was as near perfection and bliss as ever can be'. Derek, admiring my 'rugged determination' and touches of the British bulldog, sent his condolences to Thalia for marrying beneath her. 'Oh and by the way, did you force the parental hand in the usual way? Are you marrying to save the girl's good name?'

At the end of January I met Mother at a hotel for the first time in nearly two and a half years. We went on to the grandparents' flat, where Thalia was waiting. This all went off happily; Mother liked

Thalia, but rebuked me for springing her on her without warning. Our engagement to some extent softened the family's attitude to me. A meeting with Martin in December had elicited two long and decidedly pompous letters to the effect that, as he had come half way by consenting to see me, it was now up to me to admit my past disloyalty and other sins against the moral code (Eugene of course being a model of loyalty and friendliness); he even cited Sir Thomas More and the Earl of Clarendon, and ended by ascribing my attitude to vanity. There was no hope on these lines. In February, writing to congratulate me, Tellie reported that Oxford had already done Martin a lot of good and 'unstiffened his neck very considerably'. He certainly met us on friendly terms at Hambledon during the summer; but my renewed attempts to straighten things with Mother merely brought out all the old accusations: conspiracy, 'dirty little lies', slandering her by saying that she had lost her personality, and insulting Eugene and 'kicking him in the stomach'. All this I was required to renounce. I could do nothing of the sort; but something I said in a letter of July – possibly that no man can be a judge of his own actions – unexpectedly broke the deadlock. I think they must have realised that there was no hope of a confession, and that I was prepared to build my life without them, as evidenced by my engagement to Thalia. At all events Eugene wrote that my letter, although guarded in its phrasing, had removed the principal stumbling-block, and he invited me to meet them at Châtel-Guyon in the first week of September.

One result of the engagement was that I was at least *persona non ingrata* in Lowndes Square, and dined several times with the family before going to a play or concert, sometimes with Jean or Ruth or Lady Craigmyle as well as Thalia. One occasion I particularly remember. Thalia, Jean, Tom Wheeler and I saw Shaw's *Geneva*, after which on Tom's suggestion we went to a night club called (I think) Paradise. There we found Lady Craigmyle's brother Lord

Marriage

Inchcape with his second wife Nonie (Leonora) watching a striptease act. Lord Inchcape, a shy man in contrast to his ebullient wife, looked distinctly sheepish, the more so when Nonie turned to me and said: 'He insisted on bringing me to this. What does he think *I* get out of it?' Thalia and I travelled up from Cambridge to Ruth's coming-out dance at Claridge's. This produced a tricky moment when Hilary, who had been invited to dine at our table, turned up with her latest boyfriend, bringing the complement to thirteen. Fortunately no one else noticed. I had to watch my countenance when Lord Craigmyle, after several attempts to eat asparagus with a pair of tongs, finally threw down the implement in disgust and set to with his fingers.

Our life at this period seems to have been an endless round of parties, plays and concerts, in Cambridge and London. We often went to the little Torch Theatre, where Vie was helping Gerald Cooper to run a repertory club. We saw T.S. Eliot's second play *The Family Reunion*, a fine production of *The Doctor's Dilemma* in which my Harrow contemporary Michael Denison made one of his first professional performances, and the first night of *Johnson over Jordan*. Basil gave us a special engagement dinner at the Ivy beforehand, and we sat in his box. Though not a commercial success, this seemed to me one of Priestley's most interesting plays: Britten's music was admirable, with a particularly fine overture. Basil at this time was bombarding the War Office with memoranda about the employment of the theatrical profession in war time, as a result of which he was put in charge of what became ENSA. He urged me to 'take up a man's size job' and join the Territorials, which would bring me 'into contact with humanity' and greatly help my writing. When I replied that I would obviously be of little use in the forces and intended to finish my dissertation, he began to play the heavy father and called me 'a young man excusing himself from an obvious duty'. In July he astonished me by saying that he was selling the Manor – a decision he regretted for the rest of his life – and expected to work a good deal in America.

On 29 March I went to two concerts, each of which supplies a non-musical memory. The first was a song recital by a young soprano, a friend of the Craigmyles, who was studying with Elena Gerhardt. That splendid artist was much in evidence, discoursing with all and sundry: she then sat down near me. Luckily there were two vacant chairs; she comfortably straddled both. In the evening there was one of Ernest Makower's London Museum concerts, to which admission was free. A few seats on the platform were reserved for selected guests; the rest of the audience expanded into adjacent rooms, sitting on the floor and even under tables. Mother and Eugene were there on the platform but I did not reveal myself. A few days later Vie took me to tea with Adrian Boult and his family; we went on to the BBC Maida Vale studios to hear a broadcast concert he was conducting. I was thrilled by Dvořák's D minor Symphony, but found Frank Bridge's *Oration* for cello and orchestra depressing. I was introduced to Bridge, a strange-looking whiskery man, but fortunately did not have to comment on his work. Boult, who as usual paid more attention to my opinions than they deserved, was most charming. He told me that Cyril Rootham's Second Symphony, dictated on his deathbed, which he had recently conducted, did not make sense.

My enthusiasm for opera was beginning to catch fire, chiefly from performances at Sadler's Wells. I saw *Don Carlos*, *Rigoletto*, *Tannhäuser* and *Il Trovatore* during the winter, and *Don Giovanni* and *Fidelio* when the company came to Cambridge in the summer. My lengthy comments now seem a strange mixture of penetration and obtuseness; I was still struggling to reconcile myself to the form. One stumbling-block was that I approached Verdi through *Falstaff* and Wagner through *Die Meistersinger*, and was consequently too aware of the comparative crudity of their earlier work. Another was that some of the performances were insecure. *Don Carlos*, a rare novelty on the English stage, was given in the contracted 1884 version (with further cuts), which left obscurities in the plot, especially in the first and last scenes, as well as inconsistencies in the music; but I surrendered completely to the great moments, especially the Escurial scene and Edith Coates's singing of 'O don fatale'. Much of *Tannhäuser* sounded to me like vulgarised Weber, and I was impatient with the slow pace of the action and the woodenness of the characters, Venus excepted. The opera that roused the most conflicting feelings was *Don Giovanni*. I could not then reconcile the jocularity of Da Ponte, accentuated by some flippancies in Dent's translation, with the tragic grandeur of nearly all the music. At that stage in my education the mixed genres, to which so much of opera's fascination is due, still struck me as incongruous. To some extent this applied to *Fidelio* as well, though I was fully aware of its sublimity. The performance suffered from Tudor Davies's unsuitability as Florestan, not merely in his ample proportions. His aria, which he sang extended at full length on the floor, deteriorated at the end into a series of agitated gasps. When I met him at a party afterwards, his first words were 'Beethoven should have been strangled at birth'.

In June I heard *Otello* for the first time, at Covent Garden in a performance so inadequate (except for the orchestra) that it is surprising that I could grasp its stature. Melchior (Otello) seldom sang in tune, and his Italian was unrecognisable; Caniglia (Desdemona) was hard as nails; Mario Basiola (Iago) took no apparent pleasure in his villainy; the chorus was ragged, and the production, obviously unrehearsed, so inept as scarcely to exist. Otello's first entrance was totally muffed. I was constantly struck, as in *Falstaff*, by the extraordinary subtlety and variety of Verdi's manipulation of cadence figures, a point to which I have never seen justice done.

The triennial Greek play this year was the *Antigone* of Sophocles, for which Paddy Hadley wrote the incidental music. In Dent's absence in America Philip gave the introductory public lecture in King's. He began by discussing and illustrating Mendelssohn's music to the play, ending with the statement 'Mendelssohn's treatment, you will have observed, is the essence of Victorian propriety and respectability'. Then, with a change of voice, 'Dr Hadley on the other hand –' at which point the audience collapsed with laughter, and it was some time before Philip was able to resume.

In the spring Thalia and I spent several days with Derek and Anne Clifford near Rochester in Kent, and we were brought abruptly into contact with world events when an airman friend, who dropped in for a drink, told us that he and his colleagues had to sleep near their aircraft. That particular crisis, coming soon after Hitler's demolition of Czechoslovakia, was caused by Mussolini's invasion of Albania. We attended various point-to-point meetings, in which Derek's brother was riding, but I was again afflicted by an abscess in the ear and in no position to enjoy them. Derek had a fine power of invective: when a woman stepped off the pavement in front of the car, he shouted: 'Get out of the way, you illegitimate daughter of a nine-nippled washerwoman!'

The summer passed easily at Hambledon and Cambridge, with the usual round of week-end visits from my friends, cricket matches, tennis and church expeditions. Thalia took Part I of the English Tripos, the last exam she was destined to take. I made some new friends, including Wilfred Noyce, an inarticulate climber who subsequently joined the successful Everest expedition in 1953 and lost his life on a mountain in Soviet Russia, and Wilfrid Mellers, then reading English under F.R. Leavis and attended by a wife, known as Pussy, considerably larger than himself. One day Dent brought Egon Wellesz to tea with me, a refugee from the Nazis in Austria;

Marriage

he had an engaging Viennese charm, but I lost touch when he moved to Oxford. Vie introduced me to Hesketh Pearson, Henry's father, then engaged on a biography of Bernard Shaw, for which I lent him Shaw's letters to Alfred Sutro. He quoted some examples of Shaw's delight in leg-pulling, not always without malice: he disliked St John Ervine, whose first name he insisted on pronouncing like the evangelist.

Now released from emotional turmoil, I was much less troubled by the family quarrels. But the international situation was a louring presence in the background. I had felt a great sense of relief at the Munich settlement in the previous autumn, though uneasily aware that it was an inglorious escape that only put off the evil day. I wrote a poem full of guilt on the subject. Meanwhile I was struggling through the immensely copious works of Landor and, with less pleasure, John Forster's prolix and puritanically defensive biography. Thalia and I went again to the King's May Week Ball, and to the Lord's Test Match against the West Indies. Again I struck a lucky day, with centuries by Hutton and Compton. After one of the Hambledon home matches the grandparents invited the whole team in to celebrate our engagement with a party in the orchard, where we held a darts completion with the board nailed to an apple tree.

If the summer passed peacefully, the autumn brought a prolonged crisis, and not only in the capitals of Europe. My pocket diary for the last ten days of August and the first ten of September is a palimpsest of plans superimposed one upon another. The original scheme seems to have combined cricket at Hambledon, a week with Philip and others in the Lake District, a visit to Lichfield Cathedral, *Richard III* at Stratford, and the Three Choirs Festival at Hereford. This was partly supplemented and partly replaced by a visit to Mother and Eugene (now married) at Châtel-Guyon, for which I was to leave on 4 September. I was a little apprehensive as to how this would turn out, but it was not put to the test. In the event none of these plans came to maturity, and something very different occurred on 4 September.

On 21 August I began my second visit to Fairnilee. The house was full as usual, with a Newnham friend of Thalia's and a large shooting party. We spent as much time as possible away from the house, a day in Edinburgh, visits to Jedburgh, Haddington and other places to look at churches. Nevertheless, as the international temperature rose, so did the emotional temperature in the household. When towards the end of the month it became obvious that war was inevitable, Thalia and I asked if we could be married before the end of the year, a request we would never have made had she not reached the age of 21 earlier in the month. We were summoned to Lord Craigmyle's study, a room I had not previously entered, and subjected to the stormiest interview it has ever been my lot to encounter. Both Craigmyles were there, but he did most of the talking. He lost his temper completely, abusing not only my character in every possible respect but that of my family as well, none of whom he had met. The charges were: that my father was connected with the theatre, an unsavoury profession; that he had been married three times and twice divorced, which argued bad blood and instability of character; that I was a slacker and never intended to do any work; and that all I wanted was his money. The fact that my uncle Rufus had been a close friend of Lady Craigmyle's father, the first Earl of Inchcape, who had lent him his yacht to travel round the Mediterranean when he was seriously ill, was dismissed as irrelevant. All this culminated in an ultimatum: we could await his pleasure, or we could go off and get married and never receive a penny of his or his wife's money.

Thalia replied at once that in that case we would go south that night. He was flabbergasted. He said we must be mad, adding that it was an infatuation that would not last five years. We left the

Marriage

room, feeling very shaky – his rages were truly terrifying, indeed notoriously so; senior business associates had been known to quake in their shoes; Anthea Craigmyle told me many years later that his sisters sometimes doubted his sanity - and were revived by Miss Peakall, the old family nanny, with sal volatile, the only time I have ever sampled that restorative. Thalia then had her trunk sent up, and we began to pack.

As soon as Lord Craigmyle realised that we meant what we said, he raised heaven and earth and a considerable part of Scotland to stop us. Legally he could do nothing. We had deliberately not forced the issue until Thalia came of age; otherwise it would certainly have become a matter for the Court of Chancery. Lawyers, doctors and clergymen were summoned from all parts of the Kingdom to persuade us to change our mind. There were at least five of them: Mr Jacobson, the Craigmyles' London solicitor, who had been staying at Fairnilee the previous week and was required to double back (by an odd coincidence he was the father of one of our Cambridge friends); David Marshall, Lord Craigmyle's cousin, a Scottish solicitor at Dunfermline; Dr Fleming, the Church of Scotland minister at St Columba's, Pont Street; Dr Kirkpatrick, the minister of the local church at Caddonfoot; and Dr Graham, the family's doctor in Scotland. During the next 36 hours there was a constant coming and going, and the swish of the gravel outside the front door as Lord Craigmyle furiously turned his car became a familiar sound. The atmosphere was electric. There was a dreadful moment when I opened the door of one of the loos, whose lock was defective, and found Lord Craigmyle on the throne. Inevitably the staff and the house party were fully aware of what was going on. One of the shooting guests, Anthony Gascoyne, who had been at Elstree and Harrow with me, gave me a wink and wished us luck.

The five emissaries appeared one by one over the next two days and talked to us quite politely. The outcome was that we won them all round to our point of view, though we agreed not to go south at once and to postpone marriage for a month or so. Lord Craigmyle was heard to mutter: 'They've bewitched Jacobson'. Various financial arrangements were made, about which we knew nothing and cared less. The upshot was that any money Thalia inherited on her parents' death was so strictly tied up by a marriage settlement that she could not touch the capital or convey any of it to me; while her parents lived she was to receive nothing but the small allowance she had been receiving since her schooldays. That was the situation until we had been married for nearly five years. The atmosphere grew so oppressive that Mr Jacobson proposed a temporary remedy: 'Let's get out of this and have a game of golf'. Neither Thalia nor I had ever played golf in our lives, and of course we had no clubs. 'Never mind', said Jacobson, 'you can use mine' He took us to the nine-hole course at Torwoodlee, four or five miles away, which then witnessed one of the strangest games of golf imaginable. At first, when I addressed the ball, I either smote the air and missed it altogether or uprooted large divots of turf, or both. When at last I did establish connection, the ball travelled not down the fairway but in the direction of extra-cover, where it disturbed the players at another hole. Nevertheless much of the tension was eased. Neither of us ever tried to play golf again.

I received some welcome encouragement through the post. Mother applauded our resolve to elope without a penny. Peter Lucas wrote: 'You can always take the law, and the lady, into your own hands. I don't of course suggest anything rash – conveniently near Gretna Green though you are. But, when the time comes, "on saute par le fenêtre". Indeed it is a classical procedure, with romantic advantages over pink bridesmaids and confetti that Landor would certainly have appreciated too'. Vie, who had suggested I tell Lord

Craigmyle that we wanted to get married at once if there was a Hitler crisis and at Christmas if there was not, was anxious that I should start fair with Thalia's parents and did not believe we would want for money. Basil refused to offer advice 'because experience has always shown that youth only profits by its <u>own</u> experience and not by other people's! The sincerest thing I can say is that I hope you'll manage better than I did'. Ben Muirhead sent her recipe for a happy marriage: 'Remember that it is better to have a good row and to get it over than to let grievances rankle, bottling up is useless and a good old breeze clears the air'.

I had originally planned to go south on the evening of 1 September. That morning Hitler invaded Poland, the British and French ultimatum followed, and it was clearly only a matter of hours before the country was at war. Everyone expected it to begin with air attacks, and there seemed no certainty that we would be alive by the end of the year. We therefore asked the Craigmyles if we could get married at once in Scotland. They were weary of the struggle and agreed, provided we could get round the legal and clerical obstacles, with which they declined to help. We needed the signature of a Justice of the Peace (I cannot remember why) as well as the consent of the minister and the registrar to the waiving of the second reading of the banns; the first would be on Sunday the 3rd. There was also a possible difficulty in that I was not resident in Scotland.

At this point we hit another snag. Lord Craigmyle's first action when war became inevitable was to have all the seven motor vehicles filled with petrol (more was stockpiled at various strategic points round the estate); his second was to order many hundreds of packets of toilet paper, some of which were still to be found in remoter loos 25 years later. He would not allow us to use any of the cars in case the petrol was required for a more important purpose. As a compromise we were offered the pony trap. The groom, whose name was John

Knox, was therefore summoned, and we went trotting round the countryside, first to Yair on the opposite bank of the Tweed, whose owner, Sir Kenneth Anderson, was a Justice of the Peace, then to the manse at Caddonfoot a mile along the road. Dr Kirkpatrick was not at home; we ran him to earth eventually in the police station at Clovenfords, the next village. He was willing to waive the second banns if the registrar agreed. By this time the latter's office in Galashiels was closed. We had to make a second journey in the same conveyance on Saturday morning, and were much relieved when the registrar, on hearing that Dr Kirkpatrick was willing to waive the second banns, agreed to do the same. I bought a wedding ring, and we trotted back to Fairnilee to listen to the radio news. Dr Kirkpatrick came round in the afternoon and agreed to marry us at 11.45 on Monday morning, the 4th – the day I had planned to spend first in the Lakes, then at Stratford, then at Hereford, and then on the way to the south of France.

We all listened to Chamberlain's broadcast on the Sunday morning, after which Lady Craigmyle burst into tears, saying that we young people had no idea of the horrors of war. Then the air raid warning sounded, and Lord Craigmyle said, 'Let's go out on the terrace and see the fun'. Needless to say, it was a false alarm. The Craigmyles told me it would be more proper for me to spend the night in a hotel. I refused to do this, I forget on what pretext, but agreed not to see Thalia at breakfast. That evening Lord Craigmyle told us that a German submarine had sunk the passenger liner *Athenia* with considerable loss of life.

On the Monday morning I felt as if I were about to take part in a play, or even a charade. Nothing seemed real – least of all when Thalia came up the aisle to the strains of the *Lohengrin* Wedding March. Apart from the minister and the organist, the only persons present were Thalia's parents, Ruth, Donald and Miss Peakall. Jean was staying with the Millington-Drakes in Montevideo, where her uncle Sir Eugen Millington-Drake was the British Minister; she received a constant stream of letters and communiqués from the family. I had asked Donald to be best man; he obliged by pretending to lose the ring. I remember Lady Craigmyle peering round to watch me putting the ring on Thalia's finger, but nothing else until we went to the vestry to sign the register. Here occurred the most agonising moment of all. While Dr Kirkpatrick was preparing the book and a pen, Lord Craigmyle turned round to show Donald the organ, which he had presented to the church, opening a door to display its interior workings. Dr Kirkpatrick asked him to sign, and he closed the door without engaging the catch. As he turned and bent down towards the book, the door flew open and administered a sharp tap on his buttocks, whereupon he looked at me with a ferocious and accusative glare. I had to bite my lip and dig my fingernails into my palms to strangle the laugh that very nearly came.

Although I had my camera with me, as did most of the others, no one thought to take a photograph. If this reflects the precarious start of our marriage, ample photographs celebrate the silver, golden and diamond anniversaries that followed. More than sixty years later, towards the end of Thalia's life, I said to her that I could not imagine how I could have had a happier marriage. She replied that she felt the same. We were given a glass of sherry, and the Rolls Royce to convey us to Galashiels station. George, the old chauffeur, who in the remote past had been Lord Craigmyle's coachman, told us that he had driven Thalia to her christening. Since we expected the railways to be bombed, we did not attempt to reach Hambledon but spent a day and night at Carlisle. The strain of the previous fortnight had been so great that we were both in a dream; I had to remind myself again and again that I was really married. Had the thought ever occurred to us that we might one day be the owners of the Fairnilee estate, we would have considered ourselves ripe for the madhouse.

CHAPTER 13

War

At the start of the month Hambledon Hurst had been empty. Within the next few days the Grandparents arrived from St Margaret's Bay, the staff from their annual holiday, Martin and Joe from Châtel-Guyon, and Thalia and I from Scotland. Gran wrote to Mother that Thalia and I were sleeping in the best bedroom without mentioning that we were married. There was a strange air of suspense; we all expected something to happen, but nothing did – beyond an issue of gas-masks. Tommy put one on, and the expulsion of air from his cheeks made a farting noise that helped to reduce the tension. Thalia and I had a brief honeymoon, if it deserves that title, in and around Chichester, where we inspected the cathedral and neighbouring churches and spent a night at the Hitchcocks' West Wittering bungalow, sleeping on the floor as there were no vacant beds.

We decided to settle for the time being in Cambridge, and took a year's lease of a flat at 2 Trinity Street above the bookshop Bowes & Bowes. It had one peculiarity. Our front door was up a staircase on the second floor, but the bathroom was outside it between us and the shop. The bath was operated by a gas geyser that delivered the hot water so slowly that we used to leave it to fill while we did other things. One Sunday morning we turned it on and went out to breakfast, forgetting to turn it off. On our return we found the water just lapping one corner of the bath and assumed we were in time to turn it off. On Monday morning an embarrassed figure appeared and informed us that a flood had penetrated the ceiling of the shop and ruined a stack of valuable books. This was Denis Payne, the co-owner and manager. He was sympathetic, even apologetic, and charged us as little as possible – less than £25 – for the damage. Such was the remarkable start of a friendship between us and the Payne family – Denis, his wife Joan, four daughters and a son Sebastian (Basty) for whom Thalia was asked to be godmother.

On the approach of war I had consulted the Provost on what I ought to do (my college studentship had been extended for a second year). He advised me to carry on with my dissertation. I had been struck by the extreme contrast between classical calm and romantic violence in Landor's life and work. His output in a long life had been enormous, and I discovered that while all his poetry was complete in the many-volumed 'complete' edition, this was not the case with his huge output of Imaginary Conversations. In pursuing and attempting to master this mass of material, while at the same time dealing with family quarrels on two fronts, I had lost a lot of time. Dissertations had to be sent in by the end of term in early December. Hence for the first ten weeks of our residence in Cambridge I was working all day till about 2.30 a.m. and only just managed to get the thing finished in time. I noted the time of completion at 3.33 a.m. on 5 December. One of Thalia's first actions, after we had bought enough furniture to equip the flat, was to take typing lessons. I did not inflict the dissertation on her, but from this time until she was disabled by a stroke in 1987 she typed everything I wrote.

It is not easy to describe those early days of the war. On the surface things seemed to continue as normal, yet there was a whiff of 'Let us eat, drink and be merry, for tomorrow we die'. The BBC ceased to broadcast music, but bulletins and newspapers were full of air raid precautions (ARP) and arrangements for women and children to leave London for the country, with special instructions for expectant mothers with pink cards. Then there was the blackout, the source of much confusion and a proliferation of incidents both tragic and comic. Philip, who was short-sighted and a trifle absent-minded, was crossing the market square with us one evening when he collided with a lamp-post and apologised to it. Another memory is of a restaurant where we used to dine, with a door inscribed LADIES TOILET from which some joker had painted out the second I. In the world outside little seemed to be happening except at sea and in Finland, where the Russians were engaged in a private war of aggression.

In December we spent a few days at the Eccleston Hotel in Victoria, shopping for Christmas and listening on the radio to progress reports on the Battle of the River Plate and the sinking of the German pocket battleship *Graf Spee*, supplemented presently by accounts from Jean in Montevideo. Mother came over to Hambledon for Christmas, as well as Martin from Oxford and Joe from Harrow. It was the last time we were all together. The house was so full that in the evenings we sat in the big room (hoping the fire would refrain from smoking), where Joe slept on a camp bed behind the sofa. There was no mention of the quarrel.

I recall the early months of 1940 as bitterly cold. We had no heating in our Cambridge bedroom, and the bed-clothes seemed to be frozen stiff until softened by hot water bottles. But a greater shock was the announcement of the Fellowship results in March. The only awards were to two of my contemporaries. I had probably allowed my hopes to rise too high, relying on a Fellowship to allow time for me to establish myself as a writer. In time I ceased to feel aggrieved, realising that I had been in too much of a rush to think everything out, though less happy to be told unofficially that, although the regulations permitted a second attempt a year later, I would not be elected whatever I submitted. This was my first inkling that the College's manoeuvres could be something less than straightforward.

We spent Easter with the Wilsons at West Walton, where I read the lessons in church and began collecting material for a booklet on the history of that beautiful Early English building. Although I did further research in the University Library, other things intervened and it was never finished. In May I had a medical examination with a view to eventual call-up for the Services. The doctor who examined me brought an unpleasant whiff of the public school prefect. The fact that I submitted medical certificates from Cregan and Squires, including results of an X-ray the previous autumn, apparently convinced him that I was trying to shirk my duty, and he classed me in a kind of limbo whereby I was liable to be called up in emergency but civilian departments would be chary of engaging me. I consulted the distinguished explorer James Wordie, a don in St John's and University adviser on careers. He was sympathetic and advised me to wait, belying his name by a singular economy of speech.

The German conquest of Belgium and the Netherlands, followed by the Dunkirk evacuation and the collapse of France, created an air of trepidation and suspense in which it was difficult to concentrate on anything. To occupy the time Thalia and I explored Cambridgeshire churches on bicycles (as we had done in the Sevenoaks area in March), half expecting to jump into ditches if German bombers appeared overhead, or to hear on the radio that German troops had landed. Beautiful sunny weather seemed to favour an invasion. Nevertheless public entertainments continued. We attended many plays and concerts in Cambridge and on occasional visits to London. I recall being deeply impressed by Robert Ardrey's play *Thunder Rock* at the little Torch Theatre, where Vie had some sort of job.

We saw much of new friends: the economic historian Charles Wilson, who had played the violin in *The Frogs* orchestra and was soon summoned to the Admiralty, and his wife Angela; Robin Orr, organist of St John's, composer and later Professor of Music at the University, and his first wife Margaret, who had just enriched the world with twins; and the Catalan composer Roberto Gerhard and his Austrian wife Poldi, refugees from Franco's Spain. Roberto was a pupil of Schoenberg, whose music then stuck in my throat. We had many friendly arguments. Another Spanish refugee was Jesus Bal, likewise taken under Trend's wing. I recall meeting JB one day 'just off to help Jesus with his income tax'. I also met E.M. Forster, then resident in King's, a number of times; he was friendly enough, but I was disappointed when he did not answer a letter in which I consulted him on a point of literary syntax.

During this summer we alternated between Cambridge and Hambledon, and I played for the village in a number of cricket matches. I remember two games in particular, both for my personal part in them and for their links with national events. On 15 June we played Chiddingfold away. This was a few days after the evacuation at Dunkirk. As we boarded the coach at Lane End I remember Bert Jeffery saying: 'France has packed up!' It was a marvellous match. Chiddingfold batted first and were bowled out for 75, Bert (a very good bowler) taking seven for thirty-one. One of the Chiddingfold players, Soapy Gill (his real name was William) used to play for Hambledon but had moved down the road. He was a left-hander, and a tremendous hitter. He took up an aggressive stance and smote what ought to have been a six, except that the ball shot straight upwards, to an appalling height, and I was underneath it. The Chiddingfold players tried to put me off, shouting 'You'll never catch that!' but I did catch it, to my great satisfaction. I had one of my better matches with the bat too, scoring 31 and hitting a six (a rare event).

On 25 August, at the height of the Battle of Britain, we played Merrow away. While Hambledon were fielding an air battle broke out high above us – we could hear machine gun fire but could see little, apart from vapour trails. At this point the Merrow captain came out and said to Sid Marsh, 'Don't you think we should stop?' Sid replied, 'Bugger that, we're playing cricket!' and we carried on. At the same time a little man emerged from behind the pavilion and manned an anti-aircraft gun, which we didn't know was there. It did not fire, I think. This was another thrilling match and again I did well with the bat. These were two of my best matches.

In the autumn I wrote the libretto of an operetta, *Cats and Dogs*, set to music by Philip. It satirized the Nazi-Soviet pact of August 1939 that led to the invasion of Poland from both sides. The dogs represented the Nazis, the cats the Russians; the neutral Americans appeared as badgers. Fiddler, 'an insignificant little man carrying a violin', who plays Wagner motives on his fiddle, stood for Hitler, Rattin (Stalin) is distinguished by a luxuriant moustache. Among Fiddler's henchmen are Dropabrick (Ribbentrop), 'a master of diplomacy and cunning', and Boring (Göring), his chest encrusted with medals. The plot involved the lovers Fido and Kitty, under threat of execution, foiling the dictators by seizing Fiddler's violin and excising Rattin's moustache, the sources of their strength. Philip started work on the music before I had finished the text. Dadie, a director of the Arts Theatre, was enthusiastic. He put us in touch with Norman Higgins, the general manager, and it was hoped to stage the opera at the Arts the following year, with Camille Prior as producer and Harold Darke (deputising for Boris while he was serving in the R.A.F.) as conductor. Donald Beves agreed to play Boring; he had the right figure, a useful voice and was brilliant in comic roles. We approached Margaret Field-Hyde to sing Kitty while Diccon Shaw, a King's choral scholar, son of the composer Martin Shaw, agreed to take on Fido.

By the spring Philip had completed the vocal score, writing in a light style, full of parodies, in the manner of Sullivan, and embarked on the overture. I suggested he insert a couple of his earlier pieces, including a jaunty setting of Landor's 'I strove with none, for none was worth my strife', and a habanera to accompany a parody striptease by Madame Macaroni, 'a beguiling and exotic creature', at the Amorous Peacock Night Club run by the badgers. (This gravely offended Philip's Aunt Linda.) Rehearsals were held in Philip's rooms at 7 Peas Hill on 8 and 10 March 1941, followed by a 'chamber performance' with Philip at the piano that evening. Ena Mitchell sang the female solo parts; the chorus comprised singers from the Madrigal Society (Philip thought they would find the choral parts 'quite insultingly easy'). Philip calculated timings for the three acts; I noted the possible composition of the chorus and orchestra, including two trumpets, and theatre expenses. Then a thunderbolt struck. Philip had to submit the text to the Lord Chamberlain for approval. After a delay he received a letter from the Lord Chamberlain's office objecting to the parts dealing with the Russians (cats) and the Americans (badgers). They also demurred at Diabolo, the elderly president of the badgers, being described in the stage directions as bearing 'a certain resemblance to Mr Bernard Shaw'. At this stage of the war (May 1941) it was not thought politic to make fun of the Russians or the Americans, who it was hoped would come in on our side (at the beginning of Act II I had roundly attacked the Americans for their neutrality). This torpedoed the opera. That autumn I attempted to rewrite the libretto, substituting the Japanese for the Russians and men for the Americans (and inserting a crack at my father and ENSA) but this did not really work and the project came to nothing. Philip's music survives at King's.

The German victory in France had caused my mother and Eugene (married since April 1938) to beat a hasty retreat over the Pyrenees to Spain and thence to Portugal, where they remained for some weeks before crossing the Atlantic to New York. There had been some question whether Eugene retained his US citizenship, which he had allowed to lapse. Their stay in New York was largely financed by Somerset Maugham, to whom appeal had been made on the score of his friendship with Alfred Sutro. Before leaving France Eugene claimed to have destroyed a book about Hitler that he had virtually completed. I doubt if it ever existed; but on reaching New York he did utter a book with the characteristic title *The Heathen are Wrong*, published in America and Britain, dealing among other things with his escape. I have not re-read it, and remember only a reference to 'two step-sons'.

* * * * *

On the last day of September 1940 a capacious lorry transported Thalia and me, mounted on our furniture and effects, from Cambridge to Godalming, where we rented the ground floor and basement of Underbank, a tall semi-detached house at 100 Peperharow Road at the base of the hill on which Charterhouse School stands. This had the double advantage of being only four miles from Hambledon, and therefore accessible by bicycle, and only a few doors away from Philip Radcliffe's house, inhabited by his mother and sister Susan. Our landlady, who lived in the upper floors of Underbank, was Mrs Dora Minett, a retired nurse who had recently been left a widow with seven step-children, of whom only the youngest, Helen aged seventeen, lived at home. The others came and went at intervals, and the upper floors, which seemed infinitely flexible, held further paying guests, including an elderly couple named Hicks and Miriam Girvan, the newly married wife of an airman. Miriam belonged to another large family whose parents and youngest daughter Una (strange name for the youngest of twelve!) had been evacuated from Southend-on-Sea to the house of another member of the family two doors down the road. Both Miriam and Una became close friends of ours.

Mrs Minett was a kindly soul, with whom we had only a (very mild) dispute over the shared telephone. Each household was supposed to make a note of its calls, but there was usually a discrepancy when the bill came in. My suggestion that we split the difference was not always received with equanimity. Two fertile female cats were further members of the Minett household, and they were regularly courted by three ginger toms whom we called Hitler, Musso and Franco. I waged war on them, but they usually won; oddly enough they seemed to have an alliance, like their namesakes. We received one of the kittens, whom we called Sammy till 'he' turned out to be female and once produced a litter of seven. We always kept two from each litter and I had to drown the rest, which I loathed. Sammy's greatest achievement was a smooth-haired grey kitten – a 'Russian blue' – whom we called Timoshenko after a Russian general then in the news, until 'he' too turned out to be female and became Shenka (not to be confused with Schenker). I got better at sexing after this. She was with us until years after the war and became a great favourite and mother of a dynasty. In 1940 we also gave sanctuary to a feline refugee from the London Blitz, a doctored tom whom we called Pip. He proved to be the most intelligent and amusing of all our cats. He used to bring livestock, including young rabbits, into the house; on one occasion he put his head in a paper bag and careered round the room, and on seeing us open doors by turning the handle stood on his hind legs and tried to do the same. He met a sad fate in Oxford.

For the next three years I was pulled in different directions. A further medical examination in Guildford in October released me from military service, but I was not a conscientious objector and expected some sort of call-up. After waiting for a year, during which

War

I wrote my one completed novel, *Through the Maze*, I made repeated applications for a civilian war job, to a Civil Service Commission, to the Admiralty (my preference, partly because Charles Wilson was working there), to the War Office, and even to the Jewish Agency (supported by Uncle Rufus's widow Stella) – all with negative results, though I was called each time to an interview. At one point I gave up, wrote a number of short stories and began an ambitious play based on Malory's *Morte D'Arthur*. But it was not easy to concentrate. Basil, now busy with ENSA, assumed the role of heavy father and demanded to know what I was doing to serve my country. It was of course characteristic of him to throw his weight about after taking no responsibility for his family, financial or otherwise. My reply did not satisfy him, and he sent a pompous and abusive letter which I must have destroyed as I cannot find it.

There were of course various Civil Defence activities. I took my turn at fire-watching, and with Thalia and Miriam formed a stirrup-pump team in the event of a fire-bombing attack on Godalming. No such thing occurred, but we had rehearsals made as realistic as possible by the construction of a large pile of old timber and rubbish which was then set on fire. Two teams were ordered into action. Mine got there first, and after prostrating myself in a suitable position I produced such a powerful jet of water that it passed through the flames and gave the second team a drenching before they were in position. At the same time camouflaged concrete structures sprang up at strategic points in preparation for the invasion that never came.

But we were on one of the routes taken by German bombers on their way to the heavy attacks on London, and we had our share of incidents. The buildings of Charterhouse on the hill above us must have been conspicuous and could have been mistaken for some sort of military establishment. One night a raider dropped a stick of bombs right across them. Fortunately the bombs fell in the gaps between the buildings and did little damage – and a subsequent friend of mine (Frank Parsons) then at the school got into trouble for investigating the craters. Another night some oil bombs fell on one of the cricket grounds, hurting nobody but offending Philip's sensitive nose; he complained loudly of the smell which I could not detect. This may have been the occasion when I heard the whistle of bombs immediately overhead, pushed Thalia onto the floor and lay on top of her.

Hambledon did not escape. On 23 October 1940 a heavy bomb demolished one of the cottages near the top of the Grandparents' garden, killing the wife and child of the occupier and a refugee couple lodging with them; their baby was found on the common yards away, unharmed. The occupant, Leslie Phillips, owner with his brother of the local garage, was on his way back from the pub and found his home no longer there. (I based a short story on this incident.) I found fragments of the bomb in the Grandparents' damaged greenhouse. In April 1941 two German planes crashed in the neighbourhood. One of them we passed in a pond at Busbridge while bicycling to Hambledon. The other exploded almost overhead at 2 a.m. five nights later. I was at Hambledon while Thalia was attending Nanny Peakall's funeral at Fairnilee. I was at the open window watching the battle, unaware that the bomber, when attacked by a night fighter, had released a large parachute bomb, which put me on my back and blew out a wall at nearby Hambledon Homes. The occupant of the nearest bed summoned a nurse and complained of the draught.

We also chanced to be in Cambridge in July 1942 when it suffered an air raid that damaged the Norman Round Church and the Union building. I was woken by the warning siren at 2 a.m. and on the way down passed the open door of a room containing the greater part of an airman sitting cheerfully on the bed. The remainder, a leg equipped with shoe, sock and suspenders, lay separately on a chair. This was not, as I momentarily supposed, the result of the current raid but of an earlier repair. The damage to the Union came back to mind when I subsequently borrowed fire-damaged scores of operas.

In early December 1941 I went into Westminster Hospital to have the septum bone in my nose cut back to stop it blocking one nostril – a very minor operation, but memorable for more than one reason. I awoke from the anaesthetic to find a pretty nurse kneeling on my chest to prevent me pulling out the plug. I had no objection to this, but was baffled on turning on the radio to hear gloomy reports of sunk battleships American and British at Pearl Harbor and off Malaya. On the following day I felt unwell and came out in spots. The pretty nurse was withdrawn and replaced by one less favoured, and a whispered conference outside the door indicated that something serious was afoot. They thought I had smallpox, but the diagnosis was soon changed to chickenpox, acquired apparently in Cambridge a week or two before. The result was a longer stay in hospital, with more spots in inconvenient places, followed by a luxurious journey back to Godalming in an ambulance. There I passed my infection to Philip, who came out with a spectacular pimple on the end of his nose.

Throughout this period we lived on very little. I kept careful accounts, and find that in the first four years of our marriage our average expenditure was £536, and that covered furniture (originally for 2 Trinity Street), a small trousseau for Thalia, the damages paid to Bowes & Bowes, the cost of my septum operation and maternity preparations for our first child. Yet we were perfectly happy, and of course luxuries became less obtainable as the war continued. I remember rejoicing when Lady Craigmyle sent us a consignment of Tiptree jam when we arrived at Underbank. I grew vegetables on our little patch of garden, and extended it (with the approval of Mrs Minett and Charterhouse) by enclosing a small area of adjacent land and digging out shrubs and small trees. (I also tried my hand at making pastry). Thalia still had the small allowance from her Newnham days, and earned a little from running the Godalming Citizens Advice Bureau, which she did almost from its foundation. (On one occasion she took pity on an Irish girl who claimed to be homeless and allowed her to sleep on our couch, only for her to prove a thief, stealing Thalia's smartest coat and skirt.) I was not earning after my studentship ran out, but Gran gave me a little.

Relations with Fairnilee were still cool. The Craigmyles several times invited Thalia to stay without me. She refused to go, except for a single night for her old nanny's funeral. Eventually we were both invited for a week in October 1942. It was not a happy occasion, despite the presence of other visitors. One day at tea Lord Craigmyle suddenly lost his temper and began abusing me with a fertile selection of epithets in the presence of the Rector of Woldingham and the Bishop of Edinburgh. My crime had been to look at him with what I thought was a friendly expression. Thalia and I at once left the room, followed by Ruth and Lady Craigmyle. For the remaining four days of our visit he shut himself in his study and did not even appear at meals. I never saw him again. The opinion of some of his relatives was that he was not quite sane. My relationship with Margaret Craigmyle thenceforward was increasingly friendly, though she sometimes confessed to finding me a little odd.

We spent one night in London during the Blitz (12 March 1941) on our way back from Cambridge. It was a somewhat hectic experience. Vie took us to a night club (the Nightlight), where one Ord Hamilton sang cabaret songs. The refrain of one of them – 'Bang Crash Sausage and Mash It's Fanny the Fairy Queen' – has haunted my memory ever since. Vie found us a bed at the top of a tall building, were we were kept awake for most of the night by the sound of explosions, more I believe from anti-aircraft fire than bombs, but no less disturbing for that. Daytime visits to London were more frequent, to plays (mostly Shakespeare), operas (*The Tales of Hoffman*, *Sorotchintsy Fair* and *The Bartered Bride* with a memorable performance by Peter Pears as Vašek) and the lunchtime recitals at the National Gallery that ran daily throughout the war. There were also visits to Haslemere for *Idomeneo* with the same delightful soprano Idamante as at Cambridge, and Petersfield, where I had a pleasant talk with Adrian Boult arising from the programme.

We made two quite separate groups of friends during these years. One was connected with Charterhouse, the other with cricket, and one individual (Bob Arrowsmith) with both. The first group included Ewings, Lee-Uffs (each with a German wife), Murray-Rusts (a short man with a very tall wife), Lees, Morgans, Arthur Trew (a music master and friend of Philip) and John Rideout. Through the Radcliffes we met the Headmaster, Robert Birley, a man of mighty stature whose activity at a tennis net was a formidable deterrent, and Mr Honeywill, a retired neighbour, who took me to dine at Brooke Hall, a masters' dining-club, where I met Sellar, the part-author of that masterpiece *1066 and All That*. John Rideout, with whom we shared many common interests – music and classics in particular – later became an interpreter in Japanese and met a mysterious death by drowning in Hong Kong. We saw a good deal of Philip's mother and sister Susan, who between them earned a black mark for bowdlerising a review I had written for the *Surrey Times* of a local CEMA concert without my permission. I never quite trusted them after that.

The second group of friends was connected with cricket. When after 1941 Hambledon was unable to raise a team, I played for Farncombe, and sometimes for Godalming's Sunday side, whose captain was Fred Neller, a local builder. I was playing for the latter at Milford on the day Hitler invaded Russia. We had matches at the delightful little ground at Thorncombe Street (where I once nearly hit a six by mistake over the wicket-keeper's head) and against the staff of Brookwood Asylum. Here the less dangerous inmates were allowed to watch matches. One of them was armed with a golf club with which, a look of intense concentration on his face, he periodically took a swipe at an imaginary ball. Most of both teams were artisans of one sort or another. Our particular friends were Jack Spence, later foreman of the Hambledon brickworks, and his wife Minnie, and Harry Smith and his wife Marjorie. We had some good times, including bridge sessions at the Farncombe Conservative Club, but unfortunately I lost touch with most of them after the war.

One of the Farncombe fixtures stood out. This was against the Harrodian club, whose ground with a luxurious pavilion was at Barnes. The match there was an all-day affair to which we travelled in a bus full of supporters. The return at Farncombe became a two-day match over the August Bank Holiday weekend. The festivities after the game were loud and long, and many friendships resulted, including ours with John and Edith Woodard. John had been an opening batsman for the Club Cricket Conference before the war, in which he served in the RAF; he was shot down in the Mediterranean and imprisoned by the French in North Africa. This had damaged his health, and his hands were so swollen that he had difficulty holding a bat. But he had a sense of humour: I remember a beautifully executed off-drive that sent the ball down to fine leg and the language that followed it. Edith was an ornament of the Women's League of Health and Beauty; we later saw her perform at the Albert Hall.

I was twice injured while batting for Farncombe, though not against the Harrodians. Stan Maskell, the Godalming Relieving

Officer and a fast bowler, relieved me of my senses by hitting me on the side of the head with a bouncer, and a year or two later I mis-hooked a short ball on to my nose and broke it. I had to retire on both occasions but without permanent damage.

When opportunity offered I climbed the hill to watch Charterhouse 1st XI matches, where it was easy to spot the coolness and skill of the 15-year-old Peter May, and I had interesting talks with the cricket master W.W. Timms, who had played an innings of 150 for Northamptonshire while still at school. Sometimes he or Bob Arrowsmith arranged for me to have a net. In local matches I had the experience of batting against three former England Test Match bowlers, George Geary, Jim Sims and Charlie Parker. Needless to say, they soon found methods of getting me out.

As well as visits to Cambridge Thalia and I made several excursions during this period, two of them linked with our new friends the Paynes. Denis had been called up by the Navy, and Joan and the children moved to the family home at Geldeston in Suffolk, where we spent a pleasant week boating on the Waveney and bicycling to a few of the splendid East Anglian churches. A year later, when Denis was in an escort destroyer based at Sheerness, Joan rented a house at Minster in Sheppey, where she was taken ill with suspected TB. It proved to be a false alarm, but she was in no condition to run a household with two little girls under five, and Thalia offered to help her. Although unauthorised persons were forbidden to go within a few miles of the coast, I went too and occupied myself with gardening and weeding an asparagus bed. We bicycled to Warden, where we found our old bungalow derelict, with a hole in the wall and signs of having been hastily abandoned on the outbreak of war. The only plants in the garden, which we had not bothered to cultivate, were three sorry-looking pear trees. We also called on the surviving sister of Mrs Campion, who had been so kind to us as children.

A little later in the year (August 1942) we put our bicycles on a train to Reading and explored the Chilterns, visiting the Hitchcocks in a remote cottage, where we found Hilary with a newly married husband (Martin Haywood, on leave from the RAF) and a newly born baby, Carol. About this time we exchanged visits with Thalia's cousin Tom Wheeler, also newly married to Pat, at Woldingham, and with Charles and Angela Wilson at Cockfosters.

The great event of this period was the birth of our first child, a daughter, conceived on Sheppey, at 5.15 a.m. on 14 March 1943 at Mount Alvernia in Godalming. We called her Brigid Miriam. That she was named after my first love has caused an occasional raised eyebrow, but Thalia, who knew the full story of what I owed to Brigid, was in full agreement. She was christened at Hambledon Church on 4 May by the rector, Canon Seymour, who years before had picked up his crumbs on my instruction at a rectory tea. Brigid's godparents were Joe, who was in the army and unable to be present, Thalia's sister Jean and Miriam Girvan, whose husband of a few weeks had been drowned when his ship was torpedoed. Lady Craigmyle had come down from Scotland for the birth and stayed at the Lake Hotel. From this time she was much more friendly to me. The reconciliation owed something to Headley and Phyllis Ferris, friends of the Craigmyles from the first war and popular with the children. And the death of Lord Craigmyle from cancer on 29 September 1944 removed a major cause of friction.

Although our only spare bed was a couch in the sitting-room we had plenty of visitors. Jean was now in the ATS, Ruth working in the Aircraft Inspection Department, with the initials AID on her badge. Donald was still at Eton; on one occasion Lady Craigmyle took us to visit him there. We regained touch with Haricot, in service with a neighbouring family, and with Brenda Stanley, an orphan from a poor and broken family whom Thalia had supported through her school (St Felix at Southwold) and with whom (and her husband and children) we remained in close touch till her death in 2006. My brothers, both now in the army, divided their leave between us and Hambledon, where Tommy died in October 1941 and Gran suffered a stroke a year or two later, though she made a partial recovery and lived till 1956. We cycled over frequently and maintained touch with my mother, now established in the Bahamas for the duration of the war.

Thalia's doctor at this time was Dr Winsome Grantham, the middle-aged sister of a well-known admiral, who persuaded me to consult an elderly and old-fashioned Guildford doctor called Tredgold. This was a mistake: when I tried to explain my situation, he denounced me in a pompous lecture and demanded five guineas. Unfortunately as it turned out, Thalia retained faith in Dr Grantham.

* * * * *

At last in January 1944 came the offer of a job, thanks to a link through Joe to his former tutor at Merton, Robert Levens, who was working in a department of Admiralty Intelligence at Oxford, known as ISTD or NID 6. The initials stood for Inter Service Topographical Department; its function was to prepare and issue detailed reports on facilities and conditions in enemy-occupied territories to assist the planners in preparation for raids or invasion. The seed had been sown by a Royal Marines officer, Sam Bassett, and an Oxford don working in a disused Admiralty lavatory in 1940, and had been expanding in arithmetical progression ever since. It now occupied Manchester College, the University Geography School, the newly built extension to the Bodleian Library, and a series of temporary huts off Holywell Street on the edge of the Balliol cricket ground. One of these was to be my place of work.

Before I could start it was necessary to find somewhere to sleep. This proved no easy matter. The city was packed, not only with students in term-time and the denizens of various official bodies evacuated from London, but with an increasing number of American officers brought over in preparation for the invasion of Europe. (It was at this period that they earned notoriety for being overpaid, oversexed and over here.) I tried to get a bed in New College, which had some sort of mutual arrangement with King's, but to no avail. At various times I had one-night beds in Merton, Balliol, and a whole series of lodging-houses in St John Street, eating meals in restaurants and canteens. At first I commuted between Oxford and Godalming, spending alternate weekends at home – each journey involving three trains (Oxford – Reading – Guildford – Godalming). On one of my returns I found that my landlady, though she had promised to keep the room for me, had let it to an American officer, no doubt for a substantially larger fee. For three weeks the elderly widow of the physicist J.S. Haldane gave me refuge at her home in Linton Road, which had a charming garden full of primroses, grape-hyacinths and other spring flowers. When she could no longer have me I resumed my wanderings and spent four consecutive nights in different buildings. In one of them a man I was talking to and whom I had never met before suddenly collapsed in an epileptic fit, a terrifying sight if one has not encountered it before. By the time a doctor arrived he had calmed down. The doctor simply looked at him and said: 'You bloody fool, why didn't you take your pill?'

When I joined ISTD the personnel in Oxford (there were offshoots elsewhere, including a branch in Ceylon) numbered many hundreds, about equally divided between civilians and the armed forces, but including only two regular civil servants, under the command of Colonel Bassett. It was a remarkable cross-section of humanity, involving half a dozen Allied nationalities, all three services, both sexes, many ranks from junior Wrens to senior

Commanders, lance-corporals to majors, and aircraftmen to a Wing-Commander, together with civilians of almost any conceivable age and profession: retired University professors, school teachers, travel agents, geography students, secretaries and typists – covering incidentally a wide spectrum of native intelligence.

The department was organised in sections, some geographical, some technical, including a large photographic library to deal with the many photographs submitted by the public in response to a broadcast appeal, a drawing office to prepare plans of beaches and towns, an engineering section to deal with railways and bridges, and perhaps others that I have forgotten. Each geographical section, generally under a retired naval Commander, covered a particular country or area and contained would-be specialists to report on relevant aspects – beaches, ports, towns, roads, geographical features, etc. – collected from maps, Admiralty charts, guide-books, town plans, press reports, technical treatises of all kinds, ground and air photographs if available, and contacts – people familiar with the country concerned, especially if they had lived or worked there in recent years – together with any other sources that he might discover for himself.

His work was then passed to an editor in the section, whose task it was to check it for clarity, relevance, accuracy (where possible) and consistency, to remove obscurities and redundancies and to present it in a form suited to the requirements and demands of planners and combatants in the field. We were given examples of blunders that had crept into earlier reports. Sicily had been credited with a lighthouse a thousand feet high, and an earlier editor, finding on a map a building marked *Suores di Purificacione* (a convent), had reported it as a sewage works. This was the task to which I was assigned, first as an assistant editor under a colleague, then on my own. It was well suited to my frame of mind. My classical education, as well as my self-training as a writer had made me fastidious about clarity of expression and accuracy of detail. Whenever in the course of reading I spotted a misprint, a clumsy expression or a factual error my instinct was always to correct or adjust it, mentally if not physically. I had developed a natural antipathy to slipshod constructions, linguistic solecisms, floating participles, split infinitives, and any kinds of obscurity or ambiguity. All this was to come in very useful.

The section to which I was assigned covered Malaya and the Dutch East Indies (now Indonesia). Its members included two Dutch naval officers, one of whom was quick to pounce on any hint that his service might not be at least the equal of the Royal Navy, several Army officers, one a former game-warden in Malaya, a Flight Lieutenant, two good ports writers and a bevy of young female geographers, as well as secretaries and typists. One of the ports writers, Ellis Gummer, who became a close friend, had a scholarly mind and a power of accurate expression so acute that his reports, however complex, required no editing at all. They sometimes contained useful extra details; his report on Djambi in Central Sumatra, I remember, ended with the sentence 'The river is infested with crocodiles'. I was mostly concerned with the towns and transport systems of Northern and Central Sumatra, especially the roads, which were served by Army officers. Their talents (and sometimes their application) varied considerably, and I had gradually to familiarise myself with their individual foibles. After a while it became evident that I sometimes needed to assess the sources as well as their interpretations, and I picked up a range of technical information in several languages, including the fact that the word 'Bagger' in Dutch meant dredger. Towards the end of my time I was given as assistant the retiring headmaster of Shrewsbury, H.H. Hardy, who was accustomed to take a nap after lunch. He sat opposite me on the other side of the hut, and I would see him writing more and more slowly, till his hand stopped with the nib still on the paper in the middle of a word. Ten minutes later it would begin to move slowly, continuing the same word and gradually regaining its original speed. On another occasion I heard a sudden exclamation: 'Oh dear! I'm all over government mucilage!'

(Occasionally after the war some chance incidence threw my mind back to the hut on the Balliol cricket ground. When a Dutch music critic who before the war had been a church minister in Medan, the capital of Sumatra, came over to interview me about Handel, I startled him by naming the street in which he had lived. Later, when my daughter and son-in-law travelled to Australia by easy stages, I was able to guide them to the beauties of Lake Toba in North Sumatra. On our flight to Australia in 1985 Thalia and I passed close to Sabang off the northern tip and some places whose names became familiar in reports of the *tsunami* in December 2005.)

Things became very lively, at home and abroad, in the summer of 1944. Everyone of course was on tenterhooks waiting for D-Day. When it came (6 June) one of the least competent of the military officers in my section brought a portable radio into the hut and insisted on turning it on at intervals to catch the latest bulletin. This was too much for Ellis Gummer, who blew up like a miniature Krakatoa demanding to know how (expletive) anyone was expected to get any work done when distracted by that infernal machine. Five days later my nose was broken in a cricket match at Farncombe (my own fault for mis-timing a hook) and I was kept at home for a week; on the 13th my brother Joe was wounded near Caen (a telegram informed me as next of kin, Mother now being in the Bahamas). Meanwhile the Germans had begun to send over flying bombs (one of the earliest fell in Godalming). On the 15th I was having a technical discussion with Philip at Underbank when Thalia, hearing a noise and looking out of the window, suddenly shouted: 'Look out! It's one of those buggers!' – the only time I ever heard her use that word. Philip took no notice: 'We are discussing Bach' – and the bomb fell harmlessly in a field at Shackleford. On the 17th we visited Joe in hospital at Farnborough. He was under sedation, but not permanently damaged.

During this spring Thalia paid two short visits to Oxford in search of somewhere to live, leaving Miriam in charge of Brigid. We settled on a small house in North Oxford, 45 Oakthorpe Road, which the Craigmyles agreed to pay for (£1,450). It already had temporary residents in Beryl Emptage and a baby; we were happy to let them stay for a month while the father, who had acquired a business in Bournemouth, sought fresh lodgings, and Beryl became a friend. Negotiations for our purchase involved a meeting with a melodramatic solicitor who pranced round the room striking attitudes and abusing his subordinates – perhaps for our benefit.

For a month before we moved in on 19 July I lodged with the historian A.J.P. Taylor at Holywell Ford by the river. I only saw him at breakfast, but that was enough to leave a strong impression. I have never met a man more sure of himself. He regularly set the world to rights, telling us what Hitler or Stalin was sure to do next, and if they didn't he would point out where they went wrong. His wife, whose appearance had a flower-like delicacy, said very little; my fellow lodger Commander Bickford, who also worked at ISTD, said even less, and I seldom ventured to open my mouth. A week-end visit from Stephen Spender and his wife brought a certain balance and greater breadth to the conversation.

As the war moved to the Far East I became increasingly aware of the importance of our section's work and of my responsibility – also that I had something to make up, having so far contributed little to the war effort. I continued to work in the evenings after office hours, and must have put too much pressure on my resources. During the night of Christmas Eve I was taken ill with a violent digestive upset, followed and combined with the sort of panic attack that had assailed me at the same season nine years earlier. I remained in bed over Christmas and the New Year, and then consulted Squires, but was not able to travel to London. He put me on to Dr Stella Churchill, a Jungian psychologist who happened to be the aunt of a King's friend. I saw her at regular intervals over the next five months, and she certainly helped to calm me down. An attack of flu at the end of January did not help. After a week at Hambledon to recuperate I found Thalia in the throes of a miscarriage (after nine weeks). Miriam, followed by Jean, came to help with Brigid, who was now going to an infants' class, whereupon I had another bout of flu – and helped to deliver Shenka of a litter of kittens. I did not return to work till 26 February.

In the late spring and early summer our section was galvanised into urgent activity. The pressure from above had varied from time to time according to what the politicians and planners demanded. They might make urgent requests for intelligence on a particular island or district and then as rapidly shift their attention elsewhere. The demands of course were not addressed to us as individuals, but inevitably we felt the rebound. One poor fellow in our section, brought in as an assistant editor, found it all too much and committed suicide. After General Slim's victory in Burma the Allies planned a landing on the northern tip of Sumatra, and Colonel Bassett was rung up at intervals by Churchill, the Prime Minister, demanding reports and details. In the event of course the Americans dropped atom bombs, the Japanese surrendered, and the landing was transferred to the Malay Peninsula. General Sir Philip Christison, who commanded the Corps involved, later became a family friend in the Scottish Borders through a common interest in shooting and music (and lived to be 100). I asked him if ISTD's publications were any use; he gave them a good report. Our section's work however was never put to the test of war.

An Engagement with Time

* * * * *

There were a number of extra-curricular events at ISTD. In October 1944 a group of us were conveyed to Southampton, where we met various naval personnel and were shown over a destroyer, HMS *Rapid*, I think. I was astonished to see how slender she was. Captain Edney-Hayter, the ex-game-warden, organised a shoot in Gloucestershire with some of our Wrens as beaters, but I had not then been initiated into that enjoyable sport. I had many interests in common with Ellis Gummer. In June 1945 we went to the London Docks to inspect the surrendered German submarine *U776* and also the Biber miniature. As we were leaving, Ellis struck a large container with his stick, and a number of huge black birds (?ravens) flew out. A scratch mixed-sex hockey team made its appearance during the winter, and a cricket XI for which I played a few matches in the summer on a number of different College grounds. I also played occasionally for the University Press. My chief recollection is of the ground at Eynsham, where only the square was mown, the outfield remaining under long grass. At one point play was held up while a squadron of young pigs ran across the pitch; at another a fielder attempted to catch a ball that pitched just in front of him in a cowpat, and retired bespattered. There were several Americans in our unit. We tried baseball on one or two occasions. We also attempted to teach them cricket, which was rather more amusing. They began by taking a tremendous swing at every ball, throwing down the bat, and dashing off into the deep like a hare pursued by a greyhound.

We had quite an active social life at Oxford. Philip paid several visits from Cambridge, on trains that moved so slowly that he was able to memorise the names of all the obscure stations on this cross-country route, since abolished by the infamous Dr Beeching. His spidery handwriting could have accounted for the alternative claim that the train passed a number of obscene statues. Other old friends who made welcome and sometimes unexpected appearances were John Williams, a pupil of Philip's who became organist at the Tower of London, J.B. Trend, Diccon Shaw, who was to have sung the tenor lead in *Cats and Dogs*, Marjorie and Bobby Holmes from the cast of *The Cherry Orchard*, and Denis and Joan Payne. Philip was best man at John Williams's marriage to Valerie Trimble, clad in a morning coat, 'fancy' trousers and an every-day shirt and tie.

Our new friends, besides Ellis, included Mary Woodward, a jolly girl who disappeared to America, Fred Mason, a musical schoolmaster, with whom we also subsequently lost touch, and Owen Nicholls, who was subsequently to play for Sydenhurst Ramblers as a left-arm bowler, from ISTD; Norman Platt, the future founder of Kent Opera (barbarously killed off by the Arts Council), and the writer Roger Lancelyn Green, who had a bad stammer in private life, but lost it completely on the stage. In the summer of 1945 our house seemed to become a focal point or cross-roads for family meetings, both mine and Thalia's. My Aunt Ruby, whom I hadn't seen for years (and who lived to be 102), came to stay, as did the Woodards and both my brothers, now out of the army. Others who appeared were Michael Van Gruisen, Vie and Michael Balkwill, Basil (who came to view a play, *Jacobowsky and the Colonel*, and took many photos of Brigid), Thalia's sisters and her cousin Isabel Forrester-Paton. I even ran into Halsey Colchester driving an armoured vehicle through the town. Particularly welcome was my half-sister Tessa, whom I had not seen since she was a child, but who was now at the University and a very live spark. She turned up one day with Vickie and at another with her mother Lady Mercy – much changed since I last saw her at Easton – and a Welsh vet, who (I learned later) was her mother's lover but attempting to transfer his affections to Tessa.

For me the most memorable day was 22 August, when I made contact with Brigid Rees for the first time in nine years (apart from a chance meeting in King's for a moment in 1938). We had corresponded: I had written to congratulate her on the birth of her daughters Teresa and Biffy (Elizabeth) and told her of my marriage, which nearly coincided with Teresa's birth. I now rose early in the morning and travelled to East Bridgeford (where she was living, while her husband Lorimer was serving as an RAF chaplain in the Azores) via three trains and a bus, eating a snack lunch at Nottingham. I only had three or four hours with her, which included tea, a swim in a pool and making the acquaintance of Teresa and Biffy, before returning to Oxford by the same route. But I walked from the station to Oakthorpe Road, a distance of a mile and a half, in a mood of great happiness and elation – not that I was still in love with her, but because she was indeed the delightful person I had in my memory. A few days later I wrote a short story for Teresa and Biffy.

On 12 September Ruth and Archie Macdonald were married in London. We spent the previous night at the Rembrandt Hotel, taking Brigid with us (on the train from Oxford she flirted with Lord David Cecil). The one sad event this month was that poor Pip had to be put down; a savage tom had torn the flesh off his back, and whenever the vet applied medication he had insisted on licking it off.

I had been given the option of a continued job under the Admiralty, but decided to return to the neighbourhood of Hambledon and resume my writing career. We had looked at a house in Brook and found it unsatisfactory, but Thalia reported enthusiastically on The White House, Milford. The price was £6,000, which her mother agreed to pay (her father had died the previous year). Oakthorpe Road was sold on 22 September. On 1 October I obtained my release from ISTD and promptly went down with another dose of flu, but recovered in time to attend the wedding in London of Thalia's Newnham friend Elizabeth Dewart ('Zee') to Ian Scott-Kilvert, who had been at Harrow with me.

War

On the next day I was in the garden when I heard Thalia cry out in a voice of panic: 'What shall I do? What shall I do?' I rushed round and found Brigid lying on the ground next to the earth from the radio set, which she had inadvertently touched. I picked her up; she gave a big sigh and died in my arms. A woman doctor, hastily summoned, confirmed that she was beyond help. It was characteristic of Thalia that she thought first of me. 'I'm afraid for my husband. She was the apple of his eye!'

That was indeed true. I was immensely proud of her, filled with wonder that I was partly responsible for the existence of such a fascinating little creature, a source of constant joy after the horrors of the break-up at Cumberland Terrace. She had just begun to put sentences together, and would rush into my arms when I returned from the office. She had an echo of the elusive charm that I sensed in Thalia when I first set eyes on her. Of course I told myself that countless others had suffered a similar or an even greater loss, but that did not make it any more tolerable. She still haunts my memory more than sixty years later.

There was a triple irony about the event. On the previous day a man had come to mend a defect in the radio and had by some inadvertence electrified the whole set. A gate at the side of the house, which we kept closed to prevent Brigid straying on to the road, had been left open by a tradesman making a delivery; otherwise Brigid could not have reached the earth. And we were due to leave the house a week later.

Our friends did all they could to comfort us, especially Natalie Hodgson from the office, who stayed the night, Ellis, Tessa, Oliver Zangwill, who had just taken a temporary job in Oxford, and our next-door neighbours the Allens. The nuns who lived in the next house gave me a nip of whisky, but refused my request for a little more. Margaret Craigmyle and Jean stayed for a few days. The inquest, at which of course I had to give evidence, was adjourned till after the funeral, attended by both families, including Basil. She was cremated at Headington cemetery. I had a plaque with her name and dates and the words 'A happy child' placed low on the memorial wall.

Many years later, on our second visit to California in 1977, sleeping in a strange house in Berkeley, I had a particularly vivid dream, which I wrote down immediately on waking:

The time was back during the war. Thalia was with a doctor or nurse, and I was waiting to see our daughter Brigid, apparently just after her birth. But when they brought her to me she was as I remember her at the end of her life and could walk and talk. I held her in my arms (as at the moment of her death). She looked at me and said: 'Daddy, what is going to happen to me?' I knew the answer, and was too shaken to speak. Brigid looked at me with great tenderness and said: 'Don't cry, dear Daddy – please don't cry'. Then I woke up, feeling very desolated. I suddenly remembered that the date was 10 October, the 32nd anniversary of her death.

CHAPTER 14

Milford

On 18 October Thalia and I took the train from Oxford to Paddington, leaving Jean to travel with Shenka and our furniture in the removal van. Ellis met us at Paddington with a car and drove us to Milford, where we found The White House empty save for a telephone and a vast bookcase, which we had bought from the previous owner and called the Archdeacon after him. It still stands in my study at Hambledon today. The White House was much larger than our previous dwellings, with four downstairs rooms and six bedrooms (not to mention an attractive walled garden and a large orchard on the other side of the road), and we filled some of its empty spaces with furniture from the Craigmyles' house at Woldingham, which had just been sold. There was some competition over this, since Ruth and Archie were furnishing their newly acquired house in Hampstead, and Archie was decidedly acquisitive, especially over the pictures. I remember Margaret telling him that we should have the portrait of Lockhart attributed to Raeburn since I was a writer.

Our friends did all they could to make life tolerable, and so did our new next-door neighbours David and Audrey Geddes. Gran stayed for a week after a cataract operation. But it was a very bleak period. I tried to resume work on the King Arthur play, but found imaginative or creative work too distressing, and decided that I needed to get my teeth into something solid and factual if I was not to sink into useless gloom. Philip had been urging me for some time to follow up my interest in Bizet. I decided to embark on solid research for a full biography, since the French lives without exception were inadequate or hostile or both.

Margaret Craigmyle, Thalia's mother, helped me in another way, though this was not immediately apparent. She invited us to Fairnilee for a fortnight (we began by missing the train and had to travel the following night) and, since she was employing a keeper and there was no one interested in the game (Donald, who had succeeded his father, was away in the Navy) I might like to take up shooting. Her motive was to give me a new interest to stop me brooding; she could not have thought of anything more efficacious.

My start was far from impressive. Peter Dods, the keeper, took me into a large turnip field and put up a series of partridges and pheasants, and I missed the lot. The only shooting I had done at school was at a miniature range with a fixed target, and I poked at the birds, missing behind every time. However I did not intend to be beaten, and the following two days Peter and his son Wattie (then a young boy with red hair but later my keeper for many years) took me to a rabbit-warren and put in a ferret. I had to shoot the rabbit in the few seconds it took to pop out of one hole into another. This was a good test, and after a number of misses I began to score hits. All this was in preparation for a pheasant shoot. There were six guns, including Archie and two whom I later came to know well, Derrick Milligan and Dick Lund, the latter a former factor, expert salmon fisher and lover of music. There were five drives, and would have been more, but we stopped at lunch as Peter was sickening for flu. I managed to shoot two pheasants at the first drive (despite Archie claiming one of them) and one or two more later.

From that time I was hooked, not by a lust for killing as many birds or other creatures as possible (I never estimated the day by the size of the bag), but by the fascination of trying to co-ordinate eye and finger, by the wide variety of participants whom I would never otherwise have met, by the range of attractive country – moors, woods, marshes – into which it took me, and above all by its never-failing efficaciousness in banishing from my mind anxieties and preoccupations of every kind, sometimes for days on end. It never failed in this till old age and infirmity condemned me to an armchair. I never became a first-class shot, but in time I could hit fast-flying grouse and high pheasants – on one occasion being congratulated by Brian Johnson, the Duke of Buccleuch's head-keeper, on killing as high a pheasant as he had seen that year.

It was on this occasion that Margaret and David Marshall, Lord Craigmyle's first cousin, and one of those who had been summoned to block our marriage, took steps by a Deed of Variation to relax the restrictions that Lord Craigmyle had imposed on Thalia's Marriage Settlement. David said that he had never seen any such document so tightly clamped; it had not only restricted the amount of the Settlement (which derived not from him but from Margaret's father the first Earl of Inchcape) but prevented more than a fraction of it coming to me in the event of Thalia's death. On this visit we also made contact with Kathleen Betterton (née Baron), then living in Edinburgh, who had coached Thalia for her Cambridge entrance, while staying at Fairnilee in the autumn of 1936. She was a gifted writer; her unpublished autobiography, of which she sent us a chapter, included a vivid account of the family, a devastating description of Thalia's father (who had not yet succeeded to the title) acting the domestic tyrant, sacking a butler for a trivial offence at dinner, intolerant of even the slightest hint of disagreement (which would lead to sudden explosions of anger) and always insisting on holding the floor. She called him 'a caricature of a capitalist', who even talked of the abundance of his pheasants 'as if he was responsible for their procreation', and was sure that Thalia would get into Newnham because he knew the Principal.

1946 was a grim year, though lightened towards the end by the birth of our son Stephen. We were very pleased with our new house and garden with its many fruit trees, which allowed us to entertain many friends and relations, sometimes several staying in the house at the same time. Martin and Tessa both got engaged, Tessa to Peter Thomas, later MP for Conway, Secretary of State for Wales, Chairman of the Conservative Party and Lord Thomas of Gwydir. That was a happy marriage, though like ours it suffered the untimely death of children; but Martin's engagement to Monique Viner, another lawyer and later a Circuit Judge, did not last.

In June 1945 I had written to Eric Blom, inquiring whether a volume on Bizet was planned for the Master Musicians series, which he edited. Blom was music critic of the Birmingham Post and editor of *Music & Letters* and a man of immense industry who had already embarked on the fifth edition of Grove's Dictionary. He had a deformity of the spine that gave him a hunch-backed appearance. I had encountered him before the War in unusual circumstances, when Boris invited him to breakfast in his rooms at King's to meet me. Blom remembered the occasion and was encouraging about Bizet – did I intend to write a book myself? – but could not promise that Dents would publish one at that stage; new and replacement volumes were piling up and the paper shortage seemed as bad as ever.

Later I sent him my first article on Bizet, 'Carmen – An Attempt at a True Evaluation', but he rejected it for *Music & Letters*, saying that it contained nothing new (this was probably true). Subsequently a revised version appeared in *Music Review*. I kept in touch with him and at the beginning of 1946 set to work in earnest. Late in January Thalia and I stayed with Ruth and Archie at Hampstead. I was hoping to unearth Bizet material at Foyles, and at the same time plug gaps in the family library. I met Blom at the Piccadilly Hotel and next day I had a long talk with Edward Dent at his flat in Cromwell Place. Vie had arranged tickets for a Mozart recital at the Wigmore Hall. Afterwards we dined at the Moulin d'Or with Vie and her friend Constant Lambert. Philip and I had recently played through Bizet's overture *Patrie*, which employs, besides harps and a battery of percussion, both cornets and trumpets – and an ophicleide, an instrument I had not come across before. What did it look like? Lambert, in exuberant mood, at once whipped out a pen and drew a representation of an ophicleide on the tablecloth. 'Now, now, Mr Lambert!' said the waiter.

In February I sent Blom a couple of specimen chapters, about which Dents were at first dubious. I went to Cambridge to examine volumes in the Hirsch Collection at the University Library. Later Hirsch allowed me to borrow many books, sometimes entrusting them to the post. By the time I came to study his full score of *Djamileh* it had been transferred to the British Museum. On 1st April I heard that Dents had accepted my proposal – on the same day that Thalia's pregnancy was confirmed. The terms were not generous: £75 outright and no royalties. That autumn and winter I paid regular visits to the British Museum, sometimes accompanied by Philip. In November I examined full scores of the early operas in the Angelina Goetz Collection at the Royal Academy of Music – the British Museum did not possess copies at that time – and met my old piano tutor, R.S. Thatcher, the Warden, in very different circumstances, as recounted earlier. On 4 January 1947 Philip came to dinner – a frequent occurrence until the end of his life – and we played through *Noé*, a biblical opera by Bizet's father-in-law Halévy that Bizet completed.

Our baby was due in late October but was reluctant to appear. Margaret Craigmyle came down two weekends in succession in expectation of the birth but on the third weekend gave up and returned to Scotland. Ellis Gummer arrived on the evening of 16 November and flung a large lobster on the kitchen table. That did it. Next day Thalia went into labour and was conveyed to Mount Alvernia Nursing Home in Godalming, where our son Stephen was born at 4.15 a.m. on 18 November. Stephen was a sickly baby, yellow with jaundice because of the Rhesus factor, not fully understood at that time. Thalia, like her sister Ruth, had rhesus negative blood, which reacted with the blood of the baby. The first child is not affected but the condition becomes progressively worse with each succeeding pregnancy. This was to cause us terrible grief later. Thalia and Stephen did not come home until 2 December.

That winter was unusually severe. There was no central heating in the White House. Coal was in short supply but from somewhere we acquired a load of peat. On 26 January my pocket diary records: 'fearful cold and snow'; two days later I noted 31 degrees of frost (Fahrenheit), the next night 41 degrees. The agonising chilblains that had made my life such a misery at Harrow returned in full measure. Partial thaws were followed by further snow and blizzards over the next six weeks. Margaret came down for Stephen's christening in Milford Church on 9 February, a day of intense snow; Ellis, one of Stephen's godfathers (the other was Philip), started a snowball fight in the churchyard. On 14 February it was 'still hellish cold'. Towards the end of the month I went to Cambridge, partly for a revival of *The Frogs* with Walter Leigh's incidental music. I thought the production inferior to that of 1936 but was again struck by the brilliance of Leigh's music. Thalia and Stephen joined me two days later. On the 24 February I noted: 'Zero temperatures. Longest Feb. frost in history. Sea frozen', and the next day '8°[F] in Cambridge'. On 10 March a thaw started but on the 15th there were 'snowstorms again!' Finally, on 17 March, the day before my birthday, I noted with relief: 'Spring at last!'

In April the cellar at the White House flooded, water rising dangerously close to the electric meters on the wall. We summoned the Fire Brigade to pump the water out, not for the last time. It was a large dark cellar, accessed by brick steps with an unmortared brick floor and vestiges of gas lighting. The firemen prised up bricks in the middle of the floor to allow the remaining water to drain away into the sandy ground beneath.

About this time we acquired our first car, a second hand Morris of doubtful pedigree. It was obtained through Charlie Izzard, a cricketing pal from Witley. On one of our first trips, exploring churches with Ellis Gummer, the car broke down, stopping in the middle of the road from Milford to Haslemere. Luckily there was very little traffic; few people possessed cars just after the War. We pushed the car to the side and Ellis, a man of enterprise and practical *nous*, crawled underneath. A link had become detached, making the vehicle impossible to steer. Ellis effected a repair and soon we were on our way again. Sometimes we employed Mr Tombs, the elderly Milford taxi driver. His ancient black taxi had the letters PO in its number plate – we always referred to it as Po. Mr Tombs wore a black cap and drove at a stately pace. One of his ears was permanently stuffed with cotton wool.

In late March Philip and I set off on a ten day trip to Paris for research. We stayed at the Hotel d'Artois. We went first to the library of the Conservatoire, where we were welcomed by the very helpful Mlle. Annette Dieudonné. We worked long hours examining mostly unpublished music, including the fragmentary opera *La coupe du roi de Thulé* (a fascinating work with pre-echoes of *L'Arlésienne* and *Carmen*), *Carmen*, *Ivan IV* and other operas. One day I laboured for seven hours without lunch. I made contact with my relations Paul Turot and his sister Renée, a lively and spirited couple, the grandchildren of Aunt Fran (1856-1939), eldest of the Isaacs brood and sister to Rufus and my grandmother. I had met Fran in Paris in 1935, when she was being looked after by her elderly bachelor son Louis. Paul introduced me to his wife, Jacqueline, and we dined with them on several evenings; once we were joined by Jean Périer, a distinguished old singer who had created the role of Pelléas in 1902. We worked too in the Bilbiothèque de l'Opéra. Philip's assistance was invaluable, drawing my attention to many points I might have missed and copying much unpublished music.

On our last evening we went to *Carmen* at the Opéra-Comique. It was interesting to see the opera in its proper habitat but it was an erratic performance. Carmen herself (Solange Michel) was good, a real little nut-brown gypsy, and José (René Verdière), though static and plump, put plenty of passion into his singing, but the other principals were weak. I found the spoken dialogue an immense improvement, though it was heavily abbreviated and for some reason Guiraud's recitative before Micaela's air in Act III was included. We heard certain passages normally cut, including the orchestral coda to the opening chorus in Act IV, which appears in the 1875 vocal score. A few days earlier we saw Chabrier's *Le roi malgré lui*, an opera full of wonderful music but hamstrung by an inconsequent libretto.

The early summer of 1947 brought a heatwave, temperatures rising to 90° at the end of May and 94° on 3 June ('hottest day since Aug. 1933'). In May Blom accepted my article on *La coupe du roi de Thulé* for *Music & Letters*. Later I arranged a short suite from the music; it was broadcast on the BBC Third Programme in 1955. The book was finished on 5th June 1947; that afternoon I travelled to London and delivered the typescript to Blom over tea. After this I resumed work on my Malory-inspired play, *The Splendour Falls*. In August Paul and Jacqueline Turot came to stay at Milford. From late 1947 Blom began to send me books to review for *Music & Letters*. One of the first was a dim volume on Bach (in the Master Musicians series) by Eva

Mary and Sydney Grew, followed by a revised edition of the fanciful biography of Handel by Sir Newman Flower, whom I likened to Mr Jingle. This did not go down well with Flower; later he denied me access to his important collection of Handel scores. I made contact with Gerald Abraham, then Professor of Music at the University of Liverpool, which led to articles in *Monthly Musical Record* and for the music page of *The Listener*, both of which he edited. My first piece for *The Listener* was on Handel's operas – about which I knew little at that time – ahead of a broadcast of Act I of *Giulio Cesare* on the Third Programme. I met Abraham later at Blom's house in Allen Street, where he and Pat were staying. Pat (who was pregnant) had gone to bed but was kept awake by howls of laughter from below.

In July 1948 a party for Master Musicians authors was held at Eric Blom's house. This was my idea. It was here that I first met Martin Cooper. I was a little apprehensive because I had criticised his writings on Bizet but he was friendly and very complimentary about my book, which he had been reading for review. Arthur Hutchings (Schubert) was there; that month I had attacked his book on Delius in *Music & Letters* for carelessness and gross infelicities of style. He was not a man to bear grudges and later wrote me a charming letter asking for help on matters of grammar. Norman Demuth (Ravel) was an even worse writer. Another ungainly writer (not present) was A.E.F. Dickinson. I once saw a shabby-looking fellow at the opera and remarked to my companion: 'That man looks exactly the way Dickinson writes!' To which the reply came: 'That *is* Dickinson!' Philip and I encountered Mrs Peter Latham, who steamed into the room with her husband and announced: 'We have just finished Brahms'. I talked to Marion M. Scott (Beethoven), a mild-mannered elderly lady. Norman Suckling (Fauré) was also a woolly writer; Dent remarked to me of this book: 'As to Suckling, is it not time that he was weaned?' I met Percy Young (Handel) and Joan Chissell (Schumann) for the first time. It was a very jolly party.

By the end both Demuth and Hutchings were the worse for wear. A few days later Demuth wrote to me: 'I enjoyed the Party and arrived home very late and slightly bent. Someone appeared to have moved the front gate to one side ---'. I last saw Hutchings wandering down the middle of the street shouting: 'I'm as pissed as a newt!'

* * * * *

Summer weekends in these years were taken up with cricket. The Hambledon club was reconstituted in 1946, with many of the same players, including Jack Probert, Harold Wood and three of the Jeffery brothers. Sid Marsh stayed on as Captain for two years and I was made Vice-Captain. One notable cricketer was Mike Gauntlett, who I first encountered playing for Dunsfold at Hambledon in August 1941. He was an enormous man, but he was shaking like a leaf. Shortly before he had been invalided out of the army. I believe he had been at Dunkirk. Everyone called him Mike but his actual first names were Walter Herbert Frank Tremayne. Before the war he had been sports master at a prep school near London. In 1934 he persuaded Jack Hobbs to come down to the school, a match recorded in Wisden: Hobbs scored 181 for F.T. Gauntlett's XI v. Ewell Castle School. Mike had an outsize personality but he was a highly neurotic character who paid regular visits to a psychiatrist in Wimpole Street, Dr Noel Gordon Harris, 'a very good man'.

Mike worked for an industrial paints company, Docker Brothers, operating from a little office next to Jordon's Garage in Milford. His work involved much travelling by car, delivering samples to clients all over the south of England, but he hated to travel alone. From 1943 I sometimes accompanied him on these journeys, which usually ended in a pub crawl, visiting hostelries in places such as Portsmouth, Fareham, Petersfield, Liphook, Haslemere and Brook. He much preferred convivial evenings in the pub to life at home, especially after cricket matches. His wife Joan came too; when she got bored she retreated to the car. Mike was a useful chap for getting hold of items in short supply, such as wartime whisky or French wine. He stowed bottles in the back of his car, using them to ease business transactions.

Later in the war Mike ran a scratch cricket team. Joan and their two sons came to watch the matches. Mike was a slow left-arm bowler but batted right-handed. His stance at the wicket brought to mind W.G. Grace – minus the beard; he must have weighed 18 or 19 stone. When in the mood he hit titanic sixes. Once he took a tumble in the field and one of his sons piped up: 'Daddy's made a hole in the ground!' After the war Mike was prime mover in the establishment of a 'rambling' cricket team. Its origins were curious. Before the war Chiddingfold fielded two clubs. One played at Sydenhurst, a country estate situated behind St Mary's Church. Chiddingfold Working Men's Cricket Club played next to the village school. There was intense rivalry between the two teams. During the war the Sydenhurst ground was ploughed up to aid the 'war effort'. Afterwards returning members felt it would be too costly to re-lay. From now on the club would be 'playing away' but it retained the name Sydenhurst. The first match was on 7 July 1946 against Farncombe, a strong team who we beat by 8 wickets. The club was founded amid high celebration in the pub after the match. Mike was captain, Harold Cooper from Cooper's Stick Factory in Wormley chairman and I took on the post as Hon. Secretary. A fortnight later the Ramblers trounced Brook and Sandhills by 146 runs. Mike had good connections with the Kennington Oval and on this occasion the team included Jack Parker, the Surrey batsman who had been selected for the cancelled M.C.C. tour of India in 1939-40. He scored 84 runs.

The Ramblers played on Sundays, Hambledon and other local teams on Saturdays. I introduced a few players from Hambledon, Bert Jeffery, Tom Hammond and Tony and Lionel Wood. Mike played on Saturdays for Brook, others for Dunsfold, Chiddingfold or Milford. Harold Cooper was a useful fast bowler; Norman Mullins, a tall wicket-keeper and good batsman, a friend of Mike's, lived in Godalming. Ivan Roberts, the architect at Friary Brewery, smoked a pipe. Once he strode out to bat with a pipe jutting from his mouth; he reached the wicket before one of the fielders made a remark and he noticed. Charlie Izzard from Witley, Mike's dogsbody at work, was an obstinate left-hander who stuck there but seldom scored many runs. This irritated some opposing teams. The secretary of the Bognor club, a small pompous man, asked Mike 'not to bring Izzard in future because he is such a dull player'. Mike laughed. On this occasion Charlie went in first and scored 60. Charlie's brother Harry was a better cricketer but Mike never liked him. Our leading player for the first season or two was G.P.D. Blackmore (Blackie), a commercial traveller who had served in the army in India. Subsequently he played two first-class matches for Kent. He was a good fast bowler and a forcing batsman but a slightly slippery personality. Mike suspected him of stealing money from the players' changing room and I was instructed to write a letter dismissing him from the club. I received a rude post card in reply.

Following the death of little Brigid my emotional state was not good. In 1946 Mike suggested I went to see his psychiatrist, Dr Harris, at his rooms at Devonshire Place, Wimpole Street. I stayed the night with Ruth in Hampstead and Mike drove me back to Milford afterwards. Harris recommended I consult Dr Frederick Mayo Wingate, a psychiatrist connected with the Middlesex Hospital. Next month I visited him in Harley Street for the first time. Dr Wingate was a small dapper man who looked very young; I suspect he had only recently graduated. He spoke in a quiet Scots accent. I am not clear now what school of psychiatry he followed. I settled down on a couch and we would chat about anything that came to mind, following the trail wherever it led. He was friendly and helped in a way. I saw him regularly, sometimes twice a week at the start, for the next few years.

With a colleague Dr Wingate founded the Marriage Society, an introduction agency for gentlefolk seeking spouses. I joined the advisory committee and sometimes attended meetings after my sessions on the couch. Committee members would recommend applicants and give a report about them but Wingate made all the decisions. At about this time Thalia's elder sister Jean was lodging with us at Milford and helping with Stephen. Jean had been in Montevideo at the time of the Battle of the River Plate, acting as secretary to her uncle, Sir Eugen Millington-Drake, the British Minister to Uruguay. She joined the ATS and later contracted TB. Ruth had married Archie Macdonald in 1945. Jean, the eldest of the family, was by 1949 feeling very unmarried. I believe I recommended her to the Society. The first candidate selected by Wingate was not a success. Then Jean was introduced to Shirl Mussell, a widower with a grown up son. They got on splendidly. In August Shirl came to lunch at Milford. On 25 September the couple were engaged. In mid-October Shirl arrived at Fairnilee. There were financial confabulations with David Marshall, the family solicitor. Next day Jean, Shirl and David departed together. The afternoon before the wedding Margaret held a party in London at Charles Street. After attending a piano recital by Gulda at the Wigmore Hall we travelled back to Milford. The wedding took place at Milford Church on 10 December. Donald being unavoidably absent in India, the bride was given away by David Marshall, a cousin of her father. Shirl's son Peter was best man and her cousin, little Mairin Wheeler, bridesmaid. Jean, the *Surrey Times* reported, was dressed in blue and wool georgette, with diamante belt and hat to match. Pink roses formed her bouquet. The reception was held at The Refectory, an olde-worlde eating establishment on the road to Godalming. The couple spent their honeymoon in Wales.

* * * * *

The White House was an interesting old building, partly perhaps 18th century but a portion much older. Most of the exterior was either rendered or tile-hung but a small section at the back outside the larder showed exposed beams. A narrow winding stair gave access to two attic rooms, lit by dormer windows that looked on to another section of the roof. It was possible to climb out on to the leads. There was a dizzying drop to the ground. Many of Clare's belongings were stored up here after the family moved from Godalming to the United States. The attic floor was severely worm-eaten and had to be renewed. After we moved to Hambledon the new owner made extensive alterations. We were invited back to tea and could barely recognise our surroundings. There was an air of mystery about the cellar; grills outside suggested it had once been more extensive. The new owner reported that they had uncovered a second cellar under my study that had been filled in with rubble.

There was a wonderful walled garden behind the house, with a large lawn, where in the summer our weekend guests would relax on easy chairs. The more active of them, such as Frank Walker and Jeremy Noble, were sometimes persuaded to play cricket with Stephen, often before breakfast. This involved bowling a soft ball for Stephen to smite. The garden was on a slightly higher level than the house and could be approached via the dining-room French windows up steps bordered by a pair of ferns. There were flowerbeds on two sides, flanked by a gravel path, and a greenhouse with a water butt swimming with minute larvae. Near this we put up a trellis, and at the time of the Coronation erected a make-shift flag-pole. A magnificent horse chestnut tree, equipped with a swing, dominated one side of the garden. Old Mr Dance tended the flowerbeds and his nephew Maurice, an AA man with a yellow motor-bike and sidecar, came to mow the grass. On his occasional visits Thalia's brother Donald would march up and down the lawn playing the bagpipes.

Across the road was a large orchard with a vegetable garden and fruit cage to one side. Beyond the orchard, an area of rough ground, nettles and brambles led to a short section of the River Ock, a grand designation for what was no more than a stream. Near the road we had a chicken house and chicken run. In these early days we did not possess a refrigerator; surplus eggs were preserved in water-glass in a glazed earthenware container in the larder. I enjoyed tending the fruit trees, a very fine collection, including a medlar, and acquired a long pruner and a clever device on a pole for picking the topmost fruit. Most years I harvested an enormous quantity of apples, which we stored in stacks of trays and on the floor of the loft above the garage, hauling the fruit up in baskets. We were indignant when some apples in the orchard were pinched. We decided to acquire a flock of geese, hoping that their noisy honking would deter intruders. Unfortunately the geese themselves snaffled the fruit. They were good to eat, however.

Even sixty years ago the road outside the White House was busy. Our cats would cross the road to reach the orchard on the other side and at least two died as a result – Rimsky-Korsakov and Dido. Dido was killed while we were staying with Frank and Jane Thistlethwaite at Cambridge in 1950. Their cat had recently had kittens and we brought a kitten home as a replacement. Stephen looked after her – perhaps a little roughly – in the back of the car. This was Susanna, or Susie, a beautiful tabby, rather nervous, who lived to a ripe old age and moved with us to Hambledon in 1957.

Margaret began to invite us regularly to Fairnilee in the shooting season, though I was annoyed to miss our autumn visit in 1951 because Archie had taken over the house as his headquarters for the General Election. Archie had won Roxburgh Selkirk and Peebles for the Liberals in 1950 but lost the seat by 829 votes in 1951. The Borders was full of retired colonels and other ex military personnel left over from the War. They all shot. Two who were particular friends of ours, Laurie Loch and John Lowis, both Indian Army colonels, had married sisters. Their lives seemed to run in parallel – each had a son and a daughter – though in character they were very unalike: Laurie Loch was generally calm but John Lowis could be explosive. He did not suffer fools gladly (that sometimes included his wife). For years they took a little moor at Langhope. The bags were never large but these days were tremendously enjoyable. Later Laurie's son Johnnie joined the team and once Stephen appeared, letting fly with Johnnie's air rifle to no effect whatever. My first appearance on television occurred on one of these shoots. Border TV wanted a story about the opening of the grouse shooting season. It was a misty, drizzly day, very wet under foot. We were accompanied by a puffing cameraman. That evening on Border News there was brief black and white footage of me discharging my gun in the direction of a grouse.

Other regulars on Fairnilee shoots were Major Jock Sprot and Colonel Jack Hankey. Jock Sprot's sister Celia married William Whitelaw, the Conservative politician, who cast eyes in Thalia's direction before the war. Jack Hankey bred gun dogs, not very good ones, which he would press on his neighbours, accompanied by an invoice. Whelping took place in his house; afterwards torn newspapers were tossed into the garden from his bedroom window. Major Simon Baillie, a small man not endowed with much humour, was persuaded to take on Shiel, an enormous, unruly black Labrador. In training he employed a very long lead, which unwisely he secured round his waist. When a bird fell to earth Shiel galloped forwards, reached the end of his line and spun the Major round like a top. One peppery colonel had an enthusiastic and energetic spaniel called Bruce-you-bugger – at least that was how he invariably addressed him.

Dick Lund was a tall, gaunt man who had been sacked as factor at Fairnilee by my father-in-law. He was an excellent shot. Major Albert Arkwright, an old friend of the family, had escaped from a German prisoner of war camp, Oflag VI B, got back to England, and later recorded his experiences in *Return Journey*. His years as a prisoner had taken a toll on his health. General Sir Philip Christison was an officer of great distinction who commanded an army corps in Burma and accepted the surrender of Japanese forces in Singapore. When I first met him he astonished me by asking: 'What do you know about the operas of Schreker?' He had made a quiet inquiry to another member of the team as to my profession. He had encountered Schreker's operas in Germany after the Great War. Vice Admiral Sir Conolly Abel Smith commanded the escort carrier *Biter* during the Allied invasion of North Africa ('Operation Torch'). I was aware of his exploits through my interest in naval history. His seat was at Ashiestiel, adjoining Peel Farm. His final command after the war was of the Royal Yacht Britannia.

Jack Hankey took a shoot at Lindean on the outskirts of Selkirk. On a mixed partridge and pheasant day in the early Fifties we were surprised when a small clattering goods train came steaming along the middle of a field near the river on the branch line from Galashiels to Selkirk. This had already been reduced to freight only and in 1964 the single-track line was closed entirely. The stone piers of the dismantled bridge over the Tweed remained for some years, before they too disappeared when the new road bridge was built.

An Engagement with Time

* * * * *

I first met Diana McVeagh, with Tessa, at the Green Lizard café in London shortly after the war. It was the kind of establishment favoured by typists, according to Diana. She and Tessa had been at school together. Diana was studying at the Royal College of Music under Frank Howes and doing some teaching. On 20 December 1947 Thalia and I travelled to London for Tessa's wedding to Peter Thomas at St Saviour's, Walton Street. They were a very good-looking couple. Basil made a maudlin speech at the reception, much too long. Tessa smiled sweetly throughout. I caught Diana's eye. Tessa's mother, Lady Mercy, now married to her third husband, Richard Marter, looked older than when I last saw her and not entirely sober. Peter had just been called to the Bar. His legal studies had begun at Oxford before the war. He joined the RAF in 1939 and served as a bomber pilot but was shot down in 1941 and spent the next four years as a prisoner-of-war in Germany. He continued his legal studies while imprisoned, assisting inmates, and also shone as an actor.

By late 1947 Thalia was pregnant again. We were apprehensive after Stephen's difficult birth, but were reassured by Thalia's doctor, Dr Winsome Grantham. At that time the Rhesus factor, which had affected Stephen, was not properly understood, and certainly not by Dr Grantham, who held old-fashioned views. Jean was staying with us, helping with Stephen. Margaret came down for the day on Sunday 21st March. That evening Thalia unexpectedly went into labour: 'Great Medical Excitement' I noted in my pocket diary. Our daughter Diana Margaret was born at the White House at 3 a.m. next morning. Like Stephen she was yellow with jaundice. The next day I registered the birth in Witley. Philip came to dinner. Two days later, Maundy Thursday, Diana was ill. Gran appeared in the morning, Margaret came to tea and Philip was again with us for supper. Over the next two days little Diana's condition worsened. She was attended by a nurse. Diana died at 10.45 on Easter morning. If she had been born in hospital and received an immediate blood transfusion – as was the case with Ruth's second son Ian two years later – her life might have been saved. But Dr Grantham was not cognisant of these new ideas. There was a post-mortem the following morning. I made contact with the Rector and rang the undertakers. Gran, Martin and Joe appeared in the afternoon. The next day I registered Diana's death at Witley, exactly a week after I had registered her birth. The grim funeral took place at Milford Church, with the interment at Milford Cemetery along the road, the next afternoon. The fine weather had broken. Brigid came down from London, Joe, Jean, Sheila Morgan (Stephen's godmother) and Philip were with us, but Thalia was too ill to attend. It was two days before she got up for the first time. The nurse left the next day.

In February 1948 I went to Cambridge, partly for research but more importantly for a staged production of *Solomon* at the Guildhall, mounted by the same team that put on *Saul* before the war. Of all the great Old Testament oratorios, *Solomon* would seem the least likely to benefit from such treatment. It has longer, more numerous and more elaborate choruses than any of its fellows; except in the second act there is almost no plot or conflict. Yet its theatrical impact was overwhelming. It was this production, even more than that of *Saul* nine years earlier, that impelled me to write my book on the oratorios, and attempt to identify the springs of Handel's dramatic genius. The producer, Camille Prior, gave dramatic projection to the choruses by means of ceremonial processions, mime, dancing and a beautifully contrived end to Act I, with Solomon and his Queen escorted to bed, as the light faded, by a group of Moorish pages carrying magic lanterns, while the unseen pit chorus sang 'May no rash intruder'.

I did not set to work immediately. Later in the month I dealt with the proofs of *Bizet* and went through the hard labour of compiling the index. In April, shortly after the death of Diana, I resumed work on my chronicle play, *The Splendour Falls*. As soon as it was finished I sent a copy to Dadie. He sat on it for months. His verdict, when it came, was not enthusiastic. My father was more encouraging, though he commented that it was much too long. He warned me against literary jokes or 'conceits' in the theatre. 'They never succeed.' Someone (I forget who) showed it to a literary agent, who commented that the play had many good points but was too long and cumbersome. In January 1949 I delivered a copy of the play to the firm of H.M. Tennant. They promptly lost the script. I heard nothing for months. Eventually I received a discouraging letter, animadverting that it was a 'rather leaden modernisation of the Arthurian legend'. The Lancelot-Guinevere story was more successful and some episodes, 'particularly the one introducing Elaine, have poignancy and dramatic tension'. But it was 'a cheap and easy kind of humour which introduces into this kind of play references to such things as the B.B.C., Karl Marx and the Caledonian Market'. I considered the tone of this letter unnecessarily contemptuous. Peter and Tessa Thomas visited us shortly afterwards and we brought out bell, book and candle and pronounced a solemn curse on its author. Within six weeks he was dead from sudden kidney failure. I have never dared to curse anyone since.

Early in 1951 I made extensive revisions, cutting nearly 50 pages, including three whole scenes, and returned it to the agent, who found it 'tremendously improved'; she promised to send it to the BBC 'with my best sales letter'. Nearly a year later the BBC was still considering it. I never heard from the agent or the BBC again and – despairing – let the thing drop.

The reviews of *Bizet*, published in June 1948, were extremely favourable. The book was a success. The reception encouraged me to start work that month on the Handel oratorio project I had been contemplating for some time. My original title was 'The Dramatic Handel: A Study of the Jewish Oratorios and Masques'. It began as a short study of Handel's dramatic style. As usual, in the Cambridge vacations, Philip came to dinner frequently: sometimes he arrived at tea time. We went through each of the oratorios in turn, Philip at the upright piano, I sitting next to him, turning the pages, concentrating hard on the score. After each movement there was a pause while I scribbled notes. The first two works we played through were *Alexander Balus* and *Belshazzar*. Philip brought scores from Cambridge of the oratorios I did not possess. It soon became apparent that the published texts, words and music, were inaccurate, and sometimes seriously misleading. No systematic examination of Handel's dramatic music, whether opera or oratorio, had ever been undertaken. We had on our doorstep the autograph manuscripts of nearly everything Handel wrote, countless sketches, rejected drafts and unpublished pieces in his hand, and an even more voluminous store of manuscript copies and other documents. Nearly all of this material was conveniently accessible in the Royal Music Library (for long deposited at the British Museum, and in 1957 presented to the nation by Her Majesty the Queen) and in the Fitzwilliam Museum at Cambridge. It had never been used for a critical study of Handel's work or any major part of it.

In July I spent a few days in Cambridge, staying with Philip at St Clement's Gardens. I started work in the Rowe Library at King's, examining Handel scores and librettos in the A.H. Mann Collection. Later I acquired librettos on microfilm and devised a make-shift reader using a small V-shaped bookshelf, two pieces of flat glass, a bright light and a magnifying glass. In October I completed a short book on Bizet for Dennis Dobson, followed in November by the entry on Bizet for the 5th edition of Grove's Dictionary (Eric Blom protested that it was much too long. His heavy cuts in the typescript appeared in green ink.) In December I began a study of *Carmen*, libretto and music, for a Folio Society edition of Mérimée's novel in English translation, illustrated with Goya drawings. Around this time I composed a couple of short stories and some comic verses, including *The Ballad of Aunt Geranium and the Milkman*.

At the beginning of 1949 Thalia was expecting another baby. Because of the disaster with Diana it was arranged that she should enter a nursing home in London well in advance of the birth. In January Clare and her three boys stayed for a few days while waiting for their cottage in Godalming to be made ready. In February I wrote a little booklet on César Franck, commissioned by William McNaught for the Novello series. Early in March we went to Cambridge, staying with the Paynes, leaving Jean to take care of Stephen at Milford. I needed to undertake further research in the Rowe Library. Philip and I played through more Handel works, including *Il Trionfo del Tempo, Aci, Galatea e Polifemo, The Choice of Hercules* and *La Resurrezione*. Thalia returned to Milford on the 11th but I stayed on until 16 March, returning via London, where I had a session with Dr Wingate, followed by a Marriage Society meeting. I got back to Milford late that evening to find Thalia unwell. The next day she was ill in bed. The doctor came and diagnosed toxaemia. Four days later she was removed by ambulance to the Garrett Anderson Maternity Home at 40 Belsize Grove. Jean visited her the next day. At 5.30 a.m. on Sunday 27 March Thalia gave birth to a premature still-born son. I saw her that afternoon, dining afterwards with Margaret at the Ladies Carlton Club. Jean went up to see her two days later. I visited her again on Friday, after seeing Wingate, then dined with Brigid and Lorimer at Barnes. Thalia came home the following Monday, after a two week stay in the nursing home. Thalia's Rhesus negative blood made it increasingly improbable that she would ever have another successful pregnancy. These were grim days for us both.

That spring my mother, who was living with Eugene in Portugal, came over alone for Martin's wedding to an Irish girl, Nancy Lynch, at the Brompton Oratory. Two days later there was a shocking incident at Hambledon when my mother was savagely attacked and injured on the Common by a young man in blue running shorts. It was soon after midday and she was walking with Gran and Gran's dog on the lower footpath, near the road. Gran, aged 85, went for assistance but by the time help arrived the ruffian had vanished. According to the *Surrey Times*, police scoured the lonely lanes and hamlets around Hambledon – Gran and my mother were able to give a detailed description – but the assailant was never found. The affair occasioned great alarm in the village, and parents were afraid for their girls to go out. 'We are naturally very much concerned,' said the owner of the village shop. 'The man must be a maniac.' My mother was not seriously hurt but the emotional impact must have been severe. She never spoke about the incident later.

In July I was approached by Dents with a proposal for a new type of opera book, in collaboration with the American firm of Pellegini and Cudahy, dealing with one hundred of the most famous and frequently performed operas, avoiding tedious plot summaries and putting musical and dramatic values to the fore. This caught my interest. I wrote a prospectus, placing emphasis on one unique feature of opera, its power by means of music to express infinite shades of dramatic characterisation. This, and my sample chapter on *Un Ballo in Maschera*, impressed Dents and Eric Blom but the Americans expressed doubts, fearing that the approach was too 'scholarly'. I drafted five more chapters, on Cimaroso's *Il Matrimonio Segreto*, *Norma*, *Simon Boccanegra*, *Parsifal* and *Salome*. In 1951

Pellegrini and Cudahy decided not to risk their money on the book and the project fell through.

Early in the New Year Thalia and I travelled to London, staying at Margaret's flat in Hill Street. I needed to do intensive work on the Handel autographs in the Royal Music Library. We left Stephen in the hands of Nurse Thomas, hired for the occasion, and Mrs Graves, the cook. I slogged in the Library for nine days. The weather was horribly cold; on the 25th the temperature fell to 10F, the coldest January day for three years. I took the opportunity to see Dr Wingate on two occasions. We caught up with family and friends, going to tea with Martin and Nan; Joe, now a struggling barrister, came in one evening. Shortly after the war Joe looked in on us at the White House, accompanied by a new girlfriend, of whom, it seemed to me, he was excessively protective. It was fairly early in the morning and I was in the middle of breakfast. When Joe saw that I was wearing pyjamas he insisted that his girlfriend should remain in the car.

Towards the end of February we spent an even longer period in London, again staying at Margaret's flat. We left Stephen in the care of a nanny, who arrived shortly before we drove off. She was a dour middle aged woman with a brown patch on her arm where she had been scalded as a child, as she explained to Mrs Graves. Unfortunately Stephen did not like her. This time I laboured for 12 days at the BM. I encountered William C. Smith, already an elderly man, who had joined the staff of the Museum in 1900. He followed Barclay Squire as Assistant Keeper of Printed Music in 1920 and retired in 1944. He was at daggers drawn with his successor, Alec Hyatt King, who I got to know well. Willie dealt almost exclusively with printed material. I was never clear whether he could actually read music. I saw Dr Wingate twice, handing him a copy of my play; so, on separate occasions, did Thalia. We went to the Albert Hall for a performance of Britten's *Spring Symphony*, a thrilling work that set my marrow tingling. While we were away Shenka gave birth to four kittens, three of them grey.

The weather was appalling towards the end of April, with three days of heavy snow, culminating in a tremendous snowstorm. I measured ten inches of snow in the garden. The fruit cage collapsed. A thaw followed quickly and the cellar at the White House was flooded once more. In the spring and summer we made further trips to Cambridge, mixing social activity with research. We attended a performance of Monteverdi's *Orfeo* at Girton, done in the open air with some competition from nature's songsters. I met Otto Erich Deutsch at the Rowe Library. He had fled Austria in 1938 and was now living in Cambridge. He was in the final stages of preparing his Documentary Biography of Handel; a year later he sent me the proofs and we were soon to begin a prolonged correspondence. I thought him amiable, if a little dry. He loathed Willie Smith and the feeling was reciprocated. Sometimes these trips were combined with church visits, including churches at Thorpe, Stevenage, Newton, Thriplow, Fowlmere and Welwyn (the last barbarously restored).

I first met Lennox Berkeley, with Britten, before the war. I was struck at once by his personal charm, modesty and air of sweet reason, though I had not much liked the only music of his I had heard, the Psalm 'Domini est terra' at the 1938 Three Choirs Festival in Worcester Cathedral. The works he composed during the war, in which his distinctive lyrical gift began to ripen, gave me more pleasure; I admired the String Trio and Divertimento, and in May 1947 greatly enjoyed the first Symphony. On the spur of the moment I wrote to tell him so, reminded him of our Cambridge meeting, and asked if I could go and see him. He gave me a warm welcome at his flat in Warwick Square; this was the start of a friendship that lasted until his death.

My chief memory of this occasion was the appearance of Freda, a strikingly attractive woman, while we were talking. Lennox did not introduce her, and I was not clear whether she was his wife or his mistress. They had in fact recently married. Lennox and Freda paid their first visit to Milford in May 1950 and I took a photograph of them in the garden, with Freda palpably pregnant. In late March the following year they stayed for the weekend, the first of many such visits, first to Milford, then to Hambledon. Michael and Julian left their squiggles in the Visitors' Book.

Lennox was then heavily engaged on his opera *Nelson*. I was thrilled to find a modern composer whose views coincided very much with my own. His acclaimed model was Verdi; his methods were traditional in that he made regular but flexible use of arias and ensembles; and he wrote memorable and even haunting tunes. The voices carried the drama and were not mere filling or, as in many modern operas, a prickly thicket of angular intervals. On each visit Lennox played through what he had written, sometimes with Philip sight-reading when the music exceeded the reach of two hands, and all three of us endeavouring to sing the voice parts. In this way I became familiar with the music long before the performance; a little of it was composed at Milford. Lennox's voice was so deep that he seemed to sing almost everything an octave or even two octaves below pitch; we felt it was quite an achievement when he rose to the bass stave.

We had endless discussions about the problems of operatic form and particularly about dramatic timing. I lent him my score of *Un ballo in maschera* when he was debating whether to use a backstage band for the dance music in Act I, and if so how to combine it with the pit orchestra. A little later he borrowed *Simon Boccanegra*, and discovered after some months that he had forgotten to return it. I felt that Alan Pryce-Jones's libretto, though admirable in many ways, sometimes failed to make the most of the dramatic possibilities and hung fire when it should be moving on. Encouraged by Lennox, I made a number of suggestions for improvement. The outcome of all this, two years later, was the introduction of an Admiralty representative, Lord Minto, in the second scene of Act II.

CHAPTER 15

The Dramatic Handel

By 1950 the old cricket pavilion on the green at Hambledon was in a sadly dilapidated state. The original thatched roof had long been replaced by leaky corrugated iron. The changing facilities and the lavatories at the back were inadequate, to say the least. In April I and other members of the Committee met Fred Neller, the Milford builder (who had run a cricket team during the war). It was resolved that the pavilion should be rebuilt, but funds were wanting. As part of my contribution, I decided to write a little booklet on the Hambledon v Feathercombe matches, with any profits going towards the cost of rebuilding. It was hoped to enlarge the pavilion and to move it to a more central position. In the end Fred Neller was not chosen for the job.

The green formed part of the Common land acquired by Tommy in 1932. In the eighteenth century it was known as 'Brick Kiln Common' because of a small adjacent brickworks. No one knew how long cricket had been played there. The green linked Hambledon Common to the Hurst woodland. In 1950 Harry persuaded Gran to donate it to the village (not the cricket club), to ensure its preservation for all time. The gift included land on the other side of the road and a magnificent clump of oak trees, beneath which people assembled to watch matches or to shelter from the rain. On August Bank Holiday, Thalia's birthday, in the middle of an all-day match against Thornton

Heath, a presentation ceremony took place in front of an enormous crowd. Harry made a short speech. Gran as Lady of the Manor handed the trust deed to the Rector, the Rev. A.E. Borthwick, a sporty figure dressed in mufti, one of three trustees. After the ceremony the match was resumed and Jack Probert, a skilful bowler, took two wickets in successive balls. Hambledon won the match by 97 runs. In the evening there was a jolly party on the green.

Over the years we employed a series of cooks at the White House. One of the first, Betty Tarbet, was half Chinese, a friendly, cheerful woman who came with her daughter Joan. They did not stay long but kept in touch by letter for years afterwards. Thalia remembered her affectionately as 'Chinese Betty'. Mrs Dyer, who arrived in 1946, was short and had weak ankles, causing her to stump about the kitchen. At first she lived in a hut in the side garden – this may have been a quarantine measure because her husband, who appeared from time to time, had TB. Eventually she moved into the house. Mrs Dyer was a convivial soul. When she left they found accommodation in a pre-fab in Shamley Green, where Thalia and Stephen visited her. By this stage she had acquired an invalid carriage. Mrs Upton also had a little girl, Valerie, and a semi-detached husband. After leaving Milford they moved to Saskatchewan in Canada, from where the kindly Mrs Upton sent us parcels of dried fruit, tea and nuts and Polish stamps for my collection. Mrs Graves and her son Robert arrived in March 1949 and were with us for some years. Stephen and Robert became playmates, knocking nails into pieces of wood in a large room adjoining the potting shed. Mr Graves sometimes sat Stephen on his knee in the kitchen. He too had TB and indeed died of it. We were all tested for the disease at Milford Sanatorium and for a time the door of the Graves's bedroom was sealed off with strips of brown paper. In late 1952 Mrs Graves, Mr Graves and Robert moved to a Council flat on the new Milford Lodge estate. Mrs Coomber, the next cook, was a woman of vast circumference;

her daughter was of similar proportions. Within a day or two she had lodged a complaint about their beds, which they found very hard and uncomfortable. We thought her a difficult, neurotic woman and were relieved when she departed a few weeks later. Edith Manley was very thin. She brought a dark-haired eight-year-old daughter called Jacqueline, who we introduced to Stephen as he was playing in the sandpit. Luckily they got on. Jacqueline helped Stephen with his construction projects in the garden. The next year Mrs Manley took them on holiday to Shanklin on the Isle of Wight, the first of several such adventures.

I was still working on the oratorio book. I completed a first chapter – on *Jephtha*, Handel's last oratorio – in October 1950. I was in touch with Alan Frank, Music Editor at Oxford University Press. He had admired my book on Bizet and requested I send a sample chapter and outline of the new book. I received his response on 10 November. He was enthusiastic. He felt it was 'just the sort of book the OUP ought to publish'; when completed 'it will receive the most sympathetic consideration'. He was rather horrified at the projected length – 140,000 words. Need it be so long? Or so detailed? He found the chapter on *Jephtha* 'extremely difficult to read' and suggested 'pruning a certain amount of lesser detail'. He looked forward to receiving the completed manuscript 'some time in the latter part of next year'. In this he was to be disappointed.

I finished *Esther* in January 1951. There was then a delay. An American writer, Mina Curtiss, wrote to me unexpectedly from Massachusetts in September 1950. While pursuing the correspondence between Marcel Proust and Bizet's widow, she came upon the surviving papers of Bizet and his father-in-law Halévy, including diaries and a large collection of family letters, in circumstances that pointed to their imminent dispersal. She was projecting a book on the composer, incorporating all this new information, but was not herself a musician or musicologist. She arrived in France in November, intending to burrow into the National Archives. Could she see me as soon as possible? She promised to bring nine lost manuscript pages from the fragmentary opera *La coupe du roi de Thulé*, a batch of proof sheets of the piano score of *Carmen* and other treasures. She arrived in England in early January and I was summoned to the Ritz, where an exuberant middle-aged lady greeted me. As I examined her haul of Bizet letters and papers I felt like Howard Carter on first looking into Tutankhamun's tomb. We dined at the Ritz and I returned to Milford late that evening with a stack of fascinating photostats. I worked on the material intensively for the next two days. Mrs Curtiss had found the originals of the two most important published collections of Bizet's correspondence, and by restoring many deleted passages was able to straighten the record. Bizet's character was thrown into fresh perspective. In particular, the suppression of the sad story of his marriage, hitherto accepted as a blissful idyll, had distorted the picture and deprived us of revealing evidence of his character in maturity. On 12 January I took the train to London and met Mrs Curtiss once again at the Ritz. In February she returned to the States. After this we kept up a prolific correspondence for a number of years. Her book, *Bizet and his World*, was published in 1958. We had lunch with her in New York on our way to Berkeley in August 1965. On our return a year later we again stopped in New York and spent a convivial day with Mrs Curtiss at her house at Bethel.

Early in February, inspired by Mrs Curtiss's discovery of a little more of the music, I decided to put together 'a Suite for voices and orchestra' from the opera *La coupe du roi de Thulé*. Bizet finished the score but sadly much of the music was lost. I talked to Philip's sister Susan, a cellist in the Godalming Orchestra, about the Suite and the next day she appeared for tea, accompanied by the pianist Leonard Halcrow, a master at Charterhouse. Together they tried out part of the suite. There were gaps that needed to be filled. Lennox gave me helpful practical advice when the Berkeleys came for the weekend at the end of March. After they left I spent two days in the throes of composition. Next day – when my mother and Eugene drove over from Hambledon for a drink - I stayed in bed. Extracts from the suite were broadcast on the BBC Third Programme on 12 and 13 July 1955.

In February I paid my first visit to Gerald Coke's library at his stately house in Bentley, Hampshire. Since the mid-1930s Coke had amassed a rich collection of early Handel scores and other important material, including a copy of Handel's will. Coke was a charming, hospitable man who was happy to open his collection to serious scholars. I paid many visits to Jenkyn Place over the next thirty years. In May we were again in London, staying at Margaret's flat. I attended a meeting of the Royal Musical Association at which Gerald Finzi read a paper on John Stanley. I remember nothing about the talk but recall bumping into Finzi in the Gents. I spent two days studying librettos at the Royal College of Music. We attended Basil's new production of *Hassan* at the small Cambridge Theatre. Alas, it was not a success. Not all the actors were up to their parts. Basil had hoped to engage Laurence Olivier for Hassan. The play seemed much too long, with a plethora of dancing, and Flecker's high-flown language and exoticism seemed out of place in the austere post-war world.

Rather late in the day Blom asked me to contribute an article on Criticism to Grove. This occupied me, off and on, from April to August 1951. In May Stephen came home from school with mumps. After a few days I too began to feel unwell. On 21 May I wrote '?Mumps' in my pocket diary but managed to get to Hambledon to pick the team for Saturday. Next day Dr Booker confirmed that I indeed had mumps. I was confined to bed for five days. In July I gave my first talk on the BBC Third Programme, an extended review of Martin Cooper's book on French Music. I had to send my script in advance to be vetted. A few days later I travelled to London to record the talk. It was broadcast the following week. Joe heard it and sent his compliments. At the end of August I gave a second talk, a half hour disquisition on Bizet and the Stage. Occasionally later I was asked to broadcast live, a nerve-wracking experience that required rehearsal.

On the evening of 19 August we took the train to Scotland. Brigid and Lorimer Rees and the children arrived at Milford the following day to house-sit while Mrs Graves was on holiday. The cats presented no difficulty but one of the hens was off colour. Brigid wrote to Thalia that the bird appeared to be on the mend, although her comb was still a little faint. The children enjoyed playing in the large garden. Lorimer picked one of the plum trees, under the supervision of the excellent Mr Dance. On my instructions the plums were weighed. Mrs Graves and Robert and Mr Graves returned towards the end of the month and after that Brigid and family were well looked after. One morning ladies from the Milford gardening circle arrived to instruct each other on horticultural matters in the teeming rain, with Teresa, Biffy and Charles watching from the house. This occasioned great hilarity from Mrs Graves and Mrs Freeman in the kitchen.

I wrote my first review for *Opera* in May 1951, a notice of a staged production of *Belshazzar* at Cranleigh School. The magazine had been founded the year before by George Harewood, with whom I was on friendly terms. Late in the year George asked me to give my 'first impressions' of *Billy Budd*. I attended both the dress rehearsal and the première at Covent Garden on 1 December. I greatly admired the work, with a few reservations. I thought the first act a little weak and Claggart crudely drawn but was gripped by the later acts. I pointed to a couple of naval solecisms. I finished my review in Scotland the day before a successful pheasant shoot at Fairnilee.

Soon after we returned to Milford I set to work on the synopsis of a libretto on the theme of Agamemnon. I wrote to George about my idea, suggesting that it might interest Britten. George was a friend of Britten at the time. He thought it would be necessary to know a few more details before putting the idea to the composer. He was certain that the suggestion was well worth pursuing, 'particularly as Britten's latest idea for an opera libretto has come up against serious copyright difficulties'. In January 1952 I resumed work on the libretto and sent off the synopsis to George. I lunched with the Harewoods at Orme Square to discuss the project. I heard nothing more for eighteen months. Eventually I wrote again. I received a letter from George in September 1953, apologising for being 'rather remiss about your *Agamemnon* libretto. As you will have guessed, Ben stopped all consideration of other work when he embarked on *Gloriana* and now he is concentrating on *The Turn of the Screw* which is likely to be done in Venice in 12 months' time. Erwin Stein was here when your letter arrived and we both thought the best plan was to send you back the synopsis, meanwhile waiting to see if the idea seemed likely to fit in with Britten's plans some time in the future … it is, as you probably will guess, curiously difficult to persuade a composer to think seriously about something when he has his mind on something else!'

* * * * *

Following Sid Marsh's retirement I took on the captaincy of Hambledon 1st Eleven and held the post for four years. Bert Jeffery, who had also retired as a player, prepared the wicket, undertook mowing and acted as umpire. I went over to Hambledon from Milford each week to select teams, organise the rolling of the

The Dramatic Handel

square, the cleaning of the pavilion, etc. Around this time Tony Harcourt-Williams came live at Admers Cottage on the green. He was a pleasant chap but he had a pushy wife, bigger than himself and a dominating character. Like me he was a wicket-keeper. I had kept wicket at Harrow and took over the job at Hambledon when Harold Wood hung up his gloves after the war. It was a useful position for a captain because you could see what the bowlers were doing. A number of non-players, mostly local gentry, urged me to give way to Harcourt-Williams as wicket-keeper. No doubt they had been stirred up by his wife. I did on one occasion. Harcourt-Williams was not a bad keeper but no better than I was. The situation was embarrassing. I consulted two or three senior members, including Bert and Harold Wood, and they urged me to hold my ground, which I did. Meanwhile the 2nd Eleven had developed a team culture of their own, so much so that at least one member resisted promotion to the 1st Eleven.

The Annual General Meeting in February 1952, held at the Merry Harriers, had a larger attendance than usual. Major Hill was in the chair. He had been a professor at London University, a botanist, a nice old chap but one of those people who – if there is any dispute – say 'least said, soonest mended', a fatal attitude. Ted Peer proposed me as captain. Then Commander MacRae, another of the local gentry, a very tall man, who had never played for the club, proposed Tony Harcourt-Williams. The matter was put to the vote. The 2nd Eleven voted to a man for Harcourt-Williams. I suspected dirty work; their numbers seemed to have been swelled by non-players. The first team was not fully represented and the vote was lost. I was out. My colleagues were not happy and all refused the position of vice captain. In the end Dick Farnfield, a fair bowler but a feeble personality, was elected. He was the player I had tried to promote to the 1st Eleven. One of the most prominent members of the second team was Nigel Fish, a taxi-driver and agitator who

I suspected of stirring up much of the trouble. Shortly afterwards four or five 1st Eleven members left the club, including Ted Peer, the husband of the village school mistress and a very nice man. Partly because of this, and partly through pressure of work, I decided not to play at all that year, though I still turned out for the Ramblers Sunday matches.

Fewer people appeared at the 1953 AGM. I did not stand. Lionel Wood, an excellent player, was elected captain and a tiresome little man called Leach, who ran the village shop with his sister, vice-captain. Leach was a busy-body and not very much use at anything, but liked to be involved. The entire committee seemed to have changed. I hoped to play again but in early May I received a note from the club secretary, Tom Hammond, informing me that I was no longer welcome. This had been decided by the Committee, some of whom I did not know, in my absence. I learned later that the voting had gone 4/5. One of those who voted against me was the wretched Leach. I was extremely angry and wrote a blistering letter in reply. After this I resolved to have nothing more to do with the club.

In January 1952 I received an invitation from Wilfrid Mellers, then working in the Extra Mural Department of Birmingham University, to deliver two lectures at the University in December. I had met Mellers in Cambridge before the war with his first wife, known as Pussy. The subjects were French Grand Opera from 1800-1875 and French Opéra Comique and Operetta covering the same dates. On a chilly day at the beginning of December I took the train to Birmingham for the first lecture, which I had written in a hurry, barely giving Thalia time to type it. I met Wilfrid at the Midland Hotel, where I had been booked in for the night. It was a slightly dowdy establishment of the type favoured by commercial travellers. After the lecture, illustrated with gramophone records,

I dined with Wilfrid and his second wife Peggy. Wilfrid was a lively character. Like Pussy, Peggy was considerably larger than he was. Over the years I encountered Wilfrid with a series of ladies, all bigger than himself and all, it seemed, with names beginning with the letter P. I travelled to Birmingham for the second lecture – again dashed off in a day – a week later, taking gramophone records and a couple of scores.

In October we drove to London for *Un ballo in maschera* at Covent Garden. This was the first performance of Dent's new translation, which restored the Swedish background. This enormously strengthened the opera, making it clear that Verdi was striving for a new compound of tragedy and comedy. But the performance was so poor that it was difficult to estimate his success. Dent was there (with Trend), deaf as a post and denouncing the musicality of the first-night audience in the loudest and most strident tones.

The New Year began badly with both Thalia and Stephen ill. Thalia was pregnant again and we had grave forebodings. Shortly after Christmas Thalia developed a high temperature, a very sore throat and swollen ankles. It looked like toxaemia – which she had had before – which would almost certainly have meant losing the baby. However, as I wrote to Margaret in Calcutta on 5 January, 'the doctor now thinks it is only a bad attack of flu, and that the baby is all right. She is much better now and has got rid of the temperature, but is still being kept in bed in a rather depressed condition. Meanwhile Stephen contracted a form of dysentery, and has had diarrhoea for four days and nights. The doctor has been pumping M&B into him (and penicillin into Thalia), and he is now recovering …' All this occurred while Thalia was negotiating for a new cook, so far without success. Mrs Graves, who had left late the previous year, and Mrs Freeman the daily both came in and had been very helpful about meals, etc. I tried to combine work with carrying trays and running errands but was not very good at it. The weather was horrible – very cold and windy with alternate sleet and snow-storms. Three days later Stephen was ill again, having apparently caught Thalia's flu. The doctor put him on penicillin as well as M&B, both tablets taken without protest in a teaspoon of golden syrup.

While Margaret was away, Mr Bruce, the head gardener, sent us chrysanthemums from the greenhouses at Fairnilee. Thalia followed Margaret's recommended hot water treatment and they lasted very well. From the farms we received welcome butter and eggs. Margaret gave Thalia a pressure cooker for Christmas, a useful if rather alarming present. Later in the month both Thalia and Stephen were up and about again. Stephen returned to school. Thalia reported to her mother on 20 January: 'I can feel the baby moving, but gently, not any really vigorous kicks. I get tired awfully quickly if I'm on my feet a lot but now Mrs Graves comes in & prepares supper too & that makes an enormous difference.' Two days later she visited her consultant, Dr Hill, in London. There was more cheerful news. Dr Hill could find no trace of toxaemia and as far as she could tell the baby was developing quite normally.

On 28 January Thalia was taken ill once more. The doctor was called and diagnosed toxaemia and that afternoon she travelled by train and taxi to a nursing home in London. I reported to Margaret: 'She says she doesn't feel nearly so bad as last time, but her ankles are all puffy and apparently her urine is by no means what it should be … I don't think she herself is in any danger, but the chances for the baby must be pretty poor. It still has nearly 10 weeks to run, and apparently they don't want it to be more than four weeks premature (if it is to survive) because of the rhesus. I think she is prepared for the idea of losing it, but it seems a terrible shame.'

This occurred just as we were about to go to London for five or six days. We had already arranged for Mrs Graves to come to look after Stephen. The next day my mother and Eugene called in. That evening I travelled to London for two operas at Toynbee Hall, Wolf-Ferrari's *Susanna's Secret*, insufferably long-drawn-out and shockingly performed, and Mozart's unfinished German singspiel *Zaide*, its first English stage performance, an interesting work with strong prognostications of *Die Entführung aus dem Serail*. I went with Diana McVeagh. I travelled to London again on 1 February, staying with Diana at 42A Bedford Gardens. That morning there were reports of the worst floods of the century on the east coast of England with over 300 people drowned, as I noted in my diary. On 3 February I was due to give my paper on 'The Dramatic Element in Handel's Oratorios' to the Royal Musical Association. On the evening of the 1st I went to Norman Platt's house for rehearsals of the singers, including Norman and Gerald English, who were to provide the illustrations for my lecture, accompanied by Dr Bergmann on the piano. The next morning I was at Covent Garden for the dress rehearsal of Gluck's *Orfeo*, sung in English, which I had agreed to review for *Opera*. In the evening I visited Thalia at the nursing home in Belsize Grove, the same one as in 1949. She was very low. Afterwards I had dinner with Diana.

Everything boiled up the next day. I did not attend a scheduled meeting of the Marriage Society in the early afternoon. After tea I made my way to the Guildhall School. I was in a complete daze when I gave my lecture, which I am told went very well. I already knew that there was little chance of the baby's survival, but was worried to distraction at the thought of poor Thalia going through all that for nothing. It brought back all the horror of the former disasters. That evening I went to *Orfeo* at Covent Garden with Hilary. Kathleen Ferrier (who I had been told was dying of cancer) gave a most lovely performance but the production was ballet-ridden and undramatic. I found the melody and sublimity of this music very soothing in a time of affliction. At 8.40 that evening Thalia gave birth to a still-born son.

I returned to Diana's flat late that evening in deep gloom. I visited a very depressed Thalia, who had been put under a strong anaesthetic, twice in the next two days, then returned to Milford. When I told Stephen about the baby his eyes filled with tears and he ran away and hid behind the sofa. At the beginning of the following week Mrs Coomber, the new cook, arrived with her daughter. I returned to London on Tuesday, contacted the Registrar and an undertaker and saw Thalia, who seemed much better. Stephen dictated and signed two letters to her and embellished them with illustrations, one of a witch's house and one of me digging in the garden in a top hat. He also gave me drawings to take her, one an elaborate design for the house plumbing (h. and c.) worked out in the most extraordinary detail.

On Saturday I was back in London. There was a run-through of about two thirds of *Nelson* at the Wigmore Hall, without chorus or orchestra. This was a risky thing to undertake, as both the dramatic and the musical schemes were pulled out of place. I was at an advantage, having known most of the music for upwards of two years (and even being responsible for one of the characters). I longed for the stage to sort out my impressions, but felt that, following Verdi, he had got the drama into the voices. I thought it an extremely lyrical opera, full of tunes to haunt the memory. That evening I paid another visit to Thalia, followed by dinner with the Berkeleys. Thalia returned to Milford on Tuesday 17 February, two weeks after she had entered the nursing home.

* * * * *

I completed three more chapters of the oratorio book during 1952 – *Alexander Balus*, *Deborah* and *Athalia* – and in 1953 the pace quickened: *Saul, Belshazzar, The Choice of Hercules, Susanna, Joseph, Hercules, Judas Maccabaeus* and *Theodora* were put to bed. In December I began another, *Joshua*. I did not of course go into such detail, or explore the textural background so thoroughly, as I did with the opera book thirty years later. I had not then mastered the copyists. The location of some scores and librettos made them difficult to consult, I was unaware of many others and Newman Flower refused me access to his collection. I felt sometimes that I was operating in a quicksand.

One of my first pieces for *Musical Times*, a review of *Benjamin Britten*, 'a Commentary on his works from a group of specialists', edited by Donald Mitchell and Hans Keller, appeared in April 1953. I was a great admirer of Britten's music and found some of the essays illuminating, in particular George Harewood's sketch of Britten the man and Peter Pears and Hans Redlich on the non-dramatic vocal music, but I was irritated by Hans Keller's eccentric final chapter on 'The Musical Character', an astonishing amalgam of penetration and irrelevance, close argument and arrant swashbuckling, likening his approach to the bombinations of a bluebottle in a jam-jar.

In late April Eric Blom came down for the weekend. He was alone. Sadly his wife Molly had died of cancer the previous November. After lunch we drove to Hindhead and explored the Devil's Punchbowl. Next day Gran, my mother and Eugene came to tea. They had returned from Portugal and were now living with Gran at Hambledon. They spent the war in the Bahamas and then a few years in hotels in Portugal. Eugene was a great admirer of – and propagandist for – Dr Salazar and his authoritarian regime in Portugal but he hated living there, just as he had detested life in Nassau. Eugene seemed a diminished figure. His health was not good. He had diabetes. He was writing less. American Catholic journals were no longer so willing to publish his trenchant articles.

There were rejection slips (I learned much later). His biography of Stendhal had long fallen by the wayside, his great work on 'The Sovereign Ego' was nowhere near completion. Another *magnum opus*, 'Knowledge and Destiny', remained mere notes and fragments, a projected volume of short character studies, ranging from Henry James to Hemingway, not even that. Going through his papers decades later I came upon a draft letter, dated 9 May 1953, apparently written to a Hungarian relation (it begins: 'Darling' and short passages are in Hungarian). It is highly revealing. Eugene explains 'why I am not a success', putting this down to 'lack of staying power: I have always been an excellent starter but a very bad finisher ... My great defect is that I have not got enough will power and like to get hold of the easiest end of the stick ... I was always at the top of my class at school ... and <u>never</u> worked for it ... I never wanted anything badly enough to work hard for it.' He admits to being a failure, but only 'comparatively speaking'. 'I must have all comforts, good food, good clothes, quiet, in order to work. Dostoevsky did not need any of these things ... I am lazy, and have always been.'

Donald offered us places in the House of Lords' stand for the Coronation on 2 June. It meant rising at a fantastically early hour to be in position at the intersection of Elizabeth Street and Ebury Street for Donald to pick us up at 6.45 a.m. Thalia acquired some union jack bunting which she arranged on the new trellis in the garden. Somehow, with the help of Stephen, we tied a large union flag to the makeshift flagpole. We drove to London the day before, staying with Thalia's friend Elizabeth Scott-Kilvert (Zee). That evening I listened to Rossini's obscure opera *Elisabetta, Regina d'Inghilterra*, broadcast specially for the occasion on the Third Programme. The overture at least was familiar since Rossini re-used it in *The Barber of Seville*. The weather next morning was chilly, wet and overcast. Most people were wearing raincoats. Everywhere there were enormous crowds. We found our places in Stand 77 by the Houses of Parliament opposite the Victoria Embankment. There followed a longish wait. A buffet was available in Westminster Hall, we were informed. I had brought my camera and took photographs of the Lord Mayor's State Coach, the trotting Household Cavalry, the limousines of foreign diplomats and other notables and the Prime Ministers' horse-drawn carriages. Most of the crowd in our stand were wearing hats, the men in bowlers or light toppers. The Foot Guards came marching by, then the tension rose as the Sovereign's Escort of Household Calvary clattered past. I was able to snatch a blurred shot of the Queen's Coach – by this time everyone was standing and cheering wildly – between heads and waving arms.

We returned to Zee's in the afternoon and watched a recording of the service in the Abbey on television, I device I had not encountered before. Later we looked in on the Berkeleys and I gave back the score of *Nelson* Lennox had lent me. That evening Basil held a supper party at Norfolk Road for family and friends. Afterwards we drove to the Thomases and watched the fireworks from the Temple roof. We stayed another night with Zee, who as an American had been bubbling with the excitement of it all. After lunching with Margaret and Donald at the English Speaking Union we drove back to Milford. The following day I started work on the *Belshazzar* chapter.

On 8 June I listened to the first performance of Britten's *Gloriana* on the radio; I saw the opera at Covent Garden at the end of the month. I was shocked by its hostile reception in the press and wrote a trenchant letter to *The Times* on the subject, which they failed to print. I did not review it but set down my thoughts in my music diary. I was very taken with much of the music – 'perhaps the richest of his operas' – but felt there were dramatic weaknesses and that the ending, with part spoken dialogue, was a bad miscalculation. Yet the second scene of each act 'overflows with the lava of genius, and my marrow has not yet recovered from the effect'. The tune 'Green Leaves' 'will haunt me to my dying day'.

I owned a score of Donizetti's *Roberto Devereux* and suggested to George Harewood that an article on this earlier version of the Elizabeth and Essex story might be of interest. A great success in its day, the opera had not been revived since 1882. Philip and I played through the score on the piano. I thought it, in part, a very fine work and worthy of revival. My article, 'Donizetti and Queen Elizabeth', appeared in the June number of *Opera*, shortly after the Covent Garden production of *Norma* with Callas (November 1952) but some years before the first signs of renewed interest in Donizetti's serious operas. *Roberto Devereux* was revived by Welsh National Opera in October 2013.

On 6 July Thalia entered the Royal Free Hospital, Liverpool Road, for a sterilization operation. After the horror of February we knew there was no chance of another successful pregnancy. For Thalia to become pregnant again would be a catastrophe. The operation took place two days later. I caught the train to London and visited her the following afternoon. Mrs Manley, who had arrived at the beginning of May, looked after Stephen. He had taken to her daughter Jacqueline immediately but held aloof from Mrs Manley for about a fortnight, then melted and was now affectionate towards her. Next week I visited Thalia again, after lunch with Basil and David Webster at the Garrick. I stayed with Hilary. At 12 the following day we collected Thalia from the hospital. I saw Eric in the afternoon. In the evening I attended an indifferent performance of *Hercules* at the Foundling Hospital, maimed by heavy and unintelligent cutting – the loss of 6½ of Dejanira's seven airs knocked out the central tragedy.

There was a crisis at the White House one day when a long, soft-covered stool was left too near the gas fire in our bedroom. After a while it began to smoulder and the bedroom filled with smoke. Thalia was out shopping, I was in my study below and having no sense of smell could detect nothing. Mrs Manley assumed the smell came from the kitchen boiler. The fire brigade was called when smoke was seen billowing down the stairs. The firemen pushed the smoking stool through the window out on to the little roof above the projecting study window. Repaired and re-covered, the stool has served as a convenient table by my study chair at Hambledon for nearly sixty years.

In August, while we were in Scotland, Shenka gave birth to a single kitten, whom I named Theodora. This was one of Shenka's last kittens; she was now an elderly cat with leathery ears. At night the cats slept in the garage, which was where we encouraged Shenka to have her kittens. We did not want this to happen too frequently so prowling tomcats were chased away. Once Stephen trapped one in the dining-room and the tiger went berserk. When Shenka's time was approaching her behaviour changed: she would prepare a nest in a pile of old copies of *The Times* in my study.

In October we returned from another stay at Fairnilee via Jean and Shirl's farm near Ravenglass in Cumberland. This involved a long train journey from Galashiels to Carlisle (where we had lunch) and then another train to Whitehaven. At Dyke Croft (I wrote to Philip) we found tremendous energy and hard work in progress in what seemed to me an intolerably bleak and uninviting countryside. The house was continually besieged by livestock, labourers, vets, commercial travellers and mud; but they seemed to find this restful. The previous year they had obtained an explosives licence to blast away boulders that impeded ploughing on a particularly rocky pasture.

In the middle of November we were invited by Thalia's Aunt Nan (Margaret's sister) for a weekend at her grand Elizabethan house,

Lake, in Wiltshire. A partridge shoot had been arranged, with a remarkable assembly of guns: a colonel who wrote funny books (I told Philip), a fashionable portrait painter, an aristocratic Old Harrovian, a convivial brigadier, a taxidermist, a veteran of 83 and a nephew of Dyneley Hussey, the music critic. It was a perfect day, mild, cloudy, almost windless. There were vast quantities of birds, flying high and very fast – much too good for my marksmanship. Later we were provided with a sumptuous dinner and a great deal to drink, but were rather overwhelmed by small talk. We were also made to play Canasta, a form of purgatory which I do not recommend.

One day at Milford we were startled by an appalling crash and found that the William Redmore Bigg painting of a cottage scene that hung in the dining-room had fallen off the wall. It landed on the sideboard, smashing the glass and a vase. The heavy frame had caused the string to snap. When we had the frame repaired sturdy chains were attached to the top corners. The painting has hung in the dining-room at Hambledon for fifty-six years without further incident.

* * * * *

Towards the end of January 1954 we spent a few days in London, leaving Stephen in the care of Mrs Manley. We stayed at Margaret's flat in Hill Street. I saw Rimsky-Korsakov's *The Golden Cockerel* at Covent Garden. Despite the lavish and entertaining production I found this a bore, sickened by the repetition of a few themes and the endless two-bar phrases. I found myself longing for the 'incompetence' of Borodin or Mussorgsky. I spent the whole of the next day in the B.M. That evening we attended a performance of Flotow's *Martha* at King George's Hall, Great Russell Street. I enjoyed this rather more than *The Golden Cockerel*, for all that it was superficial, sentimental and wholly conventional. Some of the catchy tunes suggested pre-echoes of Sullivan. Next morning I returned to the British Museum. In the afternoon I attended an Extraordinary Meeting of the Marriage Society, which after six years as a non-profit-making public concern was being wound up. In its first two years it had received 5,000 applications for match-making and was responsible for thousands of marriages, according to Dr Wingate, but recently the supply of men had dried up.

At the beginning of March we drove to Cambridge for a staged production of *Athalia* by Girton College Musical Society. We stayed at the Garden House Hotel. The previous October I had received a lively letter from Jill Vlasto, director of studies in music: 'I need your help & shall do so for the next few months'. We had known Jill and her husband Alexis at Cambridge before the war; they were not then married. Jill was expecting a baby, which would put her out of action for some time. They had decided not to mount an opera in June; instead 'we want to do a Handel oratorio in costume ... in Lent, all v. correctly'. Jill would not be able to do anything herself but fortunately she had two first-rate girls, one to conduct, the other to tackle the stage side. They were unsure which oratorio to choose – 'we want a fair number of women's parts to use our Girtonians'. My suggestion of *Athalia*, which had not been heard in England for years, was greeted with enthusiasm. I sent Jill a copy of my RMA paper, which impressed her as being in direct descent from Dent, both in writing and conception of form. It was passed from conductor to producer to the sceptical Mistress of Girton. Jill asked me to suggest cuts and to write the programme notes. Ena Mitchell was to sing Athalia; none of Jill's girls possessed sufficient venom! Ena was the only professional singer. A small on-stage chorus of virgins, priests, Levites and attendants would be reinforced by a larger body off the stage.

We arrived in time for me to attend the dress rehearsal (Jill urged me to offer 'Helpful Hints'). Next day I laboured in the Fitzwilliam. In the evening I talked to the young producer, Flora MacLeod, over sherry. We had dinner at Girton and coffee with Lady Jeffreys, a highly distinguished physicist as well as a lover of music. The first performance was at 8.30. There were two performances the following day. In between we were invited to tea with the Mistress, Mary Cartwright, a renowned mathematician. According to Jill she strongly disapproved of staging *Athalia* and took a dim view of music critics 'swooping down on Girton – (poor fish!)'.

I attended all three performances. They confirmed my expectation that this was a dramatic masterpiece of the first order. The construction was extraordinarily original, with endless variety in the length, shape and continuity of the individual scenes and choruses, all conditioned by the drama. Equally memorable was the characterisation: not only the fiery Queen, the slippery apostate Mathan and the bluff soldier Abner, but the tender domestic ties between Joad, Josabeth and Joas and the political ties between Joad and the priestly chorus were expressed in the music with a memorable subtlety and sureness of touch.

We stayed on in Cambridge for three more days. On Sunday evening we went to a concert at King's, a mixed bag of pieces by Beethoven, Berkeley, Radcliffe, Ireland and Morley. Of Philip's three songs, 'Summer Dawn', influenced by early Vaughan Williams and Stanford, seemed to me too long. 'The Lake Isle of Innisfree' had an attractive rippling accompaniment and a nice sense of climax. 'Requiescat' (on Oscar Wilde's poem) was the best, with more power and a fine end. Before we drove back to Milford I gave an informal supervision to Ann Eminton, the conductor of *Athalia*, and Angus Watson, one of the violinists.

The Dramatic Handel

The Thomases came down to Milford for the Easter weekend. Tessa was pregnant with their third child. Since 1951 Peter had been MP for Conway. Their car was not particularly smart and the lettering on its metal number plates had faded and needed to be refreshed. A pot of white paint was produced and seven-year-old Stephen volunteered to undertake the task. Peter looked on apprehensively as Stephen wielded a large paintbrush. On Easter Sunday Basil appeared for lunch and was photographed admiring his grandchildren on the patio we had constructed out of bricks at the top of the garden, apple, pear and plum blossoming on the wall behind.

After the Hambledon debacle, I played a few matches for Brook, Mike's Saturday side, as well as regularly for the Ramblers. In June Gerald and Pat Abraham and their young daughter Frances came for the Whitsun weekend. There was tremendous talk about music (mostly Handel). On the Saturday I turned out for Brook against Albury at home. In the evening the Abrahams drove Thalia and Stephen to Brook for drinks and baby sausages outside the Dog and Pheasant. An exuberant Frank Walker arrived next day, bringing with him a Hugo Wolf autograph – a fair copy of a song – and Wolf's own copies of the *Italienisches* and *Spanisches Liederbuchen*. Frank's fine book on Wolf had been published three years before. Frank was a brilliant scholar, with an exceptional flair for unearthing fresh material. He toiled at a humdrum job with the GPO, working long hours and difficult shifts. All his scholarly work was undertaken in his free time. He looked forward to his annual leave, when he sallied forth on research trips to Germany, Austria and Italy. A whole chapter and other passages relating to Wolf's lover Melanie Köchert were suppressed from his book for fear of offending her three daughters, all of whom Frank knew. Frank was divorced, but remained on reasonably friendly terms with his ex-wife. Once he came down to Milford with his younger daughter Sally. Sometimes, if work interfered with a luncheon appointment or a visit of friends, he did 'a Whitley' – that is, phoned in sick. He did not like using the telephone; Thalia rang for him on a couple of occasions. On Monday Thalia drove Pat and the children, including Jacqueline, to a gymkhana. I suspect Pat found this more fun than endless talk about music. The Abrahams had known Archie Macdonald at Frognal before his marriage to Ruth.

In the middle of June Thalia and I drove to Aldeburgh for the Festival, staying at the Brudenell Hotel. Next evening we attended the first performance of Lennox's one-act opera *A Dinner Engagement* at the Jubilee Hall. This was very light but a brilliant success, I thought, though musically not on the same level as *Nelson*. The libretto, by Paul Dehn, was highly amusing, and the score full of felicitous touches that at the same time illumined the drama and the characters. It was preceded by a dismal performance of Arne's *Love in a Village* arranged by Arthur Oldham. Next morning we went to a Janáček concert in the Jubilee Hall – mostly short pieces, including seven irresistible folk songs, with Britten at the piano – followed by drinks at the Wentworth Hotel with the Berkeleys, Paul Dehn and others. In the afternoon we explored a swath of Suffolk churches, taking in Rendham, Sweffling, Cransford, Bruisyard, Badingham, Laxfield and Ubbeston. The pick of these was perhaps Badingham, with a magnificent hammerbeam roof with angels and a superb Seven Sacrament Font. One panel showed mourners gathered round the bedside of a dying man. So realistic was the carving that the man's shoes and chamber pot were shown under his bed. The next day we attended Bach's *St John Passion* in Aldeburgh Church. For the first time I was conscious of excessive elaboration here, especially in Part II, but this may have been due to a hard seat on a hot Saturday afternoon. The performance was in excellent style. That evening we explored churches at Saxmundham, Kelsale and Carlton. The following afternoon we drove to Southwold, visiting Thalia's old school, St Felix, and St Edmund's Church, a vast Perpendicular building with many notable features, including a remarkable screen with 36 painted panels across nave and aisles (which I attempted to photograph). There were choir stalls with misericords and exquisitely carved animals and musicians. The Festival closed on Sunday evening with an 'Opera Concert' in the Jubilee Hall, introduced by George Harewood. Monday – the Longest Day – was devoted entirely to churches, Benhall, Little Glemham, Marlesford and Hacheston in the morning, Wenhaston (with its astonishing 15th century painting of doom with leering devils), Darsham, Sibton, Peasenhall, Heveningham and Huntingfield in the afternoon. We drove back to Milford on Tuesday, stopping to take in further churches at Copdock, Braintree and Little Easton (Basil's old stamping ground).

The next day we travelled to London for *Judas Maccabaeus* at the Foundling Hospital, a rather naughty performance under Hubert Langley with continuo on piano (and no string bass), a re-arranged orchestra (no flutes, bassoons or horns) and the omission of some of the better pieces in favour of the worse. I still felt this was one of the dullest of the oratorios, with a few great moments. Afterwards we had supper with Eric at the Garrick. About this time, at Eric's request, I compiled an Addendum to the article on Postage Stamps in Grove's Dictionary.

On Sunday 18 July Jean came to stay at Milford with her three-week-old daughter Anabel. Since her marriage to Shirl in December 1949 Jean had suffered at least two miscarriages. There was a gathering of the clans. Donald stayed the night on Thursday and the following afternoon Shirl and Margaret arrived for Anabel's christening at Milford Church. A cross represented Anabel's mark in the Visitors' Book.

In August, when Philip came to dinner, we played through *Nelson* (I had again borrowed the score from Lennox). Gerald Abraham had asked me to write an article on the opera for *The Listener* ahead of its first performance and broadcast on 22 September. We travelled to Fairnilee in the middle of August. The first shoot on Peel Moor, walking up, was a fair success, marred by heavy rain in the last hour. I shot better than usual, scoring two rights and lefts in the afternoon. While at dinner with Margaret a week later we were startled by an appalling explosion in the yard below. Stephen, who had been asleep in one of the tower rooms, appeared white-faced at the door in his dressing-gown to ask what had happened. Wattie Dods, the son of game-keeper Peter, was courting June, who worked in the kitchen. He had spied a fox entering the yard to raid the dustbins and discharged both barrels of his shotgun simultaneously at the beast.

We travelled back to Milford at the beginning of September. The next day I was picking fruit. On 20 September we took the train to London for the dress rehearsal of *Nelson* at Sadler's Wells. Stephen came too. We sat in the front of the balcony and I pointed out the instruments of the orchestra to him. A technician edged along in front of us and adjusted one of the spotlights, muttering that he hoped he wouldn't have to do this on the night. Half way through the performance the orchestra lights fused and proceedings came to a ragged halt. Stephen asked solemnly: 'Was that supposed to happen?'

We drove to London for the first performance two days later, staying the night at Margaret's flat. Afterwards there was a party at the Savoy. Next day Thalia saw Dr Wingate. In the evening we went to Basil's staging of *A Diary of a Nobody* at the Arts Theatre. Again Basil seemed to have misjudged his audience. With the help of his secretary Berta Nicoll he had laboured to convert the uneventful Grossmith novel into a 3 act play. In his memoirs Basil claimed that the single set was based on a recollection of his grandmother's drawing-room. I found the play mildly amusing, but soporific. It was well done, but was it worth doing? Afterwards we dined with Basil at the Ivy, when I kept these thoughts to myself.

I reviewed *Nelson* for the *Spectator*. I thought the opera wonderfully rich in vocal melody and characterisation but felt that Lennox was less successful in conveying the broad sweep of the historical background, the pageantry of a great naval war, and the sense of Nelson's unique value to his country. The performance on the first night scarcely did the work justice. For all my admiration for the music, I felt that the story was not the perfect vehicle for Lennox. What was required, it seemed to me, was a comedy with a strong lyrical or romantic content. An idea was beginning to form at the back of my mind, and the excitement attending the production of *Nelson* gave it a push. I at once dropped a hint to Lennox. His reply was enthusiastic: 'I'm longing to know what your idea is, it sounds the right sort of thing for me – lyrical with opportunities for humour (and a nice cosy ghost who is not frightening!)' I then sat down to draft a scenario; but the subject ran away with me, and to my astonishment the complete libretto of *The Park* came out in less than three weeks. The whole thing had been thrown up with great force from my subconscious mind; it had virtually written itself. For a long time I was unable to account for this, or to discover the source of the central idea: a girl and a young man separated in time and beyond each other's reach, yet united by a spiritual link that not only conquers time but solves the apparently intractable problems that corrode their happiness and inhibit the development of both their characters. Eventually it dawned on me that it was an idealised transference of the strange and wonderful relationship that obtained between Brigid and me nearly twenty years earlier.

Lennox's reaction on reading the libretto was a mixture of fascination and alarm. He was attracted by the subject, but shrank from the necessary labour and what he saw as certain difficulties in the treatment, in particular the numerous ensembles ('I am not Mozart'). I made various amendments at his suggestion, including an aria for Barbara shortly before the final curtain, and he considered this a great improvement (July 1955). He did not know when he would be able to think about it seriously as other projects kept cropping up, including a request by the English Opera Group for a piece with Eric Crozier, resulting in the short opera *Ruth*. After the production of *Ruth* the following year – it was a fair success – Lennox wrote: 'Yes, I do hope some day to embark on an opera again. I will then think about your libretto. I do not want to do another just yet, though, because I have various other things that I want to write first.' It was another twenty years before he finally set to work on my libretto, renamed *Faldon Park* and much revised. By then, alas, it was too late. The circumstances that prevented its fruition were to cause me acute disappointment.

CHAPTER 16

Hambledon

After the sad events of the previous year, and the earlier tragedies, Thalia and I were turning our thoughts to adopting a little girl. Thalia had already discussed this possibility with Margaret. We made inquiries. In November Thalia visited an Adoption Society in London. Obviously they required to see us both and on 2 December we visited their offices at 4 Baker Street together. There were forms to be filled in and we were asked to supply references. We did not tell Stephen about our plans at this stage. Around the same time Thalia visited possible Prep Schools for Stephen next year. This was becoming urgent because St Hilary's in Godalming did not take boys after the age of eight. Thalia liked Mr and Mrs Cameron at Little Abbey School, set in the country near Newbury, though it was a long drive via Basingstoke. A week later we both returned to Little Abbey, with Stephen, and were given tea and cake in the Camerons' sitting-room. Mr Cameron was a charming, good-humoured man of forty with a dark moustache. He had been a navigator during the war in RAF Transport Command. He doted on his two golden Labradors. Mrs Cameron, grieving the recent loss of a kitten, had acquired a pair of Siamese cats. There was a lovely view from the gravelled terrace down to a lake, embowered in woodland, with fields, more distant woods and Beacon Hill grey on the horizon.

In December Brigid wrote to Thalia from Malta about our plans for adoption, agreeing to take on the guardianship of Stephen and the baby in the event of our deaths. 'Of course! Use our names as if they were your own. We will recommend you to all and sundry Societies ... Lorimer had a form sent him a few days ago, which he dealt with at great speed and sent back. I do hope everything will go in a straightforward manner, and you will achieve your adopted daughter soon. I feel that once the machinery has been put in motion, the period of waiting must be almost unbearable. <u>Please</u> keep telling us all that happens.'

On 28 January 1955 Eric wrote: 'I did have a letter and a form to fill in from the Adoption Society, with a request for further particulars if there was anything to be said in addition to the questions on the form. There was, quite a lot. I gave them plenty of reasons for seeing that any child adopted by you would be an exceptionally fortunate one. What a splendid idea! ... I <u>am</u> very glad, so much so that I am afraid I blurted it out to Philip Radcliffe at the R.M.A., feeling certain that he already knew. I do hope you don't mind. But when I spoke to your Father at the Garrick I did manage to bite it back!'

At first progress was discouraging. Brigid wrote in early March: 'I do hope you are having more hopeful comments from the Adoption Societies. It seems to me very silly that any Society should object to you approaching another. It can't be any hardship to cross off your name, if you find you can get your baby elsewhere. I think the Knightsbridge Society seem very unhelpful, and I do hope that the other two do better.'

When we told Stephen that we were thinking of adopting a baby girl he intimated carefully that he would reserve judgement about this until he saw her. Luckily the judgement was favourable. In fact, he took to his little sister whole-heartedly. Early in January Stephen came to a matinée of Humperdinck's *Hansel and Gretel* at Sadler's

Wells. I found I could still enjoy this, especially in the company of the younger generation – though what most appealed to Stephen was the explosion of the witch. I was less enthusiastic about Walton's *Troilus and Cressida*, first heard on the Third Programme, then seen at Covent Garden a few days later. Despite some lovely music and an excellent libretto I thought the characterisation weak, with much tedious declamation and not a little fustian. I suspected that between composing the first two acts Walton had heard *Peter Grimes*, for the beginning of Act II was strongly influenced by Britten – an invigorating healthy influence.

At the end of February Eugene died of cancer at a nursing home in Guildford. He had been unwell since the previous year and in uncertain health for much longer. In July 1954 he wrote to Dr Tavares de Almeida in Lisbon complaining of a fluctuating temperature, tiredness, high irritability alternating with lethargy. A planned operation at Guy's Hospital – 'by one of the best surgeons in England' – was postponed, but seemed inevitable. His doctors were unable to discover the root of the trouble, despite 15 X-rays, 13 blood tests and assorted other investigations. Two teeth were extracted. It was even suggested that he had brucellosis or a virus akin to it unknown to science: 'It seems I shall become a cause célèbre in textbooks of pathology'. All this was very expensive – for my mother – because Eugene would have nothing to do with the National Health Service.

On 17 March Miss Luther from the National Children's Home came to see us. By an extraordinary coincidence, this was the day our adopted daughter Diana was born. At the end of the month I attended the Ramblers Annual General Meeting at the Dog and Pheasant, but because of my struggle to finish the book I played no cricket at all this year. I had already retired as Club secretary. In April, after pleading from Stephen, who loved the Beatrix Potter books, we bought a pair of pet rabbits, a white rabbit Stephen named Peter and a piebald one called Belinda for Jacqueline. A portable run that could be moved about the lawn was constructed for them. Stephen biffed it with a hammer in a professional manner. Stephen and Jacqueline tended the rabbits assiduously for a time. They had separate hutches and we were concerned when they embarked on mating activity. Fortunately nothing came of it. A month or two later old Mr Dance the gardener picked up Belinda by the ears, scrutinised her underparts and pronounced: 'That bain't no female!' We need not have worried.

At the end of April we drove an apprehensive Stephen, dressed in his new uniform, with trunk, tuck-box and blue overnight case crammed in the boot, to Little Abbey School. On the way home we took the opportunity to stop off at Kingsclere Church. In May we spent a few days in Bath. I was looking forward to Grétry's *Zémire et Azor*, conducted by Beecham at the Theatre Royal. It proved a big disappointment. Though charmingly staged and sung, it was scarcely worth revival. The story and music were both slight. There was little vitality of invention, no characterisation, and (one or two numbers apart) no dramatic continuity. It suggested debilitated Mozart. Beecham had clearly tinkered with the orchestration. A ballet of hairy beasts in Act II, a sequence of pretty tunes, no doubt gingered up by Beecham, showed Grétry's slender gifts to best advantage. Some of it approached the statuesque quality of Gluck.

On the way to Bath we stopped at Devizes, where I explored two fine churches, both Norman in origin. The following morning we toured the Roman baths. Later I sent Stephen a post card of the Great Bath, which lies below street level, claiming I had seen fishes in it. In the afternoon we drove to Gloucester and I took photos of the Cathedral with my box camera. Next evening Handel's 'Water Music' and 'Fireworks Music' were performed in costume on an illuminated barge on the Avon; but the pretty picture was marred by the use of the Harty arrangements, which not only tamed the music but sounded thin and insipid in texture out of doors. Most of the next day was spent on church expeditions, to Marksbury, Chelford, West Harptree and Compton Martin in the morning, Bristol Cathedral in the afternoon. Compton Martin was by far the most interesting of the parish churches, with a superb Norman nave and tall clerestory windows, a vaulted chancel, flattened chancel arch and a twisted pillar, suggesting a stick of barley sugar, which I photographed from several angles. Bristol Cathedral had Norman origins as an abbey church but the nave was Victorian. I was interested to find a Berkeley Chapel and photographed two of Lennox's knightly ancestors, lying in full armour above their tombs.

On 3 June we drove to London for Handel's *Deidamia* at St Pancras Town Hall. This was the first venture of the newly formed Handel Opera Society and marked the start of the revival of Handel's operas in this country. The inspiration came from Dent. I am not clear why he chose *Deidamia*, Handel's last opera and one of the weakest, though it has a few superb numbers. Perhaps he was attracted by the equivocal tone of the libretto, which he translated. Unlike most Handel operas, it required a small chorus. The conductor was Charles Farncombe, director of the Board of Trade Choir, whose secretary, Gwyneth McCleary, possessed formidable administrative skills, which she put at the service of the new Society. A small grant had been obtained from the Arts Council.

The opera was considerably shortened, with nearly all the da capos reduced to their ritornellos. Dent converted the Act III duet into a trio. The castrato part of Ulysses was sung by John Kentish, a tenor. It held my attention better than I expected (I noted in my music diary). The press were not enthusiastic. Colin Mason in the *Spectator* found the opera boring, the convention dead beyond redemption, the singing 'of the kind politely known as gallant (though by no means worse than the orchestral playing)'. Other critics were kinder. Martin Cooper thought the Chandos Orchestra 'full of good intentions but the intonation was rough'.

Nonetheless the reception was sufficiently encouraging for the Society to contemplate another production next year. At the middle of June I attended a meeting of the Society in London. I joined the Committee as musical advisor and for the next five years chose the works to be performed. There were difficulties. Charles was a nice man and a competent conductor but not a strong personality and tended to be brow-beaten by Gwyneth, a forceful woman whose knowledge of music was limited. Early on she did not see why a piano could not stand in for a harpsichord as a continuo instrument. There were explosions later. In 1960 I resigned from the Committee when Gwyneth banned me from attending rehearsals for suggesting vocal ornamentation, which according to her 'upset the singers'.

In June Shenka gave birth to four stripy kittens, one of which we kept, Mordecai Thomas. On 1 July we drove to Oxford for a Musicology Congress, staying at the Randolph. Here we encountered Nigel Fortune, Jeremy Noble and Tim Neighbour, who were to become life-long friends. I already knew Tim from the Music Room at the BM, where he worked with Alec King. I met Stanley Sadie for the first time and older scholars such as Marc Pincherle, Jens Peter Larsen, Frits Noske and Paul Henry Lang. We had a lively lunch with Jill Vlasto at the Randolph. Lectures and papers – some rather dry – were spread over three days, interspersed with social gatherings and concerts in the evening. A Purcell concert at Rhodes House included the cantata 'If ever I more riches did desire', a wonderful work, and 'Come, ye sons of art', an exuberant piece with an all but Handelian splendour. I noted that 'Sound the trumpet' should never be sung by women; it was a thousand times better with countertenors (a rare breed in 1955). A 17th Century Chamber Concert at Rhodes House featured works by Morley, Gibbons, Dowland, Purcell, Blow, Simpson, Farnaby and others. Alfred Deller sang songs by Morley and Robert Johnson, accompanied by a lute. Morley's settings of 'It was a lover and his lass' and 'O mistress mine' have never been equalled. Jeremiah Clarke's 'The Prince of Denmark's March' for harpsichord was the original form of the so-called 'Trumpet Voluntary', and I preferred it. Next afternoon, with Nigel, Jeremy and an American called Bill Burge, we visited Blenheim Palace and later took in churches at Charlbury and Shipton-under-Wychwood, stopping at Burford for tea. That evening we attended a concert of sacred music at the Cathedral encompassing works by Byrd, Morley, Dowland, Gibbons, Blow, Humfrey and Purcell. I enjoyed this more than I expected, though not all the pieces were well sung.

I had at last persuaded the BBC to broadcast parts of my suite from Bizet's fragmentary opera *La coupe du roi de Thulé*. The conductor was Stanford Robinson. Earlier we had hoped for Beecham, but he proved impossible to tie down, though apparently interested. I wrote an article for the *Listener*, 'A Lost Bizet Opera', and a shorter piece for *Radio Times*. As well as the prelude (posthumously published as *Marche funèbre*), three fragments were broadcast, all from Act I: the air for the jester Paddock, the brief but exquisitely beautiful scene of Myrrha's first entry, where a melody depicting her fascination of Yorick winds its way through the orchestra, and the Legend of the Golden Cup, sung by Myrrha with the chorus joining in a magnificent tune in the refrain. On 9 July I travelled to London for an orchestral rehearsal at the Camden Theatre. There was another rehearsal on the morning of 12 July, followed by a live broadcast with my introduction on the Third Programme that evening. The broadcast was repeated the following day. The BBC gave me credit neither for discovering nor completing this, and I had the greatest difficulty in extracting a fee. But I found the music wonderfully moving – more so than I had dared to hope – especially the last two movements. Or was it that I had lived with the music so long that I could not help identifying myself with it?

We kept Brigid in touch with our struggles to find a baby. At the end of April she wrote: 'What are the Societies doing for you, and what is the latest news?' We considered several babies before we settled on Diana. We heard a little about their background but were particularly interested in Diana's. Her mother Sheilah O'Reilly was a dancer with Sadler's Wells Theatre Ballet, nicknamed The Swallow. She had danced in Weinberger's *Schwanda the Bagpiper*, an opera we had seen at Sadler's Wells in December 1948. (I described it in my music diary as a shocking opera, uninspired, tedious and incompetent.) Her father Armand was French but he had been living in South Africa, where Sadler's Wells Theatre Ballet toured in 1954. This artistic background seemed promising. Diana was a cheery, smiling baby. By July a decision had been made. On the 22nd Brigid wrote from Malta: 'We are most excited about your wonderful news, and are longing to know more'. Thalia visited Diana again at the National Children's Home in Limpsfield.

Stephen came home from his first term at Little Abbey on 26 July. Two days later Thalia drove to Limpsfield to fetch Diana. Brigid in her letter imagined the scene: 'You must be feeling on top of the world!' There was tremendous excitement when Thalia returned with the baby. I placed the green carrycot on the stool by my study chair (the same stool that had been badly burnt the year before). With Mrs Manley and Jacqueline we gathered round to admire our new daughter. Diana smiled up at us. Soon Thalia was busy preparing her first bottle. Life at Milford had changed.

In September Gran, as Lady of the Manor, no doubt egged on by Harry, paid for Hambledon village pond to be dug out and restored. Many people were unaware that there had ever been a pond by the shop. Thirty foot oak trees grew from the middle of what had become a tangled and rubbishy thicket. Bert Jeffery had an old photo showing cattle standing in the water and a flock of geese. He remembered when the pond was in daily use. Before the first war he worked in the bakery (now the shop); the baker's horse was watered there every day at one o'clock after the morning bread round. Horses were brought from Lower Farm and Malthouse Farm and several people grazed cattle on the Common. They wandered at liberty – except on cricket days, when they were chivied off the pitch. Mrs Karn's geese kept the long grass by the shop in check, enabling fielders to be placed across the road. After the war the upkeep of the pond lapsed. With more motor traffic it became less safe to graze cattle on the unfenced Common. Fewer people used the pond to water their stock and it became a convenient dump. Encroaching rushes and accumulating silt made it narrower and shallower and by 1955 the ground there was scarcely even damp.

In July Donald had introduced us to his fiancée Anthea Rich at a dinner with her brother at the Berkeley Hotel. On 22 September we were in London for Donald and Anthea's wedding at St James's, Spanish Place. It was a grand affair. I hired a morning suit from Clarke's in Godalming. Stephen wore his Sunday best. Three Catholic priests officiated in the long and elaborate ceremony (though Donald was not yet a Catholic). Anthea, looking lovely, was given away by her brother Lawrence. Donald wore Highland dress. Thalia's nephew Michael Macdonald, in kilt and cream silk shirt, was one of the page boys. After the service the couple were piped from the church. As they emerged on the street rose petals specially collected from the rose garden at Fairnilee were thrown as confetti. In the evening we took Stephen to Britten's *Let's Make an Opera* at the Scala Theatre. I thought it a weaker performance than the one I heard in 1949, which tended to show it up. But it was much appreciated by Stephen.

I continued to receive voluminous correspondence from Mrs Curtiss about her planned Bizet book, on which she still hoped I might collaborate. In September she sent me thirteen draft chapters, typed on thin paper. I found them too discursive; the background was not sufficiently related to Bizet the musician. Mrs Curtiss sailed for Europe late that month, paying a visit to Italy to trace Bizet's footsteps. She arrived in London on 27 October and established herself at the Ritz. On the 30th she descended on us at Milford, accompanied by her assistant Liliane, bringing more fascinating Bizet material. Two days later Thalia and I drove to Diana McVeagh's flat in Bedford Gardens, where we listened to a tape recording of the *La coupe* broadcast with Mrs Curtiss, Lennox and Eric Blom. Afterwards we took tea with Mrs Curtiss at the Ritz.

Diana had now been with us for four months but there were still one or two hurdles to overcome. In September Miss Luther from the National Children's Home had paid us another visit. In early November Miss Wells called to tie up details of the adoption. The following week Thalia and I, together with Diana, were summoned to attend the County Court in Guildford, where we were gently interrogated by Judge Gordon Clark, a kindly man who smiled down at little Diana. Under the name Cyril Hare, the judge was the author of a number of fine detective novels, including *Tragedy at Law*.

A couple of days later I was in London for an RMA meeting, followed by dinner with Frank Walker at the Duck Inn. Afterwards I went to *Solomon* at the Festival Hall. This was Beecham's 1928 arrangement, which I had never heard before. I found it nauseating, all the more so because the singing and playing were first-rate. Beecham reduced the work to a shambles – indeed to artistic gibberish – partly by cuts and rearrangement and partly by rescoring. Some of the cuts could be defended but the excision of the entire judgement scene – the heart of the work – made nonsense of the oratorio. The rescoring was even worse, nearly every number being arranged à la Schumann with a thick wadding of tone supplied by held notes on clarinets and horns. There was a battery of brass (including five horns and a tuba – and cymbals!), which was continually used to fatten the cadences. All the wonderful sparkle and contrast of Handel's scoring was expunged. Not a single secco recitative was given correctly. Most were scored for strings, others had the organ, while two were consigned to three solo horns. The defilement went much further than the repainting of an old master. In culinary terms it was like serving warm hock with beef.

November was marked by a sad event. Our cat Shenka was found to have cancer and had to be put to sleep, aged 13 years and 8 months. She had been with us since our days at Underbank in Godalming and was the redoubtable mother of many kittens. Later in the month I gave an introductory talk to a programme of Handel's Latin Church music, including 'Laudate Pueri' and 'Salve Regina', by the Handel Opera Society at the Arts Council's drawing room, St James's Square. We went to Oxford for *The Fair Maid of Perth*, given by the University Opera Club at the Town Hall. Jack Westrup conducted. It was a great success on the stage, especially the first two acts; Act III was spoiled by bad production; nothing could save Act IV from being a flop. I was disappointed that Westrup did not revert more often to Bizet's 1868 vocal score. The original form of the serenade, played here, was vastly superior to the emasculated version given in later Choudens scores.

Our Hillman Minx was proving unreliable and broke down on several occasions this year. Once we crawled back from London at 3 a.m. On 13 December Thalia collided with a lorry on a bend at the Devil's Punchbowl near Hindhead and that was the end of it. Luckily she was unhurt, though shaken. After this we acquired a green Morris Oxford, which survived relatively unscathed until we sailed for America in 1965. Diana's christening took place at Milford Church on 27 December. In contrast to Stephen's winter baptism eight years earlier, it was an exceptionally mild day. Lorimer, in his canonicals, performed the ceremony. Brigid and Diana McVeagh (now married to Bill Morley) agreed to become godmothers, Donald her godfather. Afterwards there was a lively party at the White House, with Ruth and Archie Macdonald, Brigid and Lorimer, Donald and Anthea, Margaret (who thought Lorimer 'a charming man'), my mother, my brother Joe and the Vicar.

In late November Gran suffered another stroke. We visited her at Stoneycrest nursing-home in Hindhead. This brought back grim memories for me, for this was the nursing-home where I had been confined during my breakdown in July 1937, and where Gran had visited me. She made a partial recovery and was back at Hambledon Hurst, very frail, shortly before Christmas. She was attended by a companion, Mrs Stainer. My mother, following the death of Eugene, was still living at Hambledon. In February Gran celebrated her 92nd birthday, but the end was near. She died at Hambledon at 1.45 p.m. on 20 March. The funeral was held at Woking Crematorium three days later. Martin stayed with us at Milford the night before. Afterwards the family gathered at Hambledon Hurst for a reflective lunch.

The house and Common had been left to Harry but, having a house of his own, he did not want them. I had known Hambledon all my life and the house was full of happy associations. The next day Harry looked in at Milford and we discussed his plans to dispose of the property. Though we were happy at the White House, I was eager that we should not lose the chance to move to Hambledon. Harry was amenable. Within a few days we went over the house with a surveyor. Less than a month later a price in the region of £9,000 for both house and Common had been agreed. The latter came with a black metal trunk of Manor deeds, some written in bad Latin, many with elaborate seals, one or two dating from the reign of Elizabeth I. In addition there was a large-scale framed map of the Manor of Hambledon dated 1763.

It was obvious that we would have to make major alterations to the house, in particular to Voysey's enormous sitting-room, its beams sagging under the weight of a concrete floor above, small windows to the south and smoking fireplace. In the winter this room was seldom used because it was impossible to heat. A young architect called Philip Jebb was recommended to us. He was a grandson of Hilaire Belloc; his school master father took his wife and four children to live with his tetchy father-in-law. Philip had recently returned from a couple of years in New York and San Francisco and had set up in London with his brother-in-law Francis Pollen. It was Pollen we met first, in July. In the next few months we had many meetings with the architects, usually Jebb, not yet thirty, a slight figure who we found sympathetic and helpful.

Jebb designed new stairs up to the music room in light oak and replaced many of the doors. I disliked Voysey's original steps, with their long balusters rising to the ceiling, because they left a gap between the staircase and the window, a space for dust to accumulate and spiders to construct elaborate webs. Voysey favoured rush matting and green and orange carpeting. One of his green carpets, no doubt dating from 1919, survives in our dining room at Fairnilee. Stephen uses a fragment of orange carpet to help him negotiate barbed wire fences on the estate. A new window was added to the kitchen and the others raised and replaced (from the outside they look original), part of a wall dividing the kitchen was taken down and a well sealed with a concrete slab. Jebb proposed two quite different fireplaces for the music room and study, one a Classical design in pine with fluted columns, marble-backed, that for my study a more robust structure in stone and tiles. He provided a sample of the type of wood and staining. Double doors to my study, lined on the inside in baize studded with brass tacks, were intended to muffle sounds coming from the other room. The entire upper floor, including our bedroom, was renewed in wood, new panelled doors replaced Voysey's rustic originals, and polished oak supplanted some of the green-tiled window sills.

I listened to much music, not only opera, on the Third Programme, but there were difficulties. In January I wrote to Philip: 'I heard [Rimsky-Korsakov's] *May Night* yesterday and thought it delightful – much fresher and more melodious than the *Cockerel* – but the wireless made disagreeable noises from time to time which blotted out the announcement of the story of the last act. So I am hazy about the plot.' A fortnight later I told Philip: 'We have a new wireless, which works by frequency modulation and gets everything far more clearly than the old one, or indeed than any machine of the ordinary type'. Its disgraced predecessor was cast out into the kitchen.

Pressed by Alan Frank, I was struggling to finish the oratorio book. I again played no cricket this year, though I watched the occasional match. I kept turning up new information and chasing hares. Every one of the oratorio chapters required revision, sometimes very extensive. I wrote to Philip in Cambridge on 18 February: 'I have been having a dreadful time with *Acis & Galatea*. The chapter I wrote in 1950 had to be scrapped completely, and an enormous new one is now in process of construction … Charles Cud[worth] helped matters by lending me a score of the Italian version from the Pendlebury, but you have no idea of the manifold complexities that have arisen. The battle has been going on for a fortnight or more, and I am now bedridden with a poisoned throat … I also had a dream that I was hauled up before a Puritan divine of fearsome aspect who went by the name of Pastor Fido. He was pedantic and sententious and most unpleasant.'

On 4 March I wrote again to Philip: 'The *Acis* chapter is nearly finished; it looks like taking up more than 70 pages!! I don't know if it is readable – even though it has one or two obscene footnotes.' After this I set to work rewriting the chapter on *Deborah*. Towards the end of April I finished correcting the typescript of Part I of the book. The next day I sent it off to Alan Frank at OUP.

Philip suggested that Bob Dart, based at Jesus College, would be a good person to look through my finished chapters. Thurston Dart was a man of protean abilities, a penetrating scholar and a brilliant performer on the harpsichord. (Later he played harpsichord continuo in several Handel Opera Society productions.) He had a lively and iconoclastic mind. He was contemptuous of modern German scholarship, referring privately to the Hallische Händel-Ausgabe as the 'Hellish Handel Outgive'. He took a violent dislike to my proposed title, 'The Dramatic Handel', envisaging a series of companion volumes, such as 'The Eclectic Handel', 'The Fanatic Handel' and 'The Pneumatic Handel'. It suggested that I was concerned *only* with drama, which I was not. On this and on many other matters, encompassing both content and style, I took his advice.

March 17 was Diana's first birthday. I turned 40 the following day. I wrote to Stephen at Little Abbey: 'Diana had five cards yesterday. She likes to play with them and then throw them on the floor. She now has two teeth, and makes a lot of new noises'. We had looked out the old wartime high-chair that had served first Brigid, then Stephen. Various repairs were needed. Cleverly, it could be converted into a wheeled low-chair with tray. On a sunny day in late April a professional photographer came to the White House and took a charming photograph of Stephen and Diana in the small front garden.

At the beginning of January I attended a meeting of the Handel Opera Society at the Board of Trade, Gwyneth's place of work. I had persuaded them to mount *Hercules* this year. I suggested cuts to the long score and wrote the programme notes. There was to be one performance at St Pancras Town Hall on 2 May. In early March I received a desperate communication from the Society appealing for costumes and enquiring if any Cambridge opera company might be able to supply them. It occurred to me that those used in the *Bacchae* might do. In the event they borrowed costumes from Glyndebourne Festival Opera. On 21 April I took the train to London to attend rehearsals, which lasted all day. The dress rehearsals at St Pancras on the 30th went on long into the evening. The performance two days later was on a higher level than that of *Deidamia*. Though the execution was imperfect, it confirmed my estimate that this was one of the greatest masterpieces in dramatic music before Mozart. Monica Sinclair as Dejanira was magnificent, singing with intensity and fiery command. Iris Kells was a touching Iole. John Noble overshot the mark with the bluff and cheery Hercules, making him hilariously comic. They were plenty of other gaucheries inseparable from amateur chorus and dancers, but none of them could obscure the power of Handel's music.

The following week I revised my chapter on *Hercules*. In early June we stayed a night at Margaret's flat in Hill Street. In the evening I attended a replay of a tape recording of *Hercules* at St Saviour's Hall, Walton Street. Next morning I saw Alan Frank at the OUP offices in Conduit Street to report on the progress of the book, about which he continued to agitate. He was anxious that it should be published in time for the 200th anniversary of Handel's death in 1959. In the afternoon Charles Farncombe came to the flat to discuss *Alcina*, which was to be the Society's offering in 1957. Again this was my choice. The opera had not been heard in London for 219 years. That evening we went to a pair of operas at the Guildhall School, first Mozart's *Sposo Deluso*, a patching up of fragments to make a short one-act work. This amounted to very little, and was not helped by a stale and silly plot. Stanford's *The Critic*, a setting of Sheridan's satirical play, is a very entertaining parody of grand opera in all its forms. I found the music extraordinarily clever and witty, depending not so much on quotation – though there were choice echoes of Beethoven, Wagner and Parry – as on suggestion.

Sadly, in July, Mordecai Thomas was run over while crossing the road to the orchard. On 27 July Diana, now sixteen months old, took her first steps. She made rapid progress in this and other departments. I wrote to Philip in November: 'Diana is becoming a perfect menace. The other day she threw three chamber-pots downstairs and locked Mrs Manley in the kitchen. She is becoming a great student of the Illustrated London News.' In October I wrote to Stephen at Little Abbey: 'I have been picking more apples with the contrivance, and one fell down and bounced on my head. Diana has learned to steal apples and pears off the side-board. She sends you a kiss through the banisters.'

In August I received a letter from Alan Frank announcing that OUP had finally agreed to publish my book. There had been a certain amount of perturbation at its size, and the enormous expense involved in producing it. But these hurdles had been overcome. I signed the 'Memorandum of Agreement' in September, agreeing to deliver the completed text and illustrations 'in a fit state for the printer' by 1 March 1957. I was to receive a lump sum of £75 on delivery of the typescript and a further £75 on publication. I demurred at a proposed starting royalty of 7½% for copies sold in

Great Britain, pointing to the considerable expenses I had borne. In the contract this was raised to 10%.

We had seen little of Dr Wingate in the last years. The Marriage Society had folded at the beginning of 1954, though Wingate still gave advice to couples contemplating matrimony in the pages of a woman's magazine. In September I was startled to read a story in the *Daily Mail* under the headline: 'Wife of marriage expert is suing for divorce'. Dr Wingate's own marriage, it seemed, had 'gone on the rocks'. A later report, after his wife, a former actress, had been granted a decree nisi on the ground of cruelty, added further details. Dr Wingate was happy to be interviewed, discoursing 'in his best couch-side manner' about where he had gone wrong. The case had not affected his practice, he claimed. He was not a marriage guidance counsellor but in his psychiatric work had 'come across many patients with troubles caused by unhappy marriages'. There was a photo of a smiling Beryl Wingate holding a snub-nosed mutt.

The beginning of October found us in London again, where we stayed with Donald and Anthea at their grand new house in The Boltons. I put in a couple of days work at the British Museum. In the evening we attended a double bill at the Scala Theatre. A dreary performance of Blow's *Venus and Adonis* under Mackerras sent everyone to sleep. It came alive briefly in the jolly huntsmen's chorus then passed out till the superb final scene. Lennox's *Ruth* received its first performance. Musically this seemed to me his best work to date. It had a fresh and abundant lyricism, was sensitively scored for small orchestra and went to the heart of its subject with an inspired simplicity. Its weakness was dramatic. There was only one moment of dramatic conflict (not in the Bible), but that was enough to inspire a very fine scene. A weak production, an indifferent conductor and revolting sets and costumes which fought against the music (Boaz in Scene 3 was got up like a cross between a Welsh magician and the Witch in *Hansel and Gretel*) did poor service to a charming little opera.

My mother had stayed on at Hambledon but in November she moved to a modern house at Sandhills, a couple of miles away. She took some of the Hambledon furniture with her, and an old single-handed grandfather clock that had survived from the time of Miss Sichel and Miss Ritchie. We selected a few items, including two Voysey mirrors, an adjustable bedroom mirror and a wall mirror with a little drawer under it in the cloakroom. The ancient dining-room table, according to my mother, had been bought by her parents at an auction early in their marriage. It had been the auctioneer's table and not in the sale but Tommy's offer for it was accepted. We had been employing Gran's two gardeners, Bert and Ernie Jeffery, since June. Bert had other skills. For years I had gone to Hambledon for Bert to cut my hair. In the summer this took place in the orchard. Bert trimmed hair in much the same fashion as he dealt with hedges. I became aware of my future responsibilities as Lord of the Manor. One evening Bert and I sallied forth to look at Manor land adjoining the Chiddingfold Road. Bert cycled over to attend my mother's small garden at Sandhills a couple of times a week.

In late November I took the train to London for the Annual General Meeting of the Handel Opera Society, held in Handel's house at 25 Brook Street, then empty ahead of renovation. It was to be many years before the house was restored and opened as the Handel House Museum. Three days later I picked the last of the medlars in the orchard at Milford, the season's final harvest. Alas, there was no medlar tree at Hambledon. In the middle of December we drove to London with my mother for Basil's latest production, *Who Cares?*, by the Jewish émigré writer Leo Lehman. Despite a good cast, including Denholm Elliott and Alec Clunes, it was a dismal failure. Basil in his memoirs blamed a taxi strike and a week of impenetrable fog 'as black as Newgate's knocker'. Afterwards we dined with Basil at the Garrick. My parents, long after their bitter divorce, had since the war re-established cordial relations.

We travelled to Fairnilee on 23 December, dining at St Pancras Station as usual and boarding the sleeper to Edinburgh. At 7 a.m. we got out at Galashiels and were met by Workman, Margaret's chauffeur. It was intensely cold on Christmas Day. We shot Fairnilee and Rink on Boxing Day, hampered by continuous snow. Some of the marksmanship was deplorable. Next day we looked out on thick snow. Most of the family were gathered in the Library with Margaret when Donald reported the shocking news that Shirl had died that morning of a sudden heart attack. The shoot with Christopher Scott, Laird of Gala, was cancelled the following day and Thalia and Donald travelled down to Cumberland to be with Jean, whose second child Lisabel was only four months old.

* * * * *

I had been appointed to the Music Advisory Panel of the Arts Council. In January 1957 I attended my first meeting at their headquarters in St James's Square. I am not clear whose idea it was that I should join; a few years later I was unceremoniously bumped off the panel with no explanation. Towards the end of the month I posted 20 completed chapters of the oratorio book to OUP and resumed my struggle with *Jephtha*. We paid a trip to Cambridge, taking in a production of *Saul* at Girton, a dreadful performance under a girl who clearly had not tried to understand the music. The composer's instructions for scoring and dynamics were consistently disobeyed.

The 1st of February was the warmest February night since before 1870 (I noted in my diary). That morning, in my role as Lord of the

Manor, I went to Hambledon to see Bert about timber in the Hurst. Philip Jebb called later in the day. He returned on 12 February, when the building contract for Hambledon was signed. The project was too big for my old cricketing companion Fred Neller. Instead the Guildford firm of T. Swayne was appointed. Work started the following week. Meanwhile, feeling under increasing pressure, I was attempting to finish the oratorio book. I completed the revision of *Jephtha*, the last chapter, in the middle of February, and embarked on the copying of music examples. At the beginning of March I received another hurry-up letter from Alan Frank ('by no means wishing to stampede you …'). The following day I finished correcting the typescript of the main text and started on the Appendices, including the substantial Appendix of Oratorio Singers. I completed the last of these, the Short Bibliography, working in bed with papers all over the counterpane, on 15 March.

On 18 March, my birthday, we drove to London for the dress rehearsals of the Handel Opera Society production of *Alcina* at St Pancras. These went on for a very long time. This year there was a better orchestra (the Boyd Neel Orchestra) and an excellent producer, Anthony Besch, who made the most of the tiny St Pancras stage. Joan Sutherland, a stalwart of Covent Garden but relatively unknown to the wider pubic, took the part of Alcina, Monica Sinclair Bradamante. At six Charles Farncombe broke off and we dined together at a pub. Rehearsals were resumed afterwards. Late that evening Charles, his father and Gwyneth came to Hill Street for a drink. I had further urgent discussions with Charles at noon the following day. In the afternoon I attended a concert at the Royal Academy of Music, including Haydn's Symphony No. 100 ('Military'). The student orchestra stamped through it accurately but heavily, proving once more what a test 18th century music is. The first performance of *Alcina* took place at St Pancras Town Hall that evening.

Alcina was performed in a version cut by me; but the expense of two horns compelled the exclusion of one aria ('Sta nell'Ircana') and the insufficiency of the singers two more ('Mi lusinga' and 'Mi restano') – violently against my wishes (I noted after the first performance). The production was a spectacular success, and it gave great and genuine delight. I was impressed by the characterisation within the arias, especially those of Alcina, but at that stage could not see that it built up. Bradamante's fiery vengeance aria in Act II stopped the show: the stalls set up a prolonged bellow and compelled an encore. On the first night Joan Sutherland did not know her part and left out one of her arias. Luckily the weekend critics came to the second night and her performance (this time including her hauntingly beautiful final aria, 'Mi restano') was hailed as a triumph. The employment of two countertenors, including the Jamaican John Carvalho as Ruggiero, attracted much comment. After attending both performances as well as two full rehearsals even the duller pieces seemed to me to sprout wings. I spent the following morning checking librettos at the Royal College of Music. Charles came to lunch at Hill Street. In the afternoon I delivered the final chapters of the book to Alan Frank at Conduit Street. After the second performance of *Alcina* that evening there was a jolly party at the Town Hall.

The beginning of April found me cutting the score of *Theodora* for the Handel Opera Society's production the following year. On 9 April I saw *Benvenuto Cellini* at Sadler's Wells, its second performance in London; the first was in 1853. I thought the opera a mess, but Act II at least was a wonderful experience in the theatre, and the music throughout full of character and surprise. As usual Berlioz showed no feeling for dramatic structure or continuity, moving abruptly from one set piece to another without bothering to win conviction for the order of events or even for the characters. Act

III went hopelessly to pieces, partly I suspected because Berlioz in altering the story could not bear to sacrifice any of his music.

Stephen came home from Little Abbey for the holidays. I had long promised to play toy soldiers with him and on Easter Day I did so. My redcoat army fell like nine-pins to his 155 mm howitzer, but not before I had inflicted severe casualties on his Commandos. Donald and Anthea had given him a Sherman tank, powered by clockwork, which was a wonder. It was capable of surmounting cushions. A driver popped up and down in the rotating turret and the gun ejected puffs of white smoke. Shenka's son Hercules viewed this monster with suspicion and when the gun turned and fired at him fled in terror.

We were over at Hambledon on the afternoon of 1 May. There was high drama at Milford that evening when an old weather-boarded barn at Secretts market garden the other side of the road – adjacent to our vegetable garden and orchard – caught fire; soon flames had enveloped the roof and tiles were clattering down. Brigades from Godalming, Guildford, Chiddingfold and Chilworth attended. Extra water was pumped from the River Ock a quarter of a mile away. A neighbouring cottage was threatened and villagers helped remove furniture into the front garden. A piano was brought to safety and placed next to the cabbage patch. Children rescued a cat and three kittens. The cottage was saved but the great barn, a smaller barn and a chaff-shed were reduced to smouldering ruins. At the height of the fire loud reports came from exploding rook-scaring cartridges.

At Hambledon work was proceeding rapidly. Huge holes had been knocked in the front of the house – protected by corrugated iron sheeting – prior to the installation of the new windows and door. Joe had expressed interest in acquiring the redundant beams but with nowhere to store them this proved impracticable. On

May 2 I began my last attack on the Handel typescript. At the end of the month we returned to St Pancras for Glinka's *Ruslan and Ludmilla*, unfortunately in a barbarously unprepared and inadequate performance. It is a fascinating opera, uneven, episodic, too long, conventional in parts but also powerfully original and full of beauty and surprise and clearly haunted later Russian composers.

On 8 June Thalia collected the Abrahams from Milford station for the weekend. Stephen was away at school but Frances resumed her friendship with Jacqueline. After tea it was sunny and we all sat in the garden. Nigel Fortune arrived just before dinner. Thalia and Pat retired early but we stayed up chatting until 1.30. Nigel had a wonderful nose for musicological gossip. Gerry told a rueful story of how he had come upon a score of *Le médecin malgré lui* in Foyles, which I also sometimes patronised. It was inscribed on the title page by Gounod to his English mistress Georgina Weldon. Gerry was tempted to buy it but the score seemed pricey; he decided to think about it over lunch. When he returned to the shop he found that 'some bugger' had snaffled it in the interval! At this point I got up and produced the score from my shelves. The following afternoon, Whit Sunday, joined by Thalia's Newnham friend Diana Bromley, we took a picnic to Hambledon. We looked round the empty echoing house, with its bare boards and unpainted walls, then toured the garden. A cement mixer, planks, scaffolding, bricks, pipework and knobbly sacks overflowing with debris encumbered the drive near the front door.

I had been asked by *Opera* to write an introductory article on *Les Troyens* ahead of its first professional production in Britain, at Covent Garden on 6 June. Philip and I spent two evenings going through the score on the piano. We went to one of the later performances, staying the night at Hill Street. This was to be our last visit; with Donald and Anthea established in The Boltons Margaret had decided to sell the flat. I found the musical performance patchy, the production in places downright insensitive; but it was a thrilling experience – it even melted a slab of chocolate in my pocket. Gielgud, like all producers from the straight theatre, thought he knew better than the composer, and ruined at least five of the best scenes. On the other hand I thought the horse was well managed. I was overwhelmed again and again by the scoring. The big octet in Act I scene 2 was shattering; likewise the approach of the horse (and the clash of arms from within), which made my blood seethe. Hylas's wonderful song seemed to have haunted Britten, to judge by Billy Budd's air at the beginning of the last act of that opera.

Two days later we drove to Glyndebourne for Rossini's *Italiana in Algeri*, rattling good entertainment, all sparkle, wit, high spirits and absurdity, if no depth of emotion. The production, by Carl Ebert, was fussy at times but there were brilliant sets and costumes by Osbert Lancaster. In the interval I talked to Anthony Besch, the successful producer of *Alcina*, about *Rodelinda*, which the Handel Opera Society hoped to put on in 1959. A few days earlier I had heard a Third Programme broadcast of *Rodelinda* in Oskar Hagen's German edition of 1920. Hagen seemed to think the plot more important than the music, retaining nearly all the recitative but butchering the airs. Sometimes we had aria without ritornello, sometimes ritornello without aria. In Act II only three truncated movements were left. Eduige and Unulfo lost all their solos. The latter was sung by a bass, and Bertarido by a baritone. Even the loveliest arias lost their da capos, and some were reduced to bleeding fragments.

Meanwhile we were attempting to sell the White House. There were no takers at the asking price of £5,500. On the advice of Bernard Grillo of Baverstocks in Godalming we reduced this to £5,250, stating that we would be prepared to consider an offer of

£5,000 for a quick sale. Planning consent had been obtained for the land opposite, markedly increasing its potential value.

Prospective buyers trooped round the house, shepherded by Mr Grillo, an exceptionally small man but a pillar of the community; this year he served as Mayor of Godalming. A surveyor called from the Halifax Building Society. His report on the repairs and redecoration needed frightened off another buyer. A Schedule of Fixtures and Fittings noted 'curtain railways', roller blinds and linoleum (pink in the rear corridor, red in the kitchen and scullery, black and white in our bathroom). We took the new linoleum from the staff room to reuse in Mrs Manley's sitting room at Hambledon. Again we were forced to lower the price. Eventually Mr Grillo suggested sale by auction. The house was not finally sold until November, immediately following the auction, for £4,450. The same buyer acquired the land opposite for £1,500. He proposed to build only one house there, on our vegetable garden, as staff accommodation, retaining the orchard. Later this disappeared under a housing estate.

There was a heat-wave in the second half of June. Mid-day temperatures rarely fell below 80F. On 17 June Thalia attended a Mass for Donald and Anthea's son Alexander, who had been born prematurely and lived for only one day. I sent Chapters 1-9 of the oratorio book to be printed. Thalia went to London to look at furniture in the flat, some of which Margaret had offered us. The following week Charles Farncombe came for the night. We had much to discuss, in particular *Theodora*. He left next morning. At lunchtime Clare and her three boys, George, Richard and Mark, arrived for the weekend. This was the first time they had been back to England since they quit Godalming for Berkeley in 1951. It was wonderful to see them again, especially Clare. Theirs are the last names in our Milford Visitors' Book. The weather was exceptionally hot – 95 F, I noted in my diary. That evening Thalia and I drove to London for Boito's *Mefistofele* at Sadler's Wells. I found this a very odd opera, deficient in musical invention and dramatic power but with impressive moments. The following afternoon we all went to Hambledon, picnicking under a cherry tree overlooking the rose garden. Thalia and Clare inspected the kitchen garden, much more extensive and open then than it is today, with sweetcorn, strawberries, an asparagus bed and row upon row of cabbages. They picked fruit, assisted by Diana (who gobbled the raspberries).

On Tuesday it was still extremely hot (89F). Philip Jebb came down to discuss the proposed bookcases in my new study and the room next door. The bottom shelves in the study were designed to accommodate my opera scores; the ones above were adjustable; the cupboards and lower shelves in the Music Room would take my gramophone records. A few years earlier we had commissioned a long white-painted bookcase with cupboards at either end to house my scores and books at Milford. With Jebb's new bookshelves there would be no room or need for this in my study; Jebb suggested it should be cut in two unequal parts, one to fit in the Blue Room, the other for the Nursery upstairs.

Thunder crashed above Milford all the following night; I was worried that the house might be struck by lightning. It remained very hot for the next four days. I took the train to London for a meeting of the Arts Council Music Panel; Humphrey Searle (an acquaintance of my father's) was one of the artists under consideration. Philip came to dinner on successive nights and we played through *Rodelinda*. We drove to London for *Deborah* at the Foundling Hospital, an unsatisfactory performance of a poor work. The best choruses were included but there was an unintelligent selection of airs. All were reduced to their first half except the dullest. The performance, with noisy choruses and the recitative taken far too slowly, emphasised the faults. It was here that I encountered Merrill Knapp, a tall, affable

American scholar from Princeton, for the first time. He had written to me a month earlier, having heard of my Handel project from staff at the British Museum. A term off had allowed him to come to London to examine the autographs and other source material at the Museum and the Fitzwilliam. He was particularly interested in the oratorios, he told me. It was partly at my suggestion that he turned his attention to Handel's operas, about which I had no intention of writing at length.

In July Basil turned up at Milford to collect a delightful set of George Harris designs for *Fifinella*. He had given them to us but to our fury changed his mind, saying he now wished to donate them to a museum. In compensation we were presented with three uncomfortable wooden benches he had picked up long ago in Florence, probably originating in a church. One of Harris's water-colours, of a laughing harlequin, was being reframed and this still hangs in the Blue Room. By July we were preparing to move to Hambledon, even though work there was not completed. The mantelpiece in the Music Room was not fitted until September; for weeks we had to make do with bare boards and mats in some rooms. On the 21st I packed my stamp albums, coin collection and other treasures. Two days later the first furniture was transferred to Hambledon. On that day there is a bold note in my diary: '<u>FINISHED HANDEL</u> – & sent off last chapters'.

On 31 July, assisted by Mr Dance, I dug up a few favourite plants in the garden at Milford, including lily of the valley and camellias, to transfer to Hambledon. (One of the camellias, planted in front of the house and grown enormously, flourishes still.) In the afternoon Thalia drove me to Brook, where I watched the Ramblers play Stoner, followed by a convivial evening with old friends at the Dog and Pheasant. I drove back with Mike. I hoped to resume my cricketing career next season. The following day we sent out change of address cards and went to Hambledon for a meeting with Francis Pollen and Swayne. A reporter from Guildford came to see me. This resulted in a short article under the headline 'Winton Dean Leaves Milford' in a local publication called *The Outlook*. Next day we began shipping loads of papers, gramophone records, etc. to Hambledon. A second load went on Sunday, followed by another picnic in the garden, with Tom and Diana Bromley and their two boys, Martin and Stephen. The pace quickened the following day, Bank Holiday Monday. We crammed a third load in the car in the morning. We had been invited to a drink with Tony Harcourt Williams and his wife at Admers Cottage. By now I had mended my fences with Tony. After a fourth load I stayed to watch the cricket, Hambledon v. Thornton Heath, followed by drinks in the pavilion. On Tuesday Blackburns transported a second load of furniture to Hambledon while we conveyed vocal scores and papers in the car in two lifts. Stephen insisted on bringing sections of his dismantled brick wall, which, in the spirit of Sir Winston, he had constructed in the garden a couple of years earlier.

Wednesday, 7 August, Thalia's birthday, was moving-in day. At 9 a.m. Bernard Grillo's minion Bennett called to see us about the sale of the house. Bert cycled over from Hambledon to help Dance dismantle the fruit cage. Posts and wire and the door were loaded into Blackburn's van. While the removal men manoeuvred the last of the furniture, including our beds, down the stairs, we had a last picnic lunch in the empty White House. Doors banged and we watched the removal van disappear heavily down the road. Earlier we had rounded up Susie and Hercules – we did not possess a cat basket – and now we took them with us in the car. On arrival Stephen carried the nervous Susie while Diana clutched Hercules, who had always been a placid, good-natured cat. Just as she was entering the front door Hercules yelped, leapt from her arms, scratching her, and fled. We did not see him again for a fortnight. The move had been an immense strain. Thalia sat down amid unopened packaging and disarranged furniture in the Blue Room and burst into tears, much to Stephen's puzzlement and concern. We thought Hercules might attempt to find his way back to Milford. After he returned, thin and dishevelled, he seemed little the worse. He continued to submit to Diana's attentions, her attempts to dress him in dolls' clothes or shut him in drawers. Susie became calmer, and lived to a serene old age. A week later we left for a holiday with Margaret at Fairnilee and all the sharp anxieties of the previous months dissolved on the hills and windy moors of Southern Scotland.

* * * * *

Fairnilee at this time of year was convenient for the Edinburgh Festival. On 26 August we drove to Edinburgh for *La Sonnambula*. I found this disappointing in the theatre, despite Callas and a good performance. It was too monotonous and lacking in tension. The quick tunes without exception were weak. Bellini had little gift for characterisation; everyone sang the same sort of music without regard to the dramatic point, and no one really came to life. There was little left save the beautiful slow melodies, a graceful mode of expression, and an occasional flash in the ensembles. The one really great passage in the opera was the 12/8 E flat ensemble in the finale (Scene 2), which haunted Verdi: compare the finale of Act I of *Macbeth*. Bellini treated the rotten plank episode effectively by harmonic suggestion; but the producer muffed the suspense by bringing Amina over the bridge at her first entry, and so demonstrating its ample solidity. Four days later we went to *Il Turco in Italia*, this time with General Christison. I enjoyed this very much more. Again and again Rossini seemed to have been visited by the spirit of Mozart; the whole score was a delight.

We took the train South at the end of August. On 5 September we had a meeting with Philip Jebb and Swayne about finishing touches to the house, which according to Thalia smelled strongly of fresh paint. The following week the mantelpiece for the Music Room was installed. On the same day a man with a long extending ladder came to fix the aerial for the FM radio high on the Voysey chimney in the front. A second aerial socket was fitted in our bedroom so I could listen to the radio up there if confined to bed. Ten days later the last of the carpets were fitted to the accompaniment of much banging and loud chatter.

I started work on the galley proofs on 18 November. I found this an appalling labour. For the next six days I kept to my bed, felled by a poisoned throat and a heavy cold. Eric Blom, a stalwart of the Garrick Club, invited us to dine there with Frank Walker and his young daughter Sally. Such a meal had been contemplated for months but for one reason or another had to be postponed. Eric wrote on 25 June: 'I am sure I still owe Thalia and you lunch or dinner at the Garrick (the former would have to be on a Sunday, the only day on which we can have ladies to lunch: dinner any evening but Thursdays).' We drove to London in the afternoon of 27 November. I had a discussion with Alan Frank and Anthony Mulgan at Conduit Street about further projects once the oratorio book was out of the way. Rashly, I had agreed to write a substantial chapter for Volume 10 of the *New Oxford History of Music* on 'Opera, Ballet, &c. (1890-1926)'. Eric was the section editor. Alan had been angling for a biography of Handel that would finally scupper Newman Flower's fanciful *Life*. I was in no position to undertake either in the short term, however.

The move to Hambledon gave me opportunities for rough shooting. On 28 November I shot a grey squirrel in the front garden. Next morning I bagged 7 squirrels, 2 jays and a pigeon in the Hurst.

The Ministry of Agriculture encouraged the control of squirrels, as vermin, by offering a bounty of two shillings a tail. I collected a fair number. At the beginning of December we motored to Oxford for a performance of Verdi's *Ernani* at the Town Hall. Though an early and in some respects a crude work, this came off brilliantly in the theatre. The richness of melody and rhythmic drive acted like a spiritual dose of salts – the perfect antidote after too much Strauss or Wagner! We stayed the night at the Randolph. After that it was back to Hambledon and the interminable proofs, which I had been urged to return as soon as possible. I was starting to find the pressure intolerable and on 6 December I was prostrated by a severe nerve attack. I stayed in bed for two days. Dr Booker called twice. He advised me to leave off work entirely for the moment. I informed Anthony Mulgan of a possible delay to the proofs and he sent his sympathy. I did manage to return the proofs of the music examples by Christmas. We drove to London on 8 December, dining early with Donald and Anthea at The Boltons. Afterwards we went to Park Lane House for a double bill. I did not greatly enjoy Milhaud's *Le Pauvre Matelot*, let down by Cocteau's novelettish libretto. I had never seen Bizet's early *Le Docteur Miracle* in the theatre. It was done, alas! with a two-piano accompaniment, omitting the delightful overture and Silvio's weak air. But the opera came to life, a little joy of its kind.

This year we had seen a good deal of the Bromleys, who had moved to a pleasant house above Haslemere. Thalia's friend Diana was dark, beautiful and intense (her grandfather was Anglo-Indian). Her father, Sir John Pratt, a distinguished diplomatist, had served for many years in the British Consular Service in China. His brother, Billy Pratt, found fame as the Hollywood actor Boris Karloff. Tom was also in the diplomatic service. He had served in Japan (up to 1941), Washington and Bagdad. At present he was based at the Foreign Office in London. He was a cultured sensitive man whom we liked enormously. They had two sons, Martin, who was dark like his mother, and Stephen. Our Stephen always enjoyed their visits. Often the three boys would stay indoors, conducting elaborate battles with their toy soldiers.

Sadly, Diana suffered bouts of depression, when she had to be confined. On 2 November Tom came to tea and dinner alone. We walked to the gate to watch the fireworks on the Green. The boys were at Prep school in Kent but after they broke up they stayed with us at Hambledon for ten days, leaving on Christmas Eve. They brought their toy soldiers and their fort. Stephen got home from Little Abbey two days later. Tom came to supper. The boys played and ragged together very happily, oblivious apparently of the dark clouds.

Some of the paths in the Hurst had become overgrown. One morning just before Christmas I crossed the Green and trudged down the muddy track armed with bow-saw and loppers, intent on opening up the ride. I found satisfaction is such physical activity. Dr Booker visited me in the afternoon. Shooting of course was another outlet. On 30 December I organised the first (and only) shoot over Hambledon Common. My companions were Commander Brodie Hoare, our next-door neighbour at Chart Cottage, and Major-General J.M. Martin from Great Meadow down the road. Jim was a retired Indian Army officer whose grandfather had been born before the French Revolution. It was a fine sunny day. We shot in the afternoon only, bagging six jays and a grey squirrel. But there were too many humans about for comfortable shooting.

* * * * *

On 3 January 1958 we drove to London, where I saw Dr Wingate at his rooms at 38 Finchley Road for the first time since 1952. For the next three years I visited him at regular, sometimes at weekly, intervals. In the evening we went to the Lyric Theatre, Hammersmith, for a double bill of *The Cooper* (Arne) and *Three's Company* (Anthony Hopkins). *The Cooper* was a charming piece, full of catchy tunes that kept their freshness wonderfully. The orchestra was represented by a piano and a harpsichord, a surprisingly successful combination. This was said to be its first London revival since the original production of 1772. *Three's Company* was pure farce and owed more to its hilarious libretto (by Michael Flanders) than to its nondescript music, a compound of Puccini, Hindemith, music-hall ballad and cinema, with an occasional echo of Sullivan.

On Sunday I attempted to write an article on *Theodora* for *The Listener*. Two days later Thalia shepherded Stephen and the Bromley boys to the dentist in London. I was having dental problems myself. I saw Mr Pilcher in Godalming, the first of three appointments in January. In the evening we took the sleeper to Scotland. I sallied out next morning for one of Jack Hankey's bits and pieces shoots. It was a dreadful day. Icy westerly gales blasted the birds about the sky. There had been a 100 m.p.h. hurricane in the night. The following day was wet but Saturday dawned fine and frosty. Attended by Peter Dods and his son Billy, I shot a duck below Caddonfoot Church. The bird landed in the water and was carried away, Billy retrieving it two miles downstream – after I had attempted to do so myself and toppled into the river. I suffered no further accidents but this proved to be a disappointing visit. We travelled South a week later; Margaret's chauffeur ferried us to Galashiels for the 10.42 train in a blizzard. We arrived at St Pancras next morning more than two hours late. The points had iced up, we were informed. The next few days were intensely cold. Eighteen inches of snow fell in Kent.

At my suggestion, the Handel Opera Society were to mount a stage production of Handel's *Theodora* at St Pancras Town Hall in late February. Unfortunately the producer, Anthony Besch, was unenthusiastic about the work. It was broadcast two weeks in advance on the Third Programme. There was an excellent cast, with Geraint Evans as Valens, April Cantelo as Theodora, Monica Sinclair as Irene and the young Helen Watts in the castrato role of Didymus (we were 'mercifully spared a hooting counter-tenor', wrote Peter Heyworth in the *Observer*, recalling *Alcina* the previous year). We drove to London for BBC rehearsals at the Camden Theatre – at one point the new car broke down - and stayed for the live broadcast.

Next day I wrote to Philip in Cambridge: 'I was sorry you could not hear the broadcast of *Theodora*, as I particularly wanted your opinion on certain questions of tempo. We had many battles over this at the rehearsals, which went on almost continuously, or so it seemed – for more than two days. I think the performance went well on the whole, especially Act II, which made us all sweat profusely. It should be tremendous on the stage; we are going to all three performances. I hope you will order all your pupils to attend. Have you heard any reactions to the broadcast?

'The hectic weekend was probably good for me, as I had a relapse last week on returning to the proofs and had to drop them again. However I feel a little better for the change of surroundings [we stayed in London for two nights] and as a result of trying to do something practical. At the first orchestral rehearsal a shattering wrong note in a string chord was followed by the words "Forbid it Heaven!" which convulsed everyone and lowered the tension most beneficially!

'At various times in the last month we have seen (i) *The Carmelites* [Poulenc], (ii) *Der Wildschütz* [Lortzing], (iii) *La Juive* [Halévy], all of which provided more interest and enjoyment than I expected. The masterpiece among them, to my surprise, turned out to be *Der Wildschütz*, a really delightful comic opera. I have heard that operas of Orff and someone else are to be done at Cambridge in March.

Is this true, and if so when, and why have I not been informed? I might possibly come up for a night or two.

'I have reverted to A. Christie and have nearly finished a batch you lent me.'

The following week I received a sympathetic letter from Eric Blom: 'I am deeply distressed to hear that you have been so ill and still have to go carefully'. I had promised him an article on Bizet's self-borrowings, together with a review of Dennis Arundell's book *The Critic at the Opera*, for the April number of *Music & Letters* but had not been able to get down to either. (The review was published in July, but the Bizet article did not appear till July 1960, after Eric's death.) Eric concluded his letter: 'Take care of yourself, and if you must do the proofs of the book, try to *enjoy* them.' On the same day Anthony Mulgan wrote: 'I am very glad to hear that you are better and making some progress with the book'. He enclosed revised proofs of the music examples for me to look through.

In late February Thalia and I spent a few days in London for the production of *Theodora*. Gwyneth kindly put us up at her flat in Marsham Court. I attended the dress rehearsal at St Pancras Town Hall on 24 February. Next morning I worked in Gwyneth's flat. Charles came to lunch. The weather was appalling – snow and ice followed by a blizzard. I ventured out in the afternoon for an appointment with Dr Wingate. I went to all the performances of *Theodora*. It was fairly heavily cut (by me). Dramatically it was a great success, despite the handicap of absurd medieval costumes (which suggested a cross between *Comte Ory* and *The Carmelites*) and a disastrous pause after Act II scene 1, which provoked a flaming row between conductor and producer. Act I was rather slow, even with the cuts, but came off completely by the third performance. Acts II and III were profoundly moving, and so gripped the audience that nobody seemed to cough or move throughout. The orchestra played wonderfully; the singers did very well, despite at least two heavy colds – especially Helen Watts as Didymus. But the blizzard halved the first night audience, and only the third performance was full. This was my first hearing of the lovely pagan chorus 'For ever thus stands fix'd'. Before the third night we dined at the English Speaking Union with Thalia's mother Margaret. Sadly this was the last time that we were to see her.

In early March we spent two days in Cambridge. I wanted to see the operas at the Arts Theatre, combining this with a little socialising and work at the University Library and the Fitzwilliam. We dined at the theatre with Philip and his pupil Philip Brett. This was the first English production of Rolf Liebermann's *The School for Wives*. It seemed to me for the most part unmitigated rubbish. The libretto (Strobel) was based on Molière, with a lot of tiresome involutions in the Hofmannsthal manner. The music had neither style nor invention, being a pastiche of everything from Mozart to Stravinsky to Schoenberg; the love music was uniformly insipid, and the comedy lacked sparkle. A quintet towards the end sounded like a cross between Stravinsky and addled Mozart.

Orff's *Catulli Carmina* was described as a scenic cantata. The orchestra comprised four pianos and eight percussion players and made noises like the smashing of mammoth dinner services, but a good deal of the score was for unaccompanied chorus. The treatment of the lovely poems (sung in Latin) was vilely insensitive: they were bawled out with no regard for shape or sentiment, much as a newsvendor might shout the racing results. The reiteration of rhythms and slapping on of one or two primary colours did create a spell of a kind, and at least he had the courage of his convictions (unlike Liebermann). The simple plan was effective, with the chorus of old men intervening derisively after the Prologue, which returned ironically at the end. Once or twice Orff touched real eloquence. More often the Abracadabra word-setting moved me to ribaldry.

On 10 March Anthony Mulgan wrote: 'I am very glad to hear that you are feeling better, and look forward to receiving the proofs round about the end of the month. I doubt very much whether the book will appear by Christmas. We will do our best, but a volume of this size takes a good deal of producing, and "Christmas" in publishing circles means "not later than the end of October". But let us see how it goes.' The next day he added: 'On consideration I think it would be better if you return the music proofs to us before returning the text proofs. No doubt there will be further corrections to the music, and after these have been done we will have to make blocks of the examples. Not until then can we go forward to paging the text; so if you could return the music as soon as you are satisfied that it is correct, I should be most grateful.'

On 18 March, my birthday, we drove to London. I saw Dr Wingate in the afternoon. I was looking forward to Mozart's *Idomeneo* at St Pancras Town Hall, put on by the Impresario Society under Hans Ucko (a professor of endocrinology), but it was a terribly stodgy and ponderous affair. It would be difficult to kill this masterpiece, but they nearly succeeded. I did not much enjoy *The Merry Widow* at Sadler's Wells a fortnight later. Lehár had a certain vitality and a genuine melodic gift, but he was too content to sacrifice both to sentimentality, I thought. When I was seventeen I would no doubt have been ravished; now the poverty of design, elementary technique and lack of dramatic (and harmonic) variety rather depressed me. A tame performance did not help.

The Easter weekend was very cold, with heavy snow on Saturday. On Easter Day my mother drove over from Sandhills for tea. By then the snow had turned to teeming rain. It was the coldest and wettest Easter of the century, I noted in my diary. On Tuesday Stephen set off with the Manleys for a long-planned seaside holiday at Ventnor on the Isle of Wight; they must have shivered on the beaches.

I finally sent back the Handel galleys on 10 April. Gerald Abraham had asked me to write an article on *Don Carlos* for *The Listener* ahead of a BBC broadcast in May. Philip came to dinner and we played through the score. I was struggling with the article a few days later when Stephen burst in to say that the Common was on fire! From the house we could see thick smoke rising above the trees. A crowd had gathered along Malthouse Lane and soon three fire engines roared up. For additional water they ran a hose from the village pond. Luckily the fire did not spread to the adjacent houses or the school at the top. The fire crews remained on the scene for several hours, dousing the smouldering peat. Diana Bromley, now recovered and back home, came to tea next day with her two boys. Together with Stephen they dashed about the blackened Common.

In early May the Handel Opera Society was to put on a performance of *Solomon* at St James's Church, Piccadilly. On 11 April Charles wrote thanking me for my programme notes. They were using the Riddick Orchestra, cheaper than the Boyd Neel, which the Society could not afford. The press would be invited, though they did not always turn up for these concerts. Most people attributed this to the parochial name of the Choir – 'Board of Trade'. They were not as good as the Handel Chorus, Charles admitted, although the basses were better. He urged me to come to the piano rehearsal at St James's on 29 April, when I would be able to indicate if there was anything which ought to be changed. I did so, combining this with a day in the British Museum and a late afternoon session with Dr Wingate. Afterwards I had supper with Charles and Gwyneth at Marsham Court.

I took the train to London again on 2 May – the hottest May day for 17 years. I spent a further few hours in the British Museum. In the afternoon I had an appointment with Roland Gelatt, executive editor of *High Fidelity*, who was over from the States. He was seeking a contribution for their Handel bicentenary issue. I was persuaded to write an article on 'Handel in Performance' – it was published the following April under a catchpenny title – for not less than $150. Thalia travelled up with Stephen in the car and saw him off on the school train at Paddington. In the evening we were at Sadler's Wells for *Benveuto Cellini*. This was the same production as last year. Again I found it a thrilling experience, despite its disconcerting mixture of genres. I had a further appointment with Dr Wingate on 7 May. Thalia arrived later in the car, bearing necessary cushions for the stern pews of St James's Church, Piccadilly, for *Solomon*. It was a goodish performance with plenty of vigour, using my arrangement. Unfortunately the replacement Solomon (Nancy Thomas) was weak, Monica Sinclair having had to pull out. Afterwards we had a picnic supper at Gwyneth's flat in Marsham Court.

Meanwhile, Anthony Mulgan had completed his labours on the galleys and was about to send them off for paging. There were still some inconsistencies, he admitted. On 21 May Thalia and I went to *Don Carlos* at Covent Garden. Basil and Diana McVeagh came too. This was a magnificent experience in the theatre (I had listened to the Third Programme broadcast a few days earlier), with superb singing from Vickers, Gobbi and Christoff. The sets and costumes were splendid and on the whole it was an imaginative production (by Visconti), including games of shuttlecock and two enormous hounds for Philip in Act II Scene 2. I was quite exhausted by emotion at the end.

On 31 May Thalia's mother Margaret died unexpectedly in her sleep at Fairnilee. Ruth and her two boys were there, Ruth convalescing after a serious illness that had affected her heart. Both had suffered bouts of angina and found the stairs a trial. (Plans were being drawn up to convert the basement into a flat for Margaret.) Ruth wrote to Thalia at the beginning on May: 'Mum & I have concocted a method of going right down to the water garden in the car! The gardeners have been set to work clearing a turning place down there & we can enjoy ourselves without having the drag up the hill forbidden to both of us. Mum seems in wonderful form …' On May 15th Margaret wrote: 'Ruth & I have been busy by the stream planting & weeding but are most depressed by the willow-herb'. She wrote again on 24th May: 'I find I go about the garden much more with Ruth & we have been weeding the rockery part of the wall round the old house … Ruth has little heart turns now & again but is wonderfully well & progressing … I have been having that pain & tightness in my chest. I think it is the weeding!' She had domestic difficulties, being temporarily without a cook, but other domestic staff had filled the breach. On 30th May she wrote to Thalia once more: 'Ruth is much better this week … Yesterday was a lovely day & she spent a lot of time repairing the Wendy House which had got blown down in our last gale'. Next morning Margaret pottered about the garden as usual and after lunch went up for her rest. She never came down.

The funeral was arranged for 4 June. We travelled to London the day before, where I had another session with Dr Wingate. After dining at St Pancras we caught the 9 p.m. sleeping train to Scotland, encountering Effie Millington-Drake, Margaret's sister, in the same carriage. We alighted at Galashiels at 6.50 a.m. and were met by the chauffeur, Workman. At Fairnilee Annie Wilson, Margaret's devoted maid and house-keeper, greeted us at the door. We ate breakfast in the large dining-room; Ruth and the boys emerged later. Soon other limousines drew up, crackling on the gravel; the door-bell buzzed again and again. There was a big party for lunch, including Margaret's nephews Kenneth Inchcape, Alan Mackay and Nigel Bailey, Effie's troubled daughter Nellie (who was to die two years later), Tom Wheeler and Marjorie Shanks, a cousin. Margaret's second sister Lady Janet Bailey (Aunt Nan) was abroad and was 'represented' at the funeral by her son Nigel. Their sister Elsie, a dare-devil flyer, had perished attempting to cross the Atlantic from East to West in 1928.

Margaret divided her loyalties between St Peter's (Episcopal) Church in Galashiels and Caddonfoot Church on the edge of the estate, where Thalia and I had been married nineteen years earlier. Here my father-in-law Alexander was laid to rest in 1944. In brilliant sunshine the mourners gathered in Caddonfoot Church for the simple service, conducted by Donald MacCuish, the Minister, who also read the Lesson. The Rev. O.L.S. Dover of Galashiels gave the address. Afterwards the coffin was borne to the graveside by six estate workers (as recounted in the *Southern Reporter*): Mr Peter Dods, gamekeeper; Mr A. Bruce, head gardener; Mr Hastie, forester; Mr G. Kirk, Peel Farm; Mr Elliot, head forester and Mr W. Wilson from the house. I was one of the 'pall bearers' at the graveside (this did not require any heavy lifting). The others were Thalia's brother Donald, Lord Inchcape, David Marshall, Archie Macdonald, Captain Nigel Bailey, William Pate from Fairnilee Farm and Michael Glendinning from Peel. There was a large party for tea at the house afterwards. Ruth's boys Michael and Ian scurried about. Margaret had supported many local organisations and charities, whose representatives attended the funeral.

Aunt Effie and Nigel Bailey departed by sleeper that evening. (Nigel left me his card: Captain Nigel Bailey, Royal Navy.) Next day Jean returned to Dyke Croft. Ruth, who was still convalescing, stayed on at Fairnilee with Michael and Ian, who were attending St Mary's Prep School in Melrose. I took the opportunity to interrogate Dods about prospects for the coming season. On 6 June David Marshall came for lunch. David was the family solicitor, and estate factor, as well as a cousin. He was an elderly man, much respected, who wore a deaf-aid attached to his balding head like a headphone. After lunch he read Margaret's Will and its provisions were discussed. Late that evening we took the train South.

I had been asked to review the first volume Walter Serauky's continuation of Chrysander's unfinished biography of Handel (confusingly labelled Volume III). Reading this massive German tome was very hard going. My dental problems had flamed up once more. Mr Bynoe drained an abscess at the end of May. I saw him again on 17 June. A week later I was back in his chair, prepared for a long and unpleasant session. This time he extracted two rotten teeth, the cause of the abscess. I had a very painful evening. I stayed in bed next day, though I ventured downstairs in my dressing-gown when Philip came for dinner. Eric had asked me to review the Halle Handel Society score of *Alexander's Feast*, another work of befuddled German scholarship – fallen, like Darius, from its high estate. This necessitated research at the British Museum on 17 July. That evening I attended a heavily cut performance of Handel's *Joshua* at the Foundling Hospital: a stupid selection, I thought, omitting the finest movement in the work, the wonderful finale of Act II, and at least one beautiful air, but retaining some dull stuff. The scoring was botched, with no horns and no harpsichord. 'Father of mercy' and 'See the conquering hero' were ruined by being sung unaccompanied – except by the piano! – and sounded like Victorian partsongs. Before this there was a moderate performance of 'Laudate pueri', spoiled by the use of a grand piano for the continuo. I had invited Eric – he had not heard *Joshua* for well over half a century, he told me – and dined with him afterwards at Ciccio's.

I was still turning out regularly for the Ramblers. On 20 July we played Littlehampton away. This was a fair distance. I travelled down with Tony Wood. Mike and the team always enjoyed a drink afterwards, starting perhaps in the pavilion and then proceeding to one or more local pubs. On this occasion Tony deposited me back at Hambledon after 1 a.m. As a result I overslept – and missed the Arts Council Music Panel meeting at St John's Square next morning.

After completing my review of *Alexander's Feast,* I began work on the page proofs of the book, which had been arriving in batches since early July. This was a fearsome labour and required intense concentration. Eric wrote on 28 July: 'I hope your page proofs don't worry you unduly: "grappling" sounds alarming. My advice would be (if wanted, which it isn't) DON'T READ THEM. I hope the change after the 11th will do you good.'

We travelled to Scotland on 11 August. We had been looking for a cottage since before Margaret's death. As well as the Fairnilee and Peel days, and a little rough shooting, I received a good number of invitations to shoot elsewhere. Margaret was very happy to have us but we did not feel it right to trespass too far on her hospitality. There was a possibility of renting a house in Melrose. Just before her death Margaret suggested a cottage at Peel, Glenkinnon Lodge, above the river, which she was letting rent-free to Mr Orr, who worked at Peel Hospital (whose grounds she also leased to the Hospital Board rent-free). Thalia thought it unfair that Mr Orr should be uprooted, especially as we would only be occupying the cottage for part of the year. Then, following Margaret's death, when Donald and Anthea took over the estate, Calfshaw Cottage, a traditionally built shepherd's cottage on the hill, became available. Its setting was idyllic, perched by itself above the Calfshaw Burn, with a wonderful view across the valley, but it had one or two disadvantages. Access was difficult, and it had no mains electricity. We purchased a second-hand – or perhaps third-hand – canvas-topped Land Rover to negotiate the steep bumpy track. It soon broke down, and the following summer it caught fire in Galashiels while Thalia was shopping. Electricity was supplied by a diesel generator housed in a shed next to the old pigsty. This had its quirks. It was not practicable to run it continuously and care had to be taken not to overload it. When a light was switched on, the machine spluttered into life – the bulb, dim at first, slowly brightening.

There was a single bathroom and WC, off the kitchen. We supplemented this with an Elsan chemical toilet in a little attic room with a skylight – we were informed that the water pressure was insufficient to put in toilet facilities upstairs. We removed the old copper in a corner of the kitchen, together with its chimney, a source of damp. In the sitting room an open fire with a back boiler heated the water to some extent. We purchased two galvanised coal bunkers, placed outside the back door. Somehow the coal merchant was persuaded to lug sacks of coal up the hill. The former coal store was converted into a drying-room for my shooting clothes. The postman stopped on the drive, clambered over the metal fence and laboured up two fields to deliver the mail.

Every couple of days Thalia would collect a pail of milk from Fairnilee Farm. A small white meat-safe kept flies off cooked and uncooked food. The odd mouse scuttered about. Later we acquired a refrigerator powered by paraffin. A little warmth was provided upstairs by paraffin stoves. The front door opened on to an area of gravel, with rough steps down to an unkempt garden with a rhubarb patch at the bottom. Stephen hung a hammock between two small trees. I was amused to see that an old map marked the 'toun of Calfshaw'. The grassy humped remains of the original farm steading could be detected behind a drystone dyke higher up the hill.

On 23 August we moved into the cottage. A couple of days earlier our furniture and effects had been transported precariously up the hill on the back of the foresters' heavy lorry. We invited Donald and Anthea and Jean (who had arrived at Fairnilee the day before with her two girls) for a house-warming drink. Two days later we drove to Edinburgh for *Euryanthe* at the King's Theatre. Donald came too. This is a difficult opera to bring off but the new version by Kurt Honolka, though it removed certain absurdities in the plot, falsified the spirit of the music. Act III was brutally cut, the lovely orchestral introduction, the hunting chorus and the May song all disappearing. On 9 September we returned to the King's Theatre for two works by Manuel de Falla. *La Vida Breve* was put on by a Spanish company with Victoria de los Angeles. Despite ghastly sets, a scratchy production, perpetual incursions from the ballet in and out of season, and the native faults of the opera – stiffness in the joints, excess of the incidental over the essential, and a melée of stylistic influences – this came off brilliantly in the theatre. *El Sombrero de Tres Picos*, danced with tremendous energy by Antonio and his company, was an electrifying score in which energy, humour, lyricism and pathos were exquisitely combined.

We returned to Hambledon on 16 September, which meant that Diana missed her first day back at school. (I had been invited to a shoot on Caddonhead Moor the day we travelled.) Next day I resumed work on the page proofs and soon began compiling the main index, which was very hard work. Anthony Mulgan offered his sympathy in a letter of 25 September. The book would certainly be out by April – 14 April was the bicentenary of Handel's death - and they were aiming for January. However the printers had been causing difficulties: 'I am privately informed by our Production Department that they will not employ these printers again, in view of what has happened over this book'. We went to London on 27 September for dinner with Basil at 18 Norfolk Road. It was his 70th birthday and a big family gathering. My mother, Martin and Nan, Joe (not yet married) and Peter and Tessa were there. Basil was in mellow and reminiscent mood. By now his career in the theatre was coming to a close – a sad anti-climax after his great days with ReandeaN in the 1920s and his years as supremo of ENSA during the war.

We took the train to London on 30 September, leaving Diana in the hands of Edith Manley. I had lunch with Roger Fiske at the BBC, when I agreed to give a 30-minute talk on *Samson* the night before it was broadcast from Covent Garden in January. This would be with gramophone records, but they could run to a singer if I wanted one. They were also proposing to broadcast *Joseph* and Roger suggested that I rather than an impersonal announcer should introduce it. As I had not done this before, would I submit myself to 'a small studio test before we commit ourselves'? He asked me to write a paragraph or two 'and let me hear you read it into a microphone some time'. Late in the afternoon I saw Dr Wingate. We dined at St Pancras before boarding the sleeper to Scotland. I had taken up a sheaf of proofs and a couple of days later I worked on them in the library at Fairnilee, which I found more congenial than the draughty, ill-lit cottage. Rain clattered against the windows. Unfortunately the bad weather persisted, marring the shoot on Peel Moor next day: heavy rain, mist and an East wind in the morning, I noted in my game book, a gale (but no rain) in the afternoon. I did not fire in three of the five drives, and two of my birds were not picked.

On 19 October I wrote to Philip in Cambridge: 'Many thanks for your letter and the Lebanese envelope, which is most acceptable. I was delighted to hear that my works are being used for purposes of pedagogic instruction by Bob [Dart]!

'Except for a little proof correction my life here has been wholly unintellectual. Strenuous exercise in the pursuit of game has reduced my waistline to such an extent that none of my trousers will stay up without assistance. Outside the door we are surrounded by mud and cow-dung; inside we live off the fat of the land. I have taken to breakfasting off partridge followed by venison (both from the estate), which suggests the Reverend Dr Gaster in *Headlong Hall*. Last night we had a blackgame omelette, a most exotic confection.

'*Samson* seems to have been a success at Leeds, the critics of the papers I have seen (Times, Telegraph, Observer, Sunday Times) say all the right things, not without a little filching from my programme article! ... We are going to the first night at Covent Garden (Nov. 15th), and I think you ought to put in an appearance together with the various other Philips with whom you are in the habit of congregating. I am to broadcast a talk on *Samson* in January, and also one on *Joseph*, which the BBC are rather surprisingly reviving for the bicentenary.

'We return to Hambledon on the 31st for what promises to be an infernally busy month, what with proofs (still coming in) and articles for American papers and something for the British Council to put out in November.'

Back at Hambledon, I wrote to Philip again: 'I am glad you are coming to <u>Samson</u> on Saturday. My expectations are not too high: reports reach me that some sinister things have been done on the musical side, including the insertion of nonsensical da capos, e.g. in "Let the bright seraphims". This seems the more gratuitous in that the score is heavily cut: "Presuming slave" for instance is out.

'I have been labouring like a beaver since we got back from Scotland, not only on proofs (complete at last), index, preface, captions, etc. but on bicentenary articles for America and for the British Council to put out in Norway (!)

'The other day a Doctor of Oceanography appeared before me asking permission to create a path on manor land, which I allowed him to do for a fee of 10/- a year. It then transpired that he (a) knows you, (b) plays the horn. His name is Laughton. Another odd fact is that one of Thalia's godchildren, Sebastian Payne, is being taught the cello by Susan [Philip's sister]. We have the house full of Paynes at the moment, including a sister of Joan's from Canada plus issue.

'You will have seen Denis Stevens boiling up for another row with Westrup, and maintaining that the Monteverdi <u>Vespers</u> was never intended to be a single work. I missed it, but had a good dose of Mussorgsky the other night, which I much enjoyed. [*Boris Godunov*, a BBC relay from Covent Garden, in Russian.] It was interesting following the original in a score of the Rimsky-Korsakov version: the changes are by no means confined to scoring.'

On 13 November, feeling under the weather, I stayed in bed, where I concocted the couple of specimen paragraphs on *Joseph* requested by Roger Fiske. I met Roger at Broadcasting House the following afternoon. Luckily I passed my audition. That evening I was at Southwark Cathedral for Britten's *Noye's Fludde*, a setting of the Chester Miracle Play. It was simple – even naïve – and contained a minimum of music; its fifty minutes included spoken dialogue (God operating through a megaphone), patches of percussion, and three congregational hymns. Yet I found it a profoundly moving experience, a work of genius that repeatedly brought a lump to the throat.

I travelled to London again the following day. I met Gwyneth, Jack Phipps, Robin Pidcock and Ande Anderson for lunch at the Civil Service Club, Great Scotland Yard. We discussed the Handel Opera Society programme for the Handel bicentenary celebrations next June; Anderson had agreed to produce *Semele*, with Robin as designer. After a session with Wingate, and a snack at the E.S.U. with John Warrack (music critic on the *Daily Telegraph*), I took the Tube to Covent Garden, where I met Philip. *Samson*, under Raymond Leppard, was a grievous disappointment. Dramatically it was a shambles, with the chorus in costume seated motionless on the stage throughout, representing both Israelites and Philistines – so that the central conflict was always blurred and the offstage choruses in Act III lost all their point – ridiculous arty costumes (Oliver Messel), a lot of self-conscious fidgeting and a total failure to realise the music in dramatic terms. The Philistine festival at the beginning was deplorably tame, and Samson not even on the stage. Musically it was not much better (though not rescored, thank goodness!), with very little light and shade, dragged tempi, not enough harpsichord but far too much organ in the airs, so that they became ponderously sanctimonious, ruinous cuts in the most carefully planned dramatic sequences, and – ultimate horror – a nonsensical da capo in 'Let the bright Seraphims' (a sop to Joan Sutherland). Only Jon Vickers (Samson) sang well. The Dalila was atrocious and wholly lacking in vocal allure. Not till 'Traitor to love' did anything come to life; after that not even this production could shake the passion out of Handel, though the emphasis throughout seemed to be on static and 'sacred' elements, not on the drama.

I was wrestling with two long articles for *High Fidelity* and *Musical America* and at the same time still dealing with proofs. On 20 November I sent off the page proofs and the Preface. At the end of the month I at last finished the two indexes. Next day we took the sleeper to Scotland, arriving at Galashiels one and a half hours late. We stayed at Fairnilee for the first few days; Thalia spent some of them with Jean in Cumberland. The weather was icy but clear; there was snow on the hills. When she returned, Thalia went up to Calfshaw to light the fire to warm the chilly cottage and air the bedclothes. We moved up there on 11 December, after which the weather deteriorated; almost all of my remaining shoots were blighted by drenching rain, sleet or gales. We returned South on 17 December. I had developed a hellish toothache and Thalia arranged for me to see the Godalming dentist as soon as possible. Mr Bynoe diagnosed an abscessed jaw, which he attempted to drain. I saw him again after Christmas, and on three further occasions in January and early February. It was a miserable time.

On 19 December we heard the shattering news that Diana Bromley had murdered her two children, Martin (13) and Stephen (10), and tried to drown herself. Tom had come home to Haslemere the evening before and found her wandering the house in a distressed state. On 20 December a policeman visited us. We did not know what to tell twelve-year-old Stephen. When he saw Thalia at her desk, completing forms about the boys, she said on the spur of the moment that they had had a terrible accident. It was only several months later that she told him the truth. Diana was charged with murder and detained in Holloway Prison but was found unfit to plead by reason of insanity.

On the last day of the year I was in London to record my talk on *Samson* for the Third Programme. Musical illustrations were provided by John Lanigan and David Kelly, accompanied by Charles Spinks on the harpsichord. I had hoped for Vickers but Roger Fiske pointed out that Vickers 'is now demanding astronomical fees'. He assured me that John Lanigan 'is really quite good'. Afterwards 1 dined with Lennox and Freda Berkeley at their house in Warwick Avenue. Lennox wanted to do another one-act opera with Paul Dehn, as a companion to *A Dinner Engagement*, and also hoped, one day, if he felt strong enough (he wrote to me later), to compose another full-length opera: 'Incidentally I want to read again your libretto in this connection.'

CHAPTER 17

Publication

At the beginning of January 1959 Nigel Fortune, as Secretary of the Royal Musical Association, invited me to deliver one of the three lectures the RMA was planning to put on as part of the Purcell-Handel Centenary celebrations in June. This could be on any aspect of Handel I cared to suggest. 'The Arts Council don't envisage much of a fee, I'm afraid, if any: they are still being rather vague about this, on the grounds, I suppose, that distinguished authorities might be above such considerations!' He concluded: 'I hope you are now quite recovered after your long rest and that the book will be out soon … I hope, too, you are getting over the shock about Mrs Bromley – I met her at your house on my last visit but one. Even after short acquaintance such news shakes me, so I understand how you must have been feeling.'

On 2 January my talk on *Samson* was broadcast on the Third Programme. Next day *Samson*, with my introduction, was relayed from Covent Garden. The performance was not much better than before, but evidently it was a great success with the public. The chorus was ragged. Nearly all the recitatives were dragged. So were many of the airs, especially 'Total eclipse' and 'Your charms to ruin', which had a bottom-heavy bass. There was a dreadful vulgar fortissimo in the last line of the Dead March.

Early January found me writing my talk on Handel's *Joseph*. In addition, Julian Herbage had asked me to do a piece for Music Magazine on Berlioz's *Te Deum*, which was to be broadcast that week. It had snowed on 4 January and more snow fell on the 11th, when it was intensely cold. That afternoon Tom Bromley came for tea. The next day – with tremendous relief – I finished the proofs of the Preface and Index to the book. I reported arctic conditions in my diary on the 14th. Two days later we travelled to London, staying with Donald and Anthea at The Boltons. At 6 p.m. there was a rehearsal for *Joseph* at Maida Vale Studios. I was at the BBC most of the following day (when a thaw set in), in the morning at 1 Portland Place rehearsing my Music Magazine talk. Rehearsals for *Joseph* lasted all afternoon at Maida Vale. In addition to an introduction, Roger Fiske asked me to provide a summary before each scene as well as each act, which must be 'as brief as you can make it without emasculation'. He felt 'reasonably certain' that I would think Norman Stone, the editor, had selected the wrong bits, but asked me to conceal my opinions as far as possible on any infamies I might detect! ('But tell me – I shall be interested!') After the rehearsals I dined in the BBC canteen. The broadcast went out at 7.35 p.m. I was up uncomfortably early next morning for a second rehearsal at 8.45 a.m. of my Music Magazine talk. I delivered this live after Julian's introduction at 10.30. Mosco Carner was one of the other contributors (on *Madam Butterfly*). Afterwards we had coffee together. I told him I had been reading his book on Puccini, which the *New Statesman* had asked me to review. Mosco was a refugee from Hitler and never lost his pronounced central European accent. He was a delightful man. His English was not always entirely idiomatic. He once said to me ruefully: 'I feel I am a square pig in a hole!'

This was the first broadcast of *Joseph*, one of the weakest of the oratorios, a mixture of the greatest Handel with routine pedestrian stuff, hamstrung by an inconsequent libretto; the music was full of things Handel did better elsewhere. It was a good performance, under Anthony Bernard (despite one or two stupid cuts), but Norman Stone's edition was flat and shorn of ornaments, appoggiaturas, etc. A few days later I received a card from Nigel confirming the date and time of my lecture in June. He added: '*Joseph* I found rather patchy, but your introduction kept me constantly amused. Do you <u>sleep</u> at the BBC these days?'

On a foggy morning in February I took the train to London and lunched with Sir Arthur Bliss and his wife in Marlborough Place. He was to conduct a Handel programme at a Royal Philharmonic concert in June and sought my advice on a number of musical problems. One of the items was the Water Music, which he proposed to perform in Hamilton Harty's version with 'additional accompaniments', the conventional choice at that time. When I argued for Handel's original scoring he quickly saw the point and agreed. I found him a charming man and we kept in touch. Later in the afternoon I had another session with Dr Wingate and attended a Royal Musical Association talk on Janáček by Desmond Shaw-Taylor, dining afterwards with Gwyneth and Charles.

I had been asked to write programme notes for the Goldsborough Concert Society Handel Commemoration Concert in April. I did not possess all the relevant Handel scores – the Gregg Press reprints of Chrysander's edition did not appear until 1965. I had to borrow scores from the Senate House, London University, where Nigel was librarian. I picked up Handel's organ concertos and *Berenice* from Nigel at the RMA meeting. There was difficulty with the Fireworks Music, which was out. Later Nigel wrote: '*Atalanta* and *Partenope* will be awaiting you when'er you choose to call'. In the next few weeks Philip and I played through *Berenice*, *Atalanta*, the Water Music, *Partenope*, *Radamisto* and *Orlando*.

Publication

I talked to Anthony Mulgan at the RMA. The following day I received a letter from him about the *New Oxford History of Music*, already long in gestation. As well as a chapter on opera and ballet, etc. 1890-1926, for Volume 10, which Eric wrote to me about in July 1956, I had been persuaded to contribute three chapters for Volume 8 (1790-1830) on French Opera, Italian Opera and German Romantic Opera. Each was to be 12,000 words in length. Ideally, OUP would like the chapter for Volume 10 by the autumn, and the three for Volume 8 by next Spring, though this volume was 'surprisingly far advanced' and they were hoping to go ahead with it rather faster. Mulgan concluded: 'I don't want to push you in any way, but I would be glad if you could consider this timetable and decide whether you could hope to keep it'. My short biography of Handel would have to wait. In the event, I gave up the opera and ballet chapter and Volume 8 was endlessly delayed. By the time my three chapters appeared, 23 years later, the original editor and almost all the original contributors, some of whom had never produced, were in their graves.

March opened warm (64 F). The first daffodil was out in the garden. On 4 March we travelled to Birmingham for a production of Handel's *Serse* at the Barber Institute. We stayed the night at the Greyfriars Hotel. Since its first revival in Gottingen in 1924, *Serse* had been immensely popular in Germany, always performed in the corrupt Hagen edition. This was only its second revival in England since Handel's single production in 1738. Gwyneth and Charles came too. I thought it an enchanting musical entertainment but at this time I was unable to detect much dramatic impulse. Nor did I think the producer's (Brian Trowell's) attempts to introduce comic business, though sometimes very funny, always attuned to the music. Very little was cut. It was a good performance, under Anthony Lewis (Professor of Music at Birmingham), but I did not like the 1760-period costumes or the octave transposition of the parts of Xerxes and Arsamenes. This was apt to make the texture bottom-heavy and knocked the magic out of some pieces, notably 'Ombra mai fu', which all but fell flat. The performance started at 7. When we arrived back at the hotel, looking forward to a late supper, we found that the kitchen had closed so we went to bed hungry!

On March 6 we drove to London for a two-night stay at The Boltons. Julian Herbage had asked me to give a talk on 'Handel and the Italian Opera' ahead of a broadcast of *Giulio Cesare* that evening. I knew rather more about the operas – not least from experience in the theatre – than I did when I wrote about them in Chapter 2 of the oratorio book some years earlier, but the restrictive *opera seria* convention still seemed to me a stumbling block. I took the opportunity to return borrowed Handel scores to London University. I rehearsed my talk at Portland Place at noon. In the afternoon I had a further session with Dr Wingate. That evening we went to St Pancras Town Hall for a concert performance of *Alcina* put on by the Handel Opera Society. The part of Oberto and many of the choral and dance movements were cut but Ruggiero's lovely air 'Mi lusinga' was restored. This time Heather Harper sang Alcina. The performance was better than two years ago and electrified the audience. Perhaps only Mozart of all other composers could have caught the heart-break of a sorceress whose powers desert her, and the nostalgic regret of a lover who has broken free. The performance was followed by a party in the Mayor's Parlour.

I was up early next morning for another rehearsal at 8.45. My talk was the first item on Music Magazine at 10.30. Afterwards I went to Royal Avenue for a conference with Robin Pidcock (designer) and Ande Anderson (producer) about *Semele*, which the Handel Opera Society was putting on with *Rodelinda* in June. Gwyneth and Charles were also present. After lunch at The Boltons we drove home. That evening I listened to the broadcast of *Giulio Cesare*, a messy and tasteless performance in German from the Schwetzingen

Festival, clumsily cut and chopped about. It was far inferior in every respect to *Alcina* and also to *Xerxes*; the opportunity of hearing all three operas within five days was welcome and illuminating. The scoring was wrong, with far too many strings, flutes for recorders and a trumpet added to the ritornellos of 'L'empio sleale'. Worse still, the four high male parts were all put down an octave, giving an insufferably ponderous effect.

In March Nigel asked me to contribute a long essay for the Purcell-Handel Festival Book, a 'glossy publication' he was editing on behalf of the Festival Planning Committee. It should be on all Handel's dramatic works, both operas and oratorios. He trusted I would not mind appearing 'cheek-by-jowl with advertisements for Elizabeth Arden and Evenings in Paris'. Eric Walter White, Watkins Shaw, Denis Stevens, Jack Westrup, Peter Pears and Basil Lam would be among my colleagues, he hoped. The proposed fee was 7 guineas per thousand words, to be paid by the Arts Council. In a postscript he added: 'I'm so glad Mrs Bromley didn't have to go through the ordeal of a trial.' (We had been concerned that we might be called upon to appear in court.)

On 5 April Thalia drove over to see Diana Bromley in her psychiatric confinement, the first of several such visits. Next day our house-keeper Edith Manley departed with her daughter Jacqueline. Edith, Thalia felt, had become increasingly neurotic and difficult. She complained that the yew hedge outside the window of their sitting-room made the room dark and demanded that it should be removed. She muttered that I did not turn up promptly for meals. They left on a very cold and wet afternoon.

On 8 April the first copy of *Handel's Dramatic Oratorios and Masques* arrived, with a courteous covering letter from the Publisher, John Brown. I thought it looked very well produced. I was pleased with the frontispiece – of a pub, the Crown and Anchor Tavern in the Strand, scene of the first London performance of *Esther*. I showed the book to Philip when he came to dinner that evening. Philip nosed through the pages, starting at the back. It was some time before he could be persuaded to put it down and finish playing through *Radamisto*.

On 11 April the ailing Eric Blom died. This was a shock because he had been working until the end. On 26 January he wrote asking whether I could bear the idea of taking on the editorship of *Music & Letters* 'when I peg out or go completely gaga? (No immediate prospect of either, I think, but I <u>am</u> seventy.)' I felt unable to take on this responsibility. He had been suffering from bronchitis but had been much better, 'having been told of a very simple remedy … that costs about 2d a week (a small boiled onion every night, which does not repel me as it would you); but I caught a filthy cold a week ago and had something of a relapse …' On 14 March he wrote: 'I am very dithery, recovering from a ghastly bout of 'flue and find recovery worse than the complaint.' He had been sent a review copy of *Handel's Dramatic Oratorios and Masques*, which he was reading when he died.

On 14 April, the Bicentenary of Handel's death, I was in London for two short operas put on by the Peter Jones Opera Society. I particularly wanted to see Bizet's early opera *Don Procopio*. This did not quite come off, perhaps because it was too difficult for singers and orchestra. Offenbach's *La Chanson de Fortunio* was a one-act piece of considerable charm, though not up to the best of his full-length operettas. Laurette's spirited song had a striking anticipation of the 'Chanson Bohème' in Act II of *Carmen*. The ensemble for the clerks and the cook used some old dodges to good purpose: voices imitating instruments, a parody ensemble about whitebait, and a drinking song in praise of water. Thalia and I travelled back to Hambledon in the car. It was a very wet night.

Next day I returned to London. I stayed the night with Diana and Bill Morley in Bedford Gardens. I had an appointment with Dr Wingate in the afternoon, followed by a Handel Opera Society Committee meeting in Room 13 at the Board of Trade. In the evening I went with Diana to the Festival Hall for the Goldsborough Society Handel Commemoration Concert, conducted by Charles Mackerras. This was a mixed bag. The overture to *Berenice* was tamely played, with long pauses between the movements and a half-attempt at double-dotting. There was a barrack-room performance of the organ concerto in B flat major (Op.7 no.1). The concerto no. 2 for double wind band and string orchestra was most interesting. Though all six movements were arranged from oratorios (*Esther*, *Messiah* and *The Occasional*) the many slight changes and the marvellously rich scoring threw quite a new light on the music. The colour, variety and fullness exposed the feeble absurdity of Beecham's anachronistic titivations. The harp concerto in B flat major (Op.4 no.6) sounded tepid, thanks partly to an interminable cadenza in the style of Ravel after the slow movement. The recorders were too far back and inaudible – and some bloody fool (I noted in my music diary) had altered my programme note to read 'flutes'. I found out later that the culprit was Mackerras himself.

The following day Thalia joined me at Diana's. We attended Eric's grim funeral at Golder's Green Crematorium. Afterwards we went back to Eric's house at Alma Terrace, where I had a long talk with Martin Cooper, music critic of the *Daily Telegraph*. We lunched at Diana's with Andrew Porter and his sister Shirley. In the afternoon I saw Anthony Mulgan at the OUP offices in Conduit Street. It was a cheerful meeting: this was the publication day of *Handel's Dramatic Oratorios and Masques*. In the evening we met Philip, who arrived from Cambridge, at Waterloo Station. We sat and talked for a while, then set off for Morley College for a production of Gluck's *Iphigenia in Aulis* by the Opera School, a most creditable and impassioned performance of a magnificent opera. The next day I wrote a tribute to Eric for the *Observer*.

At the end of April the Godalming photographer Alexander took a charming photograph of Stephen and Diana in the garden at Hambledon. The following day Stephen accompanied me down the Hurst in search of grey squirrels but we found none. At about this time I recorded the following remark by Diana in my pocket diary: 'When I jump up and down, the trees get giddy'.

Reviews of my book were starting to come in. They were mostly extremely favourable. On 4 May Nigel wrote: 'I hasten to congratulate you on your magnificent achievement. Only the evidence of my eyes makes it possible for me to believe that such a book could be written. I'm afraid I spent a whole working-day reading parts of it, and now I can't wait to get my own copy, which I am having from OUP as part-fee for my thing in Miss Holst's Purcell symposium, which looks a very feeble production beside yours. (Or even not beside it.)' On the same day Anthony Besch came down for lunch to discuss *Rodelinda*, which he was to produce for the Handel Opera Society in June. Earlier I had received a charming letter from him about my book; it had fired him with enthusiasm to produce *all* the oratorios, one by one! He had been asked to review it for *Opera*.

On a beautiful day in early May we drove to Abingdon for Handel's *Orlando*, a semi-amateur production in the tiny Unicorn Theatre, its first English stage revival in 225 years. The orchestra of ten, without horns, was located in a gallery above the stage. This was a joint venture by Alan Kitching (producer) and Frances Kitching (conductor), the first in a series of Handel opera revivals. All the parts were sung at the original pitch, but some fine arias had to be omitted because of the limited capacity of the Berkshire singers. Alan Kitching's production was true to the period in its stylised gestures and costumes, but in trying to preserve and guy the convention at the same time he undermined the opera. Nevertheless I was deeply impressed by the bewildering wealth of invention and dramatic resource in this marvellous score.

Mina Curtiss was over from America. My review of her book *Bizet and his World* appeared in *The Listener* in February. Julian Herbage asked me to review it for *Music Magazine* on the BBC Home Service, initially yoked to the new edition of Newman Flower's biography of Handel. However, since this seemed much the same as previous editions, with a few maggots removed, Julian did not think it called for further publicity. On 11 May Mrs Curtiss, who was staying at the Savoy, drove down to Hambledon for lunch, the hottest May day for five years, I noted in my diary. A French edition of her book was to be published by Plon. It would be considerably cut. She was working with their literary editor, Massenet's grandson, she told me. The French of course wanted to omit the index, but Mrs Curtiss was being adamant.

On 26 May we travelled to London for Eric Blom's memorial service at St Sepulchre's, Holborn Viaduct, for which an elegant Order of Service had been printed. A large number of persons were present. The service began unhappily with two gloomy organ preludes by Brahms, who was *not* Eric's favourite composer. Paul Jennings, Eric's son-in-law, could be heard expostulating about this afterwards. In place of a Lesson, Dr W. Greenhouse Allt read from Walter Pater's *Marius the Epicurean*. Byrd's serenely beautiful Motet *Justorum Animae* was sung by members of the choir of Trinity College of Music. Frank Howes delivered the Address. In conclusion, the Aeolian String Quartet with Jack Brymer played the Larghetto from Mozart's Clarinet Quintet. Afterwards Thalia and I lunched at Diviani's in Holborn with Alan Frank and Diana Morley.

On 29 May Tom Bromley came for the weekend. We had also invited Nigel Fortune, who arrived in time for lunch the next day.

Earlier Nigel (an assiduous follower of the game) had written: 'I have never seen you play cricket. I look forward'. In the event, he was to be disappointed. I did not participate in the Ramblers match against Horsley. But on Saturday afternoon we drove over to watch Brook play the Outlaws. Afterwards we had a convivial drink with Mike Gauntlett and the other players in the Dog and Pheasant.

I was always eager to encounter new or unknown operas. In early June we went to the Scala Theatre for *The Borderline*, an opera by Wilfrid Mellers (whose book, *The Sonata Principle*, I had reviewed the previous year). This was one of the strangest entertainments I had encountered in many years. It was a mixture of ballad opera, pantomime and modern morality. The libretto, by David Holbrook, seemed to me unbelievably inept. The music was better than the libretto, but not much, the style a mixture of folksong, skiffle, Vaughan Williams, Delius and Orff. The opening of Act I was nothing if not eccentric: the rise of the curtain was followed by several minutes of silence, the crowing of a mechanical cock, and the entry of two persons on bicycles. (Landrace pigs were mentioned in the programme, but they failed to appear.) Later there was some attractive music among much dull matter. The transfiguring magic touch elevating *Noye's Fludde* and the harvest scenes in *Ruth* was absent. Act III had more action but a funeral was prolonged interminably. The one really charming tune came in the final ensemble.

I received a brief postcard from Gerald Abraham inviting me to write an article for *The Listener* on Cherubini's operas ahead of a BBC relay of *Medea* from Covent Garden. He had been reading my book, and added: 'Heavens, how I curse your masterpiece! I've had to review it for *The Listener* and now I'm sweating over a ½ hr. b'cast on it… But it really is a masterpiece.' In his *Listener* review he gently chided me for not dealing fully with *Messiah* and *Israel in Egypt*, while admitting that this would have destroyed the unity of the book.

The Purcell-Handel Festival opened inauspiciously with a performance of *Samson* at Covent Garden. Earlier Nigel had ruminated in a letter: 'I wonder whether this festival is going to be a popular or a financial success: I'm afraid it arrives at a time when Mahler and Bruckner and bigness are all the rage with the average RFH-goer'. Next day Thalia and I travelled to London for the unveiling of a Purcell Memorial at the Royal Festival Hall, followed by an L.C.C. reception and all-Purcell concert, with Alfred Deller as soloist. I was in London again the following day for *two* lectures by J.A. Westrup, the leading authority on Purcell. Jack Westrup (later Sir Jack), Heather Professor of Music at Oxford, was a formidable figure (though not in stature). His manner was dry but he had a sharp wit. His exuberant Swedish wife Solweig had been lovely in youth. She never entirely mastered English usage. Once a gushing woman came up to her at a party, crying: 'Oh Lady Westrup, you won't know me from Adam –'. Solweig looked puzzled: 'I think I'd know you from *Adam*'. On another occasion, when Westrup had been suffering a bout of ill-health, Solweig confided: 'Jack is having the courtesan treatment'. 'I think you mean cortisone, dear', Westrup said dryly.

Westrup's first talk, a comparison between Purcell and Handel – the theme of his essay in the Festival Book – was illustrated with gramophone records. I lunched with Alan Frank and Anthony Mulgan at the Museum Tavern; later I found my way to the City Literary Institute for a *Semele* rehearsal. The second lecture, on 'Purcell and the English Tradition', was a far grander affair, delivered in Beveridge Hall, London University. That evening I went to the Royal Philharmonic Society concert at the Festival Hall. Proceedings opened with Dame Edith Sitwell declaiming a new poem ('Praise we the Gods of Sound'), followed by a performance of Purcell's ode, 'Hail, bright Cecilia', conducted by Britten. This stuck me as the most splendid of all his works, with many subtle touches. After the interval all the Handel items were conducted by Bliss. Selections from the Water Music were given in Handel's original scoring, arranged by Anthony Baines; well done, except that the strings heavily outnumbered and all but drowned the wind in the Andante. George Thalben-Ball gave a beefy account of Handel's Organ Concerto in A, Op.7 no.2, but I had expected worse. There was a superlative performance by Bliss and the Covent Garden chorus of the Coronation Anthem 'The King shall rejoice' – the best I had ever heard of a Handel anthem. There was no stodginess, only a brilliant radiance and an athletic attack (with very lively tempi) that carried away the entire audience.

On 12 June I took the train to London once more. I had an appointment with Dr Wingate, or so I thought. In fact there had been a muddle; when I arrived at his door I found that I was not expected. I had to kick my heels for an hour or two before the Private View of the Purcell-Handel Exhibition at the BM at 5.30. Afterwards I accompanied my old girlfriend Hilary to *Samson*. It was the same production, unimproved, with a different conductor and a slightly better Dalila. Even this maimed torso was moving in parts; but what an experience it should have been!

The country was beginning to experience a heat-wave. Sunday was very hot (83F). On that day I finished my lecture, only just in time for Thalia to type it. *Semele* was to be broadcast by the BBC on 23 June (the first night). I had agreed to write an introduction and a plot summary. I finished these the following day. Donald and Anthea offered to put us up at The Boltons for the latter part of the Festival. We travelled to London on 16 June. Rehearsals of *Semele* occupied most of the afternoon. That evening we went to the Old Vic for a complete stage performance of *The Tempest*, the Dryden-Davenant adaptation of Shakespeare with Purcell's music – or so it was thought at the time. The music is now ascribed to Purcell's younger contemporary John Weldon. It was poorly sung and indifferently played. Some of Locke's pieces from an earlier production were included, notably the chromatic storm music at the beginning. Some airs gained greatly from their context, in particular the touching 'Dear pretty youth', sung by one of the speaking characters (Dorinda) over the dead Hippolito (this song really *was* by Purcell). After the performance we returned for a late supper at The Boltons.

Wednesday 17 June was the day of my lecture, 'Some Aspects of Handel's Dramatic Style', delivered in Beveridge Hall, Senate House. It was very hot (84 F) and the sunniest day of the year so far. I had been severely hampered in the music examples I could choose because so few of these works – dramatic oratorios as well as operas – had been recorded by 1959 and even fewer in reasonably authentic style. I borrowed records of *Saul* and *Belshazzar* from Anna Instone at the BBC. From *Belshazzar* I chose the great central scene in which Belshazzar, 'wallowing in excessive feast', suddenly sees the writing on the wall, 'turns pale with fear, drops the bowl of wine, falls back in his seat trembling from head to foot, and his knees knocking against each other' (to quote Handel's stage directions). Unfortunately, the only available recording was sung in German and the chorus sounded as if they were discussing the weather instead of being terrified out of their lives. The American recording of *Saul* was poorly conducted, the music broken up by rallentandos and pauses, just where it should have run on without a break. The two extracts from Anthony Lewes's *Semele* were considerably better. That morning Diana helped me transfer the examples to tape. Nigel agreed to operate the machine. Before the lecture I rehearsed with Nigel in Beveridge Hall. All seemed to go well and the audience was receptive.

In the evening we went to Cherubini's *Medea* at Covent Garden. I had heard a broadcast, also with Callas, in February and found it a most remarkable opera. I wrote a long appreciation of it in my music diary. It was a very disappointing evening, despite a fiery (but monotonously truculent) performance by Callas. The conductor (Rescigno) was miserably bad, the orchestral playing slipshod. The sets were attractive but the production came to grief in the finale, which fell flat – partly because of clumsy cuts. The Lachner recitatives of 1854 were heavily out of style, clogged the action and spoiled the transitions. Cherubini's own scheme was much more flexible, including a compound of *mélodrame*, recitative and contrasted orchestral timbres in the Act II finale. A Philistine audience, present for social reasons, increased my irritation.

Next morning I took a break from musicology and escaped to Lord's for the England v India Test Match with my old cricketing friend John Woodard. In the evening Thalia and I attended the Royal Musical Association party at Duke's Hall, Royal Academy of Music. Earlier Nigel had written: 'I'm afraid the 18 June party <u>does</u> sound more pompous than one would wish, but Creber is doing most of the work and I didn't want to be too awkward, though I did win some concessions. One was an alternative to tails, but I was defeated over the inclusion in the invitation of the word "commence", which I have an especial horror of.' I was at Lord's again the next day, this time with Freda Berkeley. I skipped Percy Young's lecture on Handel's oratorios in the afternoon, as did Nigel, who I met by the Tavern at 2. That evening I went to a long rehearsal of *Semele* at Sadler's Wells.

Increasingly frantic rehearsals of both *Semele* and *Rodelinda* took place over the next three days. I tried to attend as many as I could. On Sunday my review of *Bizet and his World* was broadcast on Music Magazine. Thalia had gone back to Hambledon. On Tuesday she returned with Stephen (it was his half term). They spent a happy afternoon at London Zoo. That evening the three of us went to the first night of *Semele* at Sadler's Wells. It was done in my arrangement and fairly heavily cut, but included Cupid's delicious unpublished air 'Come, Zephyrs, come' at the beginning of Act II scene 2 – its first performance. The Gavotte in the overture was cut against my wishes. It was also the first professional stage performance of the work anywhere! *Semele* emerged as a major masterpiece, as I knew it would, and was recognised as such by all but one or two of the more obtuse critics. This was – incredibly – my first hearing of 'My racking thoughts' – as beautiful as anything in the work – and 'Above measure'; both thrilled me. Several of the more brilliant pieces – notably Semele's 'Myself I shall adore' and 'No, no, I'll take no less' – confounded my judgement in developing far more life in the theatre than on paper. The chorus 'Now love, that everlasting boy' set the audience rocking and rolling. Heather Harper was a lovely Semele, right inside the character, and Monica Sinclair a magnificent Juno – though the chorus were apt to fall behind the beat. The tempi in the Allegro movements were far livelier than in Anthony Lewis's recording; the Act II Symphony was taken almost twice as fast.

It was even hotter next day (83F); in the afternoon there were thunderstorms. I attended Jens Peter Larsen's rather dry lecture on 'Handel traditions and Handel interpretation' at London University. In the evening we went to the first night of *Rodelinda*. I explained to Stephen about the small boy (a non-singing role) who appears as Rodelinda's son Flavio in the opera. This came off superlatively well, helped by fine singing from Joan Sutherland (Rodelinda), Raimund Herincx (Garibaldo) and Janet Baker (Eduige), and sold out the theatre on the second night. I could not then detect any overall design, merely a string of superb arias and wonderful individual scenes. As such I found it a thrilling experience. It was considerably cut, including the last three arias of Act I; eleven were reduced to their first half (a tactic I was later to deplore). In Act III the producer, Anthony Besch, taking advantage of Charles's absence in America during the early rehearsals, removed the opening ritornellos of 'Un zeffiro' and 'Vivi tiranno', utterly ruining their impact. The continental visitors to the Festival, including the East Germans, all told me that they had never heard a finer performance of a Handel opera. Seven of the nine arias in Act II I heard for the first time.

After the performance we took Stephen round to meet the cast and the conductor. We called on Joan Sutherland in her dressing-room. She was relaxed and charming. She showed Stephen how she had only to add an extension to her long auburn hair to play the part. Next day Thalia escorted Stephen to Paddington to catch the School train back to Newbury. In the early evening we went to a Handel Commemoration Concert at Westminster Abbey, sitting in the choir stalls. We heard Handel's Coronation Anthem, 'The King shall rejoice', once more. It was not a bad performance, but necessarily slower and less inspiring than Bliss's in the Festival Hall, since the harmonics tended to catch each other up during a chase round the clerestory. Could the sublime Larghetto of the Concerto Grosso in B minor (Op.6 no.12) have influenced Elgar's slow movements? I wondered. 'Their bodies are buried in peace', four wonderful short choruses in the middle of the *Funeral Anthem for Queen Caroline*, were so simple, yet so overpoweringly moving that at the end I scarcely knew where I was. Afterwards we scrambled to Sadler's Wells for the second performance of *Semele*. At the end I was introduced to Princess Alexandra. I invited Basil to the performance of *Rodelinda* on 26 June and we had supper together with his friend Humphrey Searle. Two days later we drove back to Hambledon. It had been an exhausting fortnight.

When we got home I found a troubling letter from Alan Frank: 'The printer's bills have now come in for the Handel book, and I regret to say that, not surprisingly, there is a pretty formidable charge for corrections. Not an unreasonable charge, but of course the corrections were indeed heavy.' The total bill amounted to £282, not allowing for the printer's mistakes. My share of this was £95 but they were prepared to accept £47.10.0 against my royalties or as a cheque. Even after the typescript was sent in, I had continued to uncover new information. As a consequence, many changes had to be made at proof stage. This of course was not my fault so I was not very happy about the imposition.

On 1 July Charles Farncombe stayed the night. We went through *Radamisto*, which the Handel Opera Society was proposing to mount next year. My mother came for a drink in the evening and Philip, whose skills at sight-reading were invaluable, stayed for dinner. Cuts were always an important consideration, partly for financial reasons and partly because audiences in those days could not be expected to stomach four hours or more of unfamiliar Baroque music. Charles left next morning. A few days later I received a post card from him, addressed to both myself and to Bacchus, depicting a misericord of a drunken tapster. He thanked me for all my help, which had made the first week at Sadler's Wells such a success, signing himself Charles Frideric Farncombe.

In the afternoon I went to London to the BBC studios at Maida Vale. I had been asked to take part in an impromptu discussion on 'The Staging of Handel's Oratorios' with John Amis and Arthur Jacobs, to be put out on the BBC Transcription Service. This followed a controversy I had had with Arthur on the subject in the pages of *Opera*. Next day I kept to my bed, reporting on the typescript of a dull book on Handel by Herbert Weinstock. The heatwave continued. It was 88F the following day. We had been invited to a party at the White House by the new owners, Mr and Mrs Collings, and were staggered by the extent of their internal changes, not all of which were to our taste. Sunday was very hot indeed at 94F. I listened to Anthony Lewis's approving review of my book on *Music Magazine*. Later I obtained a transcript. Jean came to stay with her daughter Anabel. I had been playing less cricket lately but I turned out for the Ramblers' match against Petersfield. Lionel Wood drove me down. After a blistering day in the field most of the team repaired for refreshment to the Sun (Petersfield), followed by the Half Moon (Sheet).

The heatwave went on, with temperatures in the 90s on Tuesday and Wednesday. Nights were uncomfortably sticky. In my pocket diary I noted that the night of 8-9 July was the hottest since 2 June 1947. The following week our new housekeeper Kathleen arrived. She was an elderly Irish lady with unruly hair, good-natured but forgetful. Her first test was the visit of Merrill Knapp, his first to Hambledon, on 17 July. Afterwards Merrill wrote promising to look out for American reviews of my book. He hoped he had not tired us with his 'incessant chatter'. Merrill was indeed voluble, asking question after question but not always waiting for a reply before ploughing on with the next.

We concerned about what public school Stephen should go to when he left Little Abbey next year. Unfortunately, he was somewhat behind in his lessons. On Sunday 19 July we collected Stephen from Little Abbey and drove over to Bradfield College, where we saw the headmaster, Anthony Chenevix-Trench. A distinguished Classical scholar, he had been educated at Shrewsbury under the headmaster H.H. Hardy (later my assistant at ISTD). His war service came to an end when Singapore fell to the Japanese in February 1942. He spent the next three and a half years in captivity under appalling conditions. He had been headmaster at Bradfield for nearly five years when we met him. He became a governor of Little Abbey School, like Thalia. Stephen encountered him there, swinging on the 'monkey bars'. Neither Thalia nor I much cared for him and were not unhappy when Stephen failed to gain a place. His move to Eton was not considered a success and he left under a cloud.

On 22 July Jeremy Noble, then a bright young music critic, came for the night. Thalia was spending a couple of days at Fairnilee so Kathleen had to manage on her own. In the evening we listened to Gerald Abraham's generally approving review of *Handel's Dramatic Oratorios and Masque* on the Third Programme. Mina Curtiss had promised to look out for any American reviews. When she came down to Hambledon in May I had presented her with a copy of my book. She wrote from Williamsburg in July: 'Although I have only read three chapters ... I am really enchanted and impressed at such a combination of scholarship, wit and brilliance of style. It makes me feel very humble indeed.' I heard from her again at the end of the month. She was having horrible difficulties over the French translation of *Bizet and his World*. 'Not only is it quite literal, a first draft with no corrections, but the woman took it upon herself to make long cuts which she chose to summarize in a sort of elementary French, omitting all the details that make the book lively.' She concluded: 'I pick my raspberries and peas and wish God had seen fit to make me a plant instead of a biographer'.

On 26 July Roger Lancelyn Green and his wife June travelled down from the Wirral for a short weekend. Thalia had first met Roger, a gentle scholarly figure, on a Hellenic cruise with his mother before the war. He published a biography of Andrew Lang in 1946 and had become well-known as a writer of stories for children. On Sunday afternoon I turned out for the Ramblers v Farncombe (my old side when we lived in Godalming during the war). This was the day the fine weather broke and the match was spoiled by heavy rain and thunderstorms.

The following day I caught the 11.25 train to London, bearing Jeremy's pyjamas, which he had left under his pillow at Hambledon. I lunched with Gwyneth and Charles at the Civil Service Club. Jeremy looked in and collected his striped nightwear. At 4.30 I called at 38 Finchley Road for another hour with Dr Wingate. That evening Thalia and I attended a double bill at Sadler's Wells. I found Dallapiccolas's *Il Prigionero*, its first stage performance in Britain, an unsatisfactory opera, though not without occasional eloquence. The best thing, as so often in dodecaphonic music, was the variety of orchestral timbres and their succession and superimposition, aided by exotic instruments like the vibraphone and the saxophone. The vocal and melodic lines had little character, and the tone was too consistently shrill, in the literal and the figurative sense. Orff's *Die Kluge* was another British première. Played without intervals, it seemed interminable and tediously unrewarding. One or two soupy bits were curiously like Sullivan. In the interval we talked to Mosco Carner. A few days later he wrote: 'It was nice seeing you and your wife at Sadler's Wells the other evening. What utter trash the Orff opera (sic!) is!'

Next day Stephen came home from Little Abbey. On the same day Alan Henderson, who was to be Stephen's tutor during the holidays, arrived in a small sports-car. Alan was a likable young Scot, recently down from Cambridge. He had been teaching for a term or two at Little Abbey. He brought with him a consignment of portable radios, which he hoped to sell at a profit. These were lined up against the wall in the garage. Unfortunately, two days later heavy thunderstorms saw water lapping across the garage floor and some of the radios were damaged.

Our old friends John and Edith Woodard came for the Bank Holiday weekend with their two boys. On Sunday I played for the Ramblers against Normandy, near Guildford. A well-stocked bar was available in the pavilion. Martin and Nan and family drove down for the day on Monday. There was a major crisis that morning when Diana, aged four, and Graham, the younger of the two Woodard brothers, disappeared. We called and called. They were nowhere to be found in the garden. A search party combed the Common. Diana had recently been given a tricycle; Graham, we learned later, had borrowed Stephen's bike. Thalia, John and Alan Henderson set out in different directions in the three cars. We were on the point of calling the Police when the pair were discovered, several miles along the back road to Godalming, near Busbridge Lakes. The mischievous Diana had wanted to show Graham her school, St Hilary's.

On the morning of 10 August we were woken by a heavy storm. Rain pelted against the front windows – 1¼ inches fell at Godalming – flooding the rose-beds in the lawn. In the evening we travelled to Scotland, accompanied by Alan Henderson. We went straight up to Calfshaw. (There were only three small bedrooms in the cottage so Alan slept at Fairnilee.) After lunch Thalia went shopping in Galashiels. What happened next was recounted in the *Southern Reporter* two days later: 'On Tuesday afternoon a fire broke out in Channel Street, Galashiels. The fire was not of the usual nature … this one started inside a stationary Land Rover. The outbreak was presumed to have been caused by petrol dripping from the petrol tank down into the engine and coming into contact with hot wires. Fortunately the flames were soon noticed by a shop-keeper whose premises were situated opposite … He managed to secure a fire-extinguisher and applied it to the flames, which were soon put out.' After this we acquired a slightly more modern vehicle, but we remained jumpy about Land Rovers.

My first shoot, on 12 August, was at Langhope Moor with the Indian Army Colonels, Laurie Loch and John Lowis (Laurie's 15-year-old son Johnnie was among the party). It was fine and warm, but cloudy. The birds were not very numerous. Kathleen arrived that morning; she too was put up at Fairnilee. I shot most days over the next two weeks, ferried hither and thither by Peter Dods (who could be contemptuous about the standard of shooting). At times the weather was very hot. Meanwhile Alan Henderson attempted to instruct a reluctant Stephen, working at the desk in his downstairs bedroom, two hours in the morning, two in the afternoon. Stephen would much rather have been out in the sunshine, resting in the hammock or flinging rocks down the gully into the Calfshaw Burn. Alan left on 19 August and Stephen had his release. Two days earlier Alan was persuaded to accompany us on a walking day at Peel. On these occasions the guns, keepers and pickers-up move in line. The weather was fine but a strong South-West wind after three stormy days made the birds wild. After a while I noticed that Alan was no longer with us. We did not see him again until we returned to the vehicles for lunch. He apologised, explaining that he had lost a contact lens and felt he must search for it in the heather, though the chances of finding it were almost non-existent. This was the first time I had heard of these devices.

On 3 September we drove to Edinburgh for *Aniara* by the Swedish composer Karl-Birger Blomdahl, its British première; I gave a long account of it in my music diary. Set aboard a spaceship heading away from Earth, it was no doubt intended as a satire on the present failings of humanity, but the symbolism was not easy to follow – the less so as it was sung in Swedish. The music was a weird mixture of styles and idioms – dodecaphony, Wagner, Stravinsky, Hindemith, jazz, and three tapes with electronic and 'concrete' effects. These were used to express the utterances of the miraculous machine Mima (a kind of super-computer). There were moments of unintentional humour: the Earth was called Doris and the space cadets resembled baseball players with an uncontrollable itch to mark time. A few passages were impressive, but much was noisy or tedious. In the middle the spaceship veered off course and the Earth was destroyed. Later a Blind Poetess appeared. She was meant to represent light and culture, but her music sounded empty. The dead commander Chefone was shot ceremonially into space. Almost all the characters were dead by the end.

The lovely weather continued. On 4 September Donald and Anthea invited us to a dinner party to celebrate our 20th wedding anniversary. We were back at Fairnilee three days later when the water supply to Calfshaw gave out. We spent two nights at the house before the problem was resolved. It was hotter than ever for the last days of our visit, with cloudless skies and temperatures in the 80s. We travelled South on 11 September, after a successful shoot on Peel Moor when the sun blazed all day. The shooting however was patchy.

Three weeks later we returned to Calfshaw, leaving Diana at Hambledon with Kathleen. The weather remained unseasonably hot. The night we travelled (according to my pocket diary) was the warmest for October ever recorded. That afternoon I spied an unwary hare from our bedroom window. It was loping about the garden near the rhubarb patch. I stalked it – the first entry in my game book for this visit. On 8 October I stayed up half the night listening to the General Election results on the portable radio. These occasions always fascinated me. Afterwards I compiled elaborate tables of statistics. The weather broke on the 17th, a drenching wet day when we were shooting again on Peel Moor. There was a southerly gale in the afternoon and the birds all but flew backwards. We headed home early. My last shoot, on 23 October, was with General Christison, a day marred by gales, driving rain and very poor light. I was the only non-military member of the small party. We took the train South late that evening, leaving my damp shooting clothes hanging in the former coal store.

By now I was thoroughly tired of writing about music. I still had creative ambitions. In November I started a detective novel, *Death of an Old Cock*, set on a Scottish sporting estate not unlike Fairnilee. I worked at it off and on for a couple of months but sadly it was never finished. In December I wrote to Mina Curtiss in New York – she had asked me what I was going to set my pen to next – and mentioned my dilemma. She replied a few weeks later: 'I do want you to know that I sympathize with and understand the struggle you are going through over your disinclination to continue writing about music. I really don't think you ought to be disturbed at all. You are a brilliant writer and there is no reason why you should not write in any field you choose. I think it only natural after the really Herculean labors on Handel that you feel a kind of revulsion against what now must seem almost a kind of slavery ...

'The rewriting I have to do on the Bizet for the French translation seems to me an intolerable burden, but I can spend hours in museums seeing, for the first time, pictures that I have been looking at for years, and I find that this breaking away from documentation to observation is wonderfully stimulating. I think that you might find that a change of field would do the same thing for you. You are, after all, very young still and there would always be time for you to go back to writing about music if you wanted to. So don't be discouraged, just be daring ... do wander in any fields that will give you joy.

'If it seems impertinent of me to offer you advice, remember that I am almost old enough to be your mother and that all my life I have known writers and painters and composers who ... have gone through the same struggle that you have.'

I was touched by her sympathetic response but, for one reason or another, I did not take her advice, something I have regretted to this day.

Publication

* * * * *

The Handel Opera Society had decided to revive *Hercules* in July and mount a new production of *Radamisto*, the first opera Handel wrote for the Royal Academy of Music in 1720. On a cold, snowy day in January 1960 Charles Farncombe came down to Hambledon to discuss both productions. Philip left for Cambridge the next day. The icy weather continued. There was heavy continuous snow on 13 January; blizzards and extreme cold the day following. Luckily Bert and Ernie kept the fire in my study well supplied with coal and logs. With grim weather outside, I sat down to tackle the second volume of Walter Serauky's turgid Life of Handel, which Jack Westrup (who had succeeded Blom as editor) had asked me to review for *Music & Letters*. Fortunately, it was not quite as bulky as his previous 1,000 page tome. January 22 saw a thaw, with the first snowdrops showing in the orchard.

In February Basil persuaded us to attend his production of *The Aspern Papers* at the restored Queen's Theatre. This had opened the previous August and was one of the more successful of his post-war productions. The play had been adapted by Michael Redgrave from the Henry James story, no doubt as a vehicle for himself. It struck me as a faded literary conceit but the acting was good, with Flora Robson and Beatrix Lehmann as well as the flamboyant Redgrave. Basil and Redgrave did not get on; Basil is silent about the production in *Mind's Eye*.

Towards the end of February I went to Cambridge, where I stayed with our friends Angela and Charles Wilson. Gerald Abraham had asked me to write an article on Berlioz's *Beatrice and Benedict* for the *Listener* and next day Philip and I played through the score in his rooms. (I had seen an amateur production at London University a few days earlier.) In the evening, with Philip, I attended a concert at Selwyn, at which Bach's Goldberg Variations for harpsichord were superbly played by Bob Dart, a noble experience in every way. I devoted the following day to research at the University Library and the Pendlebury. On my last evening I dined with Philip and Angela at the Arts and afterwards we went to a stage production of *The Damnation of Faust* by Berlioz at the Guildhall. This was an all-round catastrophe. I doubt if it can be successfully staged; certainly this was not the way to do it. The producer, a choreographer named Cossa, had rewritten the libretto to bring in as much Goethe as possible, thereby reducing much of the music to nonsense. The scenery was supplied by a magic lantern, which threw a messy collection of slides in a weird mixture of styles, from naturalism to obscure symbolism, and sometimes incorporated the chandelier, the organ pipes and the 'No Smoking' notices by mistake. The singing was indifferent, the orchestral playing noisy and ponderous. It was a sad evening; the dramatic tradition in Cambridge seemed dead.

In late April I resumed work on my detective novel. The murder took place during a pheasant shoot. Lord Bamburgh, the victim, bore more than a passing resemblance to my choleric father-in-law. I based the head keeper, Macduff, on Peter Dods, the keeper at Fairnilee. There were other parallels, some potentially libellous. I had worked out the entire plot but other writing commitments intervened and the book never progressed beyond chapter eight.

The Morris Oxford had been misbehaving and in May it was fitted with a new engine. This was a relief for Thalia, who wrote to Stephen: 'Hurrah! I need not apologise to everyone for the awful fumes from my exhaust!' On 1 June, a glorious day, we motored to Glyndebourne for *I Puritani*, Bellini's last opera, not performed in Britain since 1887. I thoroughly enjoyed this; it confirmed my impression of a great advance on Bellini's earlier operas, especially in his use of harmony to make a dramatic point. Joan Sutherland was in lovely voice. I noted many brief cuts in the performance. After Handel and Gluck, however, I found the mad scenes of this period tame. We stayed the night at the White Hart in Lewes and next day, in bright sunshine, explored ten Sussex churches, including Alfriston, West Firle and Lullington (claimed to be the smallest church in England). I made notes on each. In those happy days most parish churches were unlocked.

On 12 June we drove to Cambridge and this time stayed with Frank and Jane Thistlethwaite. That evening I went with Philip, his sister Susan and Philip Brett to Jesus College for Purcell's masque in *Timon of Athens*, a rather inadequate out-of-doors performance with choristers off pitch and competition from the local starlings and the chapel clock. The following morning I laboured in the Rowe Library. I lunched with Philip, Susan and Raymond Leppard at the Arts Theatre restaurant, followed by a relaxing afternoon in the Fellows' Garden at King's. I was aware of rehearsals going on in hall for the May Concert that evening. We dined with David Willcocks on Staircase F. The concert included Bloch's Concerto Grosso No. 1 for piano and strings, a splendidly effective and sonorous work; traditional and original in the same breath. There followed a much abbreviated performance of Handel's ode, *Alexander's Feast*. The result was sadly unbalanced: the excessive proportion of recitative and chorus had a stodgy effect. The style was not bad however and I noted wonderful touches that had not struck me before. The Newburgh Hamilton finale ('Your voices tune, and raise them high') was most attractive, a lighter conclusion than the setting of Dryden's chorus. I had never heard it before.

The next afternoon we left for the little town of Orford, where we put up in the Crown & Castle Hotel. On the way we stopped at Woolpit Church, with its superb double hammer-beam roof, fourteenth century porch and splendid pews and bench-ends in the shape of a dog with a goose in its mouth, a cat, lion, bird, bear and chained monkey. After dinner we wandered round Orford Castle. We had already taken in the Coastguard Station and the lighthouse on the shingle and now we saw its flashing beam. Over the next three days I made notes on a dozen more Suffolk churches.

On the evening of 15 June we drove over to Aldeburgh for Benjamin Britten's new opera, *A Midsummer Night's Dream*, in the Jubilee Hall. This was only its second performance, this time conducted by George Malcolm (the first night was on 11 June). At first hearing I found it impressive and full of exquisite music but was unsure whether Britten had got the balance quite right. The lovers had beautiful lyrical music, the rustics were successful on a lighter level; the fairy background (the wood, etc.) was marvellous, but I was less happy about the fairies themselves. The countertenor Oberon (Deller) was perhaps a matter of taste; the boy fairies lacked any touch of magic in their stage presence, suggesting rather a prep-school end-of-term play; Puck, who threw himself about like a young rugger player, I found insufferable. To what extent this was the fault of the production I was not sure; certainly the stage was too small for it. In my music diary I expanded on the many felicities of this marvellous score. At the end of the third act the humans beat a quick retreat, leaving the fairies in charge. Their first chorus was delicious, the ensemble led by Titania and Oberon with its haunting Scotch-snap rhythm utterly ravishing. But then it seemed to me Britten spoiled everything by bringing in Puck and the spoken word. The silly boy made things worse by forgetting his lines.

A few days later I listened to the live BBC relay of the final performance, conducted by Britten. At a second hearing the work struck me as a masterpiece. Nearly everything fell into place. No doubt I was originally prejudiced by my conception of the play. Oberon's music carried more conviction, especially its delicate orchestral envelope, and the parodies went with greater zip. In a broadcast performance one was not troubled by the sight of Puck and the fairies; but I longed to see a different production with more magic on the stage.

As before, I attended many of the rehearsals for the Handel Opera Society productions of *Hercules* and *Radamisto,* on one occasion lunching with the singers. *Hercules* opened on 5 July. This did not quite come off (though a third performance, broadcast from Goldsmiths' Hall, was conspicuously successful). Monica Sinclair was in poor voice, the chorus were incommoded by being stationed far upstage behind a gauze with dancers disturbing their view of the conductor, the leader of the orchestra missed the dress rehearsal, and the quarrel scene in Act II was far too buffo (despite being toned down at my request). Other things went wrong. However some passages cut in 1957 were restored.

Radamisto opened the next night. It was a resounding success with public and critics alike, despite a deplorably weak Zenobia (Arda Mandikian) over whose engagement I was outvoted. If the drama was sometimes stiff, the musical invention, especially in melody and scoring, was extraordinarily rich. Many of the airs were touchingly characterised, and the more brilliant went off like a series of rockets; several of them stopped the show on the last night when the house was packed. I think the audience were staggered that such music had been hidden under a bushel for more than two centuries (the last performance in England was in 1728). The score was largely my arrangement, based on Handel's first revival of December 1720 with four airs from the original version restored. A good deal of course had to be cut; I regretted the loss of Radamisto's 'Dolce bene' and 'Qual nave smarrita', both very fine airs. Radamisto's 'Vile! se mi dai vita' is a powerful piece of righteous indignation, but was too difficult for the singer (Margaret Lensky). Not so 'Barbaro! partirò' –

scarcely a striking piece on paper – which Jennifer Vyvyan sang with such fire, brilliance and accuracy of coloratura that it was some time before the opera could be resumed. Bob Dart played harpsichord continuo in both productions and after the first night of *Radamisto* we drove him home.

I had heard that Rossini's early one-act opera *Il Signor Bruschino* was to be put on (as part of a double bill) by the Kentish Opera Group at Orpington, which was where Frank Walker lived. I asked Frank to make inquiries and received a long and lively letter in reply. He had been engaged for some years on a *magnum opus* on Verdi, which he was '*almost* confident' would be finished in the autumn. Verdi had been 'hanging over my head, breathing down my neck and standing on my chest'. He had just returned from his annual outing – three weeks – in Sicily, northern Italy and Austria. 'I went back, after three years, to Busseto, where everyone was, or seemed to be, pleased to see me, from the hostess of the local inn, whose name, of course, is <u>Aida</u>, to Gabriella Carrara-Verdi, guardian of the treasures of Sant'Agata. You suggested once that it was my duty to marry her … But I like her too much to wish her such a fate.'

On 14 July we drove to Orpington, lunched with Frank at the Country Club and spent a convivial afternoon at his little house in Darrick Wood Road. His seventeen-year-old daughter Sally came over and cooked us supper. Meanwhile Frank, whose hours of work were inconvenient and onerous, had asked Thalia to ring the office to say he was unwell. The operas were staged at the Civic Hall. *Il Signor Bruschino*, a farce, began slowly but soon became highly enjoyable. This was said to have been its first performance in Britain. The best part of Menotti's *The Old Maid and the Thief* was the libretto (by the composer). The action was amusing enough and the performance was a fine effort on the part of amateurs.

Two days later we drove over to Newbury with Nigel Fortune (who was down from Birmingham for the weekend) for the Fathers' Match at Little Abbey. The game took place at the Burghclere village ground a mile from the school. Stephen had hoped to play for the 1st Eleven but was not selected by Mr Sharp. The fathers were at a disadvantage, being supplied only with schoolboy bats. I wasn't asked to keep wicket. When it was my turn to bat I smote a four and a six off successive balls but was then clean bowled. Nigel sat in the shade wearing sunglasses against the hay fever he suffered from at that time.

Next week Jeremy Noble, now a music critic on *The Times*, came down to Hambledon for the day, bringing with him the American musical scholar Joseph Kerman and his wife Vivian, both of whom I was to get to know very well later. Kerman (who was born in London) had joined the faculty of music at the University of California, Berkeley, in 1951 and was to be the leading figure there for many years. I had recently read, and admired, his controversial book *Opera as Drama*, while violently disagreeing with parts of it. He spoke warmly of *Handel's Dramatic Oratorios and Masques*. Five years later, very unexpectedly, Thalia and I found ourselves on our way to America for a ten-month sojourn at Berkeley, where I had been invited to take up the Ernest Bloch Professorship of Music.

We travelled to Scotland on 10 August, dining as usual at St Pancras before we boarded the night train (I kept an appointment with Dr Wingate at 5.30). We soon settled back into Calfshaw Cottage. I had been asked to a good many shoots. Much the most memorable was the first outing on Peel Moor, a perfect day, sunny, with a little cloud and a cool NW wind. The bag of 184 grouse almost doubled the moor's record for walking up. Needless to say the marksmanship was excellent. Sadly, adjacent moors were already being ploughed up and planted with conifers, which in time ruined the shooting at Peel. Alan Henderson arrived a couple of days earlier and together with Thalia, Stephen and a mischievous Diana joined the guns for a picnic lunch above the sheep pens.

Alan had brought his tape recorder and one evening we played his recording of *Hercules* to our musical shooting friends the Lunds and the Christisons. Alan did not have to tutor Stephen this time as he had secured a place at Seaford College. Instead, they set off on a little tour of Scotland, taking in Edinburgh and South Queensferry, where they saw the twin towers of the unfinished Forth Road Bridge, then on to Stirling, Pitlochry, Blair Castle and Loch Ness (where Stephen claimed to have photographed the monster).

We arrived South on 9 September. That evening I went to *Alcina* at Covent Garden with Hilary Haywood. This was a Stockholm Opera production. It was a ghastly disappointment. They used the Roth version of 1928, hacked up the airs without mercy, and turned the whole thing into an excuse for ballet and spectacle (of a demure and pedantic kind). Not one da capo air was done complete, and most were reduced to torsos. This was one of the most misguided performances of any Handel opera that I had heard. It became a tame formal divertissement without a trace of life.

CHAPTER 18

Romantic Opera

In the middle of September 1960 I began work on my New Oxford History chapters, which covered the years 1790-1830. I embarked first on French Opera. Philip was able to obtain many of the scores from libraries in Cambridge and brought them down in batches in the vacs. We played through opera after opera, starting with Méhul's *Stratonice* and *Uthal*. This was more congenial work than minute textual labours on Handel's oratorios. Méhul and Le Sueur in particular, though forgotten today, were striking innovators, extraordinarily rich in new ideas (but deficient in technique and melodic invention). Together with Cherubini, they laid down a stock of technical innovations that was not exhausted for fifty years.

There had been rumblings at the Handel Opera Society and towards the end of September I received two letters from Charles Farncombe, one a friendly note on blue paper, the other a typewritten missive. I had been an advisor to the Society for five years but was now informed that, though the Committee valued my help, I was no longer welcome at rehearsals. In particular, I must not talk 'direct to the singers' (they sometimes asked my advice on matters of ornamentation, etc.) or make suggestions to producers. Most members of the Committee were non-musicians with no expertise in artistic matters. They were willing to offer me the title of 'Specialist Adviser' or 'Counsellor on Handelian Studies'. These were not terms

I could accept and I wrote back withdrawing from the activities of the Society. Luckily I retained my friendship with Charles, who, as chairman, was the unhappy messenger.

The beginning of October found us back at Calfshaw Cottage. The previous day we had caught an early train to London, depositing our luggage at St Pancras. We lunched with Hilary at Monmouth Road and then changed for Teresa Rees's wedding to Freddie Bircher at St Clement Danes, the RAF church where Lorimer was rector. The reception was held at the Basil Street Hotel. Stephen, in his first term at Seaford College, was unable to attend but gave the happy couple a wedding present of a plastic bucket. In due course he received a letter of thanks.

A fortnight later Thalia was ill and kept to her bed. Luckily it was not a shooting day. I contrived to relight the fire in the sitting room and cooked myself an excellent omelette for lunch. Anthea Craigmyle, Thalia's sister-in-law, was expecting a baby and on 19 October the news came that Donald's son and heir had been born. An estate party in celebration was arranged. I was shooting on the neighbouring estate of Philiphaugh. We walked many miles on a grey, misty day, in drizzle, after a few very wild partridges. Afterwards I was given tea at Philiphaugh. Dods drove me back to Calfshaw, where I changed as rapidly as I could. A huge throng had assembled in the Garden Room at Fairnilee – the tenants from Fairnilee, Rink, Peel and Williamhope Farms with their families and work people, Dods and Wattie, the foresters, house staff, wives and children. A simple repast of tea and buns had been prepared, with a glass of sherry for everyone to toast the baby's health. Then Mr Pate, the Fairnilee farmer, announced that it was time to light the beacon. We trooped along the avenue in the twilight. The foresters had prepared an enormous bonfire in the field above the drive. Well dosed with paraffin, it went up spectacularly, despite the drizzle. One or two people passing along the road below guessed its significance. Boys from the farm brought fireworks, rockets, stars, squibs and Catherine wheels, which shot off in all directions and added to the excitement.

At the end of November we drove to Oxford for Alan Bush's *Men of Blackmoor*, staged by the University Opera Club at the Town Hall. It was a long, wearisome journey in heavy traffic. We dined with Alan Henderson at the Randolph and he accompanied us to the opera. He was taking a teachers' training course in Oxford and angling for a post at Abingdon School. This was the first performance in Britain of Bush's opera – and ought to have been the last. I thought it a deplorable work, folky, muddle-headed and tendentious. Jack Westrup conducted. We stayed the night at the Randolph and returned to Hambledon the following day.

On 6 December I took the train to London for the Royal Musical Association's A.G.M. at Trinity College, followed by a paper on Arne by Julian Herbage. Jack Westrup was in the chair. Afterwards I sallied forth with Gerald Abraham (newly elected Vice President) and Martin Cooper for a cold supper (with Châteauneuf du Pape) at the Mandeville Hotel to discuss our opera chapters for *The New Oxford History of Music* (Abraham had succeeded Blom as editor). Gerry accompanied me on the train to Witley, where Thalia met us in the car. It was a foggy night. We sat up chatting till after 1 a.m. Gerry drew my attention to Dent's unpublished lectures on the Rise of Romantic Opera, delivered at Cornell University shortly before the War, which survived in typescript at the Rowe Library at King's. Obviously they were relevant to my chapters.

Early in January 1961 Thalia and Stephen returned from a stay in London bearing a large heavy tape recorder purchased in Harrods. Egged on by Stephen, Thalia recorded a few welcoming words at the beginning of the tape. We set the machine to work immediately and that evening recorded a BBC broadcast of *Billy Budd*, which had not been revived in Britain since its opening at Covent Garden in 1951. For this studio performance, conducted by the composer, Britten reduced the four acts to two and made a number of cuts.

Unfortunately the machine proved temperamental. Within a few days it was making an intermittent squeaking noise on playback, though this disappeared when the tape was rewound. I consulted Alan Henderson, now at Abingdon School. He had kindly agreed to record opera broadcasts I was unable to hear.

For some time I had been suffering from a rheumatic shoulder. Thalia rubbed in Bengue's Balsam, which had a certain efficacy. In addition, periodically, I visited a physiotherapist in Godalming, Miss Barton. Philip left for Cambridge on 14 January. A day later I noticed the first snowdrop in the garden. Since the start of the month we had played through Le Sueur's *Paul et Virginie*, Grétry's *Anacréon chez Polycrate*, Méhul's *Mélidore et Phrosine* and Le Sueur's *Ossian* and *La Mort d'Adam*, the last one of the most comprehensive and spectacular operas ever conceived, embracing not only the entire human race but the total population of heaven and hell.

I wrote to Philip on 29 January: 'Yes, Feb. 18th will do very well [for a visit]. Could you bring with you (i) Catel's *Sémiramis* (Rowe or Pendlebury – I think I ought to have a look at it) (ii) Boieldieu's *Béniowski* (Rowe), (iii) Handel's *Imeneo*, (iv) Abraham's *100 Years of Music* – rather a pretty selection, don't you think? I do not propose to go through them all during the week-end, but rather to examine them at leisure and bring them to Cambridge at the beginning of March, when I am planning a visit.

'I have been through the *Death of Adam* again, sorting out my notes, and found a few more thematic reminiscences that we did not notice – also an important one in *Mélidore et Phrosine*. Last week a performance of *L'Enfance du Christ* kept reminding me of Le Sueur, especially the modal touches and sudden drops into octaves in choruses.

'I see that the Chelsea Opera Group are going to do what Maurits Sillem believes to be the ur-*Carmen* in Cambridge, restoring various things Bizet cut out of the autograph or altered. I am rather suspicious about this, since I mistrust Sillem's judgment and find some of his arguments tendentious. You might listen and see just what he does do. He has shown me some things, and others I remember noticing in the autograph.

'Did you hear Henze's opera last Sunday [*Der Prinz von Homburg*]? I found it pretty detestable in style, an unoriginal mixture of Berg, Schönberg & Stravinsky, and disliked the treatment of the libretto. At the moment I am feeling rather bolshie about going to his new opera at Glyndebourne [*Elegy for Young Lovers*].

'The new *Music and Letters* contains a devastating exposure by Westrup of the methods of Stravinsky with Gesualdo and of Britten with Purcell, which gave me a certain amusement.

'Milner [Dean of King's, Cambridge, in my time] has written me a charming letter calling the Handel book the best ever written in English on a musical subject, which seems to me pitching it a bit steep!'

There was a crisis at Hambledon at the end of February: Diana went down with mumps! Ernie Jeffery's delightful wife Alice came in and read and chatted to her. Thalia had been planning a short break with Jean in Cumberland. She decided not to postpone it; Diana seemed on the mend by the weekend and Alice would be able to look after her. The weather was unseasonably warm. Already wallflowers were out in the front garden; the day Thalia returned pear trees broke into blossom.

On 11 March I went to London for three short oratorios by Carissimi at St Pancras Town Hall. Much the best was the last, *Jephte*, in which Carissimi made considerably more use of the chorus, which helped to get the drama into the music. But this scarcely emerged in the performance; the chorus were not on stage and were deprived of their continuo, since the organist got up to conduct! The music of Jephtha's daughter, often echoed by another soprano, was beautifully expressive throughout; her touching acceptance of her fate inevitably reminded one of Handel's Iphis.

Later in March we stayed two nights in London at a little mews house belonging to Thalia's school-friend Rachel Gee. I was suffering from a poisoned throat and not feeling at all well but was determined not to miss two operas enjoying their belated British premières on successive nights. Verdi's early *Un Giorno di Regno* (1840) was mounted at St Pancras by the Impresario Society, conducted by Hans Ucko. Unfortunately it was a very indifferent performance. Throughout the work, the slow tunes were conspicuously superior to the quick, though the latter dispensed a shameless zip which it was difficult to condemn out of hand. The following day my throat was even worse and my neck badly swollen. Janáček's *Cunning Little Vixen* at Sadler's Wells was conducted by Colin Davis. I found this a fascinating, haunting opera and wrote about it at length in my music diary. The next day, still feeling groggy, I took the train to Birmingham for Handel's *Imeneo* at the Barber Institute. This was its first English performance since 1742. I was a little surprised that Anthony Lewis chose this lesser work rather than one of the earlier masterpieces. The plot was all but negligible; the music light in tone and texture. Yet the score was full of exquisite melody. I penned my notice for the *Sunday Telegraph* in the train to London the following morning. The performance was a credit to all concerned. Lewis's scholarship and taste seemed impeccable, though he sometimes set dangerously comatose tempos. Brian Trowell's production turned the conventions to amusing use at the risk of provoking laughs in unsuitable places. Looking back, I underestimated the opera and was unaware of its manifold textual complexities. I stayed the night with Nigel Fortune at Philip Victor Road.

When I returned to Hambledon the next afternoon I retired to bed. I had mumps – for the second time! I languished upstairs for nearly a week. I managed to produce a longer review of *Imeneo* for *Musical Times,* then fell back on detective fiction. Nigel wrote sympathetically from Birmingham: 'I am sorry indeed to hear of your prolonged idleness. They say the second lot of mumps is worse than the first, but I hope this is not being so in your case. I am sure that after the first unpleasant days you will have a very agreeable recovering and reading. I think it takes three weeks or so to incubate, so it is too early to start telling you of gaps in our ranks: Maybe Tony Lewis will be struck down on some remote Greek island (whither he disappeared yesterday). I also believe that those who have been in contact with the disease tend to be carriers and not catch it themselves; I see myself in this role.'

When I got up on 31 March the wisteria on the front of the house had broken into flower and the first rose was blooming. A week later I attended a Critics' Circle lunch at the Connaught Rooms to celebrate Frank Howes's 70th birthday. Frank had recently laid down his pen after a long stint as chief music critic of *The Times*. Gerald Abraham, Diana McVeagh, Andrew Porter, William Mann (Frank's successor), Ursula Vaughan Williams, Deryck Cooke, Keith Falkner, Neville Cardus and many others were present, together with a sprinkling of spouses. Arthur Bliss made a rather pompous speech, Frank a good one but emotional at the end and his voice broke. I left with Gerry and Deryck Cooke and accompanied Gerry on the train as far as Guildford.

I had begun to modulate from French to Italian opera. Over the next fortnight Philip and I played through operas by Mayr and Paer as well as Hérold, Boieldieu and Dalayrac. In the middle of April Philip returned to Cambridge but he agreed to accompany me to a pair of operas at Sadler's Wells. I asked him to bring vocal scores of Meyerbeer's *Margherita d'Anjou* and *Crociato in Egitto* from the Rowe, and receive in exchange two that I had at Hambledon. I dined with Philip at the Ballerina Restaurant (after another session with Dr Wingate). I did not much enjoy Dallapiccola's *Il Prigioniero* but found Ravel's *L'Heure Espagnole* delicious in the theatre, conscious only of the perfect congruity of music, words and action. The translator (Viola Tunnard) enlivened the proceedings with such rhymes as 'He has a torso Just like Apollo only more so'.

At the beginning of May I wrote to Philip: 'There must be two ends to Rossini's *Otello* – (a) unhappy, (b) happy – as with Spontini's *Olympia* and certain other operas of the period. I am now imbedded in a heavy German dissertation on the unpublished operas of Spontini's youth, one by Schubert. The silly chump describes every fragment in detail with diagrams etc but does not quote a note of the music.' Two days later Thalia and I drove to Abingdon for the Kitchings' production of Handel's *Partenope* at the Unicorn Theatre. This was its first English revival since 1737. It was a creditable performance and all the parts were sung at the correct pitch but the opera was heavily cut. The castrato hero, played by the countertenor John Horrex, a natural comedian, retained only 2½ of his ten arias, making him appear even more ineffective; everyone abuses him and he remains comically mute. The orchestra was sadly truncated: no horns, trumpets or bassoons, only one flute (which played the oboe part in the ritornellos) and one oboe (which did the like for the trumpet).

Romantic Opera

I was in London again the following week for Rimsky-Korsakov's comic opera *May Night* at Sadler's Wells. This made excellent entertainment and improved as it went on. The music was often genuinely funny as well as attractive in lyrical invention and scoring. Before the performance I dined with Diana Morley and stayed the night with her and Bill at 7 Holland Park Villas. The next day I met Thalia and we moved to Rachel's flat at 20 Ovington Mews. I skipped Donald Mitchell's Royal Musical Association paper on Mahler, a composer I detested. That evening we saw Verdi's *Battaglia di Legano* at Sadler's Wells. This was done in modern dress as *The Battle* with the scene set in the last war and the patriots turned into resistance fighters against the Germans – a conception that falsified the entire opera, emphasising every improbability in the plot and making the music seem clumsy and old-fashioned. A dreadful slangy translation and poor production made things worse.

On Saturday I took myself off to the Oval to watch Surrey play the Australians. It was a balmy day – the hottest in London since September. That evening we dined with Alan Frank and his wife Phyllis Tate (whose opera *The Lodger* I had admired at the Royal Academy of Music the previous July). Alan, head of music at Oxford University Press, was a man of many talents with a lively gift for anecdote. We met the American film composer Bernard Herrmann.

After our return to Hambledon I wrote to Philip: 'Our week in London was eventful but exhausting. I contrived to hear no fewer than seven operas, five of them in the theatre, and all had many points of interest. Rossini's *Otello* [at St Pancras] is an astonishing mixture of the superb and the preposterous. It contains two startling incursions from the *Barber* in solemn contexts. The Handel [Opera Society] season was odd. *Rinaldo* went quite well, though it is far inferior to the last three Italian operas the Society has done, but the performance of *Semele* was deplorable. I am heartily thankful it was not broadcast. I can play you a tape of *Rinaldo*, and also of [Bellini's] *Beatrice di Tenda*, an opera that seems to me underrated. The audience on the first night of *Rinaldo* was packed with familiar figures, including Bob [Dart], Hubert [Langley] and Charles Cudworth [Curator of the Pendlebury Library]. Can you scrutinise the weeklies for reviews, beginning with this last week?

'We are looking forward to seeing you on the 5th. I suggest you bring Paisiello's *Nina* from the Rowe, and remove *Zampa* and the Boieldieu when you go. Are your books (Cooper and Einstein) in Cambridge or at Riverdale [Philip's house in Godalming]? I should like to borrow them for my Iphigenia article, but this will do when you come down at the end of term.'

On 23 May Gerald Abraham, his wife Pat and 11-year-old daughter Frances came to Hambledon for lunch and tea. According to Gerald's diary: 'The little 6-year-old adopted Diana was very lively and talkative and nearly wore out Franny. After lunch Winton and I talked, while Thalia took Pat and the children on the Common.' Unfortunately Diana had not been in the best of health and a few days later she went down with measles. Alice Jeffery helped Thalia care for her.

I wrote to Philip on 27 May: 'Can you bring a copy of the Waldstein sonata with you on the 5th? Or alternatively if there is one at Riverdale we could pick it up. I am not introducing it into an opera by Auber, but have to write a programme note on it for Edinburgh at the request of the Most Honourable George [Harewood, Director of the Festival].

'Frank Walker is coming tonight for the week-end. He has been bombarding us with ebullient postcards from all over Europe for the last month, so we are expecting some lively news. I gather he has finished his book on Verdi.'

Romantic Opera

My cricketing career was drawing to a close. The Ramblers had found another wicket keeper. Latterly I had not been available to play for much of August and September, when we were in Scotland, or at other times. The situation was awkward. I turned out for a few matches up to July, after which Mike Gauntlet did not pick me. Later he urged me, not too tactfully, to retire. In May our old opening bat Charlie Izzard died. Thalia and I attended his funeral at Walton with Mike and other members of the team; the match against King Edward's School, Witley, was cancelled.

In the middle of June Andrew Porter came to stay at Hambledon for the first time. Andrew, who had been born in South Africa, was music critic for the *Financial Times* and had recently taken on the editorship of *Musical Times*. We shared a mutual passion for opera and talked endlessly about it. He brought with him records of several Bellini operas (his passion at the time). While Thalia and I were lodging at Overton Mews in May Andrew came to tea and together we listened to my tape of *Beatrice di Tenda*. Andrew evidently admired my work and from this time most of my opera notices and articles were written for *Musical Times*.

Nigel wrote from Birmingham concerning the next Handel production at the Barber: 'In August I shall be starting joint translating again with [Brian] Trowell. It is almost certain that we will be doing *Ariodante*, ballet notwithstanding …

'I am sorry you've had such a wearing summer: I hope you are all well by now and that you have got your notes done. Are you embarking on another big work yet?'

The weather towards the end of June was extremely hot, rising to 93F on 1 July. We were enjoying copious strawberries and raspberries from the garden. Thalia wrote to Stephen: 'We've eaten lots & I have bottled one jar of raspberries. A great bowl of gooseberries awaits bottling, each one to be topped & tailed *and* the mildew scraped off!' A week later I received a card from Nigel: 'A *volte face* to report. It will be *Tamerlano*! 22/23 March. This was chosen without our knowing that the Barber Institute owns the 1724 score with complete *verse* translation. We must see if this will do or can be adapted. I was looking forward to translating and hope this version is abysmal. So far we can't find it!'

On 10 July Philip came to lunch and we finished playing through Cherubini's *Ali Baba*, his last opera. Late in the day Merrill and Libby Knapp, both tall and very affable, arrived with their 15-year-old daughter Joan for a two nights' stay. They had been to the Handel Festival in Halle, where the Handel Opera Society scored a hit with *Rinaldo*. I had been in correspondence with Merrill on Handelian matters for several years. He was writing a book on Handel's operas but teaching and administrative commitments at Princeton meant that he had not got very far with it.

Later in the month we drove to Glyndebourne for Henze's *Elegy for Young Lovers*. In advance, I listened to the Third Programme broadcast. I had been disappointed. I was particularly irritated by Auden and Kallman's slick and pretentious libretto. The stage made a considerable difference: aided by a striking set and first-rate production (Günther Rennert) the opera developed at times a good deal of dramatic tension. But it was fitful, owing to defects in both libretto and music. We stayed at the Esplanade Hotel in Seaford, which we thought a dreary town. The next day was devoted to exploring a further nine Sussex churches. At Friston, perched high on the Downs overlooking the Channel, I noted many ancient graffiti in the Early English porch and a 16th century oak chair carved with strange beasts. The following day we looked in at Holleyman & Treacher, the antiquarian bookshop in Brighton. In the afternoon, driving westward, we took in three more churches, before calling on

Frank and Joan Sargeant at Bosham. Frank was in the diplomatic service and served under Tom Bromley in Somalia. Their son John was at Seaford College with Stephen and often appeared with him on exeats. Tom, who had lost his own family so tragically, took the Sargeants and their two children under his wing.

We put up at the Brockenhurst Hotel in the New Forest, splashing through a tiny ford and bumping over a cattle grid to reach it. Ponies and donkeys wandered at liberty, apparently impervious to motor traffic. After dinner we strolled round the garden. Hearing whinnying, we looked over the fence: ponies were grazing on the verges of the road, including several delightful foals. Next morning we boarded the ferry from Lymington to Yarmouth on the Isle of Wight, where we were greeted by Gerry and Pat Abraham and their young daughter Frances. They took us to an exhibition of Julia Margaret Cameron's photographs; later we inspected Yarmouth Church and toured the Castle. We ate lunch at Farringford Hotel. The grand house had once been the home of Tennyson. Gerry showed us the poet's library and other features. Their cottage in Brighstone was too small to accommodate us; instead we lodged at nearby Pitt Place. On Sunday Gerry ran me to the little village of Shorewell, where I scrutinised the church, taking detailed notes, and then on to Northcourt, a fine Jacobean manor house. Pat supplied coffee on the lawn next morning before Gerry and Frances drove us to Yarmouth to catch the ferry. We returned to Hambledon circuitously by way of seven more parish churches, including Hambledon, Hampshire.

Thalia had been looking for a student to help in the house and assist with Diana. On 25 July Pauline Thompson arrived. She accompanied us to Calfshaw; at the end of August she was replaced by a fair-haired girl called Gillian Fawcett. Two days later we drove to Orpington, dining with Frank Walker and Alec and Eve King. Alec King, an old friend, was Superintendent of the Music Room at the British Museum, a lively personality and a distinguished scholar. He had preceded me at King's, Cambridge. Afterwards we trooped to the Civic Hall, where Kentish Opera were putting on *Susannah* by Carlisle Floyd, its first performance in Britain. This celebrated work had been chosen to represent American music and culture at the World's Fair in Brussels in 1958. I thought it a dreadful opera, in Menotti's manner. The plot, adapted from the Apocrypha, was set in modern Tennessee but instead of preserving the lines of the story the author debased and sentimentalised it, substituting a cheap sensationalism for what could have been a moving parable. The next day I kept to my bed with a chill.

In August Thalia received a strange rambling letter from Frank Walker. We were thinking of employing a Sicilian couple to help in the house. Frank kindly offered to translate the Italian documents and to write a letter from us to the couple in Italian (he enclosed a translation 'so that you know what you have said!') This part of his letter was typed; the following eight pages were hand-written, evidently in the office, partly on P.O. Cable & Wireless Services paper. Frank, a divorcé, had fallen in love with a lady who lived at Tring. She was a widow with two children. He talked about her when he stayed at Hambledon in May. All that summer and autumn he was in a state of intense and almost unnatural elation. He was making improvements to his house, he wrote a little later: 'My green carpets have arrived & yellow curtains for behind the Bechstein – magnificent! Tomorrow the paper in the front room is to be changed. But now I'm beginning to think I shall go & live in Tring on my retirement! (nine months or ten to go). I could easily sell this place and make a profit. Would you come & see me at Tring?' The contract for his book, *The Man Verdi*, had been signed; it was down for publication late next year: 'A quarter of a million words, they say! Ah well.'

On 11 August we boarded the sleeper to Scotland, arriving at Galashiels next morning an hour late. This time there were two shotguns. Stephen, now 15, had expressed an interest in taking up shooting; we bought him a second-hand 20-bore in a smart green case. After unpacking at Calfshaw we went in search of pigeons – it was really an exercise in gun-handling for Stephen – but there were few to be had. Stephen fired his first shot. As usual the opening shoot of the season was on the little moor at Langhope with Laurie Loch and John Lowis, both retired Colonels. Laurie's son Johnnie, two years older than Stephen, was also out. It seemed too soon for Stephen to bear his gun but Johnnie lent him his air-rifle and he popped away at anything that got up. Next evening Alan Henderson arrived with the Morris Oxford, which Thalia found much easier to drive than the heavy Land Rover. It was parked at the stables. Thalia did not attempt to drive it up the bumpy track to Calfshaw.

On 21 August we went to Edinburgh for Gluck's *Iphigénie en Tauride*. This was the first night of the first Covent Garden production since 1840! Solti's conducting combined fire with delicacy but the producer (Göran Gentele) grievously mishandled the climax of Act IV: instead of Thoas being killed by Pylades and the returning Greek crew, he was polished off in advance by Orestes with the sacrificial knife while the Scythian guards stood by and did nothing. This made nonsense of music and drama alike. Act II from first bar to last was almost unbearably moving; the later acts did not consistently retain this level.

Two days later I arranged a boys' shoot at Fairnilee on Heather Flat and Neidpath, Stephen's first. A stiff westerly wind made the birds wild but they were fairly numerous. Afterwards the boys had tea at Calfshaw Cottage. A week later Martin and Nan came to stay at Fairnilee. They shared Catholic interests with Donald and Anthea. The weather was lovely. On 31 August we shot Peel Moor for the second time. This was Martin's introduction to grouse shooting. He barely troubled the scorer, but there were one or two incidents: his gun went off accidentally as he was negotiating a dyke – and he shot an owl!

On 2 September we walked Heather Flat and Neidpath once more, this time with more success. It was another boys' shoot, but with reinforcements, including Col. Loch and two keepers (Peter and Wattie Dods). It was very hot and close. Soon Stephen was lagging behind and he gave up at lunch. I attempted to encourage him: 'Can you find another gear, Stephen?' Ian Lowis was heard to mutter to his cousin Johnnie Loch: 'Try reverse?' Three days later Stephen and I walked over to the Roman Camp on Rink and assaulted the pigeons coming in to the wood. They were less numerous than expected. Stephen claimed his first kill. On the walk back I tripped and fell and damaged my shoulder.

We were back at Hambledon in the middle of September. Next day Alan Henderson arrived with the Morris. The Hurst, garden and Common were swarming with grey squirrels feeding on acorns; I shot a good many. It was still very warm. On one day I bagged 13 squirrels in the Hurst. Philip came to dinner and we played through the Halle Handel Society's vocal score of *Ariodante*, which Andrew had asked me to review for *Musical Times*. As usual with Halle, some vocal parts were printed in the wrong clef. Near the end of the month I went to *Carmen* at Sadler's Wells, accompanied by Thalia and Philip. I was glad to hear the spoken dialogue – some of it, for the first time in this theatre! – instead of Guiraud's posthumous recitatives. A number of passages cancelled in the autograph, collated by Maurits Sillem, were also restored. Sillem assumed without evidence that these were removed without Bizet's consent. In fact their omission in nearly every case was an improvement and a tribute to Bizet's second thoughts. Their general effect was to destroy the brilliant economy and concentration we know in the usual version.

We were at Calfshaw again at the beginning of October. The visit began badly when I was stricken with rheumatism. This affected my shooting: out with General Christison at Howford, I missed six consecutive shots in the turnips! The next day I was totally incapacitated by rheumatism in the neck. By the following week however I was feeling rather better. I wrote to Philip on 19 October: 'I have heard no music here whatever, which has probably been very good for me. It appears that one of my friends with whom I shoot has been making quite a pile of money by laying bets that none of his acquaintance can guess my profession. So far he has won every time. I am thinking of demanding a royalty.

'On Friday the 13th I duly noted your first lecture. That evening another friend [Alan Ramsay] celebrated his 35th birthday with a dinner party for 25 people. This involved the consumption of a great quantity of champagne and included charades, in the course of which I was required (a) to enact the part of King Charles II with a doormat over my head representing a full-bottomed wig, (b) to assist in the delivery of a baby with an enormous pair of fire-tongs. The proceedings I believe continued all night, but we left at 2 a.m. as I had to get up at 6.45 to shoot grouse. In the circumstances my marksmanship was surprisingly accurate.

'Will you ask Charles Cudworth to send me the Handel-Gesellschaft volume containing the *Dixit Dominus*, timed to arrive on or about the 26th? Not earlier in case it is superfluously forwarded up here – a fate that has just befallen three volumes of Beethoven's letters.

'We have had gales, hailstones and hurricanes this week, but last week was as hot as the middle of August. I was in the open air for five days out of six and developed such a healthy countenance that Thalia said I looked like a ruddy colonel.

'I must now go to bed, as early action is required tomorrow.'

Our house-keeper Kathleen had departed. As soon as we arrived back at Hambledon a Sicilian couple, Lillo and Gina, were installed. They were willing and enthusiastic but had very little English. Thalia bought a Teach Yourself Italian book and a course on long-playing Gramophone records. The next week saw me reviewing the Halle Handel Society's full score of *Dixit Dominus*. Hambledon was still swarming with squirrels. At the end of the week I had an ulcerated throat and retired to bed for two days, where however I resumed work on romantic opera.

I wrote again to Philip on 5 November: 'Thank you for your letter. The Weber article [for *The Listener*] was too long and some appetising details had to be cut, which was a pity. I heard the broadcast of *Freischütz* from Covent Garden, an ill-sung and disappointing performance.

'What did [David] Cairns say about *Carmen* in the *Spectator*? I have not bought a copy and am not clear if it is necessary to do so. Also what were John Barton's [the producer's] views? You will find mine in the current *Musical Times*, which I dare say will provoke some sort of reaction from Sillem …

'Here are two alleged kittens [borrowings] for you to follow up. How much of the ballet at the end of Act I of *Ariodante* was used in the trio sonata op 5 no 2? And is it true that the ground bass of Daniel's recitative (accomp.) in Act I Scene 3 of *Belshazzar* comes from the Queen Anne Birthday Ode? You did not tell me the result of your enquiries into the Chorus of Hags in Spohr's *Zemire und Azor*. Talking of *Faust*, I was amused by the violently discrepant notices of Schumann's setting. Judging by the broadcast I should range myself between the two extremes: some of the choruses were intolerably square, but I liked the solos and most of the finale, especially the end.

'Our Italians have arrived and are a great success, though their fragmentary English is apt to yield a pair of Wellington boots instead of salt or cheese. They are exactly my idea of Figaro and Susanna, and the whole atmosphere is delightfully operatic. Frank Walker is coming down next week-end, which should make it even more so.'

Frank arrived on 11 November. He was in a strange state. He had completed his book on Verdi but had yet to perform the grinding task of compiling the index. In the summer he decided to rejoin the Royal Musical Association, asking particularly that I should second Alec King's proposal; now he had withdrawn his application. He was due to retire from the GPO in 1962 but claimed he had finished with musical scholarship, turning down work which would normally have interested him. He told us that he was selling his house in Orpington and moving to Tring in Hertfordshire, where he had agreed to purchase the house of the widow with whom he was involved. He spoke about her a good deal, showing us various letters. I felt a little anxious that he might be expecting too much; he had only met her in the summer and she did not seem to share his main interests.

In December we paid another brief visit to Fairnilee. Calfshaw was not a comfortable place at this time of year. There had been snow on the ground, and hard frost, for a week. Thalia's brother Donald came up for the day for the Fairnilee pheasant shoot. A slow thaw set in, with mist and a slight drizzle; it was slippery under foot. We ended almost in darkness. The shooting varied from the brilliant to the lamentable. We travelled South on 13 December. That morning I squeezed in a half day at Peel and Williamhope with the keeper and his cousin. We walked and drove burns, roots and stubbles. It was mild but indescribably wet, both above and below.

Two days later I was in bed at Hambledon with rheumatism and a sore throat. Dr Booker came to see me on Sunday. On Tuesday Thalia drove me to Guildford for an X-ray. I saw Miss Barton, the physiotherapist, twice during the following week. The weather was bleak, especially after Christmas, when the Thames froze at Reading. It snowed heavily all day on 31 December; I measured over 7 inches in the garden. New Year's Day marked the start of a great freeze-up – the temperature sank to 3F in London, the lowest for 95 years, while Birmingham endured its coldest night since 1888. One more trip to Scotland for the Fairnilee pheasant shoot on 2 January had to be cancelled. Instead Philip came to dinner and we embarked on Marschner's *Der Vampyr*.

Shortly before Christmas I received a letter from Phyllis Hartnoll, editor of *The Oxford Companion to the Theatre*, who was editing for Macmillans a book on Shakespeare and World Music. Would I be willing to undertake the section on opera? This was a subject that had long interested me. The deadline however was December 1962. Research would be required; I had many other commitments, principally the New Oxford History chapters, and it did not seem likely that I would be able to start work till late in 1962. Hartnoll granted me an extension to the end of March 1963, just giving time for the book to be published before April 1964, Shakespeare's 400th birthday.

* * * * *

On 4 January 1962, despite a vile cold, I went to London for Brian Trowell's Royal Musical Association paper on Handel's operas, 'Handel as a Man of the Theatre', the fruit of his experience as producer (and co-editor and translator) of *Serse* and *Imeneo* at the Barber Institute. By now the revival of Handelian opera in this country was well under way. Trowell called Handel 'one of the most under-rated figures in the history of opera'. He made many shrewd points but was reluctant to assign all heroic high male roles to women – still less to countertenors – and advised their transposition for tenor or high baritone. Catherine Wilson sang Tirinto's spectacular aria 'Sorge nell' alma mia' from *Imeneo*, in English translation, with embellishments (her part in the Barber production). Afterwards we dined at Kristof's with Nigel Fortune, Jeremy Noble, Brian and Rhianon Trowell, Peter Wishart (répétiteur for *Imeneo*), Paul Doe (leader of the orchestra), Catherine Wilson and Bob Dart.

Philip came to dinner four more times before he returned to Cambridge. We finished *Der Vampyr* and played through operas by Spontini, Cherubini and Sacchini. My rheumatism was still troubling me. Over the next weeks I made regular trips to Miss Barton in Godalming, sometimes combining these with less pleasant sessions with Mr Bynoe, the dentist. I continued to predate grey squirrels in the Hurst and behind the Village Shop. The garden was coming back to life: by late January the first snowdrops, pansies and wall-flowers were showing. But the last day of the month saw snow once more.

On 29 January I wrote to Philip: 'We are both coming to Cambridge for three or four days on or about the 27th Feb, probably staying with friends. I hoped we might come the previous week-end and so take in the Greek play as well as the opera, but it happens to be Diana's half-term and Stephen will be here on the Sunday. I gather too that Susan [Philip's sister] will be up then, and she might not appreciate a dose of Spohr and Marschner! Which night we shall go to the opera [*The Tender Land* by Aaron Copland] I don't yet know; but we are expecting you here on the 10th and we can discuss it then.

'Romantic opera is falling behind the clock owing to other events. It took me a fortnight to digest and pronounce upon the Beethoven letters [translated and edited by Emily Anderson]. In the end I got interested in them and wrote far too much. I have also written a somewhat jocose introduction to *Deidamia* and a letter to the *Listener* on the subject of Marschner, Mozart, Wagner, the raping of virgins and other kindred subjects.

'Why you should write a conventional peroration just because it pleases Dennis Arundell I don't know. Have you asked Philip Brett to make a recording of the music? If so, we shall not so much mind missing the play. [*The Clouds* by Aristophanes, produced by Dennis Arundell, with music by Philip, directed by Simon Preston.]

'At Diana McVeagh's party we met a young man who has been studying under Dallapiccola and also now under George Guest [organist and choirmaster at St John's College, Cambridge] – a juxtaposition that amused us, rather to his dismay! His name was Selkirk or Roxburgh or Peebles, I can't remember which [Edwin Roxburgh, composer, conductor and oboist].

'If you are going to Italy in April, will you give me the dates as soon as possible so that I can plan accordingly?'

I was determined that we should have a hard tennis court in the garden. I had barely played since my time at Cambridge (when Alan Turing was my tennis partner). I had recently given up cricket; the exercise would be beneficial. At the beginning of February a man appeared from a company called Fernden. We surveyed the field beyond the kitchen garden and worked out the best position. After that we would plant more trees between the tennis court and the Council houses at the end.

On 6 February we drove to London for Cherubini's *Lodoiska* at University College. This was too difficult for amateurs, and they made the mistake of placing the orchestra behind and below the stage, with the result that the most important parts of the score were often drowned and much of the performance was out of tune. Nevertheless it was possible to grasp both the great historical importance of the opera and its essential grandeur; with more lyrical invention it could stand in the repertory beside Gluck and Mozart. The most striking affinity was with Beethoven, who found here not only the model for Pizarro (in Dourlinski) and the plan and spiritual temper of *Fidelio* but the basis of his whole orchestral style.

Philip stayed the night on 10 February. We resumed our labours on Marschner, playing through *Der Templer und die Jüdin* and *Hans Heiling*. The tape recorder was misbehaving again. It worked perfectly with my own tapes but uttered periodic high-pitched screeches during those made by Alan Henderson. The first chionadoxa, lovely blue early spring flowers, were out in the little bed by the front gate. The evening Philip left I listened to Handel's *Deidamia* on the Third Programme, a dull heavy performance under Arnold Goldsbrough, who completely missed the ironical, almost cynical tone that throws Deidamia's pangs into relief. Ulysses was sung by a tenor. Some meddling fool at the BBC had tinkered with my narration, introducing a fact that was untrue, making me give an opinion I did not hold and reducing one sentence to illiterate nonsense. I sent off a furious letter of protest.

On the last day of February we travelled to London for a grand family wedding. Camilla Rumbold, a descendant of Thalia's Aunt Nan, was marrying Christopher Brett. We lunched with Anthea and Julian Jebb, Philip's artistic brother, a Kingsman, at The Boltons, and changed into our wedding garb. I had a pain and Anthea was waiting for Donald, who was at a meeting, so Thalia and her sister Jean set off for St Martin's in the Fields alone. Camilla was a cheerful, bouncing 18-year-old, in an elaborate white dress with a long, long train. Thalia thought there were far too many tiny bridal attendants, most of whom cried at one point or another; one little page boy positively *yelled*! I shared a taxi with Donald and Anthea to the reception at Claridges, where there was a vast crowd, the ladies in an assortment of outrageous dresses and hats.

We met the formidable Aunt Nan, Camilla's grandmother, whom Donald addressed in ringing tones: 'Oh there is our formidable Aunt!' However such was the babble of voices that she doubtless did not hear the adjective! Anthea looked lovely in a red suit & black curly lamb hat. We talked to other more remote family members whom one only ever encounters on these occasions. Afterwards we dined with Donald and Anthea and Jean at a little restaurant in Ebury Street called The Jabberwocky. We had an excellent meal and then Donald drove us at great speed in their little Austin 7 – Thalia, Anthea and Jean compressed in the back - to Liverpool Street Station, where we caught the train to Cambridge.

We were met by Jane Thistlethwaite after midnight and she drove us to their house at 11 Park Terrace. Frank was in Norwich, as he usually was at this time. He had been appointed the first Vice Chancellor of the University of East Anglia, not yet built or opened. He had to start from scratch, planning buildings, devising University courses, hiring staff, and so on, which he was enjoying enormously. They were looking for a house in Norwich. Next morning we rang the delightful Tess Rothschild, who as Tess Mayor had been up at Newnham with Thalia; later she married Lord Rothschild. She came round for coffee. In the afternoon Philip and I played through Spohr's *Jessonda*, the best of his operas, whose furious finales however revealed the composer as a sheep in wolf's clothing. The following morning I worked in the Pendlebury; I lunched with Thalia and Philip and returned to Philip's rooms to finish off Spohr. We dined with the Thistlethwaithes and Philip at the Arts before the opera, Aaron Copland's *The Tender Land*. The American theme seemed appropriate: Frank was a pioneer in the teaching of American history; Jane was American. This was another American folk opera, fortunately without the meretricious element of *Susannah*, but hardly a success. The naïve plot was slight; none of the characters came alive in their music. There were attractive tunes but the folky style seemed less fresh than in *Appalachian Spring*.

The next day it was snowing and horribly cold. Thalia was concerned about Stephen at school and sent him a string vest. Her sister-in-law Anthea wore one, claiming it kept out the bitter wind. We lunched with Philip and Philip Brett and then headed home.

A few days later we had a severe shock. On 6 March I received a brief letter from Frank Walker's brother (who I did not know) informing me that Frank had died suddenly the previous week, that there was to be an inquest and that his funeral would be at Tring at 2 p.m. the next day. It soon became evident that Frank had taken his own life. William Mann from *The Times* rang for help with the obituary. Thalia ordered flowers and we embarked on the long drive to Tring. There was a desolatingly small attendance at Tring Cemetery Chapel. Frank's two daughters were in Canada. We talked to his brother Alec, who told us something of the circumstances. Frank had left the proofs of *The Man Verdi* lying on his table.

On 12 March I wrote to Philip: 'Can you keep yourself as free as possible after your return [from Cambridge], and come on the evening of the 24th? I observe with horror that there are still about twelve operas which I hoped to get through before you go abroad – a situation for which Euclid had a word.

'*Alcina* [at Covent Garden, with Joan Sutherland, produced by Franco Zeffirelli] was quite immeasurably awful, the more so as the damage was wilful and the cast potentially excellent. I saw Forster there with Carlos van Hasselt, but not Philip Brett. The first sentence of Andrew Porter's notice in the *Financial Times* will make you laugh

['It would need the pen of an Addison, a Dent or a Dean to transfix the silliness of this show …']. All the reviews I have seen have been more or less unanimous, though they have varied in politeness. Will you take note of what the weeklies say and issue a report?

'The Birmingham *Moses* [Rossini] was far more rewarding, though the singers were amateurs. It contains some music worthy of Verdi and even Berlioz, together with one or two lapses into the style of the second subject of the *Semiramide* Overture, which is scarcely suitable for a row between Pharaoh & his son about the latter's marriage. I am looking forward to making a comparison between the two scores, if you can bring the French version. The Italian original, which I have here, includes some of the best pieces, but in a different order and with divers additions and subtractions.

'We also saw a Swedish opera [*The Crane Feathers*] on a Japanese subject by one Bäck, a sort of serial lollipop with a fantastic assembly of odd percussion instruments scraping, blipping and wheezing. The critics were all put next to them!'

On 20 March I went to Emily Anderson's talk on Beethoven's Operatic Plans at the Royal Musical Association. This saw the first performance in Britain of *Vestas Feuer*, the opening scene of an opera on a libretto by Schikaneder (1803). It was performed with piano accompaniment. The music was mature and characteristic; the main material of the trio was later adapted for the duet 'O namenlose Freude' in *Fidelio*. Afterwards I went with Diana Morley to St Pancras for Verdi's *I Masnadieri*, its first performance in England since the original production of 1847. This was a barnstorming melodrama with little consistent characterisation and a preposterous end. Some of the male choruses took us straight into the world of Sullivan's parodies in *The Pirates of Penzance*. Yet the thing moved; indeed it was irresistible. The animal vigour of Verdi's rhythms and melodies was so potent, his instinctive sense of what would succeed in the theatre so infallible, that the opera bounced the judgement of some grave seniors into the wildest hyperbole.

The Morleys kindly put me up for the night. The next day I took the train for Birmingham for Handel's *Tamerlano* at the Barber Institute. This was the opera's first performance in England since 1731 – and an absolute revelation. The score led me to expect some thrills, but not the overwhelming impression I received from a very fine production, easily the best of any Handel operas I had seen. Tamerlano's music, I felt, was the weakest. The part was transposed down for a baritone, transforming a mental sadist into an ineffective blusterer. But the other characters were superbly drawn, especially Bajazet and Asteria, who (as the imprisoned and oppressed) inevitably ran away with Handel's sympathy. Both had the most wonderful music throughout, predominantly in minor keys, tragic in tone, and with startling resemblances in mood and style to the sublimest moments in Bach's Passions. Most striking of all was the way the drama knitted together. Both Acts II and III end with a complex and beautifully linked sequence of movements building up to a profoundly satisfying organic whole. I was prepared for this in Act III, but the shattering effect of the last six movements in Act II took me completely by surprise. Though many pieces were shortened or reduced to their first half, very few were cut – none at all in the first two acts. Janet Baker, in the comparatively small part of Irene, was exquisite, both musically and dramatically, with firm tone, a beautiful line and a perfect stage presence. Alexander Young rose to the challenge of Bajazet's music and gave a performance that he can seldom have surpassed. Anthony Lewis's conducting was admirable in style and execution. Brian Trowell and the designer, Kerry Downes, overcame the limitations of the tiny stage most ingeniously with the aid of sliding sets and brilliant colours. I stayed two nights with Nigel and attended both performances.

At the beginning of April I received a cordial letter from Merrill Knapp, regretting that his new job at Princeton did not leave him much time for Handel. I wrote back, making a rash suggestion. Towards the end of April a second letter arrived: 'I was most interested to read the reviews of *Tamerlano* plus your own comments and delighted to know it went so well with the added effect of your getting on fire again about Handel and his dramatic gifts ... I was very flattered by your idea of possible collaboration [on a book on Handel's operas] ... I am afraid I could only be a most junior partner when it comes to writing skill, in which you far surpass me; but I might be able to supply a good deal of the basic research, which, as you know, I have gone into fairly thoroughly.'

My brother Joe was to be married at last – over a decade after Martin tied the knot with Nan and nearly 23 years after I married Thalia. On 7 April we drove London with Stephen and Diana, lunching at Ovington Mews. The Catholic wedding was held at St Etheldreda's, Ely Place, one of the very few surviving medieval churches in London. His charming bride, Jenefer Mills, worked at the BBC. She was not a Catholic. The reception was held amid the Victorian Gothic splendour of the Livery Hall, Guildhall. Our dear old nurse Haricot came back with us to Hambledon and stayed for two nights.

By 13 April the first tulip was out at Hambledon. That day a bulldozer arrived to begin work on the tennis court in the field. Because the ground was on a slight slope, soil had to be dug from the far end and built up to the South. Once the turf had been removed, however, the sandy ground proved to be unexpectedly spongy. Soon the machine got bogged down and work came to a halt.

On the last day of April I attended Philip Brett's RMA paper on English Consort Song at the Royal College of Music. Afterwards I was expecting to dine with Jeremy Noble but things did not take place as expected. To begin with, Nigel Fortune and an arch-Midlands composer named Alan Ridout missed their train to Birmingham. Then Tim Neighbour (Alec King's deputy at the British Museum) was found wandering vaguely in the street. Then we went to the Saville Club, where a treble viol in the Gent's Cloakroom revealed the presence of Bob Dart. Finally a fair quantity of good wine disappeared most congenially.

The next day I began to write my New Oxford History chapter on French opera – a fiendish job, as there was enough material for a book. Progress was sluggish and confused. At the beginning of May Philip wrote from Cambridge that Patrick Hadley had announced his retirement as Professor of Music. I replied on 8 May: 'Thank you for that startling piece of information. What is the next move? And what is the betting? The electors will have to get a move on if they are to find someone to take office in October.' Philip was half tempted to apply himself. I did not think this a good idea: 'the administrative side would drive you squiffy, and you would probably be paying repeated visits to Turkey Street'. This was a running joke. Philip once absent-mindedly boarded the wrong train from London to Cambridge, slumbered for a while, and awoke in consternation to find it stopped at a mysterious station of that name.

On 9 May the Thistlethwaites came for the night. The next day we set off for Abingdon for the Kitchings' production of *Floridante* at the Unicorn Theatre. This was its first performance anywhere since 1733, astonishing in view of the quality of the music. It was a pretty fair performance, with some enterprising vocal ornament; the castrato parts were sung at the correct pitch. Unfortunately, though Handel wrote for trumpets, horns, bassoons, oboes and recorders, we only had the last – in a single piece. The plot had more than the usual number of absurdities but Handel contrived to bring at least three of the characters to life; two episodes illustrated his astonishingly resourceful and dramatic treatment of *da capo* form. Later I wrote to Philip: 'We enjoyed *Floridante* at Abingdon, where we found ourselves sitting next to Frank Howes, looking very retired and bloogey. The Times review (rather good) was perpetrated by Stanley Sadie, who picked my brains in the interval.'

The next week I went to London for *William Tell* put on by Welsh National Opera at Sadler's Wells. The performance was exuberant but unimaginatively produced and spoiled by a painfully cliché-ridden translation. There was also a somewhat chaotic ballet. At one point one of the men picked up the wrong girl, hastily put her down, and then picked up another. At least that is what it looked like! Meanwhile my French chapter had got into a tangle and was making singularly little progress.

The following weekend my Cambridge friend Derek Clifford and his wife Anne came to stay. There was much hilarity. Derek was a lively character who had been a good poet in youth. They lived in a fine house near Sittingbourne. Derek was proprietor of a nursery specialising in geraniums and had written two scholarly books on the subject, one of which I promised to study. I afflicted them with a little Handel. We were looking for a boarding school for Diana, who was now seven. Anne recommended Leelands at Walmer, run by two redoubtable ladies, Miss Belshaw and Miss Taylor. Unfortunately it was a long drive from Hambledon.

On 26 May I wrote to Philip: 'Glad to hear your pupils are winning scholarships for jazz. It is wonderful what a little syncopation and Delius will do.

'I don't think Robin [Orr] would be a suitable professor, much as I like him. Let me know when there are any developments. I mentioned Paddy's retirement in a letter to Brian Trowell, which apparently caused great gloom in the Birmingham faculty.

Presumably they are afraid of losing Tony, but since he has just bought a house in Birmingham he may not apply.

'No news here. I have produced thousands of words on Grétry, Cherubini, etc. but the scale is all wrong and the thing will have to be done again. When you come down, can you bring *Maometto Secondo* from the Pendlebury and *The Siege of Corinth* from the University Library or the Union?

'The [Raymond] Leppard has perpetrated a most slovenly & tendentious article on the *Coronation of Poppea* in the Glyndebourne programme – but for goodness sake don't tell him I said so! He appears to have edited the music, and I rather fear for the result.'

Late May was unusually cold. On the last day of the month the two may trees outside my study, one pink, one white, were coming into flower. That night 11° of frost were recorded in the Midlands! On 1 June I travelled to London for *Euryanthe* at St Pancras Town Hall. Weber's opera has always been renowned for the superb and prophetic quality of the music – it was not only the model for *Lohengrin* but contains the seeds of even riper Wagner – and the feeble inconsequence of the libretto. Those who revive it can seldom resist the temptation to produce a new version. This one by Franz Manton of the Philopera Circle as usual made things worse rather than better. Euryanthe was represented as Adolar's wife – a psychological blunder – and Emma's ring replaced by a goblet. Lysiart was played as a grimacing hunchback, a compound of Richard III, Hagen, Claggart and Dick Deadeye, instead of a plausible candidate for Euryanthe's hand. The opera needed heroic voices and a steady tone over the whole compass. If the cast did not always achieve this, they made a creditable attempt.

The weather improved in early June, the temperature rising into the 70s. June 6 was the first day without a fire in my study. There was still no news about the Professorship. Anthony Lewis was in Cambridge for Part I of the Tripos. 'I should be interested to hear if you extracted any oracular pronouncements from Tony Lewis', I wrote to Philip on 9 June. 'I don't see why he should be dictatorial as Professor – he never gives that impression, nor is it the opinion of the Birmingham staff. What you do need after Paddy is a capable scholar and administrator. Bob I can see might annoy some people, but he would produce plenty of drive.

'Did you hear the new works from Coventry? Everyone seems agreed that the Bliss is poor (a mixture of Hereford and Hollywood is one description) and the Britten Requiem a major masterpiece. I missed the former by mistake, but was completely bowled over by the latter. The Tippett [*King Priam*] seems to have split opinion down the middle. We heard the broadcast and saw the first performance at Covent Garden, and I must say I was profoundly disappointed by the opera itself, though the production and performance were magnificent. There are beautiful moments of course, many of them very Brittenesque, but the style is much scrappier than in *The Midsummer Marriage* and the drama, while superficially less impenetrable, is no more convincing. Indeed it seems to make less sense the more one looks into it ...

'You seem to be having a little melodrama in College in the authentic revolutionary manner. I suggest you wear a crash helmet in bed, in case some poor wretch whom you failed in the Tripos decides to avenge his honour.'

Thalia was hoping to find a student to help with Diana at Calfshaw in August, ideally one who could drive and cook. Since the cottage only had three small bedrooms, additional accommodation would be needed. In June Thalia and Stephen went to inspect a caravan offered for sale by a Mr Skidmore, a weaselly man with a shifty manner. The long blue caravan seemed to be constructed largely of wood.

Mr Skidmore volunteered to drive it over to Hambledon, where it sat lopsidedly on the drive outside the kitchen. Bert and Stephen attempted to deploy its legs, without success. Later Lillo and Thalia got two of the flimsy legs down, reinforced with a large log. Mr Skidmore had promised wooden blocks but they failed to appear. Nigel kindly offered to assist in finding a student, putting up a notice advertising our requirements in the Birmingham music department. Later in the month he wrote: 'Only one of our female students is free and / or willing to go and attend upon you in Scotland. She is a somewhat vague and naïve girl … I don't know anything about her as a Domestic. She *might* be careless or absent-minded. She never writes an exercise without leaving out at least one accidental: I don't know if this means that there would always be a spoon or a plate or salt-cellar lacking from your table …' If she failed her exams she would of course not be available.

We stayed in London for the Handel Opera Society week in the middle of July. I reported to Philip on the 28th: 'We went to two performances of *Jephtha*. The first was very bad indeed, the second rather better but still patchy in my opinion. A lot of things irritated me – the cadenzas, the organ in 'Waft her angels' and even in a recitative, several of the tempi (too fast), the cutting of the 12/8 Symphony. I am afraid Charles Farncombe's conducting is getting worse rather than better. I was fitfully moved by the music, but not bowled over as I should have been. What was your opinion? *Radamisto* also misfired, despite one or two improvements over the 1960 cast. They cut three of the finest arias that were sung then, and inserted one that seemed to me much less interesting.

'We were both completely carried away by *Poppea* [at Glyndebourne], a splendid performance both musically and visually. I heard it again on the following Sunday and took a tape. I thought the Leppard did his stuff very well; indeed his realisation was much better than his defence of it in the programme. After this we visited Diana's future prep school [Leelands] and spent a hilarious day with the Cliffords, who have a very beautiful Georgian house.'

Towards the end of July Sheila Miller arrived to help with Diana. She was a brisk, sensible girl (not the Birmingham student suggested by Nigel). Alan Henderson had agreed to drive the caravan to Scotland. This involved collecting the Land Rover from Fairnilee, fitting it with a towing bar and driving South. He appeared with it on 4 August. The next day Denis and Sheila Stevens came to lunch. Stevens, who had worked as a BBC music producer and took on the task of completing the Supplementary Volume of *Grove's Dictionary* after Eric Blom's death, could raise hackles; there had been rows with Jack Westrup and others. However I always got on with him perfectly amicably. Sheila was the first of his three wives. The next day, August Bank Holiday, was very wet and rather cold. My mother and her brother Harry came to lunch. On 7 August Alan set off cheerfully for Calfshaw. He had a difficult journey; half way up the A1 the caravan lost a wheel. On the same day, men from Fernden reappeared and work resumed on the tennis court.

On 9 August I wrote to Philip: 'I am a little doubtful where you are at the moment, but hope to catch you passing through Turkey Street. We go to Scotland tomorrow night, and I am ready for it, having quite flattened myself out trying to finish the first draft of my French chapter. I merely got it into a fearful muddle and had to stop and relapse into a blooge.

'After various alarums and excursions Diana had her tonsils out last week, which we hope will put an end to her continued temperatures and sore throats. She has taken to writing voluble letters to everyone, including the cats, without regard to orthography. One of them from the nursing home contained the memorable sentence: "Ples tak me hom I hat this bludy plac".

'In the confusion caused by this I forgot to listen to the Berkeley violin pieces. Last night I heard Stravinsky's *Agon*, which seemed to me an incoherent mixture of styles – spirited rhythms and sonorities interspersed with lavatory noises.

'Had you been here last Sunday you would have seen the quaint spectacle of Mr and Mrs Denis Stevens picking raspberries and in the manner of the Ancient Mariner eating one of three. The Abrahams were supposed to come to lunch on Tuesday, but owing to some administrative muddle failed to turn up.'

The day before we left for Scotland, to improve Stephen's marksmanship, I accompanied him to a shooting school at Shalford. I shot first and to my annoyance failed to make contact with a number of the clays; Stephen on the other hand hit several. The machine was supposedly set up to mimic driven grouse, which speed up in flight; clays slow down. I was aiming ahead of the target each time. Next day we caught the train to London. I took the opportunity to visit Thomas Heinitz in Queensway about acquiring a new gramophone and amplifier, with matching speakers, to work with my FM radio. Diana travelled with Sheila four days later.

At Calfshaw, we found the caravan parked on a flattish piece of ground above the cottage. That afternoon I had a long confabulation with Peter Dods by the rearing pens in Calfshaw Wood. I was a rather more enthusiastic about striding the moor than Thalia's brother Donald and so this year he agreed to let the Peel shooting to me. In addition, he expected to be away in the States sailing his 12-Metre yacht Norsaga in trials for the America's Cup. The first shoot was on 14 August, a walking day, with keepers but no beaters. Apart from Donald and myself, the team was entirely naval or military, comprising an Admiral, a naval Captain, a Commander, two Colonels and a Major. The birds were patchy – the heather on South and Middle Hills had been badly frosted in the spring – but the shooting was mostly on target. A vast party came up for lunch on the moor.

Two days later there was a boys' shoot, with Donald, at Fairnilee. It was a sunny day with showers and a stiff westerly wind. There was a splendid show of birds, despite the wrong wind. Stephen shot his first grouse and hare. However he found the steep and uneven going on Neidpath hard. From here, I am afraid, his enthusiasm for shooting waned. Donald and the boys, including Johnnie Loch and Ian Lowis, came to tea at Calfshaw.

There were operas I wished to see at the Edinburgh Festival, two on successive evenings, so towards the end of August we booked a room at the George Hotel. *The Love of Three Oranges* was the first staging in Britain of Prokofiev's opera. Unfortunately it was sung in Serbo-Croat, which made the words and the cross-talk on which the satire depends inaccessible. An indifferent production and wobbly singing did not help. The work had a certain brittle vitality. Next day we lunched with Tony and Lesley Lewis at the George. Massenet's *Don Quixote* was another second-rate opera, redeemed by great professional skill, a sense of theatre and deft orchestration. Four days later we were in Edinburgh once more for Prokofiev's *The Gambler*, based on Dostoyevsky's novel. It was one of the dullest evenings I have ever endured in the theatre. We ate a picnic supper in the car afterwards, then retreated to Calfshaw.

We had several other outings on Peel Moor, not all of them successful. The shoot on 3 September fielded an impressive team, led by Admiral Sir Conolly Abel Smith and General Sir Philip Christison. It was a miserable day. We gave up after one drive in thick mist – the beaters lost, the guns unable to fire – whereupon it promptly cleared. The bag was two grouse. Most of the team reassembled three days later, when the weather was again foul. Amateur beaters, of both sexes, had to be employed. The mist

Romantic Opera

reduced the morning drives to two and an east wind made the birds uncontrollable but more were seen than before. The bag of 52 grouse was not bad in the circumstances. Sometimes one of the Land Rovers was taken up on to the moor, but there were hazards. On one occasion the Admiral drove his elderly vehicle into a bog and got stuck. Inevitably he was ribbed for 'poor navigation'!

Towards the end of our stay I arranged another small shoot for Stephen. Together with Wattie Dods we walked Heather Flat and Neidpath. It was a grey, drizzling day. The drives were not successful and the birds impossibly wild. We drove them nicely over the dyke to Stephen – who after a long wait in the rain had deserted and gone home!

We arrived back at Hambledon on 16 September. The next day there was snow in Surrey! Stephen and Diana returned to school. Philip came to dinner and we played through Rossini's *La Gazza Ladra* and part of *Semiramide*. Diana continued on her tempestuous way at St Hilary's. She found school very trying and got over-excited, according to her teacher, who however she liked. We hoped she would settle down soon. On Sunday Mrs Manley's daughter Jacqueline brought her fiancé to see us. We thought him cocksure and aggressive. The marriage did not last.

On 1 October I went with Philip to Berg's *Lulu* at Sadler's Wells. This was its first British performance, and a very good one by the Hamburg Opera. Slides were projected on a screen between the two scenes of Act II and again to supply the missing part of Act III. An odd feature of the production was the constant ringing of door-bells, etc., possibly intended to make an obsessive effect. I stayed the night with Diana and Bill Morley. We set off for Scotland the next day but for once we did not take the sleeper from St Pancras. Thalia travelled up from Witley with most of the luggage (after taking Diana to the doctor) and we met at Euston. We caught the 'Mid-day Scot' and had an excellent lunch (third sitting) at 3.30. We changed at Carlisle. There were wearying delays. It was not until 11 p.m. that we reached a dark and chilly Calfshaw, where we supped on scrambled eggs.

Towards the middle of October there was a mishap with the generator, which had to be tended daily. Thalia went to the shed and topped up the sump with engine oil. She was careful to replace the cap on the red can but neglected to screw back that on the engine. We ran the machine that evening and again next day till 10.30 a.m. – it was a dark morning. When I went to refill the diesel I found an indescribable mess – *everything* coated in oil. We were lucky the engine did not seize. We used copious newspapers to clean it up and then had a terrific bonfire in the garden.

Thalia had bought a ciné camera, a Kodak 'Automatic' with a built-in light meter. It took colour film. The first wonderfully evocative footage was of harvesting in the field by Calfshaw. Later in the month there were brief glimpses of shoots at Rink and Peel.

Thalia made enquiries about installing mains electricity. 'It would be wonderful not to have to worry about the engine, wouldn't it!' she said wistfully. A man from the Electricity Board came to investigate. There were difficulties. A long run of poles would be needed to carry the line up the hill from East Lodge, with a transformer at the cottage. No doubt it would be expensive. In the end we let the matter drop. After we left the cottage in 1964 our friends Rachel and John Gee installed back-up gas lighting. Many years later an underground cable was laid at minimum expense.

We returned to Hambledon on 29 October. While at Calfshaw I had been reading a proof copy, without index, of Frank Walker's *The Man Verdi*. Now I set down to review it at length for *Musical Times*. It was a very fine book, not a conventional biography but a series of oblique but minutely detailed impressions of Verdi's life, each treated from a specific angle involving his relationship with one or more individuals, such as his second wife Giuseppina Strepponi and the conductor Mariani. Walker had a genius for uncovering new information; he possessed a mind clear of fog and prejudice, constantly able to draw fresh conclusions from old facts, and an imperturbable sense of proportion. The book destroyed for ever the sentimentalised Verdi of legend. He emerged as hard, suspicious and vindictive, a man who never forgot and seldom forgave an injury, even a fancied one. Walker began his eighth chapter with admirable reflections on the biographer's task, on the credibility of eyewitnesses and the endless possibilities of self-deception and unwitting misrepresentation. His tragic death removed one of the most talented of musical scholars.

In the middle of November I resumed work on the Oxford History chapters. Mr Heinitz came to install the bulky new stereo gramophone and speakers. Work was progressing slowly on the tennis court with the digging of an elaborate system of drains. We had decided to cut down the fir trees that formed a not very adequate screen on the West side of the field and hoped to sell the timber to offset the cost.

Philip wrote from Cambridge on 16 November that the lot had fallen on Bob Dart as Professor of Music. Philip had mixed feelings about this. I replied: 'I feel quite satisfied by the election of Bob, who would have been one of two candidates. How soon does he take over? I don't really see why you should be worried, since your presence is obviously necessary to balance the Faculty, and a musicologist was needed to succeed Paddy. What has Raymond Leppard got against Bob? The idea of you acting as an Advocatus Diaboli is a comic thought. It would certainly be pleasant if Philip Brett occupied the vacancy – and I imagine Bob would be all in favour of this – but how soon will the appointment be made? Will he be able to have his full year in America?

'Why cannot those scores be taken out of the University Library? Is there a new regulation? I shall not be able to visit Cambridge this term, but it looks as if an expedition will be necessary in the spring. At the moment I am resuming my struggles with Le Sueur and Spontini, which got into such a tangle during the summer, and I am not very hopeful of quick results …

'Diana has been to see her future boarding school (at Walmer) and is positively thrilled by the prospect – much to our surprise.' [She soon changed her mind!]

Philip replied on 20 November that he now felt far happier about the Professorship. Raymond Leppard's objections to Bob seemed to be personal rather than musical: 'his rather pompous manner, which is regarded with friendly amusement by the undergraduates & by middle-aged birds like you & me, undoubtedly gets on the nerves of his slightly junior colleagues.'

I had been asked to take part in the BBC Music Quiz, always broadcast on the Third Programme on Christmas Day. We were due to travel to Scotland once more. I arranged to meet the producer, Robert Layton, at Broadcasting House on the afternoon of 5 December. My fellow guests for the recording were George Harewood and Martin Cooper, both of whom I knew well. Afterwards I had a drink with Roger Fiske, the question-master. We caught the train from St Pancras that evening. The weather was appallingly cold. Instead of going to Calfshaw, we had been invited to stay at Bowland, a grand mansion a few miles north of Fairnilee, by Alan Ramsay and his American wife Frances. Alan, the laird of the large estate, was an able man, a kinsman of Lord Beaverbrook, but rather too fond of the bottle. The train reached Galashiels two hours late.

I was looking forward to the Fairnilee pheasant shoot on Saturday but after a hurricane in the night and teeming rain next morning it was cancelled, much to my disgust. The guns had already assembled and most stayed for lunch at Fairnilee. Afterwards I drove back to Bowland with Alan. The shoot was rearranged for Monday, when the weather was kinder. Not for the first or last time, the greenhouses became a casualty. We were spoiled at Bowland – breakfast was delivered to us in bed – but the social whirl was rather a strain: Saturday night's dinner party ended at 1 a.m. and next day guests were invited for lunch, tea, drinks and a larger party in the evening. We had looked in at Calfshaw on our first day: everything was terribly damp. Thalia discovered three mice in traps and signs of their activity elsewhere, including the kitchen. Later she went over to light the fire to air cushions and curtains before putting them away in drawers. We returned South on 12 December, another bitterly cold and snowy day.

At this point I had to put aside romantic opera. A year earlier, Phyllis Hartnoll asked me to contribute a long essay on operas based on Shakespeare's plays. The deadline was the end of March 1963. I had made a rough list of 125 operas, of which I had some acquaintance with about twenty. Many of the others were very obscure, and a number no doubt unpublished. Research could yield interesting results, especially in the treatment of librettos at different periods, though it might not unearth a great deal of musical significance. Again, Philip was able to bring down scores from Cambridge, and I obtained others from the BBC Music Library. Philip came to dinner on 20 December and we embarked on Smetana's unfinished *Viola* and Goldmark's *Wintermärchen*, the work of his old age and as over-ripe as a fallen peach.

Next day I disposed of three squirrels and a jay in the Hurst. On Saturday Jim Martin, the amiable General who lived at Great Meadow bordering the Common, invited me to a shoot at Shillinglee just over the Sussex border. The eight guns included a Brigadier and an Indian Prince. It was a fine frosty day, beginning and ending in fog. There were beautiful coverts but few birds, many foxes and an insufficiency of beaters. We saw a roe deer and a kingfisher but few genuine targets. Jim severed the telephone communications with Plaistow.

It was intensely cold over Christmas. At 6.50 p.m. on Christmas Day we sat down to listen to the Music Quiz on the Third Programme. It was considerably shortened. I was a little miffed that some of my correct answers had been cut. My brother Martin and family came to lunch on Boxing Day, together with Basil and my mother, and Sheila Miller arrived to help with Diana. Towards evening it started to snow. I watched the slow flakes falling into the orchard from my study window, little suspecting that we would not see green grass again for two and a half months. The following day the snow came heavily and lay thick. Philip was due to come to dinner but cried off. He made it to dinner on 29 December, when we tackled Malipiero's *Giulio Cesare* – which suggested a cross between Vaughan Williams and later Puccini – and started Blacher's *Romeo and Juliet*. On the 30th there was a blizzard and more snow – I measured at least eleven inches outside my study. A visit by my sister Tessa and family was cancelled. Philip dined with us again on New Year's Eve; we finished *Romeo and Juliet* and embarked on Malipiero's *Anthony and Cleopatra*. When the time came for him to leave it was snowing heavily once more and he was stranded. Thalia lent him a pair of my pyjamas and a face flannel and put him up in the spare room. So it was that Philip stayed the night at Hambledon and returned home to Godalming the following year!

CHAPTER 19

Shakespeare and Opera

On New Year's Day we awoke to more snowfalls. I measured 14 inches in the garden. This was the heaviest snow in Southern England since 1881 (I noted in my diary). A few days earlier Phillips Garage fitted chains to the tyres of the car to help it negotiate the treacherous roads. Next morning Bert and Ernie were busy clearing the drive. Thalia drove me to Guildford, where I caught the train to London; I had much work to do at the B.M. on Shakespeare operas. Later I looked in at the BBC to drop off borrowed scores. In the evening I attended Denis Arnold's RMA paper on Venetian Conservatories at Trinity College. Gerald Abraham was in the chair. He had struggled up that morning from Brighstone on the Isle of Wight, where the snowdrifts were hedge-high, leaving Pat and their daughter Frances without coal or wood.

Philip and I played through more Shakespeare operas. I was impressed by Ernest Bloch's *Macbeth*, where a leitmotif system is employed with great skill and subtlety to illuminate the drama. Wagner's early *Das Liebesverbot*, based on *Measure for Measure*, was full of French and Italian tricks and ornaments and did all the things he was later to denounce with particular fury in other people's operas. Further snow fell, followed by partial thaws. Then there was another freeze-up; 38º of frost (-21 C) was reported in Scotland; the sea froze near Ramsgate, and later at Herne Bay (for the first time since

1947) and the Thames iced over at Kingston. Every morning we woke in the icy bedroom and looked out at the bleak scene, rubbing frost-ferns from the window-panes. Stephen was not unhappy when the start of his term at Seaford College was postponed by a week.

Philip left for Cambridge on January 14, when there was a slight thaw; two days later more snow fell and the temperature plummeted again. I took the train to London and did another stint at the B.M. Thalia joined me at Lyons Corner House. Afterwards we went to Sadler's Wells for Weill's *The Rise and Fall of the City of Mahagonny*, its first performance in Britain. This struck me as a minor opera by a composer of small but curiously individual talent. I found it amusing for one act but then became progressively bored, partly by Brecht's cheap and tiresome libretto, a sort of Communist journalese, partly by the limitations of the musical idiom.

It was colder than ever. Thalia took Diana and her friend Nicola Baldry to the frozen water meadows at Shalford, where they slid around on sledges. The Thames froze at Windsor. I trudged out in the snow with my gun and bagged a pigeon by the gate and a magpie in the Hurst. My last shoot of the season was at Oxenford Grange near Elstead. The snow lay thick on the ground and an icy north wind blasted our faces. The temperature never rose above 10F. Understandably the pheasants would not get up. In the afternoon we attacked pigeons on a kale field. I shot the only pheasant but we could not pick it. Three red deer were seen bounding away in the distance. The day ended in another heavy snowstorm.

Our French friends Michel and Madeleine Poupet came to stay for the weekend. Michel was a Bizet fanatic and (unusual for a Frenchman) determined to uncover the truth about the composer, not to perpetuate myths. He worked in a government job in Paris but was on secondment to the French Embassy in London. Michel was a nice man, with pretty good English, but exceedingly garrulous. He wrote me voluminous letters concerning Bizet in a large untidy hand. That Sunday icebergs in the Channel kept the ferries in port. The night of 22-23 January was the coldest yet. I retired to bed with flu.

Three days later a slow thaw began. I took the train to London and worked in the B.M. After depositing me at Guildford Station, Thalia visited Roy and Una Hawkswell, whose car was still frozen up. They were short of fuel. Thalia volunteered to transport coal, if needed, in the boot of the Morris Oxford. She joined me later for Brigid and Lorimer's Silver Wedding party at Marloes Road, Kensington. We stayed two nights at the English Speaking Union, in comfort but at considerable expense. While we were away, Alice Jeffery looked after Diana and put her to bed. Next day we had a drink with Edmund Tracey, Peter Heyworth's number two on *The Observer* and music editor of the *Times Educational Supplement*. I returned his records of Zandonai's *verismo Romeo and Juliet*. We lunched with Joe and Jenny at their tiny flat in The Temple – up four flights of stone stairs. Joe had installed additional shelves, altered mantelpieces and made other impressive home improvements. That evening we went to a party given by Arthur Jacobs and his wife in North London. Arthur, deputy editor of *Opera*, was a good linguist and a prolific translator of opera librettos. In November, at his request, I had read a bulky typescript of opera synopses he had produced in collaboration with Stanley Sadie. It was a convivial party. We drank warm punch. I came away with a vocal score and a Russian recording of Shebalin's *The Taming of the Shrew*.

Over the next days there was more snow. Thalia investigated the little wooden fruit shed. Most of the apples were frosted to the core. A few, though wizened, still seemed good. Ernie was set to work sorting them out. He said he had never known the frost do so much damage. Diana was away from school with a cold; she played *HMS Pinafore* on a gramophone interminably. I still had a large number of Shakespeare operas to tackle and persuaded Philip to come down from Cambridge; he stayed a night over the weekend. The day he arrived there was another heavy snowstorm. We worked hard, playing through Orff's *Sommernachtstraum* and Reynaldo Hahn's and Adrian Beecham's diverse versions of *The Merchant of Venice*. Beecham's opera suggested a cross between *Trial by Jury* and Edwardian balladry, with some grotesque word-setting, inconsequent harmony and a total inability to construct ensembles.

I laboured in the B.M. all day the following Wednesday. Thalia drove me to Witley Station in a blizzard. We met in the evening and went to Verdi's *I due Foscari* at University College. It was a pretty fair amateur performance, though the producer did not help by using a combination of modern dress, cloaks and spears. The libretto was all but incomprehensible without prior study but the emotional predicament of the three leading characters obviously fired Verdi's imagination. The male choruses, though crude, had an undeniable dramatic potency.

I kept to my bed for the next two days with a sore throat. For a short time it was markedly warmer. On Sunday, however, when Stephen and John Sargeant came for the day on exeat from Seaford College, there was yet another blizzard. I was getting very tired of looking out at whiteness. Luckily I had a blazing fire in my study, which Bert Jeffery kept supplied the coal and logs. Elsewhere in the house the inadequate central heating was supplemented by gas fires and paraffin stoves. On Thursday it snowed hard all day. Diana had returned to school but had picked up the latest St Hilary's bug and was in bed with a throat infection, tended by Thalia and Alice Jeffery. The day before had been sunny. Men came to remove the spruce trees on the west side of the field. We had hoped to sell the timber but had received no offers. Instead of being felled the trees were toppled by a bulldozer and then burnt – in the face of furious expostulations about the smoke from Councillor Main next door. The tennis court was still not finished. The contractors promised to send a detailed estimate for a retaining wall and an elaborate system of drains under the court.

Philip came down from Cambridge for a second weekend. We played through the *Romeo and Juliet* operas of Georg Benda, J.E. Barkworth and Harry R. Shelley. Gotter's libretto for Benda belonged to the *Sturm und Drang* school, half realistic and half sentimental, with far too much spoken dialogue, some of it concerned with superfluities such as Juliet's Aunt Camilla. Shelley was an American organist, the composer of innumerable sentimental and religious ballads. His opera suggested a mixture of Gounod, Barnby and Johann Strauss, with occasional whiffs of Wagner. Philip left on Sunday afternoon and I retired to bed with a temperature and a nasty cough. I stayed there for much of the week. Lillo also was taken ill but after two days appeared downstairs again as bouncy as ever. There was more snow. Diana was still unwell and recovering rather slowly. Thalia moved her from her little bedroom to the nursery. She had been prescribed penicillin, dosed every six hours by Thalia, who had to wake her at 5 a.m. Luckily she took the sugar-coated pills like an angel and was soon asleep again.

I listened to a sound but rather plodding performance of Handel's *Orlando* under Goldsbrough on the Third Programme. It had an admirable cast. Janet Baker sang Orlando's music with superb control of line and expression. Heather Harper, as the shepherdess Dorinda, was scarcely less outstanding. I was again impressed by the manifold riches of the score, but at this stage quite failed to understand the libretto, which I damned in my review in *Opera*. The *scena* at the end of Act II, suggesting Gluck in its evocation of Cerberus, Purcell in its use of ground base, and even Weber in some of its romantic flights of harmony, was surely the greatest of all operatic mad scenes.

Tragically, Alice Jeffery, Ernie's wife, who until a few days earlier had been helping to care for Diana, seemed to have picked up her infection, which developed into pneumonia. She grew progressively worse and on Wednesday 19 February was taken to hospital at Hydestile, where she died two days later, aged only 53. We all attended her funeral at Hambledon Church. (Stephen had come home to recuperate after an outbreak of flu at Seaford College.) It was Ash Wednesday and the churchyard was still covered in snow.

On 28 February I paid another working trip to Cambridge, lodging at Kings. On the first evening I dined with Philip at the Arts and called on Bob Dart in Jesus. Over the next three days I studied a number of very obscure and dim Shakespeare operas in the Rowe Library and the Fitzwilliam Museum, playing through some of them with Philip in his rooms. There was a good deal of unintended humour to be found in the librettos. Edmond Audran's *Gillette de Narbonne*, based remotely on *All's Well that Ends Well*, consisted almost entirely of waltzes and polkas in the manner of Offenbach. The character corresponding to Shakespeare's Diana, that virtuous Florentine, became a promiscuous gipsy who declared that a man had only to whisper the word 'Turlututu' in her ear for her virtue instantly to collapse.

Sunday 3 March was bitterly cold. Thalia reported that the first snowdrops were showing through the snow at Hambledon. That evening I dined in Hall with Noel Annan (Provost of King's), Dadie Rylands and E.M. Forster. On Monday I worked in the Pendlebury, travelling home by train in the afternoon. A real thaw had begun at last. Aconites and crocuses were springing up in the garden. On 7 March the garden was clear of snow for the first time since Christmas. I kept to my bed for three days with a heavy cold, then ventured downstairs in my dressing gown, sitting in the music room with a rug wrapped round my lower half. According to Thalia, I only wanted a nightcap to resemble an illustration from a Dickens novel.

In the middle of March I spent another week in London, staying at the English Speaking Union. Sheila Miller had come to us again, enabling Thalia to join me later in the week. I worked solidly on Shakespeare operas in the B.M. for six days. Philip, back in Godalming, came to assist me on two days – just as he had helped me in Paris with my Bizet researches sixteen years earlier. On the first evening I dined with John and Catkin Warrack. John was music critic for the *Sunday Telegraph*. Afterwards we went round to see the composer Joseph Horovitz – an old friend of John's - who played through his edition of Cherubini's one-act opera *Pimmalione*, upon which he had laboured for two years. It was an old-fashioned work, written to please Napoleon, with a castrato hero. The next evening I was at St Pancras Town Hall for Rossini's *La Pietrà del Paragone* (1812), its English première. This made good entertainment but sounded like a preliminary shot at its superior successors, notably *L'Italiana in Algeri* and *Il Turco in Italia*. Music and libretto often suggested the latter, which had the same intricate sort of plot and similar jokes about Turks and poets. Thalia drove up in the car, which however was misbehaving once more – a slight petrol leak – and she had to seek the assistance of a garage. Philip and I were at the B.M. again on 26 March. In the evening I had dinner with Alec and Eve King at Rudall Crescent. Here I met two distinguished American music librarians and their spouses – D.W. Krummel, lately of the Library of Congress, and Vincent Duckles, from the University of California at Berkeley. Would I be interested in coming to Berkeley, he wondered?

Thalia was in contact with Mr Coombs of Jackman's Nursery about replanting the strip alongside the tennis court following the demolition of the spruce trees. Instead of Thuja (Western

Red Cedar), recommended by Mary Parker at Feathercombe, Mr Coombs suggested Lawson's cypress as easier to transplant. It would be quick-growing and provide a satisfactory screen. This proved to be bad advice. In front we planned groups of shrubs and a few small trees. At the far end of the field he advised a laurel hedge – Thalia couldn't bear cypresses on two sides of the garden. Work on the tennis court had been suspended for the winter. It was by no means finished. Thalia attempted to rouse the contractors from their hibernation.

A few Shakespeare operas remained. I had missed the deadline of 31 March. On 8 April Philip came to stay. He was put to work at once, playing through Fibich's Wagnerian *Tempest*, Charles Silver's amiably insipid setting of *The Taming of the Shrew* and the 1847 version of Verdi's *Macbeth*. Next day we tackled Winfried Zillig's *Troilus und Cressida* (1951), the only opera I could discover on that play. An opera on *The Tempest* by the English composer A.M. Hale was chaotic in style and remarkable for some extraordinary aberrations of language. Stephano says of Caliban 'He's still in a funk' – apparently to supply a rhyme for 'drunk'. Stanford's *Much Ado About Nothing*, though thoroughly competent, seemed pedestrian after Berlioz's sparkling *Béatrice et Bénédict*. I was impressed by Holst's one-act *At the Boar's Head*, on his own clever libretto based on the tavern scenes in both parts of *Henry IV*. The music, 'founded on old English melodies', was ingenious and something more. Few composers have come closer than Holst to matching the authentic bite of Shakespeare's language. Ambroise Thomas's *Hamlet*, a compound of the impressive and the deplorable, was written for the Swedish soprano Christine Nilsson, hence the expansion of Ophelia's part beyond the demands of the drama. After three days' hard labour, Philip departed for Cambridge.

Easter Saturday found me cutting back gorse on the Common. Next day Martin and Nan and family drove down from Sutton for lunch and tea. Alan Henderson arrived in a green sports car, accompanied by a charming striped kitten named Bosch. Susie tolerated him, except when he tried to share her saucer of milk. Two days later I began work on the final version of my Shakespeare chapter. In the same week I heard the first cuckoo (18 April). We filmed Alan and Bosch departing in the sports car. He left twice, for the benefit of the camera. At long last, work resumed on the tennis court. The following week, the new trees and hedging plants arrived.

On 5 May Thalia went to London to meet the Swiss au pair at Victoria Coach Station. Rosemarie was German-speaking but apparently knew French too. She was very shy and at first hardly uttered a word in any language, despite Thalia's attempts to converse with her in French. It was all rather a strain. Next day I filmed her on the swing under the blossoming cherry tree. Thalia consulted Jackmans about the cypress plants, which were going brown at the tips. They should be sprayed in the evenings, we were advised, despite the wet weather. A new hose and extension were bought for this purpose. Lillo had acquired a motor scooter, but not a licence or insurance. He set off illicitly down Vann Lane – where he was unlikely to encounter the Surrey Police – with brave Gina riding pillion.

On 10 May Gerald and Pat Abraham arrived for the weekend. The wisteria, wreathing above the Music Room window, had burst into flower and looked wonderful. That morning I had another painful appointment with Mr Bynoe, who stopped several teeth. The Abrahams were house hunting. Gerald had a new job at the BBC; they were anxious to find somewhere nearer London than the Isle of Wight. Gerry observed in his diary: 'Thalia met us at the station. Nice dinner and talk but very late to bed. This morning Diana was much in evidence: very pretty and vivacious, now eight. Winton's mother came to lunch; we liked her very much – very entertaining, too. Afterwards Thalia drove her home and then took us to see The Farmhouse, Enton, which proved another disappointment.' After tea I led Gerry and Pat to the top of the Common, with wonderful views over the wooded Weald to the South Downs (with Chanctonbury Ring easily recognisable). Then Thalia joined us and we strolled back, and round the garden, where the lilacs were coming out beyond the bowling green. In the evening I played the tape of the Birmingham *Tamerlano*, recorded in the theatre (the BBC declined to broadcast it). Gerry, who knew Russian, took me through the vocal score of Shebalin's *The Taming of the Shrew*, explaining the action. We finished it next morning. After lunch we chatted and slumbered and later went for a walk round the lanes. We had supper in the Music Room, listening to Prokofiev's *The Duenna* on the Third Programme, but the Abrahams had to depart for the station after the first act. Towards the end of June they found the Old Schoolhouse in the remote Sussex hamlet of Ebernoe, a few miles down the Petworth road.

Summer arrived with a sudden heat-wave. The temperature rose to 82F on the last day of May, the hottest since September. Basil came to tea and dinner on Whit Sunday. We relaxed outside in the sun, Basil in benign mood. Diana pranced around the lawn. The first rose was out; behind us, the pink honeysuckle on the veranda was in exuberant flower. On 7 June I finished a draft of my Shakespeare essay – after anxious inquiries from Phyllis Hartnoll a couple of days earlier. Derek and Anne Clifford came for the weekend. Derek had recently brought out another book, *A History of Garden Design*. The weather was gloriously hot. We played rudimentary tennis on the lawn (the tennis court was still not finished), all the males shirtless. Diana pursued Rosemarie with a hose-pipe.

I had been receiving feelers from California. At the beginning of June a letter arrived from David Boyden. He was staying in Oxford, struggling to finish a book on the history of violins and violin playing. He wrote: 'I have just received a letter from Joseph Kerman with the splendid news that you are interested in coming to Berkeley. I am glad, but not surprised, to learn that the Music Department (which I headed for six years prior to Dr Kerman's tenure) had the good sense to invite you to hold the Bloch Professorship.

'Naturally, you will have a number of questions about Berkeley before you embark on what is a long trip and considerable undertaking … and I should be glad to come to you at Godalming, and try to tell you about Berkeley and how we work in the Music Department.'

Boyden and his wife Ruth appeared for tea and dinner on 11 June. The Ernest Bloch Professorship had been established to bring distinguished figures in music to Berkeley, where Bloch taught from 1940 until his death in 1959. I would be the second holder of the post. The duties involved teaching graduate students for two semesters and delivering a series of lectures. Although I was used to giving lectures I had never done any teaching. The subject would be Handel's operas, which in my study of the oratorios I had referred to in terms that scarcely did them justice. I needed to make my peace with the mighty shade of the composer. For the second semester I chose romantic opera as my subject. It was in Berkeley that my old girlfriend Clare, now a widow with three sons, chose to settle. I had recommended Philip Brett for a fellowship at Berkeley, where he studied under Kerman. There was much to think about.

On 18 June we drove to London, staying with Donald and Anthea at The Boltons. We went to Smetana's *The Two Widows* at the Guildhall School, its first production in Britain. The simple-minded libretto had little dramatic interest; the music fell between stools, the romantic side – more pretentious than in *The Bartered Bride* –

threatening to weigh down the comic. The following night we saw Handel's *Xerxes* at Sadler's Wells. This was the 1959 Birmingham production with a few changes of cast and Arsamenes played by a woman – an immense improvement. Unfortunately, Xerxes was still sung by a tenor. Otherwise the performance, under Anthony Lewis, was musically first-rate. Only one aria was cut altogether. The next day, working at The Boltons, I finished the revision of my Shakespeare essay.

Giulio Cesare that evening was a much less satisfactory performance. Joan Sutherland was miscast as Cleopatra, lacking youth, kittenishness and voluptuousness in her voice (and her person); though she sang the more serious arias well she destroyed the effect of 'V'adoro pupille' by rushing ahead of the beat. Much else was wrong with the production, visually and musically. Ptolemy and Nireno (a eunuch!) were sung by basses, Curio by a tenor. Most of Ptolemy's part was cut. The orchestral playing under Charles Farncombe was heavy and inflexible, the ornaments and cadenzas often badly out of style. The score was severely shortened, but at least we were spared the meaningless mutilations usual in contemporary German performances.

The final Handel Opera Society offering, *Jephtha*, opened on 25 June. It was last year's production with a new cast. The chorus (though not the soloists) sang better and the continuo was more in style (without the intrusive organ), so that at least some of the grandeur came across. I still thought the production, by Anthony Besch, sacrificed too much of the drama to the formal detachment of the Greek chorus. That morning I sent off my Shakespeare essay – three months late and over 10,000 words too long. Later, at Phyllis Hartnoll's pleading, I attempted to cut it.

On 27 June we drove to Abingdon for *Agrippina* at the minute Unicorn Theatre. This was the opera's English première after 250 years! The recitatives were sung in English, the airs in Italian. The performance was not at all bad; we had all the specified instruments except trumpets and drums, and the vocal parts were sung at the correct pitch with a woman as Nero and a countertenor Narciso (John Horrex, tempted to pull faces during other people's arias). Fourteen arias were omitted, and nine reduced to their first part. Agrippina's irresistible waltz song at the end of Act II set the audience rocking. After the performance the Kitchings gave a jolly party for the performers and the critics, including Andrew Porter, Stanley and Adele Sadie, Colin Mason and Diana Morley. We stayed the night at the Queen's Hotel.

A few weeks later Nigel Fortune came down from Birmingham for his annual visit. We also asked Edmund Tracey, who occupied Stephen's room at the top of the house. On Sunday my mother drove over from Brook for breakfast. She was in lively form. The discourse ranged from Jung on archetypal dreams to opera in the 1890s. There was a faint background noise after swarms of Lillo's Italian relatives arrived from Woking, rather to his horror. It was a lovely day. It was still very hot when we drove to Orpington on Tuesday for Kentish Opera's revival of Dittersdorf's *Doktor und Apotheker*, one of the most popular operas of the late 18th century. Dittersdorf's style was so like Mozart's, without the genius, that odious comparisons were difficult to avoid. However the opera was a pleasant entertainment in its own right.

On 28 July Tony and Lesley Lewis came to stay at Hambledon. It was again extremely hot – 84F in places on Monday. We sat in the garden outside the loggia. Tony had a booming voice but the impression of stateliness and pomposity was misleading: in his shirt-sleeves, he bent down and let the exuberant Diana ride piggy-back on his shoulders. She rode him round the garden. (Once at Birmingham I heard imitation Tonys booming away.) In the afternoon we drove to Winkworth Arboretum, near Godalming, where the lake was a tremendous attraction for bathers. Diana, her friend Nicky and Rosemarie (who held badges for life-saving) promptly jumped in, Diana splashing about supported by a blue rubber ring. Later I played my tape of the Goldsbrough *Orlando*. Half way through the telephone rang. It was Lina Lalandi, founder and director, with Sir Jack Westrup, of the English Bach Festival at Oxford. Lina was Greek, a harpsichordist and singer – and a force of nature. They had decided to put on Handel's *Athalia* in the Sheldonian next summer. Would Professor Anthony Lewis agree to conduct it, did I think? 'If you hold on a minute, Lina, I'll ask him – he's sitting next to me!'

At the beginning of August the tennis court was finally finished. It looked magnificent. I played my first game of tennis since 1940! The prospect of Scotland cheered my spirits. I contacted guns about the forthcoming Peel shoots. We arrived at Galashiels early on 12 August and in the afternoon I reconnoitred the moor with Wattie and Peter Dods. That evening Donald and Anthea invited us for a drink at Fairnilee – when we learned to our horror that Donald had decided to sell the estate!

CHAPTER 20

Fairnilee

The news fell like a thunderbolt. Since shortly after the war, Fairnilee and Peel had been a vital part of my existence, which I could scarcely bear to lose. They had helped make life tolerable at a time of great distress, after the death of little Brigid. I had virtually no shooting in the South. Donald did not make clear *why* he wanted to sell Fairnilee. Admittedly he was not such an enthusiastic shot as I was. Yachting and the pursuit of the America's Cup, which over the last years had taken him to Cowes and the States, had become a highly expensive obsession. Donald was the youngest of the family. Fairnilee, haunted by the shade of a tyrannical father, may have held unhappy associations for him. A sensitive boy, naturally left-handed, he had been bullied into wielding a pen in his right hand, with the consequence that his adult writing was almost completely illegible. For the last two years I had leased the shooting on Peel from him, sharing it with the neighbour across the march at Ashiestiel, Admiral Sir Conolly Abel Smith. Even before this, I often made the arrangements, with Donald not arriving until just before the shoot. I knew the land intimately and had worked happily with the keepers, Peter and Wattie Dods, from the time just after the war when Peter taught me to shoot.

On 26 August we drove to Edinburgh for Verdi's *Luisa Miller* at the King's Theatre. I found this less moving than at Sadler's Wells in 1953, partly because the staging was all wrong, with clumsy sets and no social distinctions drawn between the Millers and the courtiers – everyone was dressed to the nines. We stayed the night at the Caledonian Hotel. Next evening we went to *Adriana Lecouvreur*, the first performance of Cilea's opera in Britain since 1906. It came off well in the theatre and though the music never rose above the second rate was a better work than many others of its period in Italy, apart from Puccini. The scoring throughout was admirable. We got back to Calfshaw after midnight. Two days later Donald Mitchell and his wife (whom we had lunched with at the Festival Club) came to tea at the cottage. Donald was a critic on the *Daily Telegraph* and had a finger in many another musical pie. We sat outside on the little gravel terrace in the sunshine, talking of Benjamin Britten (but steering clear of Mahler).

At the beginning of September I received a letter from Dadie Rylands, with whom I had discussed my Shakespeare project while working on the operas at Cambridge in March: 'I suggested to the Editorial Board of SHAKESPEARE SURVEY that you should be invited to contribute an article to the special centenary number on either serious or comical musical adaptations and travesties of the Bard; of course you might prefer to write about Verdi's Shakespearian masterpieces. I know that you will be both scholarly and original and entertaining. The Board welcomed the suggestion. The payment is very modest but think of the prestige!

'If you are willing, would you write to Professor Terence Spencer [at Birmingham University] who is mainly in charge of the number and who is also the Director of the Shakespeare Institute at Stratford – a most dear, delightful man: and tell him what you would like to do – about 5000 words I imagine – perhaps a little more. As long as it is concerned with the musical history of Shakespeare on the stage I am sure that you can follow your own bent and humour.'

Dadie had been active on my behalf elsewhere. A little earlier a letter arrived from Robert P. Heller of Associated Television: 'I have invited George Rylands to act as our consultant for special programmes during 1964 in observance of the Shakespeare Quatercentenary …

'One avenue of fresh approach, suggested by Rylands, might be the re-creation, in part, of productions of Shakespeare in music through the centuries. Rylands has recommended that we should approach you, in his opinion the greatest expert and the liveliest mind in this field of research, to discover whether you would be willing to discuss the practical possibilities.

'Would you let me know if this interests you?'

This was a new field for me. I had rarely seen television; we did not possess a set. We travelled South on 11 September, after a fourth shoot at Peel, an excellent day. For once we did not get wet. As well as the usual military and naval personnel, the party included two lairds, the bluff, red-faced Christopher Scott of Gala and Sir William Strang Steel ('Willow') from Philliphaugh, a tall, delightful baronet with a dry sense of humour. At Hambledon, over the next week, I disposed of 31 grey squirrels in the Hurst after the vermin had taken all my nuts!

Gerald and Pat Abraham had just moved to the Old School House at Ebernoe, a tiny village lost in the Sussex Weald and – I suspected – somewhere in the previous century. They came to dinner a few days later. Both were a little glum, having delivered Frances back to her boarding school. The previous day Thalia drove Diana to her new school at Walmer. Shortly before the Abrahams arrived the Italians returned from their holiday in Sicily, full of good spirits and looking very well and sunburned. They brought wine made by Lillo's father, in a beer bottle, which they insisted on our sharing at dinner. It was surprisingly good. We began the meal with corn-on-the-cob from the garden, followed by grouse from Fairnilee. Altogether it was a hilarious evening. Lillo and Gina gave us each a little gift, a tiny gold heart for a necklace or bracelet for Thalia and Diana, a belt for Stephen and a plate with a picture of an old castle at Naro for me to hang in the study.

There were problems with the tennis court. Thalia asked the local builder Neller to extend the retaining wall adjoining the path, as it was obvious that the first heavy rain would wash quantities of sand onto the court. The au pair Rosemarie had been a great success but sadly she was now returning to Switzerland to sort out problems with parents and boyfriend. In her place Poppett Sutton, a girl who lived in the village and had just left school, agreed to assist Thalia at Calfshaw.

I travelled to London to meet Robert Heller and other A.T.V. executives, together with Dadie, at Great Cumberland Place. It was an extremely wet afternoon. For a modest fee I agreed to prepare a list of excerpts from Shakespeare operas. The next day an article appeared in *The Times* under the headline **Craigmyle Estates in Market**. It read in part: 'Lord Craigmyle is selling his Fairnilee and Peel estates in Scotland, two properties on opposite sides of the Tweed, near Clovenfords, which together total about 3,860 acres. They are in the market for private sale, and offers in the region of £150,000 for the whole are expected by the agents, C.W. Ingram and Sons, of Edinburgh.'

In a rather depressed state of mind we caught the sleeper to Scotland the following evening. Poppett accompanied us, together with about fifteen items of luggage. She was a lovely girl and proved to be a great help to Thalia at Calfshaw but unfortunately had to go South a fortnight later to have her appendix removed. At Dadie's suggestion, I had written to Professor Spencer at Birmingham. I now heard from him. He invited me to give one of the main lectures at the Eleventh International Shakespeare Conference at Stratford in early September next year, unfortunately during the grouse shooting season when we hoped to be in Scotland. Nonetheless I accepted.

We had sad news from Hambledon about Hercules, Shenka's son, as Thalia recounted to Stephen: 'Bert wrote that he found him dead in his box in the garage on Wednesday morning. Poor old Hercules. I think he must have passed away quite peacefully in his sleep thank goodness. I must say I did wonder when we came away if I would see him again. He was so thin and seemed to have so little interest in life – even in milk.' An epistle also arrived from Lillo, beginning: 'Today I have received your letter tell me that you and Mr Dean live very well. Same we it here.' Diana wrote a pathetic pleading letter from Leelands and Thalia at once decided to visit her, involving a very long and complicated journey to Walmer. When she arrived however Diana seemed comparatively cheerful, though not keen on her dormitory companions or on making her bed. I stayed with Alan and Frances Ramsay at Bowland over the weekend. Meanwhile I had been endeavouring to concoct information about Shakespeare operas likely to amuse an A.T.V. audience. I found this an arduous task – and not only because I was compelled to work from memory and notes in the absence of the scores at Hambledon. Thalia borrowed a typewriter from the Ramsays.

By now all my shooting friends knew about the proposed sale of Fairnilee. Alex Seton, an amazingly vigorous figure who strode the moor in shorts, generally ahead of the line, wrote on 18 October: 'I am very sorry at the thought that you may lose all your shooting, it is very bad luck and I do not suppose that you have any in Surrey … I am sure that "getting away from it all" to the Borders does you an awful lot of good, and I wonder how you will replace it in the future.' Eric Lloyd wrote from Bowland: 'It is a great pity for you if the place is sold & I can feel how unhappy you must be. I only hope that perhaps someone will buy it who can still be willing to give you a chance with the shooting – it may still be if the price is not put too far up in the sky.'

With this in mind I approached John Gee, husband of Thalia's school-friend Rachel, who lived in some style in Sussex. He knew the estate; I had invited him to shoot at Peel last October. With no space at Calfshaw they put up at Peel Farmhouse, attended by Annie Wilson, Margaret's former housekeeper, who had a little flat there. John employed an agent to assess the land, raising our hopes, but they were soon dashed. John wrote on 20 October: 'Re Fairnilee …. I am advised that I should not make an offer over 100,000 … But after giving the whole thing an immense amount of thought I really do not think that even at that price the return would be at all good. Furthermore one has got to face a considerable outgoing, in the way of management fees, etc. …

'I frankly, on reflection, do not think that I have the energy to put into this. So for these reasons I have not made an offer – and I'm afraid do not feel inclined to do so.

'I am terribly sorry from your point of view, but I really feel that this is the right course for me, as I have very heavy commitments at this end as you will know.'

John suggested we could talk further when we came South but I rang him at once. Unfortunately he was out. The next day I was up early for a shoot at Peel. It was agreed that John would call at 8.55 a.m. I had a short agitated conversation with him but he was not to be moved. Thalia drove me to Peel. It was a perfect October day, warm, sunny, a gentle South-West breeze – the best day of the season – but nearly all the birds had gone. That evening I got into

Fairnilee

a panic over the sale of Fairnilee. Thalia tried to reassure me. There might be other avenues …

The following day the weather was again glorious. In the morning Thalia and I drove to the Buccleuch Estate Office to consult Jamie Galbraith, the Duke's factor. Jamie was another shooting companion. He had lost a hand and an eye while serving on a destroyer during the engagement with the *Bismark* in 1941. These disabilities did not much hamper his shooting; his 20 bore was equipped with a special hook and the stock modified to sight on his good eye. Jamie was brisk and made some helpful suggestions. Why not make an offer for Fairnilee ourselves, in partnership with others? We did not have the funds to make an outright purchase, we believed. In the evening I rang Eric Lloyd and Thalia's sister Jean.

Christopher Scott, the Laird of Gala, had also expressed interest. This year we had shot the Fairnilee and Gala House moors together. But now he wrote from London: 'This is just a note to say that I have decided not to go ahead with my project to buy Fairnilee. I am very, very sorry about this, but I really do feel it is beyond my resources. I hope I did not buoy your hopes up in vain, but I feel I must withdraw – the stakes are too high!' On the Sunday before we travelled South we held a small drinks party at Calfshaw. It was a convivial occasion. Afterwards Alan Ramsay missed the turning at the bridge and drove his Land Rover into the burn. As a result, we had an unexpected guest for supper – and for the night.

The day after we got back to Hambledon we followed up one aspect of Jamie Galbraith's advice: we travelled to London to consult Mr Pearce of Jackson-Stops in Curzon Street about a possible purchase of the estate. At the beginning of November I received another communication from Christopher Scott: 'I am writing this letter to say Scott is still in the Fairnilee Stakes. Since my last letter

I have heard that somebody, very interested, has been round Gala. So I may be in a position to offer for part of Fairnilee after all.

'Can I be considered as a member of your group? Basically my interests are
- a) The Rink [Farm] (& tenant)
- b) Any fishing going
- c) Any woods

but of course I might come in on a bigger scheme, if need be.

'Could you bear this in mind? I think it is most noble of Donald not to sell to a Speculator, & I do feel we must try & make an offer. If you have some friends who want bits – well, count me in!'

On 10 November I wrote to Philip in Cambridge: 'I hope you are doing some work. I have far too much, thanks to the importunity of editors and the disappearance for several weeks of the Shakespeare proofs, which I hoped to tackle at Calfshaw. They have now been unearthed and dealt with, but have held everything else up. The next major job is the revision of the Master Musicians Bizet, but there is a whole stream of articles to be tackled before I can get back to the New Oxford History.

'We have had both children home for half-term, and they evince an equal and emphatic distaste for mathematics. I am not sure this is a wholly unhealthy symptom. Last Sunday there was quite a ceremony in the garden, when my father planted an Oaktree he had grown in London from a Scottish acorn. We feel a plaque ought to be put up recording the occasion.

'Did you hear the original version of Beethoven's *Leonora* [on the Third Programme]? It was interesting (I had heard it before), but Basil Lam's introductory talk, besides making inflated claims for it as a masterpiece in its own right, completely missed the links with Gaveaux and the French Revolution, which explain a lot of the curious details in the libretto.

'When do you come back? Michel Poupet wants you to accompany him in some Bizet songs, but they go back to Paris at the end of the year. He talks so incessantly that you won't get a word in edgeways.'

In the middle of November Lillo and Gina unexpectedly gave notice. They had found more lucrative employment at Guildford Hospital - £20 a week between them – and a flat in Guildford for £3 a week. They departed on 22 November, the day President Kennedy was assassinated. We were sorry to see them go. After this we never again had live-in staff, apart from au pairs. The stuffy bedroom at the top of the house became an increasingly cluttered box room, and eventually – after the installation of elaborate shelving – a last resting place for my overflowing journals and magazines.

On 26 November Thalia and I took the train to London. I went to Wilfrid Mellers' R.M.A. paper on 'The Avant-garde in America' while Thalia called on Anthea and the children at The Boltons. We both attended Verdi's *Attila* at Sadler's Wells, its first performance in Britain since 1848. This was well sung, but the dramatic imbecility of Solera's libretto was not softened by unimaginative production, drab sets and an awkward translation. It was a weaker opera than many of Donizetti's later works, which clearly influenced it. Nevertheless the score contained some fine things, especially in the first act, which began with an exquisite *Romanza* for the heroine and ended with a splendid scene in which the superstitious Attila quails before Pope Leo and a band of Christian maidens outside Rome. We ate a picnic supper on the train home. I had encountered Gerald Abraham at the meeting. Two days later I received a stern note from him: 'When I saw you last night I forgot to mention that I should be very glad to have your copy for N.O.H.M. VIII in the very near future.' At about this time I asked Thalia to pack a consignment of grey squirrel tails to send to Wattie Dods at Fairnilee to make into fishing flies.

On 2 December I went to Covent Garden for Shostakovich's *Katerina Ismailova*, the opera originally produced in 1934 as *Lady Macbeth of the Mtsensk District* and subsequently banned by Stalin. It was not a very shocking opera and not a very good one. The libretto was a sorry debasement of a fine story by Leskov. The musical style was chaotic, in approach and substance. I was reminded of Janáček's *Katya Kabanova*, a work however of infinitely superior dramatic and musical stature.

Next day we had arranged to see Jamie Galbraith at the United Services Club, Pall Mall. In the event I went alone; Thalia had a fearful headache after driving to Walmer and back to see Diana at the weekend. Jamie advised that we make an offer for the entire estate, though we could not afford to keep it all; parts would have to be sold off. That could be decided later. Afterwards, feeling very much happier, I dined with Donald and Anthea at The Boltons. It was past midnight before I got back to Hambledon and talked it over with Thalia. By the morning the matter had been decided. Thalia contacted Ingrams, the Edinburgh selling agents, and (as advised by Jamie) made an offer of a little over £142, 000 for the Fairnilee and Peel estates.

Two days later we heard that our offer had been accepted. We were grateful to Donald for giving us the chance. An estate-breaker would undoubtedly have offered him more. A few days later we travelled to London to discuss arrangements for the purchase with my brother Martin, the family solicitor. Next morning Thalia was greeted by Mr Evans in the Cricket Green Stores with a copy of the previous night's *Evening Standard*, with a small paragraph concerning the sale of Fairnilee and Peel, which would 'remain in the family'. The news spread quickly. Wattie Dods wrote: 'Congratulations! We got the news from Mr Marshall [Donald's factor] on Thursday of your purchase, and were very glad to hear it.

'I will only be too glad to continue here [as keeper], of course with new management there is always a few minor details to see to but will see to these when I see you personally ... P.S. Thank you for squirrel tails.'

Laurie Loch, one of my oldest shooting friends, also wrote to congratulate us. He had heard a rumour too that I was going to California 'on a professional job'. When would they next see us in the Borders?

Just before Christmas our French friends Michel and Madeleine Poupet visited us for the weekend. On Saturday Philip came to dinner, together with Gerald Abraham (Pat was unwell). Thalia also asked Jerry Jarratt, Stephen's French master, a highly civilised and entertaining man. No doubt she hoped he would talk to Madeleine, whose English was much less good than Michel's. After dinner we held a small Bizet Festival! Michel possessed a serviceable tenor voice. He had brought a sheaf of Bizet songs; Philip accompanied him at the piano. I looked out my material on Bizet's fragmentary opera *La Coupe du Roi de Thulé* and they played and sang through that too. It was a memorable evening. Philip reappeared the following afternoon and this time we recorded the songs and other items. Philip played resolutely. At a dramatic point in one of the songs the microphone tumbled off the piano on to the floor.

Basil spent Christmas Day with us but departed the following morning. Sheila Miller arrived in the afternoon. Thanks to John Gee I had obtained a half gun in a shoot at Goodwood. As in Scotland, there was a strong military element among the participants. Sometimes I shot with *three* generals. Jim Martin collected me at 9 a.m. for the Boxing Day shoot. It was exceedingly wet and we gave up at noon after three drives, everyone soaked. A replacement day was arranged for 28 December, over different ground. This was much more successful, though curtailed by thickening mist. I put a large cock pheasant though the keeper's roof!

Nigel Fortune wrote with news from Birmingham. After considering *Scipione* and *Poro* they had settled on *Ariodante* for the next Handel opera, in May, at the Barber. Tony Lewis was not pleased to discover that the BBC were doing their own Third Programme production of *Ariodante* – in March, Nigel thought: 'So you will have to do a comparative review. It is stupid of them not to check first with the obvious places.

'No doubt you will have heard that Jeremy [Noble] will by May be a new figure on our campus. I also hear that Berkeley is to have a temporary addition to *its* campus …

'I am counting on you to dine as my guest after the [R.M.A.] Purcell paper on 9 January. We will be a dozen or so – at Laytons, I hope … I am glad – if Rumour in the person of Jeremy be correct – to be on your side over the Shostakovich opera: no doubt he is indignant with both of us.

'Looking forward to seeing you – maybe even at the Bach paper on the 2nd [*Bach and the Bible*]? Perhaps not really you …'

We travelled to Fairnilee on 9 January. I caught an earlier train to Waterloo in order to attend Margaret Laurie's paper at Trinity College, 'Did Purcell set *The Tempest?*' Anthony Lewis was in the chair. Laurie cast doubt on Purcell's authorship and attributed the work to John Weldon. I was highly sceptical about this at the time. Jack Westrup thought it was nonsense. Nigel took the opposite view. I dined at Laytons with Nigel, Anthony and Lesley Lewis, Westrup, Dennis Arundell, Charles Cudworth, Brian and Rhianon Trowell and Margaret Laurie. I had to scurry off early to meet Thalia and the children, with our luggage, at St Pancras.

Donald and Anthea greeted us at Fairnilee. We stayed in the flat Anthea had created in the nursery wing, which had its own entrance, rather than at Calfshaw. We shot Rink and Fairnilee on 11 January. As well as Donald, Jamie Galbraith and Christopher Scott were among the party. It was a fine, still day and very mild (too much so – the birds were out in the fields and hedgerows). The bag was evenly distributed between cocks and hens: 33½ each, according to my Game Book (including one hermaphrodite). Next morning I sallied out with Wattie and Peter Dods and the dogs to search for any unpicked birds (we found four). That afternoon the Galbraiths came to tea. The question of how we would fund the purchase of Fairnilee had still not been resolved. Even with a mortgage advance secured on the estate from Thalia's Marriage Settlement, we still had insufficient funds. Something would have to be sold. If it helped, Jamie would be happy to purchase the salmon fishing, over 3½ miles from Caddonfoot Church to Tweed Bridge, leaving us with the farms and the shooting (I had little interest in fishing at the time). Willow Strang Steel looked in at 6. Earlier he had written to me congratulating us on the purchase of Fairnilee. 'We will now have to make you a member of all the landowning, fishing, game & forestry organisations! This will cost you a little but is one of the pleasures of being a Laird! You may remember that I mentioned to you that Robert Jackson, my factor, would be available and delighted to help with the management and/or supervision of anything you want; my own opinion is that he is sound & pretty good & conscientious …' Willow was knowledgeable and sympathetic – and not angling to buy any portion of the estate. We discussed the fishing and other matters. Two days later I met Jackson at a cold and damp shoot at Philliphaugh. We travelled South the next day. We decided not to accept Jamie's offer – very fortunately, as it turned out. The salmon fishing proved to be by far the most profitable part of the estate. Later I became an assiduous fisher for salmon, catching more than 60 in the course of a long career.

Back at Hambledon, I returned to the revision of my Master Musicians *Bizet*. There was a great deal to do. Since 1947 the quantity of material bearing on Bizet's life had more than doubled, thanks chiefly to the serendipity of Mina Curtiss. Her book *Bizet and his World* (1958) put all earlier biographies out of court, and I had to rethink mine from the beginning. What was intended to be a revised edition of an old book was to become to a large extent a new one.

At the end of January we paid another visit to Fairnilee. On the way through London we called on Martin at his office. Afterwards we had a drink with Christopher Scott at Essex Villas. Christopher's head was still buzzing with schemes for the estate, all involving himself. His latest was that we should become partners in farming 'Fairnilee Home Farm'. We arrived at Galashiels early next morning. It was still dark. At Willow's recommendation, we had asked Robert Jackson to become the estate factor. We held a long conference with him in the afternoon. William Pate, the tenant of Fairnilee Farm, was retiring in May. Jackson was confident we would find applicants willing to take on the tenancy and pay a good rent. He would vet these for us. Rink Farm was to be sold to Mr Bayne, the sitting tenant, but we would retain the fishing and shooting. We liked Jackson and were relieved to have found someone to undertake such tricky matters, about which we knew little. What my father-in-law would have said had he known that I was to become Laird of Fairnilee I struggle to think.

I was delighted to find that a Keepers' shoot had been arranged for Fairnilee and Rink next day. Mr Bayne, Robert Jackson and Laurie Loch came too. It was a cocks only day (the four hens were mostly shot by the keepers!), cold, with a blustery wind, squally sleet showers alternating with periods of sunshine. There were not many cocks but a fine show of hens emerged from several of the coverts. Three generations of the Dods family turned out, including eight-year-old Peter. Peter Dods senior had now retired as head keeper. The following evening I called on him at his new quarters in the Bothy.

Thalia was making plans for the flat, still filled with Donald and Anthea's furnishings. She wasn't very happy with the dark sitting room with its one North-facing window. The flat could be extended along the corridor to take in three more small bedrooms, another lavatory and bathroom. An architect would be needed to devise a means of separating it from the main house, which we intended to let, together with the garden. We had already received inquiries. On Monday Mr Stewart-Clark, a rich bachelor who worked in Edinburgh, appeared with his sister. He was an enthusiastic shot and fisherman, though we doubted whether there was enough of either to suit him. We had agreed to take on Wattie Dods as gamekeeper from 1 March. Back in the South, Thalia and I visited Martin at his office in Carlos Place. He introduced us to an accountant, a curious species of individual, Thalia thought, but doubtless necessary to advise on tax.

At the beginning of February I received a slightly worried letter from Merrill Knapp. I had informed him about the Berkeley professorship. The terms involved my delivering six public lectures on Handel's Operas, to be published by the University of California Press. Would these queer the pitch for our joint book? He wrote to Joe Kerman, chairman of the department, who was able to reassure him that there was unlikely to be a conflict between neat lectures and a magisterial comprehensive book. Merrill proposed to come over with his family for a few weeks in the summer.

On 12 February Thalia and I went to Sadler's Wells for *The Makropulos Case*, its first performance in England. I was looking forward to this. Čapek's fascinating play had haunted me ever since I saw it at the Embassy Theatre in 1931. Janáček's opera completed the miracle. Like all his late works it made an impression of unity by breaking all the rules – the vocal writing was fragmented and unlyrical, the instrumental fell likewise into a mosaic of short phrases. Yet so close was his sympathy with the characters and so intense his grasp of the spiritual themes that the opera gripped from start to finish. The central figure of a woman 300 years old was an extraordinary creation, as indeed she was in the play. This was surely one of the great operas of the century. Marie Collier, confronted with the unique task of playing a prima donna to whom the whole history of the art of singing is an open book, gave an impressive performance as Emilia Marty.

In February I received a charming letter from Charles and Sally Farncombe. They were thrilled to hear about my appointment at Berkeley. Sally (who was American) would be only too happy to help with any information: 'Usually, she says, you are able to take over the house of a professor who is on a year's sabbatical leave.' In the event we took over the house of the late Professor Potter, whose widow was away.

Later in the month Philip arrived for the weekend, laden with scores. With the prospect of Berkeley looming, we began to play through Handel operas. I made detailed notes. I did not possess many of the scores. The invaluable Gregg Press reprint of Chrysander's 19th century edition only became available in 1965. Three days later we attended *Aroldo* at St Pancras. This was the first performance in England of an opera of Verdi's maturity, dating from 1857. It was easy to see why. The original version (*Stiffelio*, 1850), a domestic tragedy after the manner of *Luisa Miller* and *La Traviata*, concerned the divorce of a 19th century German pastor – a very odd choice in a Catholic country. In superimposing a new libretto, putting back the action 600 years to the 'heroic' period of the Crusades, and transferring the scene to Kent and the banks of Loch Lomond, Verdi and his librettist Piave produced a monumental absurdity. This was surely one of the silliest librettos ever conceived. But there was some fine music, by no means all belonging to the revision.

In the middle of March we stayed two nights with Donald and Anthea at The Boltons. We saw Gluck's *Iphigenia in Aulis* at St Pancras Town Hall. Sadly it was a limp and depressing performance, with a weak cast and a bad conductor. The wonderful opening failed to ignite the opera, which never left the ground. The next day Anthea and the children went down with mumps! In the afternoon we had a conference with Martin and our new accountant Richard Moss, mostly concerning Fairnilee. We dined with Christopher and Anne Scott at Essex Villas. Christopher had been tempted to bid for the tenancy of Fairnilee Farm but – perhaps fortunately – had decided against it. We heard from Leelands that Diana had caught chicken pox. I worked in the B.M. all day on Friday. In the evening we were at St Pancras again for Cherubini's one-act *Pygmalion*, unfortunately a concert performance only, conducted by Joseph Horovitz, the editor of the score; he had played it to me on the piano the previous year. It was a slight work with little action or conflict. The airs were mostly short and marred by a lack of sustained melody, though there were many phrases of great eloquence. In the same concert Horovitz conducted the Philomusica of London in Haydn's symphony No. 83 ('The Hen'), a far more sensitive performance than a recent widely publicised effort by Boulez. Afterwards we drove home. Next day the first daffodils were out in the garden. It was 14 March. This would have been little Brigid's 21st birthday.

The weather turned colder. It snowed on 18 March, my birthday. In the evening we went to Haydn's *L'Infedeltà Delusa* at St Pancras, a Handel Opera Society production conducted by Charles Farncombe. This was said to be its first British stage performance. Unfortunately Haydn had little feeling for the theatre. The musical resource, though ample, was governed by a logic outside the drama, with which it did not synchronise. Nonetheless there was some delightful music. The opera had no chorus, but it was evidently thought inexpedient to allow the Handel Opera Society chorus to gather rust, and they were superimposed on the ensembles, involving much silly business to keep them occupied. It was good to find (in Cherubini and Haydn, though not in Gluck) that the St Pancras rates now ran to a more liberal distribution of appoggiaturas.

On 23 March we drove to Seaford College for the school play, *Julius Caesar*, produced by Jerry Jarratt. We were accompanied by Danielle, a French-speaking Swiss au pair, who had arrived the day before. It was a pretty fair effort for schoolboys and Stephen made his mark as a quavering Cinna the Poet. The next week the weather was miserable. My pocket diary records that it was the coldest and dullest Easter weekend *ever* in some parts. For three icy days at the start of April the temperature never reached 40F. April 8 saw the first real spring day. Philip came to dinner and we finished playing through *Alessandro*. On 10 April a dinner was held at Bertorelli's in honour of Gerald Abraham's 60th birthday. Pat accompanied us in the car. Unfortunately we were caught up in traffic and arrived half an hour late – much to Gerald's agitation – missing the drinks and chat beforehand. There were about forty persons present, critics, Russian specialists, University people, a contingent from the BBC and *The Listener*. Gerald gave an account of the occasion in his diary: 'We sat with Jack and Solweig [Westrup] at the head of the table. Nigel Fortune and Denis Arnold had made rather a mess of the seating (as of the rest of the organisation!) but we enjoyed it more than we'd expected to ... Jack said a few words and I thanked.' Afterwards Thalia drove Gerry and Pat to Waterloo, where they caught the last train. We had arranged to stay two nights with Valerie Williams at Drayton Gardens. The following evening we were at Covent Garden for Verdi's *Otello* under Solti. This was chiefly remarkable for Gobbi's superb Iago, one of the great performances of our time.

A few days later Stephen accompanied me to *L'Arlésienne*, the first English stage production of Daudet's play since 1888, with all Bizet's music in the original scoring. This was a joint effort by the musical and dramatic societies of the John Lewis Partnership. The play strayed now and then across the borders of sentimentality, but the music was so superbly integrated that I found it a profoundly moving experience, sometimes almost unbearably so. Towards the end of April I finished the revision of my book on Bizet.

In early May we drove to Birmingham for *Ariodante* at the Barber Institute, its first stage revival in England since 1736. It had been narrowly anticipated by a BBC Third Programme performance under Arnold Goldsbrough, with three of the same singers, including Janet Baker (as Ariodante). She was in superb voice. The contrast between Anthony Lewis's and Goldsbrough's reading of the score was sometimes startling. Whereas the latter tended to drag the slower movements, Lewis once or twice went in the opposite extreme, especially in the Romantic sinfonia depicting the rising of the moon at the beginning of Act II. Many arias were reduced to their first half; others were cut entirely. Despite this, the opera seemed excessively long, especially the static first act. All the ballet music was included. Nor did it suit the small stage; the chorus and the band for the spectacular last scene had to be accommodated in the wings while the stage was left to four dancers. Brian Trowell made good use of the available resources, but missed a unique opportunity of suggesting the Scottish background (the scene is set in Edinburgh); the 18th century after all saw the revival of Highland dress.

Afterwards we had supper with the Lewises and cast at Sir Hugh Casson's new Staff House. We stayed the night with Nigel in Handsworth. Next morning I met Tony Lewis at the Barber and discussed cuts for his forthcoming performance of *Athalia* in Oxford. After lunch we set off to Abingdon for the Kitchings' revival of *Admeto*, last staged in England in 1754. It was a considerably less skilful performance than that of *Ariodante* but I was more impressed by the opera, particularly the first two acts. Unfortunately it was clumsily cut, the superb second act being ruthlessly shortened instead of the weaker third. Hercules's first air was clowned, which made the audience think the Hades scene a huge joke. The opera had more drama and genuine emotion than I thought in 1947, when I heard a broadcast performance with Admeto sung by a baritone; the Euripides scenes being markedly superior to the rest. We put up at the Queen's Hotel and stayed up late chatting with Andrew Porter, Diana Morley and Stanley and Adele Sadie. We drove home next day, packed rapidly and that evening dined at St Pancras Station on the way to Fairnilee.

We had much to do. A sale by auction of the contents of the mansion, including pictures, furniture, silver, china, books and bric-a-brac, was to take place on 19 and 20 May, when unfortunately we could not be present. We needed many items for the flat, not only furniture but curtains, beds, mattresses, eiderdowns, blankets, pillows and the like. We were able to purchase some of these in advance; we put in low bids for others. One day an organ-builder arrived about the removal of the organ, which Donald had resolved to donate to a church in Aberdeen. The organ was a folly of Thalia's father. None of the family was particularly musical and it was little played. The console sat in the hall; the pipes occupied a large space on the landing leading to the nursery wing; the works encumbered a dark room in the basement. Latterly, when Margaret was out of earshot, Stephen essayed the keys, pulling out the stops and making an appalling racket.

Robert Jackson had found a tenant for Fairnilee Farm. John Pate was the nephew of the retiring farmer, William Pate. He was a tall, sturdy man, one of several farming Pates in the district, all strong characters. He came to see us one evening. On our last day Robert arrived with an architect, Kathleen Veitch, from Melrose, whom we liked very much. Thalia noted though that she had expensive ideas, like most architects. We were delighted when Wattie Dods caught a 5½ lb. salmon, which accompanied us on the train, swaddled in newspaper.

It was gloriously hot in the south. Rhododendrons were already flowering in the garden. A few days later we went to London for a party given by Gwyneth McCleary and Sally Farncombe. Before this we called in on Martin at Carlos Place, where there were formidable documents to be signed and witnessed in connection with the purchase of Fairnilee. After the party we met David Hubback, a friend from my Cambridge days, now at the Treasury. He took us to a pub called The Sherlock Holmes in Northumberland Street. We enjoyed an excellent meal in the Grill Room above the bar. Through a huge glass screen we found ourselves peering into Sherlock Holmes's study, with appropriate furniture, his pipes, books, violin, syringes, greatcoat and deerstalker hanging from a peg.

That weekend we set out early in the car to visit Diana at Leelands. It was a long drive to the windy Kent coast. We took her out to lunch. Later we talked to the Principal, Mrs Varcoe. Poor Diana did not much care for education. We stayed at a large hotel overlooking St Margaret's Bay. On Sunday Diana and two friends came out for the day and played on the beach in the afternoon. In the evening we dined with Dr James Hall and his wife at their house on the Dover Road in Walmer. Hall was a remarkable man, a GP, a retired sea surgeon, a choirmaster and a passionate Handelian. Over the years he had assembled an important collection of early printed editions of Handel's works (and also contemporary manuscripts); he had generously lent me items from time to time. His book *Sea Surgeon* gives a vivid account of his exploits during the war and after, jumping on and off ships in the stormy English Channel to perform emergency operations, notably during the evacuation from Dunkirk.

The next day we lunched at The Maiden's Head in Uckfield. Donald Mitchell and his wife had kindly allowed us to change at their cottage near Lewes, after which we drove to Glyndebourne for Verdi's *Macbeth*. This was a new production, and a very good one, apart from a weak and wobbly Lady Macbeth (a replacement). The Greek baritone Paskalis, who played Macbeth, was quite outstanding and the producer (Franco Enriquez) scarcely put a foot wrong. His motionless groupings for the big ensembles were admirable, and his treatment of Duncan's dumbshow entry all but converted me to the music: its tinkling tune conveyed a strange irony. The whole thing was several grades above Zeffirelli.

On 28 May I noted in my diary: 'Fairnilee becomes ours'. Stephen was doing rather better at school. He wrote us short but trenchant letters. He had recently been invited to join the Aquila, an exclusive society for senior boys with intellectual pretensions. They spent a good deal of time debating important matters in pubs, I gathered. At the end of May my Balkwill 'cousins', their wives and several of their offspring, dined with us at Hambledon. Michael and John were the sons of my Aunt Vie by her first husband, before she married Basil's brother Vernon. Stephen, wearing his blue Aquila tie, was home from Seaford for half term. I took a little ciné footage as the party strolled round the garden, which with hawthorn, azaleas, rhododendrons, peonies and honeysuckle all in flower, was looking lovely. Michael worked at the BBC. He was editor of a new programme, *Westminster at Work*, presented by Ian Trethowan, an up-and-coming man, according to Michael. Trethowan duly progressed up the rungs of the Corporation, becoming Director General in 1977. By this time he had come to live in Hambledon. I remember conversing with him in our garage (he was an opera lover), which had been requisitioned to accommodate a small exhibition during the village celebrations for the Queen's Silver Jubilee in 1977.

On 2 June Philip wrote from Cambridge: 'His Bobship [Bob Dart] is on the whole in good form, though liable to bouts of pontifical self-dramatization which are liable to put up the backs of divers of his colleagues. However we survive!' Two days later we drove to Oxford for John Eccles' *Semele*, put on by amateur forces at the Holywell Music Room. This was billed as the first production of England's first full-length opera. Congreve's libretto was later set in modified form by Handel. It was a much better work than I expected, occasionally almost rivalling Handel's setting. It made one regret the composer's abandonment of the theatre for fishing in the Thames (he lived until 1735). There was no chorus and the defective score was patched up in places by the editor, Stoddard Lincoln, who played harpsichord continuo. Earlier I asked Bob Dart about Lincoln; he found him an agreeable fellow but '*not* the brightest & best of the sons of the m., I'd say'. Unfortunately licencing regulations prevented the use of full scenery and costumes in the Music Room. Tokens and gesture were substituted; a bearded Jupiter in a scarlet and black opera cloak neatly suggested the immortal tycoon.

Our new accountant Richard Moss recommended setting up a company to manage the Fairnilee estate. This would help alleviate the tax burden, he assured us. In recognition of Stephen's success at school, we named it the Aquila Estate Company. Thalia and I became directors, my brother Martin company secretary, with Robert Jackson an additional director and general manager.

On 2 July we drove to Oxford for *Athalia* in the Sheldonian Theatre, where Handel first performed the work in 1733; had it ever been done there since? It was an almost uncut performance under Anthony Lewis and, except for one or two details, a very good one. We had the full instrumentation, including theorbo and recorders, and the choral singing was magnificent. The explosion of brass, drums and double chorus in 'The mighty Power' was shattering. The brevity of all the solo movements in Act III intensified the effect of dramatic precipitation. It was a great experience; I had not been so moved for years. Before the performance we dined with the Paynes at Woodstock Road. On the way home the car broke down and we had to be rescued by the AA. We did not reach Hambledon until 3 a.m.

The next day Thalia drove to Ashford to stay with Joe and Jenny, who had moved to a fine house in West Brabourne. From there she visited Diana at Leelands. Afterwards she wrote to Stephen: 'I arrived home from Deal late Sunday night to find Daddy surviving after his weekend in Danielle's [the au pair's] care though he had meals at even odder times than usual. Danielle had done several vases of flowers which were extremely artistic. I forbore to point out that it would have been nice if I hadn't had to make Daddy's bed when I arrived! All the doors and windows were wide open when I got here and just as I was going up to bed the black cat [an uninvited visitor] darted through the house. Daddy with indignant glee gave chase with a tennis racquet and Danielle ran after him pleading "No, no". The cat was so scared that it entirely failed to see the obvious exit and ran upstairs. I felt I couldn't face all this at this juncture, being quite exhausted with a beastly long drive, so I took myself off upstairs with the remains of the brandy bottle (about ¼ glass!) and disassociated myself from the affair. The cat cleverly did so too as a prolonged and thorough search of the house failed to reveal it and Daddy decided in the end that it must have run downstairs while he was looking in one of the upstairs rooms.'

Merrill and Libby Knapp arrived in London in time for the Handel Opera Society season in July. We had an early supper with them at Wellington Square, off the King's Road – we were told to look out for a yellow door. Then we wound through the traffic in two cars to Sadler's Wells. *Semele,* under Peter Gellhorn, began shakily but improved throughout the evening and was very good indeed by the last scene. Elizabeth Harwood had enriched her portrait of Semele, always well sung, with the right suggestion of sensual abandonment. Ino and Juno were taken by the same singer, Helen Watts, to the great advantage of the impersonation scene. We stayed the night with Anthea at The Boltons; I laboured all next day in the B.M. on Handel librettos. In the evening we saw *Riccardo Primo*, its first performance anywhere since 1735. It was worth doing, though it is not one of Handel's best operas, hampered by a clumsy libretto tailored to a patriotic occasion. Two of Costanza's finest arias were cut. Unfortunately Riccardo's part was transposed for a tenor. Richard Lewis sang very well but the coloratura, intended for Senesino, fell in the least expressive part of his voice, making the arias seem heavier and more pedestrian than they are.

We were in London again the following week for the first meeting of the Aquila Estate Company – attended by Martin and the accountant Richard Moss, who was appointed auditor – at Carlos Place. That evening we went to Southwark Cathedral for Britten's new 'church parable' *Curlew River.* I had heard the broadcast from Orford Church a few weeks earlier. At the end, as we genteelly pushed our way towards the bottle-neck of the door, everyone round us was full of praise. Despite the great beauty of much of the music, the work left me unmoved. The emotion rang false, because I suspected it was not at all about what it purported to be, and the final miracle came over as a fake. Afterwards we had a very lively and convivial dinner at the Garrick Club with Denis and Sheila Stevens and Neville and Molly Marriner, who we had not met before (they were delightful). Neville had just recorded Handel's Op. 3 concertos. Denis had a fair experience of American music departments and their personalities. The meal began with avocado pears (a particular favourite) and concluded with brandy, and cigars for the men. At the end the Marriners gave us a lift to Waterloo in their two-door Volkswagen. The two Stevenses and Molly squeezed somehow into the back while Thalia perched on my knees in the front, clinging to the open sunshine roof.

On 19 July Philip wrote from Cambridge with a rather startling piece of news: 'London University has at last decided to have a full-time Professorship of Music. It has been offered to Bob [Dart], who has accepted it. It is all very odd: though I have often felt critical of Bob, I am fully aware of all that we owe to him here, and I am sure that he will be missed. Meanwhile I imagine that before long the electors will have to meet.' Dart had been in post for less than two years. On this occasion I was asked to become one of the electors.

Two days later I kept to my bed, struggling to finish my lecture on Shakespeare and Opera for Stratford. Merrill Knapp came for a night and we laboured on Handel's operas. He returned for another session shortly before we departed for Scotland. One evening we trooped round to the Baldrys next door to watch General Christison discoursing on the Battle of Bannockburn on BBC television. This was to be the last time we stayed at Calfshaw Cottage. The main part of the mansion had been denuded of furniture, paintings, carpets and curtains – apart from the great red plush curtains on the main stairs. The organ had been removed, leaving a huge space on the landing. Donald had inherited a wonderful collection of paintings. Portraits by Allan Ramsay hung in the Library; elsewhere there were portraits by Raeburn, Reynolds, Gainsborough, Beechey and Lawrence; Romney's 'Lady Hamilton as a Welsh Girl' hung over the fireplace in the dining room. There were many other lovely pictures, including two works by J.W.M. Turner: a watercolour of The Rialto – Venice (1820) and a watercolour drawing of Ashiestiel, the former home of Sir Walter Scott. Not all were sold at the auction; many were retained by the family. Shadows on walls and electric sockets (for picture lights) were the only indications of their former presence. Latterly some had been shifted to make room for Anthea's own large canvases. A portrait by Stanley Cursiter of the three Shaw sisters, Jean, Thalia and Ruth, with old Fairnilee House behind, was considered so dreadful that there were no takers among the family. (Eventually it was taken in by Donald's eldest, Alison.)

We were not able to attend the auction in May, which occupied two days. We put in bids for a few extra items; most exceeded our limit, including a barometer hanging in the outer hall and one of four bear-skin rugs. We were successful in acquiring two bathroom chairs with cork seats, fire-irons, an electric kettle and the Bendix washing machine that thundered in a little room at the top of the back stairs. Thalia was upset to discover that items we had reserved, such as Andrew Lang's *The Gold of Fairnilee*, had been sold in error. In advance we secured Margaret Wrightson's marble bust of Thalia's sister Jean – but not its wooden stand – and her charming bronze statuette of Thalia as a dancer.

The day after we arrived Miss Veitch the architect came to see us. We had decided to take the old nursery into the flat as our sitting room. Anthea had converted it into a bedroom. Now the organ pipes had gone we could divide the flat from the rest of the house at the landing, panelled to match the original, Miss Veitch suggested. The service lift would have to be removed, since it rose through both parts of the house. The old-fashioned internal telephone system had also gone. At the back of a cupboard in Mr Huckle's basement office Stephen discovered my father-in-law's passport, with a grim photograph, well-stamped up to 1938; also a quantity of red tape.

Stormy weather hampered several of my shoots. More than once I returned to Calfshaw drenched. Our first outing on the Fairnilee and Gala House moors produced a record bag but was too strenuous for Stephen, who gave up at lunch. There was a serious incident on Alan Ramsay's shoot at Caddonhead – on an otherwise successful day – when one of the guns swung down the line and peppered two of the other guests. The culprit was sent home in disgrace.

On 28 August we drove to Edinburgh. I spent the day in the National Library of Scotland studying Handel opera librettos. In the evening we saw *From the House of the Dead*, Janáček's last opera, based on the Dostoyevsky novel. This was its British premiere. I found it a profoundly moving experience. The Prague orchestra played superbly and the production on the whole was sensitive. As an opera it was another miraculous triumph over apparently hopeless limitations. There was virtually no story, and no conventional symphonic method; merely the repetition and variation of brief germ phrases. Yet the atmosphere was intensely potent and dramatic. Both the claustrophobia of the prison camp and the compassion of the composer came over with extraordinary vividness.

Before we travelled to Scotland Danielle had returned to Switzerland. She found Hambledon rather quiet. Sheila Miller accompanied us to Calfshaw but could only stay for two weeks. She was replaced by another student, Susan Gibson. On 31 August we set out with Stephen for the Eleventh International Shakespeare Conference at Stratford-upon-Avon, leaving Diana in the care of

Susan. Thalia couldn't face the long car journey so we decided to fly from Edinburgh's Turnhouse Airport. This was a novel experience for us. We changed planes at Glasgow for Birmingham, where we hired a car. We stayed at the Grosvenor House Hotel. Next morning we found our way to the Shakespeare Institute, Church Street, where among the scholarly crowd we met the director, Professor Terence Spencer. The morning's main lecture was given by Charlton Hinman, from the University of Kansas, who discoursed learnedly on Shakespeare's Text. He had a little trouble reading his script because light from the window behind reflected on the back of his spectacles. An adjustment to the curtains solved the problem. He talked of compositors and their vagaries. He had devised a clever machine for comparing different printings of the First Folio, the 'Hinman Collator'. After lunch we explored Shakespeare sites in the town, starting with Holy Trinity Church and Shakespeare's funerary monument and effigy. Among other features, I noted the good stalls with 26 misericords of striking imagination and impropriety. This was one of the last entries in my Register of Parish Churches, begun in 1936. In the evening we went to a highly enjoyable production of *Henry IV Part 1* at the Memorial Theatre.

My lecture on 'Shakespeare and Opera' next morning found an appreciative audience. Dadie congratulated me heartily – he especially enjoyed the jokes. In the afternoon we flew back to Edinburgh, stopping for dinner at Glasgow Airport. When we got back to Calfshaw we found Frank and Joan Sargeant's camper van parked above the cottage. Frank was on leave from his diplomatic duties. Thalia's sister Jean arrived with her three girls and they stayed in the flat. Next day (4 September) was our Silver Wedding Day. Stephen photographed us outside the cottage in the sunshine. Despite my father-in-law's dire prognostications, our marriage had been a success. Later I walked down to the river to watch the Sargeants fish. In the evening there was a large drinks party in the dining room of the empty house. The only item of furniture was a kitchen table. Stephen and John Sargeant ran amuck with a fire hose and threatened to douse the guests. Afterwards Jean and the Sargeants came for supper at the cottage.

We returned South in the middle of September; the children had to go back to school. Philip came to dinner and we played through more Handel operas. Soon we were back at Fairnilee. A little sadly, we decided to give up Calfshaw and move permanently to the much more comfortable and convenient flat. It was a relief not to have to worry about the generator. We went up to the cottage and collected my shooting gear and boots. Later Wattie Dods helped Thalia bring down the Calor gas cooker, spin dryer, clothes airer and other items in the Land Rover. We had important matters to decide concerning the management of the estate. Robert Jackson appeared with Mr Goose from Tilhill Forestry and we spent two days going round the woods – divided into 'compartments' on the Tilhill plan, with recommendations for thinning, felling, weeding, 'brashing' and replanting. We still had not found anyone to take on the main part of the house. We wanted to keep sufficient of it to allow us to ask friends to stay. The servant's wing under our flat would become a second flat, with its own kitchen but connected to ours by the back stairs. Thalia discovered a cache of 78 rpm gramophone records in one of the cupboards in the Library. She transferred them, two heavy albums at a time, to the flat. It was unclear if anyone would ever play through the complete recording of King George VI's Coronation. The weather was becoming colder. Thalia froze when going round the proposed lower flat with Miss Veitch. She made regular trips to Calfshaw, compiling an inventory and fetching things down. Wattie Dods helped with the furniture; Thalia acquired a few other items at a sale in Galashiels. On Election Night (15 October) I sat up until 3.30 listening to the results on our portable radio. General Elections held a particular fascination for me. I spent the next day

Fairnilee

or two compiling statistics and colouring in maps. I returned to Handel during a break in shooting. We drove to Edinburgh and I had another long session in the National Library of Scotland, only emerging when they shut their doors at 8.30, eating a picnic supper in the car on the way home. The last shoot at Peel and Ashiestiel was a disaster. Thick mist ruined one drive – nothing was shot; another was spoiled by incompetent flanking. Despite seeing a fair number of birds in the afternoon it was decided to abandon shooting for the season – I suspected mistakenly.

There were compensations. The autumn colours on the estate were lovely. We could barely believe that all these trees and fields were now ours. On her last trip to the cottage Thalia walked round one of the woods above Calfshaw and as she left an enormous moon was rising above the trees.

We returned to Hambledon at the end of the month for the children's half term holidays. As already mentioned, I had been asked to be one of the Electors of the Cambridge Professorship of Music following Bob Dart's resignation. Near the end of October – on a highly confidential basis – I received copies of applications and curricula vitae for Ivor Keys, Ian Parrott and F.W. Sternfeld. Parrott had been an exact contemporary of mine at Harrow. He was a pillar of the musical establishment in Wales, but more a composer than a scholar. He named Sir Jack Westrup as one of his referees. This was not a wise choice. Westrup wrote a devastating letter to the Registrary, concluding: 'It is difficult to admire [Parrott] as a person, but easy to feel sympathy'

I travelled to Cambridge on 9 November, lodging for the first two nights at King's. Philip and I went through *Arminio* and *Muzio Scevola*. The first Electors' meeting on was held in the Old Schools on 11 November. Our friend Charles Wilson, the historian, was a fellow elector. Thalia arrived that evening and we stayed with the Wilsons at Queen's Road. The second Electors' meeting was at 9.30 the following morning. In the event we chose Robin Orr, Professor of Music at Glasgow and a composer, who had come under consideration two years earlier. Thalia and I returned to Hambledon the following afternoon.

I received a letter from Vincent Duckles, Music Librarian at Berkeley: 'I am here in London for a few days, and I wonder if we might possibly get together to discuss Handel sources and other matters that might concern your teaching at Berkeley next Fall.' I took the train to London the following week, working all day at the B.M. and meeting Duckles at the English Speaking Union at 5. I found him extremely helpful. He agreed to order all the materials for at least six Handel operas for my students to study on microfilm. Afterwards I met Diana Morley and we went to *Il Trovatore* at Covent Garden, the first night of the new Visconti-Giulini production. It was nothing like as good as their *Don Carlos* in 1958, one of the supreme achievements of post-war Covent Garden, perhaps because of defects in the work. Surely no libretto in operatic history omits so many of the essential links in the plot. *Il Trovatore* is a succession of dramatic highlights with superb tunes. The characters are jerked scene by scene into palpitating life; they do not, like those of Verdi's late operas, seem to have developed during the intervals. The singing was only moderate. Most of the cabalettas were much shortened.

We returned to Scotland on 4 December, but only for a week. I had invited John Gee, Jamie Galbraith and Thalia's brother Donald, Lord Craigmyle, to the shoot at Fairnilee and Rink. The morning before, I went round the stands with Wattie Dods. The Gees returned to Annie Wilson at Peel Farm while Donald and Anthea stayed with Christopher and Anne Scott at Gala House. It was a successful day, though the weather broke too soon after several days' frost. By far the most successful stand was Raewiel Burn. This was the covert where I imagined Lord Bamburgh meeting his end in my unfinished detective story. The following week saw me studying Handel opera librettos (*Tamerlano* and *Siroe*) and tackling the proofs of my revised book on Bizet.

We decided to spend Christmas at Fairnilee this year, arriving with Stephen and Diana on 22 December. In between shoots, I worked on Handel librettos. We invited Basil once again; he arrived by train on Christmas Eve. Though 76, he was still in pretty good health. He had heard that Faith Celli, a young actress he directed in *The Blue Lagoon* in 1921 (when she protested about the skimpiness of her dress of imitation plantain leaves), was buried in Caddonfoot Churchyard. She had quit the stage after her marriage to Arthur Murray, the future Viscount Elibank, a local landowner. Basil walked the mile and a half down the main road to Caddonfoot Church to visit her grave. For the most part, Basil was in mellow and reminiscent mood. He talked of the playwright Clemence Dane, now sadly in failing health, with whom he enjoyed a striking success with *A Bill of Divorcement* in 1921. At Christmas dinner Basil presided in my place at the head of the table. On 28 December, a very cold day, he departed for Dunfermline, and from thence to his friend John Drummond of Megginch at Megginch Castle in Perthshire.

My last shoot was with Willow Strang Steel at Philliphaugh. The rain was almost continuous with mist and thaw and melting ice under foot. Otherwise it was a marvellous day. There were eight stands, nearly all with superb high birds. The shooting was poor in the morning but improved dramatically after lunch and whisky. On 2 January we caught the 10.58 p.m. train at Galashiels. This involved Thalia putting Diana to bed early and then rousing her. Not for the first time, we arrived at St Pancras very late.

CHAPTER 21

Heading for Berkeley

There were now only eight months before we sailed for America. We would be away for almost a year. I did not feel at all prepared. The day after we got back to Hambledon I took an early train to London and worked solidly at the B.M. Before Philip returned to Cambridge we played through three more Handel operas, *Arianna*, *Ezio* and *Faramondo*. I was still mired in the proofs of the Bizet book, including the appendices. By 19 January the first snowdrops were emerging in the garden. There followed a heavy fall of snow. Diana ventured out next morning wearing four pairs of socks and Thalia's snow boots. Later she accompanied Thalia to the shop, hauling the sledge through the slush in the face of an icy wind. I had agreed to give a lecture on Handel's Operas at Cambridge at the beginning of March. One day I stayed in bed and began work on it.

Near the end of January we paid a brief visit to Fairnilee. The flat was very cold when we arrived but electric fires and paraffin heaters made it habitable. There was snow on the ground and brilliant sunshine. In the morning I reconnoitred the Neidpath woodland with Wattie; in the afternoon I worked on *Sosarme*. Electricians were to start the following week separating the electrical system of the flat from that of the main house. Thalia laboured on her hands and knees pulling up carpet tacks in the bedrooms and rolling up the carpets to allow access to the floor-boards.

It was a glorious day for the shoot at Fairnilee and Rink, continuous sunshine and frost with snow under foot. Four keepers bore arms as well as the regular guns, Peter and Wattie Dods, Bald from Gala House and the rascally Jimmy Bruce from Yair across the river. Robert Jackson joined the team for part of the afternoon. Afterwards the guns came in for a sociable late picnic lunch. It was inconvenient not having a garage up at the house. Each evening Wattie collected the car and drove it down to the garages at Robin's Nest a quarter of a mile away. Unlike Thalia's mother Margaret and Donald and Anthea – and my grandfather Tommy – we did not of course employ a chauffeur. On one evening we went out to dinner and had to walk up the icy drive in the dark. We discussed this problem with Miss Veitch. The only practicable solution was to convert my father-in-law's finely panelled business room into a triple garage, inserting three tip-up doors, removing the panelling – it was sold to Brigadier Anthony Farrar-Hockley, later Commander of Land Forces, Northern Ireland – but retaining the parquet flooring.

I persuaded Philip to come down from Cambridge for the weekend early in February, when we played through more Handel operas. In the middle of the month I met old Willie Smith at the B.M. He was bearing his prized 1717 edition of the libretto of *Rinaldo*. He would not let me alone with it for a moment. He assured me it would not take long to note the additional songs. We went through it together, page by page. I was delighted to find an aria Willie had not spotted, as well as other changes. In the afternoon I went to Macmillans at St Martin's Street. I had been asked to give advice on the future of Grove's Dictionary. I talked to the directors; Maurice Macmillan, the son of Harold, was in the chair. I liked them all and a useful discussion ensued. The 5th edition, published eleven years before, had a number of grave shortcomings, despite Eric Blom's herculean labours. It was clear to me that a wholly new edition would be required. Afterwards I met Thalia at University

College for *Das Liebesverbot*, a British première. This was Wagner's second opera, written at the age of 21. The libretto turned *Measure for Measure* into an undergraduate manifesto in praise of free love and coarsened the plot and characters beyond recognition. The music was an extraordinary hotchpotch of French, German and Italian styles, with rare hints of the later Wagner, notably one melody used again in *Tannhäuser*. The numerous ensembles sometimes had a flavour of Sullivan, an unwitting tribute to the latter's nice ear in parodying the idiom of romantic opera. The student performance was much cut. We rolled home after midnight.

On 26 February Thalia and I attended Richard Rodney Bennett's new opera *The Mines of Sulphur* at Sadler's Wells. To my surprise, I was most impressed by this. It had a superb sense of theatre: libretto and music worked hand in hand, the timing was astonishingly good for a first full-length opera, and the whole was taut and professional. The plot, on the surface a sordid eighteenth-century murder, was also a ghost story and a subtly integrated study of the inner working of guilt. It was brilliantly worked out; the two levels met and merged in the shattering last act. After listening to the radio broadcast a week later a few doubts set in.

The next day I took the train to Cambridge, where I was to give my lecture on 1 March. I lodged at King's. The following day Philip and I played through Handel's short opera *Silla*. I dined in Hall and afterwards we stayed for a concert put on by the Musical Society. I was in the wrong mood for Brahms's *Four Serious Songs* (Op. 121), having imbibed port and other good cheer. The unrelieved earnestness and gloom, especially of the first two songs, jarred on me. Philip Brett agreed to help with my taped music examples. We held a rehearsal on Monday morning. Unfortunately, the numeration of the Cambridge machine was different from that of my own tape recorder, making the examples hard to locate; it was not always clear to Philip when to stop the tape. However the lecture in the Cambridge Music Faculty late that afternoon went off fairly satisfactorily. Later I attended a concert in the Senate House given by the University String Players. Britten's *Les Illuminations* seemed to have grown an extra song since I heard it before – the fourth, 'Antique', a particularly lovely piece with scoring for solo violin foreshadowing the operas. The soprano was not good enough to put across Rimbaud's words. Afterwards I had a drink with both Philips.

I returned to Hambledon next morning. It was snowing and intensely cold. Two days later about a foot of snow fell in the night. There were blizzards. On Sunday Stephen came home on exeat with John Sargeant. I had agreed to give the lecture again at Goldsmiths' College, New Cross. After the debacle at Cambridge, I asked Stephen to transfer all the examples to a single tape. This proved much more satisfactory but unfortunately the student audience was very small. My brother Joe came for the night. He sallied out on the Common and unearthed numerous small trees for the copse he was planning at his home in Kent. My mother remarked that his car looked as if Birnam Wood was on the move again! On Sunday, while Thalia was visiting Diana at Deal, Basil and my mother looked in on me. They ambled up the drive together. It was more than forty years since their divorce.

In the middle of March Thalia and I went to St Pancras Town Hall for Monteverdi's *Il Ritorno d'Ulisse in Patria*, incredibly its first stage performance in Britain. This was a most rewarding experience, and not at all badly done. Only an imbecile would doubt Monteverdi's authorship. Act II in particular was on the highest level of genius throughout, and some of the characters were as vivid as those of *Poppea*, though the opera did not quite hold this level of inspiration. As usual, there were three planes, gods, heroes and comic servants, and each had its mead of attention. I found the gods the least memorable: it was in revelation of human emotion that Monteverdi was supreme.

On the first day of April Philip accompanied us to Seaford College for *Hamlet*, put on in the School Hall. There was a fine Hamlet and Stephen distinguished himself as a grey-haired, bumbling Polonius. John Sargeant played Rosencrantz. Near the end of the month, after a long slog, I finished the page proofs and index of *Bizet*. At last I was able to start on my lectures for Berkeley. A day or two later I took Stephen to the Guildhall School for Suppé's *Boccaccio*, its first English revival since 1885. Though lacking Sullivan's technique and Offenbach's wit, this stood up well. The libretto was genially improper, if a little too complex. Suppé could write catchy tunes with plenty of rhythmic bite. An octet for three pairs of lovers and two cuckolded husbands (one in a barrel, the other up a tree) was well sustained and more imaginative in harmony than the rest of the score, besides being very funny. On 3 May Thalia and I had our passport photos taken at Muddles in Godalming. That evening we were at Covent Garden for *Lucia di Lammermoor*, a limp performance under Bonynge, who endeavoured to make Donizetti sound like Bellini instead of emphasising the links with Verdi. Joan Sutherland was in fine voice, but the others produced an orgy of wobbly singing. The next week Thalia went to London, visiting the Chartered Bank and a travel agent to make arrangements for our journey to America. We had decided to sail rather than fly.

On 13 May, a very hot day, we travelled to Birmingham. Hitherto the Barber Institute had concentrated on the Italian baroque for its opera productions. This year, as a better-late-than-never tribute to the bicentenary of Rameau's death, Anthony Lewis gave us *Hippolyte et Aricie*, only the second of his operas to appear on the English stage. This was Rameau's first opera, written at the age of 50 after a career devoted to church, chamber and keyboard music.

Perhaps as a result, it was more a series of blown up miniatures than a work of commanding architectural span. The finest music – and it was magnificent – occurred in the second of the five acts, which had nothing to do with the story. The tiny stage only allowed a token representation of the spectacular, ballet and choral scenes. Nevertheless Brian Trowell's production and Mark Haddon's sets ensured that the eye was not starved. There were superb performances from Janet Baker as Phaedra (though the tessitura was a little high for her) and John Shirley-Quirk as Theseus.

I had been having what Philip called internal troubles and a week after our return from Birmingham I consulted a surgeon in Guildford, Mr Boulter, who recommended a small operation. On the evening of Sunday 30 May Thalia drove me to Mount Alvernia Nursing Home at Guildford. The operation was at 8.30 the following morning. Next day I wrote to Stephen: 'Thank you very much for your amusing letter, which helped to cheer me up. I am not feeling too bad today, though still rather uncomfortable. Yesterday they gave me a lot of dope, etc, and I could not stand up. Eventually I had to be escorted along the passage by two nuns to spend a penny, but could produce nothing. Instead I was violently sick. The journey then took place in reverse, and I was hoisted back to bed. I am hoping the surgeon will let me go home tomorrow. He is a nice cheerful man with a taste for opera. He is going to the same opera as us at Glyndebourne later in the month, but unfortunately not on the same night.'

Thalia collected me the next morning, when advance copies of my new Bizet book arrived. This edition was outside the Master Musicians series and in a larger format, with a drawing of the composer on the front cover. The following day I was able to resume work on my Berkeley lectures. One evening Susie, the last of our cats, did not come in for her supper. Late next afternoon Verena the

Swiss girl saw her lying in the front border in the sunshine. She was dead. It was fifteen years since we brought her back with us from Cambridge as a kitten.

On 16 June, a very wet day, we drove to Glyndebourne for *Anna Bolena*. This came off splendidly in the theatre. It would have been even better if several big pieces had not been severely abbreviated. The march for Henry's wedding to Jane in the last scene was cut altogether, destroying a superb stroke of dramatic irony. It was refreshing to see so many of my colleagues eating their words about Donizetti! We joined John and Rachel Gee. Rachel supplied a delicious picnic supper, which we consumed under a covered way leading to the opera house while the rain fell in splashing torrents. I was the only one to get really wet, while retrieving my medicines from the car. I came back with trouser bottoms soaked and water dripping off my mackintosh and cloth cap.

We stayed with Donald and Anthea in London for the two Handel Opera Society productions. Before we set out I paid another visit to Mr Bynoe, who stopped three teeth. *Rinaldo* was a revival of the 1961 production, improved in one or two details. Despite many fine arias the drama never gathered momentum, or gripped as a whole, thanks partly to Handel's inexperience and a weak libretto. The next day Thalia and I lunched at the ESU with Clorinda Stockalper and her sister Viviane, who we had not met before. They were descendants of my great aunt Kate, Tommy's elder sister. Both were charming, intelligent girls; Clorinda, the elder and shyer, hoped to forge a career as a concert pianist. She showed us laudatory reviews of her concerts at Bristol. She practiced for seven or eight hours a day, she told us. We heard nothing more from either girl. Later we learned that Clorinda had become a nun. *Saul* that evening was a disappointment, the tension repeatedly broken by dropping the curtain in the middle of an act. The chorus was handled with an apologetic lack of conviction. There were some deplorable lapses of taste, notably in the ornamentation. Geraint Evans however was a magnificent Saul, immensely potent in voice and gesture; he dominated the stage and did full justice to the rich characterisation of the music.

At the end of June I was at Covent Garden for *Moses and Aaron*, which Andrew Porter had asked me to review for *Musical Times*. Thalia was reluctant to make another trip to London but Philip bravely agreed to accompany me (Schoenberg was not his cup of tea). This was the opera's first English production (by Peter Hall). Long study of the libretto, by Schoenberg himself, had convinced me of the greatness of the conception; whether it was fully realised in terms of music and theatre I was not sure. The performance threw everything in – dozens of supers and dancers, two horses, a highland cow and several small goats, besides a huge chorus (the advertised camel failed to pass its stage test). The big choral scenes were splendidly effective and the Golden Calf episode (with the best music in the opera) gripping. The duets for Moses and Aaron were inhibited by the difficulty of building an opera round a character (Moses) who does not sing.

The next day Thalia drove me to Guildford for a check-up with Mr Boulter, the cheerful surgeon. I endured another grim session with Mr Bynoe, who stopped four more teeth. A visit to the oculist followed; Mr Stabach, the Godalming tailor, measured me for a new pair of trousers. There were necessary vaccinations ahead of our departure. Mine had a most peculiar result – it left me temporarily crippled. According to Dr Coupland, this was because it had not been done for many years – and when it was done (I was about 18) it had not taken properly. We advertised Hambledon Hurst for let in the Personal Column of *The Times*. Poppett Sutton agreed to accompany us to California to help with Diana. It would be an adventure for her. Poppett's parents, Ted and Trottie, who lived nearby at Bryony Hill, would take in Stephen, who was still at school – and at the moment suffering exams. Ted was a tall amiable dentist with a practice in Guildford. A few days later we signed a lease with Mr Voakey, an American, and his English wife. Bert and Ernie Jeffery would continue to tend the garden. My study was shut off and various precious items stowed in Lillo and Gina's former bedroom at the top of the house, to which a padlock was applied. Unfortunately this was left unlocked; when we returned a year later a number of items had disappeared.

Thalia couldn't face a further trip to London for *The Fiery Angel* at Sadler's Wells (27 July), its first English performance. Instead I asked Diana Morley to accompany me. It made a very mixed impression. The demonic passages had real power and gripped the attention almost continuously; Prokofiev's fondness for ostinato became an apt symbol for obsession. But the human episodes were feeble and derivative. The success of the New Opera Company's performance owed much to Marie Collier's vivid re-creation of the taxing part of Renata. She had a remarkable gift for sexually obsessed and distracted heroines, as she showed in *Katerina Ismailova* and *The Makropulos Case*.

I had hoped to make significant progress with my lectures for Berkeley but found myself continually blocked by more immediate commitments. This was to have very unfortunate consequences later. In 1964 Bärenreiter published a new full score of *Carmen*, edited by Fritz Oeser, together with a critical report. I asked Andrew Porter to obtain a copy for me to review in *Musical Times*; unfortunately it arrived much later than expected, near the end of July. This turned out to be a long and extremely arduous task. Oeser's edition was a musicological disaster of the first magnitude, an arbitrary conflation, based on random principles of selection, of what Bizet intended, what he rejected, and what the editor thought he would have done better to write. Michel Poupet checked a number of points for me in Paris. When Diana Morley (who was assisting Andrew in the MT office) came down for the day we sat on the sofa together and I pointed out some of Oeser's more egregious errors. I managed to complete a rough draft of the article two days before we sailed for America and put the final touches to it in Berkeley.

I was determined not to miss the opening of the grouse season. On 11 August, rather than take the train, Thalia and I flew to Edinburgh for a brief visit. We stayed with my shooting friend Col. John Lowis and his wife Muriel. Wattie Dods met us at Edinburgh. The weather was lovely. We shot Peel on 13 August, an entirely military party of guns, apart from the factor Robert Jackson and myself. It was a perfect sunny day but a brisk S.E. wind spoiled all five drives. There were fewer birds than I had ever seen at Peel (though some refused to fly). This proved to be the start of the moor's long decline. On Saturday we shot the much smaller Fairnilee moor. The day was warm, rather close and cloudy. The S.E. wind suited Neidpath. It was a most successful and enjoyable day, the bag (44 grouse, double that on Peel) easily a record for the ground. The next morning we deposited my shooting clothes and boots at the flat and talked to Mr Bruce, Margaret's retired head gardener, who still pottered about the garden and kept an eye on the house. We had made no progress in finding a tenant for the main part. That would have to wait. In the evening Wattie drove us to Turnhouse Airport, Edinburgh, and we flew home.

I had placed a large order with Gregg Press for reprints of Chrysander's edition of Handel's Works. It was particularly anxious to receive the operas. There had been difficulty with the binder, I was informed. At last, at the beginning of August, the volumes started to arrive. They were very well printed, in handy reduced format, with blue paperback covers. The remaining titles would be forwarded to me in Berkeley.

For our last days in England the weather was glorious. We said goodbye to our neighbours Brian and Pat Baldry. My mother came to dinner. Dr Coupland looked in. Bert Jeffery cut my hair in the orchard. Philip appeared for dinner three times. On the last occasion we took him to the Dog and Pheasant at Brook, opposite the cricket ground, scene of many a convivial post-match evening with Mike Gauntlett. Early on the morning of 26 August the Suttons collected us in two cars and drove us to Southampton, where Thalia and I boarded the Queen Mary with Diana and Poppett. Stephen joined us briefly as we found our cabins. At 12.30 the horn snorted three times and the great ship edged away from the dock.

CHAPTER 22

Berkeley

We started three quarters of an hour late, leaving Stephen and the Suttons hanging about impatiently. Stephen's blue pullover was in view from well out in Southampton Water. I photographed some cocooned minesweepers and inspected a castle on the Isle of Wight. The Channel was foggy. We called in at Cherbourg around 5.0 p.m. and sent off letters and post cards. (Later at Berkeley I compiled a log of our voyage from 26 August to 1 September.)

Diana felt sick the next morning but still swam enormous distances in the pool. I plunged in several times. Thalia and I retained our sea legs. We discovered that James Grayson and his wife were travelling in the next cabin; Jimmy was the managing director of Westminster Records and keen to record some of Handel's dramatic works, operas as well as oratorios. There was much gossip about Handel, singers, conductors, etc.

We were all photographed on our way down to dinner – reminding Thalia of a similar occasion in 1938. Next morning, while shaving, I filled in the answers to a Quiz, which I won. Later the Steward presented me with my prize, an alarm clock. In the middle of the afternoon, the Queen Elizabeth returning from New York passed close along the port side – a magnificent sight. Jimmy Grayson had a six minutes' telephone conversation with his sister on board her.

I experimented with an American film, *How to Murder your Wife*, but left before the murder. Two nuns sitting near the front were lapping it up.

On Sunday the ship ran into mist; the foghorn sounded bleakly all day. Jimmy Grayson complained of ear-ache, attributing it to an excess of unsuitable music played on a Hammond organ in the lounge (including selections from *The Mikado* and *Swan Lake*). We attended a bizarre Fancy Hats Competition, and later Thalia and I took to the floor. I purchased five bottles of Scotch whisky free of duty (at £1 each) to set us up in Berkeley.

We reached New York at 9.30 a.m. on 31 August and disembarked in a great scramble. We were met by Mina Curtiss's chauffeur in a Cunard-sized Rolls Royce and conveyed with our baggage to her grand apartment in the Stanhope Hotel, where we stayed in comfort and luxury. Poppett and Diana went up the Empire State Building, travelled on a street-car and visited the Zoo in Central Park. Thalia and I spent a very enjoyable evening with Denis and Sheila Stevens, dining in an Italian restaurant and being driven round New York.

The following day we flew to San Francisco (5½ hours). I peered out of the window, catching glimpses of the Great Lakes, the Missouri River, the Rockies (including the snow-capped Wind River Range) and the Great Salt Lake. Clare Millikan was at the airport to greet us with her sons George and Mark and Lawrence Moe, Chairman of the Music Department. We were installed in the Berkeley Hills on the North side of campus at 1151 Euclid Avenue, a pleasant house but darkened by a grove of redwoods. We dined with the Moe family and fell early into bed.

Two days later Larry Moe, who was University Organist as well as Chairman, showed me round the Faculty buildings and Library. My duties were to teach graduate students in seminars, and in the spring to deliver the Ernest Bloch lectures, a series of public lectures on Handel and the Opera Seria. I had hoped to complete these before we arrived but unfortunately this was very far from the case. First I had to touch up the two *Carmen* articles before sending them off to Andrew Porter at the *Musical Times*. The next day we were invited round for a drink by Joseph Kerman and his wife Vivian. We had first met the Kermans five years earlier, when Jeremy Noble brought them down to Hambledon. Joe was the leading musical scholar at Berkeley, a man of strong opinions and formidable intellect. He was then in his early forties, with a neat moustache that later expanded into a beard. Fortunately, I got on very well with him.

Our house was built in a canyon, the ground falling away steeply on one side. I worked in Professor Potter's study downstairs, but the crowding redwoods meant I had to have a light on all day and chatter and footsteps in the room above sounded through the thin wooden floor. I resumed work on the Bloch lectures; a few days later the first lecture began to move. We had arranged for the airmail edition of *The Times*, printed on thin paper, to be forwarded to Berkeley, allowing us to keep up with news from home, and world events – local papers were useless in this respect. Clare and Mark found us a car, a 1964 Dodge; it took Thalia a little time to get the hang of the different controls, and to driving on the right. Later the car suffered a flat tyre, and on one unfortunate occasion Thalia lost the key.

Soon the household was augmented by a diminutive grey kitten, which Diana christened Tinkerbell. She was a mischievous creature, looking exactly like our old cat Shenka; she climbed up people as if they were trees and liked to tangle with Thalia's knitting and scatter her papers on the floor. Later, in maturity, she would settle comfortably on Thalia's back while Thalia was sunbathing on the patio. Sadly, because of quarantine regulations, we had to leave her behind, heavily pregnant, when we left Berkeley near the end of June.

Luckily she did not interfere with the tape recorder (we had shipped out a substantial quantity of my tapes), a large stately instrument which the University bought for me – though I would have to pass it on to my successor. Its method of operation was different from mine at Hambledon. The University assigned Jack Swackhamer, a colleague in the Music Department, to unravel its peculiarities.

The weather was beautiful – sun every day and no rain, though mist in the morning rather spoiled the view over San Francisco Bay, full of bridges and islands. The University was enormous, like a small town; there were about 28,000 students altogether, I reported to Stephen. The architecture and design of the town was wildly eccentric. Every house tried to be as different as possible from its neighbour, and was on a different level because of the hills.

We were invited to an elegant dinner with the Moes at Miller Avenue and met other members of the Music Department. After the meal the talk turned to Berkeley campus politics, provoking laughter and acid comments, but rather leaving us out of the conversation, as one of the other guests, the composer Seymour Shifrin, remarked more than once.

I met my graduate students for the first time in a Music Department office on 20 September. There were six of them, three women and three men. They treated me with great respect. Each was set to unravel the source materials and genesis of a different Handel opera. The first of my weekly seminars was held the next day. I found teaching very enjoyable; the students were all intelligent and keenly interested in the work. Vincent Duckles, the Librarian, told me that they had been monopolising the microfilm readers and trying to obtain keys to the Library in order to work after hours. Every Friday I made myself available in the office for those seeking help or advice.

Berkeley

We went to dinner with the Duckles', at their weather-boarded house on Eucalyptus Path, in the hills on the South side of the Berkeley campus, and were introduced to their five enormously tall sons. Here I met Daniel Heartz, another colleague, a specialist in sixteenth-century music and society; later he stayed with us at Hambledon. After the meal we stepped out on to the patio for coffee. It was a lovely warm night. From this coign of vantage we looked down on the lights of Berkeley, the Bay Bridge and the Bay of San Francisco. A new moon emerged from behind the eucalyptus trees that framed the view but sank all too soon behind San Francisco.

In the middle of October Thalia and I went to *Lohengrin* at the open-air Greek Theatre of the University. The sun was blazing hot but a little breeze kept it from being unbearable. I wore my cloth cap as protection and Thalia borrowed Poppett's red straw hat. The variety of headgear among the audience was astonishing; many resorted to the Programme fixed over the head at an appropriate angle. The performance was excellent, though the sound of the orchestra was dispersed and augmented by jays, dogs and aircraft. I enjoyed it far more than I expected. The drama was thin, the vocal writing square and rhythmically deficient, but there was a great deal of wonderful music, especially on the orchestral and harmonic side.

Towards the end of the month I invited my six students to our home at Euclid Avenue to listen to a private recording of the Birmingham *Tamerlano* of 1962. Joe Kerman and Clare and Mark came too. This was the first of a number of 'Tape Parties' we held over the following months, with intervals for tea and buns, often concluding with drinks and a buffet supper. Sometimes I played tapes to my colleagues, setting the machine going but not telling them what they were listening to! They were all stumped by Janáček, barely known in America at that time – except Swackhamer, who guessed. He taught musicianship and harmony and seemed to hold a lower academic rank than others in the Department, but he had a wider knowledge of opera. Puzzled faces greeted the overture to *L'Africaine*; Swankhamer plumped for Meyerbeer, at the second attempt.

Many of my colleagues were composers (including Swackhamer), writing in a variety of styles – I heard some of their pieces in concerts and recitals at the Music Department performance venue, Hertz Hall. We got to know Andrew Imbrie and his wife well; later they visited us at Hambledon. His music owed something to Bartok and Stravinsky but possessed a flavour of its own. He went to Paris before the war and (like Lennox) studied composition briefly with Nadia Boulanger.

I could not get on at all with Arnold Elston's *String Quartet* (1961), a grim work that I liked much less than its composer. Its unrelenting seriousness suggested a man straining to scratch an inaccessible spot in the middle of his back. Elston had been a pupil of Webern, but missed his virtue of terseness. Once at a drinks party Elston's wife, who was Viennese, complained that their dog had eaten one of Arnold's socks, which when it emerged had changed colour, spoiling the match with its mate. I suggested that she should feed the other sock to the dog, to obtain a matching pair. I fear the refined Mrs Elston was not amused!

William Denny's *String Trio* (1965), a thoroughly well-made work, was more conservative but far more rewarding than most of the modern American music I had heard. It reminded me a little of Roussel (a point appreciated by the composer, who turned out to have been a pupil of Dukas). Charles Cushing, nearing retirement, was also very French in his tastes; he had studied under Nadia Boulanger for two years; his wife Charlotte was half-French. Their daughter Jennifer married Alan Curtis, another of my scholarly colleagues. Jack Swackhamer was a small man with a slightly grizzled untidy black beard. He reminded me of pictures of the young Tchaikovsky. He was extremely good company. He had served as a US Army medic in the Colorado ski troops during the war, he told us.

On 18 October, early in the morning, there was a minor earthquake. Two days later I kept to my bed, feeling weak. The weather was extremely hot – 88F in San Francisco. The heat continued until the end of the month, when I was felled by gastric flu. We visited the Berkeley Rose Garden on Euclid Avenue, bathed in the pool at Strawberry Canyon and took long walks in Tilden Park, a lovely nature reserve with lakes, many paths and trails and wonderful views. Once I was followed by a tame deer. On another occasion I watched two deer coming down to drink in a winding stream.

In November my health took a turn for the worse – and so did the weather. We had seen no rain apart from a slight shower in the middle of October but now it came down in bucketloads. I felt very unwell on 24 November; the next day – Thanksgiving Day – thunder shook the house and hail clattered down. My Tuesday seminars continued and the students came to further tape sessions – *Xerxes* (unfortunately with a tenor Xerxes) in November and *Orlando* the following month. I called on John Roberts, perhaps the brightest of my students, at his apartment at 14½ Hillside Court on the South side of campus, bearing the tape of *Ariodante*, a 1964 BBC broadcast under Arnold Goldsbrough, with Janet Baker incomparable in the title role. She was barely known in America then. In the second week of December, we lit the wood fire for the first time. For my last seminar of the year the countertenor John Thomas, a Berkeley student, sang Handel airs in the departmental rehearsal room.

We felt cut off from our friends over Christmas; we missed Stephen. Most of the cards from England arrived late. All the manifold preparations – including a stately Christmas tree with coloured lights – put a strain on Thalia, though she was assisted by the ever-cheerful Poppett, who baked an excellent cake. Clare and Mark looked in after lunch on Christmas Day and another of my students, the delightful Charlotte Greenspan, stayed for supper. The atmosphere in that small, dark house had become oppressive.

The New Year opened bleakly. Joe Kerman assisted at my seminar on 4 January. That evening I collapsed and for the next two days I stayed in bed, feeling awful. Larry Moe came to visit me. He was wonderfully sympathetic and understanding. He offered to take my next seminar, the last in the Handel series, if necessary. He recommended a psychiatrist, Dr Saxton Pope, at Cowell Hospital on College Avenue. I saw Dr Pope that afternoon, and liked him immediately, feeling sure he could help me. He prescribed a cessation of all mental work, walks in the countryside, tennis and gardening. I was still struggling with the lectures, though I had most of them in draft, and had a little work to do preparing the seminars on Romantic Opera, due to begin in February. Joe Kerman kindly agreed to take these over for the time being.

For the next weeks I saw Dr Pope regularly and gradually began to feel better, despite severe setbacks. I went for long walks with Thalia in Tilden Park. Though still January, it was often warmer than Fairnilee in August. Sometimes we would lie back in the grass and look up at the clear blue sky. I found a little gardening to do, though the cultivated garden at the house was tiny, the rest a steep canyon with redwood trees. I cut back some of the redwoods with great satisfaction, trimmed the hedge and pulled out brambles. Later a professional called Al Constantine came to tackle the redwoods. He wielded a saw on a long pole, similar to the device I used at Milford, while a colleague shinned up the trees like a monkey, lopping off branches with a handsaw at Thalia's direction.

Camellias were flowering in the garden, and fruit beginning to ripen on the lemon tree – though why it should choose do so at that time of year was unclear. We encountered strange animals and birds. One evening I spotted an enormous stag as big as a cow eating our roses. Poppett came upon a remarkable beast with a long nose and a long tail in the kitchen late one night. It had squeezed through Tinkerbell's small door in search of scraps. It turned out to be an opossum, a native American marsupial. After we had all inspected it the creature trotted off along the path like a small pig.

Thalia came down one morning to find the kitchen covered in feathers and a dishevelled-looking American robin sitting on the clothes-line. It had evidently had a tussle with Tinkerbell, which the robin must have won as Tinkerbell was nowhere to be seen. The bird hopped out when Thalia opened the big door and flew away, despite its lack of feathers.

I was touched to receive an elaborate 'Get Well Soon' card from my six students from the Handel seminar. It featured a motley collection of comic Ronald Searle characters – each of the students signed his or her name under an 'appropriate' figure! Old fears had returned. Unlike many of my colleagues, I was neither a performer nor a composer, nor had I been trained in the technicalities of musical scholarship. In February Philip wrote from Cambridge: 'I sincerely hope that the worst is now over. I think I can understand how the trouble arose, especially if you are surrounded by lots of aggressively practical musicians. But you have obviously been able, in your seminars, to arouse interest and enthusiasm in a manner beyond the reach of many practical musicians, & have every reason to feel proud of having done all you have done without the aid of the usual technical training: it has been a triumph of intelligence and sensitiveness over early difficulties.'

On 15 February I noted in my diary: 'worked a little for first time!' I finished the draft of the final lecture the next day. A fair bit of re-arranging and polishing was still needed. I had been commissioned to deliver six lectures but found I had material for seven and a half! Seven would be fine, said Joe, but the additional half might be a problem. In the end I combined Orchestration with Modern Revivals in my last lecture. At about this time someone lent me a tape of a dreadful performance of *Serse* from Milan. I had a very bad night.

On 23 February, Handel's birthday, we invited John Roberts round for coffee. John was a particularly gifted student and later a distinguished Handelian, visiting us at Hambledon and in Scotland. We talked Handel and played parts of my tape of the 1960 Handel Opera Society production of *Hercules*. I was feeling a little more ready for small social gatherings. Next evening Joe Kerman and Alan Curtis looked in. The following week, after a bad relapse, four of my old class, John, Peggy Radin, Sally Fuller and Charlotte Greenspan, came in to listen to Handel's *Imeneo*, a tape of extracts from the 1961 Birmingham production. Next day Thalia and I took the East Ridge Trail in Redwood Regional Park. Over the next fortnight I completed the second revision of all seven lectures.

We varied our walks, on one occasion taking the paved and relatively flat Nimitz Way, an old road constructed to access a redundant missile site, now returned to nature. We sun-bathed by a patch of wild lupins in Laurel Canyon, ambled round Lake Anza and struggled up the Wildcat Peak Trail, partly in sun and partly in shade, leading to a knoll with panoramic views of San Francisco and the Bay Area bridges.

On 14 March I wrote to Stephen (who was planning to visit Berkeley for three weeks during his school holidays in April): 'You will be able to hear my first two lectures – unfortunately not the most hilarious of the set. But they are all to be published. I am pretty sure of finishing them now, though I only work in the mornings. Some days I feel perfectly well, but there are still occasional bad patches.

Berkeley

'Yesterday we went for a walk in the hills and saw a strange meteorological phenomenon. It was sunny and warm at first, and then long tentacles of black mist started creeping in from the Pacific. The temperature suddenly dropped about 20 degrees and a mighty susurration began in the pines. Yet to the east there was still bright sunshine, with the tops of mountains floating about in a disconnected manner in the sky, and far to the west beyond the mist was a strip of gold light on the sea, so dazzling that it was impossible to look at.'

The garden and the surrounding countryside held unsuspected hazards. Thalia became infected by a plant called poison oak, which grew in profusion in the canyon below the house. It caused rashes and intolerable itching, which after a few days got worse rather than better. She began to feel quite leprous! A doctor gave her cortisone shots to prevent the sores blistering, assuring her cheerfully that the infection would last at least a fortnight. She was prescribed an ointment containing iron to smear on her chin and arms.

On 17 March (Diana's 11th Birthday) Sally Fuller, another extremely able student, came for the evening and dinner. The opera she had been assigned was *Giulio Cesare*; she has done a brilliant job. She became a good friend and years later we edited the opera together for Oxford University Press. After supper next evening (my 50th birthday – alas!), we were summoned to John Roberts' apartment at 14½ Hillside Court for a party given by the students to celebrate my half century. I knew nothing about this in advance. There was a birthday cake, and Champagne; the students performed a delicious little part-song, adapted from a Mozart canon, with a replacement text (supplied by Sally Fuller) 'Filicitas tibi Wintonius et jocunda nativitas'. Other delightful performances followed. At the end I was presented with a bottle of sherry and six avocado pears (a particular favourite of mine). They had even organised a sitter-in so that Poppett could come along too. I was deeply touched, and reluctant to leave.

I had abandoned Professor Potter's downstairs study – chatter and heavy footsteps reverberating through the wooden floor became intolerable – and migrated to the small bedroom destined for Stephen. I finished the lectures ready for typing on 22 March. Thalia undertook this arduous task, though work was suspended for a couple of days while Joe Kerman read through my manuscript. I spent three days selecting and timing music examples from my tapes and records – hampered when the tape machine broke down. The following Tuesday I felt well enough to take my first seminar on Romantic Opera. The four brightest students from the previous semester – Peggy, Charlotte, Sally and John – had been joined by Dan Coren and Marvin Tartak. In the afternoon we invited Dan Heartz, who had helped with the seminar in my absence, and all the students to a tape party – this time Traetta's 1772 opera *Antigone* – concluding with a convivial buffet supper provided by Thalia and Poppett.

On 31 March, a very hot day, I was frustrated not to be able to follow the General Election results in Britain, in which Peter Thomas lost his seat at Conway. I had a bad setback the following week; my appointment with Dr Pope was rushed forward to Monday. A technician in the office transferred my music examples on to seven separate reels. Few of the operas, apart from *Alcina*, had been commercially recorded then; Alan Curtis supplied some of the gaps with vigorous renditions on the harpsichord. The descent of the goddess Fortune on a wheel in *Giustino* was particularly effective: the music, suggesting the rotation of a wheel, seemed to evoke a picture of the goddess mounted on a bicycle!

We greeted Stephen at San Francisco Airport on 6 April; Thalia burst into tears. Stephen enjoyed his three weeks in Berkeley. We went to Tilden Park, where I photographed him interrogating a large goose by Jewel Lake. Sometimes he was content to retreat to the study downstairs (which I had vacated), browsing among Professor

Potter's rich collection of English poetry. Some days were very hot indeed; at the same time, in Britain, blizzards were reported: April 14 was the coldest April day in London since 1911, I noted in my diary.

My first Bloch lecture, on the Opera Seria Convention, was to take place in Room 155, Dwinelle Hall, a vast, labyrinthine building dating from the early 1950s. I saw Dr Pope in the afternoon. Before the lecture, Joe Kerman took us for a meal at the Faculty Club. We drank a glass or two of wine, including Stephen; Joe looked round anxiously as at 19 Stephen was under-age according to the laws of California. A fair audience, including all my students and a sprinkling of my colleagues, had assembled in the well-appointed lecture theatre. Joe introduced me in very flattering terms as the author of the best book on music published since the war.

The lecture went without a hitch. I felt very tired afterwards, but immense relief (as I reported to Dr Pope the next day). The taped examples came over very well. Much of the music would have been unfamiliar – except the first example, 'Handel's Largo', not a sacred piece, despite finding favour with church organists, and not marked 'Largo', but the opening arioso of the opera *Serse*, sung by an Oriental monarch (a soprano castrato) who falls in love with a tree. Handel's operas, until very recent times, had scarcely met with more comprehension.

Postscript

Winton's lectures, after his severe breakdown in the winter, were a success. In between he gave additional talks at Santa Barbara (where they breakfasted with the composer Peter Racine Fricker), a round trip of 883 miles, he noted in his diary, and at Stanford University at Palo Alto. On 3 May an article by Peggy Radin, one of Winton's students, appeared in the *Daily Californian*: 'Dean's lectures are to be published … But do not wait to read them instead of coming to listen; you will be deprived of some wonderful musical examples; and of the pleasure of knowing Winton Dean … For he is in the noble tradition of English men of letters: he speaks and writes with ease, eloquence, erudition – and delight … here is a man of impeccable scholarly acumen who presents his material with surpassing warmth; whose love of the music he talks about is almost palpable.'

In 2023 Sally Fuller and Charlotte Greenspan wrote: 'Winton Dean's Berkeley Handel Opera seminar was memorable on several counts, but two in particular stand out. One was his incomparable passion for his subject and his ability to convey to his students his keen insights into the dramatic and emotional core of Handel's operas. Through him, they took on life for us, not least because he brought with him many private tape recordings that allowed us to hear complete operas often interpreted by eminent singers of the day. And we were also touched by his and Thalia's hospitality and generosity in inviting us to their house for extended listening sessions that involved tea and biscuits and often dinner. We were

Postscript

most graciously welcomed by them, unusual in our graduate student experience. To this day, decades later, viewing or listening to a Handel opera, or even hearing a single aria, conjures up that remarkable Berkeley seminar and Winton and Thalia's supportive presence.'

Index

Abel Smith, Vice-Admiral Sir Conolly 409, 566, 567, 587
Abercrombie, Lascelles 34
Abraham, Frances 441, 470, 540, 543, 573, 589
Abraham, Gerald 318-19, 401, 441, 442, 443-4, 470, 485, 508-9, 517, 523, 533, 534, 537, 540, 543, 565, 573, 581-2, 589, 595, 597, 604-5
Abraham, Pat 441, 442, 470, 540, 543, 565, 573, 581-2, 589, 597, 604-5
Adamson, Myrtle 13, 148-9
Adcock, F.E 163, 164
Addison, Joseph 285, 556
Adler, Alfred 180, 207
Aeschylus 147, 213, 214, 222
Alcira 38-9, 40, 261
Alexander (photographer) 506
Alexandra, Princess 514
Alice (maid) 288
Allen, Mr and Mrs 391
Allingham, William 73
Ambariotis, Mr 253
Amery, L.S. 291
Ames, Leslie 94
Amis, John 515
Anderson, Ande 495, 502
Anderson, Emily 552, 556
Anderson, Sir Kenneth 362
Anderson, Mary 123
Annan, Noel 282, 318, 578
Anning Bell, Laura 525
Anning Bell, Robert 525
Antonio (dancer) 492
Archibald, John 95
Ardrey, Robert 367
Aristophanes 105, 118, 147, 200, 552
Arkwright, Major Albert 409
Armand (Diana's father) 454
Arne, Thomas 350, 442, 480, 533
Arnold, Denis 573, 604
Arrowsmith, Bob 377, 379
Arundell, Dennis 270, 482, 552, 598
Ashby, Rev. Norman 75
Ashdown, Arthur 53
Ashton, Frederick 223
Aspasia 143
Asquith, H.H. 67
Atkins, Ivor 341-2
Atkinson, B.G.W. 144-5
Auber, Daniel 540
Auden, W.H. 162, 163, 288, 345, 542
Audran, Edmond 578
Avgherinos (Greek family) 84
Aylmer, Felix 270

Index

Bach, Johann Sebastian 198, 199, 232, 265, 290, 324, 386, 400, 442, 524, 557, 598
Bäck, Sven-Erik 556
Bacon, Charlotte (Lota) 29-30, 35, 82, 88, 195
Bacon, Lewis 88
Bacon, Roger 35
Bacon, Sewell 35, 82
Bagger, Enid 169, 179, 180
Bagger, Esther, née Van Gruisen, formerly Dean 12, 13, 23, 24, 25, 26, 27-37, 38, 39, 40, 41, 45, 47, 48, 49, 50, 51-52, 53, 54, 55, 58, 61, 62, 64, 65, 74, 77-96 *passim*, 109, 110, 114, 128-36 *passim*, 141, 143-8 *passim*, 151, 157, 170, 177-85 *passim*, 191, 192, 193-4, 196-7, 203-9 *passim*, 211, 216, 217-18, 219, 220, 224, 227, 260-3, 264, 268, 288, 291, 296, 314, 319-20, 332, 335, 336, 351-2, 354, 357, 360, 364, 366, 370-1, 381, 385, 415, 424, 431, 433, 449, 458, 465-6, 484, 492, 515, 564, 572, 582, 585, 623, 630
Bagger, Eugene 28, 82, 179 and n., 180, 182, 189-90, 191, 192, 193-6, 197, 202-3, 205, 206, 207, 217, 219, 224, 227, 234, 260-1, 262, 263, 268, 291, 319-20, 335, 336, 338-9, 352, 354, 357, 370-1, 415, 424, 431, 433-4, 449, 458
Bagger, Palline 179
Bailey, Lady Janet (Aunt Nan) 437, 488, 553, 554
Bailey, Nigel 487, 488
Bailey, Rupert 270, 300-1
Baillie, Isobel 317
Baillie, Major Simon 408-9

Baines, Anthony 510
Baker, Janet 513, 557, 577, 605, 625, 637
Bakewell, Fred 95-6
Bal, Jesus 368
Balaskas, Xenophon 189
Bald, Mr 621
Baldry, Brian 612, 630
Baldry, Nicola 574
Baldry, Pat 612, 630
Balkwill, John 90, 177, 271, 608
Balkwill, Michael 90, 177, 264, 389, 608, 609
Balkwill, Violet (Vie), see Dean
Banks, Sergeant-Major 107
Barkworth, J.E. 577
Barlow, Christopher 212
Barnby, Sir Joseph 577
Barrie, J.M. 104
Barrington-Ward, Sir Lancelot 216
Bartered Bride, The (Smetana) 339, 377, 583
Bartlett, Ethel 103
Bartley, Brigid, later Rees 184-5, 190-1, 193, 202, 203-8 *passim*, 212, 216, 217, 218, 220, 221, 293, 312, 315, 330, 331, 348-9, 380, 389-90, 411, 414, 425, 445, 448, 454, 458, 575
Bartley, Mrs 207
Bartók, Béla 323, 636
Barton, John 548
Barton, Miss 534, 550, 551
Basiola, Mario 355
Baylis, Lilian 146
Bayne, J. 600
Beale, Mr (farmer) 85
Beaverbrook, Max Aitken, 1st Baron 570

Becker, Amelia (Nan) 27-8,
  32, 50, 53
Beddoes, Thomas Lovell 290
Beecham, Adrian 576
Beecham, Sir Thomas 36, 173,
  187, 266, 316, 325, 326, 450, 453,
  456-7, 505
Beeching, Dr Richard 40, 388
Beechey, William 613
Beethoven, Ludwig van vi, 4, 19,
  143, 169, 173, 198, 207, 232, 233,
  264, 265, 266, 273-4, 280, 281,
  286-7, 316, 317, 321, 325, 327, 341,
  355, 401, 440, 463, 547, 551-2,
  553, 556, 594
Belasco, David 6
Bell, Julian 161
Bellini, Vincenzo 467, 524,
  540, 541, 624
Belloc, Hilaire 459
Belshaw, Miss 560
Benda, Georg 577
Ben Hur (1925 film) 68, 93
Bennett, Richard Rodney 622
Bennett, Mr 475
Benninger, Rosemarie 581,
  582, 585, 590
Berdyaev, Nikolai 312
Beresford, Lord Charles 224
Berg, Alban 264, 535, 567
Bergmann, Dr 431
Berkeley, Freda 418, 424, 432,
  442, 497, 512,
Berkeley, Julian 417
Berkeley, Lennox v, 342, 345, 417-19,
  424, 432, 435, 440, 442, 443, 445,
  446, 451, 456, 464-5, 497, 636
– *Nelson* 418-19, 432, 435, 442,
  443-4, 445

Berkeley, Michael 417
Berlioz, Hector 468-9, 499, 523,
  524, 556, 580
Bernac, Pierre 325
Bernard, Anthony 329, 500
Berridge, Rosamond 334, 351
Berridge, Rev. 334
Berryman, John 302
Besch, Anthony 467, 471, 480-1,
  506, 514, 584
Betterton, Kathleen 395-6
Betty (Tommy's intended) 23
Beveridge, Hal 13
Beves, Donald 166-7, 172, 188, 202,
  212, 213, 215, 276, 288, 318, 339,
  340, 432, 369
Bewley, Neville 161, 175-6
Bickford, Commander 386
Bigg, William Redmore 438
Binks, Martin 328
Bircher, Freddie 532
Birley, Robert 298-9, 377
Birtwistle, Harrison 118
Bizet, Geneviève 422, 423
Bizet, Georges 66, 79, 101, 201, 232,
  272, 318, 326, 346, 394, 396, 397,
  401, 412, 413-14, 422-3, 425, 456,
  457, 478, 482, 504, 507, 512, 517,
  522, 535, 546-7, 574, 575, 579, 594,
  595, 597, 599, 605, 619, 620, 624,
  625, 628-9
– *L'Arlésienne* 605
– *Carmen* 77, 78, 79, 146, 174, 222,
  240, 281, 289, 346, 396, 399, 400,
  414, 423, 504, 535, 546-7, 548,
  628-9, 633
– *La Coupe du Roi de Thulé* 399, 400,
  423-4, 453-4, 456, 597
Blacher, Boris 572

Index

Blackball, Bishop Offspring 285
Blackmore, G.P.D. 404
Blackmore, R.D. 24
Blake, William 134, 175
Bliss, Sir Arthur 500, 510, 514, 537, 562
Bloch, Ernest 525, 529, 573, 583, 633, 643
Blom, Eric 328, 396, 397, 400, 401, 414, 415, 424, 433, 436, 443, 448, 456, 477, 482, 489, 490, 501, 504, 505, 506, 507, 523, 533, 564, 621
Blom, Molly 433
Blomdahl, Karl-Birger 520
Blomfield, Sir Reginald 187
Blow, John 453, 464
Blumenfeld, R. D. 223
Blunt, Anthony 161
Boas, Philip 104-5
Boieldieu, François-Adrién 534, 538, 540
Boissier, A.P. 105
Boissier, June, later Marchioness of Aberdeen 105-6
Boito, Arrigo 473
Bonynge, Richard 624
Booker, Dr Frederick 424, 478, 479, 550
Borgioli, Dino 233, 267
Boris Godunov (Mussorgsky) 261
Borodin, Alexander 318, 438
Borthwick, Rev. A.E. 421
Bostock, John 99, 100, 106-7, 109, 114, 115, 116, 117, 118, 120, 125, 127, 128, 129
Boulanger, Nadia 636
Boulez, Pierre 603
Boult, Adrian 181, 201, 271-2, 317, 325, 354, 377
Boulter, Mr 625, 627
Bourne, Roland 190
Bowra, Maurice 167
Boyden, David 583
Boyden, Ruth 583
Bowland 570, 571, 591
Bradley, A.C. 306
Bradman, Donald 145
Bradshaw, T.E.J. 104, 105
Bradshaw, Mrs 105
Brahms, Johannes 173, 190, 230, 266, 287, 303, 307, 317, 324, 325, 341, 346, 401, 507, 622
Brearley, Walter 71
Brecht, Bertolt 574
Brett, Christopher 553
Brett, Philip 483, 525, 552, 555, 558, 569, 583, 622, 623
Brett, Miss 54, 55, 58
Brice, Mitford 82, 95-7, 178
Bridge, Frank 325, 354
Bridie, James 123
Brierley, Major 71
Briggs, Lizzie 45
Britten, Benjamin 174, 324-5, 345-6, 353, 416-17, 426, 433, 435-6, 442, 449, 455, 471, 495, 510, 526-7, 534, 535, 562, 588, 611-12, 623
Broadwood, Captain Evelyn 318
Bromley, Diana, née Pratt 470, 475, 478, 479, 480, 485, 497, 498, 503
Bromley, Martin 475, 479, 480, 485, 497
Bromley, Stephen 475, 479, 480, 485, 497
Bromley, Tom 475, 478-9, 497, 499, 507, 543
Brontë, Emily 316
Brooke, Rupert 68, 268

Brown, Coral 270
Brown, Ivor 125
Brown, John 503
Browning, Robert 165, 274
Brownlee, John 267
Bruce, Archibald 430, 488, 629
Bruce, Jimmy 621
Bruckner, Anton 199, 232, 272, 509
Buccleuch, 8th Duke of 395
Buccleuch Estate Office 593
Buck, Sir Percy 318
Buckingham, Duke of 121
Burge, Bill 453
Busbridge 154, 343, 374, 519
Busch, Adolf 325
Bush, Alan 533
Busoni, Ferruccio 199, 280
Butt, Dame Clara 157
Bynoe, Mr (dentist) 489, 496-7, 551, 581, 626, 627
Byrd, William 453, 507
Brymer, Jack 507
Byron, Lord 243, 292

Caclamanos, Mr 215
Cairns, David 548
Calfshaw Cottage 490-1, 496, 519, 520, 521, 529, 532, 543, 545, 546, 549, 562, 564, 565, 566, 568, 570, 571, 588, 590, 592, 593, 594, 599, 612, 614, 615, 616, 617
Callas, Maria 436, 476, 512
Calvert, Wilkie 95
Calvin 112
Cambridge Handel Festival (1935) 187-8
Cameron, C.J.G. 447
Cameron, Julia Margaret 543
Cameron, Mariel 447

Campion, Mrs 85, 379
Caniglia, Maria 355
Cantelo, April 481
Čapek, Karel 145, 602
Cardus, Neville 537
Carey, Clive 146
Carissimi, Giacomo 536
Carner, Mosco 326, 499, 518
Caroline, Queen 167
Carrara-Verdi, Gabriella 528
Carroll, Madeleine 36
Carroll, Sydney 139
Cartwright, Mary 440
Carvalho, John 468
Casals, Pablo 316
Casson, Sir Hugh 606
Catel, Charles-Simon 534
Cathcart, Marie (Mrs Harry Isaacs 1) 18, 22
Catullus 147, 237
Cecil, Lord David 390
Celli, Faith 49, 619
Chabrier, Emmanuel 400
Chaliapin, Feodor 231
Chamberlain, Neville 343, 362
Chance, Michael 95
Chaplin, Charlie 74, 309
Charles II 339-40, 547
Charles, Prince of Wales vii
Charterhouse School 79, 173, 225, 298, 321, 371, 373-4, 375, 377, 379, 423
Chaucer, Geoffrey 285
Chekhov, Anton 330, 331, 332
Chenevix-Trench, Anthony 516-17
Cherubini, Luigi 508, 512, 531, 542, 551, 552-3, 561, 579, 603, 604
Chester, Frederick 73
Chesterton, G.K. 104

Index

Chick, Mr 140
Chissell, Joan 401
Chopin, Frédéric 293, 327
Christie, Agatha 482
Christie, J.M. (Kibosh) 68-9, 76
Christison, General Sir Philip 387, 409, 476, 521, 530, 547, 566, 612
Christoff, Boris 486
Christson, Christ 253
Chrysander, Friedrich 489, 500, 602, 629
Church, Richard 272-3
Churchill, Dr Stella 287
Churchill, Sir Winston 108, 118-19, 387, 475
Cicero 189, 205
Cilea, Francesco 588
Clapham, Jana 185, 188, 222, 268
Clapham, J.H. 183, 184
Clapham, Michael 183
Clapham, Lady 184
Clarendon, Edward Hyde, 1st Earl of 352
Clark, Judge Gordon (Cyril Hare) 456
Clarke, Jeremiah 453
Clayton, Rev. P.B. 116
Clifford, Anne 338, 356, 560, 564, 582
Clifford, Derek 215, 273, 338, 356, 560, 564, 582
Clifford, Timothy 274
Clunes, Alec 465
Coade, T.F. 106
Coates, Albert 266, 325
Coates, Edith 355
Coates, John 103
Cockerell, Lady Florence 175
Cockerell, Sir Sydney 174-5

Cocteau, Jean 478
Cohen, Alice, later Marchioness of Reading 20-1
Coke, Gerald 424
Colchester, Halsey 344-5, 351, 389
Coleridge, Samuel Taylor 105
Collier, Marie 602, 628
Collings, Mr and Mrs 515
Collingwood, Lawrance 289
Colville, Jock 108, 175
Compton, Denis 357
Congreve, William 609
Conrad, Joseph 62
Constable, John 186-7
Constantine, Al 638
Cooke, Deryck 537
Coomber, Mrs Florence 421-2, 432
Coombs, Mr 579-80
Cooper, Gerald 353
Cooper, Harold 403, 404
Cooper, Martin 346, 401, 425, 452, 505, 533, 540, 570
Copeland, Miss 85
Copland, Aaron 551, 554-5
Coren, Dan 642
Cornford, John 161
Coronation of Poppea (Monteverdi) 561, 563, 623
Cortot, Alfred 280
Cossa, Gabor 524
Coupland, Dr G.M. 627, 630
Coward, Noel 210
Cox, Sister 64-5, 115
Craig-Jones, Douglas 237-8
Craigmyle, Alexander Shaw, 2nd Baron 332, 333-4, 337, 343, 344, 345, 353, 354, 358, 359, 360-1, 362, 363, 376, 380, 386, 391, 393, 395, 488, 606, 614, 615, 621

Craigmyle, Anthea, née Rich 359, 455, 458, 464, 469, 470, 472, 478, 490, 491, 499, 510, 521, 532, 545, 553, 554, 555, 583, 586, 595, 596, 599, 601, 603, 611, 613, 618, 621, 626
Craigmyle, Donald Shaw, 3rd Baron 333-4, 345, 362, 363, 380, 394, 405, 407, 434, 435, 443, 455, 458, 464, 466, 469, 470, 472, 478, 488, 490, 491-2, 499, 510, 521, 532, 545, 549, 553, 554, 565, 566, 583, 586, 587, 590, 594, 596, 597, 599, 601, 603, 606, 613, 618, 621, 626
Craigmyle, Margaret v, 179n, 332, 333, 337, 339, 343, 344, 348, 351, 352, 354, 358, 359, 361, 362, 363, 375, 376, 380, 386, 391, 393, 394, 395, 397-8, 405, 408, 410, 414, 416, 424, 429, 430, 435, 437, 438, 443, 444, 447, 458, 462, 466, 470, 472, 476, 480, 483, 486-8, 489, 490, 592, 607, 621, 629
Craigmyle, Thomas Shaw, 1st Baron 331
Cranmer, Arthur 187
Cravcenko, Angelica 304
Creber, Mr 512
Cregan, Dr 207, 216, 367
Cripps, Sir Stafford 143
Cross, Joan 289
Cross, John 103
Crozier, Eric 446
Cudworth, Charles 540, 547, 598
Cumberland Terrace 129-30, 144, 182, 193, 202, 203, 204, 206, 207, 219, 220, 260, 362, 391
Cunliffe-Lister, Philip 72-3
Cursiter, Stanley 613

Curtis, Alan 636, 640, 642
Curtiss, Mina 422-3, 456, 507, 517, 522, 600, 632
Curzon, Clifford 234-5, 264, 281, 282, 286, 303, 306-7, 327, 347-8
Curzon, George 136
Cushing, Charles 636
Cushing, Charlotte 636
Cushing, Jennifer, later Curtis 636

Dalayrac, Nicolas 538
Dale, Benjamin 318
Dallapiccola, Luigi 518, 538, 552
Dalmeny, Lord, later 6th Earl of Rosebery 71
Dance, Maurice 406
Dance, W. 406, 425, 450, 474, 475
Dane, Clemence 146-7, 619
Daniel, Samuel 79
Danielle (au pair) 604, 610, 614
Da Ponte, Lorenzo 355
Darbishire, Elizabeth 328
Darke, Harold 342, 369
Dart, Thurston (Bob) 461, 493, 524, 528, 540, 551, 559, 562, 569, 570, 578, 609, 612, 617
Daudet, Alphonse 605
Davenant, Sir William 511
David, Dick 214
Davies, Fanny 42
Davies, Tudor 289, 355
Davies, Miss 73, 74, 76, 78-9
Davis, Beatrice 15
Davis, Colin 536
Davis, Daniel 14-15
Davis, Esther, later Miller 16
Davis, Fanny 15
Davis, Godfrey 15
Davis, Jane 15

Index

Davis, Lizzie, later Miller 15, 16
Davis, Philip 95
Davis, Phoebe, later Miller 15, 16
Davison, Barbara, later Balkwill 271
Davison, John 271, 283, 299, 308, 314, 334, 338, 345
Dawson, Peter 77
Dean, Basil 5, 8, 27, 28-37, 38, 46, 48-50, 53, 61, 62, 77, 82, 93, 96, 114, 120, 132, 136-140, 146, 177, 178, 180, 183, 197, 203, 208-11, 214-15, 216-17, 222, 223, 224, 260, 261-2, 263, 267, 269, 282, 291-2, 319-20, 330, 336, 338-9, 345-6, 353-4, 361, 373, 389, 392, 410, 424, 435, 436, 441, 443, 444-5, 448, 465-6, 473, 474, 486, 492-3, 514, 523, 572, 582, 594, 597, 608, 619, 623
– *The Blue Lagoon* 48-9, 619
– *Fifinella* 34, 49, 474
Dean, Brigid Miriam 49, 135, 380, 386, 387, 389, 390, 391-2, 404, 461, 587, 603
Dean, Catherine (Aunt Kate) 8, 9
Dean, Clara Ellen, see Dunbar-Smith (Aunt Nellie)
Dean, Diana Margaret 410-11, 414
Dean, Diana Rosamund Thalia, later Bracewell 385, 449, 454, 456, 458, 461-2, 463, 473, 475, 492, 493, 506, 519, 521, 530, 535, 540, 562, 564, 565, 567, 570, 574, 575, 576, 577, 581-2, 585, 586, 589, 591, 596, 603, 607, 610, 614-15, 619, 620, 623, 630, 631, 632, 633
Dean, Dorothy 11
Dean, Duncan 11

Dean, Elizabeth Mary, née Winton 6, 9, 10, 11, 12, 31, 51, 77, 140-1, 174, 178, 217, 218, 260, 263
Dean, Harding Hewer 5, 6, 9-11, 12, 31, 51, 77, 140-1, 174, 178, 217, 218, 260
Dean, Jenefer, née Mills, 558, 575, 610
Dean, Johnson 8
Dean, Joseph (baker) 6, 8
Dean, Joseph (1816-1895) 6, 9
Dean, Joseph (1921-2010) 9-10, 33, 46, 50, 51, 53, 57, 58, 60, 61, 62, 74, 75, 84-92 *passim*, 94, 127, 128, 130, 139-40, 142, 147, 149, 150, 153, 157, 182- 3, 186, 187, 191, 194, 196, 203, 204, 206, 207, 209, 215, 217-18, 219, 220, 221, 224, 260, 263, 291-2, 314, 335-6, 364, 366, 380, 381, 385, 386, 411, 416, 425, 458, 469, 492, 558, 575, 610, 623
Dean, Madeline 11, 141, 143
Dean, Martin 33, 46, 47, 50, 52, 53, 58, 59, 60, 61, 62, 72, 74, 75, 77, 83, 84, 87, 88, 91, 92, 27, 130, 137-8, 139, 141, 142, 149, 150, 153, 182-3, 186-7, 196, 203, 204, 217-18, 219, 224, 260, 262, 263, 291, 314, 335, 336, 339, 352, 364, 366, 396, 411, 415, 416, 458, 492, 519, 545-6, 558, 572, 581, 596, 600, 601, 603, 607, 610, 611
Dean, Nancy (Nan) née Lynch 415, 416, 492, 519, 545, 558, 581
Dean, Pinkerton Jenns 6
Dean, Stephen 55, 170, 396, 398, 405-11 *passim*, 414, 416, 421, 422, 424, 429- 38 *passim*, 441, 444, 447-50, 454, 455, 458, 459, 461-2, 463, 469, 470, 475, 476, 479, 480,

484-5, 486, 491, 497, 506, 513-20 *passim*, 524, 529, 530, 532, 533, 541, 543, 545, 546, 551, 555, 558, 562, 563, 565, 567, 574, 576, 578, 585, 590, 591, 597, 604-10 *passim*, 614, 615, 616, 619, 623, 624, 625, 628, 630, 631, 634, 637, 640, 642-3
Dean, Tessa, later Thomas 80, 136-7, 139, 219, 224, 389, 391, 396, 410, 412, 435, 441, 492, 572
Dean, Thalia, née Shaw vi, vii, 62, 89, 179 and n., 330-4, 337-41, 343-53, 356, 357, 358-63, 364-68, 371, 373-77, 379-81, 385-7, 389-92, 393-98, 405, 407, 408, 410-11, 414-16, 420-1, 425, 428-32, 434-7, 441-4, 447, 448, 454, 455, 456, 457, 466, 470-80 *passim*, 482, 483, 486-91 *passim*, 494, 496, 497, 503-19 *passim*, 524, 528, 529, 530, 532-50 *passim*, 553-4, 555, 558, 562, 563, 565, 567, 568, 571, 572, 573-82 *passim*, 589, 590, 591, 592, 593, 595, 596, 597, 599, 601, 602, 605-30 *passim*, 631, 632, 633, 635, 637, 638, 639, 640, 641, 642, 644, 645
Dean, Vernon 11, 90, 96, 143, 177-8, 180, 208, 217, 224, 282, 291, 319, 608
Dean, Violet (Vie), formerly Balkwill 11, 90, 94, 177, 178, 179-80, 181-2, 193, 206, 208, 209, 217, 218, 219, 222, 224, 234, 260, 261, 262, 264, 268, 269, 270, 271, 272, 283, 294, 319, 331, 336, 349, 351, 353, 354, 357, 360-1, 367, 376-7, 389, 397, 608
Dean, William 8
Dean, William Boswell 6-8, 9
Deane, Richard, Admiral 8

Dean-Smith, Margaret 174, 331
Defoe, Daniel 143
Degas, Edgar 169
Dehn, Paul 442, 497
Delius, Frederick 36, 326, 341, 401, 508, 560
Deller, Alfred 453, 509, 526
Demuth, Norman 401, 402
De Navarro, Toty 122
Denison, Michael 120
Denny, William 636
Dent, Edward J. vi, 146, 187, 188, 198-9, 200, 215, 265, 275, 276, 278, 280-1, 289, 318, 327, 328, 339, 341, 343, 355, 356, 397, 401, 429, 439, 451, 533, 556
Denyer, Mr 42
Dermota, Anton 304
De Selincourt, Hugh 264
Deutsch, Otto Erich 417
De Vere Stacpoole, Henry 48
Deviot, Gordon 146
Dewart, Elizabeth (Zee) 390, 434, 435
Diaghilev, Sergei 31
Diana, Princess of Wales vii
Dickens, Charles 66, 579
Dickinson, A.E.F. 401
D'Indy, Vincent 235
Dietrich, Marlene 231
Dieudonné, Annette 399
Dilke, Ossie 214
Disraeli, Benjamin 14
Dittersdorf, Karl Ditters von 585
Dmitrov, Mesdemoiselles 239, 240, 257
Doble, Frances 36
Dobson, Dennis 413

Index

Dobson, Meric 237, 238, 239, 249, 251, 253, 254, 257, 258, 269
Dods, Billy 480
Dods, June, née Sowman 444
Dods, Peter 394, 444, 480, 488, 520, 524, 532, 546, 565, 586, 587, 599, 601, 621
Dods, Peter (junior) 601
Dods, Wattie 394, 444, 532, 546, 567, 586, 587, 596-7, 599, 601, 607, 616, 618, 620, 621, 629
Doe, Paul 551
Domgraf-Fassbaender, Willi 304
Donizetti, Gaetano vi, 214, 436, 595, 624, 626
Doone, Rupert 288
Dorothy (cook) 45
Dostoyevsky, Fyodor 434, 566, 614
Dover, Rev. O.L.S. 488
Dowland, John 453
Downes, Kerry 557
Draper, Ruth 215
Drinkwater, John 120, 271, 274
Drummond of Megginch, John 619
Dryden, John 285, 349, 511, 525
Ducat, Andy 152
Duckles, Vincent 579, 618, 634, 635
Dugdale, Captain 125
Dukas, Paul 235, 636
Duleepsinhji, Kumar Shri 95
Dumas, Alexandre 336
Dunbar-Smith, Arnold 5, 174-5
Dunbar-Smith, Nellie 5, 174, 264
Dunn, Geoffrey 328
Dunn, J.W. 123-4
Dunning, G.C. 122
Dunovan, Margaret 45
Dürer, Albrecht 312
Duveen, Claude 314

Dvořák, Antonín 90, 354
Dyer, Mr 421
Dyer, Mrs Kay 421

Ealing Studios 139-40, 210-11
Easton Lodge 93, 137, 223-4
Ebert, Carl 471
Eccles, John 609
Edney-Hayter, Captain Frederick Charles 388
Edward IV 93, 139
Edward VII 137, 224
Edward VIII 231, 271
Edwards, Fred 297
Eeman, Beryl 302
Einstein, Alfred 540
Elgar, Sir Edward 103, 199, 325, 326, 341, 514
– *Enigma Variations* 103, 117, 341
Elibank, Arthur Murray, 3rd Viscount 49, 619
Eliot, T.S. 162, 222, 270, 272, 290, 353
Elizabeth I 459
Elliot, Mr 488
Elliott, Denholm 465
Elston, Anne 636
Elston, Arnold 636
Elstree School 62-81, 115
Eminent Victorians (Lytton Strachey) 147
Eminton, Ann 440
Emptage, Beryl 356
English, Gerald 431
English, Miss 64
Enriquez, Franco 608
ENSA 32, 210, 353, 370, 373, 493
Epstein, Jacob 15, 143
Ervine, St John Greer 27

Euclid 555
Euripides 163, 213, 214, 269, 606
Evans, B. Ifor 156
Evans, Edwin 342-3
Evans, Geraint 481, 627
Evans, Peter 275
Evans, W. D. 596
Ewing, Mr and Mrs 377

Fairnilee 49, 343-5, 358-63, 374, 376, 394, 395, 405, 408, 409, 426, 428, 437, 444, 455, 459, 466, 476, 486-9, 490, 491, 493, 496, 517, 519, 520, 521, 522, 524, 532-3, 545, 549, 550, 564, 566, 570, 571, 586, 587, 590-4, 596-7, 598, 599-601, 603, 606-7, 608, 609, 612-14, 615-17, 618-19, 620-1, 629, 638
Falkner, Keith 537
Falla, Manuel de 492
Fane, Lady Augusta 223
Farnaby, Giles 453
Farncombe, Charles 451, 452, 462, 467, 468, 472, 482, 485, 500, 501, 502, 514, 515, 518, 523, 531, 532, 563, 584, 602, 604
Farncombe, Sally 602, 607
Farnfield, Dick 427
Fauré, Gabriel 401
Fawcett, Gillian 543
Fell, Clare Isobel 123
Ferrier, Kathleen 431
Ferris, Headley 380
Ferris, Phyllis 380
Fibich, Zdeněk 580
Fielden, Thomas 321
Fielder, Mr & Mrs 85, 95
Field-Hyde, Margaret 327, 369
Fields, Gracie 140, 210

Finzi, Gerald 424
Fischer, Edwin 280, 325
Fish, James 345
Fish, Nigel 427-8
Fiske, Roger 493, 495, 497, 499, 570
Fitzgerald, Mr 82, 84, 88
Flanders, Michael 480
Flecker, James Elroy 31, 33, 67, 424
Fleming, Dr 359
Fletcher, B.A. 110
Flint, Russell 141
Flotow, Friedrich von 438
Flower, Sir Newman 401, 433, 477, 507
Floyd, Carlisle 544
Foch, Ferdinand 67
Fontanne, Lynn (Lunt) 330
Fonteyn, Margot 317
Forbes-Robertson, Jean 214
Forbes-Robertson, Sir Johnson 171
Forester, C.S. 104
Formby, George 210
Forres, Lord 226
Forrester-Paton, Isabel 389
Forster, E.M. 368, 555, 578
Forster, John 357
Fortescue, Sir John 119
Fortune, Nigel 452, 453, 470, 498, 500, 503, 506, 507-8, 509, 511, 512, 529, 537, 541, 542, 551, 557, 559, 563, 564, 585, 598, 604, 606
Forty, Lieutenant-Colonel 110, 112
Fox, Mr 86
Frank, Alan 422, 460, 461, 462, 463, 467, 468, 477, 507, 509, 514-15, 539
Franklin, David 275, 277
Franck, César 232, 326, 414
Franco, Francisco 196, 265, 312, 368, 372

Index

Franz Joseph, Emperor 179
Freeman, Rosemary 299
Freeman, Mrs 425, 429
Freud, Sigmund 1, 180
Fricker, Peter Racine 644
Friedrich, Karl 305
Fry, Miss 89-90
Fučik, Julius 77
Fuller, Sarah vi, 640, 641, 642, 644
Furtwängler, Wilhelm 266, 286-7, 303

Gainsborough, Thomas 613
Galbraith, Jamie 593, 596, 599, 618
Galsworthy, John 62, 104, 147
Gamble, Patrick 137
Gandy, Christopher 269
Gardiner, Henry Balfour 101
Gardner, Mrs 223
Garnett, J.C. Maxwell 110, 113
Gascoyne, Anthony 359
Gaubert, Philippe 286
Gauntlett, Joan 403
Gauntlett, Mike 402-3, 404, 441, 474, 489, 508, 541, 630
Gaveaux, Pierre 595
Geary, George 379
Geddes, Audrey 393
Geddes, David 393
Gee, John 568, 592, 597, 618, 626
Gee, Rachel 536, 539, 568, 592, 618, 626
Gelatt, Roland 486
Gellhorn, Peter 611
Gentele, Göran 545
George V 175, 208, 209
George VI 616
Gerhard, Poldi 368
Gerhard, Roberto 265, 368

Gerhardt, Elena 286, 354
Gertrude (housemaid) 45
Gesualdo, Carlo 535
General, The (film) 93, 104
Ghost Goes West, The (film) 204
Gibbons, Orlando 453
Gibbs, Cecil Armstrong 147
Gibson, Susan 614-15
Gielgud, Sir John 103-4, 146, 471
Gigli, Beniamino 232
Gilbert, W.S. 105
Gill, Soapy 368
Gina 548, 549, 581, 590, 595, 628
Giraudoux, Jean 330
Girvan, Miriam 371-2, 373, 380, 386, 387
Giulini, Carlo Maria 618
Glendinning, Michael 488
Glock, William 326
Gluck, Christoph Willibald 232, 286, 431, 450, 505-6, 525, 545, 553, 577, 603, 604
Gobbi, Tito 486, 605
Goebbels, Dr Josef 256
Goethe, Johann Wolfgang von 118, 188, 524
Goldmark, Carl 232, 571
Goldsbrough, Arnold 553, 577, 586, 605, 637
Goodall, Reginald 326, 349
Goose, Mr 616
Goossens, Mrs 'Booney' 33
Goossens, Eugene 33
Gordon, Mrs 281
Gore, Bishop Charles 116
Göring, Hermann 369
Gosse, Edmund 24
Gotter, F.W. 577
Gounod, Charles 201, 232, 470, 577

Gover, Alf 144-5
Goya, Francisco 312, 414
Grace, W.G. 403
Graham, Dr 359
Graham, Mr 305
Gran, see Van Gruisen, Florence Angela
Grant, Michael 119, 186
Grantham, Dr Winsome 381, 410, 411
Graves, Robert 421, 425
Graves, M.P. 421, 425
Graves, Mrs Louisa 416, 421, 425, 429, 430-1
Granville Barker, Harley 270, 330
Gray, Thomas 267
Grayson, James 631, 632
Green, June 517
Green, Phyllis 179 and n., 517
Green, Roger Lancelyn 179n., 389, 517
Greenhouse Allt, Dr W. 507
Greenspan, Charlotte 638, 640, 642, 644
Greig, Geoffrey 71, 76
Greig, John, Bishop of Guildford 76
Grétry, André 450, 534, 561
Greville, Lady Mercy (Nancy Parsons), later Dean, Gamble, Marter 34, 35, 36, 93, 137, 224, 389, 410
Greville family 137
Grew, Eva Mary 400-1
Grew, Sydney 400-1
Grillo, Bernard 471-2, 475
Grimthorpe, Ralph Beckett, 3rd Baron 71
Grossmith, George and Weedon 444-5

Gudgeon, Sergeant-Major 107
Guedalla, Philip 217
Guest, George 552
Guillebaud, Mr & Mrs 185
Guiraud, Ernest 400, 546
Gulda, Friedrich 405
Gummer, Ellis 384, 385, 388, 398, 399

Hackforth, Mrs 198
Haddon, Mark 625
Hadley, Patrick (Paddy) 324, 356, 559, 560, 562, 569
Hahn, Reynaldo 576
Haig, Douglas, 1st Earl of 67
Haines, Mr 122
Halcrow, Leonard 423
Haldane, Mrs J.S. 382
Hale, A.M. 580
Halévy, Fromental 397, 422, 481
Halifax, Edward Wood, 1st Earl of 125
Hall, Dr James S. 608
Hall, Peter 627
Hall-Neale, George 45
Hall-Neale, Maud 45
Hambledon Hurst 41-6, 53, 135, 151, 364, 374, 458-60, 467, 469, 470, 473, 474, 477, 627
Hambourg, Mark 325
Hambourg, Michal 325
Hamilton, Hamish 170
Hamilton, Newburgh 525
Hamilton, Ord 376
Hammond, Elsie, née Jeffery 321
Hammond, Robin 222
Hammond, Tom 321, 404, 428
Handel, George Frideric vi, vii, 38, 147, 166-7, 188, 198, 199, 232,

Index

274-8, 290, 324, 328, 329, 349, 350, 385, 401, 411-17 *passim*, 422, 424, 431, 432-3, 439, 441, 450-2, 457, 461, 462, 465, 470, 474, 477, 485, 486, 489, 492, 495, 498-515 *passim*, 522, 523, 525, 531, 534, 535, 536, 541, 542, 547, 548, 550- 1, 557, 558, 560, 583, 601, 602, 608-19 *passim*, 620, 621, 622, 629, 631, 633, 634, 637, 638, 639, 640, 643, 644-5
– *Acis and Galatea* 342, 460-1
– *Admeto* 606
– *Agrippina* 584-5
– *Alcina* 462-3, 467-8, 481, 502, 530, 555-6, 642
– *Apollo e Dafni* 202
– *Ariodante* 188, 199, 541, 546, 598, 605-6, 637
– *Athalia* 439-40, 586, 606, 610
– *Belshazzar* 329, 511
– *Berenice* 167, 188, 505
– *The Choice of Hercules* 187, 275
– *Deborah* 473
– *Deidamia* 451-2, 553
– *Floridante* 559-60
– *Giulio Cesare* vi, 401, 502-3, 584, 641
– *Giustino* 642
– *Hercules* 147, 436, 462, 523, 527, 530, 640
– *Imeneo* 536-7, 551, 640
– *Jephtha* 275, 422, 563, 584
– *Joseph* 499-500
– *Joshua* 489
– *Judas Maccabaeus* 443
– *Messiah* 316-17
– *Orlando* vi, 506-7, 577, 637
– *Partenope* 538
– *Radamisto* 523, 527-8, 563
– *Ricardo Primo* 611
– *Rinaldo* 539-40, 542, 626
– *Rodelinda* 471, 506, 512, 513-14
– *Samson* 275, 493, 494, 495-6, 498, 510
– *Saul* 205, 274-8, 341, 411, 466, 511, 626-7
– *Semele* 275, 449, 510, 511, 512-13, 539-40, 609, 611
– *Serse (Xerxes)* 501-2, 503, 584, 637, 640, 643
– *Solomon* 411, 456-7, 485, 486
– *Susanna* 187-6, 316
– *Tamerlano* 542, 557, 558, 582, 635
– *Theodora* 350, 480-1, 482-3
Handel Opera Society 451, 457, 461, 462, 465, 467, 468, 471, 480, 485, 495, 502, 505, 506, 515, 523, 527, 531, 539, 542, 563, 584, 604, 611, 626, 640
Hankey, Col. Jack 408, 409, 480
Hannibal 221
Hann, V. 85
Hannen, Nicholas 270
Harcourt-Williams, Tony 427, 475
Harcourt-Williams, Mrs 427, 475
Hardy, H.H. 384, 516
Hardy, Thomas 175
Harewood, George Lascelles, 7th Earl of 146, 425, 426, 433, 436, 443, 540, 570
Haricot, see Harrison
Harker, Mr 67
Harper, Heather 502, 513, 577
Harris, Augustus 24
Harris, Frank 24
Harris, George 34, 48, 474
Harris, Dr Noel Gordon 402, 404
Harrison, Sir Edward 12

Harrison, Kenneth 212, 216, 221, 265, 290, 338
Harrison, Laura (Haricot) 47-8, 50, 52, 53, 58, 60, 61, 84, 85, 86, 87, 91, 137, 196, 262-3, 380, 558
Harrow School 62, 78, 79, 80, 98-129 *passim*, 150, 296, 398
Harrow Football 106, 126
Hartnoll, Phyllis 550, 571, 582, 584
Harty, Sir Hamilton 451, 500
Harvey, A.D. 96
Harwood, Elizabeth 611
Haslock, Philadelphia 6
Hasselt, Carlos van 555
Hastie, Mr 488
Hauptmann, Gerhart 30
Hawkins, Mr (Malthouse Farm) 53
Hawkins, Mr (Sheringham House School) 55
Hawkswell, Roy 575
Hawkswell, Una 371-2, 575
Haydn, Joseph 169, 173, 232, 264, 303, 326, 327, 467, 603, 604
Haydn, Michael 232
Haywood, Carol 380
Haywood, Hilary, see Hitchcock
Haywood, Jeremy 186
Haywood, Martin 380
Headlong Hall (T.L. Peacock) 494
Heartz, Daniel 635, 642
Heath, Geoffrey 301-2
Heinitz, Thomas 565, 569
Heller, Robert P. 589, 590
Hemingway, Ernest 434
Henderson, Alan 518, 519, 520, 530, 533, 534, 545, 546, 553, 564, 581
Hendren, Patsy 144
Henry VIII 139
Henryson, Robert 285

Henschel, Helen 103
Henze, Han Werner 535, 542
Herbage, Julian 499, 502, 507, 533
Herbert, A.P. 60
Hercules (cat) 469, 475, 476, 591
Herincx, Raymund 513
Hérold, Ferdinand 538
Herodotus 164
Herrmann, Bernard 539
Hess, Myra 264, 325
Heygate, Mr 84
Heyworth, Peter 481, 575
Hicks, Dr Nugent 213
Hicks, Seymour 131
Hicks, Mr and Mrs 371
Higgins, Norman 369
Hill, Dr 430
Hill, Major 427
Hindemith, Paul 208, 214, 480, 520
Hinman, Charlton 615
Hirsch, Paul 397
Hitchcock, Hilary, later Haywood 157-9, 185-6, 270, 282, 331, 338, 339, 353, 380, 431, 436, 510, 530, 532
Hitchcock, Mrs 158
Hitler, Adolf 118, 124, 154, 178, 214, 313, 343, 356, 361, 369, 371, 372, 378, 386, 499
Hoare, Commander Brodie 479
Hoare, Major Brodie 299
Hoare, Sir Samuel 291
Hobbs, Sir Jack 402
Hobsbawm, Eric 162
Hofmann, Ludwig 233
Hofmannsthal, Hugo von 483
Hoggard (maternity nurse) 51
Holbrook, David 508
Holland, J.F.M. 106, 114

Hollis, Lady 222
Holmes, Bobby (Cecil) 282, 389
Holmes, Marjorie 389
Holmes, Mr 54, 55-6, 57
Holmes, Mrs 54, 58
Holst, Gustav 580
Holst, Imogen 506
Homer 147, 155, 241, 296
Honeywill, Mr 377
Honolka, Kurt 492
Hopkins, Anthony 480
Hopkins, Gerard Manley 162
Hopper, Victoria, later Dean 93, 102, 139, 208, 216, 223, 224, 292, 330, 389
Horace 159
Horder, Thomas, 1st Baron 339
Horniman, Annie 29
Horovitz, Joseph 579, 603
Horrex, John 538, 585
Horszowski, Mieczyslaw 316
Housman, A.E 159, 216
Howes, Frank 267, 272, 278, 410, 507, 537, 560
Hubback, David 160, 182, 185, 188, 228, 231, 279, 284, 302, 331, 607
Hubback, Eva 160
Hubback, Rachel 284
Huckle, W.B. 344, 614
Hulme, Joe 95
Humby, Betty, later Beecham 326-7
Humfrey, Pelham 453
Humperdinck, Engelbert 448
Hunt, John 173
Hunt, Leigh 183
Hussey, Dyneley 438
Hutchings, Arthur 401, 402
Hutton, Len 341, 357

Ibsen, Henrik 214, 281-2
Ictinus 253
Imbrie, Andrew 636
Inchcape, James Mackay, 1st Earl of 332, 333, 358, 395
Inchcape, Kenneth James William Mackay, 3rd Earl of 487, 488
Inchcape, Kenneth Mackay, 2nd Earl of 352-3
Inchcape, Leonora (Nonie) 353
Instone, Anna 511
Ireland, John 440
Isaacs, Nelly 17, 18
Isaacs, Eleanor, née Rowland 17
Isaacs, Esther (Essie), see Sutro
Isaacs, Florence Angela, see Van Gruisen
Issacs, Frances (Fran), later Keyzer 17, 18
Isaacs, Fred 17
Isaacs, Gerald, see Reading
Isaacs, Godfrey 17
Isaacs, Harry 15, 17, 18-19, 22, 23, 26, 171
Isaacs, Harry (pianist) 19
Isaacs, Sir Henry Aaron 14, 17, 23
Isaacs (Isaac) 14
Isaacs, Joan, later Zuckerman 226
Isaacs, Joseph 14, 16, 17
Isaacs, Marcel 19
Isaacs, Michael (fruit-broker) 14
Isaacs, Michael, later 3rd Marquess of Reading 20, 226, 229, 307
Isaacs, Nellie, later Detmold 14, 17, 18
Isaacs, Rufus, see Reading
Isaacs, Sara, née Davis 14, 16-17, 22
Isaacs, Sara, née Mendoza 14
Isaacs, Stella, see Reading

Isherwood, Christopher 288, 345
Izzard, Charlie 399, 404, 541
Izzard, Harry 404

Jackson, Barry 34
Jackson, Robert 599, 600, 607, 610, 616, 621, 629
Jackson Knight, W.F. 290
Jacobs, Arthur 515, 575
Jacobson, Mr 359, 360
James, Henry 133, 170, 181, 190, 434, 523
James, Dr Thomas 268
James, Miss 120
Janáček, Leoš 2, 145-6, 442, 500, 536, 596, 602, 614, 635
Jarratt, L.A. (Jerry) 597, 604
Jebb, Julian 553
Jebb, Philip 459-60, 467, 473, 477, 553
Jeffery, Albert (senior) 135, 297, 320-1
Jeffery, Alice 535, 540, 575, 576, 578
Jeffery, Bert 44, 46, 151-2, 153, 192, 220, 286, 297, 320, 321, 334, 350, 368, 402, 404, 426, 427, 455, 465, 467, 475, 523, 562, 573, 576, 591, 628, 630
Jeffery, Ernie 44, 91, 151, 402, 465, 523, 535, 573, 575, 578, 628
Jeffery, Fanny 46, 220, 286, 320, 334, 350
Jeffreys, Bertha 440
Jenkins, Newell 305-6
Jenkinson, Anne Clegg 12
Jennings, Paul 507
Jerger, Alfred 233, 304
Johnson, Brian 395
Johnson, Robert 453

Johnson, Dr Samuel 167, 257, 267, 268, 285
Jones, Henry Arthur 24
Jones, Inigo vii
Jones, James 8-9
Jones, Morgan 327
Jones, Miss 16
Josef (waiter) 305
Joseph, Anne 339
Joseph, Peter 54, 111, 219, 228, 283, 299, 338, 339
Jung, Carl 387, 585

Kafka, Mr 309
Kalenburg, Josef 233
Kallman, Chester 542
Karn, Mrs 455
Kathleen (house-keeper) 516, 517, 520, 521, 548
Keaton, Buster 93, 104
Keats, John 30, 270
Keller, Hans 433
Kells, Iris 462
Kelly, David 497
Kennedy, Daisy 271
Kennedy, President John F. 595
Kennedy, Margaret 222
Kent, Prince George, Duke of 231
Kent, Princess Marina, Duchess of 231
Kentish, John 451
Kentner, Louis 325
Kerman, Joseph 529, 583, 601, 633, 635, 638, 640, 642, 643
Kerman, Vivian 529, 633
Ketèlbey, Albert 77
Kettle, Arnold 56
Keynes, J.M. 289, 345
Keynes, Lydia (Lopokova) 214, 289

Index

Keys, Ivor 617
Keyzer, Louis 192
Kimber, Sergeant-Major 107
King, Alec Hyatt 416, 452, 543-4, 549, 559, 579
King, Eve 543, 579
King's College, Cambridge 116, 125, 159-63, 167, 168, 169, 172, 174, 183, 187, 197, 198, 200, 351, 367, 368, 370, 396, 440
King Solomon's Mines (H. Rider Haggard) 65
Kipling, Rudyard 208
Kipnis, Alexander 303, 304
Kirby, Percival 318
Kirk, G. 488
Kirkpatrick, Dr 359, 362, 363
Kitchener, Herbert 63
Kitching, Alan 506-7, 538, 559, 585, 606
Kitching, Frances 506, 538, 559, 585, 606
Kittermaster, D.B 115
Kitto, Francis 160, 162, 182
Knapp, Joan 542
Knapp, John Merrill vi, 473-4, 516, 542, 558, 601, 611, 612
Knapp, Libby 542, 611
Knappertsbusch, Hans 304
Knox, John (groom) 361-2
Köchert, Melanie 441
Kodály, Zoltán 341
Konetzni, Anny 233
Konetzni, Hilde 304
Korda, Alexander 292
Kratina, Rudolf Josef 266
Kreisler, Fritz 325, 326
Krummel, D.W. 579
Kubelík, Rafael 316

Kunz, Zinka (Milanov) 303
Kyriakos, Mr 251
Laborde, Charles 120, 121
Lachner, Franz 512
Lalandi, Lina 586
Lam, Basil 594
Lambert, Constant 223, 267, 293, 297
Lamberti, Mario 186, 237
Lancaster, Osbert 471
Landor, Walter Savage 315, 339, 357, 360, 365, 370
Landowska, Wanda 325, 327
Lang, Andrew 517, 613
Lang, Matheson 93
Lang, Paul Henry 452
Langland, William 285
Langley, Hubert 188, 275, 349-50, 443, 540
Lanigan, John 497
Lansbury, George 118-9
Larsen, Jens Peter 452, 513
Larwood, Harold 189
Latham, Peter 401
Latham, Mrs Peter 401
Laughton, Tony 494
Laurie, Margaret 598, 599
Lawless, Mrs 90
Lawrence, D.H. 131
Lawrence, Sir Thomas 613
Laycock, Sir Joseph 224
Layton, Robert 570
Lazzari, Virgilio 304
Leach, Mr 428
League of Nations 109-13
Lear, Edward 135
Leavis, F.R. 274, 256
Leavis, Q.D. 274

Lee, Mr and Mrs 377
Lee-Uff, Mr & Mrs 377
Lefébure, Yvonne 303
Lehár, Franz 484
Lehman, Leo 465
Lehmann, Beatrix 523
Lehmann, Lotte 233, 236
Lehmann, Rosamond 306
Leigh, Walter 174, 200, 212-13, 214, 215, 398
Leigh-Mallory, Beridge 315
Leigh-Mallory, Christina Ruth, née Turner 295, 298
Leigh-Mallory, George 31, 185, 225
Leigh-Mallory, Rev. Herbert 31, 225
Lensky, Margaret 527
Leoncavallo, Ruggero 15
Leonie, Adrienne 15
Leppard, Raymond 495, 525, 561, 563-4, 569, 570
Leskov, Nikolai 596
Le Sueur, Jean-François 531, 534, 535, 570
Levens, Robert 381
Levin, Bernard 56
Lewis, Anthony 501, 513, 516, 536, 537, 557, 562, 566, 584, 585, 586, 598, 605, 606, 610, 624
Lewis, Lesley 566, 585, 598, 606
Lewis, Richard 611
Liebermann, Rolf 483
Liliane (Mina Curtiss's assistant) 456
Lillo 548, 549, 563, 577, 581, 585, 589, 590, 501, 595, 628
Lincoln, Stoddard 609
Linda (Philip Radcliffe's aunt) 370
Liszt, Franz 21, 199, 308
Little Abbey School 447, 450, 516, 529

Little Easton Manor 36, 80, 93-4, 136, 138-9, 210, 216, 217, 223, 224, 353-4
Liverpool Repertory Company 29, 34, 183
Llewellyn, Redvers 289
Lloyd, Eric 591-2, 593
Lloyd, Geoffrey 125
Loch, Johnnie 408, 519, 545, 546, 566
Loch, Col. Laurie 408, 519, 545, 546, 597, 600
Locke, Matthew 511
Lockhart, John Gibson 393
Loder, John 140
Long, Kathleen 325
Lonsdale, Frederick 131
Lope de Vega, Félix 17
Lopokova, Lydia, see Keynes
Lortzing, Albert 481
Los Angeles, Victoria de 492
Lowis, Ian 546, 566
Lowis, Col. John 408, 519, 545, 629
Lowis, Muriel 408, 629
Lubin, Germaine 286
Lucas, Donald 163, 220, 221
Lucas, F.L. (Peter) 163, 221, 267, 268, 290, 315-5, 328, 360
Lucas, Mary 163
Lucretius 147
Lund, Dick 394, 406, 530
Lunt, Alfred 330
Lush, Rev. Vicesimus 285
Luther, Miss 449, 456
Lutyens, Edwin 135
Lynch, Nancy, see Dean
Lynn Linton, Eliza 24
Lyon, M.D. 76
Lyon, P.H.B. 110

Index

McBurney, Charles, 269
McCarthy, Lillah (Lady Keeble) 171
McCleary, Gwyneth 451, 452, 462, 467, 482, 485, 486, 495, 500, 501, 502, 518, 607
MacCuish, Rev. Donald 488
Macdonald, Archie 390, 393, 394, 396, 405, 408, 442, 458, 488
Macdonald, Ian 410, 486, 487, 488
Macdonald, Michael 455, 486, 487, 488
Macdonald, Ruth, née Shaw 333, 352, 353, 362, 376, 380, 390, 393, 396, 398, 404, 405, 410, 442, 458, 486-7, 488, 613
Mackail, J.W. 131
Mackay, Alan 487
Mackay, Elsie 488
Mackerras, Charles 464, 505
McLaughlin, Gibb 270
MacLeod, Flora 440
Macmillan, Harold 621
Macmillan, Maurice 621
MacMurray, John 230
MacMurray, Lois 230
MacMurray, Lois (Bisi) 231
McNaught, William 414
MacNeice, Louis 162
MacRae, Commander Kenneth 427
McVeagh, Diana, see Morley
Maeterlinck, Maurice 131, 170, 326
Mahler, Gustav 190, 199, 346, 509, 539, 588
Main, A.C. 577
Makower, Ernest 87, 148, 173, 306-7, 354
Makower, John 52
Makower, Rachel 148
Malcolm, George 526

Malipiero, Gian Francesco 572
Malko, Nikolai 103
Mallory, Clare, later Millikan 185, 201, 202, 225-6, 279-80, 290, 292-6, 297-8, 300, 315, 321, 330, 331, 338, 346, 406, 414, 472, 473, 583, 632, 633, 635, 638
Mallory, George, see Leigh-Mallory
Mallory, Mrs, see Leigh-Mallory
Malory, Thomas 267, 373, 400
Malthouse Farm 53, 89, 455
Mandikan, Arda 527
Manifold, John 273-4
Manley, Edith 422, 436, 437, 438, 454, 463, 472, 485, 493, 503, 567
Manley, Jacqueline 422, 436, 442, 450, 454, 470, 485, 503, 567
Mann, William 537, 555
Manton, Franz 561
Manzano, Toto 230, 302
Manzano, Count 229, 230, 236, 302
Manzano, Countess 229, 230, 236, 302
Marchant, Sir Herbert 118
Marchant, Stanley 318
Mariani, Angelo 569
Marks, Claude 113
Marks, Frances 14, 17
Marlborough, John Churchill, 1st Duke of 119
Marlowe Society 167, 282
Marriner, Molly 612
Marriner, Neville 612
Marriott, C.S. 94
Marschner, Heinrich 550, 551, 552, 553
Marsh, Sid 368, 402, 426
Marshall, Arthur 215
Marshall, David 359, 395, 405, 488-9

Marshall, James 597
Marter, Richard 137, 410
Martin, Hugh 72-3, 79, 104, 120
Martin, Major-General J. M.
    479, 573, 597
Martin, Dr (Blob) 63-4
Masefield 101, 349
Maskell, Stan 378-9
Mason, Colin 451-2, 585
Mason, Fred 389
Mason, Stewart 119, 121
Massenet, Jules 507, 566
Massey, Raymond 217
Massingham, Dorothy 144
Matters, Arnold 289
Maugham, W. Somerset
    172, 197, 371
Max-Müller, Friedrich 24
May, Peter 379
Mayer, Sir Robert 306-7
Mayor, Tess, later Rothschild
    80, 282, 283, 285, 299, 315,
    331, 338, 554
Mayr, Simon 538
Medley, Robert 288
Méhul, Étienne-Nicolas 531, 534
Melchior, Lauritz 355
Mellers, Peggy 429
Mellers, Pussy 356, 428
Mellers, Wilfrid 356, 428-9, 508, 595
Mencken, H.L. 27
Mendelssohn, Felix 272, 289, 356
Mendoza, Daniel 14
Mendoza, Sara, see Isaacs
Menotti, Gian Carlo 528, 544
Menuhin, Hephzibah 325
Menuhin, Yehudi 325
Mérimée, Prosper 414
Merrick, Leonard 16

Messel, Oliver 496
Meyerbeer, Giacomo 18,
    293, 538, 636
Michel, Solange 400
Miles, Margaret 47, 48, 52, 84, 85,
    88, 91, 130, 196
Milhaud, Darius 478
Milkina, Nina 235
Mill, J.S. 20
Mills, Dicky 50, 135
Mills, Jenefer, see Dean
Miller, Edgar 15
Miller, Esther, née Davis
    (1836-1864) 16
Miller, Esther (1867-1926) 16
Miller, Henry 16
Miller, Hugh 271
Miller, Olgar (Sagittarius) 271
Miller, Sheila 564, 572, 579, 597, 614
Miller, Victor 15
Miller, William 16
Milligan, Derrick 394
Millikan, Clare, see Mallory
Millikan, George 472, 632
Millikan, Glenn 293, 294, 315,
    330, 338, 346
Millikan, Mark 472, 632,
    633, 635, 638
Millikan, Richard 472
Millin, Elizabeth 8
Millin, James 8
Millington-Drake, Lady Effie 344,
    363, 487, 488
Millington-Drake, Sir
    Eugen 363, 405
Millington-Drake, Nellie 487-8
Milner-White, Rev. Eric 165-6,
    222, 276, 535
Milton, John 267

Minett, Dora 371, 372, 375
Minett, Helen 371
Ming (Oliver Zangwill's cat) 168
Mitchell, Donald 433, 539, 588, 608
Mitchell, Ena 275, 370, 439
Modigliani, Amedeo 187
Moe, Lawrence 632, 634, 638
Moir, James 104, 105
Moiseiwitsch, Benno 198
Molière 483
Monk (chauffeur), 148, 149, 296, 345
Monro, Mrs Harold 272-3
Monteux, Pierre 232
Monteverdi, Claudio 417, 495, 623-4
Montgomery, Peter 236
Moore, Gerald 198, 381
Moore, Grace 231
Moore, Tom 176
More, Sir Thomas 352
Morgan, Charles 291
Morgan, Sheila 377, 411
Morley, Bill 458, 505, 507, 539, 557, 567, 585, 606, 618, 628, 629
Morley, Diana, née McVeagh 410, 431, 456, 458, 486, 505, 507, 537, 539, 552, 505, 507, 556, 557, 567, 585, 606, 618, 628, 629
Morley, Thomas 440, 453
Morton, J.B. (Beachcomber) 14
Moss, Richard 603, 609, 611
Mozart, Wolfgang Amadeus 101, 102, 151, 169, 173, 207, 208, 214, 222, 224, 231, 232, 233, 235, 273, 303, 305, 316, 326, 327, 328, 397, 431, 446, 450, 462, 463, 476, 483, 502, 507, 552, 553, 585, 641
– *Idomeneo* 328-9, 484
Muirhead, Benedetta (Ben) 89, 143, 144, 145, 157, 361

Muirhead, Litellus (Tellie) 89, 143-4, 157, 185, 196, 290, 352
Muirhead, Simon 89, 144
Mulgan, Anthony 477, 478, 482, 483, 486, 492, 501, 505, 509
Mullins, Norman 404
Munby, Tim 183
Murray, Arthur, see Elibank
Murray, Sir David 141
Murray-Rust, Mr & Mrs 377
Muspratt family 47
Mussell, Anabel 443, 516
Mussell, Jean, née Shaw 333, 352, 362-3, 366, 380, 387, 391, 393, 405-6, 410, 411, 414, 437, 443, 466, 488, 491-2, 496, 516, 535, 553, 554, 593, 613, 615, 616
Mussell, Lisabel 466
Mussell, Peter 405
Mussell, Shirl 405, 406, 437, 443, 466
Mussolini, Benito 124-5, 126, 195, 356
Mussorgsky, Modest 438, 495

Naismith, Edna (Mrs Harry Isaacs 2) 18
Napoleon Bonaparte 579
Nash, John 129, 187
Nathan, George Jean 27
Nayudu, C.K. 94
Neel, Boyd 281, 467, 485
Neighbour, Oliver (Tim) 452, 559
Neller, Fred 378, 420, 467, 590
Nicolai, Otto 103, 232
Nicoll, Berta 444
Nicholls, Owen 389
Nilsson, Christine 580

Noble, Jeremy 406, 452, 453, 517, 518, 529, 551, 558, 598, 633
Noble, John 462
Nordau, Max 24
Northcott, Honor 141, 193, 194
Norwood, Catherine 155, 156
Norwood, Dr Cyril 79, 99, 102, 106, 107, 109, 116, 118, 125-6, 128, 129, 155-6
Noske, Frits 452
Novotna, Jamila 233, 304
Noyce, Wilfred 356
Nugent Hicks, Dr Frederick 203

Ochs (diamond millionaire) 20
Ochs, Miss 20
Oeser, Fritz 628-9
Offenbach, Jacques 504, 578, 624
Oldham, Arthur 285, 442
Olivier, Laurence 424
Oltrabella, Augusta 234
O'Neill, Eugene 330
Ord, Boris 200-1, 212, 215, 265, 266, 269, 271, 274, 275, 276, 278, 289, 291, 302, 304, 326, 327, 328, 339-40, 347, 369, 396
O'Reilly, Shielah 454
Orestes (inn-keeper) 245, 246
Orff, Carl 481, 483-4, 508, 518, 576
Ormrod, Pim 93
Orr, Margaret 368
Orr, Robin 368, 560, 618
Orr, Mr 490
Owen, Wilfred 162

Paderewski, Ignacy Jan 289
Paer, Ferdinando 538
Paisiello, Giovanni 540
Palestrina, Giovanni 349
Paravicini, Livia 302

Pares, Sir Bernard 125
Parker, Charlie 379
Parker, D.C. 318
Parker, Eric 53, 153, 296
Parker, Eric (junior) 296-7
Parker, Jack 403
Parker, Mary 580
Parrott, Ian 617
Parry, Sir Hubert 463
Parsons, Frank 374
Parsons, Nancy, see Greville, Lady Mercy
Part, Anthony 113
Paskalis, Kostas 608
Patáky, Koloman von 234
Pate, John 607
Pate, William 488, 532, 600, 607
Pater, Walter 507
Paul, Herbert 131
Pauly, Rose 304
Payne, Denis 365, 379, 389, 414, 610
Payne, Joan 365, 379, 389, 414, 610
Payne, Sebastian 365, 494-5
Peakall, Miss 344, 359, 362, 374, 376
Pearce, Mr 593
Pears, Peter 325, 329, 377, 433
Pearson, Henry 161-2, 357
Pearson, Hesketh 170, 357
Peer, Ted 427, 428
Pelléas et Mélisande (Debussy) 169, 400
Périer, Jean 400
Perosi, Lorenzo 232
Petri, Egon 198, 199, 280, 325
Pfitzner, Hans 199
Phipps, Jack 495
Piave, Francesco Maria 603
Pidcock, Robin 495, 502
Piggot, Mary 307

Index

Pigou, Arthur Cecil 227, 228, 273, 283
Pilcher, Mr (dentist) 480
Pincherle, Marc 452
Pinza, Ezio 304
Pip (cat) 372, 390
Pitt, William 14
Phillips, Leslie 374
Platt, Norman 389, 431
Playfair, Nigel 131
Plumptre, E.V.C. (Plum) 104, 117, 119-20, 125-6, 186, 215, 220
Pollen, Francis 459, 475
Pope, Alexander 267, 290
Pope, Dr Saxton 638, 642, 643
Porter, Andrew 505, 537, 541, 546, 555-6, 585, 606, 627, 628, 629, 633
Porter, Shirley 505
Potter, Beatrix 449-50
Potter, Prof. George Reuben 602, 633, 642-3
Poulenc, Francis 325, 481
Pound, Ezra 162, 290
Poupet, Madeleine 574, 597
Poupet, Michel 574-5, 595, 597, 629
Poussin, Nicolas 17, 186
Pratt, Billy (Boris Karloff) 478
Pratt, Sir John 478
Praxiteles 254
Preston, Kerrison 134
Preston, Simon 552
Priestley, J.B. 141, 330, 345, 353
Prior, Camille 212, 213, 274, 276, 337, 339, 369, 411
Probert, Jack 402, 421
Profumo, Jack 120
Prokofiev, Sergei 566, 582, 628
Proust, Marcel 422
Pryce-Jones, Alan 418-9

Puccini, Giacomo 6, 267, 289, 480, 499, 572, 588
Purcell, Henry 452, 453, 498, 503, 506, 509, 510, 511, 525, 535, 577, 598

Queen's Road 34, 41, 46, 51, 56, 57, 58, 89, 129, 143, 144, 149
Queen Mary (Consort) 135
Queen Mary (liner) 630
Quiller-Couch, Sir Arthur 216

Rachmaninov, Sergie 235-6, 342
Radcliffe, Philip v, 148, 160, 165, 173-4, 196, 198, 199-200, 222, 229-30, 231, 235, 236, 264, 265, 266, 281, 286, 287-8, 292, 294, 295, 315, 318, 319, 323, 324, 325, 330, 331, 332, 336-42 *passim*, 346, 350, 356, 357, 366, 371, 374, 375, 377, 385-6, 388-9, 394, 397-401 *passim*, 410-11, 413, 414, 418, 436, 437, 438, 440, 443, 448, 460-1, 463, 470, 473, 481-2, 483, 485, 489, 493-5, 500, 504, 505, 515, 523-4, 525, 531, 534-5, 538, 539-40, 542, 546, 547-9, 550, 551-2, 553, 554-6, 559-80 *passim*, 594-5, 597, 602, 604, 609, 612, 616, 617, 620, 621, 622, 623, 624, 625, 627, 630, 639
– *Cats and Dogs* 369-70
Radcliffe, Susan 222, 371, 377, 423-4, 495, 525, 551
Radcliffe, Mr (Philip's father) 174
Radcliffe, Mrs (Philip's mother) 148, 371, 377
Radford, Evelyn 328
Radford, Winifred 328
Radin, Peggy 640, 642, 644
Raeburn, Sir Henry 393, 613

Rameau, Jean-Philippe 624-5
Ramsay, Alan 547, 570-1, 591, 593, 614
Ramsay, Allan 613
Ramsay, Frances 570, 591
Ranczak, Hildegaede 267
Rattigan, Terence 80, 316
Rautawaara, Aulikki 304
Ravel, Maurice 505, 538
Raverat, Gwen 276
Rea, Alec 27, 89, 183, 210
Rea, Mrs Alec 35, 58
Rea, Elizabeth (Leeby), later Clapham 183, 184, 185, 212, 293
Rea, Lorna 156, 264, 332
Rea, Philip 156
Reading, Eva, Marchioness of 226
Reading, Gerald Isaacs, 2nd Marquess of 14, 20
Reading, Rufus Isaacs, 1st Marquess of 1-2, 14, 15, 17, 18, 20-1, 35, 125, 128, 132-3, 142, 171-2, 205, 219, 286, 333, 358, 373, 400
Reading, Stella, Marchioness of 125, 132-3, 142, 171-2, 219, 286, 294, 351, 373
Redgrave, Michael 523
Redlich, Hans 433
Reed, Carol 211
Rees, Biffy 390, 425
Rees, Brigid, see Bartley
Rees, Charles 425
Rees, Rev. Lorimer 218, 330, 390, 414, 425, 448, 458, 532, 575
Rees, Teresa 390, 425, 532
Reger, Max 199
Reining, Maria 305
Rennert, Günther 542
Rescigno, Nicola 512

Réthy, Esther 304
Revenger's Tragedy, The (Thomas Middleton) 282
Reynolds, Sir Joshua 613
Reynolds, Mr 258
Rhodes, Wilfred 77
Ribbentrop, Joachim von 369
Rich, Anthea, see Craigmyle
Rich, Lawrence 455
Richards, Mr and Mrs 83, 84
Richards, Master 84
Ridgeway, Rev. Vibert 75
Ridout, Alan 559
Rideout, John 377
Rimbaud, Arthur 623
Rimsky-Korsakov, Nikolai 438, 460, 495, 539
Rimsky-Korsakov (cat) 407
Ritchie, Emily 42, 465
Ritchie, Mabel (Margaret) 275
Roberts, Ivan 404
Roberts, John H. vii, 637, 640, 641
Robertson, Rae 103
Robertson, W. Graham 133-5, 170, 189
Robinson, Stanford 453
Robson, Flora 330, 523
Romney, George 613
Ronald, Landon 201, 289
Rootham, Cyril 201, 274, 354
Rooting Manor 90, 94, 177, 319
Rosemarie, see Benninger
Rossini, Gioachino 232, 288, 293, 434, 471, 476, 528, 538, 539, 556, 567, 579
Roswaenge, Helge 303
Roth, Herman 530
Roth, Herr 266
Rothenstein, Sir William 291

Index

Rothschild, Tess, see Mayor
Rothschild, Victor, Lord 80, 554
Roussel, Albert 636
Roxburgh, Edwin 552
Rubbra, Antoinette 325
Rubbra, Edmund 325
Rumbold, Camilla 553
Rycroft, Charles 284
Rylands, George (Dadie) 167, 172, 212, 265, 318, 578, 588-9, 615

Sacchini, Antonio 551
Sack, Erna 266
Sadie, Adele 585, 606
Sadie, Stanley 452, 560, 575, 585, 606
Salazar, António de Oliveira 433
Salfi, Francesco 267
Salmonsbury Camp 122
Saltmarsh, John 185, 268
Samuel, H.D. 118, 121, 122
Sanderson, E.L. (Bags) 62-3, 64, 65, 66, 69-70, 71, 72-73, 76, 79, 80, 81, 114, 150
Sanderson, Mrs E.L. 65, 66, 71, 74, 79, 80, 81
Sanderson, Rev. Lancelot 63
Sandham, Andrew 144, 145
Sappho 216
Sargeant, Frank 543, 615, 616
Sargeant, Joan 543, 576, 615, 616
Sargeant, John 543, 616, 623, 624
Sargent, John Singer 134
Sayers, Dorothy L. 111, 208, 270, 271
Sawin, Lewis 170-1
Schallgruber, Gerda 230, 312
Schenker, Heinrich 372
Schikaneder, Emanuel 556
Schnabel, Artur 280, 325, 327
Schnitzler, Arthur 330

Schoenberg, Arnold 200, 214, 323, 368, 483, 627
Scholfield, A.F. 265
Schreker, Franz 409
Schubert, Franz 207, 232, 236, 264, 266, 289, 317, 324, 325, 326, 327, 401
Schubert, K. 538
Schumann, Elisabeth 233
Schumann, Robert 39, 234, 401, 457, 548-9
Scott, Anne 603, 618
Scott, Christopher 466, 589, 593-4, 599, 600, 603, 618
Scott, C.W.A. 220
Scott, Marion M. 401
Scott, Sir Walter 66, 613
Scott-Kilvert, Elizabeth (Zee), née Dewart 390, 434, 435
Scott-Kilvert, Ian 390
Scriabin, Alexander 325
Schuschnigg, Kurt 326
Seaford College 530, 532, 543, 574, 576, 578, 604, 624
Searle, Humphrey 473, 514
Searle, Ronald 639
Seaton, George John 15
Sellar, W.C. 377
Sellers, Peter 14
Senesino (Francesco Bernardi) 611
Serauky, Walter 489, 523
Serkin, Rudolf 325
Seton, Alex 591
Sewell, Ernest 73
Seymour, Rev. Canon Edward J. 380
Shaftesbury, Earls of 135
Shairp, Mordaunt 121
Shakespeare, William 92, 103-4, 117, 167, 197, 285, 288, 292, 312, 319,

330, 377, 511, 550, 571, 573, 576, 578, 579, 580, 581, 582, 584, 588, 589, 590, 591, 594, 612, 614, 615
Shanks, Marjorie 488
Sharp, N.H.G. 529
Shaw, Alexander, see Craigmyle
Shaw, Alexander 472
Shaw, Alison, later Heggs 613
Shaw, Diccon 369, 389
Shaw, Donald, see Craigmyle
Shaw, George Bernard 104, 146, 170, 175, 222, 278, 286, 330, 352, 357, 370
Shaw, H. Watkins 503
Shaw, Jean, see Mussell
Shaw, Margaret, see Craigmyle
Shaw, Martin 369
Shaw, Ruth, see Macdonald
Shaw, Thalia, see Dean
Shaw, Tom 532
Shaw-Taylor, Desmond 500
Shebalin, Vissarion 575, 582
Shelley, Harry R. 577
Shenka (cat) 372, 387, 393, 417, 437, 452, 457, 469, 591, 633
Sheppard, J.T. 163-4, 212, 213, 214, 215, 220, 268, 269
Sheridan, Richard Brinsley 463
Sheringham House School 54-8, 62, 64, 87, 160, 161
Sherwin, Amy 8
Shifrin, Seymour 634
Shirley-Quirke, John 625
Shostakovich, Dmitri 287, 596, 598
Shurland Castle 83, 86
Sibelius, Jean 302, 316, 326
Sichel, Edith 42, 465
Sillem, Maurits 535, 546, 548
Sills, H.H. 163, 164, 168, 220

Silver, Charles 580
Simon, Brian 284
Simon, John 284
Simpson, Thomas 453
Simpson, Wallis 271
Sims, Jim 379
Sinclair, Monica 462, 467, 481, 486, 513, 527
Sitwell, Dame Edith 509-10
Skidmore, Mr 562-3
Slim, General William 387
Smetana, Bedřich 232, 571, 583
Smeterlin, Jan 103
Smith, Dodie 30, 146, 204, 211
Smith, Harry 378
Smith, Marjorie 378
Smith, William C. 416, 417, 621
Solera, Temistocle 595
Solti, Georg 545, 605
Somervell, Sir Donald 318
Sophocles 147, 356
Sousa, John Philip 24
Sparrow, John 162
Spence, Jack 378
Spence, Minnie 378
Spencer, Terence 588, 590-1, 615
Spender, Natasha 386
Spender, Stephen 208, 318, 386
Spenser, Edmund 259, 312, 316
Spenser Society 216, 273, 274
Spinks, Charles 497
Spohr, Louis 548, 551, 554
Spontini, Gaspare 538, 551, 570
Sprague, Master 55
Sprot, Celia 408
Sprot, Major Jock 408
Squire, William Barclay 416
Squires, H.C. 207, 219-20, 261, 294, 295, 296, 367, 387

Index

Stabach, Mr (tailor) 627
Stabile, Mariana 233, 304
Staggins, Nicholas 339
Stainer, Mrs 458
Stalin, Joseph 369, 386, 596
Stanley, Brenda, later Watson 380-1
Stanley, John 424
Stanford, Charles Villiers 440, 463, 580
Stein, Erwin 426
Stein, Gertrude 4-5, 274
Stendhal 434
Stephenson, George 244
Sternfeld, F.W. 617
Stevens, Denis 495, 503, 564, 565, 612, 632
Stevens, Sheila 564, 565, 612, 632
Stevenson, R.L. 95
Stewart-Brown, David 99
Stewart-Clark, Mr 601
Stockalper, Clorinda 626
Stockalper, Viviane 626
Stone, Norman 499, 500
Stradella, Alessandro 232
Strang Steel, Sir William (Willow) 589, 599, 600, 619
Strauss, Johann 577
Strauss, Richard 265-266, 267, 287, 478
Stravinsky, Igor 323, 342, 345, 483, 520, 535, 565, 636
Strepponi, Giuseppina 569
Strobel, Heinrich 483
Strohbach, Leopold Hans 266
Stubbs, Sergeant 72
Suckling, Norman 401
Suggia, Guilhermina 425
Sullivan, Sir Arthur 102, 105, 370, 439, 480, 518, 556, 622, 624

Suppé, Franz von 624
Susie (cat) 407, 475, 476, 581, 625-6
Sutcliffe, Herbert 95-96
Sutherland, Joan 8, 467, 468, 496, 513, 514, 524-5, 555, 584, 624
Sutro, Alfred 17, 21-2, 25, 29, 42, 59, 60, 91, 92, 130-2, 133, 134, 141, 160, 169-71, 189, 190, 225, 274, 357, 371
Sutro, Esther (Essie) 1-2, 17, 20, 21, 22, 23, 25, 27, 29, 31, 42, 130, 132, 133, 141, 149, 160, 169, 173, 179, 181, 182, 186-7, 189
Sutro, John 170, 189
Sutro, Leopold 60, 145, 170
Sutro, Violet 60, 145
Sutton, Poppett 590, 627-8, 630, 632, 635, 638, 639, 641, 642
Sutton, Ted 628, 630, 631
Sutton, Trottie 628, 630, 631
Sved, Alexander 305, 317
Swackhamer, Jack 634, 635-6, 636-7
Swayne, T. 467, 475, 477
Szigeti, Joseph 325

Tallack, Philip 120-1, 286
Tarbet, Betty 421
Tarbet, Joan 421
Tartak, Marvin 642
Tate, Beatrice (Botter) 64, 66, 67
Tate, Maurice 189
Tate, Phyllis 539
Tavares de Almeida, Dr 449
Taylor, A.J.P. 386
Taylor, Cecil, née Fitzgerald, later Woodham-Smith 84, 94
Taylor, Margaret 386
Taylor, Miss 560
Taylor, Mr 84, 94

Tchaikovsky, Pyotr Ilyich 236, 308, 324, 349, 537, 637
Tedder, Air Chief Marshall Lord 29
Telford, Mrs 42
Ten Club 172, 197, 281-2, 317
Tennyson, Alfred, Lord 165, 534
Testament of Beauty, The (Bridges) 257, 318
Terry, Ellen 42, 134
Thackeray, W.M. 42
Thackeray Turner, Hugh 226
Thalben-Ball, George 510
Thatcher, Dr R.S. 78, 100-2, 103, 397
Thistlethwaite, Frank 290, 338, 407, 525, 554-5, 559
Thistlethwaite, Jane 407, 525, 554-5, 559
Thomas, Ambroise 580
Thomas, John 637
Thomas, Nancy 486
Thomas, Peter 396, 410, 416, 435, 441, 642
Thomas, Tessa, see Dean
Thomas, Nurse 416
Thompson, D.C. 73
Thompson, Francis 175
Thompson, Sir John 125
Thompson, Pauline 543
Thorborg, Kerstin 233, 303, 304, 305
Thucydides 125, 164
Tiepolo, Giovanni Battista 238
Tiger (wire-haired terrier) 58-9, 189
Timms, W.W. 379
Timoshenko, Semyon 372
Tinkerbell (cat) 633-4, 639
Tippett, Michael 562
Tolstoy, Leo 17
Tombs, Mr 399

Toppan, Cushing 229-30, 295-6, 302, 305
Toscanini, Arturo 232-3, 234, 236, 286, 287, 294, 303-4, 306, 317, 325, 346
Tovey, Sir Donald 282
Toye, Francis 278
Tracey, Edmund 575, 585
Traetta, Tommaso 642
Tredgold, Dr 381
Tree, Sir Herbert 31
Trend, J.B. 199-200, 265, 293, 316, 346, 268, 389, 429
Tresham, Millicent 137, 224
Trethowan, Ian 609
Trew, Arthur 377
Trimble, Valerie, later Williams 389, 605
Trouncer, Cecil 270
Trowell, Brian 501, 536-7, 541, 550-1, 557, 560, 598, 605-6, 625
Trowell, Rhianon 551, 598
Tunnard, Viola 538
Turgenev, Ivan 131, 330
Turing, Alan 160-1, 552
Turner, Eva 267
Turner, J.W.M. 613
Turot, Jacqueline 400
Turot, Paul 399, 400
Turot, Renée 399
Tynan, Anne 110, 113

Ucko, Hans 484, 536
Umberto, Prince of Piedmont 231
Upton, Valerie 421
Upton, Mrs Violet 421
Upward, Edward 163
Utrillo, Maurice 169

Vanbrugh, Sir John 165, 172

Index

Vanbrugh, Violet 349
Van Gogh, Vincent 18, 106, 169-70
Van Gruisen, Agatha (Aggie) 13, 30, 148
Van Gruisen, Albert Henry (Tommy) 12, 13, 23, 24-5, 29, 30, 31, 35, 38-45 *passim*, 53, 59, 62, 84, 124, 126, 128, 130, 135, 142, 147-9, 151, 168, 180, 183, 185, 186, 187, 191, 192, 194, 195, 216, 217, 219, 226, 269, 282, 286, 288, 291, 295, 299, 314, 319, 331, 336, 345, 364, 374, 381, 420, 465, 621, 626
Van Gruisen, Albertus (1741-1824) 12
Van Gruisen, Albertus (1786-1831) 12
Van Gruisen, Emmy 13
Van Gruisen, Esther, later Dean, see Bagger
Van Gruisen, Florence Angela, née Isaacs (Gran) I, 12, 16, 17, 18, 20-30 *passim*, 35, 38-9, 41-6 *passim*, 51, 53, 58, 62, 87, 89, 90, 91, 92, 126, 128, 130, 132, 133, 135, 141, 147-9, 151, 160, 169, 170, 171, 173, 179, 180, 181, 183, 185, 186, 187, 189, 191, 192, 194, 195, 205, 207, 216, 217, 219, 224, 225, 226, 229, 260-1, 263, 268, 269, 282, 286, 288, 291, 294, 295, 299, 314, 316, 317, 319, 328, 331, 332, 338, 351, 364, 374, 376, 381, 394, 400, 410, 411, 415, 420, 421, 433, 454, 458, 465
Van Gruisen, Harry 26-7, 33, 45, 261, 282, 286, 312, 420, 421, 454, 458, 564
Van Gruisen, Horace 13
Van Gruisen, Kate 13, 295, 626
Van Gruisen, Lottie 30
Van Gruisen, Michael 27, 31, 142, 389
Van Gruisen, Nicolaas Laurentius (1824-1898) 12
Van Gruisen, Nicholas (1856-1912) 12
Van Gruisen, Ruby, née McKay 26, 45, 389
Van Gruisen, Wilfred 26, 27, 34
Varcoe, Mrs 607
Vaughan Williams, Ralph 199, 222, 286, 328, 341, 440, 508, 572
Vaughan Williams, Ursula 537
Veitch, Kathleen 607, 613, 614, 616, 621
Verdi, Giuseppe 17, 38, 214, 232, 281, 303, 329, 345, 355, 418, 429, 432, 476, 478, 528, 536, 539, 540, 544, 549, 555, 556-7, 568-9, 576, 580, 587-8, 595, 602-3, 605, 608, 618, 624
Verdière, René 400
Verena (au pair) 625-6
Verity, Hedley 145
Vermeer, Johannes 308
Veronese, Paolo 238
Vickers, Jon 486, 496, 497
Viner, Monique 396
Visconti, Luchino 486, 618
Vlasto, Alexis 439
Vlasto, Jill 439, 452
Voakey, Mr 628
Voysey, C.F.A. 22, 39, 42-3, 459, 460, 465, 477
Vyvyan, Jennifer 528

Waghorn, Anne 89
Waghorn, Mark 89
Waghorn, Mrs 89

Wagner, Richard 24, 101, 198-9, 232, 233, 234, 286, 303, 304, 305, 317, 354-5, 369, 463, 478, 520, 552, 561, 573, 577, 622, 635
Walker, Alec 555
Walker, Frank 406, 441-2, 456, 477, 528, 540, 543, 544, 549, 555, 568-9
Walker, Sally 441, 447, 528
Walkley, A.B. 22
Wallace, Edgar 257
Wallace, Kitty 88
Wallace, Lucille 234-5, 264, 281, 282, 306, 307, 347-8
Wallace, Mrs 307
Walmsley, J.F. 67-8, 76, 105, 151
Walpole, Sir Robert 167
Walter, Bruno 230-1, 232, 233-4, 235, 303, 304, 325
Walton, Sir William 449
Warden 82-90 *passim*, 95, 144, 157, 177, 379
Warrack, Catkin 579
Warrack, John 495, 579
Warwick, Daisy Greville, Countess of 34, 36, 93, 137-8, 217, 223, 224
Watkins, Ronald 114, 117-18, 119, 129
Watson, Alister 161
Watson, Angus 440
Watson, Bill 381
Watts, Helen 481, 483, 611
Weber, Carl Maria von vi, 305, 327, 355, 548, 561, 577
– *Euryanthe* 304, 305, 306, 492, 561
Webern, Anton 200, 636
Webster, David 436
Wedd, Nathaniel 163, 164-5
Weill, Kurt 574
Weinberger, Jaromír 454
Weingartner, Felix 232, 233, 325
Weinstock, Herbert 515
Weldon, Georgina 470
Weldon, John 511, 598
Wellesz, Egon 231, 356-7
Wellington, Arthur Wellesley, 1st Duke of 183
Wells, H.G. 216
Wells, Miss 456
Westrup, Sir Jack 278, 326, 342, 457, 495, 503, 509, 523, 533, 535, 564, 586, 598, 604-5, 617
Westrup, Solweig 509, 604-5
Wheeler, Chrisopher 269-70, 272
Wheeler, Mairin 405
Wheeler, Mortimer 123
Wheeler, Pat 380
Wheeler, Penelope 269-70
Wheeler, Tessa 123
Wheeler, Tom 337, 339, 344, 352, 380, 488
Whelan, Frederick 110, 111-12, 113
Whimster, D.C. 118, 119, 122
Whistler, James McNeill 24, 187
White, Eric Walter 503
White House 390, 393, 398, 399, 406-7, 410, 416, 417, 421, 436-7, 458, 461-2, 471-2, 475, 515
Whitelaw, William 408
Wiggin, Frances 204
Wilbye, John 340
Wilde, Oscar 24, 167, 440
Wilkins, Mr 71, 78
Wilkinson, Patrick 163, 186, 220, 276
Willcocks, David 525
Williams, Dorian 120
Williams, Emlyn 211
Williams, Harcourt 270

Index

Williams, Harold 266
Williams, John 389
Williams, Judy 302
Williamson, Sir Hedworth 135
Willis, Constance 267
Wilson, Angela 380, 523, 618
Wilson, Annie 487, 592, 618
Wilson, Catherine 551
Wilson, Charles 368, 373, 380, 523, 617-18
Wilson, E.L. 86
Wilson, Peggy 201, 221, 227, 292, 299, 338, 340, 341, 346
Wilson, Steuart 201
Wilson, Willie 488
Wilson, Mrs (Peggy's mother) 227, 334, 346-7, 367
Wingate, Beryl 464
Wingate, Dr Frederick Mayo 404-5, 414, 416, 439, 444, 464, 479, 482, 484, 485, 486, 487, 493, 495, 500, 502, 505, 510, 518, 529, 538
Wings (1927 film) 93
Winton, Elizabeth Mary, see Dean
Winton, Mrs 10
Wishart, Peter 551
Wolf, Hugo 232, 441
Wolfe, Humbert 274
Wolf-Ferrari, Ermanno 431
Wolfit, Donald 103
Wong, Anna May 145
Wood, Harold 402, 427
Wood, Sir Henry 201, 325

Wood, Lionel 404, 428, 516
Wood, Tony 404, 489
Woodard, Edith 378, 389, 518
Woodard, John 378, 389, 512, 518-19
Woodard, Graham 519
Woodgate, Mr 74
Woodham-Smith, G.I. 82, 83, 84, 94, 95
Woodhouse, Frederick 187-8
Woodward, Mary 389
Woolley, Frank 94
Wordie, James 367
Workman, Alexander 466, 487
Wright, Geoffrey 212
Wrightson, Margaret 613
Wuthering Heights (Emily Brontë) 146
Wyatt, Sir Thomas 316
Wyss, Sophie 325

Xenophon 150

Yealland, Dr Lewis 205, 206, 207
Yearp, A.E. 122
Young, Alexander 557
Young, Percy M. 401, 512

Zandonai, Riccardo 575
Zangwill, Edith 189
Zangwill, Israel 160, 189
Zangwill, Oliver 160, 168, 299, 338, 391
Zeffirelli, Franco 555, 608
Zilliacus, Konni 111-12
Zillig, Winfried 580